THE CHINESE
Their History and Culture

BY KENNETH SCOTT LATOURETTE

D. WILLIS JAMES PROFESSOR OF MISSIONS AND
ORIENTAL HISTORY AND FELLOW OF BERKELEY
COLLEGE IN YALE UNIVERSITY

Third Edition Revised
Two Volumes in One

NEW YORK
THE MACMILLAN COMPANY
1951

Copyright, 1934 and 1946, by
THE MACMILLAN COMPANY.

All rights reserved—no part of this book may be reproduced in any form without permission in writing from the publisher, except by a reviewer who wishes to quote brief passages in connection with a review written for inclusion in magazine or newspaper.

Sixth Printing, 1951.

Printed in the United States of America

IN MEMORY OF
FREDERICK WELLS WILLIAMS
1857–1928

PREFACE TO THE THIRD EDITION

It is, naturally, gratifying to the author that the continued sales of this book make a further revised edition possible. In the nearly eleven years since the last revision, the advance of scholarship has revealed some new facts and has disclosed fresh angles on old views. Advantage has been taken of this progress to alter a number of the existing pages. Friends, both in private letters and in published reviews, have pointed out mistakes. These have been rectified. The changes have been mainly in the first volume, but several have been made in the second. In these nearly eleven years, moreover, striking developments have occurred in China. The struggle with Japan which began in 1931 has been intensified through the penetration by the invader of much of China Proper. China has become a participant in a second world war. Indeed, instead of being on the periphery of that struggle, as in the First World War of the twentieth century, China was the scene of the first stages of the contest which later assumed world-wide proportions and has suffered fully as much as any of the other combatants. The revolution in all phases of Chinese culture which has been so momentous a feature of the twentieth century has been accelerated. To take account of these developments it has been necessary to add a number of pages to the first volume, to rewrite certain other pages toward the close of that volume, and to modify pages in the second volume which deal with the changes of the present century. The bibliographies have been thoroughly reworked. Some titles have been deleted and many have been added, particularly of books and articles which have appeared since the last revision. The effort has been made, then, to bring the book fully down to date—in its summary of existing knowledge of the history and culture of the Chinese, in its account of recent events, and in bibliography. It is to be hoped that the usefulness of the book will be not only prolonged but also enhanced. The author would express his thanks to Professors J. J. L. Duyvendak, L. C.

Goodrich, and C. H. Peake, and to Dr. H. H. Hart for careful lists of corrections and additions. He would also record his gratitude to the many others, too numerous to list here, who, either in private letter or in published review, have offered suggestions and pointed out errors. To them is due much of whatever improvement over earlier editions the present edition displays.

K. S. LATOURETTE

New Haven, Conn.,
   March, 1945.

PREFACE

THE importance of China is only dimly appreciated by the modern Occident. Here live approximately four hundred millions of people, the largest fairly homogeneous group of mankind. Nearly a fourth of the human race, the Chinese outnumber the entire population of the Western Hemisphere. Their total is probably greater than that of populous India and is only slightly less than that of all Europe. In blood and culture China is much more nearly uniform than India, Europe, or the Americas.

Until recently separated from the rest of the world by barriers of mountain, desert, and water which could be traversed only with difficulty, the Chinese developed their political and social institutions, their philosophy, and their economic life with fewer contributions from without than has any other major civilized group of mankind—except perhaps the pre-Columbian cultures in Mexico, Central America, and Peru.

Chinese culture has been noteworthy both for its excellence and for its influence upon its immediate neighbors. In philosophy it has displayed originality and has had marked social effects. The older political structure endured longer than any other ever devised by man, and, when measured by the area and the number of people governed, was one of the most successful in history. In quality and volume Chinese literature ranks among the greatest produced by the human race. China's art is being more and more enthusiastically acclaimed by Western experts. The economic organization of the Empire made possible the existence of an enormous population. Chinese culture influenced profoundly all its immediate neighbors—notably the Japanese, the Koreans, the semi-nomadic peoples to the north and west, and the Asiatic peoples to the south, and to a somewhat lesser degree the civilized peoples of Central Asia.

In itself such a civilization deserves study. It is particularly valuable, however, for the perspective which it gives upon our own. In any well balanced consideration of human institutions the comparative method must be included, and here is a great group of mankind, highly civilized, until recently remote from the Occident, whose experience should prove of no little use to the rest of the race.

Moreover, the Chinese, so numerous and so highly cultured, for almost a generation have been in process of change. All phases of life are being affected, with results for the moment chaotic and with an outcome as yet unpredictable. Whatever the future, it cannot be without marked significance for all the world.

An understanding of the Chinese, therefore, their history, their culture, and their present problems, is of prime importance for Europe and America.

Not since the last revision of Samuel Wells Williams, *The Middle Kingdom*, made in 1883, have we had in a European language a satisfactory large, comprehensive book on China and the Chinese. Many short works have appeared, some of them excellent, and a few fairly large volumes have been published; but so far none has done for the present generation of the English-speaking world quite what *The Middle Kingdom* did for our parents and grandparents. Recent years have witnessed a great advance in many phases of our knowledge of the Chinese. Numerous monographs and still more numerous articles in scholarly periodicals have rapidly expanded the West's fund of information concerning them. Fully as interesting and even more important are the changes which have been altering every portion of the nation's life.

The need exists, consequently, for a work which will endeavor to picture afresh the Chinese, their history and civilization, bringing into its composition all our knowledge concerning them, both old and new. This the following chapters essay to do. The proportions of the picture will inevitably be influenced by the author's own perspective and to many may seem faulty. The attempt has been made, however, to portray the various features of Chinese life, remote and recent, in their relative importance as molders of the nation.

As will be seen by a glance at the table of contents, the geography and natural resources of China are first described, and their influence upon the people. Then follows a summary, comprising more than half of the work, of the nation's history from the beginning to the present. This is succeeded by chapters on population and on each of the main phases of the culture and institutions of the country—political, economic, philosophical and religious, social, æsthetic, and intellectual. Under most of these topics a description is given of the structure of Chinese life as it developed before the coming of the European, and is followed by an account of the modifications of the past few years. To each chapter is appended a brief bibliography (by no means exhaustive) of the more important books and articles on the subject. Some standard Chinese works are included, not because the reader is likely to consult them or because the author has gone through them all (for he has not), but to give some slight indication of the wealth of Chinese material which exists and to suggest some of the places in which original research in the sources must begin. The order of each bibliography is usually (1) works in Chinese and translations of Chinese material, (2) books in European languages on the general subject of the chapter, and (3) articles and books on special phases of the subject of the chapter arranged in the sequence in which these phases are treated. The paraphernalia of footnotes will be missed by some, but references for particular paragraphs can usually be quickly discovered either in the books which cover in general the subject of the chapter or in the special articles and monographs, listed as are these latter in the order in which the topics occur. At the end of the second volume, just before the index, a list of the Chinese names in the text will be found, arranged alphabetically according to their romanization and each with its corresponding Chinese characters. No one system of romanization meets with the approval of all sinologists, but in the main the one most frequently used in books in English, that of Sir Thomas Wade, has here been followed.

The book is in no sense either a repetition or an enlargement of the author's *The Development of China*, but is an entirely independent work meant to perform a different function. *The Development of China* is intended as the shortest possible introduction to China and its history and as a text for brief, elementary courses on the Far East. The present work is meant to be a fairly full summary and interpretation of what is known about the Chinese, both for the general reader and for longer, more detailed college and university courses on China.

The sinologist will discover in the volumes little, if anything, which he does not already know, but it is hoped that he will find them an accurate and useful summary. The value of such a work rests not on fresh research in specialized fields, but on the summary and interpretation of results available in detailed but unconnected studies. For the general reader or for the foreign resident or traveller in China who desires a more than fleeting view of the country the work may prove of value.

To those to whom the volumes are their first introduction to China, much of the text may seem to be overloaded and confused with strange names. The effort has been made, however, to reduce these to the minimum which all who seek to be familiar with the main features of the history and culture of the Chinese must know. The expert, indeed, may feel that too many names have been omitted.

No one can be more conscious than is the author of the inevitable defects of such a work. It must be brief. Many fields which it attempts to cover lack the necessary spade-work of specialized monographs and later researches will invalidate or modify the conclusions reached. Even at its best it cannot hope to be standard for many decades. New studies, both by Chinese and by Occidentals, will quickly make great portions of it obsolete. Such advance in our knowledge, indeed, is not only to be welcomed but encouraged. China, too, is moving so rapidly that those sections of the book which attempt to portray and interpret contemporary conditions and movements will soon be out of date. Even measured by our present knowledge some mistakes will almost inevitably creep in. It is hoped, however, that the following pages have succeeded in achieving a fairly well-balanced summary of what is now familiar to experts, and that they will aid in encouraging further investigation in many of the fields covered.

More and more Chinese are interpreting their country to the West—a movement to be greeted most warmly. There must always remain, however, as for every nation, need for the sort of appraisal which the foreigner, with his different and often more detached perspective, can give.

It is, of course, too much to hope that these volumes will take as prominent a place as that once held by *The Middle Kingdom*. It may not be unduly presumptuous, however, to dedicate them to the memory of Frederick Wells Williams, the distinguished son of the distinguished author of that monumental work. Frederick Wells Williams was born and spent his boyhood days in China, aided in the final revision of *The Middle Kingdom*, and during more than thirty years on the teaching staff of Yale gave courses on China and helped to stimulate that scholarly interest in the land of his birth which is now, fortunately, so markedly on the increase in the United States. To him the author owes his introduction to and much of his love for Chinese lore.

The author wishes to record his gratitude to Doctors A. W. Hummel and B. Laufer and to Professors M. S. Bates, K. L. Chen, Lewis Hodous, William Hung, Ellsworth Huntington, Frank W. Price, and L. S. C. Smythe, each of whom read longer or shorter portions of the manuscript and to all of whom he is indebted for invaluable suggestions. But for their generous assistance the book would be guilty of many more mistakes and omissions than is now the case. He also is under deep obligation to Mrs. L. F. Lincoln, whose efficient typing of the manuscript from his often nearly unintelligible drafts and whose suggestions for improvements in style have been indispensable, and to Dr. Luther C. S. Shao for copying into graceful form from the author's crabbed script the Chinese characters of the text and the index. The author, too, is indebted to the libraries of Yale University for the use of books which their ample facilities have afforded.

In addition to the bibliographies included at the end of the various chapters, the author has made extensive use of H. Cordier, *Bibliotheca Sinica* (second edition, Paris, 1904–1908, Supplement, Paris, 1924), the most nearly complete bibliography of writings on China in Western languages, and of Samuel Couling, *The Encyclopædia Sinica* (London, 1917), which, while avowedly incomplete and at times inaccurate, is an extraordinarily useful book of reference.[1]

No history can be freed from the writer's preconceptions. The very selection of facts involves a judgment as to the relative importance of the myriad actions and events which constitute the

---

[1] Since the first edition was published, another excellent bibliography has appeared—R. J. Kerner, *Northeastern Asia: a Selected Bibliography* (2 vols., Berkeley, 1939). It devotes approximately half its space to China and includes works in Chinese as well as those in Western languages.

Current exhaustive bibliographies are in *The Far Eastern Quarterly* (New York, 1941 ff.).

crude stuff from which history is composed. The present author has made an honest attempt to achieve an attitude of detachment—the avowed ideal of most of modern scholarship. He is conscious, however, that in his choice of material he has stressed the political aspects of his story more than some sinologists will approve. He is also aware that at times his warm sympathy with the Chinese may have betrayed him into seeming to be an apologist for them. His constant endeavor, however, has been to avoid the rôle of the advocate and to be simply an impartial observer and recorder.

New Haven, Conn.
June, 1933

CONTENTS

VOLUME I

CHAPTER		PAGE
	PREFACE TO THE THIRD EDITION	vii
	PREFACE	ix
I	GEOGRAPHY AND ITS INFLUENCE ON THE CHINESE	3
II	THE BEGINNINGS OF CHINESE CIVILIZATION (TO B.C. 221)	32
III	THE FORMATION OF THE EMPIRE: THE CH'IN AND HAN DYNASTIES (B.C. 221–A.D. 220)	88
IV	DIVISIONS AND FOREIGN INVASIONS: FROM THE CLOSE OF THE HAN TO THE BEGINNING OF THE SUI DYNASTY (A.D. 220–589)	143
V	REUNION AND RENEWED ADVANCE: THE SUI (A.D. 589–618) AND T'ANG (A.D. 618–907) DYNASTIES	177
VI	POLITICAL WEAKNESS BUT CULTURAL BRILLIANCE: THE FIVE DYNASTIES (A.D. 907–960) AND THE SUNG DYNASTY (A.D. 960–1279)	222
VII	CHINA UNDER THE RULE OF THE MONGOLS (A.D. 1279–1368)	262
VIII	CHINA AGAIN UNDER CHINESE RULE: THE MING DYNASTY (A.D. 1368–1644)	283
IX	THE CH'ING (MANCHU) DYNASTY: ITS HEYDAY AND THE BEGINNING OF ITS DECLINE (A.D. 1644–1838)	309
X	THE TRANSFORMATION WROUGHT BY THE IMPACT OF THE OCCIDENT	
	I. The Empire Is Shaken by Wars with Western European Powers and the Resulting Treaties and by Accompanying Internal Rebellion (A.D. 1839–1860)	340

CHAPTER		PAGE
XI	THE TRANSFORMATION WROUGHT BY THE IMPACT OF THE OCCIDENT	
	II. Partial Recovery from the Shocks of the Preceding Two Decades: the Restoration of Internal Order but the Slow Permeation of the Empire by Occidental Trade and Ideas (A.D. 1861–1893)	360
XII	THE TRANSFORMATION WROUGHT BY THE IMPACT OF THE OCCIDENT	
	III. The Crumbling of the Structure of the Old Chinese Culture and Foreshadowings of the New (A.D. 1894–1944)	376

Volume II

XIII	THE CHINESE PEOPLE	495
XIV	GOVERNMENT	513
XV	ECONOMIC LIFE AND ORGANIZATION	555
XVI	RELIGION	607
XVII	SOCIAL LIFE AND ORGANIZATION	665
XVIII	ART	722
XIX	LANGUAGE, LITERATURE, AND EDUCATION	765
XX	BY WAY OF SUMMARY	806
	PROPER NAMES AND CHINESE WORDS USED IN THE TEXT AND THEIR CORRESPONDING CHINESE CHARACTERS	817
	INDEX	833

THE CHINESE
THEIR HISTORY AND CULTURE
VOLUME I

CHAPTER I

GEOGRAPHY AND ITS INFLUENCE ON THE CHINESE

THE NAME

THE name China is a foreign appellation, probably derived from a dynasty which reigned over the Empire in the third century B.C. The Chinese long held it as an ideal that there should be only one political administration for civilized mankind and regarded their own as that government. Hence no pressing need existed to distinguish their country from another. They might speak of China as *T'ien Hsia*—"Under Heaven." The most frequent name employed was *Chung Kuo*—"The Middle Kingdom." The Chinese often denominated themselves *Han Jên*, or the "Men of Han," after a famous dynasty of that name. *T'ang Jên*, or the "Men of T'ang," after another famous dynasty, was frequently on the lips of the Chinese in the South. The name officially adopted by the Republic is *Chung Hua Min Kuo*, literally, "Central Flowery People's Country," or, better, "Central Flowery Republic."

THE TWO MAIN DIVISIONS OF CHINA

What now appears on the map as China falls into two main parts, China proper, where the major proportion of the population has long been Chinese, and what, intermittently, have been the outlying sections of the Empire, where until recently the Chinese have been in the minority.[1] The distinction between the two divisions is not so closely drawn as in the nineteenth century. Indeed, it is fading and no longer conforms strictly with administrative and racial realities. Large parts of the dependencies have been officially organized as provinces, with the same status as those of China proper. Chinese have migrated extensively into

---

[1] In Manchuria and in portions of Inner Mongolia, as we shall see later, Chinese now form the major part of the population.

some of them. Even now, however, the division preserves a degree of rough approximation to the facts which renders it a useful framework for classification.

CHINA PROPER

China proper is made up chiefly of the valleys of two great rivers, the Yellow and the Yangtze, and one smaller one, the Hsi Kiang, which, taking their rise in the vast table-lands and mountain fastnesses to the west, flow eastward into an arm of the Pacific. In fertile plains along the middle and lower course of the Yellow River is the traditional seat of primitive Chinese culture, and in comparatively early times the Chinese state incorporated the middle and lower reaches of the Yangtze basin. Later, in the centuries just before and just after the Christian era, the Chinese occupied the basins of both rivers and of their tributaries up to the mountains and plateaus of the West and annexed the coastal regions to the south, where numerous smaller valleys, notably that of the Hsi Kiang ("West River") and its confluents, afforded inviting homes. Migration, settlement, and more or less complete amalgamation with earlier stocks followed occupation and annexation, although in some sections very tardily. The area of China proper is approximately a million and a half square miles [2] —about half the size of the United States without Alaska and two-fifths that of Europe.

A more detailed description of this region will disclose the features which have made it a natural unit and the seat of a numerous and civilized people, and which have helped to give to the Chinese some of their outstanding characteristics.

Politically the Chinese to-day divide their country into twenty-eight provinces. These do not include Outer Mongolia and Tibet, which, although technically still under Chinese suzerainty, for most practical purposes have been lost to the Republic. China proper includes, roughly, eighteen of the twenty-eight. Not all of the political boundaries of the provinces correspond to the natural contour of the land and an intelligible picture can better be obtained by treating the country according to its topography than by its administrative units.

[2] We do not have exact measurements and the total is probably above rather than below this figure.

Nature has divided China proper into four main sections, the North, made up chiefly of the valley of the Yellow River (Huang Ho) and its tributaries, the upper portion of the Yangtze Valley and the adjoining mountains and table-lands, the lower part of the valley of the Yangtze River, and the coastal regions south of the Yangtze. Each of these, in turn, has natural subdivisions.

CHINA PROPER: THE NORTH

The North of China proper comprises most of the provinces of Shantung, Hopei (formerly Chihli), Honan, Shansi, Shensi, and Kansu and the northern portions of Anhui and Kiangsu. Topographically it shades off into a tier of new provinces, Jehol, Chahar, Suiyüan, and Ninghsia, which have been carved out partly from some of the older northern provinces and partly from what is often denominated Inner Mongolia. Its major stream is the Huang Ho ("Yellow River"), which, rising in the mountains and plateaus that fringe Tibet, by a devious route flows into the Yellow Sea. Its name describes its color, and this in turn is due to the vast amount of sediment which the river carries and which, lodged in shifting bars, in spite of the size of the stream, makes difficult or impossible navigation by all but the smaller craft.

With this sediment the Yellow River and some smaller adjacent streams—principally the Pai Ho on the north and the Huai Ho on the south—have built up a vast alluvial plain on either side of the Shantung promontory. This plain, which extends over much of Honan, Hopei, and Shantung, and over the northern portions of Kiangsu and Anhui, and which on the south merges with the delta of the Yangtze, was laid down in what was once sea bottom. It is very level and extends for scores of miles without prominent hills or valleys.

In common with other fluvial heavy carriers of sediment, along its lower reaches the Huang Ho has tended to raise for itself natural dykes and a bed higher than the adjoining plain. This tendency, reënforced by the embankments built by man, leads to devastating floods. As its bed rises higher and higher between its dyke-like banks the stream inevitably breaks its bounds, and, spreading its waters over the surrounding country, seeks a new bed on a lower level. As a result its mouth has been now south and now north of the Shantung mountains, by shiftings which have brought untold distress to the dense population of the adjacent area.

The northern plain has been, however, the friend of civilization, because, except for a few stretches marred by alkali or sand, it is very fertile. Together with a smaller plain in the valley of the Wei, a tributary of the Huang Ho, it was the scene of the development of the culture which shaped the rest of China. On it rose most of China's ancient capitals, and on it to-day stand several of her largest cities—notably Peking (lately also Peiping), Tientsin (near the mouth of the Pai Ho), and Tsinanfu, the capital of Shantung.

The sediment that furnishes the material for the plain is derived largely from a peculiar type of soil, the loess, which blankets many of the regions of North China. Loess occurs from the borders of Mongolia on the north and the Tarim basin in Sinkiang on the west into Shantung on the east and in spots into the Yangtze Valley on the south. Often scores of feet in depth, in some places it forms plateaus and in others fills valleys. It is very friable and, while of varying texture, is usually reducible by rubbing to a fine powder. Extremely fertile and easily cultivated, it is the source of much of the agricultural wealth of North China. It has a vertical cleavage and often is worn down into gullies and canyons with steep walls. It is also easily eroded and accordingly chokes the rivers that drain it. The loess is probably of wind-borne origin and apparently the product of thousands of years of dust storms not greatly dissimilar to those now familiar to the inhabitants of North China. It is of varying ages, the rate of deposition seemingly having been much more rapid in some eras than in others. In some places it can still be seen in process of formation. While originally laid down by the wind, streams have carved into it and have redeposited a large proportion of it, so that much of it is now in alluvial strata.

The fertility of the northern plain has been partly offset by deficient and irregular rainfall, especially inland. From the dawn of history, droughts and floods have repeatedly scourged with famine larger or smaller sections of the plain and the adjoining highlands.

Parts of the eastern boundary of the North China plain is formed by the mountains of Shantung. These consist chiefly of ancient rocks of the same formation as the hills of the Liaotung Peninsula, just to the north, in Manchuria. Erosion has rounded their contours and broadened their valleys. The most famous peak is T'ai Shan, slightly over five thousand feet high, the chief of the sacred mountains of China. To it for centuries the Chinese have looked with veneration and to it continue to come thousands of pilgrims. Thanks to its rocky formation and to the subsidence of the coast, the Shantung promontory possesses excellent harbors, notably Kiaochow Bay.

To the north of the North China plain high hills lead up to the Mongolian table-land. To the west rise first the mountains and plateaus of Shansi and then the mountains and valleys of Shensi and Kansu. Loess blankets much of the country, but the cultivated land is largely in the valleys and on the adjacent terraced hillsides. There are a few plains. How much of the land was wooded in primitive times we do not know. It seems fairly certain that over large portions of the area trees were sparse or entirely lacking. However, forests once covered much more of the country than now. Where they were cut the hillsides were rapidly eroded and the valleys often gutted with débris.

Most of the valleys are narrow, but there are exceptions. The chief of these is where the Wei, just above its confluence with the Yellow River as the latter breaks out of the mountains on the southern leg of its great northern bend to turn sharply to the east, flows through a broad and fertile plain. Here was an early seat of Chinese culture. Here, too, have been some of China's capitals, notably Hsianfu (Ch'angan), and here have been enacted many of the most famous scenes of China's history.

Shansi is, as has been said, made up largely of mountains and plateaus. These buttress the Mongolian highland and contain extensive coal measures. The most notable peak, and one of the chief Buddhist sacred mountains, is Wu T'ai Shan, near the northeastern border of the province. The chief river, the Fên, drains southwestward into the Huang Ho—above the junction of the latter with the Wei.

West of Shansi the mountains become higher until in parts of Kansu they attain to elevations of twenty thousand feet and more. As one proceeds westward, moreover, the valleys become narrower and the population more sparse than in the East. The Yellow River encloses in its northern bend the Ordos, a plateau which is mostly desert. The river itself is navigable as far as Lanchow in Kansu, but above its junction with the Wei many rapids interrupt its course.

To the southeast the North China plain shades off imperceptibly into the delta of the Yangtze River. However, a series of mountains and hills, with gradually diminishing heights, reaches eastward from the great ranges and table-lands of the West and forms an effective watershed between nearly all the lower length of the Yangtze—to the south—and the Huai and Yellow Rivers —to the north. The Huai River, draining much of the territory between the lower courses of its mightier neighbors, the Huang Ho and the Yangtze, constitutes one of China's major engineering problems, for it has no adequate mouth and any unusually rainy season sends its waters over the neighboring thickly settled countryside.

CHINA PROPER: THE UPPER PART OF THE YANGTZE VALLEY

The Yangtze is one of the greatest of the world's waterways. Rising in Tibet, the streams that go to make it cut their way in enormous canyons off the roof of the world to form, still in rugged country, what in its upper reaches is poetically called the River of the Golden Sand. To the south of this upper course, and partly drained by it, lies the southwesternmost province of China, Yünnan—literally, "South of the Clouds." The table-land which forms the most populous portion of Yünnan is high enough to have a salubrious climate and is well watered by streams and lakes. Its natural outlet is to the southeast and this was facilitated in the twentieth century by a railway built by the French. From Yünnan, also, a pass by way of Bhamo leads into the valley of the Irrawaddy and so into Burma—a route traversed through the centuries by merchants and armies. To Yünnan led, in the second world war of the twentieth century, the "Burma Road" and the "Ledo Road" which gave "free" China land access to the outside world.

Next on the course of the Yangtze is the great province of Szechwan (the "Four Streams"), the largest of the eighteen, and an empire in itself. The heart of Szechwan is a hilly, arable region known as the Red Basin—from the underlying sandstone.

Toward the western edge of the Red Basin is a fertile plain, watered by an ancient irrigation system, and the seat of the chief city of the province, Chengtu. The Basin has an abundant rainfall and a sub-tropical climate and hence supports a dense population. It is also rich in minerals. It is cut by several rapid rivers, notably the Min, which waters the Chengtu plain.

To the southeast, Szechwan is bounded by the mountainous province of Kweichow, to the west stretches Tibet with its great ranges and high plateaus, to the southwest lies Yünnan, to the north Shensi and Kansu are reached only through passes over a fairly formidable chain of mountains, and to the east rise more curtaining hills. Szechwan is, therefore, a geographical entity. The Yangtze provides it with its most important gateway to the outer world. That river, on leaving the most thickly populated parts of the province, for scores of miles cuts its way through the opposing hills in a series of huge gorges. The accompanying rapids make navigation hazardous, but for centuries boatmen have traversed them, and, of late years, especially constructed steamers have regularly made the run.

CHINA PROPER: THE LOWER PART OF THE YANGTZE VALLEY

From the gorges eastward the valley of the Yangtze begins to widen, only occasionally to be constricted by hills. More tributaries enter. On the south are two lakes, the T'ung-t'ing and the P'o-yang. These are practically continuous with the Yangtze and serve as reservoirs of the flood waters of the great river. Into each empty streams from the hinterland. The basin of the T'ung-t'ing Lake and of its affluents is roughly coterminous with the province of Hunan ("South of the Lake"). Hunan is largely mountainous and wooded, but numerous streams provide it with many fertile valleys. The P'o-yang Lake and the valleys of the streams which flow into it are nearly identical with the province of Kiangsi ("West of the River"). Kiangsi, like Hunan, is hilly, and also possesses valleys which support an extensive population. From the upper reaches of the Hsiang, the chief stream of Hunan, and of the Kan, the main river of Kiangsi, important passes across the hills give access to the south coast.

From the north, the chief tributary of the Yangtze is the Han, and at its junction with the main river lie the three cities, Hankow, Wuchang, and Hanyang, or, as they are known collectively, Wuhan. The province of which these three constitute the metropolis is Hupeh ("North of the [T'ung-t'ing] Lake"). Wuhan forms a natural commercial center, and so huge is the Yangtze that at high water ocean-going steamers make it a port of call, nearly six hundred miles from the coast. East of Hupeh and Kiangsi lie the two provinces of Anhui and Kiangsu, both of them spanning the river.

From the point where it leaves the gorges, the Yangtze is flanked by fertile alluvial plains of varying width and of its own building. At Chinkiang, about a hundred and fifty miles from its mouth, these broaden out into a delta and are being steadily extended by the silt-laden waters. Kiangsu possesses, as might be expected, several large cities—among them Nanking, on several occasions the capital of China, Soochow, Wusih, Ch'angchow, Yangchow, and the modern commercial metropolis of China, Shanghai. Shanghai, the result of the ocean-borne trade with the Occident, sprawls along the Huang-p'u, a small river which empties into the mouth of the Yangtze. In the Kiangsu delta are several lakes, among them the T'ai Hu. From the gorges eastward the Yangtze and its main tributaries lend themselves to navigation. For this purpose they are supplemented, especially on the delta, by an elaborate network of canals. The Grand Canal, connecting the South and the North, begins at Hangchow and runs northward, originally to the outskirts of Peking (Peiping). Through traffic is no longer able to traverse its entire length, but sections of it are still in use, in some places very extensively so.

CHINA PROPER: THE SOUTH COAST

South of the mouth of the Yangtze, the coast of China becomes rugged and deeply indented and the main mountain ranges run parallel to the coast. The cultivated land lies in the valleys or on artificially terraced hillsides. The ancient rocks which compose most of the region have been much eroded. Subsidence of the coast has given rise to islands and estuaries. The coastal region, divided politically into the four provinces Chêkiang, Fukien, Kwangtung, and Kwangsi, is separated from the basin of the Yangtze by barriers of hills, most of them averaging from three to six thousand feet in height. Many of the hills are covered with small timber and bamboo. The region is traversed by numerous streams, most of them comparatively short and punctuated by rapids, and, accordingly, is divided into many little valleys. These valleys favor the development of clans and of local dialects, so that it is not strange (although geography is not the sole cause) that the greatest variations in language occur here. The most considerable valley is that of the Hsi Kiang ("West River"). Its broad delta is fertile and densely populated. On its estuary (near where it is joined by other streams from the North) stands the city of Canton. The Hsi Kiang is navigable to the borders of Yünnan. Next in importance ranks the Min, which empties into the sea just below the city of Foochow. The scenery along its banks is famous.

The northern portion of Chêkiang encloses a section of the Yangtze delta. The major part of the province is mountainous. Its chief cities are Hangchow and Ningpo. Hangchow, near the mouth of the chief river of the province, the Ch'ien-t'ang, and flanked on one side by the beautiful West Lake, has been renowned for many centuries. Ningpo, on a plain near the mouth of a stream farther east, is a populous and well-known port. The Chusan archipelago, to the north of Ningpo, owes its fame chiefly to the island of P'u-t'o, one of the sacred centers of Buddhism. Fukien is almost entirely mountainous, and its largest city, Foochow, has already been noted. A second port, Amoy, to the south, has supplanted as a commercial center the nearby medieval mart of Ch'üanchow. Since its foundation over a century ago as a British colony, Hongkong, on a rocky island (late in 1941 captured by the Japanese), has been an important commercial rival of Canton. On the populous delta of the West River are still other cities, and on a plain near the mouth of another stream, the Han, near the Kwangtung-Fukien border, is Swatow, the entrepôt to a larger metropolis, Ch'aochow. Kwangtung, save for the delta of which Canton is the metropolis, is chiefly mountainous. To the south of Kwangtung, separated by a narrow strait, lies the rugged island of Hainan. The mountainous province of Kwangsi is really a westward extension of Kwangtung, being made up principally of the upper part of the valleys of the West River and its tributaries. Better supplied with harbors than most of the north coast and nearer to the East Indies, the Malay Peninsula, Siam,

India, and Europe, the south coast has had most of the ports for ocean-borne commerce.

CHINA PROPER: CLIMATE

As to climate, China proper lies almost entirely in the temperate zone. Only portions of the three southernmost provinces, Yünnan, Kwangsi, and Kwangtung, are within the tropics. Seasonal differences are marked. In the spring and summer, the arid land-masses to the north and northwest of China proper heat more quickly than do the seas to the east and south, and the warm air, rising, creates areas of low pressure. As a result, moisture-laden winds sweep northward from the ocean, bringing rain. In the autumn and winter the process is reversed. The air over the great northern and western land-barriers cools more rapidly than that over the tropical and sub-tropical seas to the south, and, moving southward, brings clear skies and lower temperatures. Consequently, China proper has most of its rain in the spring and summer.

To the south, nearer the sources of the cloud-carrying winds, and where the coast is backed by mountains which precipitate the moisture as it comes in from the ocean, the rainfall is heavy. At Hongkong it amounts to more than eighty inches a year and along the south coast it averages almost sixty inches. In Central China the precipitation averages about forty inches a year and in the Yangtze delta forty-five. In both South and Central China the summer humidity is high, ranging in the sixties, seventies, and eighties. In the North, farther from the sources of moisture, the rainfall declines, usually being between twenty and thirty inches on the coast and much less inland.

Torrential rains are known in the summer, both in the North and the South. In Southwest Hopei (Chihli) twenty-three inches fell in thirty-three hours in the summer of 1924, and more than once Hongkong has had over twenty inches in twenty-four hours. The heavy summer rains account in part for the rapid rise of the rivers in that season and for the frequent floods.

Throughout China, because of this monsoonal climate, the autumns are usually bracing and the winters cool or cold. Ice occasionally forms as far south as Canton—about the latitude of Havana and Calcutta. No other large seacoast tropical city in the world has so cool a winter. Light falls of snow are common in Central China—about the latitude of Cairo and New Orleans and with only a slightly higher elevation. In North China the winters are cold. Peking, at approximately the same latitude as Athens, Washington, and San Francisco, and not far inland, has much lower temperatures in January and February than any of them.

So marked a difference between North and South in rainfall and temperature helps to make North China quite distinct from the Yangtze Valley and the south coast in appearance and crops. In the South the plains and hills are green, the growing season is six to nine months in length, two or three crops a year are raised, and the prevailing grain is rice. In the North the hills and plains are brown and dust-blown during the winter, the growing season is shorter (four to six months), no more than two crops a year are obtained, wheat, kaoliang, and millet form the staple grains, and beans are raised extensively. The North suffers periodically from drought and the subsequent famines. North China, too, shades off gradually into regions where true desert conditions prevail. Indeed, semi-arid and even desert conditions here and there extend southward into the northernmost tier of the eighteen provinces. In the North, moreover, the heat and the rain of the summer encourage a luxuriant growth, but the cold and dry winters kill off all but the hardier plants. Trees, accordingly, do not easily start, and the characteristic forest is of broad-leaved, deciduous varieties. Because of climate and the nature of the soil only parts of North China seem ever to have been heavily timbered. On the other hand, the longer growing season and the heavier rains of the South favor trees. Vegetation is much more luxuriant and forests grow more quickly.

The difference in climate between the North on the one hand and the Yangtze Valley and the South on the other accounts in part for other contrasts between the two sections. In the North the slight rainfall with its frequent failure means numerous famines. The cold winters militate against health. The cold and the dust storms tend to keep people indoors, in an unsanitary atmosphere. Since fuel is dear, houses remain poorly heated. Heavy clothing is customary, and winter laundry and bathing difficult. Under such circumstances disease flourishes. Moreover, the short growing season makes for intense activity during part of the year and enforced idleness during much of the remainder. Home industries only partially occupy the time of the slack seasons. For a large proportion of the rural population lack of occupation encourages a relaxing of morale in the long interval between the harvest and the spring plowing. The frequent famines in the North tend also to lower the quality of the population. In the Yangtze Valley and the South, on the other hand, the winter temperatures are milder, dust storms do not occur, and outdoor life and frequent bathing are possible. The longer growing season shortens or eliminates the winter idleness of the farmer. Famines are less frequent. The undoubted fact that of late centuries the Chinese of the Yangtze and the South average much higher in initiative and leadership can, therefore, probably be attributed in part to the climatic contrasts between the great sections of the land.

Even in the Yangtze Valley and the South the climate is not altogether favorable. The enervating humid heat of the summers partly counterbalances the benefits of the cool winters.

Throughout China the concentration of the rainfall in the spring and summer reduces the productivity of the fields. A more evenly distributed precipitation would make for better crops. In the North, where the total annual precipitation is scanty, much of the rain comes in torrential downpours and runs off into the rivers before it can penetrate the soil.

To the climate, too, may be ascribed in part (but not entirely) the paucity of such domestic animals as the cow, the sheep, and the horse, which depend largely upon pasture and hay for food. The rank growth in the humid, damp summers makes for coarse grasses which prove difficult to eat and digest. The dependence for animal food on such scavengers as the pig and the chicken may have a climatic factor back of it. More than the North the Yangtze Valley and the South, with their hot, wet summers, show the effects of this absence of pasture grasses.

To the monsoonal nature of the climate must be assigned, too, some of the floods which so often afflict China. The concentration of the rain in a few months frequently means torrential downpours and the consequent over-congestion of the drainage system.

It is possible that Chinese architecture has been to a certain extent determined by the climate. The heavy summer rains make necessary sound, sturdy roofs if the house is to be protected, and one of the most prominent features of the Chinese building is the heavy tiled or thatched roof.

How far climatic conditions have altered within historic times we do not know. It is sometimes asserted that the North is drying up, but there seems to be no conclusive evidence of progressive desiccation during the past three thousand years.

CHINA PROPER: MINERAL RESOURCES

China proper is rather poorly stocked with useful minerals. Gold, silver, and copper are found in several of the provinces, but not in the rich deposits characteristic of some other countries. The relative dearth of the precious metals, especially of gold, may account in part for the failure to use gold for currency and for the frequent recourse to paper money. China's store of sulphur, lead, and zinc is widely distributed but is probably inadequate to supply the needs of an extensive industrial development. China also possesses some tin—just how much is not known. She has important stores of tungsten and in antimony she dominates the world's markets. Coal is found in every one of the eighteen provinces of China proper, and in some of the other ten. Experts' figures for the extent of these deposits vary greatly, but it seems probable that China possesses by far the largest coal reserves in the Far East. However, even the most enthusiastic recent estimates give her only a fourth of those of the United States. The more conservative appraisals—which are probably very much too low—credit her with less than one per cent. of the reserves of the United States. Estimates as to the amounts to be found in the various provinces differ widely. Shensi and Shansi are said to have eighty-five per cent. of the whole. Other well-stocked provinces are Hopei, Hunan, Szechwan, Shensi, Kweichow, Yünnan, Honan, and Shantung. So far, no very great stores of petroleum have been discovered. Faulting appears to have drained away and metamorphism to have destroyed most of what natural reservoirs may once have existed. Iron ores are widely distributed. However, they are only a fraction of those of some of the great steel-producing countries of the Occident and as a rule are ill-adapted in quality and quantity to large scale production and inadequate to supply the needs of any such mammoth industries as flourish in the United States and Western Europe. Bauxite, important for aluminum, is reported to be plentiful. Moreover, with the coming of plastics steel may not be so much in demand.

CHINA PROPER: FLORA AND FAUNA

China has an abundant stock of plants. One expert botanist has declared that she has the richest temperate flora in the world. Competent authorities believe that there are fifteen thousand species, fully half of them peculiar to the country. Many of these plants and trees are useful to man and the number has been enlarged by the introduction through the centuries of scores of others. The great variety in the flora makes for an almost equally rich fauna. The waters of China, too, teem with fish, a large proportion of them edible. A few of the many kinds of domesticated animals may have been indigenous to China and made subject to man there. More of them seem to have been introduced from abroad, some in prehistoric or early historic times.

THE OUTLYING SECTIONS

The second main division of China, what we have called the outlying sections, is made up chiefly of what are usually known politically as Tibet, the New Dominion (Sinkiang), Mongolia, and Manchuria.

The political organization and boundaries of these districts have varied greatly from time to time, even during the past two hundred years. The classification here given is only a rough one and to it exceptions can probably be taken. Kokonor, for instance, might well be grouped as a separate division. Moreover, as we have suggested, for a generation Sinkiang has been classed as a province, on a par with the eighteen of China proper, and parts of what the older maps show as Tibet and Mongolia have recently been organized into provinces. In spite of Japanese occupation, the Chinese bitterly resent, too, any implication that Manchuria is politically in any way distinct from the China which lies south of the Great Wall.

THE OUTLYING SECTIONS: TIBET

Tibet is a vast plateau, probably between seven hundred thousand and a million square miles in extent, a large proportion of it—possibly half—over fifteen thousand feet in height. It is thus the most extensive region of such an elevation on the planet. Tibet is a land of rounded hills and great plains, presumably the result of long erosion in an earlier geological era. It contains many lakes, the chief of them being the Kokonor, with a surface of probably something less than two thousand square miles. Numbers of the lakes are salt, and most of them show marked signs of shrinkage. The rainfall apparently was once much greater than now—although this is disputed. On the northern borders of Tibet rise the K'un Lun and the connecting Altyn Tagh and Nan Shan ranges, some of whose peaks soar to heights of twenty thousand feet or more and are crowned by snow fields and glaciers. They form the natural boundary between Tibet and Kansu and the New Dominion. To the south of Tibet rise the Himalayas, the loftiest mountain range on the earth, and, geologically speaking, comparatively young. In deep canyons to the north of the Himalayas and in the eastern portions of Tibet flow the upper waters of the chief rivers of Northern India, Burma, Siam, Indo-China, and China. High mountains border the Tibetan plateau on the east, separating that region from China proper, notably from Szechwan. Politically, the portions of Tibet next to India are now virtually independent of China, and along the borders of China, in the new provinces (formerly the special administrative districts) of Kokonor (or Ch'ing Hai) and Hsi K'ang, largely carved out of what was once Tibet, Chinese authority is in many places very shadowy.

THE OUTLYING SECTIONS: THE NEW DOMINION

The New Dominion (Sinkiang), so called because it was the last of the major outlying districts to be brought into the Manchu Empire, but also known as Chinese or Eastern Turkestan, in average elevation is decidedly lower than Tibet. In contrast with the high plateau to the south, much of it seems to the traveller a great depression in the earth's crust. One oasis, indeed, Turfan, is slightly below the level of the sea. The New Dominion is made up of two main divisions separated by a range of mountains, the T'ien Shan. That south of the T'ien Shan is geographically an extension of the Gobi Desert. Most of it constitutes a huge basin drained by the Tarim River eastward into a marshy lake, the Lob Nor. In many places once extensive oases supporting prosperous populations have become desert in historic times, but whether this indicates progressive desiccation is still debated by travellers and experts on climate. To the north of the T'ien Shan stretch more desert and semi-desert plains and valleys (not as forbidding as the Tarim basin) known politically as Ili or Kuldja and Zungaria. To the west and northwest, mountains form a natural boundary between the New Dominion and Central Asia.

Across Sinkiang have run for untold centuries overland trade routes between China and the outside world. One main route follows the northern side of the Tarim basin to such cities as Kashgar and Yarkand, at the eastern foot of the Pamirs—the barrier between China and India and the trans-Caspian regions. Another leads north of the T'ien Shan to Kuldja, near the head of the Ili River, and thence down the valley of the Ili to the steppes east of the Aral Sea.

THE OUTLYING SECTIONS: MONGOLIA

To the north of China proper and to the north and east of the New Dominion lies Mongolia. Much of Mongolia is a tableland of from three to five thousand feet elevation. The area immediately north of the Eighteen Provinces—the so-called "Inner Mongolia" and divided politically into the new provinces (formerly the special administrative districts) Jehol, Chahar, Suiyüan, and Ninghsia—is much of it only semi-arid, a transitional region between the lands to the south and the Gobi. The Gobi and the adjacent Ordos are for the most part rocky, gravelly, and sandy wastes traversed by low mountains and hills. To the north and west steppes, mountains, and valleys occupy much of what is called Outer Mongolia. A good deal of the North and West possesses grazing land and parts of it are fairly well watered by rivers. The higher mountains in the Northwest are forested.

THE OUTLYING SECTIONS: MANCHURIA

Manchuria, the most easterly of the outlying portions of China, is also the best endowed for human habitation. Divided into the three provinces of Liaoning (also called Fengtien and Shengking), Kirin, and Heilungchiang, it is often known as the "Three Eastern Provinces." Since, however, a portion of Eastern Inner Mongolia, notably the province of Jehol, is sometimes included, many Chinese prefer to denominate Manchuria simply as "The Eastern Provinces."

To the west Manchuria is bounded by Mongolia, from which it is separated by the escarpment which ascends to the Mongolian plateau and which is crowned by the Hsinganling (Khingan) mountains—a range which averages about four thousand feet in height. To the north rise more mountains and, just north of them, the Amur River (or the Heilungchiang) forms a convenient boundary. On the east mountains separate Manchuria from the valley of the Ussuri and the Japan Sea. To the south the gulf of Chihli and the Yellow Sea afford access to the Pacific. The only easy land route into China proper lies along the coast where spurs reaching out from the hills which divide the province of Hopei (Chihli) from Mongolia recede only far enough to allow a narrow pass. Manchuria, therefore, has usually been distinct politically from the rest of China—not so much so, however, but that it has repeatedly been a part of the Empire. In spite of the Japanese occupation and the Japanese-supported state of Manchoukuo, it is still accounted by the Chinese as legitimately as much a part of their country as China proper.

Extensive plains, valleys, and low hills largely make up the central portion of Manchuria. Several rivers furnish the drainage, chief among them the Liao, running southward, and the Sungari, with its leading tributary, the Nonni, running northeastward into the Amur. The area of level, arable land in Central Manchuria probably totals somewhat less than in the North China plain. East of the mouth of the Liao juts the Liaotung Peninsula, geologically a continuation of the mountains of Shantung. To the east of the Liaotung Peninsula, in turn, flows the Yalu River, the natural boundary between Manchuria and the Korean peninsula. Korea, as we shall see, has in whole or in part been at various times politically a dependency of China.

The valleys and plains of Manchuria are fertile and fairly well watered. Forests cover many of the mountains, and deposits of minerals, notably coal, and some gold tempt the miner. Rigorous winters and hot summers make the climate one of extremes. Agriculture prospers. Until late in the last century the land was sparsely settled, but for the two decades or so before the Japanese *coup d'état* of 1931 Chinese were pouring in at the rate of hundreds of thousands a year. Koreans, seeking escape from the economic pressure in their native land, have been crossing the borders by the tens of thousands. Thousands of Japanese are to be found, principally as merchants, officials, and soldiers. While some regions in Manchuria now display familiar and distressing signs of overcrowding, large portions of it remain relatively undeveloped and constitute a land of opportunity.

LANDS TO THE SOUTH

To the south of China proper lie other lands, to-day not claimed by the Chinese but formerly from time to time politically subordinate to the Empire.

The valleys of the Irrawaddy and the Salween, streams which rise in the mountains and highlands in the southeastern portion of the Tibetan *massif* and flow southward into the Bay of Bengal, are politically known as Burma. Roads from Yünnan penetrate them, and, until the latter part of the nineteenth century, for many decades Burma made periodical gifts to Peking which the Chinese regarded as tribute. Siam, included principally in the valley of the Menam, is so separated from China by mountains that only infrequently and vaguely was it politically an appendage of the Middle Kingdom.

What we now call French Indo-China comprises several states, the northern ones of which have long oscillated between political independence of and subjection to China. The chief districts are Tongking (the heart of which is the delta and valley of the Red River, a stream which flows southeastward from the Yünnan table-land), Annam (the seacoast and mountains south of Tongking), Laos (the mountains and hills and the upper part of the valley of the Mekong to the west of Annam) and Cambodia and Cochin-China (on the fertile delta and lower portion of the

Mekong River, a stream which, like the Yangtze, the Salween, and the Irrawaddy, rises in the great mountains and plateaus to the west of China proper). The boundaries and political relations of Tongking, Annam, Laos, Cambodia, and Cochin-China have been subject to many changes. The French and the Japanese have been only the latest of many conquering invaders. As might be expected, the region shows the effect of Chinese and Indian cultural influences, the Chinese strain being strongest toward the north.

The Island of Formosa, just southeast of the China coast, must also be mentioned. Conquered and made a part of the Chinese Empire in the seventeenth century, and to-day predominantly Chinese in population, in 1895 it was ceded to Japan.

EFFECTS ON THE CHINESE OF THEIR ENVIRONMENT: CHINA PROPER

From the foregoing description of the face and climate of China the effects of geographic environment upon the Chinese must be at least partially apparent.

In the first place, China proper is fitted by nature to be the home of a great, fairly unified culture. It possesses extensive, fertile valleys. It displays a marked diversity and a rich supply of plants, many of them useful for food, clothing, and shelter. Its fauna shows variety and a large degree of serviceability to man. Its mineral resources suffice for all the more pressing needs of civilization—at least before the recent development of industrialism. Except for the Northwest, Szechwan, and the Southwest, the internal barriers of hills do not seriously discourage the spread of peoples and extensive intercommunication. Along the south coast the hills offer something of an obstacle, enough to account for the differences in language between that region and the North, but not enough to prevent political and cultural unity with the rest of the country. Navigable streams, particularly those of the Yangtze system, penetrate most of the land and facilitate internal commerce. China proper is one of the regions of the globe fitted to be the seat of a great empire.

Possessing a home so richly endowed with the physical bases of civilization, as a rule the Chinese have been economically all but self-sufficient. The country is so large that they have had their energies chiefly engrossed in occupying, developing, and defending it. With some marked exceptions, only recently have they begun to look outside for an outlet for their surplus population. Not until the seventeenth and eighteenth centuries did the Chinese go in numbers to Formosa and not until the twentieth did they begin to flood Manchuria.

Certain qualifications, due partly to the natural features of the country, must be noted. Natural obstacles to an integrated country are fully as great as in Western Europe, where they have helped to give rise to separate nations. India, too, with no more formidable internal barriers presents an almost infinite diversity and never until the British forced it on them did all its inhabitants submit to one imperial rule. But for their political genius and the remarkable system of government which they devised, a similar fate might have overtaken the Chinese. Cultural and political unity, while not forbidden by the natural environment, must be ascribed chiefly to the Chinese themselves.

Even with their extraordinarily successful machinery of empire, the Chinese have frequently suffered from temporary divisions which have arisen in part from topography. At best their unity, while marked, is by no means complete. Barriers of hills and of mountains outside the great alluvial plains form obstacles to intercommunication, favor variations in culture, and make difficult the achievement of political empire. It was centuries before the civilized dwellers in the plains of North China could conquer and assimilate their neighbors in the adjoining highlands. In North China commerce and movements of troops must be mostly overland rather than by streams, for the lower course of the Yellow River is obstructed by sediment, and the upper course—above the juncture of the Wei—is rendered difficult by rapids. Much of the Yangtze, that natural artery of communication, is precarious for traffic, as we have seen, because of the rapids through the hills which separate its lower reaches from the province of Szechwan, and above the gorges the rate of fall renders navigation difficult. The hills and mountains along the south coast and in the Southwest have made these regions somewhat hard to hold and have favored rebellions. Even yet the Chinese have not fully occupied the hills in the Southwest, but for the most part have pushed their non-Chinese neighbors only out of the valleys.

The very size of the country militates against unity. Nowhere else has any group of mankind succeeded for so long a time as have the Chinese in holding together under a single rule so large a section of the earth. The Roman and Spanish empires did not endure for as many centuries. The extensive domains ruled by the Persians, Alexander, the Arabs, the Mongols, and the Turks broke apart, at most after a few hundred years. China, in spite of periodic internal disruption and occasional conquests by foreigners, has continued. Of the modern empires, with the railroad, the steamship, and the telegraph to tie them together, only five— the British, the Russian, the French, the American, and the Brazilian—surpass it in area, and only one, the British, is more populous. Europe west of Russia, an area not far from the size of China proper, has never been politically unified and is split into many tongues and states. It is not surprising, therefore, that provincial feeling runs high, that much more power has been wielded by local and sectional and provincial governments, the clan, and the guild than in some highly centralized modern states, and that from time to time the country has been politically divided.

Moreover, variations in climate and in physical surroundings favor a certain diversity in culture and in national characteristics. Some of these have been stated earlier. It must be added that the Chinese of the North are more stolid and conservative than those of the South. This is probably due in part to a difference in blood, but it may also be ascribed to the famines which, because of drought and flood, have periodically devastated the North. The phlegmatic seem better adapted to surviving times of prolonged dearth, and the highly strung and energetic who do not perish apparently are inclined to migrate to regions of less forbidding climate. Through the centuries, therefore, this selective process may well have produced a variation in type. Differences in the staple grains are accompanied by divergences in tillage. Domestic animals vary, donkeys and mules being characteristic of the North and the water buffalo of the Yangtze Valley and the South. Probably allied to this is the fact that in the North freight is moved partly by carts, and elsewhere by river, canal, and wheelbarrow, and that in the North roads and streets are broad and adapted to the wagon, the cart, and horses and that in the South even the highways are narrow tracks between rice fields or over the hills, suited only to the wheelbarrow, the sedan chair, the burden-carrying coolie, or, occasionally, the donkey. Then, too, the Yangtze Valley and the South, with mist-crowned hills and mountains and with abundant verdure, in contrast to the semi-arid and brown North, may well have stimulated differences in the expression of the æsthetic feelings, both in the painter and the poet.

Still again, China's natural resources, while heretofore ample for almost all her needs, have ceased, or are about to cease, to be so. Her population has caught up with and congested her arable lands, fertile and extensive though these are. Certainly within the last two or three centuries it has begun to spill over into adjoining regions. Improvement in agricultural methods and scientific seed selection may, as we shall see in a later chapter, enable the Chinese to utilize types of lands, very extensive, which now produce little, and to increase the yield from land now cultivated. In Manchuria and possibly in Inner Mongolia some virgin soil remains. Much of this, however must be classed as marginal—tillable in seasons of more than average rainfall, but failing to yield a paying crop when the precipitation does not rise above its normal median. A stable and efficient government and improved methods of transportation would afford much relief from the pressure of population. These possible solutions, however, at best offer merely a reprieve. At the rate of increase maintained under the comparative peace and prosperity of the latter part of the seventeenth and of the eighteenth century, the leeway afforded by them would soon be taken up. Increasing famines, therefore, and a further accentuation of the present grinding poverty can be avoided only by one or more of three expedients—emigration on a scale such as the world has never seen, an extensive industrialization of the country and the exchange of the products of factories for foodstuffs, or a drastic restriction in the birth rate. Other nations have already restricted Chinese immigration to most of the more salubrious, relatively unoccupied areas of the globe, such as the United States, Canada, and Australia, and are likely to continue to do so—if they can. China does not possess sufficient resources of coal and iron to sustain an industrial development as extensive as that in the United States and in Western

Europe—although in some sections water power may partially overcome this handicap. Industry, moreover, does not permanently solve the population problem: witness Great Britain and Japan. The structure of Chinese social and religious life has so far encouraged rather than discouraged a high birth rate. It seems obvious, therefore, that the limit of China's natural resources is in sight, and that only a revolution in the Chinese family system and ethical ideals, with widespread teaching and practice of birth control, can ward off disaster.

EFFECTS ON THE CHINESE OF THEIR ENVIRONMENT: THE OUTLYING SECTIONS

When the effect of China proper upon the Chinese people has been appraised, only part of the story has been told. It still remains to recount the influence upon them of the outlying territories.

First of all, these regions have, as we have seen, a marked effect upon the climate of China proper. The heating of the great arid land masses to the north in the summer and the cooling of them in the winter help to determine the direction of China's winds and with them the regularity or irregularity of the rainfall. Upon rainfall, of course, China's food supply largely depends.

Then, too, these territories, especially Tibet (including the new provinces carved from it), are the sources of China's main rivers.

In the next place, the outlying territories have been the origin of repeated invasions. What are now Mongolia and Sinkiang are, as we have seen, arid or semi-arid, and except for occasional oases their populations have, perforce, been chiefly limited for their livelihood to the herds which pasture on the grasses nourished by the scanty and uncertain rainfall. These peoples, accordingly, have been nomadic or semi-nomadic, with the hardiness and capacity for quick movements and great sudden physical exertion which such a manner of life begets. They have also, as is the habit of such peoples, been warlike. Moreover, they have looked with envy upon the fertile and prosperous valleys toward the east and south and repeatedly have attempted to force their way into them. When a series of unusually dry years diminished the pastures, these invasions appear to have been particularly marked, but they have occurred at many other times.

Invasions from Mongolia and Sinkiang have been encouraged by the possibility of access to China proper from these regions. From the Mongolian plateau several passes lead down into the plains and valleys of China. Sinkiang is comparatively low, and is provided, in the Tarim basin and oases to the eastward and in the valleys to the north of the T'ien Shan, with natural highways, relatively unimpeded by mountains, into the valley of the Yellow River. It has, accordingly, been both an avenue and a source of invasions.

Manchuria, too, has been a menace. While its valleys are fertile and its climate much more favorable to civilization than that of Mongolia, it was much slower—possibly because of its rigorous winters and perhaps for other geographic reasons—to develop a civilization than was the Yellow River Valley. Its peoples, therefore, have been lured by the charm of the lands to the south, and the narrow route along the seashore has resounded again and again with the tramp of marching armies—from early historic times down into the most recent years.

There have been times, moreover, although less frequently, when the Tibetans have invaded China. For centuries border struggles between Chinese and Tibetans have been a fairly constant feature of Chinese history.

The Chinese, therefore, have had almost constantly to be on their guard against their neighbors to the north and west. Until the nineteenth century the security of their northern frontiers loomed as their chief foreign problem. This problem they handled in a variety of ways—partly by attempting to play off one "barbarian" tribe against another (a policy which they later tried with Occidental peoples, and with some success), partly by garrisons reënforced by extensive fortifications, often by treaties with potential invaders, and occasionally by carrying the war into the enemies' territories and holding them in subjection. This last policy was particularly effective under the Manchus.

Fortunately for the Chinese, the peoples to the north have not always been able to form effective coalitions. By their nomadic manner of life they are condemned to warring tribal divisions. Repeatedly, however, a line of rulers has welded into a fighting force a sufficient number of them to seize part or all of the coveted prize to the south. At varying intervals, therefore—

either because of internal weakness in the Empire or because of the generalship of the invaders—all defensive measures have broken down and China proper, particularly the North, has been overrun. Again and again peoples from the north have set up dynasties which have ruled part or all of China. We shall run across the more prominent of them in succeeding chapters— several of them in the third, fourth, fifth, and sixth centuries of the Christian era, the Liao, the Chin, and the Hsia in the eleventh, twelfth, and thirteenth centuries, then the Mongols, and finally the Manchus. In some respects the Russians fall in this same succession, for they, too, are from the north and have attempted to absorb part of China.

Of the main outlying territories, only the lands to the south— in the present Burma and Indo-China—have never been a major threat. The distances from them to the chief centers of Chinese civilization have been too great or the natural barriers too formidable to permit of conquest. These lands, indeed, possibly because of their tropical climate, have been mastered by the Chinese rather than the Chinese from them.

The land boundaries of China have not only influenced climate, given rise to the main rivers of the country, and been the source of repeated invasions, but they have also proved an obstacle (although by no means an insuperable one) to intimate contacts with other civilized portions of the globe. The other leading centers of early cultures—the valleys of Northern India, the highlands of Persia, the Tigris-Euphrates Valley, the Nile Valley, and the basin of the Mediterranean—were separated from the valleys of the Huang Ho and the Yangtze by vast distances and barriers of mountains, deserts, and seas. Some intercourse there was. Archeology, indeed, more and more leads us to believe that we formerly underestimated both its quantity and its influence. The further research proceeds, the more we are impressed with the contributions of the Chinese to the peoples to the west of them, especially in Central Asia, and of these peoples to the Chinese. Trade was maintained overland, most of it by the natural routes across Sinkiang. In the Tarim basin lived cultured peoples who acted as intermediaries between China and the West. Commerce was carried on with lands to the south and west by way of the sea through the ports of South China, but distances proved so great and until the last century the means of navigation remained so crude, that water-borne foreign trade was not extensive. Through all the centuries, however, while ideas filtered in from the outside world, and occasionally political conditions made possible a somewhat extensive intercourse, the Chinese, compared with most other civilized peoples, have been isolated.

Isolation probably contributed toward the formation of a number of the familiar characteristics of the Chinese. To it may partly be ascribed their intense national pride. All other civilizations with which the Chinese had close contacts were derived from themselves and, they thought, were inferior to theirs. They were the source of the culture of most of their neighbors, but although they repeatedly profited by contributions from abroad, with the exception of Buddhism they thought of themselves as having received but little. Theirs was the Middle Kingdom and all other peoples were barbarous. Even when conquered, they gave their culture to their rulers and eventually either absorbed them or drove them out. Their land was large, and during most of their recorded history was under one administration. So far as they knew, except for reports, often vague, of other lands to the west, theirs was the mightiest realm on earth. Their experience with peoples on their borders and especially with other invaders helps to account for the fact that when Western nations forced their way into the country the Chinese long regarded them as simply a new group of barbarians and, while willing to learn a few details from them, for many years did not dream that the entire structure of Chinese culture would need to be recast. Lack of intimate relations with other great civilized states, too, helped to breed in the Chinese a reluctance to regard themselves as one of a family of nations or to treat with Occidental powers on the basis of equality. This hereditary attitude of superiority has been outraged by the encroachments of foreigners in the nineteenth and twentieth centuries and may account in part for the intense impatience with treaties derogatory to Chinese sovereignty.

So far we have had little to say of the effect of the ocean. However, this has been quite as important as that of the land boundaries. The sea, as we have seen, is the source of the moisture-laden winds that bring China's rains. Until the last century, moreover, the ocean was even more effective in isolating

China than were the great land masses to the north and west. To the east the only civilized peoples with whom commerce was possible were the Koreans and Japanese. Culturally both of these borrowed from rather than contributed to the Middle Kingdom. The Pacific coast of North America was too far distant to admit of much intercourse by the small ships of the earlier centuries, and until the nineteenth century was sparsely peopled and that mostly by savages. In Southeastern Asia were civilized lands, but the nearest had derived much of their culture from China and so had little to give her. India, the closest great cultural center markedly different from China, was almost as far and as difficult of access by sea as by land. No invasions were to be feared from the ocean, except by pirates, who, while often annoying, never seriously threatened a conquest of the country.

The Chinese were not greatly tempted to become a seafaring people. Until the nineteenth century their own vast land engrossed, as we have said, almost all their energies. North of the Yangtze, where were long the chief centers of civilization, the proportion of coast line to area is small, the connections (by way of the silt-laden Yellow River) between the interior and the sea are poor, and until recently there was scanty reward in commerce with neighboring islands and coasts. The South, supplied with much better harbors, was not fully incorporated into the Empire until the seventh and eighth centuries of the Christian era and even then remained on the periphery of national consciousness. From the South, to be sure, merchants ventured abroad, sometimes to fairly distant parts, and, later, partly because of limited arable land, overseas emigration from that region began. Not until the nineteenth century, however, did either have a marked effect upon the nation as a whole. China faced north and west, and not south and east.

With the nineteenth century began a great change. The sea, instead of being a barrier and a defense, became a highway and a source of danger. The Occidental, developing larger and faster ships than had ever been known, arrived in force and insisted upon being admitted. Danger still lurked on the north, for an aggressive Russia now threatened, but it had also appeared from the south and the east. The Westerner had penetrated the natural barriers of China, and from a totally unexpected direction. Japan, reorganized on Occidental models, has become a major menace. The result has been disorganization and revolution. China, accustomed to think of herself as an empire, which although occasionally overrun by barbarians or divided was yet without a peer, was now compelled to deal with other nations as equals. Always heretofore the dispenser and seldom the conscious receiver of culture, she now found the structure of her civilization antiquated and was faced with the unpleasant necessity of discarding part of it and thoroughly renovating the rest.

BIBLIOGRAPHY

The best books entirely or chiefly devoted to the geography of China are G. B. Cressey, *China's Geographic Foundations* (New York, 1934); A. Hermann, *Historical and Commercial Atlas of China* (Cambridge, 1935); G. M. H. Playfair, *The Cities and Towns of China* (Shanghai, 1910); L. Richard, *Comprehensive Geography of the Chinese Empire and Dependencies*, translated into English, revised and enlarged by M. Kennelly, S.J. (Shanghai, 1908); L. H. D. Buxton, *China, the Land and the People* (Oxford, 1929); Jules Sion, *Asie des Moussons* (Paris, 1928–1929, Vol. 9 of *Géographie Universelle*); L. D. Stamp, *Asia. An Economic and Regional Geography* (New York, 1929); Julean Arnold, *China, An Industrial and Commercial Handbook* (Washington, 1926); W. H. Mallory, *China: Land of Famine* (New York, 1926); and Marshall Broomhall, *The Chinese Empire* (London, 1907). Three volumes by Ellsworth Huntington, *West of the Pacific* (New York, 1925), *The Character of Races* (New York, 1924), and *The Pulse of Asia* (New York, 1907), contain much interesting material and many thought-provoking comments. G. B. Cressey, *Asia's Lands and Peoples* (New York, 1944), pp. 35–169, contains an excellent survey of China with good bibliographies.

On the mineral resources the best popular treatise is H. Foster Bain, *Ores and Industry in the Far East* (New York, 1933). See also Wilfred Smith, *A Geographical Study of Coal and Iron in China* (London, 1926); *China Year Book*, 1928, pp. 66–106; and J. W. Frey, *Economic Significance of the Mineral Wealth of China* (*Annals of the American Academy of Political and Social Science*, Nov., 1930, Vol. 152, pp. 116–126). On geology see also the publications of the Geological Survey of China; Geological Society of China, *Bulletin* (Peking, 1922 *et seq.*); Ferdinand von Richthofen, *China, Ergebnisse eigener Reisen und darauf gegründeter Studien* (5 vols., Berlin, 1877–1912); F. von Richthofen, *Tagebücher aus China* (2 vols., Berlin, 1907) (Although still largely quoted, and notable for his pioneer work, Richthofen is now largely out of date and displaced by later studies.); Carnegie Institution of Washington, *Research in China* (3 vols., Washington, 1907–1913); R. Pumpelly, *Geological Researches in China, Mongolia and Japan during the Years 1862–1865* (Washington, 1866); J. Gunner Andersson, *Den Gula Jordens Barns* (Stockholm, 1933).

On rainfall see L. Froe, *La Pluie en Chine* (Shanghai, 1912). On a related subject see Yao Shan-yu, *The Chronological and Seasonal Distribution of Floods and Droughts in Chinese History, 206 B.C.–A.D. 1911* (*Harvard Journal of Asiatic Studies,* Vol. 6, 273–312), and Yao Shan-yu, *The Geographical Distribution of Floods and Droughts in Chinese History* (*The Far Eastern Quarterly,* Vol. 2, pp. 357–378).

On the flora of China there are useful summaries in S. Couling, *Encyclopædia Sinica* (London, 1917), pp. 55–58, and in Ernest H. Wilson, *China, Mother of Gardens* (Boston, 1929). A bibliography can be found in H. Cordier, *Bibliotheca Sinica*.

On the outlying dependencies consult Fernand Grenard, *La Haute Asie* (Paris, 1929, Vol. 8 of *Géographie Universelle*), V. Karamysher, *Mongolia and Western China: Social and Economic Study* (Tientsin, 1925) and Owen Lattimore, *Inner Asian Frontiers of China* (Oxford University Press, 1940). On Tibet see Sir Charles Bell, *Tibet. Past and Present* (Oxford, 1924). On Sinkiang see Owen Lattimore, *The Desert Road to Turkestan* (London, 1928) and M. R. Norins, *Gateway to Asia: Sinkiang* (New York, 1944). On Manchuria see Owen Lattimore, *Manchuria, Cradle of Conflict* (New York, 1932). On Mongolia, see Owen Lattimore, *The Desert Road to Turkestan* (London, 1928), Roy Chapman Andrews, *Across Mongolian Plains* (London, 1921), and Sven A. Hedin, *Across the Gobi Desert* (London, 1931).

CHAPTER II

THE BEGINNINGS OF CHINESE CIVILIZATION
(TO B.C. 221)

ORIGIN OF THE CHINESE

THE beginnings of the Chinese, like those of other ancient peoples, are shrouded in obscurity. Chinese literature, although voluminous during most of the past twenty-three or twenty-four centuries, gives us little incontestable information concerning the origins of the people and their culture. What many modern scholars hold to be the earliest written documents that have come down to us—contained chiefly in the collection known as the *Shih Ching*, or Classic of Poetry, and in portions of the *Shu Ching*, or Classic of History [1]—show a culture which was far from primitive and was presumably the result of centuries of development. Within the last few years, archeology has unearthed important information, but as yet this is too fragmentary to be made the basis for much more than interesting conjectures. Future discoveries may revolutionize present theories. Some scholars have sought light in an analysis of the primitive Chinese written characters, or in deductions from the nature of the earliest known civilization. The Chinese myths akin to those by which other peoples have sought to account for the existence of the universe and of mankind, and for the origin of themselves and of their culture, probably complicate rather than simplify the confusion. Until very recently Chinese scholars—so deeply concerned with most other periods of their history—were but little interested in the question of beginnings. It has been Western scholars of the past two and a half centuries and Chinese scholars of the present century who have been the most exercised by it.

The theories advanced by the Occidental savants have been

---

[1] Even the earliest sections of the *Shu Ching* are now thought by many scholars not to be so ancient as the oldest poems of the *Shih Ching*.

many and ingenious. An early hypothesis long favored in certain quarters was that Chinese civilization owed its beginnings to Egypt. This has faded into the background and during the past generation or more the majority of Western students who have sought an answer to the riddle have looked to the overland routes which debouch in what is now known as Kansu and Shensi for the paths by which the Chinese and their culture first entered the territory which is now theirs. Terrien de Lacouperie stoutly advocated an early migration from Babylonia. The French sinologist Biot suggested that China was inhabited initially by savages, and that into these moved a black-haired race from the Northwest. Another scholar has professed to find in Sumerian the prototype of the system of Chinese writing. Others are inclined to postulate in ancient cultures in Central Asia the common birthplace of the civilizations of the Tigris-Euphrates Valley and of the Chinese. Another sees the peoples of the steppes and deserts of Central Asia both as transmitters of culture from Mesopotamia and other fertile valleys and as originators. He attempts to give dates for some of the irruptions of these peoples into the North China plain. Still other sinologists maintain that while it may not be necessary to look westward for all of early Chinese culture, some influences certainly entered from that direction. One scholar has argued for the European origin of the earliest Chinese civilization. Another has professed to see in the primitive culture several elements from the outside—from the West, the Northwest, and the Northeast. Still another has conjectured that rice culture and especially the use of the water buffalo entered from India. There is an able contestant for the southern origin of Chinese culture. A somewhat similar assertion is that the earliest Chinese we know are the northernmost fringes of a racial and cultural group whose western representatives are the Tibeto-Burman peoples of Tibet, Szechwan, Yünnan, and Burma, and whose central and southern representatives are the tribes which survive in the hills of Central and South China and in Indo-China. A favorite hypothesis of numbers of scholars is that there were successive waves of migration from the North and Northwest, each partly subjugating and assimilating its predecessors and partly driving them southward, and that we must look to the extreme South for the best traces discernible to-day of the most primitive inhabitants of China.

The only safe conclusion is that the facts now at our disposal form an untrustworthy guide to more than tentative opinions.

While it is true that as yet our knowledge is insufficient to frame a theory of the beginnings of the Chinese and their culture which will meet with the unanimous assent of informed scholars, certain well-established facts even now at our disposal will inevitably enter into the completed picture.

First of all, we know that when the Chinese are first discerned fairly clearly through their earliest written records they were an agricultural folk living on the North China plain and in the lower part of the valley of the Wei, slowly extending their boundaries at the expense of peoples who lived on the hills and plateaus—and even on the plains—about them and whom they regarded as barbarians. Like the oldest civilizations in the West of which history apprizes us, those of Egypt and Babylonia, and also like early civilization in Northwest India, that of China first emerges into the dim light of pre-history in a fertile river valley. In early historic times the Yellow River emptied north of the Shantung promontory. The Hopei plain was largely a delta, traversed by a number of streams, and the region may well have been less arid than it is to-day and more inviting to agriculture. Much of North China was covered with loess, great areas of which appear not to have been heavily forested, and so could, with relative ease, be reduced to cultivation.

Rich finds of inscribed bones give early forms of the Chinese written character and corroborate about three-fourths of the names of the rulers of the shadowy Shang dynasty—the second in traditional Chinese history—that have come down to us in the ancient books. Recent excavations have added much knowledge of the Shang culture and show it to have been advanced.

Japanese discoveries in Eastern Mongolia, South Manchuria, and the Korean-Manchurian border of neolithic remains probably point to early, non-Chinese culture or cultures in these regions. Implements of neolithic man have been found in many parts of China proper.

Recently, moreover, archeology has revealed extensive evidences of a culture that was probably on the border line between the stone and the bronze age—chalcolithic, as it has been dubbed. The most startling of the discoveries are in the North. In a cave in Southern Manchuria, on the site in Honan of what seems to have been an extensive village, in Kansu near Lanchowfu, and as far west as Kokonor, have been disclosed relics of what appear to be different stages of the same culture (sometimes called—especially that in Honan—by the name Yang Shao). Some of the objects are probably (although not certainly) the prototypes of implements and utensils still manufactured and in common use in China. Most of the skeletal remains of the Yang Shao culture that have been uncovered seem to be of the same stock as that of the Chinese who to-day inhabit the region. The evidence points, therefore, to some racial and cultural continuity between that age and our own. Whether any of this culture was indigenous is uncertain. We are not even sure that it is an early stage of historical Chinese civilization. Tracing a line of descent has been difficult. The latest stages of Yang Shao culture may have persisted into the third dynasty, the Chou. It seems clear that a great gulf separated this Yang Shao civilization from that of the Shang, the second of the traditional dynasties. There was also a hard, black pottery culture. Many lived in villages of partly subterranean dwellings which were enclosed by earthen walls. Millet, possibly derived from India, was the most common grain. There were horses, pigs, dogs, sheep, and cattle. The painted pottery culture seems to have antedated that of the black pottery. The bronze culture of the Shang began later than either. Sericulture was present in neolithic times and continued into the Shang.

A still earlier link in the chain is a few traces of paleolithic man, chiefly in Shensi and Mongolia. Between the paleolithic and the late stone or early bronze age no connecting stage has been found, and since some of the paleolithic relics are beneath a heavy mantle of loess the gap in time is probably very considerable. We do not know whether the paleolithic remains were left by the ancestors of the present Chinese, by a people whom the Chinese conquered or displaced, or by stocks which disappeared long before the ancestors of the Chinese entered North China. There seems to be some similarity between the products of paleolithic man in China and those in other parts of Europe and Asia—possibly indicating cultural connection.

The problem of origins is further complicated by the discovery, in recent years, near Peking, of bones (including skulls) of a still earlier type of man, one of the most primitive known, and, connected with them, of what seem to be artifacts and perhaps traces of the use of fire.

Another set of data to add to our fragmentary picture is what has been disclosed in Central Asia of a very early culture, probably greatly antedating anything of a similar grade yet found in China, and from which migrations into China, or at least cultural contributions through commerce, may have come. A possible cause of population movements may have been a decline in rainfall accompanying the retreat of the last ice sheet—perhaps twelve to twenty thousand years ago.

We also know of the early civilization of city-dwellers in the Tigris-Euphrates Valley and of an urban culture in Northwest India, probably as far back as the fourth millennium B.C. These centers seem older than anything of so high a type which has yet been found in China, and it is within the range of possibility that some impulse from them made itself felt in the North China plain.

One other group of facts is the increasingly accumulating evidence that both in historic and in prehistoric times transfers of culture occurred—partly through migrations of peoples—over the vast plains which cover much of the surface of Central and Western Asia and Eastern and Western Europe.

In the light of all these evidences, it is not strange that the majority of scholars who have recently dealt with the subject have looked westward for a clue to the sources of the Chinese and their civilization. That some early influences entered from the West appears to be well established. It is not yet clearly demonstrated whether these came through trade or the migrations of peoples or both. Neither is it known just how potent these were in shaping the civilization of historic times. It is to be hoped that archeology will later have more to tell us.

CHINESE MYTHS AND LEGENDS OF THE BEGINNINGS OF HISTORY

While the oldest records do not attempt to trace to their beginnings either the Chinese race or mankind as a whole, from time to time popular fancy has essayed to do so, with the result that we possess many tales bristling with mythical heroes. Although quite undependable as history, these stories are of importance, partly because they appear again and again in literature, mythology, and religion, and partly because by some Chinese and Westerners the more prominent figures are seriously taken as actual personages. For example, the Yellow Emperor occupies a prominent place in Taoism, and at least one recent attempt has been made to begin Chinese chronology with his accession. It is just possible, moreover, that some of the stories will eventually be found to have a basis in actual fact. They must, therefore, be mentioned.

As is natural with myths, particularly when, like these, they have varying origins, differing accounts and attempts at chronology exist. Only the chief personages that appear in one or more Chinese histories deserve mention. P'an Ku is frequently described as separating the heavens and the earth, and as forming the sun, the moon, and plants and animals. There are, however, several versions of his myth. Following him some accounts say that there appeared twelve or thirteen Celestial Sovereigns (*T'ien Huang*), all brothers, each of whom reigned 18,000 years, eleven Terrestrial Sovereigns (*Ti Huang*), again brothers, each of whom also ruled 18,000 years, and then nine Human Sovereigns (*Jên Huang*), once more brothers, who reigned a total of 45,600 years. We hear also of Yu Ch'ao, who is reputed to have taught men to build houses; of Sui Jên, who is said to have devised a way of producing fire by boring one piece of wood with another; of Fu Hsi, who is reported to have taught his people to fish with nets and rear domestic animals, to have devised musical instruments, to have substituted for writing by knots in strings the pictograms and ideograms which form the basis of the present system of characters, and to have invented the eight trigrams—*pa kua*—later used in divination. To Nü Kua—often associated closely with Fu Hsi—is attributed the regulation of marriage. Shên Nung, the "Divine Husbandman," is reported to have taught the people agriculture and to have been the father of medicine. Huang Ti (the Yellow Emperor) is credited with fighting successfully against the barbarians, with instituting the system of official historiographers, with inventing bricks for building purposes, with erecting an observatory, with correcting the calendar by adding an intercalary month, and with introducing the chronological system of reckoning by cycles of sixty years. He is also reported to have built a temple to Heaven, to have regulated the division of the land according to the "well-field" (*ching t'ien*) system (to be described a few pages below), to have invented carts drawn by oxen, to have devised several musical instruments, and in many other ways to have advanced civilization. His principal spouse is credited with having taught the people sericulture, so important to the later life of China.

After a number of other rulers is said to have come Yao, a model Emperor, who, in naming his successor, passed over his own son as incompetent and appointed Shun, whom he had selected for his skill and integrity and whom he had tested in various ways. Shun is reported to have performed sacrifices of several kinds, to have introduced uniformity into measures of length, capacity, and weight, to have travelled widely, to have subdued some of the barbarian tribes, to have divided the Empire into twelve provinces, and to have regulated some of the watercourses. Shun, so it is said, like Yao, went outside his family and chose as his successor Yü, who had drained the waters of a great flood which had afflicted the country in the days of Yao. Shun and Yü each is reported to have reigned for a time conjointly with his predecessor and then, the latter abdicating, alone.

Yü is said to have made the crown hereditary in his family and to have founded the first dynasty, that of Hsia. This dynasty, the names of whose rulers tradition essays to give, is reported to have come to an end through the excesses of its last ruler, Chieh, who, falling under the spell of a beautiful but depraved woman, engaged in debauchery and cruelty. An outraged country was at last, so the story goes, led in rebellion against him by T'ang, who, defeating and exiling the tyrant, founded the second dynasty, that of Shang or Yin—Shang being the name by which the members of the ruling house called themselves, and Yin the title by which the dynasty was denominated by the one which succeeded it.

As has been said, it is very uncertain whether these figures have actual history back of them. Some are probably entirely mythical, the creations of folk-lore and of uncritical writers in the attempt to account for the origin of the world and the beginnings of civilization. Some may be heroes or gods taken over from other peoples when they were conquered and assimilated by the Chinese. We are made suspicious by the effort to associate five of the pre-Hsia rulers—the Five Sovereigns (*Wu Ti*)—with the five elements of traditional Chinese physics—earth, wood, metal, fire, and water. The fact that these early figures are called rulers seems to indicate that the stories as we now have them date from a time when men, dwelling in an organized monarchy, read back that form of society into primitive times. Some of the monarchs, such as the rulers of the Hsia, may have arisen out of the efforts of noble families of later times to provide themselves with ancestors. Some, like Yao, Shun, and Yü, lauded as ideals by the Confucianists, may be in part the creation of this school in an endeavor to give to its teachings the sanction of antiquity. Of these three only Yü is mentioned in what is probably the earliest literary record, the *Shih Ching* (Classic of Poetry), and the first certainly authentic documents in which the names of Yao and Shun occur are of the sixth or the fifth century B.C. It has also been suggested that Yao, Shun, and Yü were heroes of peoples in the Yangtze Valley or of districts still farther south, and were taken over into Chinese lore when these regions were incorporated into the expanding Chinese cultural area. Yü himself was either later deified or was originally a deity, and seems to have been identified with a god who was lord of the harvest. P'an Ku is also very late (probably not earlier in our records than the third century B.C.) and may have come from the aborigines. Huang Ti may be to a large extent a pleasant fiction of the early Taoists, devised to give to their contentions the authority of the past. He may have been derived from peoples on the Northwest who were late in entering China, or owe his popularity to his association with thunder and lightning, as a kind of god of these phenomena. Possibly he was not widely known until the third century B.C. In the debates on philosophy which were one of the outstanding features of the centuries shortly preceding the Christian era, each of the rivals would quite naturally seek to bolster its cause by ascribing its tenets to heroic figures of the past, and to assert that in an ancient golden age the practice of its teachings had been attended by prosperity. We are not entirely sure that there ever was such a ruling line as the Hsia. It seems probable, however, that it existed. The strong tradition about it and the fact that some families of historic times claimed descent from it seem to indicate that it corresponds with a stage in Chinese history. The dates which some historians attempt to fix are, of course, untrustworthy. Those often given for the Hsia, B.C. 2205–1766, are obviously quite inaccurate.

THE SHANG OR YIN DYNASTY

In the Shang (or Yin) dynasty we have begun to emerge on fairly firm ground. About three-fourths of the names of the rulers of this line, as given in the older Chinese histories, have been, as we have suggested, confirmed by inscriptions on the "oracle bones," used for divination, discovered in Honan—on the "Waste of Yin," the site of a capital of the dynasty—at the close of the last century. It seems probable that the complete list of Shang monarchs was preserved through the ancestral observances of later rulers of a feudal principality who claimed descent from them. The sequence of the main series of Shang rulers is fairly well established. Accurate dates are still largely unobtainable. The ones often given for the beginning and end of the dynasty are B.C. 1766–1122, but the first of these is undependable. The dynasty probably took its rise sometime between the seventeenth and the thirteenth century before Christ.[2]

The culture of the Shang was already fairly far advanced. So far as we know, it was indigenous and not an importation. There was a system of writing by means of the predecessors of the present characters. Writing was on ivory or bronze, or—for purposes of divination—incised or scratched on bones and tortoise shells. It is possible, too, that slips of bamboo were already, as in later centuries, written on by means of ink or a kind of varnish. Indeed, it is certain that a brush was employed for writing. The shells of the cowry were used for money. Society was based upon agriculture, and was probably aristocratic, with a sharp division between the lower and upper classes. The patriarchal family was prominent, although matriarchy possibly had existed in more remote times. At the head of the state was the *Wang*. The succession went from older to younger brother, or, failing a younger brother, from father to son. The *Wang's* duties were both religious and civil. There were many officials. Religion, as later, was a unifying factor.

There were numerous domesticated animals—among them cattle, the sheep, the pig, the horse, the dog, and fowls. Tigers, bears, and wolves were still to be found, and were hunted. Great solici-

---

[2] Current Chinese scholarship leans toward the sixteenth century, with the seventeenth as a possibility.

tude was displayed for agriculture, the basis of the state's prosperity. Millet was the chief grain. Wheat, probably introduced from abroad, was raised. The wheel was employed in peace and war. There were buildings, some of them fairly large and with wooden pillars.

The army was organized probably, although not certainly, with cavalry, chariots, and infantry. The Shang seem to have introduced the chariot. At times fairly large forces were put in the field. We know of one army of at least five thousand. Iron was not yet in use, but some of the many implements and utensils of bronze have come down to our own day. These, especially the sacrificial vessels and bells and the designs and figures on them, display a skill in casting which has seldom, if ever, been surpassed. They are superior to those of the succeeding dynasty, and their vigor and boldness of conception and execution give indications of genius. There were stone sculptures, some of them vigorous and beautiful.

Religion continued to have a large place in the life of the state. Ancestors were greatly revered. Sacrifices were made to the rivers and the earth. Divination was extensively practiced, the wishes of the spiritual powers being consulted on every important occasion. The stars were supposed to be intimately connected with the affairs of men, and a kind of astronomy existed. Much was made of the calendar. The highest god was Shang Ti. Numerous ceremonies were maintained for ancestors and divinities. Human sacrifices, sometimes on a large scale, appear to have been common.

The territory of the Shang rulers probably included only the valley of the Yellow River from the foot of the Shansi plateau to the mountains of Shantung and to the valley of the Huai—that is to say, parts of the present provinces of Honan, Hopei, and Shantung. It is uncertain whether it reached the coast, although it had at least indirect touch with the sea. Toward the middle or close of the dynasty, colonies probably moved out into the surrounding country, conquering the barbarians and forming settlements in some of the hill country and in the valleys of the Wei and Fên, in modern Shensi and Shansi. This expansion led to the establishment of hereditary principalities on the frontiers—little states ruled by the families who had founded them. Shang culture, moreover, seems to have made its influence felt in the Yangtze Valley.

THE CHOU DYNASTY

The conventional story told of the downfall of the Shang and the establishment of the Chou dynasty resembles that by which tradition accounts for the ruin of the Hsia. It may be, indeed, that the latter is copied from the former. Here, too, an infamous ruler, this time named Chou Hsin, a man of ability, aided and incited by a favorite concubine, turned tyrant and profligate. Many cruelties and excesses are ascribed to the ill-omened pair. Chou Hsin came into conflict with Wên Wang, the ruler of Chou.

Chou, a principality in the valley of the Wei, on the western frontier of the then China, represented the growth of a new, vigorous state—its prowess strengthened by prolonged warfare with the barbarians—as contrasted with the older order. The Chou people seem to have been related to the Chinese already on the North China plain, but racially and culturally somewhat different from them. Wên Wang was, significantly, called the "Chief of the West." The Chou intermarried with the Shang, but the two were clearly not identical. Certainly, too, the coming of the Chou was attended by a fairly sharp break in cultural development. In many ways the civilization of the Chou differed from that of the Shang.

Later historians glorified Wên Wang, representing his character and administration as ideal. It seems probable that he helped to strengthen the Chou domains in preparation for the struggle for supreme power. Chou Hsin was at first successful against Wên Wang. The latter was imprisoned and was released only on the payment of a heavy fine. His son, known to later generations under the title of Wu Wang, finally led in a revolt which overthrew the tyrant. The latter set fire to his palace and perished in the flames, his corpse was decapitated by his rival, the hated concubine was executed by the victors, and Wu Wang set up a new dynasty, the Chou.

The traditional account of the overthrow of the Shang bears the earmarks of partisanship, and very possibly arose from the narrative preserved by the victorious Chou in the ceremonies of their ancestral temple. Chou Hsin may not have been nearly the cruel and dissolute tyrant that our records picture to us. It is clear, however, that the change of dynasty occurred.

The accuracy of the date usually given, B.C. 1122, is in debate, but seems to be confirmed by recent findings. The uncertainty of the chronology for the early ages of Chinese history is aggravated by the existence of at least two varying lists of dates. The Hsia, the Shang, and the Chou form the ancient period of China's history. They are properly classified together as the Three Dynasties.

We have little, if any, certain information about details of events during the initial centuries of the Chou. The ceremonies in honor of the ancestors of the family have transmitted to us names of rulers, but not much else that is dependable. Tradition has attempted to fill the gap and the supposed deeds and character of some of the early rulers of the house, lauded by the Confucian school, are part of the literary and moral heritage of China. Wu Wang, like Wên Wang, was regarded by posterity as a model. He is reported to have established his capital not far from the later Ch'angan (Hsianfu), on that broad lower portion of the valley of the Wei which, as we have seen, is the westernmost of the large fertile plains of the North and so in the region where was the original seat of the Chou power. Wu Wang is represented as having redistributed the principalities which made up the realm, entrusting to the descendants of the Shang a southern portion of their former domains, and to two of his brothers other great sections. The realm ruled over by the early monarchs of the Chou was probably more extensive than that of the Shang. China was growing.

Wu Wang was succeeded by a son, then a mere boy, known to posterity as Ch'êng Wang. During Ch'êng Wang's minority the regent was Wu Wang's brother, Chou Kung ("the Duke of Chou"), who had been of great assistance to the state during Wu Wang's lifetime. Chou Kung, esteemed a paragon by later generations, is said to have consolidated the power of the dynasty and so successfully to have trained the young monarch that the latter was able to reign acceptably after the regent's death. To him, too, is attributed the administrative organization of the realm on a pattern which for generations remained the model. To Chou Kung is ascribed the *Chou Li*, The Ritual of the Chou.

a compilation possibly dating actually from the fourth and third centuries B.C., or even later, and much or all of it the attempt of the authors to give the sanction of antiquity to an imaginary utopia of their own creation.

It must be repeated that the dependability of the stories about Wên Wang, Wu Wang, and Chou Kung is in debate. The trend of present opinion is to regard few facts about them as well established and to think of these rulers as very shadowy figures idealized by later generations and especially by Confucian scholars.

Some of the early monarchs of the Chou apparently extended the boundaries both of their domains and of Chinese culture. Chao Wang, the traditional dates of whose rule—according to one chronology—are B.C. 1052–1001, and his successor, Mu Wang, with reign dates—by the same chronology—of B.C. 1001–946, are said to have triumphed over the barbarians, and, among other regions, to have carried victoriously the arms of the Chinese into the valley of the Han, across the mountains which form the southern boundary of the valley of the Wei. Mu Wang especially is credited with having been an energetic and restless traveller, to have pursued his conquests beyond the Yangtze on the south, and to have penetrated to the far northwest, visiting a mysterious Hsi Wang Mu, literally, "West King Mother." Hsi Wang Mu has stimulated much discussion among Occidental sinologists, actuated as they are by a natural desire to ferret out all possible early connections between China and the West, and many ingenious guesses have been made as to her identity. The fullest details of Mu Wang's travels are to be found in an historical romance which probably dates from the first century A.D. and the factual basis of the account is almost certainly too tenuous to yield dependable results. It seems fairly reasonable, however, to assume that these early monarchs expanded their domains, even gaining a foothold in the Yangtze Valley. It is possible, too, that tradition is right in declaring that Mu Wang modified the administrative system and the laws of the land, for this would probably be advisable if the new territory were to be assimilated.

With the ninth and eighth centuries B.C., our knowledge of events, although still meager, increases somewhat, thanks chiefly to some of the poems in the *Shih Ching,* which probably were composed to announce to the ancestors the achievements of the monarch. The power of the Chou *Wang* had begun to decline. The Kingdom, as we have suggested, had long been divided into principalities. Some of these were ruled by collateral branches of the royal house, others by descendants of ministers and generals who had been rewarded for service to the state by hereditary fiefs, and still others by families who claimed to trace their lineage from the rulers of preceding dynasties. Probably several of the princes were extending their boundaries at the expense of the adjoining non-Chinese peoples and so were enlarging the borders of China. Weak monarchs, inevitable in any hereditary line, found difficulty in asserting their authority over powerful vassals, and privileges once conceded proved obstacles to the resumption of the power of the central government by the occasional vigorous *Wang*. Hsüan Wang, the traditional dates of whose reign are B.C. 827–781, was apparently abler than some of his immediate predecessors. Certainly he was strong enough to fight successfully against the barbarians in the modern Shansi and Northern Shensi, carrying the war into the highlands from which these enemies menaced the prosperous plains. He also invaded the valley of the Han. Such aggressiveness outside his boundaries would seem to imply that he had made progress against his own insubordinate lords.

Hsüan Wang, however, only postponed the decay of his line. His successor, Yu Wang, is declared by tradition to have been hopelessly weak and to have sacrificed the state in the attempt to satisfy the whim of a court beauty. He put her in place of his queen and disinherited the latter's son, the heir presumptive. To make her smile, so the story runs, he had the beacon fires kindled which were the signal for his vassals to rally against a raid of barbarians. When the fires were lit in earnest, the lords, fearing another practical joke, failed to respond against a joint attack of the invaders and the outraged father of the deposed queen. Yu Wang was killed and his unpopular mistress taken captive. At the beginning of the next reign, traditional dates of which are B.C. 771–720, the weakness of the Chou was openly proclaimed to the world when the capital was moved from the valley of the Wei, where it was subject to the forays of the barbarians, eastward to Loyang, near the present Honanfu, more remote from the dangerous frontier. The change marked the hopeless decline of the Chou, and while the dynasty endured for over five centuries longer, the feudal states and not the royal line now become the center of interest. The activities of the feeble *rois fainèants* were more and more restricted to their religious and ceremonial as contrasted with their political functions. The dynasty prior to the removal of the capital is known as the Western Chou and after that event as the Eastern Chou.

From the eighth century B.C. until the middle of the third China roughly resembled the Europe of the Middle Ages. Like Medieval Europe, China was a collection of states with unstable boundaries. A kind of feudalism existed, the local princes in theory owing homage, tribute, counsel, and military service to the Chou monarchs, and minor lords having similar obligations to more powerful ones. The details of organization, however, were quite different from those of Europe. As the power of the Chou declined, some semblance of security was sought, as in Europe, in alliances and leagues, and several individual states successively won a kind of hegemony. Purely Chinese states were supposed not to make war on each other—a principle often honored more in the breach than in the observance—that devastating activity being theoretically employed only against the barbarians, the peoples of non-Chinese culture. When war was waged between any of the feudal states it was often more to exhibit the prowess of individual combatants and their skill in the established rules than to annihilate the adversary.

As in the Europe of the Middle Ages, the boundaries of civilization were steadily extended to embrace new peoples. In Europe the spread was northward—into Germany, Great Britain, Scandinavia, Russia—while in China it was eastward (through Shantung), westward (into Szechwan), and especially southward (into the Yangtze Valley). As in Europe, too, a community of culture existed, but in China, although marked variations were found, especially in the frontier states which were beginning to enter the pale of Chinese culture, there seems to have been a closer approach to uniformity. The development of vernacular differences, particularly in literature, did not proceed as far as in Europe, and no religious chasm appeared such as that between the Western and Eastern churches. As in Medieval feudal Europe, so in the China of the Eastern Chou, intellectual activity was marked —although here a comparison with the era of the great Greek philosophers would be more accurate, for the Eastern Chou was the outstanding creative period of Chinese thought. Unlike the process in Europe, moreover, division was succeeded suddenly by political union, and this was accompanied and followed by increasing uniformity in culture.

THE HEGEMONY OF VARIOUS FEUDAL STATES

The China of the Eastern Chou, then, was divided into a large number of states. By the seventh century B.C., five of these had begun to emerge as somewhat more powerful than the others. In the Northeast was Ch'i, in parts of what are now Shantung and Hopei; in the North, in the modern Shansi, was Chin; in the West, in the modern Shensi, was Ch'in; on the plain, not far from the old centers of culture, Sung; and in the South, centering in the present province of Hupeh, Ch'u. Four of these five, it will be noted, were on the frontier. They could grow by expansion outward—away from the older centers of culture—and their populations probably included strong infusions of "barbarian" blood. Ch'u, indeed, appears to have been almost entirely non-Chinese in race, originally non-Chinese in speech, and partly so in culture. Some members of its ruling aristocracy probably came from the North. These frontier states strove to control the older China, largely the present Honan. Here was the traditional center of culture and of political authority. Here, too, the many small principalities constituted a tempting prey to their larger neighbors. Only one, Sung, was able to make an effective bid for power against the frontier states, and its importance was transitory.

The first of the five strong states to achieve the hegemony was Ch'i. Tradition declares it to have been under an unusually able ruler, Huan, advised by a distinguished minister, Kuan Chung, that, in the first half of the seventh century B.C., it acquired wealth and prestige. By vigorous administrative, military, and fiscal reorganization, undertaken through the leadership of these two men, the state was transformed. The wealth of the prince was increased by monopolies of staple industries, including especially the manufacture of salt and iron. Commerce was encouraged. When some of the minor states into which the older centers of Chinese culture were divided had become enfeebled, Ch'u reached out from the South and menaced them with possible absorption. At this juncture the threatened states, in self-defence, for the moment ignoring their enmities, by treaty formed a league against the invader (B.C. 681) and placed themselves under the protection of the prince of Ch'i.

The league thus formed endured for more than two centuries. The authority of its head was confirmed by investiture from the Chou *Wang*. Assemblies of the league were not held at stated intervals, but whenever need arose the heads of the allies were convoked by the president. Some convened for the purpose of undertaking a joint war and were attended by the feudal chiefs with all their armed contingents. Others, with peaceful purposes, did not bring together so large a body of men.

Late in the reign of Huan, after Kuan Chung had died (B.C. 643), Ch'i fell into internal confusion and the presidency passed out of its hands. For some years thereafter the very existence of the league was threatened. The head of Sung, one of the other member states, attempted as its president, but in vain, to give it adequate leadership, and at least one of the members sought safety in an alliance with that very Ch'u whose aggressions had brought the organization into existence.

The league, thus jeopardized, was salvaged and given renewed strength by the presidency of Wên, prince of Chin. Chin, located in the mountains and plateaus of the present Shansi, was not so easily unified as Ch'i, on the adjoining plain, for internal barriers favored the independence of the local clans. Wên, whose personal name was Ch'ung Erh, was the son of a barbarian mother. Before his accession he had learned hardihood and resourcefulness by years of wandering and adventurous exile. In B.C. 636 he succeeded in establishing himself in Chin, and during a brief reign of eight years (he died B.C. 628) he exercised the rule so ably that for a century and a half thereafter his descendants were usually the acknowledged heads of the league. By skillful administrative reorganization he welded his principality into an effective fighting unit. Then, allying himself with other states, he attacked and overwhelmingly defeated Ch'u, and was appointed by the Chou ruler as the head of the feudal chiefs.

Chin, placed at the forefront of the Chinese states by the prowess of Wên, did not hold its place without many struggles and reverses. Under weak princes and internal dissensions, indeed, it gradually, in spite of temporary revivals, declined. Ch'in, in the territory once held by the early rulers of the Chou and long a rising power, was now the guardian of the western marches. Partly barbarian in blood, apparently it acquired prowess by constant fighting, and in the second half of the seventh century, under its great prince Mu, a contemporary of Wên, it made a temporarily successful bid for the hegemony. Ch'u in the South was always to be reckoned with, and at the beginning of the sixth century defeated Chin and seemed to be on the point of replacing it.

With one of the sudden reversals of fortune which make these centuries so confusing, Ch'u, on the point of victory, suddenly declined (in the latter half of the sixth century B.C.). Chin, although not particularly strong, found an ally in Wu, a state which first emerged into prominence near the opening of the sixth century B.C. Wu, in the lower part of the Yangtze Valley and commanding the mouth of that river and the fertile plains along its lower courses, occupied most of the territory covered by the present province of Kiangsu and portions of the present Anhui, Chêkiang, and Kiangsi. Some of its rulers may have had in their veins princely blood of China, brought by the southward migration of adventurous aristocrats. Its people were possibly allied racially to the Chinese, but were late in acquiring Chinese civilization and were regarded as barbarians by their northern neighbors. During the sixth century B.C., thanks in part to the ability of its rulers, Wu became one of the most powerful states of China and continued so into the fifth century. In 482 B.C., indeed, the prince of Wu seems to have succeeded the now almost impotent princes of Chin as the real head of the league—although the titular presidency may still have remained with Chin.

Within a decade of this triumph, however, Wu collapsed (B.C. 473). The most southerly of the states of China of the later years of the Chou dynasty, Yüeh, in the modern Chêkiang, destroyed it. For a time Yüeh became the outstanding state of East China. However, although it removed its capital to a point on or near the south coast of the present Shantung (B.C. 379), it did not occupy the dominant position over inland China that some other states had had or were later to possess. It remained chiefly a coastal power. Both Wu and Yüeh seem to have depended in part upon boats for their victories, navigating these craft on the sea and on the rivers and lakes in which their possessions abounded. Wu, indeed, appears to have begun the Grand Canal, that great artificial waterway whose completion is attributed to the Mongols, nearly two millenniums later, and which, proceeding along the alluvial plain, helps to connect the valleys of the Yangtze and the Huang Ho. It is not strange that, relying so much on their water-craft, neither Wu nor Yüeh succeeded in making its authority effective over the interior.

Chin did not long survive Wu. Most of its territory being in the mountains, plains, and valleys of what is now Shansi, its internal barriers always threatened it with division into warring clans. This tendency was accentuated by the distribution of fiefs by the princes of Chin among their favorites and relatives. It is not surprising, therefore, that the authority of the princes declined and that toward the close of the fifth century Chin broke into three fragments (Han, Wei, and Chao). Neither of these was strong enough to occupy the dominant rôle in national politics formerly held by the united Chin.

THE PERIOD OF THE CONTENDING STATES AND THE TRIUMPH OF CH'IN

By the middle of the fifth century the old China was beginning to disappear and great changes were in progress. The feudal institutions of the past were disintegrating and new ideas appeared in administration, legislation, philosophy, and religion. As we shall see in a moment, the period was one of creative thought. Warfare among the many states which made up China had long been part of the ordinary course of events. Such an outline as we have given probably seems intricate enough to those for the first time introduced to the story, but compared with the complexities of the detailed narratives it is simplicity itself. The scene now becomes even more confused and belligerent. To Chinese historians the era is known as that of the *Chan Kuo*, or Contending States. The Chou rulers became increasingly feeble and the feudatories in the older China dropped more than ever into the background—the prey of the partially Chinese principalities on the border. With the breakup of Chin ended any semblance of that league and that principle of hegemony by which a measure of respect had been paid to the rights of the individual states and some protection given them. Heretofore, as we have seen, war between the feudal states had been carried on in large part according to recognized rules. Moreover, in theory it did not have as an aim the extinction of the enemy or even the annihilation of his army, but the punishment of the guilty and the giving effect to the judgments of Heaven. Now, war became a business. Military organization and technique were altered and became more efficient. The contest was one for the survival of the fittest. The strong ruthlessly overran and absorbed the weak. Some of the members of the old aristocratic houses sank to the level of the common people and many new families rose to power.

The principal combatants were the great principalities on the frontier, Ch'in, Ch'u, Yen (with its capital on the site of the present Peiping), the three fragments of Chin, and a revived Ch'i. These were known as the *Ch'i Hsiung,* or Seven Martial (States). Ch'i had not been a major figure in Chinese politics for about two centuries, but it had continued to exist, and, under the leadership of a usurping ruling house—regarded disapprovingly by scholars who favored legitimacy—it rose once more to prominence. However, Ch'in and Ch'u, with a much stronger admixture of non-Chinese blood and culture, were the chief rivals. Both were expanding at the expense of their neighbors. In the fourth century B.C., Ch'in conquered the state of Shu, in the present province of Szechwan—a section which now begins to have a part in Chinese history. In that same century Ch'u overthrew Yüeh and absorbed the northern portions of its dominions—those formerly belonging to Wu. As between Ch'u and Ch'in, the tide of fortune ebbed and flowed. Alliances centering around each were made and dissolved, the lesser states seeking safety or aggrandizement by throwing in their fortunes now with one and now with another of the more formidable combatants.

Ch'in owed much of its strength to Kung-sun Yang, also called Wei Yang or Shang Yang, who, belonging to the ruling family of Wei, in the middle of the fourth century, under Duke Hsiao—who appears to have combined ability with an ambition to control all China—became a minister of Ch'in. Under Wei Yang's direction the laws and administration of his adopted state were reorganized and the foundations laid for the eventual victory of Ch'in over its rivals.

The other six of the seven leading states were, in B.C. 333, brought together in a league to resist the prosperous Ch'in. This immediate period is often known as that of the Six Kingdoms. The alliance was not permanent, partly because its members were too jealous of each other long to hold together. With this league is associated a famous historical romance which attributes the enterprise to Su Ch'in, one of the wandering scholar-diplomats of the time and which assigns the undoing of the alliance to a former fellow-student of Su Ch'in, Chang I, in the service of Ch'in.

Many were the wars and the exploits of these troubled years, and many a story has been handed down of loyalty, of trickery and intrigue, of prowess, and of generals and statesmen successful to-day and disgraced and banished or executed tomorrow. One of the festivals of a later China, that of the Dragon Boat, is said (probably erroneously) to take its rise from the search for the body of Ch'ü Yüan, a statesman of Ch'u, who is declared to have drowned himself (B.C. 295) in despair over the failure of his prince to take his advice against the schemes of the astute Chang I.

For a time it seemed that China might never be unified, but be divided permanently among Ch'i, Ch'u, and Ch'in. In the third century Ch'in and Ch'i, in recognizing each other's spheres of influence, ratified the assumption by the two rulers of an ancient religious title, *Ti*, declared by legend to have been held by early sovereigns, the head of Ch'in becoming *Hsi Ti*, or Emperor of the West, and the head of Ch'i becoming *Tung Ti*, or Emperor of the East. They soon abandoned these designations, possibly because of the widespread opposition of their neighbors, but the pretensions they embodied were probably still cherished.

Gradually, however, and with occasional reverses, Ch'in forged its way to the front. Toward the close of the fourth century it obtained possession of two passes which insured it free exit eastward and southward. Its military organization seems to have given it an advantage. Instead of depending on chariots, the familiar war vehicle of the older China still relied on by its rivals, it formed an army in which horse and foot soldiers predominated.

THEIR HISTORY AND CULTURE

It may have adopted these from the "barbarians" with whom it fought on its western and northern frontiers. Ch'i and Ch'u occasionally stopped their own quarreling to unite against the common enemy, but formed no permanent alliance. Early in the third century Ch'i was practically eliminated as a major power. Its prince, in attacking his neighbor (possibly with the purpose of mastering China), brought down on his head a number of the other states and was disastrously defeated. The ruin of Ch'i strengthened Ch'in. In the first half of the third century Ch'in repeatedly defeated Ch'u and annexed much of its territory.

In the struggle between the great rivals, the prestige and the power of the Chou sank ever lower and lower. The rulers of the more prominent of the feudal states had for some time assumed the title of *Wang*, heretofore the exclusive designation of the Chou monarchs—thereby probably in effect declaring their equality with the house of Chou and possibly indicating their ambition to master all China. In the middle of the third century B.C., Ch'in wrested from Nan Wang, the last of the Chou to wear that title, the western portion of his small remaining territory and carried off the nine tripods which, alleged to have been handed down from the Emperor Yü, were esteemed as symbols of supreme power. On the death of Nan Wang, in B.C. 256, a relative, under the designation of Eastern Chou Prince (*Tung Chou Chun*), maintained for a short time something of a semblance of authority, until, in B.C. 249, he in his turn was defeated by Ch'in and forfeited his territory to the victor.

The extinction of the Chou was, however, by no means the last of the steps necessary to assure Ch'in the Empire. Other and more powerful rivals had to be overcome. The final victory was under the direction of one of the most important and interesting figures in all Chinese history, he who is known to posterity as Shih Huang Ti. To the birth and tutelage of this unifier of China a peculiar story is attached. In the third century B.C., a prince of Ch'in, a not particularly clever fellow, was in exile, and while he was there an unusually able man, Lü Pu-wei, a merchant, who saw in him an opportunity for advancement, attached himself to him. Lü Pu-wei, by skillful management, obtained for his princely patron the appointment to the succession to the throne of Ch'in. Lü Pu-wei had a beautiful and charming concubine, and, when the prince became infatuated with her, surrendered her to him. A son of this beauty was Chêng (born B.C. 259), later Shih Huang Ti, and malicious and perhaps ill-founded gossip has it that his father was not the prince, but the clever Lü Pu-wei. When, thanks to his friend, the prince succeeded to the rule in Ch'in, Lü Pu-wei continued as his chief adviser and remained powerful in the earlier years of the reign of Chêng—who, as a minor, followed his reputed father as head of Ch'in (B.C. 247). Lü Pu-wei is said to have been accused of complicity in amorous intrigues of and with his former concubine, now the queen-dowager. Certainly Chêng, not unwilling to be rid of so powerful a mentor, banished him (B.C. 238). Again accused of treasonable designs, Lü was banished a second time, probably to the present Honan (although just possibly he was later in Szechwan). His life seems to have been ended by poison.

Before Lü's fall, Ch'in was well on its way to its final triumph over its rivals. In the second half of the third century it annexed state after state. Ch'u was erased from the map, and in B.C. 221 the conquest of what was left of Ch'i completed the territorial unification of China under the all-powerful Ch'in. The older, classical China had been subdued by a state which was mostly Chinese in culture but which was only partially Chinese in blood. One stage of China's development had come to an end and a new era, that of imperialism, had dawned.

CULTURAL GROWTH UNDER THE CHOU

These centuries of almost incessant warfare had been accompanied by remarkable developments in civilization and, as the preceding narrative indicates, by the wide extension of Chinese culture in regions within and outside its native habitat.

The original China, it will be recalled, was on the plain formed by the Yellow River and its tributaries. At the outset of the Chou much of it was still uncultivated. It contained large fertile areas but also swamps and regions of shifting sands. At the beginning of the dynasty, and for many centuries thereafter, peoples whom the Chinese regarded as barbarians lived not only on the edges of the plain, but also in the plain itself, some of them on the seashore.

As it expanded, Chinese civilization took to itself many elements of the peoples with whom it came in contact. By the close of the Chou, and probably much earlier, the culture of the Chinese, like that of many other peoples, was becoming a synthesis of contributions from many regions, north, south, and west of the primitive seat of civilization. For instance, in the later centuries of the Chou and down into the Ch'in dynasty there are evidences of so-called "Scythian" influence on art objects, including bronzes. From the eighth to the third century B.C. the Scyths were in control in much of what is now Russia and the effect of their art on that of China argues either direct or indirect contacts of the Chinese with the peoples of the vast plain which stretches across much of Europe and Asia.

As has been said, it is not a simple matter to determine the earliest culture of the Chinese. Our written documents are comparatively few, and their dates, the purity of their present texts, and even the authenticity of numerous sections are so open to question that many of the conclusions drawn from them are disputable. As is natural, the further back we go the more open to debate our findings become. Archeological researches into this period are still, as we have said, so decidedly in their infancy that most of the deductions drawn from them must for the present be very tentative. Much of what is given below is, accordingly, conjectural and may have to be altered or even discarded as knowledge of the period advances. This is especially true of the picture of economic and social life given in the succeeding paragraphs.

ECONOMIC ORGANIZATION

In the early years of the Chou dynasty, Chinese culture, it will be recalled, was already advanced. As before, the basic industry was agriculture. Millet, rice, wheat, and barley were the chief cereals. Some of these were quite possibly of foreign origin. The ox-drawn plow appeared, possibly of alien provenance. Fermented liquor was made from both rice and millet. Vegetables were raised and fruits were cultivated. The mulberry was particularly useful, because its leaves nourished the silk-worms and so were essential in the production of the most characteristic of Chinese textiles. Several kinds of plants were employed in the production of cloth. The pig and the chicken were, with the dog, the omnipresent live stock, and there were other domestic animals. Irrigation on a large scale came in the latter part of the period.

Iron came into use sometime during the dynasty. The coming of metallic money must have wrought changes in the economy of the land.

As in the Shang, a sharp distinction seems to have existed between the lower, or peasant, and the upper, or aristocratic, classes. The lower were occupied with cultivating the soil. The upper classes did the governing. So marked was the difference that a suggestion has been made, as yet quite unproved, that the peasants were a conquered group, the descendants of the neolithic population, and the aristocracy victorious invaders, possibly of another race, owing their position in part to their more powerful organization and better material equipment. Bronze weapons and implements, for example, may originally have been the possession of the aristocracy, so helping to give them the ascendancy.

The distinction appears to have been accentuated by or at least to have had some association with the growth of towns. During the Chou urban civilization was spreading, centering in capitals of the feudal princes and of the *Wang*. Between city dwellers and the rural population a gulf tended to exist. The town, dominated by the aristocracy, seems to have had a market place, an altar to the earth—a raised mound of beaten soil—and the ancestral temple of the ruling lord. It was surrounded by a wall and a moat. This town may have succeeded in part the earlier holy place which had been the center of peasant life, an identification which may have assisted the feudal chiefs in their domination of the rural community.

Tradition asserts that land was divided according to the *ching t'ien* or "well-field" system. While some scholars regard this as an imaginary creation of later utopian philosophers, probably it had an actual basis in fact. On the other hand, presumably it was never systematically carried out on any such large scale as some writers have supposed. By this device the arable land was assigned in sections to eight peasant families each. Every section was plotted in a form resembling the Chinese character for well, *ching*, 井, the eight outer plots being cultivated in common by the eight families and the central plot being reserved for residences and the raising of the produce which went to the lord. The title was vested in the lord. Permanent individual peasant ownership appears not to have been thought of. New land was cleared as the old was exhausted, and periodical reassignment was the rule. The size of the *ching* varied with the quality of the soil. As irrigation and methods of cultivation improved, residence and boundaries between fields were of longer duration, only the poorer soil being allowed periodically to lie fallow. While the peasant did not own the soil, apparently he was permanently attached to certain districts, and so, like the European serf, enjoyed a better status than that of slavery. Probably not until toward the close of the Chou dynasty did peasant proprietorship prevail. Wei Yang is credited—possibly incorrectly —with having made it the rule in Ch'in. The *ching t'ien* system gradually disintegrated, and by the third century B.C. (probably even as early as the sixth century) it was passing away.

Much of the work of bringing waste lands into cultivation, of draining swamps and constructing canals for irrigation, seems to have been performed by the state. While possibly accelerated under some of the great feudatories in the closing years of the Chou, it had been in progress for centuries and must have entailed great labor for many generations of peasants and officials.

As towns grew and as the Chinese extended their domains and became more numerous, commerce and industry seem to have expanded. The rise to power in Ch'in of a merchant, Lü Pu-wei, may have been symptomatic of the increased importance of his class. The introduction of coined money, about the beginning of the first millennium B.C., probably had a profound effect upon the social and economic organization of the time.

SOCIAL ORGANIZATION

It was only during the season when the land was cultivated that the peasants lived on it. During the winter they were gathered into villages, where each family had its permanent and separate home. Some homes were caves dug in the loess where it rose in sharp cliffs. Others were built of mud. The villages, as we have seen, were usually walled and clustered about the residence of an official, often the seignior's home and ancestral hall.

Frequently, too, they were on heights overlooking the fields, out of the way of floods and more easily defended than on the plain. In these villages the life of the community centered around market places and public grounds.

It was in the spring, before the workers went to the fields, that the mating of young couples seems to have taken place. There were great community festivals in the spring and in the autumn when the entire village gave itself over to dancing and ceremonials.

Agriculture and the life of the peasantry were carefully regulated and directed by officials, so that China early possessed a kind of bureaucracy.

The aristocracy were chiefly distinguished from the peasants by an elaborate family and hierarchal organization. Each patrician clan professed to trace its descent through the male line to a common ancestor—a god, a hero, or a monarch. Sometimes the original progenitor was supposed to be a bird or an animal. These latter were often purely mythical creatures, such as the unicorn and the dragon. The men were careful not to take wives, or even concubines, of their own clan name. However, two houses often intermarried for many generations, and sons customarily obtained wives from their mother's family. Then, too, children of a brother and sister might marry—being of different clan names. The clan was not a territorial division and did not necessarily hold land as a unit. The effective tie was not economic but religious—the cult in honor of the ancestors and especially of the putative founder of the clan. The family organization contained interesting survivals of what was possibly a much earlier matriarchate. If, as seems possible, in primitive times the children received their mother's name and husbands were joined to their wives' families, by at least the time of the feudal system the organization of the aristocracy had become clearly patriarchal.

The aristocratic clan in turn was divided into families, each with its male head who officially represented and had authority over its members. Marriage, being the means of perpetuating the family and the clan, was of great importance and by elaborate rites. At the time of the marriage the bride was formally introduced to her husband's parents and ancestors. Secondary wives might be taken. A birth was regarded as lucky or unlucky according to the day on which it occurred. An infant which arrived on an unpropitious day might be abandoned.

One scholar has it that during much of their boyhood and adolescence the boys lived apart, in a common house, where they were educated. In practice it may be that they actually spent the time with their mother's relatives and were trained by them. The segregation of the boys and girls is, however, conjectural and is denied by other scholars.

On reaching man's estate the youth was inducted into that rank with formal ceremonies, receiving the cap which indicated that he was now recognized as an adult.

The social life and even the recreations of the aristocracy, such as archery and music, were rather rigidly controlled by custom.

From the upper classes came the lords and the great landed proprietors. By no means all those of patrician birth possessed large estates. Many were petty landowners, a kind of sturdy squirearchy from which came numbers of the thinkers and military adventurers of the later centuries of the Chou. Others were employees of the state, scribes, school-teachers, diviners, or experts on ritual. Still others were merchants, for in time, as we have said, a fairly extensive domestic and interstate commerce arose in such commodities as salt, grain, silk, horses, and cattle.

POLITICAL ORGANIZATION

Political organization had probably developed in complexity since the Shang, if for no other reasons than that the extent of territory governed had increased. It was still, however, permeated largely by the patriarchal ideal. Civilized society was regarded much as a huge family, and its units as smaller families. The religious tie was strong.

The head of the state was, of course, the *Wang,* or monarch. In theory the *Wang* ruled because of the decree of Heaven (*t'ien ming*) and the *tê* (originally meaning magical power, but later, by Confucian scholars, given the moral connotation of "virtue") of himself and his ancestors obtained through obedience to the commands of Heaven. In practice the authority of the *Wang* depended very largely upon his own ability and force of character. Time-distances were great, and the leading territorial magnates were disposed to act very much like independent sovereigns—at least in all except religious matters. As we have seen, after the first few monarchs of the Chou it was a rare *Wang* who was able to become more than a kind of high priest and a source of titles. In the earlier days of the dynasty, the monarchs had much real power and probably were more considerable potentates than those of the Shang. Later they became mere figureheads, retaining some degree of importance chiefly because of the prestige of their line and their religious functions.

The *Wang* was assisted by a chief minister and by six subordinate ministers in charge of different phases of administration —agriculture, the army, public works, religious rites, the monarch's personal affairs, and punishments. Below these appears to have been an extensive and fairly complicated officialdom of varying ranks. Some of the positions were hereditary. During the many centuries which the dynasty endured, modifications in the system inevitably occurred. As the effective power of the *Wang* declined, this officialdom ceased to have the administrative significance that apparently it once possessed. Accordingly it became more and more stereotyped and regularized. Together with the *Wang*, however, it was considered to have practical religious importance, for its continued functioning was held essential to that coöperation of Heaven, Earth, and man upon which depended the prosperity and welfare of the realm. Religious ceremonies performed by the proper functionaries were supposed to be quite as requisite to the well-being of society as the observance of ethical obligations between man and man.

The realm was divided into two main parts, the royal domains, ruled directly by the *Wang* through his officials, and the fiefs of the many feudatories. During part of the Chou dynasty, the realm, vassal states and all, appears to have been divided into nine provinces, each with a kind of governor, appointed by the *Wang* from among the local lords. These provinces, however, probably possessed little more than a ceremonial significance and later writers overstressed their actual importance. As has been customary with states organized on the feudal basis, the vassal owed his overlord homage, military service, and tribute. In return he received land. Investiture was marked by solemn ceremonies. Homage was supposed to be performed at periodical intervals, varying with the distance of the fief from the court.

Tribute was chiefly in kind—in products of the soil and the loom—for metallic money seems not to have made its appearance until the latter part of the fifth century B.C. Every lord was also bound to perform the proper sacrifices to the spirits of the land and to his ancestors and to maintain justice toward and honor among his subjects. Each feudal prince had his own officials, graded in a kind of hierarchy.

The structure was held together in part by the observance of an elaborate ritual by which inferiors honored superiors. Theoretically, too, the lords were subordinate to the *Wang* and could be promoted or demoted by him. Before the break-up of the old feudalism toward the latter part of the Chou, there seems for centuries to have been a kind of stability—uneasy and not too secure, to be sure—and a recognized order. It was overturned by the rise of the great warring states out of which Ch'in emerged triumphant.

The meager laws were largely penal, covering classes of crimes and certain acts which we in the Occident would call civil. Judged by modern standards punishments were severe, although no more so than those of many other nations of antiquity. The chief recognized ones were death, castration, amputation of the feet, cutting off the nose, and tattooing the face. Frequently they could be compounded by the payment of a fine. Contracts were regularly made and legally recognized.

As to war and defence, the Chinese employed chariots and ensconced themselves in walled towns and villages. War was cruel—as it always is. It seems possible that a victory over the barbarians was sometimes celebrated by a cannibal feast off the bodies of the vanquished, although wars between Chinese were not so terminated. In days when the feudalism of the Chou was at its height custom regulated combats between feudal states. That kind of battle, as we have suggested, was in large degree a matter of ritual—of generous sparing of life, of loyalty to one's chief, and of gaining or losing prestige by following or disobeying the rules. It was a kind of bloodless military chess. When toward the end of the Chou the struggles between the great rivals became acute the older courtesies tended to fall into desuetude.

ART

The bronzes which have survived from the Chou show a level of culture far from primitive. The sacrificial vessels especially command the admiration of experts everywhere. At the outset they displayed no sharp break with the Shang bronzes. Not far from 900 B.C. new forms, of inferior workmanship, supplanted their predecessors. About three centuries later a revival of old forms, but with more ornamentation than the latter and with inlays appeared. The new was known as the Huai style. Many samples of jade, too, show artistic taste and skill. Lacquer began to be employed.

LITERARY DEVELOPMENT

Writing by the prototypes of the present characters had been devised, as we have seen, at least as early as the Shang dynasty, and the Chou witnessed a fairly extensive and rich literary development. More characters were formed. Books were inscribed on tablets of wood or bamboo, presumably with ink. The language displayed dialectical differences, but these were not sufficiently marked, at least among the educated, to prevent a community of culture.

The earliest form of literature appears to have been religious in character—hymns sung at sacrifices, songs to accompany the dances and feasts in honor of the ancestors, and bits of prose to parallel the pantomimes performed in the ancestral temples. Poems were composed for the great ceremonial occasions at court—banquets, archery contests, receptions, and the like. To these were added folk songs—satires, laments of widows, complaints of soldiers whose officers had conducted them to defeat, dances of the young in the spring, love songs, songs at the birth of a child, for weddings, and the like. Many are included in that anthology of ancient verse, the *Shih Ching*, or Classic of Poetry, brought together in Chou times. Still others are to be found in compilations of the period which contain both poetry and prose. While the original text of the *Shih Ching* has suffered in transmission, a large proportion as we have it to-day is probably authentic.

Prose owed much to the official scribes charged with the preparation and preservation of official documents and with the arrangements for religious ceremonies and feasts. Ritual purposes required short accounts of the legends concerning the ancestors which the dancers portrayed in pantomime. The descriptions were necessarily exact, terse, minute, and rather dry. To accompany some of these outlines speeches were composed and attributed to the chief actors. Here the imagination of the scribes had greater liberty. Records were also kept of official transactions—lawsuits, the granting of fiefs, and the like—in highly technical language. Descriptions began to be written of administrative machinery and of geography—the latter from the viewpoint of the administrator and tax collector. Philosophy—particularly, as was natural, political philosophy—began to emerge.

Many of these ancient prose documents have been preserved in a collection known as the *Shu Ching,* or Classic of History. Fairly early tradition—possibly reliable—declares that Confucius edited it. Much of the text of the *Shu Ching* as we have it to-day is either corrupt or spurious. It has been clearly demonstrated, for example, that the portions of it which are only in the so-called "ancient text" are a forgery of post-Chou times. Much of that contained in the "modern text," however, is usually regarded by scholars as an authentic record of ancient traditions.

The scribes, too, charged with preserving the archives, began the custom of keeping terse annals of events, especially of official acts, with exact references to dates and persons. One of these, of the feudal state of Lu, was the basis of a history which has been preserved, thanks possibly to its association with the great name of Confucius, under the title of the *Ch'un Ch'iu,* or Spring and Autumn (Annals). It has been traditionally represented as written by Confucius, but the accuracy of this view has been boldly challenged and hotly debated. Some others of the annals of local states—of Chin and Wei—were in the *Chu Shu Chi Nien* (discovered in a tomb in the third century A.D.), freely translated, as the Bamboo Annals and so denominated because the copy then found was written on tablets of that material. It must be added, however, that the existing work which now bears that title is by no means of indubitable authenticity. Many scholars insist that it is a forgery, a compilation of quotations from other books, and that only fragments of the genuine original survive. The *Tso*

Chuan, traditionally a commentary on the *Ch'un Ch'iu,* is really of independent origin or origins, being made up of one or more histories which through the ages probably have suffered from interpolations, but which seems at least in part to be as old as the second century B.C. and perhaps older. A suggestion, as yet unsubstantiated, hints that it may be an historical romance.

Still another form of prose originated with the professional diviners, those whose task it was to give counsel, through their auspices, on important actions. The sort of divination which had been practiced under the Shang—by the application of fire to bones and the shell of the tortoise and the interpretation of the resulting cracks—fell into abeyance under the Chou and the very manner of performing it was forgotten. Under the Chou divination was by a variety of mediums, including the milfoil and the sixty-four hexagrams. The hexagrams, developed out of the lines which composed the simpler eight trigrams, had, like the latter, been devised early. Their traditional ascription to Wên Wang and Chou Kung possibly arose out of the attempt to give them the authority of two of the great heroes of the dynasty. The hexagrams, of six lines each, were made up of combinations of whole and broken lines, as, for example, in the following: ☷ ☱ ☶ ☴.

Brief interpretations of these, in technical and, to us, obscure language, were made, presumably as guides to the diviners. In commentaries on or appendices to the foregoing, and of later origin, something of a philosophy was elaborated, including principles of government. In them the terms *Yin* and *Yang,* eventually to loom prominently in speculative thought, and which even to-day hold a large part in popular concepts, make what is possibly their earliest extant appearance. The *Yin* and the *Yang* seem to have been unknown under the Shang and so possibly did not enter Chinese life until sometime in the Chou. The entire collection, comprising documents of various dates, has been transmitted to us as the *I Ching,* or Classic of Change. Tradition attributes the authorship of the older portions to Wên Wang and Chou Kung, and declares that they were composed while the former of these two worthies was a political prisoner and the latter in voluntary exile. It also assigns the appendices to the pen of Confucius. All of this is more than open to question, although at least some of the appendices were written by members of the Confucian school and it is barely possible that the sage himself wrote parts of them.

The *Shih Ching, Shu Ching, Ch'un Ch'iu,* and *I Ching* by no means exhaust the list of the literature of the Chou period. In the later centuries of the dynasty, indeed, books increased in number and in the variety of the subjects treated. The rich and varied development in philosophical thought which will be mentioned in a moment is recorded in works which are rightly among the most treasured of China's possessions. There were compilations on ritual, the most honored of which are the *Li Chi,* or the Book (more literally, the Record) of Rites, the *I Li,* and the *Chou Li.* The *Li Chi* was not collected into its present form until a later dynasty, and much of its material is of post-Chou composition. The *I Li* is probably the fragment of a larger work, of unknown origin, which presumably appeared in the second century before the Christian era—or, according to some critics, at a still earlier time. The *Chou Li,* or Rites of Chou, called in early times *Chou Kuan,* or Officials of Chou, was possibly the work of an anonymous writer of the fourth or third century B.C. and may date from as late as the first century A.D., but, as we have seen, it is traditionally—and almost certainly falsely—ascribed to Chou Kung. It is a utopian plan for the organization of government—an idealized picture of the Chou administrative system—which repeatedly has had great influence upon political and social reformers. The version which has come down to us is often said to be the product of a still later day, but a recent brilliant study learnedly contends that while many interpolations may have been made and although the political organization which it describes may never have existed in its entirety, much of the text as we now have it dates from at least as early as the second century B.C. There were histories, among them a general one of China from B.C. 722 to 450, which has been transmitted as a component part of the *Tso Chuan,* probably composed in the fourth and third centuries B.C.; the *Chan Kuo Ts'ê,* or Documents of the Fighting States (a collection of texts bearing on the last troubled years of the Chou period); and the *Kuo Yü* (perhaps older than the *Tso Chuan,* composed of material related to the latter, and possibly brought together about the fourth or third century B.C.). Historical romances were also written, usually clustering around famous individuals and combining both fact and fiction.

Toward the end of the Chou new forms of poetry appeared, possibly representing the influence of the "barbarians" who were then being assimilated into Chinese stock. Probably the most famous examples of these is by Ch'ü Yüan (whom we have already mentioned as a statesman of the partially Chinese principality of Chou and as traditionally associated with the Dragon Boat Festival). His poem, the *Li Sao,* in which he pours out his soul in lament and so discloses himself and his ideals to posterity, is one of the most famous in all Chinese literature. Some doubt has been cast on the authorship and even on the existence of Ch'ü Yüan, but the composition appears to belong to this period. It certainly registers a high-water mark of literary achievement.

In the last centuries of the Chou China was coming to have more numerous contacts with the peoples to the west. The empire of the Persians and the succeeding one of Alexander must have brought the cultures of Iran and the Occident somewhat nearer to her, and her own expanding frontiers were reaching toward Central Asia. It is not surprising, therefore, that the fringes of the two foreign civilizations should somewhere nearly touch hers in what is now the New Dominion and that along the land routes commercial intercourse should have arisen. This intercourse seems to have enlarged somewhat the Chinese knowledge of geography. It appears also to have brought in more advanced astronomical and mathematical ideas and the elements of the related pseudo-science, astrology. The modifications in the calendar and the method of reckoning time which were made more than once under the Chou may have entered from abroad.

DEVELOPMENT OF SCHOOLS OF PHILOSOPHY

The outstanding intellectual achievement of the Chou was in the realm of philosophy. Philosophy seems to have arisen in the sixth century B.C. Certainly its great development was in that and the following centuries. Why it came to birth when it did must be in part a matter of conjecture. The period roughly corresponds with the rise of Greek philosophy, with some of the most creative years of the Hebrew spirit, with the beginning of

Buddhism and Jainism, and possibly with the inception and at least with the spread of Zoroastrianism. Whether we have here more than a coincidence cannot—at least as yet—be determined. It seems clear that the political and economic organization had much to do with the intellectual activity of the times. The division of the realm into many principalities encouraged variety and individuality. Professional scholars wandered from state to state, seeking learning or employment. At the capitals of the different feudatories thinkers gathered and debated. Some of the rulers encouraged this practice and at least one established a center in which he assembled distinguished representatives of several different schools. It was an age of intellectual ferment and daring.

This flowering of the Chinese philosophical genius was profoundly influenced by early Chinese religion. In a sense, indeed, it was an outgrowth of it.

What the earliest Chinese religion was we cannot certainly tell. The subject has long been provocative of conjecture among Western sinologists, and occasionally of acrimonious debate. Evidence is as yet too fragmentary to permit of final answers. When we first obtain clear pictures of Chinese religion, during the Shang and early in the Chou, the culture of the nation was already far removed from its primitive stages. However, religion was still crude. The Chinese peopled the world with divine influences, with spirits, and with gods and goddesses of various kinds. In each little agricultural village was normally a sacred mound, early the center of life of these communities. There were house gods—for instance, of the hearth, and of the corner where the seed grain was stored. Spirits or gods of the rivers, of the mountains, of the stars, of other natural objects, and of the five elements were honored or propitiated. Some of the divine influences were scarcely personal. On the other hand, there were intensely personal spirits of the great heroes of the past. The ancestors, too, were believed to live on, sometimes for generations: one soul of each of the dead remained with the body and another ascended on high. However, it was held that in the course of time the souls of the deceased disintegrated and were absorbed into the impersonal forces of nature.

The early Chinese apparently indulged in little profound speculation about religion and were not careful that their views should be logical or consistent. By at least the close of the Chou, moreover, and probably many centuries earlier, religious beliefs and practices differed somewhat from state to state. These variations were especially marked in the frontier principalities, such as Ch'in and Ch'u, whose populations and cultures had strong elements not to be found in the older states of the North China plain.

Spirits and gods were superior to men in power, but were not almighty. They were of varying degrees of importance and of extent of jurisdiction. For example, there were many earth gods, each with only a local sphere of power, and there was the Sovereign Earth, with a much wider domain. Very early, perhaps from the beginning, a tendency existed to divide superhuman beings and influences into two groups, those terrestrial and those celestial—those of the earth and those of the air or sky. *T'ien* (Heaven) and *Ti* (Earth) formed a pair, and *Shang Ti* (the Supreme Ruler) may have been paralleled by *Hou T'u* (the Soil or Earth).[3] Supreme over both groups was one great being, variously called *T'ien* (usually translated Heaven) and *Shang Ti* (probably best translated the Supreme Ruler—although the original meaning of *Ti* is uncertain—and possibly the glorified first ancestor of the ruling house). Originally *T'ien* and *Shang Ti* were probably distinct, *T'ien* perhaps meaning the heavenly abode, or city of the dead, and *Shang Ti* having more of a personal theistic significance. If we may trust the oracle bones, *Shang Ti* was the term most used under the Shang for the Supreme Being.[4] Under the Chou, *T'ien* tended to supplant it—possibly because *T'ien* was the god of the ruling house. The Chou *Wang* was regarded as the son of *T'ien* and as reigning by the mandate of *T'ien*. Eventually *T'ien* and *Shang Ti* practically coalesced. *T'ien* or *Shang Ti* was sovereign over gods and men.

The coöperation of the spiritual beings was essential to the welfare of men, including that of groups and of society as a whole. It was to be secured by the proper performance of ritual and sacrifices in honor of these beings, and—at least in the later centuries of the Chou—by right ethical conduct. The ceremonies were often elaborate, with offerings of food, both grain and flesh,

---

[3] *Hou T'u* may at different times have been identical with *Ti* (Earth), a female deity, and *Shê* (ruler of the soil), a male god.

[4] There is a conjecture, however, that the idea of a Supreme Being came in with the Chou.

and, occasionally, of human life. In its earlier stages, religion may have had much of dread and of grim shedding of man's blood. Under the Chou, the more repulsive features appear gradually to have disappeared. Earlier, too, some phallicism probably existed. Possibly, indeed, it was quite prominent. However, it, also, apparently slipped into desuetude and its conventionalized symbols lost their original significance. Ceremonies to the ancestors were in temples constructed for them, or in special rooms or alcoves reserved for them in the dwellings of their descendants, for the dead were treated as having the needs of the living. Ancestors were represented by tablets. The others of the spirits and gods were worshipped in the open air, and near the capital particularly were altars to the most important of them. Some ceremonies appear to have been held in sacred groves. Much of the communal life of the peasants centered round the sacred place, and this, as we have seen, seems later largely to have coalesced with the power and rites of the feudal lord.

Since the proper maintenance of religious ceremonies was essential to the coöperation of spiritual beings with men and so the welfare of society, it was a matter of public concern and one of the chief functions of the state. Each of the feudal lords had ceremonies at which he must officiate, and some of the most important could be performed only by the *Wang*. No class which could strictly be called priestly existed, for the conduct of religious rites was one of the responsibilities of officials charged with administration. However, experts in ritual, who directed the officials in this phase of their duties, formed a recognized profession and were recruited from the upper classes.

Diviners, as we have seen, were also a separate profession. Moreover, a special class existed, held in much less respect than were these others, whose members claimed to act as spokesmen—or spokeswomen, for they were from both sexes—of the unseen, and who, to this end, on occasion could become possessed by the spirit with which they claimed communication.

The schools of philosophy which arose during the later centuries of the Chou were all more or less strongly tinged with these religious beliefs, some partly endorsing and partly modifying them, and some rationalizing or repudiating them in whole or in part.

The common interest which ran through most of the schools

of thought was social—the creation of an ideal human society. This emphasis was natural among a people accustomed to regard religion as primarily a matter of community utility, and particularly so since the majority of the philosophers were from the governing classes and were themselves office-holders. It cannot be too greatly emphasized that the chief problem to which most of the thinkers of the Chou addressed themselves was, how can society be saved? Cosmogony, cosmology, the nature of the gods —if any—and of man were subordinate and ancillary to this question.

From the standpoint of subsequent influence, the chief of the schools was that known to Westerners as Confucianism. The greatest figure in it was, of course, Confucius. The traditional dates of the sage, B.C. 551–479, may be in error, so at least one eminent scholar declares, by several years. The usual story of his life has it that he was born in one of the smaller of the feudal states, Lu, in the present province of Shantung, of aristocratic stock, of an aged father and a younger mother. His father died, so the story continues, during his son's infancy, and the sage was reared, in poverty, by his mother. He early showed a predilection for ceremonies and the learning of the past and achieved such proficiency in them that he attracted students. For years, the traditional accounts say, he held office in his native state, eventually rising to the highest position open to a subject, but in middle age he retired to private life, the reason usually assigned being that he resigned in protest against the unworthy conduct of his prince. During the next several years he travelled from state to state with a group of his disciples, hoping vainly that some ruler would adopt his principles of government and employ him to carry them out. In his old age he returned to Lu and there died after some years of quiet spent in study and teaching. Dignified, courteous, conscientious, high-minded, studious, a lover of antiquity, of books, of ceremonial, and of music, thoughtful, affable, calm, serenely trustful in an overruling Providence—all these are terms which immediately come to mind as descriptive of the man pictured in the discourses transmitted by his faithful disciples. So far as he is disclosed to us in the records, Confucius was somewhat lacking in what we would regard as a sense of humor and displayed little if any love for children and, except for his mother's memory, no especial regard for members of the opposite sex, even his wife; but we must not be too hasty in judging him or insisting that he conform to our own standards.

The interests of Confucius were chiefly those of the statesman and the teacher of ethics. He was concerned for the achievement of good government and held that this was to be by a return to the methods of the great sage-rulers of antiquity. Apparently he thought of himself as a transmitter and not a creator, as simply a student and a teacher of the best of China's past. The way of attaining to good government, as he believed it to have been achieved in the past, was the maintenance of the proper ceremonies, including those of a religious nature, and the exhibition by the ruling classes of a good moral example. Society was kept prosperous and at peace, so he held, not primarily by force, but by the influence of high character on the part of the monarchs and the members of the upper classes, and by adherence to customary ritual. He set himself and his followers, then, to the study and observance of the ancient ritual and to the cultivation of uprightness. As a means to saving society, he sought the cultivation of the *chün tzŭ*, or perfect man.

The fullest, although not the only record of the teachings of Confucius, is in the *Lun Yü*, or Analects, which is made up chiefly of what are said to be the sayings of the great master. Some of these are of doubtful authenticity, but the larger part appear to be authentic, although not necessarily the *ipsissima verba* of the sage, recorded by loyal followers.

Before the end of the Chou several schools of thought—one enumeration of them declares that there were eight—developed within the stream of what may be called the Confucian tradition. The immediate successors of Confucius seem not to have been men of outstanding ability and it was not until Mencius that what may be called Confucianism again included a man of first-rate caliber. Mencius, like Confucius, was a native of the state of Lu. His traditional dates, B.C. 373–288, like those of his great predecessor, are questioned. Most of his working life appears to have been in the second half of the fourth century B.C. He seems to have owed to a wise mother even more than did Confucius. Like the latter, he was a high-minded, careful scholar who attracted students. Like him, too, he was chiefly interested in government and spent much of his life as a wanderer, seeking to induce princes to adopt his standards. He also followed Confucius in teaching that government should be not by brute force but by the good example of the rulers. This he emphasized even more than did Confucius. There are scholars who insist that in some of his teachings he differed fundamentally from Confucius. He maintained, probably as a necessary corollary to his contention that a state would respond to worthy influence, that man is by nature good. Man's nature must, of course, be educated, but this was to be by an environment made favorable by good-will, by music, by art, and by the kindly care of rulers. As a further corollary, Mencius would justify rebellion against hopelessly corrupt rulers, declaring that Heaven, hearing and seeing as the people hear and see, would remove its mandate from those against whom the people persistently complained. Much more than Confucius, Mencius was a caustic critic of the princes. He was emphatic in believing that the state must encourage the material welfare of men—in promoting the provision of food and clothing. His views are preserved to us in a book, *Mêng Tzŭ Shu,* or the Book of Mencius, which seems to be a fairly authentic record of his teachings.

The other great figure of the Chou period who built upon the basis of Confucius was Hsün K'uang, or Hsün Tzŭ. He was probably a little more than thirty years younger than Mencius and his working life fell mostly in the third century B.C. Hsün Tzŭ, also concerned for good government, but living in an age when violence was even more marked than in the times of Confucius and Mencius, contended that man is by nature bad. This evil nature, however, he held to be indefinitely improvable. The change is to be wrought largely by educating men through self-effort, through practice, through acquired habit, through the regular and proper observance of ritual, through music, through the social customs come down from the past, through the example of worthy princes, and through laws. He deplored war and would have a prince win the allegiance of his enemy's people by his noble character rather than by arms. He glorified the state, which he would have enforce the right kind of education. The state, too, he wished to see achieve a balance between men's material wants —for food and clothing—which lead to strife, and the supply of these necessities. Like Mencius, he held that the economic basis of society is important. Both the principles of ethics and the correct rites he believed that he found in the words and acts of the sage-rulers of the past as recorded in the classical books. He denied, however, the existence of the spiritual beings whom the ceremonies were supposed to honor. He derided fortune-telling by reading physiognomy, and while he allowed the traditional forms of divination by the state, he regarded them as undependable. He held that Heaven is not personal, but is unvarying law which automatically and infallibly rewards the good and punishes the evil. In the face of the confusion in existing society, he was an optimist, insisting that the universe is on the side of righteousness and that man's evil nature can be modified for good. He decried dialectic—emphasized by some contemporary philosophers—and believed that man can arrive at a knowledge of the eternal principles of the universe by reflection and meditation rather than by reason.

Of the philosophical schools of the Chou period, the next to Confucianism in lasting influence has been Taoism. The traditional founder was Lao Tzŭ, reputedly an older contemporary of Confucius and the keeper of the archives of the court of the Chou. He is a very shadowy figure and may never have existed. The little book attributed to him, usually called the *Tao Tê Ching,* the most honored treatise of the school, is very possibly of the third century B.C. and is of very uncertain authorship. The most prominent Taoist author, Chuang Tzŭ, flourished in the second half of the fourth century B.C. He was master of a vivid literary style, which later exerted a marked influence. In addition to his writings, several fragments of other treatises of the school have come down to us, among them some bearing the name of Lieh Tzŭ, and possibly from the Han or Chin dynasty, several centuries later.

Taoism is so named from the *Tao,* an ancient Chinese term which the school used to represent the great reality back of and infilling the universe. In general the Taoists seem to have meant by it something akin to what Western philosophers call the Absolute. Knowledge of the *Tao,* they insisted, is not to be attained by reason and study, but by the mystic's way of contemplation and inward illumination. The real world, accordingly, is not that perceived by the physical senses. Nature was idealized and the Taoists sought to merge themselves in it. Man's conduct, they argued, should conform to the *Tao,* and this was held to be *wu wei,* often roughly translated as "inaction," but better defined as a way of "doing everything by doing nothing." It must be noted, however, that some modern scholars maintain that the mystical elements were not well developed until much later, and that their importance in Chou Taoism has been exaggerated.

The Taoists were in opposition to the elaborate ritual, the carefully reasoned codes of ethics, the earnest—and at times pedantic and painful—cultivation of character, and the intellectual approach of Confucianism. They were not exclusively concerned with the salvation of society, but when they did talk about it they maintained that it was to be achieved by abandoning the elaborate ceremonies and organization of current civilization and by returning to primitive manners and conforming to the quiet simplicity of the ceaselessly operating *Tao.* People must not be taught nor their desires awakened by learning. In their political and social theories the Taoists were closely akin to the philosophic anarchists of the Occident. The early Taoists may well have represented the protest of rural districts, of thoughtful commoners, and of aristocrats at odds with their own class, against the elaborate civilization of the towns whose growth seems to have been a feature of the middle and later centuries of the Chou and in opposition to the domination of that official aristocracy of which the Confucian school was a bulwark. It has also been suggested—although on grounds which are probably much less tenable—that Confucianism represented the civilization of the older centers in the North, and Taoism that of the Yangtze Valley, especially Ch'u. Whatever the reason for the difference, Confucianism and Taoism were certainly at variance.

It is not strange that Taoism, with its talk of the unreality of the visible world and of conformity with the *Tao,* should degenerate in popular practice to the search for an elixir by which to achieve immortality and for means of transmuting baser metals into gold. The decay seems to have begun before the end of the Chou. Certainly it proceeded very rapidly in succeeding centuries. It was not unnatural, moreover, that those who professed to master the demons with which Chinese fancy peopled the invisible world should attach themselves to and seek justification in Taoism. This crass popularization did not prevent a small minority of earnest souls from continuing to penetrate the meaning and follow the mystic way of the earlier exponents of the cult.

A variant of Taoism, dealing primarily with politics and especially with relations between the feudal states, had as its greatest teacher Kuei-ku Tzŭ, of the fourth century B.C., who is usually claimed by the Taoists. Two of his best known pupils, Su Ch'in and Chang I, have already figured in our story as skillful diplomats.

Still another school was that associated with the name and teachings of Mo Ti, or Mo Tzŭ. Mo Ti was probably, as were Confucius and Mencius, a native of the little state of Lu, and, while his dates are uncertain, seems to have done most of his work in the second and third quarters of the fifth century B.C. He came, therefore, between Confucius and Mencius. His interest, like that of these two, was in the improvement of society. He differed from them in seeking this, not through the observance of ceremonies, but by whole-hearted conformity to the will of God and by reason, aided by logic. In contrast with a tendency, already observable, to identify Heaven with unvarying, unfeeling law, he believed strongly in its personality, and employed the term *Shang Ti* more frequently than the less personal term *T'ien*. He believed that man finds his highest good in conforming to the will of this Supreme Being, and, since Heaven loves men, favoring righteousness and hating iniquity, men ought to love one another and be righteous in life. Men should, indeed, love all their fellows as they would their own blood brothers. Applying the tests of love and of logic to human institutions, he condemned war as unbrotherly and murderous. It must be noted, however, that it was chiefly offensive war which he felt to be wrong. He did not, as have some Christians, advocate opposing aggression by active good-will or by passive, unarmed resistance. With his utilitarian outlook, he condemned many of the rites so dear to the Confucianists. While emphatically believing in the existence of spirits, he set himself against extravagant funerals, elaborate ceremonies, and even music, as detracting from and not aiding the welfare of the living. He would have a regulated consumption and would confine production to the necessities. He vigorously denounced determinism and held that men could perfect themselves by their own efforts. His views were, not unnaturally, roundly condemned by the Confucianists, particularly by Mencius. Among other arguments they contended that Mo Ti's principle of universal love by denying the duty of special or exclusive affection to one's own kin would dissolve the family and so destroy society.

Mo Ti's followers remained influential for several centuries after his death and included many brilliant minds. Before long they seem to have divided into at least two sects. One, considered more orthodox, emphasized the religious features of their master's teachings, and the other—a variant, a kind of Neo- or Reformed Mohism—stressed his dialectics. The former was held together by strict discipline under successive heads who were regarded as sages. Its members were somewhat ascetic, wearing simple clothing and eating plain food, working hard, and condemning music and elaborate burial and mourning ceremonies. The other branch had as its two chief exponents Hui Tzŭ, of the fourth and third centuries B.C., and Kung-sun Lung, of the third century B.C. It attempted to give further philosophical and metaphysical justification to the principles of Mo Ti and specialized on logic. The members of this branch, with their penchant for argument and their emphasis on terms, have not inaptly been called the sophists or dialecticians of China, and are sometimes classed separately as the *Ming Chia*, or School of Names.

The sects arising out of the work of Mo Ti seem to have suffered severely in the disorders that accompanied the end of the Chou. Their principles of universal love and non-aggression were scarcely in keeping with the violence of the age. Adherents of Mo Ti, however, were to be found as late as the first century B.C. Some of the writings of Mo Ti and his followers have been preserved and the logical methods developed in them have had marked influence.

A thinker who seems to have left behind him no cult and whose teachings are known chiefly through his adversaries was Yang Chu. Yang Chu, who lived in the fourth century B.C., acknowledged allegiance to none of the great schools of the time, but was an individualist and espoused both pessimism and fatalism. He regarded life as full of woe. Any exertion to better human society, such as that made by the Confucianists and Mohists, is futile, for fate determines all. Such heroes of China's antiquity as Shun, Yü, and Chou Kung, who spent themselves in the service of the state, knew never a day of ease, and those whom the Confucianists branded as villains, like Chieh and Chou Hsin, who were said by their vices to have ended their respective dynasties, enjoyed lives of pleasure. Dead, both good and bad are equal. Yang Chu advised, accordingly, that each should take life as it comes, enduring and making the most of it for himself, and not bothering about others or the state.

Another school, a fragment of whose teachings is preserved for us in one of the appendices of the *I Ching,* seems to have arisen among the professional diviners, and is sometimes known as that of the philosophy of nature or of *yin* and *yang*. On the basis of the *yin* and the *yang* it sought to frame a cosmogony and a cosmology, holding that the eternal *Tao* expresses itself through them and that they are represented by the whole and the broken lines of the ancient trigrams. Here, too, the *t'ai chi,* or "Great Ultimate," is talked of—although it is not emphasized. Many of the ideas of this sect were not their exclusive property or creation, but were widely diffused. They were to be very influential and have reappeared repeatedly in the history of Chinese thought.

Still another group, but which some consider as not a distinct school, was the *Fa Chia* or Legalists. Living in the fourth century, when disorder was increasing, its exponents despaired of saving society and improving human nature by the moral example of the rulers, as the Confucianists would do. One can by no means be sure of having a ruler of high character to set such an example, they contended, and, even if there were such, men are not sufficiently good by nature to respond. A fixed body of law, impartially and firmly administered, will not fluctuate as does the character of princes. Men, too, with their imperfect natures, can be best restrained and guided by force expressed in law. Laws should be adapted to changing circumstances and should be framed partly on the basis of the study and rectification of terms —of which the school made much. Aristocracy and the state were exalted. One group of the Legalists stressed agriculture and the economic self-sufficiency of each principality. Another sought to encourage commerce as a source of prosperity. It wished to socialize capital and have the state undertake trade and thus prevent private manipulation of prices and inequality of wealth. The great schools, Confucianism, Taoism, and Mohism, all had their influence, different Legalists showing evidence of being molded in part by one or the other of them. Han Fei Tzŭ (of the third century B.C.), a large proportion of whose writings have come down to us, was in many respects a Taoist. He is said also to have been a pupil of Hsün Tzŭ, and so to have been subject to some Confucian ideas. Hsün Tzŭ's conception of human nature as bad, but improvable, and of education as something to be enforced by society, seems to have developed logically into Legalist ideas. Han Fei Tzŭ, it may be added, was a redoubtable sceptic who questioned the alleged facts of antiquity concerning Yao and Shun to which so many scholars appealed for authority.

Li K'uei, also called Li K'o, a minister of the state of Wei, who is classified with the Legalists, advocated the equalization of prices of agricultural products by state purchase in times of plenty and sale in times of dearth.

To another notable member of the *Fa Chia,* Wei Yang (also called Kung-sun Yang or Shang Yang and by a prominent modern Chinese scholar said not to have been a theoretical Legalist, but a practical statesman), is, as we have seen, attributed the reorganization of Ch'in, under Duke Hsiao, in the middle of the fourth century B.C., which prepared the way for the ultimate triumph of that state. Wei Yang is said to have destroyed the decentralizing feudalism which before his time prevailed in Ch'in, as elsewhere in China, substituting for it an absolute ruler governing through a bureaucracy; to have abolished the *ching t'ien* system of land-holding, replacing it with individual peasant proprietorship; to have instituted severe laws with exact rewards and punishments; and, arranging families in groups, to have made each jointly responsible for the good behavior of its members. He is reported to have decried much of the culture of the old China and to have stressed agriculture and military organization. By discouraging interstate commerce and hoarding the produce of the soil, he is said to have attempted—in a fashion resembling that of the mercantilists of later European times—to make Ch'in self-dependent. Some of this—the encouragement of agriculture and the frowning on commerce—had a distinctly Taoist tinge. By centralization under an absolute ruler governing through a bureaucracy, by severe discipline, and by military and economic

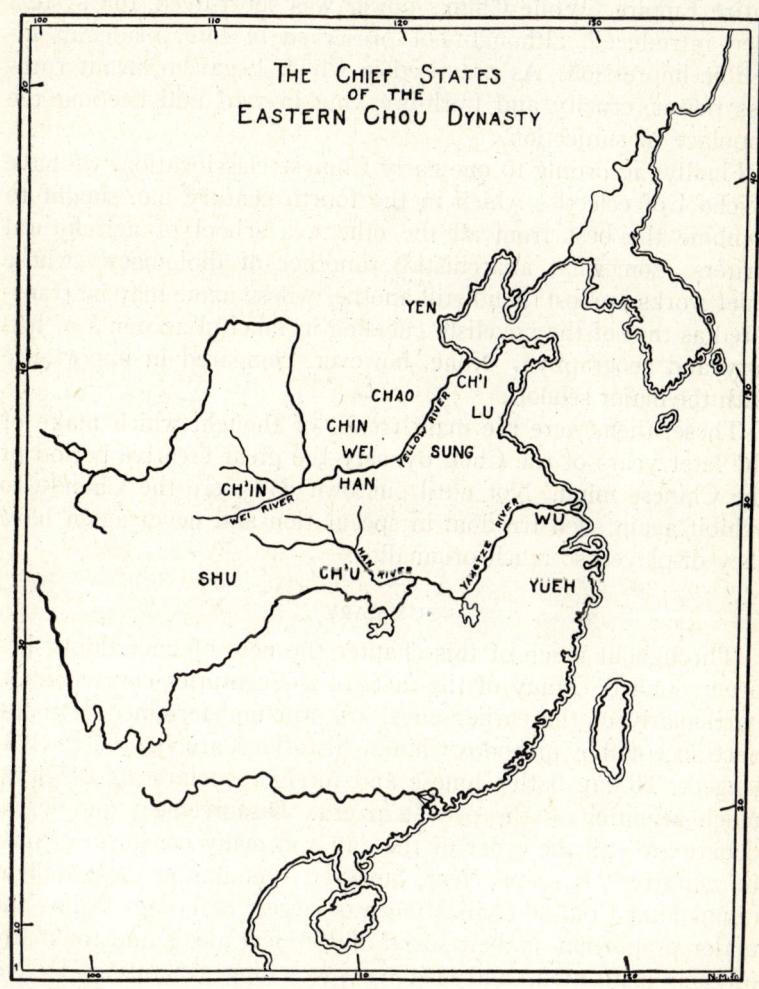

organization, he sought to weld Ch'in into an effective fighting unit.

Whether or not Wei Yang was responsible for all these changes, they were distinctly Legalistic in their conception and were carried out in Ch'in. Largely because of them, Ch'in attained to the efficiency which enabled her to master her neighbors. It is not strange that, victorious, Ch'in sought to apply them to the entire Empire. While Ch'in's power was short-lived, the system then introduced, although not preserved *in toto,* made an indelible impression. As practised in Ch'in, Legalism meant ruthless power, cruelty and faith-breaking in war, and keeping the populace in subjection.

Finally, according to one early Chinese classification, we have a school of eclectics which in the fourth century B.C. sought to combine the best from all the others, a school of agricultural writers (somewhat anarchistic), another of diplomacy (whose chief works are lost), and still another whose name may be translated as that of the novelists (dealing in fanciful accounts of history and geography). None, however, compared in importance with the major schools.

These, then, were the main trends of thought which make of the later years of the Chou dynasty the great creative period of the Chinese mind. Not until our own day were the Chinese to exhibit again such freedom in speculation and never again have they displayed so much originality.

SUMMARY

Throughout much of this chapter the note of uncertainty has been sounded. Many of the facts of the centuries covered in it, particularly of the earlier ones, are still undetermined. Others, once accepted by orthodox Chinese historians, are vigorously challenged. To-day both Chinese and foreign scholars are devoting much attention to the pre-Ch'in era. Disagreement and warm debate are still the order of the day and many conclusions must be tentative. It seems clear, however, that during these millenniums later Chinese civilization was largely determined. For the major proportion of their social and ethical ideals and for many of their institutions and customs succeeding generations looked for sanction to the China of the years before the Ch'in.

This culture, so rich and vigorous, had its original seat in the North China plain and the valley of the Wei. It did not remain there, however, but spread to the outlying districts, only partly Chinese in blood, where were those great states in whose hands lay the political destinies of the land. The agents of the spread seem chiefly to have been scholars, statesmen, and aristocratic adventurers from the older China, who, seeking employment at the hands of the powerful but semi-barbarous chieftains on the frontier, tutored these rulers in the civilization which they respected and copied while they domineered over its possessors. It was a process which, in its essence, Chinese history was often to see reproduced—the conquerors yielding to the culture of the conquered.

China was expanding, by the migration both of the Chinese and their culture. The way was being prepared for new and startling developments. Divided politically but vigorous intellectually, China was to be united under one strong rule. In doing so, it was to display fresh cultural growth. The formation of the new Empire was to be accompanied not only by marked political changes, but also by extensive alterations in the economic, social, and intellectual life of the people.

Future developments, revolutionary in many ways though they were, did not efface the cultural contributions of the Chou and its predecessors. The emphasis on ceremonial, the forms of ritual, the family system, the growing regard for certain ethical standards, were to persist, some of them studiously unaltered, to our own day. In many respects, before the final downfall of the Chou, Chinese culture had taken on its definitive ideals.

BIBLIOGRAPHY

Most of the chief Chinese sources for the period have been mentioned. The standard translations into English of the *Shu Ching, Shih Ching, Ch'un Ch'iu* (including the *Tso Chuan*) are by James Legge, in *The Chinese Classics* (5 vols., Hongkong, 1861–1872. Second edition, revised, 5 vols., Oxford, London, 1893, 1895). Translations of the *Li Chi*, the *Shu Ching*, the *I Ching*, and parts of the *Shih Ching*, by Legge (Oxford, 1879, 1882, 1885) form volumes 3, 16, 27, and 28 of *The Sacred Books of the East* . . . edited by F. Max Müller. The Jesuit missionary S. Couvreur has made translations into French and Latin of the *Li Chi* (second edition, Hochienfu, 1913), the *Shu Ching* (Hochienfu, 1897), the *Shih Ching* (Hochienfu, 1896), the *Four Books* (second edition, Hochienfu, 1910), and into French of the *Ch'un Ch'iu* (Hochienfu, 1914). An English translation of the *Chu Shu Chi Nien* (Bamboo Annals) is in Legge's prolegomena to the *Shu Ching*. The

Chou Li has been translated into French by E. Biot (*Le Tcheou-li ou Rites des Tcheou*, 3 vols., Paris, 1851). The *I Li* has been translated by John Steele, *The I Li or Book of Etiquette and Ceremonial* (2 vols., London, 1917). See Sir Everard Fraser and J. H. S. Lockhart, *Index to the Tso Chuan* (Oxford University Press, 1930). See also A. Waley, *The Book of Songs* (London, 1937).

The discussion of the authenticity of the so-called "ancient" text of the *Shu Ching*, with a list of the spurious portions, is in Edouard Chavannes, *Les Mémoires Historiques de Se-ma Ts'ien*, Vol. 1 (Paris, 1895), pp. cxiii–cxxxvi, and in Paul Pelliot, *Le Chou king et le Chang chou che wen; Mémoires concernant l'Asie Orientale*, II, Paris, 1916. Beginning with the so-called Han Learning school of savants of the Ch'ing (Manchu) dynasty, some Chinese scholars have been giving much attention to the authenticity and the dates of these early literary remains. Some have been inclined to call many of them forgeries composed under Wang Mang (first century A.D.). Others, while not going so far, hold that most of them are of much later dates and authorship than those traditionally assigned, and attempt to evaluate in a fresh way the information which they give. In this present century Liang Ch'i-ch'ao and Hu Shih have been especially active in setting in motion this kind of research. A noteworthy book by one stimulated by this school is Ku Chieh-kang, *Ku Shih Pien* (A Critical Exposition of Ancient Chinese History) (Peking, 1926). Liang Ch'i-ch'ao's views are to be found in his *Chung-kuo Li-shih Yen-chiu Fa* (Methods of Studying Chinese History) (Shanghai, 1922 and 1925), in his Collected Lectures (*Hsüeh Shu Chiang Yen Chi*) (3 vols., Shanghai, 1922, 1923, 1925), and in his *Yao Chi Chieh T'i Chi Ch'i Tu Fa* (Methods of Studying Important Classical Books) (Peking, 1925). Hu Shih's views are in his collected works, *Hu Shih Wên Ts'un* (Shanghai, 1927). An excellent short summary in English of these views is by Arthur W. Hummel, *What Chinese Historians are Doing to Their Own History* (*American Historical Review*, Vol. 34, July, 1929, pp. 715–724).

An article on the tests to determine the authenticity of the ancient texts is B. Karlgren, *The Authenticity of Ancient Chinese Texts* (*The Museum of Far Eastern Antiquities, Stockholm, Bulletin No. 1*, 1929, pp. 165–184). See also B. Karlgren, *On the Authenticity and Nature of the Tso Chuan* (Göteborg, 1926 and H. Maspero, *La Composition et la date du Tso tchouan* (*Melanges chinois et bouddhiques*, Vol. I, pp. 137–216). Karlgren continues the study of the authenticity of ancient texts in *The Early History of the Chou Li and Tso Chuan Texts* (*The Museum of Far Eastern Antiquities* (*Östasiatiska Samlingarna*) *Stockholm, Bulletin No. 3*, 1931, pp. 1–59).

The *Li Sao* has been translated several times into European languages. See Lim Boon Keng, *The Li Sao, An Elegy on Encountering Sorrows, by Ch'ü Yüan* (Shanghai, 1929), severely criticized by many. Also on the poetry of Ch'u see Ed. Erkes, *The Ta-chao*, in *Hirth Anniversary Volume* (London, 1923), pp. 67–86.

Probably the best English work on the *Lun Yü* is by Soothill, *The Analects of Confucius* (Yokohama, 1910). Also of importance is A. Waley, *The Analects of Confucius* (New York, 1939). A very good short, semi-popular account of Confucius—chiefly a translation of his life in the *Shih Chi* of Ssŭ-ma Ch'ien, a critical list of the documents containing his teachings, and a few selections from his sayings, is in R. Wilhelm, *Confucius and Confucianism*, translated from the German by G. H. and A. P. Danton (New York, 1931). The standard translation of Mencius into English and an excellent one of the *Lun Yü* are by Legge, in *The Chinese Classics*. On Mencius there are also Leonard A. Lyall, *Mencius* (London, 1932) and I. A. Richards, *Mencius on the Mind: Experiments in Multiple Definition* (London, 1932). L. S. Hsü, *The Political Philosophy of Confucianism* (New York, 1932) has many good features, but is marred by a somewhat too enthusiastic admiration for its subject.

The standard works in English on Hsün Tzŭ—although they are not without some serious defects—are H. H. Dubs, *Hsüntze, the Moulder of Ancient Confucianism* (London, 1927) and H. H. Dubs, *The Works of Hsüntze* (London, 1928). An interesting short monograph on Hsün Tzŭ is Andrew Chih-yi Cheng, *Hsüntzu's Theory of Human Nature and Its Influence on Chinese Thought* (Peking, 1928).

One translation of Mo Ti is Alfred Forké, *Mê Ti, des Socialethikers und seiner Schüler philosophische Werke* . . . (Berlin, 1922). Another translation, and a much smaller book, is Yi-Pao Mei, *The Ethical and Political Works of Motse, translated from the Original Chinese Text* (London, 1929). See also Suh Hu (Hu Shih), *The Logic of Moh Tih and His School* (*Chinese Recorder*, 1921, Vol. 52, pp. 668–677, 751–758, 833–843), Y. P. Mei, *Motse . . . the Neglected Rival of Confucius* (London, 1934) and L. Tomkinson, *The Social Teachings of Meh Tse* (*Transactions of the Asiatic Society of Japan*, 2d Series, Vol. 4, Dec. 1927).

The standard translation in English of the Tao Tê Ching and of Chuang Tzŭ are in *The Texts of Taoism*, by James Legge (2 vols., Oxford, 1891, Vols. 39 and 40 of *The Sacred Books of the East*). Another of Chuang Tzŭ is by Giles, *Chuang Tzŭ, Mystic, Moralist, and Social Reformer* (2d edition, Shanghai, 1926). Excellent on the *Tao Tê Ching* is A. Waley, *The Way and Its Power: a Study of the Tao Tê King and Its Place in Chinese Thought* (London, 1934). Still another work on Chuang Tzŭ is Fung Yu-lan, *Chuang-tzu* (Shanghai, 1932). Of Taoist texts there are also useful translations in Lionel Giles, *The Sayings of Lao Tzu* (London, 1904) and Lionel Giles, *Taoist Teachings from the Book of Lieh Tzu* (London, 1912). On the date and identity of Lao Tzŭ see H. H. Dubs in *Journal of the American Oriental Society*, Vol. LXI, pp. 215–221, Vol. LXII, pp. 300–304, and D. Bodde in *Journal of the American Oriental Society*, Vol. XLII, pp. 8–12, Vol. XLIV, pp. 24–27.

The work attributed to Wei Yang (Shang Yang) has been translated into English by J. J. L. Duyvendak, in *The Book of Lord Shang*. A

Classic of the Chinese School of Law (London, 1928). Another book on the Legalists is by the famous Liang Ch'i-ch'ao—Leang K'i-Tch'ao, *La Conception de la Loi et les Théories des Legistes à la Veille des Ts'in*. Extrait de l'*Histoire des Théories politiques à la Veille des Ts'in*, translated by J. Escarra and R. Germain (Peking, 1926). This is a translation of sections of a larger book and appears in English as Chapter VII and Appendix VI of Liang Ch'i-ch'ao, *History of Chinese Political Thought during the Early Tsin Period*, translated by L. T. Chen (New York, 1930). See also E. R. Hughes, *Political Idealists and Realists of China of the Fourth and Third Centuries B.C.* (*Journal of North China Branch of the Royal Asiatic Society*, 1932, Vol. 63, pp. 46–64). On Han Fei-Tzŭ, see W. K. Liao, *The Complete Works of Han Fei Tzŭ* (Vol. I, London, 1939).

On Yang Chu see A. Forké, *Yang Chu's Garden of Pleasure* (London, 1912).

Excerpts from the philosophers of the Chou are in L. Wieger, *A History of the Religious Beliefs and Philosophical Opinions in China*, translated by E. T. C. Werner (Hsien-hsien, 1927) and E. R. Hughes, *Chinese Philosophy in Classical Times* (London, 1942).

On the philosophers of the Chou see also Fung Yu-lan, *A History of Chinese Philosophy*, translated by D. Bodde (Peiping, 1937), an excellent product of modern Chinese scholarship; A. Waley, *Three Ways of Thought in Ancient China* (London, 1939); A. Forké, *Geschichte der alten Chinesischen Philosophie* (Hamburg, 1927); Liang Ch'i-ch'ao, *History of Chinese Political Thought during the Early Tsin Period*, translated by L. T. Chen (New York, 1930); Hu Shih, *The Development of the Logical Method in Ancient China* (Shanghai, 1922); D. T. Suzuki, *A Brief History of Early Chinese Philosophy* (London, 1914). There is a good deal of material on the philosophy of the period in Chen Huang-chang, *The Economic Principles of Confucius and His School* (2 vols., New York, 1911).

The *Shih Chi* of Ssŭ-ma Ch'ien, a famous standard general history of China giving the story from the beginning and based on earlier Chinese works, and written at the close of the second and the beginning of the first century B.C., has been in part translated into French with extremely full and valuable prolegomena, appendices, and notes, by Edouard Chavannes, in *Les Mémoires Historiques de Se-ma Ts'ien* (5 vols., Paris, 1895–1905).

The fullest general histories of China in a European language are J. A. M. de Moyriac de Mailla, *Histoire Générale de la Chine* (13 vols., Paris, 1777–1785)—based upon a famous general history, the *T'ung Chien Kang Mu*—and Henri Cordier, *Histoire Générale de la Chine* (4 vols., Paris, 1920–1921). De Mailla is, however, not always trustworthy, even as a translation of the *T'ung Chien Kang Mu* (partly because the latter was revised after he had used it), and Cordier is based in part upon de Mailla.

By all odds the best secondary account in any language on the period covered by this chapter is Henri Maspero, *La Chine Antique* (Paris, 1927), which, in addition to its excellent text, has extensive footnote references to Chinese sources and to monographs and articles by Chinese, Japanese, and Western scholars. A stimulating book, especially for the political and social organizaticn, is Marcel Granet, *La Civilisation Chinoise* (Paris, 1929), which majors on the pre-Han period. This has been translated into English (*Chinese Civilization*, New York, 1930). All of Granet's work, however, is regarded by many sinologists as putting forward suggestive but highly debatable hypotheses with too much assurance. Good secondary general accounts are in O. Franke, *Geschichte des Chinesischen Reiches*, Vol. 1 (Berlin and Leipzig, 1930), Friedrich Hirth, *The Ancient History of China to the End of the Chou Dynasty* (New York, 1911), and E. H. Parker, *Ancient China Simplified* (London, 1908). About half of R. Wilhelm, *A Short History of Chinese Civilization* (translated from the German, New York, 1929), is on this period. An essay containing the views—rather radical and not exclusively on the pre-Ch'in period—is V. K. Ting, *How China Acquired Her Civilization*, in Sophia H. Chen Zen (editor), *Symposium on Chinese Culture* (Shanghai, 1931).

Special monographs of importance are R. Britton, *Chinese Interstate Intercourse before 700 B.C.* (*American Journal of International Law*, Oct., 1935); Henri Maspero, *L'Astronomie Chinoise avant les Han* (*T'oung Pao*, Vol. 26, pp. 267–356); a view suggesting that there was a strong phallic element in early Chinese religion in B. Karlgren, *Some Fecundity Symbols in Ancient China* (*The Museum of Far Eastern Antiquities, Stockholm, Bulletin No. 2*, 1930, pp. 1–66); Marcel Granet, *Danses et Legendes de la Chine Ancienne* (2 vols., Paris, 1926); Marcel Granet, *La Polygnie Sororale et le Sororat dans la Chine Feodale* (Paris, 1920); Marcel Granet, *Fêtes et Chansons Anciennes de la Chine* (2d edition, Paris, 1929), translated into English by E. D. Edwards as *Festivals and Songs of Ancient China* (London, 1932); and O. Franke, *Der Ursprung der chinesischen Geschichtschreibung* (*Sitzunsberichte der preussischen Akademie der Wissenschaften*, 1925, pp. 27 et seq.). Albert Tschepe, *Histoire du Royaume de Tsin* and *Histoire du Royaume de Han* (*Variétés sinologiques*, Nos. 27, 31, Shanghai, 1909, 1910) contain a good deal of material, but show no very great perspective or critical acumen. On Lü Pu-wei and the rise to power of Ch'in, see D. Bodde, *Statesman, Patriot, and General in Ancient China* (New Haven, 1940).

On art an excellent brief survey is H. Ardenne de Tizac, *L'Art Chinois Classique* (Paris, 1926).

A useful summary of recent archeological finds is N. C. Nelson, *Archeological Research in North China* (*American Anthropologist*, Vol. 29, pp. 172 et seq.), and by L. H. D. Buxton in *Encyclopœdia Britannica* (14th ed., Vol. 5, pp. 524–528). On Peking man, the most primitive known in China, see F. Weidenreich, *The Skull of Sinanthropus Pekinensis* (Chungking, 1943). The chalcolithic finds are described more fully by J. G. Andersson in *An Early Chinese Culture* (*Bulletin of the*

Geological Survey of China, Oct. 1913, pp. 1–68); by J. G. Andersson in *The Cave-Deposit at Sha Kuo T'un in Fengtien* (*Palæontologia Sinica*, Series D, Vol. 1, Fas. 1, Peking, 1923); by T. J. Arne, *Painted Stone Age Pottery from the Province of Honan, China* (*Palæontologia Sinica*, Series D, Vol. 1, Fas. 2, Peking, 1925); by J. G. Andersson, *On Symbolism in the Prehistoric Painted Ceramics of China* (*The Museum of Far Eastern Antiquities, Stockholm, Bulletin No. 1*, 1929, pp. 65–70); and by J. G. Andersson in *Preliminary Report on Archæological Research in Kansu* (*Bulletin of the Geological Survey of China*, 1925). The remains of paleolithic man are described in O. Zdansky, *Preliminary notice on two teeth of a hominid from a cave in Chihli* (*Bulletin of the Geological Survey of China*, Vol. 5, Nos. 3–4 [1927], pp. 281–284); D. Black, *Discovery of further hominid remains of lower quarternary age from the Chou Kou Tien deposit* (*Science*, Vol. 67, Feb. 3, 1928, pp. 135, 136); and Chardin and Licent, *The discovery of paleolithic industry in North China* (*Bulletin of the Geological Survey of China*, Vol. 3, No. 1 [1924], pp. 45–50). There is also an important article on the prehistoric period in D. Black, *The Human Skeletal Remains from the Sha Kuo T'un Cave Deposit in Comparison with Those from Yang Shao Tsun and with Recent North China Skeletal Material* (*Paleontologia Sinica*, Series D, Vol. 1, Fas. 3). On Japanese discoveries in Manchuria of neolithic Chou, Ch'in, and Han periods, see Yoshito Harada and Kazuchika Komai, *Mu-yang-ch'eng: Han and Pre-Han Sites at the Foot of Mount Lao-t'ieh in South Manchuria* (*Archæologia Orientalis*, Vol. 2, Tokyo, 1931).

On the "oracle bones" of Honan, see L. C. Hopkins in *Journal of the Royal Asiatic Society*, 1911, pp. 1025–1034, 1915, pp. 49–61, 289–303, 1917, pp. 69–89, and L. C. Hopkins in *Hirth Anniversary Volume*, pp. 194–205.

On the Hsia see E. Erkes, *Ist die Hsia-Dynastie Geschichtlich?* (*T'oung Pao*, Vol. 33, pp. 134–149).

On the Shang see J. M. Menzies, *The Culture of the Shang Dynasty* (Smithsonian Institution, *Annual Report*, 1931, pp. 549–558); H. G. Creel, *The Birth of China* (London, 1936), scholarly and semi-popular, and which also has chapters on the Chou; and H. G. Creel, *Studies in Early Chinese Culture* (Baltimore, 1937), somewhat technical.

On some tombs of the Chou period see W. C. White, *Tombs of Old Lo-yang* (Shanghai, 1934).

On the interaction with the frontiers see O. Lattimore, *Inner Asian Frontiers of China* (Oxford University Press, 1940).

On the exchange of cultures across much of Asia and Europe in prehistoric and early historic times, see J. G. Andersson, *Der Weg über die Steppen* (*The Museum of Far Eastern Antiquities, Stockholm, Bulletin No. 1*, pp. 143–164).

On chronology see, in addition to general works listed above, Leopold de Saussure, *La Chronologie Chinoise et l'Avènement des Tcheou* (*T'oung Pao*, 1924, pp. 287–346), and C. W. Bishop, *The Chronology* of *Ancient China* (*Journal of the American Oriental Society*, Sept. 1932, Vol. 52, pp. 232–247).

On Lü Pu-wei, see Richard Wilhelm, *Frühling und Herbst des Lü Bu We, aus dem Chinesischen verdeutscht und erläutert* (Jena, 1928). Something is added in a review by P. Pelliot in *T'oung Pao*, Vol. 27, pp. 68–91.

On the language of Ch'u see E. Erkes, *Die Sprache des Alten Ch'u* (*T'oung Pao*, Vol. 27, pp. 1–11).

CHAPTER III

THE FORMATION OF THE EMPIRE: THE CH'IN AND HAN DYNASTIES (B.C. 221–A.D. 220)

THE CH'IN DYNASTY: SHIH HUANG TI

THE triumph of Ch'in, as we have suggested, was not the work of one man. Many had had a part—Duke Mu, Duke Hsiao, Wei Yang, and others whom we have not named. A system rather than an individual was victor. It is not strange, therefore, that the conqueror sought to reorganize and rule the newly won Empire by the methods which had proved so effective in his own state. In doing so he proved unable to perpetuate the power of his house, but he began a new day for Eastern Asia. He outlined an organization which, with many alterations, was that by which the Middle Kingdom was governed until A.D. 1912 and which, with occasional failures of longer or shorter duration, held together with remarkable success the vast region which is China. Moreover, in welding all China into one political unit, the conqueror, possibly quite unconsciously, brought in part to fruition the hopes of many dreamers. A large proportion of the thinkers of the Chou had conceived of China as a political whole, including all of civilized mankind. With the progressive disintegration of the power of the Chou, the aspiration had seemed to be further and further from reality. Now it was translated into fact, but in a decidedly different form from that which some of them had visualized.

The leader immediately responsible for this revolutionary development was Chêng—better known to history as Shih Huang Ti. His great assistant and chief minister was Li Ssŭ. Li Ssŭ, one of those migrant scholar-statesmen for whom the later years of the Chou had been famous, was a native of the state of Ch'u, and had, together with Han Fei Tzŭ, the distinguished Legalist, been a pupil of Hsün Tzŭ. Hsün Tzŭ, although usually classified with the Confucianists, perhaps was influenced by the Legalists. Especially did his theory of the absolute power of the prince accord with their ideals. In practice Li Ssŭ was a fairly thoroughgoing Legalist and so fitted in with the purposes of Chêng. Li Ssŭ was older than Chêng and became so prominent that he intermarried his children with the imperial family. Undoubtedly he had great influence with his prince. The latter drew from him some items in the program of the new empire.

When all China had been subdued, the energies of Chêng and Li Ssŭ were directed toward consolidating the conquests into an administrative and cultural whole, toward extending the boundaries into non-Chinese territory, and toward safeguarding the frontiers.

Chêng's organization of the Empire bears all the marks of genius—whether his or Li Ssŭ's or a heritage from the earlier rulers and ministers of Ch'in is difficult to say. It was possibly due to all three. The feudal principalities which had given the period of the Chou both its variety and its disorder were abolished. This step was presumably made easier by the decimation of the old aristocracy in the prolonged wars which preceded the triumph of Ch'in. On the advice of Li Ssŭ, a suggestion that the realm be redivided into satrapies governed by members of the imperial family was rejected. Instead of rule through the old aristocracy or through members of Chêng's family, an elaborate bureaucracy was created, with diversified functions and with carefully graded honorific titles. At the capital was a numerous administrative staff divided into several departments—among them a head of military affairs, a superintendent of the chief provincial officials, a chief of archery, a superintendent of the palace officials, a commandant of the palace guard, a superintendent of the imperial equipages, a chief justice, a supervisor of the barbarians who had submitted to the Ch'in, a chief of the police of the capital, and a head of imperial works. The Empire was divided into thirty-six—later augmented to forty or forty-one—*chün*, or provinces, and each of these in turn into *hsien*, or prefectures of varying sizes. Over every *chün* and *hsien* was placed a member of the bureaucracy. The plan, it must be added, was by no means entirely new. In name and concept both *hsien* and *chün* had come down from the Chou, although under the Chou the former had been larger than the latter. Wei Yang, moreover, had created a hierarchy with many titles. Very wisely Chêng did not depart entirely from the past.

At the head of the whole organization was the Emperor. To signalize the fact that he was making a fresh start in governmental tradition, Chêng assumed the designation of Shih Huang Ti—Shih meaning first, and Huang and Ti being titles customarily ascribed to mythical or semi-mythical rulers of antiquity—the Three Huang and the Five Ti. He thus gave fresh prestige to his reign and distinguished his office from that of the inept Chou. Had he been content with *Wang,* the designation of the Chou monarchs, he might properly have been expected to reproduce their form of government, with its disastrous decentralization.

To insure the pacification of the Empire, Shih Huang Ti had the arms collected of those who were not in his own forces and melted into bells and huge statues. Probably further to insure his own authority, he ordered the powerful and wealthy of the realm to move to the capital, Hsien Yang, not far from the later Ch'angan (Hsianfu). Here, presumably, they could be more easily kept under surveillance in case any of them contemplated sedition, and they would, too, lend dignity to the capital and so to the sovereign's power. It may be significant, moreover, that the capital was retained in the ancient territory of Ch'in, nearer to the dangerous northwest frontier than had been the capital of the Chou and where Shih Huang Ti's rule was longer established. At Hsien Yang, to the south of the River Wei and across from the main body of the city, Shih Huang Ti had constructed for himself, by the forced labor of thousands of men made eunuchs by the state, a vast palace. Around the memories of this structure interesting tales were to cluster.

Probably with the double purpose of insuring unity and prosperity, Shih Huang Ti attempted to make uniform the weights and measures of his domains. Implements and the gauges of wagons were standardized.

Under Shih Huang Ti, moreover, the private ownership of land by the peasants, which since the fourth century had prevailed in Ch'in, was extended to the entire country. Peasant proprietorship did not prove an unmixed blessing to the farmers. In the course of time many lost their lands and became slaves. The great public works, constructed by forced labor, tended further to infringe on the liberty of the lower classes. True to his Legalist training, however, the Emperor was trying to encourage agriculture.

It may be an indication of other great public works of the reign that from about now the irrigation project which makes fruitful the plain about Chengtu, in Szechwan, is said to date. It is reported that Li Ping, a Ch'in official, led the Min River through a pass which he cut in a mountain, and distributed its waters through a network of canals. Certainly the Emperor was attempting to provide unity by building an extensive system of roads centering in the capital. He also did much to improve the canals, possibly with a similar motive. Apparently with the same objective in mind, he destroyed some of the local walls and other fortifications erected by feudal princes.

The Emperor was an indefatigable traveller. Possibly from an innate restlessness and desire to see the country, and perhaps with the purpose of personally supervising his officials and so of insuring order, he spent much of his time traversing his domains.

One of Shih Huang Ti's most famous—or infamous—devices for insuring peace and unity was his attempt to suppress the criticisms of his rule by the adherents of others of the philosophical schools than the one he was following. As we have seen, the state of Ch'in had been organized by Wei Yang according to the principles of the Legalists—by severe laws, absolute autocracy, the encouragement of agriculture, and concomitant measures. To this system the rulers of Ch'in naturally attributed much of their success, and Shih Huang Ti sought to extend it to the entire Empire. The last centuries of the Chou, however, had been marked by freedom of thought and discussion and, as a corollary, by the vigorous denunciation of one school by another. The schools, moreover, concerned themselves largely with government and political theory. It is not strange, therefore, that Shih Huang Ti looked askance at the prospect of the continuation of these disputations. By them his own theories of administration would certainly be pointedly questioned and the continuation of his rule threatened. Criticism had, apparently, already begun—if, indeed, it had ever been absent—when, in response to a memorial of the influential Li Ssŭ, the opposing schools and the documents on which they based their authority were ordered suppressed. The memorial rehearsed what was almost certainly the fact—

that the scholars were condemning the laws of Ch'in and were praising the institutions of the past. The Confucianists, with their emphasis upon the moral influence of an upright ruler rather than upon strict law, and the followers of Mo Ti, with their belief in applying universally the principle of love, were especially opposed to the type of government which Shih Huang Ti was establishing. When, as they were accused of doing, they voiced their views publicly, they probably found ready listeners among those who were groaning under the heavy hand of the Emperor, with his suppression of the old feudal society, his stringent regulations, and his heavy exactions in taxes and labor. It must be added, moreover, that some Legalists tended to look askance at any wide use of literature (other than their own). There are suggestions that Wei Yang had considered a holocaust of books when he was in charge of Ch'in and that Shih Huang Ti found the idea in the writings of the great Legalist, Han Fei Tzǔ. Long before any of these, moreover, Mencius reports that princes had the custom of burning books which were obnoxious to them.

Shih Huang Ti, at the suggestion of Li Ssǔ and with Legalist severity, decreed that all the literature to which the non-Legalist scholars looked for authority be taken by the local officials and burned, including the official chronicles of the different feudal states, the Classic of Poetry (*Shih Ching*), the Classic of History (*Shu Ching*), and the discourses of the teachers of the philosophical schools. The task was not so difficult as might be supposed, for most of the books seem to have been on slips of bamboo, which were bulky and not especially easy of concealment, and the copies were probably not numerous. The only books excepted from the proscription were those on divination, on medicine, on agriculture and arboriculture, and the official chronicles of the state of Ch'in. These, it will be seen, either fitted in with the Legalist theories, which stressed agriculture, with the predilections of the Emperor, who was very credulous of superstitions, or with the desire to glorify Ch'in and its power. Copies of the prohibited books were to be preserved in the imperial library, but they could not be consulted without the consent of the proper officials. The death penalty was prescribed for those who discussed the *Shih Ching* and the *Shu Ching*—a favorite method of teaching of the members of the various schools, and especially of the Confucianists—and for those who denounced the present and praised antiquity. Punishments only slightly less drastic were decreed for those who failed to burn their books and for officials who did not enforce the edict. The conduct of the people, so it was ordered, must be regulated entirely by the officials by means of the law, and not by any books in which "the sayings of the ancient kings" were held up as an example.

Just how thoroughly the decree was enforced we do not know. It may be that the literary losses commonly ascribed to it were due more to the wars which immediately preceded the triumph of Ch'in. Certainly many of the cities were burned in these struggles and the collections of books contained in them must have suffered heavily. From the catalogue of the imperial library of the succeeding dynasty, moreover, it is clear that the sweep was by no means thorough. Some destruction there undoubtedly was, however—enough to bring down upon the memory of Shih Huang Ti the opprobrium of generations of writers of the school which under later dynasties was made orthodox, that of Confucius. Scholars who violated the command were executed and even the heir apparent was exiled to the frontier for criticizing the Emperor. Here again, however, there is some debate as to whether the number who suffered the death penalty was very large. Given the difficult problem of unification to which Shih Huang Ti had set himself, and the methods to which the victory of Ch'in seemed to owe so much, his action is quite understandable.

The reign was by no means one of complete suppression of literary advance—or at least not of the tools of scholarship. Li Ssŭ is the reported inventor of a new style of script, the "Lesser Seal." The "Lesser Seal" characters, it must be noted, were already in use in the latter part of the Chou. At most Li Ssŭ merely constructed an improved and standardized list and made it uniform throughout the realm, thus further promoting the unity of the Empire and its culture. To the commander-in-chief of the Emperor's armies, Mêng T'ien, is ascribed—incorrectly, for the brush pen had been in use for centuries—the invention of the writing brush of hair. Probably about the same time silk, presumably already employed for such purposes, was further substituted for bamboo slips as a vehicle for the written characters.

As we have suggested, Shih Huang Ti, not content with unifying China, proceeded to extend his boundaries into non-Chinese territory. Much of the coast from the present Chêkiang south into what is now Indo-China was occupied by peoples called the Yüeh, presumably related to the present Annamites. They were partially civilized, tattooing their bodies, using metals, and displaying skill as navigators. They possessed fertile and well-cultivated lands. In B.C. 221 Shih Huang Ti sent five large armies to annex the region. The more northerly territories—those in the present Chêkiang, Fukien, and Kwangtung beyond Canton—were quickly overrun. It was not until about B.C. 214, however, that the more southerly regions were conquered. By the end of that year the Ch'in boundaries seem to have been extended into the delta of the Red River and along the coastal plain beyond the site of the present Hué.

Shih Huang Ti is credited with colonizing the present Kwangtung with the idle and the vagabonds—among them probably those kept out of peaceful pursuits by the long wars and now, with the restoration of order, left restless, without regular employment and hence as actual or incipient bandits constituting a menace to the community. Some of the colonists, moreover, are said to have been criminals—those who had fallen afoul of the severe laws of Ch'in. Others very probably were those thrown out of their usual occupations by the abolition of feudalism.

Some of the main features of the Ch'in administrative organization were extended transiently and perhaps nominally to the present Kwangtung, Kwangsi, and Tongking. The Chinese, however, seem to have disturbed but little if at all the local political forms, the social institutions, and the culture of the southern portions of their new conquests. The process of assimilating the region was to be deferred until the next dynasty.

In the Center and the Central West Shih Huang Ti's domains extended into the present Hunan, Kweichow, and Szechwan. Szechwan was colonized by enforced emigration from the older China.

In the Northwest, Shih Huang Ti's forces defeated the Hsiung Nu, a pastoral, horse-using people, probably akin to the Tatars and Turks and possibly the same as or related to the Huns of European history. For several centuries we hear much of them in Chinese annals. About the time of Shih Huang Ti, but more immediately after his time than during it, the Hsiung Nu were being welded into an effective confederation. The Emperor only temporarily curbed their power, and when the Ch'in collapsed they again proved a serious menace. Shih Huang Ti's conquests against the Hsiung Nu are said to have reached as far as the present Lanchow in Kansu. Into the Northwest, too, the Emperor extended his administrative organization and settled part of the region with convicts from his older domains. The Emperor, by extensive compulsory movements of population toward the frontiers, was possibly attempting to foster an ethnic as well as a cultural unity in his domains.

In what is now Korea a prince recognized the overlordship of the Ch'in. There are hints, too, that Shih Huang Ti sketched out a maritime policy.

On the northern marches, as a protection against the forays of the Hsiung Nu and other truculent, semi-nomadic tribes, Shih Huang Ti constructed, by forced and convict labor, fortresses and barriers, extensive portions of that Great Wall which, added to and repaired during the centuries, is one of the monumental achievements of men's hands. The princes of the northern feudal states are said to have built, long before the time of Shih Huang Ti, walls along their northern frontiers as a defence against forays and invasions. Shih Huang Ti's wall, which very probably incorporated these, is reported to have extended from somewhere in the present Kansu to Shanhaikuan on the sea. The present wall follows only in part the course of that of Shih Huang Ti.

Much of the work of conquest and of the construction of fortifications was under the supervision of Mêng T'ien, who had assisted in the final subjugation of the Empire.

Such extensive public works required not only forced labor but heavy taxation. New imposts were devised—among them a poll tax, and possibly the monopoly of salt and iron. They did not serve to make the Emperor popular with his subjects.

Shih Huang Ti, conqueror and able organizer and administrator though he seems to have been, shared the religious beliefs and popular superstitions of his age. He sacrificed extensively to various divinities, carrying out a well-established custom that the state should thus insure the coöperation of the unseen powers for the welfare of man. The Ch'in brought in the worship of five gods or Heavenly Emperors—earlier four—identified with the five elements, the five directions (east, west, north, south, and center), and the five planets. It will be recalled, too, that the school of the Legalists, whose political precepts the Emperor followed, had been much influenced by Taoism, and that by the end of the Chou Taoism had in practice degenerated into magic and a search for an elixir of life. The Emperor was fearful of death and did not like to hear of it or of funerals. It is recorded that—presumably to avoid evil spirits, but possibly from fear of assassination—he did not permit any one to know the room in his great palace where he expected to spend the night, but commanded several chambers to be constantly in readiness for him. A popular belief had arisen—it has been suggested that it was an importation from the coastal races in the Northeast—in immortals who dwelt in sacred mountains and could teach mortals the secret of escaping death. Shih Huang Ti spent much energy in searching for the drug that would confer immortality. He is reported, at the suggestion of one of his advisers in this quest, to have sent into the eastern sea as a purchase price for it a company of youths and maidens of good families. These never were heard from again and it is asserted, although on no dependable grounds, that the expedition reached and colonized Japan.

This striving for immortality and this surrounding the habitation of the Emperor with mystery as well as magnificence may have been partly from the desire further to augment the imperial authority and the unity of the realm by making the monarch divine. Be that as it may, the search for the much-desired drug proved vain. Death overtook the Emperor while he was on one of his journeys, away from his capital (B.C. 210). Li Ssŭ, who was with him at the time, feared rebellion if the demise were immediately known. He managed, therefore, to keep the fact a secret until the imperial entourage, bearing with it the body, returned to Hsien Yang.

The delay gave time for some of the more powerful of the company to arrange the succession to suit themselves. One of Shih Huang Ti's last acts had been to order a message sent to his eldest son, the heir apparent—still in exile on the northern frontier—to return to the capital with the funeral cortège and conduct the interment. Li Ssŭ, Chao Kao (a powerful eunuch), and Hu Hai, the second son of Shih Huang Ti, substituted for it a letter commanding the eldest son to commit suicide. They also fabricated a decree of the late Emperor appointing Hu Hai to the succession. This cold-blooded plot was entirely successful. The eldest son accepted the spurious missive as genuine and complied with its command. Arrived at the capital, the conspirators met with no important opposition. Hu Hai mounted the throne as Êrh Shih Huang Ti, "The Second Generation Emperor," and had his father's remains placed in a huge tomb that had long been in building.

Ssŭ-ma Ch'ien, writing something over a hundred years later, tells marvelous stories of this sepulchre—saying that it was hollowed out of a mountain, that in it were a reproduction of the heavens and a map of the Empire, that it was stored with riches, that it was guarded by machines so ingeniously devised that they would discharge arrows on any intruder, that the workmen who had perfected the final arrangements were sealed alive in the tomb to prevent them from divulging its secrets, and that the place was then planted to give it the aspect of a natural mountain. How much the story grew with the telling we do not know, but a lofty tumulus is still pointed out as the remains of the grave.

THE DOWNFALL OF THE CH'IN DYNASTY

The Ch'in dynasty did not long survive the death of its first monarch. The changes introduced by the conqueror had been so drastic, his laws so severe, and the burden of his public works so heavy, that once his strong hand was removed an upheaval was almost inevitable. The former rivals of Ch'in, too, had not been so thoroughly crushed and welded into the new Empire but that adherents were found who sought to revive at least the strongest of them. Certainly only an extraordinarily able successor could have prevented or even postponed extensive rebellion. Êrh Shih Huang Ti was far from equal to the task. The eunuch Chao Kao soon completely dominated him. Êrh Shih Huang Ti added to the stringent laws of his father, continued the heavy taxation and the expensive construction of the great palace of his sire, and so severely punished those who criticized him that no official felt safe. The experienced advisers of the last reign were put out of the way, probably through the machinations of Chao Kao. Mêng

T'ien, the commander-in-chief of the armies which guarded the frontier, was ordered to commit suicide, and Li Ssŭ, after advising moderation and more attention to the marches, was thrown into prison and executed. Revolts soon broke out, Chao Kao had Êrh Shih Huang Ti killed (B.C. 207) after a brief reign of three years and buried him like a commoner. In his place the eunuch put Tzŭ Ying, a son of the eldest son of Shih Huang Ti, but simply with the title of the *Wang* of Ch'in—possibly hoping to placate the rebels by a surrender of the Empire and a return to the old divisions. Before long Tzŭ Ying found a means of having the powerful king-maker killed. After a reign of less than two months he in turn was eliminated by the head of a league of rebels, the capital was plundered, the great palace built at the cost of so much treasure and human suffering was given to the flames, and the dynasty of Ch'in was at an end. Incidentally the disaster probably entailed as great a loss of the records of the past as did the burning of the books by Shih Huang Ti.

The debacle of the family of Shih Huang Ti was overwhelming, but the work of that grand monarch and of the predecessors of his line was by no means wholly undone. The feudalism of the Chou had been effectively erased, and when, a few years later, a successful general once more united the Empire, he and his house preserved in modified form much of the administrative machinery of the Ch'in. The old states had been so thoroughly disposed of that the attempts to revive them proved few and unsuccessful. The elder China, with its picturesque feudalism, had disappeared forever. A unified Empire had been formed. Much of the old passed over into the new and left on it an indelible imprint, but the China which Shih Huang Ti helped to bring into existence henceforth differed, both in political organization and in other phases of its civilization, from that of pre-Ch'in times. A new era had dawned.

There is an interesting appropriateness in the origin of the name China. At its inception it appears to have been a designation given the country by peoples in Central Asia and to have been derived from Ch'in, with which, as the dominant state in the Northwest, the non-Chinese to the west would first come in contact.

THE FOUNDING OF THE EARLIER OR WESTERN HAN DYNASTY

The rebellions which made a sudden and violent end to the Ch'in dynasty brought an almost entirely new set of families to the fore. Here and there members of the princely houses of the later centuries of the Chou appear prominently as actors, but either the vigor of these lines had run out or most of their able members had been exterminated by Shih Huang Ti and in the wars that preceded his victories. It was largely offspring of relatively undistinguished progenitors who emerged as leaders from the free competition of the fresh period of disorder.

The most prominent of the new men were Hsiang Yü (or Hsiang Chi) and Liu Chi (or Liu Pang). Hsiang Yü was of great height, marked impetuosity and generosity, and superb physical prowess. His father had been a general of Ch'u, whose stronghold was, it will be recalled, in the Yangtze Valley, and had perished when that state was being conquered by the Ch'in. When insurrection broke out against the incompetent successor of Shih Huang Ti, Hsiang Yü took service under his uncle, Hsiang Liang, who was seeking to restore Ch'u. A member of the former ruling house of Ch'u, found living in obscurity as a shepherd, was elevated to the headship of that principality. When, in the vicissitudes of war, Hsiang Liang was defeated and lost his life, Hsiang Yü quickly rose to the supreme command of the armies of Ch'u, and, his prince being very much of a puppet, bade fair to be not only the chief man of Ch'u but of the Empire. It was he who led the forces which sacked the Ch'in capital and put to death the feeble grandson of Shih Huang Ti, and, when this had been done, it was he who proclaimed his titular master Emperor, under the title of I Ti. He parcelled out the realm among the leading generals of the victorious rebels and among some of the Ch'in generals who had submitted, giving them the title of *Wang*. He himself became the *Wang* of Ch'u (B.C. 206). This, it will be noted, was a revival of decentralization. The headquarters of the new régime were established not on the plain of the Wei but in the present Hunan, nearer the center of Ch'u, from which Hsiang Yü's support seems largely to have been derived. Hsiang Yü soon fell out with the new Emperor and had him killed. This act precipitated the inevitable struggle between the rival generals.

In the ensuing trial of strength the chief opponent of Hsiang Yü was he who was later termed Liu Pang. Under the Ch'in, Liu Pang had been a minor official in his native district. He is said to have been of an open and generous disposition, fond of his cups, and with an eye for a pretty face. He could also, as it proved, be persistent, prudent, shrewd, and cruel. Charged with conducting a group of forced laborers to the mountain where the tomb of Shih Huang Ti was being built, he set his prisoners at liberty and, putting himself at the head of a few of the boldest of them, became an outlaw in the mountains and marshes of Central China. In the disorder which succeeded the death of Shih Huang Ti, he was chosen to head his native district and attached himself to Hsiang Liang in the effort to revive the state of Ch'u. He quickly became a leading commander of the forces of that principality and was soon Hsiang Yü's major rival.

In the fighting between these two doughty generals the victory seemed to perch upon the banner first of one and then of the other. At one time Hsiang Yü offered to settle the issue in single combat with Liu Pang, but the latter, more cautious, declined. At the outset Hsiang Yü seemed to be in the lead, for he routed Liu Pang's army and captured the father and wife of his antagonist. Later the rivals made a treaty, dividing the Empire between them. This compact Liu Pang almost immediately broke (B.C. 202) and, in a great battle which followed, brought about the downfall of his enemy. Hsiang Yü fled from the field of his disaster with a few devoted followers, still desperately fighting, and, when all was obviously lost, committed suicide.

Liu Pang's subordinates—possibly not without prompting—offered the title of Emperor to their commander, now clearly the master of the country. After the ostensible reluctance and triple refusal which etiquette prescribed, Liu Pang accepted (B.C. 202), thus perpetuating the form of unity which Shih Huang Ti had begun. The date from which the new dynasty was reckoned was not B.C. 202, but B.C. 206, when Liu Pang had become *Wang* of Han.

The Han made permanent the work which the Ch'in had begun, and endured, with two marked interruptions, for over four hundred years—centuries which were among the most glorious of China's long history.

Liu Pang, whom we had better now call by his dynastic title, Kao Tsu or Kao Ti, proved a wise administrator of his conquests. He declared a general amnesty and repealed many of the severe laws of Ch'in. Kao Tsu and the earlier rulers of his house favored the minimum of state regulation and of formal etiquette. Presumably he realized that popular opinion would not tolerate the restoration of Ch'in Legalism with its grinding totalitarianism. He was a man of the people, with crude language and manners, and owed his position in part to his good judgment of men and his appeal to the commoners. Kao Tsu took steps which later led to the adoption of Confucianism by his house. He recognized in practice the Confucian theory that government must be for the benefit of the governed and as much by example as by force. He had some Confucian scholars around him, notably one of his ministers, Lu Chia. It is said that when Kao Tsu contemptuously remarked that he had won the Empire from the back of a horse and had no need for the *Shih Ching* and *Shu Ching* of the scholars, Lu Chia boldly told him that the Empire could not be administered from the back of a horse and that if the Ch'in had sought to rule by the Confucian virtues it would not so quickly have come to an end. Moreover, in the last year of his reign, Kao Tsu visited, while on one of his journeys, the tomb of Confucius and offered a sacrifice there. Although this probably merely indicated that Kao Tsu regarded the sage as one of the many great men whose spirits deserved honor, it shows that the Confucian school was no longer proscribed as in the days of Shih Huang Ti. Kao Tsu also employed Confucian scholars in drawing up a simple form of etiquette for the court, to eliminate the boorishness which characterized the actions of his entourage in the earlier years of his reign. The adoption of Confucianism was probably further foreshadowed by an order (B.C. 196) that the princes send men of ability to court for the public service, for it was a Confucian principle that government should be by able and upright officials. It must be noted, however, that filling offices with the most fit might also be a corollary of the Legalist program and so may have been in part a heritage from Ch'in.

Religiously, Kao Tsu was tolerant of tribal and local cults. They were represented at his capital by their shrines, priests, and ceremonies. This was, of course, a wise administrative measure.

Kao Tsu fixed his capital in the former domains of Ch'in, on the broad plain of the Wei River, at Ch'angan, a few miles northwest of the later Ch'angan of the T'ang and not very far from the capital which Shih Huang Ti had built. He retained, too, much of the governmental machinery of Ch'in. In at least one very important respect, however, he departed from the organization of Shih Huang Ti: he divided the realm into principalities, placing over them members of his family and military commanders who had done him marked service. The chief of these had the time-honored title of *Wang*. The provision was probably wise at the time as a means of preventing or suppressing sedition. Moreover, the *Wang* were few in number and were kept under a kind of surveillance by counselors appointed by the Emperor. Their domains did not supplant the administrative divisions of the Ch'in, but the latter were continued and were governed by the hierarchy of Shih Huang Ti, modified somewhat, but still appointed by the Emperor. In spite of safeguards, however, the creation of the *Wang* brought its problems, for it repeatedly threatened the renewed disintegration of the Empire. Feudalism, in a modified form, once more raised its head.

With all of Kao Tsu's skill and power, his authority was by no means undisputed and much of his reign was troubled by revolts. These he suppressed, however, and so successfully did he do his work—steering a middle course between the feudal anarchy of the later years of the Chou and the extreme centralization of the Ch'in—that when he died (B.C. 195) the throne passed on to his family without such a major upheaval as had followed the demise of Shih Huang Ti.

The unity of the Empire and the continuation on the throne of the line of Kao Tsu were both helped and endangered by his widow Lü Hou, who survived him fifteen years. Lü Hou had been Kao Tsu's wife from the days of his obscurity and, being a woman of masculine mind and indomitable will developed by the hardships which the pair had early undergone, she is said to have been in large part responsible for the eventual triumph of her spouse. During the later years of Kao Tsu the two saw less and less of each other, but when the change of reign came she succeeded in having her own son, a mere lad, placed on the throne. Another son, born of Kao Tsu's favorite concubine, she had poisoned and, possibly moved by the hatred and jealousy of a slighted wife, she had his mother horribly mutilated and killed. Lü Hou's own son, the Emperor Hui Ti, proved dissipated and she was practically monarch during his reign. She married him to a granddaughter of hers, and, although the union is believed to have been childless, on his death she declared Emperor successively boys whom she said were its fruits. These children were, of course, mere puppets, and Lü Hou was the real ruler. The first of them was a son of Hui Ti by a concubine. When he showed too much independence she had him imprisoned. She appointed her own relatives to high office and apparently sought to supplant permanently the Liu family. On her death, however, the house of Liu asserted itself, exterminated her kin, and placed on the throne a son of Kao Tsu, known in history as Wên Ti.

Of Wên Ti and of the succeeding Emperor Ching Ti, his son, but little need here be said. Wên Ti was an exceptionally able ruler. He favored Confucianism. The surviving prohibitions of Ch'in were still further lightened, that against criticism of the government being entirely abolished. The Ch'in edict proscribing all but certain authorized books, it should be noted, had been rescinded while the Empress Lü was in power. Capital punishment was comparatively infrequent. Taxes were reduced. Under them the Empire was recuperating from the extreme exhaustion which characterized the earlier years of the Han. Members of the Liu family were again appointed to rule over the great divisions of the Empire, but their power was more and more curtailed. One of the steps taken against them—the annexation to the central government of portions of their estates [1]—led to a concerted revolt of several of these dignitaries. Upon its suppression a further diminution of the importance of the *Wang* was effected by depriving them of some of their functions and establishing the principle that their domains should be partitioned among their children rather than passed intact to one heir.

APEX OF THE EARLIER HAN DYNASTY: THE REIGN OF WU TI

The Han dynasty reached its height under the Emperor who is best known to posterity by the title of Wu Ti (usually called Han Wu Ti to distinguish him from Wu Tis of other dynasties).

[1] The step was taken in part at the suggestion of some Legalists.

Coming to the throne in B.C. 140, at the age of sixteen, he ruled the Empire until B.C. 87, or for over fifty years. His was by far the longest reign of the dynasty, and one of the most famous in the history of China. He inherited a realm which had recovered from the exhaustion that preceded and followed the Ch'in and which was now prosperous and ready for expansion and fresh activity. The half-century is noted both for extensive foreign conquests and for marked internal developments in organization and culture.

The territorial expansion during the reign of Wu Ti was to the northwest, the northeast, and the south, and extended the boundaries and the influence of China farther than at any previous time.

In the Northwest, the chief enemies of the Chinese were the Hsiung Nu. As we have seen, this semi-nomadic people had been held at bay by Shih Huang Ti. They had taken advantage of the internal turmoil in China at the close of the Ch'in once more to become aggressive. Welded into a confederation by an able leader, they had become a formidable foe. During the earlier years of the Han they had been a fairly constant menace and had repeatedly raided Chinese territory. Wu Ti made their subjugation one of his major objectives. In doing so he established contacts with Central Asia which brought the Chinese into touch with the great civilizations to the West—with interesting consequences.

Wu Ti sought to conquer the Hsiung Nu partly by direct military campaigns, partly by establishing military colonies in their territory, and partly by diplomacy. Wu Ti's generals carried on the warfare for years and with much success. The Chinese frontier was pushed out to include most of what is now Kansu, probably beyond where it had been in Shih Huang Ti's time, and colonies, garrisons, and a westward extension of the Great Wall— first to the Jade Gate (Yü Mên) and later still farther westward—helped to give the victories permanence. Wu Ti did not entirely break the power of the Hsiung Nu, but he reduced it greatly.

In the days of their might, the Hsiung Nu had defeated some neighbors of theirs, the Yüeh Chih,[2] or Tochari, who were then living in what is now, roughly, Western Kansu. The Yüeh Chih

---

[2] Also romanized Yüeh Shih.

were probably an Indo-European people, speaking an Iranian dialect, and unrelated racially to the Hsiung Nu. Migrating westward into what is now Ili and later still farther westward and then southward, for some centuries they ruled the territory north of the Oxus, and in Bactria (in the trans-Caspian region, north and east of Persia) overthrew the kingdoms established by Greek adventurers in the wake of the armies of Alexander the Great. Later some of them invaded Northwest India and in the early part of the Christian era, under the Kushan dynasty, experienced important cultural developments. It was a mark of statesmanship on the part of Wu Ti that he attempted to form an alliance with them against their common enemy, the Hsiung Nu. The envoy whom he chose to effect this purpose was Chang Ch'ien—who seems, indeed, to have suggested the plan.

Around the name of Chang Ch'ien many later accretions of legend and fabrication have gathered. Even the standard accounts have been declared by some scholars either to be interpolations or to contain many later additions. Back of them must, however, lie at least a basis of fact. The record as we have it can be summarized as follows. In B.C. 138 Chang Ch'ien left China on his westward journey. The Hsiung Nu captured him and for ten years held him prisoner. Escaping, he reached the Yüeh Chih in Bactria and spent a year among them. The Yüeh Chih declined the proffered alliance, but Chang Ch'ien had brought the Chinese in touch with the West and had reached the outposts of the cultural influences of the Mediterranean world. The intrepid traveller succeeded in making his way back to China (B.C. 126).

While in Bactria, Chang Ch'ien found bamboo and cloth which he believed—possibly incorrectly—to have originated in what are now Szechwan and Yünnan. He learned that these were said to come through India and that they had reached that country by way of what is now the Yünnan-Burmese border. This led him to dream of opening communication between China and the West by that route instead of by the one which the Hsiung Nu had made so difficult for him. However, he found this impracticable.

A few years later Chang Ch'ien went on another embassy to the West. This time he himself did not go so far as on his first journey, but sent subordinates on the more distant missions.

Chang Ch'ien, it must also be noted, introduced into China from the West alfalfa and the cultivated grape. Later tradition was to credit him, falsely, with having brought numbers of other plants from Central Asia.

Wu Ti effectively followed up the expeditions of Chang Ch'ien and succeeded in making Chinese power felt in what is now the New Dominion. Some peoples in the Tarim basin and in Ili were reduced to submission. Horses were even asked from a state in the later Ferghana, in the valley of the Jaxartes, west of the boundaries of the present Sinkiang, and, when these were refused and the Chinese envoy killed, the general Li Kuang-li was dispatched to wreak the Emperor's vengeance. At first he was unsuccessful and was beaten back, but Wu Ti kept him and his decimated forces, in disgrace, on the Western frontier. Then, returning over the long desert road to the attack, Li Kuang-li was victorious and placed a Chinese nominee on the throne. More than ten embassies went from the country to China during the reign of Wu Ti. Li's was a noteworthy military feat, worthy of ranking with those which the Romans had been performing, only a few decades before, in the Mediterranean world to the west.

It was not only in the Northwest that Wu Ti was extending his power. In the Northeast he was gaining victories. Wu Ti's initial endeavors in that region are said to have been for the purpose of turning the flank of the Hsiung Nu. In what is now the southern part of Manchuria and the northern part of Korea, a state had arisen during the early years of the Han with its capital at what is now P'ingyang. Its name, Ch'aohsien, is to-day, under its Japanese pronunciation, Chosen, used for all Korea. Ch'aohsien acknowledged somewhat vaguely the suzerainty of China, and when it treated rather lightly its duties as a vassal Wu Ti determined to bring it more fully under his sway. The ensuing war led, in the last decade of the second century B.C., to the annexation of Ch'aohsien to the Han domains. The conquest was, naturally, followed by the infiltration of Chinese culture into the peninsula. Into the Northeast, too, in what is now the northeastern part of Hopei and South Manchuria, and even in the present Korea, Chinese settlers were moved to help hold the territory for the Empire. Near P'ingyang, for example, a wealthy Chinese colony was established in B.C. 108. For four centuries or more, until A.D. 313, it flourished and remained an outpost of Chinese imperial power, with governors appointed from China. In the tombs of the colony rich remains of civilization have been found. The effect of this settlement on the life of the adjacent Koreans must have been marked. It is possible, too, that a little Chinese culture filtered into Japan by way of Korea. Indeed, the Chinese claim that under part of the Han Japan was a vassal of China.

Wu Ti also extended his territories to the south. The peoples in the present coast provinces to the south of the Yangtze and in Annam which, under Shih Huang Ti, had been brought within the administrative system of the Ch'in and had been partially colonized by Chinese, had taken advantage of the weakness of the Empire between the First Emperor and Wu Ti again to become independent. Divided under several local rulers, they fell a comparatively easy prey to the vigorous, growing colossus of the North. A kingdom in what is now the southern part of Chêkiang was the first to be annexed—in the earlier years of Wu Ti's reign —and thousands of its people were moved into the valley of the Huai. A state in what is now Fukien was the next to submit, and much of its population is said to have been deported to the north of the Yangtze. The mixture of population was probably furthered to crush out local loyalties and, by creating one amalgamated Chinese race, to strengthen unity and the power of the Emperor.

The largest of the southern kingdoms, called Nan Yüeh, had been established by a Chinese, a former officer of Shih Huang Ti. For a time this ruler acknowledged the suzerainty of the Han, but after a few years he deemed himself strong enough to assert his independence. Nan Yüeh had its capital at what is now Canton and seems to have comprised much of the present Kwangsi and Kwangtung and of the eastern portions of what is now French Indo-China. The Han cast especially covetous eyes upon its territories when a Chinese envoy made the discovery that the products of what is now Szechwan—a Han possession— were carried to Canton by way of the West River and its tributaries. Under Wu Ti's direction Nan Yüeh was conquered (B.C. 108), its territories were added to the Han domains, and a canal was built to help connect the basin of the West River with that of the Yangtze. As under the Ch'in, however, Nan Yüeh was governed according to its old customs and through its native chiefs. No new taxes were placed on it—at least for the time. Colonization of the South—especially of the Canton region—by Chinese proceeded apace, and it and Han control were favored by placing the passes across the hills between the Yangtze and the south coast under administrative districts of the great valley.

Petty states in what is now Kweichow and Yünnan also made their submission to Wu Ti. The conquests in Yünnan were partly with the motive of opening or controlling trade with India via Burma—possibly following up a suggestion of Chang Ch'ien.

Before the death of Wu Ti, then, the Han administrative organization had been extended on the south to include much of what is now Chêkiang, Fukien, Kwangtung, Kwangsi, Hainan, the northeastern section of French Indo-China, Kweichow, and Yünnan.

Much of this success on the field of battle was due to modifications in military methods. As under the Ch'in, the old cumbersome war chariot was passing and a more mobile cavalry, supported by infantry, was coming into use.

The Han Empire was now not far from the size of that which the Roman Republic had recently been building in the Mediterranean world. The culture of this China was probably not so rich or so varied as that of the contemporary West, but, as we shall see a little later, in comparison it was by no means barbarous.

The long reign, the vigor, and the vast conquests of Wu Ti brought marked internal developments in China. Wu Ti continued the policies of his immediate predecessors and further reduced the power of the local princes and increased that of the bureaucracy which headed up in the Emperor. As had Kao Tsu, he appointed counselors to each *Wang* to watch and report to him the action of these magnates. He continued systematically to divide the great fiefs—commanding the lord to leave his estate not to one heir only, but to partition it among all his sons. Moreover, Wu Ti called into his service men of ability wherever he found them, disregarding birth and often raising to high power those of base extraction. He was an enemy of feudalism and of privilege of birth, for these threatened internal unity and his own power. The old aristocracy, already weakened by the wars that preceded the triumph of Ch'in and by the policies of Shih Huang Ti, was dealt further blows. The former distinction between it and the commoners was passing. The manners of the old nobility tended more and more to be adopted by the lower classes. New divisions between the rich and the poor were appearing.

Like Shih Huang Ti, Wu Ti strove to exalt the authority of the throne. To this end, he developed a system whose rudiments seem to have existed before his time for discovering and choosing men of promise. On at least one occasion he awarded a prize to him who gave the best advice on the art of government. He commanded local officials to recommend those in their jurisdictions who were the most virtuous and surrounded himself with men renowned for their wisdom. The beginnings of the competitive examination for the choice of the worthy for office seem to date from his reign, although Wu Ti and his successors did not utilize it as extensively as did some later dynasties. Wu Ti instituted a higher school at the capital for the training of future officials, and schools were encouraged in the local provinces and districts. This was not entirely an innovation, to be sure, for schools were to be found in the Chou dynasty and possibly earlier. It was, however, a further expansion of the time-honored system.

This policy, extended and elaborated by later rulers and dynasties, was to grow into that bureaucracy and official hierarchy which was to be one of the outstanding features of the Chinese state—the device by which the great area of China was held together and administered. It cannot be attributed solely to Wu Ti. The Ch'in, and especially Shih Huang Ti, did more to create it than he, the earlier monarchs of the Han employed the principle, and the roots of it go back into Chou and possibly into pre-Chou times. For example, some of its basic concepts are to be found in the writings of more than one of the Chou schools and probably were not original with any one man. Wu Ti, however, was astute enough to see the importance of the system and to add to its practical application.

The court presented a mixture of several of the philosophical schools. It was deeply interested in the magical side of popular Taoism, as had been Shih Huang Ti, and several of the administrative devices of the Emperor smacked strongly of Legalism. Wu Ti, however, showed favor to the adherents of Confucianism.

His principle of appointing to office the ablest, although harking back to the Legalistic Ch'in, could plead for justification Confucian precepts. He made a descendant of Confucius the superintendent of public instruction, and he encouraged the study of the Classics to which the Confucianists looked for authority. He chose at least some of his functionaries from those most skilled in the Classics. He gave a blow to the Legalist school—which continued to be influential—by refusing to appoint to the public service those trained in it. He furthered, in other words, that adoption of Confucianism by the state which was to be one of the outstanding features of later Chinese government.

This emphasis on Confucianism had the effect of carrying over to the new age the ethics and formal courtesy of the Chou feudal aristocracy. The new ruling classes were thereby encouraged to a certain refinement of life and to the maintenance of a partial continuity with the culture of the past.

Still, Legalism continued, and even after Wu Ti's death there was staged at court a debate between an official who supported certain Legalist measures inherited from Wu Ti and the Confucian opponents of that policy.

Much of the revival of Confucianism is attributed to two convinced adherents of that school, Kung-sun Hung and Tung Chung-shu. Kung-sun Hung, formerly a swineherd, took a high stand among the scholars examined by Wu Ti and, during years in public office, lived simply and gave freely of his substance to the poor. Tung Chung-shu was a diligent student much influenced by Taoism. He was the reputed founder and certainly a leader of a philosophy which declared that when the state committed evil and injustice Heaven would show its displeasure by famines, earthquakes, fires, and floods, and if these were not heeded would seek to bring the ruler to repentance by such portents as eclipses and comets. If the Emperor were still recalcitrant, final ruin would come. This theory professed to be Confucianist and was very influential under the Han and, indeed, under later dynasties.

In some respects the Confucianism of Wu Ti's reign differed decidedly from that of the Chou. It was more positively theistic than was either Confucius or Mencius, stressing the beneficent rule of Heaven in the affairs of men, and it made more of a belief in spirits than did either of these two sages—thus finding room for the superstitions of its times. How much, if at all, these modifications were due to the influence of Mo Ti's school it is impossible to say, but one distinguished modern scholar has declared the Confucianism of the Han to be "Mohism" thinly veiled under a Confucian disguise.

From the economic standpoint, the record of Wu Ti's reign was varied. Commerce appears to have flourished. Domestic peace, the reduction of the power of the local princes, and the increased administrative unity of the Empire probably promoted the growth of internal trade. This seems to have been augmented by the extensive annexations of territory, particularly those in the South. Trade with foreign countries also increased, but, although spectacular and with important cultural consequences, in proportion to that within China's boundaries presumably it was very small. Wu Ti attempted to regulate commerce and had an official whose function it was to mitigate extreme fluctuations in it—and possibly to make a profit for the state—by buying the great staples when they were cheap and placing them on the market when prices rose. This policy, as well as the state monopoly of salt and iron, to be mentioned in a moment, apparently was adopted at the advice of a minister imbued with Legalist principles. Canals were dug—among them one between the valley of the Wei, on the North, and that of the Han on the South—probably at least in part for the purpose of facilitating communication and promoting economic prosperity as well as political union, and a great road was constructed to the South and the Southwest. During a devastating famine in the North, scores of thousands of the sufferers were moved into other territory. Great irrigation works were constructed in arid regions, a dangerous flood of the Yellow River was curbed, and thus large territories were reclaimed for cultivation.

Wu Ti's many wars and his extensive public works brought with them serious financial problems, and, at times, distress. Taxes were increased, new imposts were levied, and fresh sources of revenue were sought. The government monopoly of salt and iron, which appears to have been first attempted under Shih Huang Ti, was now extended and was placed in the hands of those merchants who had operated these industries when they were private enterprises. This seems to have been at least in part because the manufacture of salt and iron was prominent as a source of private wealth. Fortunes had been amassed through it, and the state may therefore have looked with covetous eyes upon a possible large addition to its revenue. A special military nobility was created and the titles in it were sold. A regular plan of reducing the severity of punishments by the payment of a fine came into use. Levies were made on the princes for the ostensible purpose of supporting official sacrifices and then were devoted to military purposes. Either now or soon thereafter an excise was placed on liquor. The currency was debased, surviving coins of the earlier part of the reign being the merest fraction in weight of those of a similar denomination of a few years before. Wu Ti later made coinage an imperial monopoly—for previously it had been minted by various dignitaries—and endeavored to restore it to its avowed value. In the first—in part a political measure to increase the power of the throne at the expense of the local princes —he seems to have been successful, but in the latter he was only partially so, for the new coins, although far heavier than those they supplanted, as extant specimens show, were still below their nominal worth. There was an unsuccessful attempt, too, at a kind of currency made up of the skins of deer. While farmers were granted special tax exemptions, additional levies were placed on merchants—a device which seems to have been a reversion to that of the Ch'in. Freedom from taxes was promised to those who gave slaves for labor on the public works, and additional quantities of slaves were obtained through the prolonged foreign wars.

It must be noted that numbers of these actions may have been prompted quite as much by the desire to increase the power of the throne and to further centralization as by financial necessity. Certainly their trend was in that direction. Whatever their motive, the new exactions and the heavy cost of war led to much popular discontent for which Confucian scholars acted as spokesmen. The latter would have abolished many of the new financial measures of the state and advocated winning the barbarians by benevolent rule rather than by costly armed force.

In literature the reign was chiefly noteworthy for the *Shih Chi* (Historical Records), the great history of Ssŭ-ma Ch'ien. Born *ca.* B.C. 145, the son of Ssŭ-ma T'an, a court astrologer, Ssŭ-ma Ch'ien had exceptional preparation for his *magnum opus*. At an early age he memorized the texts of antiquity which provided him with much of his source material. He travelled extensively through the Empire and for a time was a government inspector in newly conquered lands in Szechwan and Yünnan. Upon the death of his father, he succeeded to the latter's office, and in that position aided in the reform of the calendar. For daring to advocate the cause of a general against whom the wrath of the Emperor was directed, he was emasculated, a common punishment of those days. His history was written both before and after this event. How much of it was from the pen of his father there is no sure way of telling, but Ssŭ-ma Ch'ien seems to have been at least the chief author. Based largely upon earlier works and documents which it often incorporates with but slight changes, it covers the history of China from the beginning to Ssŭ-ma Ch'ien's own day and includes not only the narrative of political events but biographies of prominent men, accounts of some of the chief feudal states of the Chou and of some of the foreign peoples touched by the Han, chronological tables, and treatises on such phases of culture as the rites, music, divination, the calendar, and economics. After Ssŭ-ma Ch'ien's death additions were made to the *Shih Chi*, and it was revised and possibly rearranged—alterations which provide the scholar with a major textual problem. It was deservedly regarded by later generations as a model and became a prototype of a whole series of Dynastic Histories which, taken together with the *Shih Chi*, give a voluminous and, on the whole, an authoritative record of China's past—much more extensive and reliable than that possessed by any other people over so long a period.

Wu Ti seems to have attempted to modify religion in a way that would make it ancillary to that unity and emphasis upon imperial power for which he was striving. He celebrated with great pomp two sacrifices—*fêng*, by which prayer was made by the Emperor to Heaven (*T'ien*) from the sacred mountain, T'ai Shan, with the spirit of that peak as the messenger, and *shan*, by which prayer was made to the Sovereign Earth (*Ti*). Both purported to be revivals of earlier ceremonies and are said to have been performed by Shih Huang Ti, but apparently were inventions of Wu Ti and his advisers. Probably both were ostensibly for the purpose of asking the blessing of these divinities upon the

Emperor and requesting long life for him. By emphasizing the place of Heaven, however, *fêng* would help to create the idea of a celestial unity and monarchy of which the imperial state could be held to be a counterpart. *Shan* also loaned its strength to this by stressing the supremacy of Earth (*Ti*) over the many local gods of the soil and of natural objects. The time-honored ceremonies to these latter could not well be abolished, but they tended to perpetuate the territorial particularism which was the enemy of imperialism, and anything which strengthened the preëminence of *Ti* would be a support to the monarch's authority. Possibly with a similar purpose, Wu Ti arranged the gods of heaven into a hierarchy, placing over it the five "Emperors Above" who presided over the four cardinal points and the center and who had come down from the Ch'in, and superimposing in still higher rank a supreme god called *T'ai I,* or the Great One. The general conception of the spiritual organization of the universe as a counterpart of its political organization appears not to have been new, but by stressing the idea that both halves of the spirit world are monarchical in form and by emphasizing the position of the Emperor as the head of the cult, the dignity of the visible ruling house was enhanced.

In spite of his statecraft, Wu Ti was as much fascinated by the beliefs of the popular religion of the age, and especially of the debased Taoism, as had been Shih Huang Ti. Attempts at the transmutation of metals and the search for an elixir of life and other means of achieving immortality had his endorsement, and the supposed experts in these fields exercised great influence over him. Shamanism, or its close cousin, was powerful at court, possibly strengthened by contact with peoples in the Northwest, where it seems to have been particularly at home.

THE DECLINE OF THE EARLIER HAN DYNASTY

Of the immediate successors of Wu Ti not much need here be said. For nearly a hundred years the Empire continued without any major event which should detain us in detail. Two or three of the seven monarchs whom this paragraph covers appear to have been men of some ability, although none was outstanding. At least one was a patron of literature and encouraged the editing of the ancient classics. The inevitable court intrigues which have been fairly constant factors in Chinese, as in much other history, help to give bulk to the annals of the time. Rebellions there were, too, sometimes within the older sections of the Empire and sometimes in the newly conquered domains. Part of the South that had been annexed under Wu Ti, especially the island of Hainan, was abandoned, on the ground that it cost more to hold than it was worth. To the west the Chinese continued to extend their power. Their influence seems to have been potent even on the northwestern border of India. The Hsiung Nu were defeated again and again, and their chiefs finally acknowledged Chinese suzerainty. Hsiung Nu, too, entered the military service of China. The hereditary principle of succession, however, brought with it weak and dissipated princes, and, early in the first century A.D., a crisis arose by which the dynasty was, for a time, displaced.

WANG MANG

The new threat to the Han came through a family named Wang. One of the Wang daughters became a concubine of the heir apparent who ascended the throne in B.C. 48. Having the good fortune both to win the favor of her lord and to present him with a son, she was made Empress and her son heir apparent. Upon the death of her spouse, her son became Emperor and she Empress Dowager. Her brothers and others of her kin were given high office and she and her family dominated the state.

Of the male relatives of the Empress Dowager, the most discreet was a nephew, Wang Mang. In contrast with the other influential members of his family, he was distinguished for his scholarship, his patronage of learning, his filial piety, and his temperate living. While the others were dissipated and extravagant, he lived with marked frugality and distributed nearly all his great income among his poor friends and followers. It is not strange, therefore, that while still in his thirties he became the most powerful figure in the Empire.

The Empress Dowager's son was on the throne for about a quarter of a century, long enough for the Wang family to establish itself firmly. He, however, left no heir, and the nephew who succeeded him (B.C. 6) brought with him his own mother's relatives and the Wang family was temporarily eclipsed. The new

Emperor proved a debauchee and when, after a brief reign, he was gathered to his fathers (A.D. 1), the Wang family reasserted itself and Wang Mang was made regent of the new Emperor, a boy of eight years.

Wang Mang now became more popular and powerful than ever, maintaining his simple manner of life, giving the government vast sums for distribution among the poor, founding a national university, and gathering scholars from all over the land. The boy Emperor died in A.D. 5, poisoned, so rumor declared, by the Wang family for showing too much independence. An infant was placed on the throne and Wang Mang was made Acting Emperor. Shortly, in A.D. 8, Wang Mang, with great show of reluctance, deposed the puppet and declared himself in name what he had been in fact.

Wang Mang took the title of Hsin Huang Ti, the "New Emperor," and called the dynasty which he believed he was establishing by the name of Hsin. Because his attempt soon failed, thus making it obvious that he had not received the mandate of Heaven, and because he violated one of the cardinal Confucian virtues, that of loyalty of a minister to his prince, orthodox Chinese historians have heaped anathemas upon his memory. He seems, indeed, really to have cared little for the interests of the people and to have sacrificed them ruthlessly to attain his own ends. He attempted far-reaching innovations, but these presumably must be attributed to Confucian scholars whose coöperation he won.

For more than a century an occasional voice had been raised in high places in protest against some of the obvious injustices of the times. Much of the land was held in great estates and high rentals were charged the luckless cultivators. Slaves, too, were cruelly treated. Masters had the power of life or death over them and not infrequently exercised it. Over these and other inequalities some of the educated evinced marked concern. In doing so they were true to what had been, at least since the middle of the Chou dynasty, one of the characteristics of much of Chinese scholarship at its best, devotion to the welfare of the populace. Wang Mang, who had long been surrounding himself with scholars among whom were doubtless many social idealists, endeavored to put into operation some of the suggested reforms, and in doing so became one of the most interesting figures in China's history. Yet he also continued the existing corruption of officials.

In the very first year of his reign, Wang Mang attempted a sweeping agrarian reorganization of the Empire. He declared the nationalization of the land, thus annihilating at a stroke the huge estates, and he abolished slavery. The purchase and the sale of land and retainers were henceforth forbidden. The land confiscated to the state was to be divided into equal tracts and given to the cultivators. To this wholesale and startling revolution he added others. He continued the imperial monopolies of salt, iron, and coinage—although he had wished to abolish the first two and preserved them only because he needed the revenue—and added to these wine and mines. He reorganized the currency, introducing, in place of a coin of only one value, tokens of several denominations. At least some of these were given archaic forms. He also attempted to have the state fix prices at equitable figures, thus protecting the farmers against the merchants. By continuing the policy which had appeared before under the Han of having the state enter the market, buying up surplus stocks of goods in times of plenty and selling them in times of dearth, he further attempted to equalize prices. He provided for state loans, on which no interest was to be charged, to those needing them for funeral and sacrificial purposes, and for the advance of funds, at a moderate rate of interest, to those requiring them for productive enterprises.

An interesting accompaniment of the reforms was an emphasis on the study of ancient literature. A distinguished scholar, Liu Hsin (who died in A.D. 22), is particularly noted for having sought out and edited ancient texts. Because of his zeal in his chosen task and a famous catalogue of ancient works prepared by him, he is sometimes denominated China's first bibliographer. All later Chinese scholarship owes him an incalculable debt.

Wang Mang's literary entourage is accused by some Chinese scholars of deliberately forging, in support of his contentions, important books and parts of books commonly ascribed to the Chou dynasty. The *Chou Li,* the *Tso Chuan,* portions of the *Shu Ching,* and one of the commentaries of the *Shih Ching* are among the works said thus to have been falsified. The theory is not proved to the satisfaction of all experts, but it has won many supporters and some parts of it are usually accepted as substantiated.

Wang Mang stimulated the study of the Confucian canon—even though he may have modified it. He built dormitories for thousands of students and encouraged education. He paid marked honors to Confucius—repairing his temple, granting him a posthumous title, and ennobling one of his descendants. All this he may have done to obtain the support of the powerful Confucian scholar class.

So complete a reorganization as that effected by Wang Mang inevitably met serious opposition. The wealthy and the powerful were, of course, almost all against it. The law against the purchase and sale of land and slaves had to be repealed at the end of three years, although a later decree penalized slave-owners with heavy taxes. Insurrections broke out, greatly to the distress and perhaps somewhat to the surprise of Wang Mang. He seems to have believed that if he could introduce proper institutions peace would reign in the world. He was puzzled when his innovations were followed by more rather than less disorder. Although now well along in his sixties, he continued to work long hours in the attempt to devise new and less unsuccessful measures and gave himself almost no sleep. The members of the Liu family, taking advantage of the general unrest, raised their standard against the usurper. Wang Mang aroused their ire still further by destroying the Han ancestral shrines. Other malcontents gathered into bands of brigands, some of whom, called the Red Eyebrows, became very formidable. Incidentally, these Red Eyebrows seem to have been one of those organizations which, often secret and possessing religious features, frequently through the centuries have had in China an important part in fomenting and leading revolts. Subject peoples on the frontier took the opportunity offered by the weakness of the Empire to throw off the Chinese yoke. Although, in the earlier years of his rule, Wang Mang had vigorously maintained Chinese prestige in the far Northwest, the Hsiung Nu now caused him anxiety by overrunning some of the northern provinces, and Chinese outposts in the Tarim basin had to be abandoned. In the South, what is now Tongking refused to acknowledge his rule and many adherents of the Han took refuge there. Rebellion led by the Lius finally overwhelmed Wang Mang. An old and disappointed man, in A.D. 23 he was killed in his capital, Ch'angan, and his dynasty and his innovations crumbled. He was not forgotten, however, and, although his memory was execrated by the orthodox, his bold and sweeping experiments had a lasting influence on Chinese thinkers.

THE LATER OR EASTERN HAN DYNASTY

The Liu family, as we have said, led the armies which made an end of Wang Mang, and, quite naturally, one of the most vigorous of their number placed himself on the throne. Naturally, too, the name of Han was continued. However, the capital was moved eastward, to Loyang, in the present province of Honan, and from this point the dynasty is denominated by historians the Eastern, or Later Han (in Chinese *Tung Han* or *Hou Han*).

The first of the Later Han, known as Kuang Wu Ti, spent much of his reign in restoring internal order to the Empire and in reasserting the authority of the Chinese over the outlying, tributary states. The bandits, especially the Red Eyebrows, who had sprung up during the later years of Wang Mang, gave him much trouble. However, he proved himself equal to the task. In his reign of more than thirty years he brought back to the Middle Kingdom a measure of domestic peace and made the Chinese name once more feared abroad. The former possessions of the Ch'in and the Han in the delta of the Red River and along the coast of what is now Annam were reconquered by the general Ma Yüan. This region, which previously had been permitted to retain its old customs, was now sinicized. The native *mores* were gradually but surely eradicated, schools of the Chinese type were founded, and Chinese letters and social and political rites and institutions became dominant. The cultural transformation and administrative unity under the Later Han prepared the way for the future Annamite state and civilization. In the Northwest and in what is now the New Dominion Kuang Wu Ti began the process of reëstablishing Chinese suzerainty. He retained the administrative organization of the Western Han, and, indeed, this persisted until the later years of the dynasty. Like several others of his line, moreover, Kuang Wu Ti was not only a warrier, but a patron of Confucian culture. A man of education, he enjoyed surrounding himself with scholars and founded a higher school at his capital. It was a revivified Empire which he passed on to his successor, Ming Ti.

The political history of the next century and a half need detain us but very briefly. A succession of Emperors, none of them especially noteworthy, perpetuated the Han line. Several of these at their accession were infants and most of the others came to the throne in their teens. The immaturity of the rulers encouraged court intrigues, and the power of the women of the palace and the baleful influence of the eunuchs increased. With such feeble leadership, the house of Han was obviously nearing its end. Confucian scholars persistently protested against the eunuchs and the abuses in government. At times their efforts were effective, but they could not long retard the decay. Toward the close of the second century the eunuchs were strong enough to take heavy toll from among their adversaries. Insurrections broke out, bands called the Yellow Turbans making themselves particularly obnoxious. These Yellow Turbans were a Taoist sect, and in a certain sense the downfall of the Han was due to a Taoist revolt against the Confucianism dominant in the bureaucracy.

The army asserted itself at court to control the eunuchs, and, toward the close of the second century, a general, Tung Cho, made himself master of the Emperors, supplanting one boy puppet by another. In A.D. 190 Tung Cho burned the capital, Loyang, and established himself and the futile monarch at Ch'angan. For two years he ruled with a high hand, ruthlessly crushing all opposition and giving a show of legality to his acts by declaring that they were performed in the name of the Emperor. The country did not accept him quietly, however, jealous rivals formed a coalition against him, and he was assassinated (A.D. 192) by one of his own lieutenants, an adopted son.

The struggle for power continued until Ts'ao Ts'ao, the son of the adopted son of a former chief eunuch, and an extraordinarily able but utterly unscrupulous and extremely crafty man, made himself supreme at court. The imbecile boy whom Tung Cho had placed on the throne was shorn more and more of his prerogatives, but was allowed to retain the title of Emperor, until, in A.D. 220, on Ts'ao Ts'ao's death, he was persuaded to cede the throne to Ts'ao Ts'ao's son, Ts'ao P'ei. Ts'ao P'ei founded a new dynasty, the Wei. As we shall see a little later, a member of the Liu family professed to carry on the Han dynasty in what is now Szechwan. The main line of the Han, however, had come to an end. The actors in the drama were probably quite unaware of it, but a great period in the development of the Chinese nation had closed and the Middle Kingdom was entering another era of marked transition.

One phase of the activity of the Later Han must, because of its cultural consequences, be gone into with more detail than the brief summary in the last four paragraphs has permitted. The generals of the Later Han maintained and even strengthened Chinese might on the far western frontiers in what is now the New Dominion, and so kept open the overland routes to the West. The Hsiung Nu, to the immediate north and west, continued a menace and never could long be ignored. However, connections with the Yüeh Chih were kept up, although with at least one rift in the friendship, and the petty states in what is now the New Dominion, centering around such oases as the present Kashgar, Yarkand, Khotan, and Turfan, became tributary to China as a protection against the common enemy, the Hsiung Nu. The fact that at least the ruling classes in most—and possibly all—of these states were Iranian and the Hsiung Nu were of a very different race may have been an added incentive to seek Chinese assistance.

Under Ming Ti, the Hsiung Nu who had invaded what is now Kansu were crushed and the Chinese took possession of the present Hami, west of Kansu. This helped to revive Chinese prestige in the distant West and some of the states in that region renewed their tributary connection with the Han. Chinese officials were soon appointed to supervise the subordinate principalities.

Probably the most famous of the Chinese agents in the far West was Pan Ch'ao (A.D. 32–102). Although the scion of a family noted for its literary accomplishments, brother of Pan Ku, the great historian, and of Pan Chao, China's most distinguished woman-of-letters, he was more a man of action than a scholar. Weary of literary employment and petty official appointment at the capital which barely kept the wolf from the door, he determined to seek adventure and renown on the frontier. This he did, and there displayed such daring and ability that before many years he was the leading Chinese official on the Central Asiatic edges of the Empire. He extended the Chinese power in what is now the western portion of the New Dominion. The little states here often proved recalcitrant and Pan Ch'ao's life seems to have been one of fairly constant fighting. He made Chinese power feared even farther west, across the mountains, in territories which are now Russian, and one of his diplomatic agents reached the shores of the Persian Gulf. His exploits were certainly equal to those of any of the great Roman generals and were possibly superior to them. In his late sixties, worn out, Pan Ch'ao sought and obtained the Emperor's permission to retire, but died not long after his arrival at court.

The distant posts held by Pan Ch'ao were not easily retained. A son succeeded him in his command and seems to have had fair success. However, we read of repeated revolts of the subject states, of attacks of Tibetans on Chinese outposts, and of complaints at court at the cost of the military undertakings involved. Before many years the Han began retrenchment. Retreat was not steady or uninterrupted. At least once again, led by Pan Yung, another son of Pan Ch'ao, the soldiers of the Han were seen in the oases at the foot of the mountains that separate the present New Dominion from India and Central Asia, and Chinese influence appears to have been strong there until at least the second half of the second century. For years Chinese garrisons held points in what is now Western Kansu. Modern archeology has shown that the frontier wall built west of Tunhuang toward the close of the second century B.C. was held by Chinese garrisons until the middle of the second century A.D. It was only when the increasing impotence of the Han monarchs made it difficult to maintain order even at home that these were withdrawn.

One object of all this costly military activity seems to have been to keep open the trade routes to the West. The present names of the cities and oases for which the Han strove—Hami, Aksu, Kashgar, Turfan, Khotan—indicate to any one at all familiar with the caravan routes that the Chinese were attempting to control and make safe the long roads by which their commerce passed to and from the cultural centers in the other parts of Asia.

FOREIGN TRADE UNDER THE HAN

Under the Han the natural barriers which tend to separate China from the rest of the world were being overcome by both Chinese and foreigners. The era was one which favored commerce. Not only had the Han brought prosperity and territorial expansion to China, but elsewhere powerful states were an assistance to trade. In what is now Northwest India and Afghanistan some of the Yüeh Chih had established a kingdom under the Kushan dynasty. The Parthian Empire occupied most of what is now Persia and the region immediately north of it, and in its cities Greek merchants were to be found, deposits of that eastward wave of Hellenic culture which had come with the conquest of Alexander and was only slowly subsiding. Since the last century or so of the Chou, states with Greek rulers and with strikingly Greek features had borne witness to that conquest on its Indian and Central Asian frontiers. Still farther west the Romans were unifying the Mediterranean world. In what is now the southern part of European Russia were various divisions of the Sarmatians, and here, too, on the shores of the Black Sea, were Greek cities, centers of trade. Throughout much of Asia commerce was more extensive than it had been before. Merchants passed across Central Asia into China by routes which skirted the northern and the southern slopes of the Tarim River basin. They also came to the Han Empire by way of the South—up the rivers of what is now Burma and across the hills into the present Yünnan, and, by the longer sea route, to the south coast. For a time the main port in the South was in the future Tongking, then under the control of the Han. It was not until later centuries that it was supplanted by Canton.

China's commercial contacts with the peoples on her far western frontiers were, when the distance is considered, fairly extensive. The Han knew the Yüeh Chih and the Parthians, not only by trade but by political embassies. It seems probable that merchants from India and Ceylon found their way to China by the southern routes. The Chinese, moreover, were aware of at least the eastern portion of the Roman Empire, calling it Ta Ch'in. With the Mediterranean world they had little, if any, direct contact. Traders from the West were regularly reaching India. When, about the first century B.C. or the first century A.D., they learned to take advantage of the monsoon to make the voyage across the Indian Ocean from the Red Sea, the commerce became extensive and important and was to continue so for many centuries. Few travellers from the Mediterranean world seem to have gone beyond India and Ceylon, however, although the Romans and Greeks heard vaguely of China. In A.D. 120 jugglers, sent with an embassy of one of the states on China's southern border, arrived at Loyang and professed to come from west of the sea, a region which they declared to be the same as Ta Ch'in. In A.D. 166, merchants from Ta Ch'in reached Loyang and claimed to be an embassy from their king—who is supposed to have been the Emperor Marcus Aurelius Antoninus. Aside from these somewhat dubious instances we do not hear specifically of any representatives of the Mediterranean world penetrating China, although some may have done so. Moreover, we are not sure that Chinese journeyed as far west as the Roman Empire, even though the Chinese historical records of the time give a description of Ta Ch'in which may have been derived from eyewitnesses. The envoy whom Pan Ch'ao sent—possibly with the hope of opening communication with Ta Ch'in without the intermediation of the Parthians, who, as enemies of the Romans, would not be especially eager to promote direct trade relations between China and Rome—succeeded only, as we have seen, in reaching the Persian Gulf.

The commodities exchanged through this commerce were, naturally, those which combined small bulk and weight with high value. The chief Chinese export appears to have been silk—in its raw form, as thread, and as cloth. We hear repeatedly of it, and in late years specimens of it in the form in which it was shipped have been found, preserved through centuries by the dry desert air, near the western end of the wall which the Han built to protect the overland routes. Skins, furs, rhubarb, and cinnamon are also said to have been among the merchandise which the Chinese sent westward and which eventually reached the Mediterranean world. The Middle Kingdom received in return glass, jade (although most of that used under the Han was of domestic origin), horses, precious stones (including the diamond), ivory, tortoise shell, asbestos (either now or a little later), and some fine cloths of wool and linen.

CROSS-FERTILIZATION OF CULTURES THROUGH THE COMMERCE OF THE HAN

Commerce inevitably resulted in reciprocal cultural influences. There was an interchange in art and commerce over a vast area reaching from north of the Black Sea into China. Its full extent we shall probably never know. At best our information is fragmentary. One small example of what must have been taking place over much of this wide region has come to light in recently excavated tombs not far north of Urga, in Outer Mongolia. These sepulchres, supposed to date from about the beginning of the Christian era, are within territory once under the jurisdiction of the Hsiung Nu and are possibly those of Hsiung Nu or of related peoples. They contained pottery, several kinds of cloths, and a variety of objects in stone and metal. The artistic designs were derived from Greek, Chinese, Sarmatian, Scytho-Siberian (Yüeh Chih), Persian, Babylonian, and Assyrian sources. If this was true here, quite off the main trade routes, an admixture must have occurred along the chief arteries of commerce. Recent discoveries in the Tarim basin reveal the presence of various cultural influences in Han times. Excavations by Japanese in late years in Southern Korea in tombs possibly of a post-Han date have disclosed fragments of Roman glass goblets.

China, we know, had some effect upon the cultures of other peoples. Many Chinese joined themselves to the Hsiung Nu—a migration stimulated by the grim practice of Chinese Emperors of executing generals and envoys who were unsuccessful against the enemy. These, as well as merchants, must have spread Chinese ideas and manners among the "barbarians." Silk, we have seen, went from China to the countries of Central and Western Asia and to Rome, and the peach and the apricot, of Chinese origin, reached Rome by the first century A.D. China, too, began to exert a marked influence on Tongking and Korea, and the Japanese had contacts with her.

Very notable was the effect of foreign intercourse upon China Many of its ramifications are obscure or perhaps entirely hidden, but we are aware of it in the fields of art and religion. Chinese bronzes now add to the rather stiff, symbolic, and predominantly geometrical designs of the Chou forms radically new to China. Stone sculptures, preserved in tombs, display the same general tendencies. Figures of men, heretofore rare, appear, scenes of daily life are portrayed, attempts are made to picture the spirit world, and the whole is full of action. The stone sculptures themselves were an innovation. We might believe these novelties a creation of the Chinese genius, stimulated by the vigor of the Han culture—as, indeed, they probably in large part were—but for the appearance of motives which we know to be foreign—some of them Greek, some Sarmatian, and some probably Iranian and Babylonian. Glazes may possibly (although they may have been much earlier) now have been employed for the first time by the Chinese. Glass itself is said to have been first manufactured in China under the Han. It had, however, been used as an inlay as early as the middle of the first millennium B.C. Beautiful lacquer objects were produced under state inspection, as we learn from archeological finds in a Chinese colony in Korea. Indeed, lacquer appears to have been very popular, for widely scattered examples of it have been found. Chang Ch'ien, we have seen, introduced the grape and alfalfa—the latter to feed the horses which Chinese were importing from Central Asia. Bronze mirrors of the Han show the grape as a decoration. It is possible that the Chinese derived some musical ideas from the Greeks and some notions of alchemy—although in the latter case the transfer may (not very probably) have been in the other direction. Other plants than those we have mentioned may have been brought in. It has been conjectured that some ideas of Greek medicine and mathematics entered and that the calendar was affected. Certainly Chinese ideas of geography and of the extent of the world were enlarged.

THE INTRODUCTION OF BUDDHISM

In religion there was the introduction of what later became one of the major factors in Chinese life, Buddhism. Buddhism had begun that expansion which eventually made it one of the most widespread and potent of faiths. It had originated as an off-shoot —a heresy—of older Indian religion, probably in the sixth century B.C. Its founder, of an aristocratic family, had become oppressed by the suffering of life, and, abandoning his position and his family, as so many others in India have done through the ages, had sought a solution of the problem of evil. Seeing the pain which appears to be an inevitable concomitant of consciousness, and believing, as his contemporaries did, in the transmigration of souls—that physical death is not an escape from suffering, but simply ushers in a new stage of existence which is also marked by anguish—the salvation which he sought was a way of getting rid of pain, a means of breaking the endless round of rebirths. He tried earnestly the several roads recommended by the philosophers and religious experts of the India of his time, but to no avail. Finally, when all these had failed him, and in despair he was sitting in meditation under a tree, the answer flashed into his mind and he became the Buddha, the "Enlightened." It was one of those revolutionary experiences which change the course of history. Having found for himself the secret of release, of inward peace, and of freedom from pain, the Buddha spent the rest of a long life in teaching it to others.

There is no space here to go into the Buddha's precepts in any detail. He summarized them under the four truths—that life and suffering are inseparable, that suffering is due to desire or thirst, that to get rid of suffering one must be emancipated from desire, and that the way to freedom from desire is the eightfold path. This eightfold path included right views (seeing life as it really is, always changing and with no abiding entity which can be called soul), right aspirations, right meditation, and right actions. He inculcated self-forgetfulness and kindly service—although with no passionate attachment to any one or any thing. The goal, of course, is the extinction of desire and so the end of pain—*nirvana*.

Obviously the Buddha's teaching was rather alien to Chinese thought: the mental and spiritual world in which he lived differed from that of the Middle Kingdom. His system had as its object escape from existence, which he regarded as evil. Here and there were Chinese pessimists, but the bulk of China's thinkers regarded life as worth living. They were optimistic about human nature. They deemed it either good to begin with, or, if innately bad, improvable. Some of them sought the indefinite prolongation of life. If they troubled themselves at all about the state of the dead, it was to seek to make the ancestors happy and to obtain their blessing upon their descendants. Most philosophers were absorbed in the problem of bettering existing human society. To be sure, Buddhism had some things in common with such ancient Chinese thinkers as Hsün Tzŭ. The belief in the reign of law in the universe and retribution according to strict justice were akin to the Indian conception of *karma* which Buddhism inherited. The more thoughtful among the Taoists, too, with their sympathy with meditation and their suspicion that the physical world, including the *ego*, might prove an illusion, were somewhat in accord with Buddhist aspirations. Even here, however, the similarity was by no means complete. Yet, as we shall see, Buddhism was to have some of its greatest triumphs in China and was to persist there after it had all but disappeared from the land of its birth.

After the Buddha's death, his teachings continued to spread, although at first rather slowly. Under the most powerful of its early converts, Asoka, a monarch who ruled over much of India in the third century B.C., Buddhism entered upon a period of rapid expansion. In the second century B.C., under Menander, a Greek who hewed out a principality for himself in the wake of the armies of Alexander the Great, and whose domains were in Bactria, northwest of India, and in India itself, Buddhism prospered. In the second century A.D., Kanishka, the powerful (Kushan) monarch of the branch of the Yüeh Chih who ruled in what is now Northwest India and Afghanistan, became a devoted patron of the faith. Thus Buddhism was prominent in some of those countries with which the Chinese were establishing contacts through the westward expansion and commerce of the Han. It is not strange that, an enthusiastically missionary faith, it now made its appearance in the Middle Kingdom.

In the course of its spread, Buddhism, like all great faiths, developed schools of thought. The chief divisions are known as Mahayana and Hinayana, the "Greater Vehicle" and the "Lesser Vehicle." Mahayana, sometimes called Northern Buddhism, exalts the *bodhisattva,* one who, with *nirvana* within his grasp, postpones entrance into it and is born and reborn until he can make possible the salvation of all living beings. Prayer and worship were absent from the Buddha's teachings, for he believed that each must work out his own salvation unaided by divine beings—who, like men, are still subject to rebirth and so are unsaved. They crept back into Mahayana, however. Hinayana, sometimes denominated Southern Buddhism, insists that the ideal of the Mahayanist is unattainable and is untrue to the teachings of the Buddha and emphasizes the *arhat*, he who has found enlightenment for himself. Both Mahayana and Hinayana were to be found in Northwest India in these centuries, and it was only gradually that the former prevailed in the North and the latter in the South.

Just when and by what route Buddhism first made its way to China remains uncertain. The story usually told, that its introduction was associated with a dream of Ming Ti, the second Emperor of the Eastern Han, is an invention of later years and quite undependable. The foreign religion was already in China at the time that Ming Ti is said to have had his dream. It may, indeed, have been present much more than a century before. Buddhism may have come first by any of the three trade routes from India—by Yünnan, by the south coast, or overland through the Tarim basin. Possibly it arrived both by way of the Northwest and the South. We know that in 2 B.C. a Chinese envoy heard of Buddhism from the Yüeh Chih and that as early as the first century A.D. Buddhist monks and laymen were living in China under the protection of a brother of the Emperor. We hear of the erection of a Buddhist temple in a city in the present Anhui in A.D. 190. We know, too, that in the first half of the second century of the Christian era Buddhist communities were to be found in Loyang. One of the missionaries was a Parthian prince —known in Chinese as An-shih-kao—who had renounced the succession to become a monk. With a compatriot and a Chinese, he formed a group which translated Buddhist literature into Chinese and whose members were known to the faithful as the "Inimitables." The Parthians, it may be noted, probably came by way of the Tarim basin. Others of the missionaries were from India.

Early Buddhist missionaries appear to have been welcomed by some of the more scholarly Taoists, and were, indeed, for a time popularly regarded as Taoists. As such, their faith did not seem so very alien to the Chinese.

How soon opposition developed we do not know, although it

is clear that by some the Buddhists were denounced as untrue to Chinese culture and traditions. In any event, under the Han the faith of Gautama was only gaining a foothold and was not yet especially strong. It may be that the Confucian scholars, who were shown more favors by the Later than by the Earlier Han, were strong enough to act as a check on the new religion. Not until after the downfall of the Han was Buddhism to experience its phenomenal growth.

OTHER CULTURAL DEVELOPMENTS UNDER THE HAN

The Han dynasty was notable not only for importations from alien civilizations but for marked developments in the native culture, seemingly independent of stimulus from the outside.

The most noteworthy were in the realm of thought and literature. The dynasty was distinguished for the achievements of its scholars. It was not an age of creative or original philosophic thought. To be sure, the schools of the Chou were remembered and many of their writings preserved and carefully studied. We have seen that the Legalists persisted well into the course of the dynasty and that the followers of Mo Ti were active and retained their separate existence at least as late as the first century B.C. However, only two of the schools, Taoism and Confucianism, continued strong throughout the Han.

Taoism, as we have noted, was often popular at court. Indeed, one of its greatest exponents was a grandson of Kao Tsu—Liu An, commonly known as Huai-nan Tzŭ—who, like so many of the time, sought for endless life and a means to the transmutation of metals. Perhaps he should not be classed with the Taoists, for he sought to construct a syncretic philosophy made up of elements from all the main schools of thought. Implicated in a political plot, he committed suicide, but popular tradition declares that he discovered the elixir of life, drank of it, and, rising to heaven, became an Immortal. In A.D. 163 an Emperor made official offerings at the supposed birthplace of Lao Tzŭ and the following year built a temple to him in the capital and used there in his honor the ritual employed in the imperial sacrifices to Heaven. It was in the Later Han that Chang Tao-ling, traditionally the first head of the Taoist organization, is said to have lived. Chang Tao-ling led a sect, called "Five-Bushel-Rice Taoists" from the fact that each convert was taxed that amount. Toward the close of the second century A.D. the Chang family, supported by this sect, rebelled and for some years created an independent state in the present Szechwan and Shensi, governing through a Taoist priesthood. Out of the sect arose much of the later popular Taoism. The so-called Taoist Papacy which persisted to our own day was kept in the Chang family.

Although Taoism displayed much superstition and alchemistic research, these developments did not prevent a few earnest souls from seeking in its earlier books the answer to some of the deeper questions of thoughtful minds. For example, one group of Taoists regarded the way of Heaven as ceaselessly operating, impersonal law. They opposed the absolute control of the state, reverted to the anarchistic tendencies which are so strong in the *Tao Tê Ching*, emphasized the freedom of mankind, and protested against adherence to ritual as a means of insuring order and progress. Their boldness cost some of them their lives.

Confucianism, in a modified form, as we also have suggested, was more and more espoused by the state. We have seen that the earliest rulers of the dynasty were somewhat lukewarm toward it but were forced by the exigencies of their position to show it some favor. It will also be remembered that as time passed the attitude of succeeding monarchs became more encouraging. Confucian writings were made the chief subjects of study in the schools and formed the basis of the examinations through which men of ability were recruited for the civil service. The prominence of Confucianism increased under Wang Mang and the Hou Han. Under the Earlier Han the cult of Confucius seems to have been maintained only as were those of other ancestors, by his lineal descendants, although occasional Emperors honored his memory. Under the Later Han (A.D. 59) sacrifices in honor of Confucius and Chou Kung were decreed in all the schools in large cities. In the first century A.D. official texts of the Classics were ordered established. By imperial command (A.D. 175) these were engraved on stone and placed outside the state academy in the capital. By this time the Confucian scholars were very powerful in the state. They attracted many disciples and their leaders formed a kind of ruling group which they sought to perpetuate by marriage alliances among their children. Between A.D. 175 and A.D. 179 a violent reaction against them, as we have said, led by the palace eunuchs, ousted them and killed many of their number. While during the brief remaining course of the dynasty they did not regain their former influence, the Confucian tradition was by that time too firmly established to disappear and whatever the bias of individual rulers—often Taoist or Buddhist—the state was henceforth built on what were largely (but by no means entirely) Confucian principles. This official Han Confucianism, it will be recalled, was in many respects quite different from that of the Sage and his immediate disciples and was influenced by Taoism, Mo Ti and his followers, and the Legalist School.

Why Confucianism should have been selected from among its rivals for imperial favor must be in part a matter of conjecture. Although his religious views seem to have made a deep impress upon both Confucianism and Taoism, Mo Ti's statecraft was probably held to be impracticable; the Taoist political theories may have been too incompatible with the complex civilization which was developing; and the severe reaction against the thoroughgoing application of Legalist principles by Shih Huang Ti and the opposition to them under Han Wu Ti and his successors may have discredited that school. The ritualism advocated by the Confucian school provided the forms for the type of civilized life to which the Chinese were traditionally accustomed. Moreover, they enhanced the prestige of the Emperor, a result which commended itself to the Han monarchs.

At the risk of being wearisome, however, it must be repeated that the Chinese state system of the Han and succeeding dynasties owed a debt not only to Confucianism but to others of the schools of the Chou. In it were elements traceable to the Legalists, the Taoists, and the Mohists. The Confucianism of the Later Han was in many respects a syncretic product to which all of the major schools of the Chou contributed.

In establishing this composite Confucianism as the leading philosophy of the state and making its texts the subject of study in the schools of the Empire and the basis of civil service examinations, the Han monarchs were promoting the cultural unity of their domains. The very syncretism which so characterized the Han—as contrasted with the distinct philosophic divisions of Chou times—both reflected and contributed to the political and cultural imperial structure now achieved. The Han not only welded China into a political Empire. They founded its solidarity upon a more lasting basis, that of one civilization and theory of life. It was this basis of union which China was never completely to lose and which was to hold her together in spirit even in the long periods when administratively she was divided.

Independent speculation tended to die out. Tung Chung-shu, for example, would have had Wu Ti proscribe all non-Confucian teaching and study, and, with the exception of Taoism, in the course of the Han dynasty the other schools disappeared as separate entities. One of the thinkers who stood out prominently in the memory of later generations was Wang Ch'ung, of the first century A.D. An eclectic and a sceptic, influenced by both Taoism and Confucianism and yet not blindly enamored of either, he reacted against much of the current Confucianism. He held that man is not so important as Han Confucianists declared him to be, that natural phenomena and catastrophes are not the results of man's acts, and that such events as a human birth are accidental and not the purposive deeds of the universe. He criticized Confucius and Mencius, expressed doubts about the reliability of much of the ancient literature, argued against immortality and the existence of any spirit, and made much of the *yin* and the *yang*. He was, moreover, a determinist, contending that man's lot is fixed by blind fate. Even Wang Ch'ung, however, was not so original as were many of the Chou dynasty, and most of his cardinal ideas had been held before him. Yang Hsiung, a contemporary and minister of Wang Mang and one of the noted thinkers of the Han, held that the nature of man, one of the moot points of Chinese philosophy, is a mixture of good and bad, and that each becomes what instruction and practice make him. He, too, however, was clearly not striking out on particularly new lines and was a devoted Confucianist.

Some reasons for the decline of originality seem fairly clear. One was the stern repressive measures of Shih Huang Ti. Another was probably the encouragement given under the Han by the state, now a unified empire, to Confucianism and Taoism. Even though in the first century or more of the dynasty the Legalists had state support, as time passed official preferment and social distinction were more and more gained through adherence to one of these other two schools. After the establishment of Confucianism as the official orthodoxy, the study of the members of the educated class—as quotations in their writings show—was confined chiefly to the works esteemed by that sect: the range of reading, and with it of thought, narrowed. Gone were the days of the Chou, when, in the variety of feudal states, diversities of culture were possible and even encouraged. The Emperors, to insure the political unity for which they strove, were promoting cultural uniformity. The time had passed when wandering and original scholars knew that if they and their theories were rejected at one court they would stand a chance of being accepted at another. Whether, had the old system of separate states continued, original speculation would have persisted and Chinese thought have made further progress, must ever remain unknown, but, as it was, it appears that the domination of philosophic orthodoxy was the price which China paid for political integrity. Other causes for the decline of originality of thought may have been the scepticism which had been strong since the later centuries of the Chou, a tendency in a practical age to discredit theoretical reasoning, and the popularity among the educated of superstitions and of the search for the philosopher's stone and an elixir of life.

It must be noted that a good many religious developments occurred under the Han. In addition to the introduction of Buddhism and the changes in Confucianism and Taoism, other innovations were made. For instance, the worship of great men of the past was introduced and became part of the state cult. It appears to have begun with the Emperor Hui Ti, who commanded that a temple be erected to his father, Kao Tsu, in each district and fief and that sacrifices be offered at stated intervals. This was a manifest aid to unifying the Empire and perpetuating the Han rule. By the Later Han it became customary to offer sacrifices to the memory of other distinguished men.

The energy of China's intellectuals, instead of seeking an outlet in formulating novel ideas, went largely into historical and literary studies. The surviving books of the Chou dynasty were carefully collected and edited. Among those having a large part in this work were two scions of the imperial family, Liu Hsiang and Liu Hsin, father and son, of the first century B.C. and the first century A.D. Liu Hsiang was a writer of note, with a finely polished prose style, who was markedly influenced by Taoism. Liu Hsin has already been noted. In the course of the Han thirteen of the ancient works were set up as canonical—the *I Ching*, the *Shu Ching*, the *Shih Ching*, three versions of the *Ch'un Ch'iu* with three different commentaries on it, the *Li Chi*, the *Chou Li*, the *I Li*, the *Hsiao Ching*, the *Lün Yü*, the *Êrh Ya*, and the *Mêng Tzŭ Shu*. The *Êrh Ya*, it may be noted, is often called the oldest Chinese dictionary—although considerable parts of it are at least as recent as the third century B.C.

Editorial work was especially needed, for inventions in writing materials and the new forms of the characters encouraged by them were fast making the older script intelligible only to the expert. Wooden and bamboo tablets gave place to silk fabrics and, in the Later Han, to paper. The traditional date for the first manufacture of paper, A.D. 102 or 105, is only approximate, and the new material must have grown out of many tentative experiments. However, examples of true paper dating from the Han and fabricated from the bark of the mulberry tree, from hemp, and from rags, have been discovered and show what was taking place. With the new material and with the brush pen, new forms of the characters came into common use and displaced the old. Li Ssŭ, the great minister of Shih Huang Ti, is credited with having developed, as we have seen, probably out of the form current in the state of Ch'in, a script which he and his master tried to make universal. The new styles then developed, it may be noted, were to persist: documents dating from the Han have forms of the characters which differ little from those in use to-day. In the second century A.D. the classics were engraved on stone slabs. From these slabs they could be reproduced by rubbings on paper, a technique which was in use by this time. It must be added that the invention of so perishable a writing material as paper, some centuries before printing made possible the rapid and cheap multiplication of books, was not without its disadvantages, for practically no manuscripts of early date have come down to us.

The preservation of the early literature was complicated by the disasters which civil strife brought upon the libraries of the time. When the capital was sacked at the end of the Ch'in, when more destruction overtook the palaces at the overthrow of Wang

Mang, and again in the turmoil that accompanied the end of the Later Han, quantities of books were destroyed—probably all told a very much more extensive loss than the "burning of the books" by Shih Huang Ti. The result is that works which now purport to have been handed down through and from the Han undoubtedly contain many mistakes and have suffered alterations.

As we have seen, histories were being written. Pan Piao, the father of Pan Ch'ao, began a continuation of Ssŭ-ma Ch'ien's great work. This was completed by his son, Pan Ku—who was also something of a philosopher—and by his gifted daughter, Pan Chao, and is known as the *Ch'ien Han Shu*, or Book of the Former Han. Pan Chao, it may be noted, was not only a historian, but a poetess, an essayist, and a novelist. Her advice to young women was to remain a model almost to our own day.

Among dictionaries the *Shuo Wên* was compiled (under the Later Han), and is still a source of information (although now largely superseded by archeological finds) for early Chinese forms. Many commentaries on the Chou literature were written embodying the views of the Han scholars, some of them at variance with the teachings of the original texts.

A new prose style was developed. It was simple and while not identical with the vernacular, in grammar and construction largely conformed to it. For its vigor and clarity it is even now admired and regarded as a model. Many scholars, however, tended to display their erudition by interlarding their pages with quotations from older books.

Poetry also flourished, although none of its authors attained the distinction of the greatest of their successors of later dynasties. Much of the verse of the Han was influenced by the literary traditions of the state of Ch'u. These differed decidedly from the restrained classicism of the North and had a pronounced strain of romanticism, an exuberant vocabulary, and a rather wild fancifulness. Incidentally, the painting of the Han seems also to have been molded in part by Ch'u ideals. Chang Hêng, the first Chinese painter of whom we know much, a contemporary of Wang Ch'ung, was as well an astronomer, a mathematician, and a poet.

Most of the preceding pages have concerned themselves with the achievements of the upper classes—the men and women of power and of education. One would like to know what the masses were doing and thinking. Here and there we catch glimpses of them—as in the agrarian reforms which altered their means of livelihood, in sculptures which hint at sports and games (although these may have been chiefly for the aristocracy) and at popular religious cults, and in the pages of Wang Ch'ung, where popular beliefs are described in the process of holding them up to ridicule. On the whole, however, our knowledge is most fragmentary.

SUMMARY

It was a rich age, that of the Ch'in and the Han. China, next to Rome, was the most powerful state on the planet. In a land in which was a local particularism that might later have developed into the type of divisive nationalism so characteristic of Europe, unity had been accomplished and the separatist tendency had been decisively weakened. This, one of the outstanding political achievements in the history of the race, was the work of both the Ch'in and the Han. The former began it and the latter carried it further. The means employed were partly administrative and partly cultural. The administrative machinery was largely the contribution of the Ch'in. The cultural theories by which the Ch'in tried to reënforce their organization—those of the Legalists—proved too drastic. It was due to the genius of the Han that the principles chiefly associated with a different school, that of Confucius, were adopted and made to work. This successful combination of administrative machinery with a unifying, practical philosophy of human society, proves the greatest of the Han rulers to have possessed extraordinary political capacity. Moreover, the territory of the China thus united and made strong was being greatly extended, the Chinese showing that power of assimilating and molding other peoples which has been one of their outstanding characteristics. Civilization, too, was developing and being modified—in part by foreign influences.

Like all human inventions, the Ch'in-Han system was not without defects. There was a tendency to crush originality: political unity was achieved through enforced cultural uniformity and this latter could be brought about only by stifling the brilliant individualism so characteristic of the disunited Chou. Freedom and progress were sacrificed to the ideal of domestic peace.

Then, too, the system was dependent on an hereditary imperial house. The keystone of the arch was the Emperor. If he were strong, stability was sure. When, however, as is inevitable in the course of any family, weaklings came to the fore, the entire structure weakened and eventually collapsed.

The downfall of the Han did not entirely undo the work of that dynasty and its predecessor. To the ideas, the literature, and the institutions of the period later generations recurred again and again. Even to-day the Chinese proudly call themselves *Han Jên,* "the men of Han." No radically different political system was seriously tried until the twentieth century. The China of the next two millenniums had been born. The Chinese Empire had made its appearance.

BIBLIOGRAPHY

The chief Chinese source for the Ch'in is Ssŭ-ma Ch'ien's *Shih Chi*. The *Shih Chi* continues into the reign of Wu Ti of the Former Han. This and the *Ch'ien Han Shu,* the famous work by the Pan family, noted above, are standard for the Former Han. For the Former Han there is also the *Han Chi,* or Han Annals, by Hsün Yüeh (A.D. 148–209), arranged by years, on the plan of the *Tso Chuan*. For the Later Han, the *Hou Han Shu,* compiled by Fan Yeh, of the fifth century, is the major authority (although inferior to the *Ch'ien Han Shu*). Much of the portions of the *Shih Chi* which deal with the Ch'in and the Han has been translated by E. Chavannes, in *Les Mémoires Historiques de Se-ma Ts'ien* (5 vols., Paris, 1895–1905). Chavannes' great work is not only a translation but also contains extensive prolegomena, notes, and appendices. Among these are extremely valuable essays on the lives of Ssŭ-ma Ch'ien and of his father, on the sources of the *Shih Chi,* the history of the reign of Wu Ti, the administrative organization of the Ch'in and the Han, and possible connections between Greek and Chinese music. An important translation of portions of the *Ch'ien Han Shu,* with valuable introductions, notes, and appendices, is H. H. Dubs, *The History of the Former Han Dynasty, by Pan Ku* (Baltimore, 2 vols., 1938, 1944). On the *Ch'ien Han Shu* see also C. B. Sargent, *Subsidized History. Pan Ku and the Historical Records of the Former Han Dynasty* (*The Far Eastern Quarterly,* Vol. 3, pp. 119–143).

As for the second chapter, so for the third, the most voluminous general histories in Western languages are de Mailla, *Histoire Générale de la Chine,* H. Cordier, *Histoire Générale de la Chine,* and L. Wieger, *Textes Historiques* (2 vols., Hochienfu, 1903, 1904)—which is based upon standard Chinese histories but is decidedly uncritical. Useful shorter summaries are in O. Franke, *Geschichte des chinesischen Reiches* (Vol. 1, Berlin and Leipzig, 1930); F. E. A. Krause, *Geschichte Ostasiens* (Göttingen, 1925); René Grousset, *Histoire de l'Extrême-Orient* (2 vols., Paris, 1929); and Arthur Rosthorn, *Geschichte Chinas* (Stuttgart-Gotha, 1923, Vol. 10 of *Weltgeschichte in gemeinverständlicher Darstellung*, edited by L. M. Hartmann). H. A. Giles, *A Chinese Biographical Dictionary* (London and Shanghai, 1898) is valuable because of the large time scope covered and contains useful material, although there is a lamentable lack of references to the sources from which the information is drawn, and the sketches are usually not very critically written, contain mistakes and omissions, and must be used with extreme care—wherever possible checked with other accounts.

The only special history which needs noting, besides that of Chavannes, is Albert Tschepe, *Histoire de Royaume de Ts'in* (Shanghai, 1909. *Variétés Sinologiques* No. 27). It takes traditional views.

Many special monographs and articles exist dealing in part or entirely with events under the Ch'in and the Han. M. Granet, *La Civilisation Chinoise* (Paris, 1929), translated into English as *Chinese Civilization* (New York, 1930), carries its account through the Han. Notable studies dealing with the Ch'in are D. Bodde, *China's First Unifier. A Study of the Ch'in Dynasty as Seen in the Life of Li Ssŭ* (Leiden, 1938), and D. Bodde, translator, *Statesman, Patriot, and General in Ancient China* (New Haven, 1940).

On administrative organization there are T. H. Koo, *Constitutional Development of the Western Han Dynasty* (*Journal of the American Oriental Society*, Vol. 40, pp. 170–193), Von Wilhelm Seufert, *Urkunden zur staatlichen Neuordnung unter der Han-Dynastie* (*Mitteilungen des Seminars für Orientalische Sprachen*, Berlin, 1922, pp. 1–50), and the appendix mentioned above in Chavannes, *Mémoires Historiques de Se-ma Ts'ien* (Vol. 2, pp. 513–543).

On the related topic of education, there is Édouard Biot, *Essai sur l'Histoire de l'Instruction Publique en Chine* (Paris, 1847).

On the origin of the name China, see B. Laufer in *T'oung Pao*, 1912, pp. 719–726, and P. Pelliot in *ibid.*, 1912, pp. 727–742, 1913, pp. 427, 428. Laufer's view differs from that of Pelliot. See summaries of various theories in Henry Yule, *Cathay and the Way Thither*, edited by Henri Cordier, Vol. I (London, 1918).

On chronology, see E. Chavannes, *La Chronologie Chinois de l'an 238 à l'an 87 avant J. C.* (*T'oung Pao*, 1896, pp. 1–38, 509–540).

On Wang Mang, see Hu Shih, *Wang Mang, the Socialist Emperor of Nineteen Centuries Ago* (*Journal of the North China Branch of the Royal Asiatic Society*, Vol. 59, 1928, pp. 218–230), H. O. H. Stange, *Die Monographie über Wang Mang* (*Ts'ien Han Shu Kap. 99*) (Leipzig, 1939), H. H. Dubs, *Wang Mang and His Economic Reforms* (*T'oung Pao*, Vol. 34, pp. 219–265), which vigorously presents a critical view of Wang Mang, and O. Franke, *Staatssocialistische Versuche im Alten und Mittelalterlichen China* (*Sitzungsberichte der Preus-*

sischen Akademie der Wissenschaften, Philosophisch-historische Klasse, 1931, XIII, pp. 218–242). The theory that the *Tso Chuan* and *Chou Li* as we now have them are forgeries of Wang Mang's entourage is combated by B. Karlgren in *The Early History of the Chou Li and Tso Chuan Texts* (*The Museum of Far Eastern Antiquities, Stockholm, Bulletin No. 3,* 1931, pp. 1–60).

On one phase of taxation under the Han, see S. Kato, *A Study of the Suan-Fu, the Poll Tax of the Han Dynasty* (*Memoirs of the Research Department of the Toyo Bunko,* No. 1, 1926, pp. 51–68).

On the sacrifices *Fêng* and *Shan,* see E. Chavannes, *Le T'ai Chan* (Paris, 1910).

On foreign wars and conquests there are O. Lattimore, *Inner Asian Frontiers of China* (Oxford University Press, 1940), W. M. McGovern, *The Early Empires of Central Asia* (Chapel Hill, 1939), Arthur von Rosthorn, *Die Ausbreitung der chinesischen Macht in südwestlicher Richtung bis zum vierten Jahrhundert nach Chr.* (Prague, 1895), E. H. Parker, *A Thousand Years of the Tartars* (London, 1924), E. Chavannes, *Trois Généraux Chinois de la Dynastie des Han Orientaux* (*T'oung Pao,* Ser. 2, Vol. 8, No. 2), Henri Maspero, *L'Expedition de Ma Yuan* (*Bulletin de l'École Française d'Extrême-Orient,* 1916, No. 1, pp. 49, 55), and Leonard Aurousseau, *La Première Conquête Chinoise des Pays Annamites* (*IIIe siècle avant notre ère*) (*ibid.,* 1923, pp. 137–264). On Ch'in and Han possessions in Manchuria, see Yoshito Harada and Kazuchika Komai, *Mu-yang-ch'eng: Han and Pre-Han Sites at the Foot of Mount Lao-t'ieh in South Manchuria. Archæologia Orientalis,* Vol. 2, Tokyo, 1931.

On the closely allied subject, foreign intercourse and commercial and cultural exchanges, there are E. Chavannes, *Les Pays d'Occident d'après le Heou Han Chou* (*T'oung Pao,* 1907, pp. 149–234); Albert Hermann, *Die alten Seidenstrassen zwischen China and Syrien* (*Quellen und Forschungen zur alten Geschichte und Geographie,* Berlin, 1910); an interesting map in A. Hermann, *Die Verkehrswege zwischen China, Indien und Rom um 100 nach Chr.* (Leipzig, 1922); an account of recent excavations on the site of one of the old posts on the trade route, long occupied by a Chinese garrison, in A. Hermann, *Lou-lan, China, Indien und Rom im Lichte der Ausgrabungen am Lobnor* (Leipzig, 1931); F. Hirth, *China and the Roman Orient* (Shanghai, 1885); M. P. Charlesworth, *Trade-Routes and Commerce of the Roman Empire* (Cambridge, 1924); W. H. Schoff, *Navigation to the Far East under the Roman Empire* (*Journal of the American Oriental Society,* Vol. 37, 1917, pp. 240–249); W. P. Yetts, *Discoveries of the Kozlóv Expedition* (*Burlington Magazine,* Vol. 48, 1926, pp. 168–185); E. Chavannes, *Documents Chinois Découverts par Aurel Stein dans les Sables du Turkestan Oriental* (Oxford, 1913); M. Aurel Stein, *Ruins of Desert Cathay* (2 vols., London, 1912); M. Aurel Stein, *Innermost Asia* (4 vols., Oxford, 1928); M. Aurel Stein, *Ancient Khotan* (2 vols., Oxford, 1907); M. Aurel Stein, *Central-Asian Relics of China's Ancient Silk*

Trade (*Hirth Anniversary Volume*, London, 1923, pp. 367–374); M. Aurel Stein, *Serindia* (5 vols., Oxford, 1906 et seq.); Sir Aurel Stein, *On Ancient Central Asian Tracks: A Brief Narrative of Three Expeditions in Innermost Asia and Northwestern China* (London, 1933); J. J. M. de Groot, *Chinesische Urkunden zur Geschichte Asiens* (2 vols., Berlin and Leipzig, 1921–1926); F. Hirth, *The Story of Chang K'ien, China's Pioneer in Western Asia* (*Journal of the American Oriental Society*, Vol. 37, 1919, pp. 89–152); F. Hirth and W. W. Rockhill, *Chau Ju-kua* (St. Petersburg, 1912); F. Hirth, *Ueber fremde Einflüsse in der chinesischen Kunst* (Munich and Leipzig, 1896); B. Laufer, *Jade, A Study in Chinese Archæology and Religion* (Chicago, 1912); B. Laufer, *Sino-Iranica, Chinese Contributions to the History of Civilization in Ancient Iran, with Special Reference to the History of Cultivated Plants and Products* (Chicago, 1919); Helen E. Fernald, *Rediscovered Glories of Korean Art* (*Asia*, Vol. 31, Dec. 1931, pp. 788–795, 799–802); B. Laufer, *The Diamond, A Study in Chinese and Hellenistic Folklore* (Chicago, 1915); B. Laufer, *Asbestos and Salamander* (*T'oung Pao*, 1915, pp. 299–373); A. von Le Coq, *Buried Treasures of Chinese Turkestan* (London, 1928); F. J. Teggert, *Rome and China* (University of California Press, 1939); and G. F. Hudson, *Europe and China: A Survey of their Relations from the Earliest Times to 1800* (London, 1931).

On the introduction of Buddhism, see H. Maspero, *Le Songe et l'Ambassade de l'Empereur Ming* (*Bulletin de l'École Française d'Extrême-Orient*, 1910, pp. 95–130) and H. Maspero, *Communautés et Moines Bouddhistes Chinois au IIe et IIIe Siècles* (*ibid.*, 1910, pp. 222–232).

On the history of thought see A. Forke, *Geschichte der mittelalterlichen chinesischen Philosophie* (Hamburg, 1934).

On Confucianism, see Hu Shih, *The Establishment of Confucianism as a State Religion during the Han Dynasty* (*Journal of the North China Branch of the Royal Asiatic Society*, 1929, pp. 20–41). See also J. K. Shryock, *The Origin and Development of the State Cult of Confucius* (New York, 1932); H. H. Dubs, *The Victory of Han Confucianism* (*Journal of the American Oriental Society*, Vol. LVIII, pp. 435 ff.).

An interesting debate between the Confucianists and Legalists in the first century B.C., throwing light on the administrative organization under Han Wu Ti is in E. M. Gale, *Discourses on Salt and Iron: A Debate on State Control of Commerce and Industry in Ancient China, Chapters I–XIX. Translated from the Chinese of Huan K'uan with Introduction and Notes* (Leyden, 1931).

On Buddhism, Confucianism, and Taoism, see L. Wieger, *Histoire des Croyances Religieuses et des Opinions Philosophiques en Chine, depuis l'Origine jusqu'à nos jours* (1917) (translated into English by E. T. C. Werner, Hsien-hsien, 1927).

On various forms of art, see Édouard Chavannes, *Mission Archéo-*

logique dans la Chine Septentrionale (Paris, 1909–1915), especially Tome 1, première partie. *La Sculpture à l'Epoque des Han* (Paris, 1913); R. L. Hobson and A. L. Hetherington, *The Art of the Chinese Potter from the Han Dynasty to the End of the Ming* (London, 1923); Osvald Siren, *Histoire des Arts Anciens de la Chine* (6 vols., Paris, 1929–1932); B. Laufer, *The Beginnings of Porcelain in China* (Chicago, 1917); Victor Segalen, Gilbert de Voisins et Jean Lartique, *Mission Archéologique en Chine (1914–1917)* (2 vols., Paris, 1923–1924); B. Laufer, *Chinese Grave-Sculptures of the Han Period* (London, 1911); H. Ardenne de Tizac, *L'Art Chinois Classique* (Paris, 1926); Otto Fischer, *Die chinesische Malerei der Han-Dynastie* (Berlin, 1931), in which Han art is asserted to be a purely indigenous development; M. Rostovtzeff, *Inlaid Bronzes of the Han Dynasty in the Collection of C. T. Loo* (Paris, 1927), in which foreign influences in Han art are stressed; C. Hentze, *Chinese Tomb Figures. A Study in the Beliefs and Folklore of Ancient China* (London, 1928); and W. C. White, *Tomb Tiles of Ancient China* (Toronto, 1939).

On the invention of paper and new forms of writing, see T. F. Carter, *The Invention of Printing in China and Its Spread Westward* (revised edition, New York, 1931), and Bernhard Karlgren, *Philology and Ancient China* (Oslo, 1926).

On literature, see a careful biographical study of Pan Chao with translations of some of her work by Nancy Lee Swan, *Pan Chao: The Foremost Woman of China* (New York, 1932); Paul Pelliot, *Les Classiques Gráves sur la Pierre sous les Wei en 240–248* (*T'oung Pao*, 1924, pp. 1–4); Lo Tchen-ying, *Une Famille d'Historiens et son Œuvre* (Lyon, 1931); H. A. Giles, *A History of Chinese Literature* (New York, 1909); Georges Margoulies, *Le "Fou" dans le Wensiuan* (Paris, 1926); and Georges Margoulies, *Le Kou Wen Chinois* (Paris, 1926).

On Wang Ch'ung, see A. Forke, *Lun Hêng* (*Mittheilungen des Seminars für orientalische Sprachen,* Berlin, 1906, 1907, 1908, and *Beibände zu den Mittheilungen des Seminars für orientalische Sprachen,* Berlin, 1911).

On Huai-nan Tzŭ, see E. H. Parker, *Hwai-nan Tsz, Philosopher and Prince* (*New China Review*, Vol. 1, pp. 505–521), and E. H. Parker, *Some More about Hwai-nan Tsz's Ideas* (*ibid.*, Vol. 2, pp. 551–562).

On slavery see a careful and comprehensive study, C. M. Wilbur, *Slavery in China during the Former Han Dynasty* (Chicago, 1943).

CHAPTER IV

DIVISIONS AND FOREIGN INVASIONS FROM THE CLOSE OF THE HAN TO THE BEGINNING OF THE SUI DYNASTY (A.D. 220–589)

INTRODUCTORY

WITH the end of the Han began a period of civil strife, internal division, and weakness which lasted for almost four centuries. Non-Chinese peoples on the northern and western frontiers took advantage of the dissensions among the possessors of the fertile and wealthy valleys to the east and south and invaded the land, sometimes setting up kingdoms which lasted for long periods. The administrative structure erected by the Ch'in and the Han could not be operated for the entire country, and, where preserved, was often much weakened. The cultural unity achieved by them was also threatened. Foreign influences, especially Buddhism, wrought striking modifications in the life of the country. When, at the close of the sixth and the beginning of the seventh century, the Empire once more was brought together under one ruling house, Chinese civilization had become something rather different from what it had been under the Han.

In many ways the experience of these years resembles that through which the Occident, and, especially, the Mediterranean world was then passing. In both regions were political disunion and foreign invasions. In each, important cultural changes were in progress. Between the two great movements an actual connecting link existed in the vast migrations of peoples which characterized them both: it was from Central Asia that some (although by no means all) of the wave which overwhelmed large portions of the Chinese and Roman Empires seems to have originated. The suggestion has been made, indeed, that common climatic changes lie back of them—a prolonged period of scanty rainfall in the great steppes and semi-deserts of Central Asia which set the nomadic peoples in motion in search of food.

In China, however, the anarchy was not quite so marked nor were the changes so revolutionary as in the West, and recovery was more rapid. In both regions a new faith was making rapid strides—Christianity in the West and Buddhism in the Middle Kingdom—but Buddhism was not so thoroughly to transform the civilization of China as was Christianity to mold that of the Occident. As, in the Mediterranean area, in the East the Byzantine Empire perpetuated much of the Græco-Roman world, even more in China purely Chinese states continued in the South the traditions and institutions of the past, and in no great region of the Middle Kingdom does the retrogression toward barbarism appear to have been so marked or so prolonged as in Western Europe during the Dark Ages. In the Europe of the Dark and Middle Ages, however, a proportionately larger geographical extension of civilization took place than in China during the centuries of division. In the Occident, the shock was so profound that the unity which was Rome's greatest achievement was never again fully realized over all the area which had once been included in that empire, while in China complete union was again consummated and the territory governed was fully as large as under the Han. When, in the sixth and seventh centuries, the Sui and the T'ang once more brought the Chinese together, the culture which was then theirs, while markedly different from that of the Han, was not as much so as was that of the European Middle Ages or the Renaissance from that of the Roman Empire. The China of the Ch'in and the Han more nearly succeeded in surviving the years of disintegration and in impressing itself unchanged upon foreign invaders than did the Græco-Roman world. Moreover, in flood-tide the T'ang displayed a much richer and more varied civilization than the Western Europe of the same period. From Italy westward recuperation from the invasions had begun but was not to be accomplished until several centuries after the T'ang.

Why there should have been these differences need not here engage us. Whether, on the whole, the persistence of the past in China was as desirable as were the greater variations in the Occident is a question which, while very important, must not be entered into in this volume.

THE THREE KINGDOMS (A.D. 221–265)

Following the collapse of the Later Han, for several decades the Empire was divided into three major fragments and the period, consequently, is known in Chinese records as that of the Three Kingdoms. In the Northeast, as we have seen, Ts'ao P'ei, the son of the distinguished and able but unscrupulous Ts'ao Ts'ao, persuaded the last of the Later Han to abdicate in his favor. Taking the name of the power which his famous father had exercised in fact, he called himself Emperor. His dynasty he denominated Wei. He had possession of the Han capital, but only a minority of the Han domains recognized him. In the South, Sun Ch'üan, son of an official and general of the declining years of the Later Han, declared himself Emperor and gave to his dynasty the name of Wu. He and his successors controlled most of the former possessions of the Han in the Yangtze Valley east of the gorges and on the south coast into what is now Annam. Wu established its capital first at what is now Wuchang and later at the present Nanking. In Szechwan a member of the Liu family, Liu Pei by name, a descendant of one of the Han Emperors, assumed the imperial title, and his dynasty—usually regarded by orthodox Chinese historians as the legitimate one of the time—is called the Minor or Shu Han, Shu being the designation of the state over which he ruled.

The half-century or so during which these three states existed is one of the most romantic in the history of China. Around it stories of valor and adventure have collected which have been the source of many plays and popular narratives and of what is probably China's outstanding historical novel, the *San Kuo Chih Yen I,* or Romance of the Three Kingdoms. The most famous heroes of the period are the trio, Liu Pei, Chang Fei, and Kuan Yü, and the premier of the Shu Han, Chu-ko Liang. The first three are said to have become sworn brothers by the "Peach Garden Oath" and are reputed to have performed prodigious deeds of heroism. Kuan Yü and Chang Fei perished in 219 and 220 respectively, before the abdication of the last of the Later Han, the one by assassination and the other executed by Sun Ch'üan. Liu Pei died in 223. Centuries afterward, Kuan Yü was canonized as God of War and as such has been widely worshipped as the patron of soldiers. Chu-ko Liang, who survived the other three, was noted for his stratagems and his inventions of military machines.

In spite of the personal bravery of the three heroes and the skill of Chu-ko Liang, Shu was the first of the three states to disappear. During the lifetime of Chu-ko Liang it seemed to be successful in its wars with Wei, but, some years after the death of that statesman, thanks probably to the incapacity of the successor of Liu Pei, it was conquered by its northeastern rival.

The dynasty of the house of Ts'ao did not long survive the end of Shu. As Ts'ao Ts'ao and his son first dominated and then deposed their titular masters, the last of the Later Han, so in turn their descendants fell under the control of and eventually were displaced by the family of their chief minister. In 265 Ssŭ-ma Yen, whose father had been premier of Wei, deposed the last of Ts'ao Ts'ao's descendants to bear the title of Emperor and established himself as the first Emperor of a dynasty which he called by the name of Chin (also romanized Tsin and usually denominated the Western Chin or Tsin to distinguish it from its continuing branch, the Eastern Chin). A few years later, in 280, Ssŭ-ma Yen succeeded in overthrowing the ruler of Wu. China was now nominally once more reunited under one monarch.

THE CHIN (OR TSIN) DYNASTY

Ssŭ-ma Yen managed to hold most of his domains together during his lifetime, and to his court came envoys—or at least so Chinese historians declare—from Ta Ch'in (the Roman Orient) and from distant portions of Central Asia on the extreme edge and even beyond the widest extension of the Han domains. He is known to posterity as Wu Ti, or, to distinguish him from the others under different dynasties who had been given that title, Chin Wu Ti.

Ssŭ-ma Yen died in A.D. 290 and his descendants soon fell upon evil days. His immediate successor proved incapable of maintaining peace, but, feeble and mentally incompetent, was largely under the control of a vigorous and unscrupulous wife. Civil strife ensued, chiefly among members of the imperial family. Non-Chinese peoples took advantage of the situation to extend their conquests in Chinese territory. The house of Ssŭ-ma Yen was unable to compose its differences and present a united front against the invaders, and in 316 the grandson of Wu Ti and the fourth Emperor of the line surrendered to one of the barbarian chiefs, abdicated, and shortly afterward was put to death.

AN ERA OF DIVISION: THE CHINESE STATES OF THE SOUTH

Now came a period of division. In the Yangtze Valley princes of Chinese blood ruled, and their domains extended along the south coast. Occasionally they pressed their boundaries northward beyond the confines of the basin of the Yangtze. In the North non-Chinese peoples established states. They usually adopted Chinese culture and their leaders often aspired to the title of Emperor. The time was one of great confusion, but the reader may be helped to see its main features by the somewhat artificial device of outlining first the chief political events in the South and then those in the North.

In the South a branch of the Ssŭ-ma family maintained itself somewhat precariously for a little over a century (317–420) with its capital on the Yangtze at a place denominated Chien-yeh or Chien-k'ang (now Nanking) and is known as the Eastern Chin. Much of the course of the dynasty was punctuated by revolts and intrigues—the common lot of all Chinese ruling houses—and also by wars with the states on the north. About the middle of the fourth century the throne was dominated by an unusually able general, Huan Wên, who regained for his master Szechwan (for the preceding third of a century or so largely comprised in a Chinese state in that region founded in *c.* 304 by a family who had assumed the imperial title) and for a time extended the frontiers of the Eastern Chin to include much of the North China plain. So powerful was he that he deposed the reigning Emperor and placed his own puppet, still of the Ssŭ-ma family, on the throne. This puppet, it is generally supposed, was to abdicate upon demand in favor of the king-maker. However, he died prematurely and was soon followed to the grave by the ambitious Huan Wên. The Ssŭ-ma line thus obtained a fresh reprieve and reigned for nearly half a century longer.

The end of the Eastern Chin came in 420, brought about by another ambitious general, Liu Yü. Liu Yü claimed descent from a brother of the founder of the Han dynasty but had been born and reared in poverty. Not until middle life did he achieve prominence. Then, enlisting as a soldier, he quickly displayed ability, rose rapidly to high command, subdued a number of revolts, and carried the boundaries of the Chin to the Yellow River in successful fighting against the northern states. Liu Yü took advantage of the virtual dictatorship which these victories gave him to have the feeble Emperor killed. He set up another of the Ssŭ-ma line who soon abdicated (by request) and shortly afterward was also killed. Liu Yü, who had been known as prince of Sung, now established a new dynasty by that name. To distinguish it from the later and more renowned dynasty of Sung it is often called the Liu Sung.

The fall of the Eastern Chin (420) is usually said to mark the beginning of the era known to the Chinese as the Nan Pei Ch'ao, or the Southern and Northern Dynasties, which lasted until 589. Another classification—inclusive of a longer period—employed by Chinese historians is the Six Dynasties, by which are meant the six kingdoms and dynasties between the downfall of the Han and the reunification of China in 589 which had for their capital what is now Nanking. They were Wu, the Eastern Chin, the Liu Sung, the Southern Ch'i, the Liang, and the Ch'ên. In reality the end of the Eastern Chin marked no especial revolution. China was divided, to be sure, but not much more so than it had been for decades. The confusion became only a little more confounded.

The Liu Sung quickly ran its course. Liu Yü, known to posterity by the familiar title Wu Ti, did not long enjoy the power for which he had murdered his masters, but died in 423. The seven members of his family who successively followed him on the throne were short-lived. Four came to violent ends before reaching their twentieth birthday, and the oldest, known to posterity as Wên Ti, who reigned for nearly thirty years and under whom the realm experienced a fair degree of prosperity, was put to death by his own son. Family wars and intrigues make the chronicles of the dynasty peculiarly sordid and bloody. By a certain rough justice of fate, the Liu Sung was brought to a close, as it had been begun, by a vigorous general. Hsiao Tao-ch'êng, its chief commander, slew the last two Emperors of the line and, in 479, placed himself on the throne.

Hsiao Tao-ch'êng became the first Emperor of the dynasty

known as the Southern Ch'i. This had even shorter shrift than the Liu Sung. The founder died a little less than three years after mounting the throne and of his six descendants who held the imperial title only one reigned for more than two years and four died by violence. Domestic strife and war with one of the states of the North permitted little quiet. Again a general made an end of the dynasty (502) and founded a new one, the Liang.

The first monarch of the Liang, Hsiao Yen, known to posterity as Wu Ti (or, to distinguish him from the many others of the same appellation, Liang Wu Ti), was a distant connection of the rulers of the preceding dynasty. He held the throne until his death, in 549, or for nearly half a century. Frugal, an enemy of luxury and excess, and something of a scholar, he appears to have sought conscientiously the welfare of his realm. He reduced taxation, ordered the establishment of schools, and strove for peace. At first an ardent Confucianist, in late middle life he became a devout Buddhist. In his extreme old age (for he lived to be eighty-six) misfortunes overtook him. In the South, Annam revolted (in 541—but it was soon reconquered, the return of Chinese power beginning in 545), and a famous attempt to overwhelm the northern kingdom of Wei through the prolonged siege of the strategic city on the Han, later called Hsiangyang, failed because of the disastrous collapse of the dam which the attackers were building to drown out the beleaguered. In the North a vassal prince rebelled and crossed the Yangtze, and the now feeble Liang Wu Ti died in penury in what was later to be known as Nanking.

Great confusion marked the next few years. The rebel prince sought to establish a new dynasty, but was speedily slain. Violent struggles for the succession brought several members of the family of Hsiao Yen to the throne, but one after another these were quickly killed. In 557 the Liang dynasty is said officially to have ended, although a branch of the Hsiao family retained a precarious hold upon a section of the country until 589 and is known as the Hou Liang, or Later Liang (not to be confused with a Hou Liang of the tenth century).

The last Emperor of the Liang had been compelled to abdicate by one of his officials, Ch'ên Pa-hsien, a descendant of a renowned statesman of the Han. Ch'ên Pa-hsien established at the present Nanking a dynasty called the Ch'ên, but died about two years after his accession. His descendants held the throne for approximately thirty years. Their rule was terminated by Yang Chien—of whom more below—who once more united all China and founded the Sui.

These, then, were the dynasties which reigned in the South. Probably because they were predominantly Chinese in blood, orthodox Chinese historians regard them as in the legitimate line of succession as contrasted with the kingdoms of the North, which usually had at their head princes of partially or entirely non-Chinese stock. Some of the northern states were, however, fully as powerful and civilized as were their southern neighbors and also laid claim to imperial prerogatives.

With all the division, it is significant that the title of Emperor and with it the idea of unity were not allowed to lapse. Thanks to the work of the Ch'in and the Han—and, probably, to the traditions of pre-Ch'in times—the Chinese still thought of themselves as part of a cultural whole over which there could be only a single fully legitimate supreme ruler. Civilized human society, even though at times divided, must, they thought, ultimately be politically one.

AN ERA OF DIVISION: THE NON-CHINESE STATES OF THE NORTH

During these centuries of division, events in the North were even more confused and kaleidoscopic than in the South. The many states, most of them established by invaders, usually had rapidly shifting boundaries and as a rule several were in existence at one time. Wars among them and with the dynasties of the South were frequent. Only the chief of the states and a few of the more prominent events need here be mentioned.

We have seen that the Western Chin came to its end largely through the attacks of non-Chinese peoples. These were the Hsiung Nu, so frequently mentioned in the preceding pages. Their power had been broken by the Han, but they had maintained their separate existence under their own chiefs and were numerous in the northern marches. Many of them were in the service of the Emperors. When the Chin began to show weakness they threw off its yoke. Their ruling family claimed descent from the Han through a princess of that house who had been given to one of its ancestors in marriage. Accordingly it assumed the family name of Liu, began to pay reverence at the graves of the Han, and gave the designation Han to the state which it founded—sometimes called the Pei (Northern) Han. It was obviously making a bid for the mastery of all China and was seeking to give to its aspirations the guise of legitimacy. In 308 one of the line, Liu Yüan, felt himself strong enough to take the title of Emperor. It was his son, Liu Ts'ung, who brought the Western Chin to a violent termination.

Liu Ts'ung changed the name of the Hsiung Nu dynasty from Han to Chao (after an ancient feudal state by the latter name), usually called Ch'ien (Earlier) Chao. Liu Yüan was succeeded by a kinsman, and he, in turn, was slain by one of his own generals, also a Hsiung Nu, who took the throne and whose short line is known as Hou Chao, the Later Chao. These Hsiung Nu states, it is well to note, had their strongholds in the Northwest and sometimes their capital was at Ch'angan.

The Later Chao was succeeded in the Northwest by a state established by a Mongol people, formerly supposed—incorrectly—to be Tanguts, and who gave to the brief dynasty which they founded the name of Ch'in—the same as that of the great feudal state which in the third century B.C. had united China. During its comparatively brief course it was divided into two sections called Ch'ien and Hou—the Earlier and the Later Ch'in. In the second half of the fourth century the most powerful ruler of the Earlier Ch'in, Fu Chien, extended his boundaries into what is now the New Dominion, into Szechwan, and over much of North China, overrunning, among other small states, one which had its center in North Shansi and which had been founded by a family—possibly Mongol in stock—early in the fourth century. Fu Chien came to grief in an attempt to push his conquests to the south against the Eastern Chin, and, disastrously defeated, was killed in a revolt of his own generals. One of these founded the Later Ch'in.

In the far Northwest, the general whom Fu Chien had dispatched into Central Asia, Lü Kuang, was returning from a successful campaign when he heard of the fall of his sovereign. Pausing in what is now Kansu, he carved out for himself a principality which he ultimately called Liang (Hou Liang, or the Later Liang, to distinguish it from another and slightly earlier northern principality which is called the Ch'ien, or Earlier, Liang). Not long afterward, two of Lü Kuang's own subordinates, taking advantage of a reverse which he suffered at the hands of the Later Ch'in, revolted and seized part of his territory, founding petty states which are known as North and South Liang.

While these events were taking place in the Northwest, in the Northeast another people were establishing themselves. The Hsien Pei (often written Hsien Pi), of whose racial connections we are not quite sure but who seem to have been Mongols, were widely spread in what is now North China, Manchuria, and Mongolia, having occupied, among other regions, much of the area formerly held by the Hsiung Nu. During most of the fourth and into the fifth century a portion of the Hsien Pei—whose seat was in what is now Southern Manchuria—under the leadership of several members of the Mu-jung family set up in the Northeast, with its center in the modern Hopei, a state known as Yen. This again, thanks to the vicissitudes of war, had several subdivisions—the Earlier Yen, the Later Yen, the Northern Yen, and the Southern Yen. Several members of the Mu-jung family took the title of Emperor, thus displaying both their political ambition and their desire to be thought of as in the Chinese cultural stream.

During these confusing years of division we hear also, in the first half of the fifth century, of the dynasty of Hsia, with its center in the Ordos, north of what is now Shansi. Its name was derived from the first of the Chinese dynasties, for its ruler claimed descent from that house.

The longest lived and most powerful of the states of the North was founded by the T'u Pa (or Toba). Their dynasty, the Northern Wei (or Yüan Wei), lasted from 386 to 534, and two shorter succeeding dynasties, the Western Wei (Hsi Wei) and the Eastern Wei (Tung Wei), also of the T'u Pa, persisted until 557 and 550 respectively. As is the case with so many of these northern peoples, the ethnological connections of the T'u Pa are somewhat uncertain. They are usually said, perhaps wrongly, to be a branch of the Hsien Pei and they may have been either Mongols, "proto-Mongols," or Turks. In the latter part of the fourth and in the first half of the fifth century, under a succession of able and vigorous leaders, the T'u Pa overran most of the North and united it under one rule, bringing to an end the petty states of Liang and Yen and the other principalities in that area. In the middle of the fifth century they carried their arms into what is now the New Dominion, and several of the leading oases and trading centers of that region, including Turfan and Kashgar, became tributary to them.

The T'u Pa monarchs first fixed their capital at P'ingch'êng (now Tat'ung), in Shansi, but later, in the last decade of the fifth century, moved it to Loyang in Honan. They strove to adopt and patronize Chinese institutions and culture. Eventually the T'u Pa language and costume were proscribed, conformity to the Chinese in these matters, in family names, and in court ceremonial was ordered, and intermarriage with the Chinese encouraged. The T'u Pa became defenders of Chinese civilization against fresh invasions from the North—building for that purpose at least two frontier walls. As we shall see in a moment, some of the line were especially noted for their advocacy of Buddhism, although others espoused Confucianism and still others Taoism.

Among the most powerful of the enemies on the north against which the Northern Wei strove to defend their realm were a Mongol people known to the Chinese as the Juan Juan, meaning to wriggle, like a worm, possibly a pun on their true name. They gave the northern marches much trouble. About the middle of the sixth century the Juan Juan were in turn defeated by some of their former vassals, the T'u Chüeh, a Turkish people, who thereupon, in the second half of the sixth century, proceeded to build in Mongolia and Central Asia an empire of vast dimensions. These Turks, indeed, joined in overthrowing the Hephthalites, or "White Huns," possibly related to or identical with the Juan Juan. In the middle of the fifth century the Hephthalites had become a great power centering in the valley of the Oxus and had been successful invaders of India. The T'u Chüeh were not very highly civilized and had derived such culture as they possessed probably not from Chinese but from Iranian and Aramean sources. They formed a temporary alliance with the Sassanian monarchs of Persia and obtained the territory in which are now Bokhara and Samarkand, thus controlling in part the caravan routes by which silk was carried from China to the Byzantine Empire. We find these Turks, however, soon turning against their quondam allies, demanding free passage across the Persian possessions for the commerce between China and Constantinople, seizing from the enfeebled Sassanids territory south of the Oxus, and making approaches for concerted action by the Byzantine Empire and themselves against the Persians. This action was taken, the Byzantines attacking from the west and the Turks from the east.

To return to North China and the fate of the Wei. By the middle of the fifth century the vigor of the T'u Pa line was running low. The Northern Wei, as we have seen, in 534 broke into the Western and the Eastern Wei. The Eastern Wei was set up by a powerful general who dominated its puppet prince, and in 550 the son of this general took in name the power which his father had exercised in fact, founding the Pei Ch'i, or Northern Ch'i dynasty. In like manner, the Western Wei was founded— at Ch'angan—under the direction of a general who kept on the throne a prince of the legitimate line. Similarly also, this *roi fainéant* was made to abdicate (556) and was then killed (557) and a son of the king-maker was placed on the throne as the first monarch of the Pei Chou, or Northern Chou dynasty. In 557 the Northern Chou overran and annexed the Northern Ch'i, so that most of China was divided between two ruling lines, the Ch'ên in the South and the Northern Chou in the North.

The time was now ripe for the reunification of China. Neither the Ch'ên nor the Northern Chou was especially strong and a vigorous and able schemer would meet no insuperable difficulty in overturning them both. This man appeared in the person of Yang Chien, an official under the Northern Chou and a descendant of a distinguished scholar and statesman of the Later Han. His daughter was married to his master and when the offspring of that union, his grandson, succeeded to the throne Yang Chien soon (581) persuaded him to abdicate in his favor and established himself as the first monarch of the Sui dynasty. A few years later his armies overthrew Ch'ên and he became head of a reunited China (589).

CULTURAL CHANGES: GENERAL

To those for the first time reading Chinese history, the period which we have just recorded must seem a hopelessly confused mass of names and wars. A detailed account would be even more perplexing. Not only have many important figures and events of the period not been mentioned, but several of the minor states which arose in these years of disunion—some of them with Chinese and some with non-Chinese rulers—have not been so much as named. A perusal of the annals of the period gives the impression of almost continuous strife, of wave upon wave of barbarian invasion, of a seemingly uninterrupted series of rebellions, and of widespread anarchy. A large proportion of the so-called Emperors came to violent ends, and sordid intrigue and selfish betrayal seem to have been the order of the day. Much of such literature as had survived the Han or was freshly produced was destroyed, particularly in a military catastrophe under the Wei and in the disorders that accompanied the downfall of the Liang.

Fortunately, however, this is only one phase of the story. Disorder and anarchy there were, but the very wars brought about a geographical extension of the Chinese people and their culture. Then, too, over considerable portions of time large sections of the land enjoyed comparative peace and prosperity. The partial breakdown of government and the consequent loosening of the political, social, and intellectual structure that had been developed under the Ch'in and the Han permitted a flexibility in mind and culture which had not been known since the later years of the Chou. Foreign commerce continued and may have increased. Contacts with non-Chinese peoples and civilizations multiplied. More contributions entered from the outside than in any previous period within historic times and, since China was comparatively malleable, some rather profound changes followed. To obtain a well-balanced picture of the era, therefore, we must notice the non-political side of the story somewhat in detail.

The wars and the barbarian invasions in the North brought about a southward migration of the Chinese. The movement seems to have been largely one of officials and the wealthy, but many of the country folk must also have changed their homes. Heretofore the Yangtze Valley had been on the fringes of Chinese civilization and had been occupied only partially by Chinese stock. Now, for the first time, it gradually became a chief center of Chinese culture. Indeed, as we have seen, for nearly three centuries the purely Chinese dynasties had the seat of their government there. The growth in the population of the region appears to have been rapid during the fourth and much of the fifth century, and to have slowed down only with the disorders which marked the course of the later southern dynasties. In its new environment, moreover, Chinese culture took on some fresh forms, especially in literature and art. From the South came the drinking of tea. Our first reference to that custom is from the second half of the third century. The use of tea was long confined chiefly to the southern and central parts of the Empire. Not until the eighth or ninth century did it become common in the North.

In the meanwhile, Chinese civilization did not permanently lose ground in the North. The non-Chinese conquerors almost always bowed to the civilization of their subjects, and, in time, adopted it. Intermarriages wrought, of course, modifications of racial stock and presumably there were changes in the spoken language. However, in spite of all the innovations brought by the wide acceptance of Buddhism (of which more in a moment), in the North as in the Yangtze Valley Chinese culture appears to have undergone no basic alterations and to have held its own.

Some of the Chinese attempted to keep themselves free from the taint both of alien and of plebeian blood. Great aristocratic families arose, especially in the South, who monopolized a large proportion of the chief offices and possessed extensive landed estates. They intermarried among themselves in spite of the attempts of some of the rulers to prohibit the practice. In time their ways were aped and their lineages appropriated by commoners. Their failure to conserve exclusiveness was accompanied by the spread of their culture and the preservation of many of the older Chinese ideas and customs.

The periods of peace and prosperity which large portions of the land enjoyed permitted the carrying on of the institutions of the past and the perpetuation of the arts of civilization. Many of the rulers, both Chinese and non-Chinese, were patrons of learning as interpreted by the Confucian school. In the third century, the Wei dynasty—established by the Ts'ao—had some of the classical books of antiquity engraved on stone at the capital, Loyang, alongside those set up by the Han. Repeatedly we read of monarchs founding schools, and at times Confucius appears to have been even more honored than under the Later Han. We hear of a Confucian temple built in 505, with an image of the sage in it. Some rulers favored Taoism, and Buddhism was often and, in the main, increasingly popular with the rulers. Confucian scholarship seems to have made no great gains, and to have displayed no especial creativeness, but Confucian philosophy persisted as the theory on which the state and society were supposedly chiefly grounded.

The names of some eminent men of letters have come down to us. Wang Pi, of the first half of the third century, composed commentaries on the *I Ching* and the *Tao Tê Ching*, trying to find in the former wisdom rather than divination and to make of the latter a consistent philosophic whole. The "Seven Sages of the Bamboo Grove" of the third century were free-thinking philosophers and poets who took a Taoist outlook on life, kept largely aloof from conventional society, and lived simply—albeit bibulously. It may be that some of the Taoist texts usually ascribed to great figures of the Chou dynasty are their work. They helped, moreover, to develop the verbose, superficial, and highly artificial prose style, which during the centuries of disunion and into the succeeding period largely supplanted the concise, semi-rhythmical style of antiquity. A poet still famous was T'ao Ch'ien (365–427), who had several times been in official life but who longed for quiet and retirement. Interestingly enough, late in life he made the acquaintance of Hui Yüan, who, as we shall see presently, more than any other appears to have been responsible for the early stages of the growth of the Pure Land School of Buddhism.

Poetry seems to have been stimulated to fresh life by the new southern environment of Chinese culture under the six dynasties, as well as by contact with Buddhism. Taoism, as we have suggested, had its influence. Many a man, weary and disillusioned by the disorders of the time, withdrew from public life to solitude or to his estates and sought to bring himself into harmony with nature, partly by the methods advocated by Taoism. Some of these recluses endeavored to express themselves in verse.

Wang Hsi-chih (321–379), one of China's most distinguished calligraphists, a Taoist by belief, belongs to these centuries.

Forerunners of a voluminous class of Chinese literature, local gazetteers, appeared, modeled on the *Ch'un Ch'iu*. Histories were written, some of them in the style of Ssŭ-ma Ch'ien's great work. Cartography developed. Works on botany began to be written.

A form of writing was developed, the *p'ien t'i*, or parallel style, by which sentences were so arranged that the meanings and sounds of words were balanced in pairs.

Great libraries were collected under state supervision, and although they were usually scattered or burned in the political upheavals of the times, the love of books never died out and numbers of the writings of the past survived. Some ancient literature, moreover, was conserved in anthologies of prose and poetry collected during these years.

Modifications were made in the bureaucracy developed under the Ch'in and the Han. It has been suggested that from this period dates the sharp division between military and civil officials. According to this theory the non-Chinese rulers often found it wise to continue the bureaucracy inherited from the Han and to fill its posts with Chinese. As military conquerors, however, they were inclined to restrict the functions of this bureaucracy to civil matters and to reserve posts in the army to their own people. To insure this control, they would in part parallel the civil bureaucracy with a set of military officers. This hypothesis is doubtful. Long before the period of disunion some officials existed whose duties were purely civil and some whose functions were military. It is possible, however, that the accentuation of the difference may have come about in the fashion described. Feudalism and the division of the state into numerous principalities again raised their heads—as was inevitable in periods when the central government was weak. Powerful aristocratic families rather than those who had come up through free competition in the civil service examinations tended to monopolize the chief offices. More than once, however, a strong ruler attempted to enforce his authority through some form of organization which showed the influence of the models of the past.

Innovations appeared in other phases of life. The wheelbarrow and the water mill appeared. For the first time we hear of sedan chairs and dice. Coal began to be used.

FOREIGN COMMERCE

Foreign commerce continued, both by the overland routes and by way of the ports on the south coast. Trade by the overland routes was probably often interrupted or hampered by war, but we have already seen that the Northern Wei extended its power to the extreme West of what is now the New Dominion and that the silk trade appears to have been maintained. Of the southern ports, those in Tongking, on the delta of the Red River, were earlier of chief importance, but Canton was growing as a rival.

Chinese merchants seem not to have ventured very far afield and to have left chiefly to strangers the initiative in foreign trade, but outsiders found China a profitable country with which to deal.

Now and again we obtain glimpses of this foreign commerce or its concomitants which show us something of its extent. In 226 a merchant from the Græco-Roman Orient—Ta Ch'in—arrived via Tongking at the court of the state of Wu. Other merchants from Western Asia are reported to have come in fairly large numbers to what is now Indo-China and even to Canton. Sun Ch'üan, the first Wu Emperor, made at least two attempts to get in touch with the outer world, the first through an official whom he started back with the merchant from Ta Ch'in, but who died on the way, and the other through representatives whom he sent to the countries to the south. In 433 an embassy reached China from a state in the South—either from Java or from the Malay Peninsula. Beginning with the latter part of the third century, the kings of Champa, just to the south of the Chinese domains in Indo-China, began sending envoys. Some of these rulers, indeed, recognized Chinese suzerainty, although others did not scruple to invade the adjoining imperial domains. Embassies, too, are said to have arrived from Ceylon and India to the Liu Sung court to congratulate it on the progress of Buddhism in its domains. The large number of Buddhist missionaries in China who came by sea probably indicates a fairly extensive ocean shipping. Toward the latter part of this era, Justinian (527–565) of the Byzantine Empire attempted to open a new route to the Far East which would avoid the domains of his enemies, the Sassanids. Sericulture reached Khotan from China early in the fifth century. The cultivated walnut seems to have been introduced into the northwest of China, possibly from Tibet, by the fourth century, and the pomegranate, which was probably of Iranian origin, in about the third century. The secret of manufacturing glass appears to have been brought (although not for the first time) by Syrian or Indian artisans in the first half of the fifth century, brocades came from Persia as early as 520, and commerce in walrus ivory and other northern products trickled through from the far North and perhaps even from across the Bering Straits.

It must not be thought that, compared with present-day international commerce, the bulk of this trade was very large. Measured by that standard it was a mere trifle. Possibly it was small even when contrasted with the foreign commerce of the T'ang, the great dynasty which followed. For the times, however, especially when we recall the disasters which were overtaking the Mediterranean world during the fifth and sixth centuries, it was not insignificant.

It may be noted here, although it does not bear directly on commerce, that the music of Kucha, a highly cultivated center in what is now Sinkiang, had an influence on that of China, for an orchestra was brought back from there by Lü Kuang's forces.

It must also be added that Japan was feeling the influence of Chinese civilization. In the third and fourth centuries, a strong state with Chinese rulers was established in what is now the southern portion of Manchuria and northern Korea, and Chinese culture became very potent in the Korean peninsula. In the fourth century, after the collapse of this state, the stream dwindled but by no means disappeared. Under Chinese influence and with Chinese art forms Buddhism reached even Southern Korea in the fifth century. While the Chinese were in Korea, Japan and the peninsula were very closely in touch with each other, partly through Japanese invasions, and Chinese culture flowed into the islands. Japanese envoys visited Northern China and Chinese penetrated to Japan. Chinese and Korean immigrants helped to provide that country—then very rude—with scribes, and the Chinese characters were introduced, although possibly not for the first time. In the *San Kuo Chih*, or Memoirs of the Three Kingdoms, a history written in the third century, is a description of Japan derived from a Chinese visitor or visitors, which is one of the earliest extant descriptions of that land. As the years passed, direct connections between Japan and the China of the Yangtze Valley were made. Industries, especially weaving, were introduced to Japan. Numbers of Chinese immigrants settled in the country and some of them built Buddhist temples. During part of the time Japan was regarded by the Chinese as a vassal state and in recognition of this relationship at least two Chinese dynasties conferred an honorary title on its ruler. Japan was being brought into the Chinese cultural area.

THE CONTINUED INTRODUCTION AND GROWTH OF BUDDHISM

One of the clearest evidences of Chinese contact with the outer world and at the same time the greatest foreign contribution to the China of the period was the rapid growth of Buddhism.

There is something surprising in the firm establishment, great popularity, and wide acceptance of Buddhism in China. Usually a religion spreads to another land through one or more of five agencies: (1) conquest by adherents of the faith, with the subsequent conversion of the vanquished either by force or by the material advantages which accrue to conformity with the religion of the rulers—as in most Moslem conquests and in the subjugation of what is now Latin America by the Christians of Spain and Portugal; (2) intimate commercial contacts by which merchants or professional missionaries propagate the faith (as in the acceptance of Islam in parts of Africa in our own day, and in much of the expansion of Christianity in Northern Europe in medieval times and in Japan in the sixteenth and nineteenth centuries); (3) the bringing together of peoples of different cultural strata, those of lower civilizations being ashamed of their "barbarism" and taking over the religion along with the other features of the higher civilization (religion proving the chief vehicle of the higher culture, as in the spread of Buddhism to Japan and of Christianity in Northern Europe); (4) a large body of earnest missionaries (as during much of the spread of Christianity); and (5) a deep sense of religious need which the native faiths leave unsatisfied and which the new religion gives promise of meeting. Of these five agencies the first three in this case were almost entirely lacking. There was little or no conquest of China by peoples previously Buddhist, commercial contacts, as we have seen, were comparatively slight, and Chinese culture in many respects was equal and even superior to that of the peoples of India and Central Asia from whom the Chinese received Buddhism.

It will be remembered that Buddhism had arisen in a civilization whose dominant interests were seemingly quite different from those of China. Indian culture, as represented by its intellectuals, was other-worldly, deeply concerned about the fate of the individual after death, firmly convinced of the reality of the transmigration of souls, and given to mysticism. Except for Taoism, Chinese thought was chiefly absorbed in successfully ordering human society and in such related problems as the quality of human nature. It upheld the traditional honors to ancestors, but for long it had been influenced by an undercurrent of scepticism about the reality of life after death. It had no inkling of metempsychosis. Mysticism, if present at all, was there only in rudimentary form. Why should Buddhism, which arose out of specifically Indian needs and problems, meet with such successes in a cultural atmosphere as alien to it as that of China?

Moreover, Buddhism ran counter to much that was fundamental in Chinese life. It advocated celibacy, a practice most destructive to the family, that social institution by which Confucian thought and Chinese tradition set such store. In its monastic communities it tended to create *imperia in imperio* which an autocratic state such as was China in its centuries of power must regard with suspicion and certainly must insist upon controlling. Its premium on mendicancy was obnoxious to statesmen who must have regarded sturdy beggars as parasites on society. Its asceticism was contrary to Confucian moderation and humanism.

Then again, no other foreign faith, not even Islam or Christianity, has ever obtained anything like the hold in China which Buddhism has, and that notwithstanding the fact that Islam has been continuously represented in the Middle Kingdom for eleven or twelve centuries—approximately two-thirds of the time that Buddhism has been there—and Christianity has been in the Middle Kingdom intermittently as long as Islam and continuously for as many centuries as were required to give Buddhism its wide acceptance.

On further consideration, however, at least some of the reasons for Buddhism's success become apparent. Even if limited, commercial contacts between China and Buddhist peoples existed. In some respects—as in astronomy and mathematics and in some phases of art, letters, and philosophy—the professors of Buddhism could teach the Chinese. Zealous and scholarly Buddhist missionaries came in large numbers.

Moreover, Buddhism seemed to meet some basic demands of the human spirit for which the then existing Chinese religions offered no satisfaction. Mahayana Buddhism—the type which ultimately predominated in China—presented a more definite picture of the future life than did they and could promise to all who followed its precepts the assurance of bliss beyond the grave— an ample and happy existence of which it gave glowing and specific portrayal. It also terrified the timid and warned the wicked with its hells. To be sure, the conception of *nirvana* was too abstruse for most Chinese and the problem—of escape from rebirth and suffering—for which it was the solution and which gave it an appeal to the Indian mind was alien to Chinese thought. For most Chinese Buddhists, however, *nirvana* faded into the background.

Buddhism may also have been a welcome relief from the rigid determinism of Confucianism. Its doctrine of *karma*, by which an individual's present lot is fixed by his deeds in all his previous existences, seems almost as hopelessly fatalistic as the Confucian belief in the inflexible Will of Heaven. A man by his deeds in this life, however, could modify his *karma* and so affect his lot in a future existence.

Then, too, Buddhism, with its philosophies, its pantheon and saints, its images, its stately worship, its music, its voluminous religious literature, its cosmology, and its elaborate forms of the religious life, greatly enlarged the spiritual horizons of the Chinese and made a powerful æsthetic and intellectual appeal. To some, moreover, the celibacy, the asceticism, and the authoritarian community life must have proved attractive. In an age of disorder the cloistered quiet of the monastery with its escape from the turmoil of life was compelling.

Buddhism, again, in practice exalted the individual as the native philosophies did not. Confucianism and Taoism were aristocratic, and Taoist immortality was only for the few. Buddhism was for all: any one, no matter how humble, might share in its salvation for himself, or, more popularly, through an easy reliance on monk, ceremony, saint, or savior.

Moreover, Buddhism proved adaptable and its interpreters accommodated it in large part—although never entirely—to previous Chinese prejudices and conceptions.

Finally, the time was eminently favorable for the growth of Buddhism in China. The faith was still in its heyday in the land of its birth and Buddhist missionaries were enthusiastically propagating it in new lands. Mahayana Buddhism especially was strong (although Hinayana was not unrepresented) in what is now Northwest India (Gandhara and Kashmir) and in some of the regions to the north (Kashgar, Yarkand, and other centers) across which ran the trade routes between China, Persia, and the Roman Orient. Here, then, was a great spiritual movement in the full flood of missionary enthusiasm and expansion, and in lands with which China had commercial contacts.

Just when this was true, in China the structure of society had been enfeebled by disorder. The state was not in a position to offer the effective resistance to Buddhism—even when it wished to do so—that it could under the great monarchs of the Han. Confucian orthodoxy suffered from the irregularities and partial collapse of the educational and bureaucratic structure which were its bulwarks and from the civil strife which must have taken heavy toll of its leaders. Moreover, Confucianism was burdensome, and its debility may have been greeted with a feeling of relief. To be sure, Taoism throve. It was often popular, as under the Eastern Chin, when it was dominant in court circles. However, a few Taoists, distressed by the degradation of their faith, greeted Buddhism as akin to the reform which they were seeking. Then, too, Chinese, disheartened by the chaos in society, welcomed the refuge from the world which Buddhist monasteries and Buddhist philosophy seemed to afford. In the North, finally, were non-Chinese peoples, some of whom had contacts with that Central Asia where Buddhism was now so strong, and upon most of whom the esteem for native Chinese culture rested more lightly than upon the pure Chinese.

It is not surprising, therefore, that these centuries saw Buddhism become an integral and influential part of Chinese life. Nor is it strange that Buddhism was more widely successful than

Islam and Christianity were later to be. It came and was already firmly established before these had arrived, and, by its chronological priority, made progress more difficult for the other two. It entrenched itself in China, moreover, in the one time after the third century B.C. when, over a long period, the structure of Chinese life was greatly weakened and could offer little resistance. By the time when, centuries later, Islam and Christianity appeared on the scene, the Empire was once more unified and Confucian philosophy and the Chinese social structure were in a position to oppose new and revolutionary ideas. The disorganization in every phase of Chinese life which has come in the twentieth century is, to be sure, more profound than was that of the third to the seventh century, but so far it has not been nearly so prolonged. It is significant, moreover, that during these recent years Christianity, the missionary faith of to-day, has been making phenomenal gains—in part a contemporary illustration of the way in which Buddhism won its great victories.

Buddhism was brought to China through numerous foreign missionaries. From the names that have come down to us we know that some were from Cambodia, some from Ceylon, and some from India, including South India, and that others, perhaps the larger proportion, were from what are now Northwest India and Afghanistan (where, it will be recalled, the Kushan kings, a Yüeh Chih dynasty, had espoused it), and from regions in Central Asia to which the faith had spread from that center—Parthia, for example, and what is now the New Dominion. Some came to the South by way of the sea, and others to the North by the overland trade routes.

Among the many names that we have is that of Dharmaraksha, a native of Tunhuang—near what is now the extreme western border of Kansu, and so a center where many influences were to be found coming east and west over the trade routes. He is said to have known thirty-six languages or dialects. Arriving at Loyang in 266, in the next half-century he is reported to have made translations of more than one hundred and seventy-five Buddhist works. We hear also of Kumarajiva (344–413), the son of an Indian father and of a princess of Kucha, a famous Buddhist center in what is now the New Dominion. He was educated in part in Kashmir, was brought back a captive from

Kucha by the expedition of Lü Kuang at the close of the fourth century, and labored with marked success in Ch'angan. Sometimes called the greatest translator of Buddhist texts, during nine years at Ch'angan he organized a bureau which had in it hundreds of monks and which, under his supervision, put ninety-four works into Chinese. Famous, too, is Bodhidharma, called by Chinese sources, on decidedly dubious grounds, the twenty-eighth Patriarch, or official teacher, in line from the Buddha. He is said to have come from India by way of Canton about the first half of the sixth century, to have been received with honor by Liang Wu Ti at what is now Nanking, and later to have moved to Loyang. However, the importance ascribed to him in later Buddhist writings is very probably a pious exaggeration. Not only are many of the stories told about him—such as his crossing the Yangtze on a reed—obviously unauthentic, but we have very little concerning him, even of the non-miraculous, from contemporaries or near-contemporaries.

Much of the work of the missionaries consisted in the translation of Buddhist books into Chinese—a labor in which natives shared. To no small degree, indeed, the success of Buddhism in the Middle Kingdom appears to have been due to these literary labors. Long lists of the works put into Chinese, from the Han dynasty onward, have been preserved. This voluminous literature won the respect of a people whose leaders have traditionally held the written page in high esteem.

Buddhism was further encouraged in the Middle Kingdom by the journeys to India of ardent Chinese monks who sought in the home of their religion not only inspiration but sacred books and relics as tangible aids to the faith in China. These travellers seem to have been fairly numerous. The most famous of the period covered by this chapter was he whose religious name was Fa-hsien. Fa-hsien set out in 399 with the purpose of obtaining in India more nearly perfect copies of Buddhist sacred books than were to be found in his native land. He went by one of the caravan routes across the Tarim basin, in India visited important Buddhist centers and collected copies of the works for which he was in search, and, returning by way of Ceylon and the ocean route, landed on the north coast after an absence of fifteen years. Somewhat less distinguished was Sung-yün, who, sent in 518 with a companion by an Empress Dowager of the Northern Wei to quire Buddhist books, reached India by the overland route and arrived home in 521.

Chinese monks were not content simply with translations of the Indian scriptures of their faith, but began the production of an independent native literature on Buddhism.

Through the labors of the missionaries and their converts Buddhism became extremely popular. It did not always have smooth sailing. Not until 335 did the state permit native Chinese to become monks—although many had previously done so—and on several occasions monarchs of Confucian or Taoist convictions instituted persecutions, destroying monasteries and ordering the monks back into secular life. The old order was not so moribund that it could offer no resistance. Often, however, Buddhism was espoused by the rulers, an act which could not fail to augment the popular following. Devotees of Buddhism were found both among the Chinese monarchs of the South and the non-Chinese princes of the North. Probably the most famous of the southern imperial converts was Liang Wu Ti who, as we have seen, after being an earnest Confucianist, in middle life embraced Buddhism. He publicly expounded Buddhist sutras, collected a Chinese edition of the Tripitaka, issued edicts against animal sacrifices, was a strict vegetarian, and three times retired to a monastery. Several monarchs of the Northern Wei, of the T'u Pa line, stand out as patrons of the faith. At least two of them opposed it, but the majority endorsed it. Some even took part in Buddhist ordinations and preached Buddhist sermons. We read of thousands of monasteries and of hundreds of thousands of monks, and have a report that in 381 nine-tenths of the inhabitants of Northwestern China were Buddhists. Accurate statistics are, of course, lacking, and these numbers are probably exaggerations, but taking as a whole the centuries between the Han and the Sui Buddhism undoubtedly grew in popularity. By the advent of the Sui it had become an integral and powerful part of Chinese life.

Both Hinayana and Mahayana Buddhism were found in China, but Mahayana predominated and became standard.

Buddhism had a manifold influence upon the life of the period. Religiously it introduced new conceptions, among them many gods, the transmigration of souls, and much clearer convictions about life after death. Ethically it reënforced some features of traditional Chinese morality, including kindness and regard for human life, and it also carried these particular virtues further, insisting on regard for all animate existence. In time many of its concepts crept into folklore and popular festivals, so that all, whether avowed Buddhists or not, more or less unconsciously were affected by it.

Between the third and the seventh century Taoism was largely recast under its influence, developing a liturgy, an ecclesiastical organization, and a canon of sacred writings. In the fifth century K'ou Ch'ien-chih established at Tat'ung a Taoist temple with a priesthood with rules and regulations and with rituals of worship and fasting. As early as about A.D. 300 the Taoist imitation of Buddhist writings began. At that time a Taoist composed a sutra which attempted to prove that Buddhism is a form of Taoism and that the Buddha himself was a convert of Lao Tzŭ.

In literature and language, Buddhism not only introduced many new terms, but, in their study of Chinese, Buddhist missionaries, coming with the perspective of foreigners, originated a phonetic analysis—by means of what are called initials and finals—which entered into later Chinese philology and literature.

In art especially Buddhism brought fresh contributions. It was in Northwest India, particularly in Gandhara, that statues of the Buddha were first made. Here Greek influence was still strong, so that the earliest Buddhist iconography is distinctly Hellenic in form. It was through Gandhara that the easiest—although not the shortest—of the trade routes passed by which communication was had between what is now the New Dominion and India. Hence this Græco-Buddhist art spread into Central Asia and eastward into the Tarim basin and on to China. In the oases of what is now the New Dominion and in China proper statues large and small were carved or cast in metal, frescoes were painted on the walls or rock temples, stone carvings were made, and stelæ were set up, a large proportion of them showing Græco-Buddhist features. Other, more purely Indian art came in by the shorter but more difficult route across the Pamirs. In the New Dominion, indeed, surviving examples of this period and of the centuries immediately succeeding show a mixture of many strains—Græco-Roman, Persian, Byzantine, Indian of the Gupta period (fourth and fifth centuries), Græco-Buddhist (of Gandhara), and others of as yet unknown provenance. Given the trade routes, this art could not fail to have its effect in the Middle Kingdom. Impressive survivals of Gandhara Græco-Buddhist influences in China are in the caves of Tunhuang, in Tat'ung, in a gorge called Lungmên, near Loyang, and in many monuments and images which have been brought to our museums in the Occident. The Buddhist art associated with the name of the Northern Wei is noted for its Gandhara characteristics, its beauty, and its relative simplicity. In the Yangtze Valley a current from Southern India seems to have entered. Here, too, as possibly in the North of China, the Buddhist stream merged in part with Taoist impulses. Probably the greatest painter was Ku K'ai-chih, of the fourth and fifth centuries, a native of Kiangsu, who often employed Buddhist themes. One of the stories told of him is that he paid a large subscription to a Buddhist temple by painting a picture on the temple wall and having the monks charge a fee of the throngs who flocked to see it. It must be noted that Ku K'ai-chih also painted landscapes, portraits, and scenes from daily life. He was a well-known figure of his generation, a sort of "inspired eccentric" who, in addition to his achievements in art, held office for much of his life.

BUDDHIST SECTS (OR SCHOOLS)

Not only did Buddhism make its impress on Chinese civilization: China wrought changes in Buddhism. Buddhists took over much of Taoist terminology, studied Taoist literature, and even wrote commentaries on the *Tao Tê Ching*. As a result, Taoism had its effect on the foreign faith, although to exactly what extent is difficult to trace. As any vital religion will do, Buddhism developed sects (or schools). Some were imported from India, but those most influential in China were largely of indigenous growth. The Chinese, indeed, eventually made of Buddhism something quite different from that which had come to them. Much of the intellectual and religious activity of the years of political disunion and of the immediately succeeding centuries was both stimulated by and expended upon Buddhism. The energy which under the Chou had found an outlet in the creation of the many schools of thought of that dynasty and which under the Han had gone into Taoism and into establishing Confucianism was now largely absorbed by Buddhism. Often the new developments in Buddhism professed to find their authority in Indian texts or founders: as in the case of most religions, sanctions were sought in the past. In fact, however, they showed distinctly the marks of the Chinese genius.

One of the most prominent of the Chinese sects, the Ch'an, or, to give it its better known Japanese name, Zen, declared that salvation was to be achieved by inward enlightenment. Enlightenment came, so it said, in an instant, as it had to the Buddha—by a conversion experience. Good works, asceticism, ceremonial, the study of books, and meditation were held to be at least secondary and perhaps in vain. To make contact with reality and to understand it one must look within. Knowledge, in other words, was purely subjective. The sect is reported to have been introduced into China by Bodhidharma in about the first half of the sixth century. Tradition has it that Bodhidharma spent nine years at Loyang, silently gazing at a wall in meditation. As a matter of fact, we know very little about him, for most of our accounts of him are pure legend. He appears to have arrived in the fifth century and, after about fifty years in China, to have died in 520. He was only one of the contributors to the formation of Ch'an. The sect was really the result of a long evolution. It did not come to its fullest form until the seventh and eighth centuries A.D. It began at least as far back as the fifth century, with Tao Shêng, a disciple of Kumarajiva and Hui Yüan. Tao Shêng attacked the Indian idea of merit and enunciated the principle that Buddhahood was reached by sudden enlightenment and not by the long and arduous practices of regulated and disciplined meditation. In a certain sense Ch'an was a revolt against the methods of which Bodhidharma was held to be an advocate. Ch'an appears to have been indebted at least in part for its popularity—and perhaps for some of its basic ideas—to Taoism, which had long prepared the ground by its emphasis upon quietism and simplicity. It represented, too, a reaction against the complicated ritual and philosophy by which some of the current Buddhist teaching had hedged about the road to salvation.

The T'ien T'ai sect had as its founders two Chinese known

as Chih I (or Chih K'ai), who died in 597, and Hui Ssŭ, who died in 577. Chih I, a pupil of Hui Ssŭ, had once been a teacher of Ch'an Buddhism but came to see what he believed to be its weaknesses. He declared that salvation was to be achieved not by Ch'an processes alone but by a combination of meditation, concentration, the study of books, ritual, moral discipline, and insight. He stressed particularly one of the Buddhist writings known as the Lotus Sutra, and tended to a theistic explanation of the Buddha nature. Reality was not purely subjective, as to the Ch'an, but an objective activity exerting itself for the good of all beings. The school took its name from a mountain in Chêkiang called T'ien T'ai, to which Chih I retired to teach and to practice his doctrine. Its moderation and its systematization and simplification of Buddhism appealed to many of the cultivated classes, trained by the Confucian tradition to distrust extremes and to shun intricate metaphysics. It made for tolerance and produced many scholars.

A third sect, and the most widely popular among the laity, was the Pure Land (Ch'ing T'u) or Lotus school. It is said to have been founded by Hui Yüan (333–416) of Shansi, who later established a Buddhist center in the present Kiangsi, in hills not far from Kiukiang. Its distinctive teaching, however, is much older and goes back to non-Chinese roots. It declares that salvation is by simple faith in Amitabha, or Amida (in the modern colloquial, O-mi-t'o-fo), one of the many Buddhas with which Mahayana peoples the spiritual universe. This faith, expressed in calling upon the name of Amida, is all that is necessary to secure admission after death into the Western Paradise. The Pure Land way freed the humble believer, who must needs go about the daily occupation of making his living, from the study of books, the elaborate meditation, and the ritual which could be followed only by the professionally religious. It is interesting, and possibly significant, that before his conversion Hui Yüan had been an earnest Taoist and that at least one other of the early leaders of the sect had also been a Taoist. It may be that the longing for immortality which had possessed these men, and which they had sought to satisfy through Taoism, led them to welcome and to propagate the Pure Land, which offered a future life of bliss, not to the few and at the price of long practice, as did popular Taoism, but to the many, and by the much easier road of faith. Certainly some of the more earnest Taoists of the period found in Amida the answer to their highest aspirations and Taoism influenced the terminology of the sect. It seems possible, moreover, that the disorders of these centuries bred in many a weariness of the world and caused them to seek to escape from it to a future life of bliss by a simpler method, more possible for the layman, than the difficult road of Ch'an or T'ien T'ai.

Other schools were to follow in the next century or two—upon the narrative of which we are shortly to enter. The end of the sixth century and the reunification of the Empire saw Chinese Buddhism in its heyday, prepared to take a prominent part in the brilliant era then dawning. That era was, indeed, to owe much of the distinctiveness of its culture to the contributions brought by the foreign religion.

SUMMARY

The three and a half centuries of comparative internal weakness, civil strife, and foreign invasion which followed the downfall of the Han dynasty had at last come to an end. They had been marked by almost incessant warfare. Ambitious rulers, Chinese and non-Chinese, many of them taking the title of Emperor, had sought to annihilate their rivals. The sufferings of the masses had often been intense, and for long periods extensive sections of the country had been given over to what was little better than anarchy. Civilization had by no means collapsed, however, the non-Chinese peoples were being assimilated, and in some directions advance was registered. Buddhism was winning a large place for itself, bringing with it important contributions from other lands. The breaking of the hard and fast molds of the Han and the entrance of fresh ideas may have been necessary if there was to be a new period of cultural development. It may, indeed, have been unfortunate for China that the disintegration of the old was no more extensive or prolonged. The China of the seventh and succeeding centuries, while displaying many new features, was still basically unaltered from that of the Han. The revolution was not nearly so thoroughgoing or so prolonged as in the Occident. Possibly as a consequence, the Europe of the thirteenth and sixteenth centuries differed much more from the Græco-

Roman world than did the China of the seventh to the twentieth century from that of the Ch'in and the Han. It was, however, a somewhat altered China which emerged from the years of distress.

BIBLIOGRAPHY

The best full Chinese sources for the period are the dynastic histories. The *San Kuo Chih,* or Memoir of the Three Kingdoms, was composed by Ch'ên Shou of the third century and so is practically contemporary with the events recorded. Being a subject of the Chin, the author was biased in favor of the state of Wei. Much of it is dry as to style, but it was enriched in 429 by an abundant and valuable commentary by P'ei Sung-chih, and is said to be one of the best of the Chinese historical works. The *Chin Shu,* or Book of Chin, was compiled in the T'ang dynasty by imperial order from the works of preceding authors. The *Sung Shu,* or Book of the (Liu) Sung, is by Shên Yo (441–512), as are also histories of the Chin and the Ch'i. The *Nan Ch'i Shu,* or the Book of the Southern Ch'i, is by Hsiao Tzŭ-hsien (489–537). The *Liang Shu* and the *Ch'ên Shu,* or the Book of Liang and the Book of Ch'ên, were both written by Yao Chien (died 643) at imperial order, largely on the basis of material collected and partially compiled by his father, Yao Ch'a, an official under the Ch'ên. The *Wei Shu* was written by Wei Shou (506–572), was twice revised in the next two decades, and in its present form was revised and added to from other sources under the Sung (960–1279). It is unique among the dynastic histories in having an essay on Buddhism and Taoism, for the writers of most of these histories, being orthodox Confucianists, tended to ignore the rival faiths. The *Pei Ch'i Shu,* or Book of the Northern Ch'i, in rather indifferent literary style, was written by Li Po-yao (565–648) from sources assembled by his father, Li Tê-lin, an official under the Northern Ch'i and the Northern Chou. The *Chou Shu* was compiled early in the T'ang dynasty, by imperial order, from contemporary, or nearly contemporary, material. The *Nan Shih,* or Southern History, an abbreviated account of the Sung, Southern Ch'i, Liang, and Ch'ên, was compiled by Li Yen-shou of the seventh century and revised by a contemporary, Ling-hu Tê-fên. From the literary standpoint it is inferior, but it contains some information not found in the separate histories of these dynasties. The *Pei Shih,* or Northern History, an abbreviated account of the Northern Wei, the Northern Ch'i, the Northern Chou, and the Sui, also by Li Yen-shou, is much better done than the *Nan Shih* and fills many of the *lacunæ* in the separate histories of these dynasties. In both works the author made use of his father's notes.

It is noteworthy that several of these histories were composed by imperial order. The T'ang initiated the custom of having the records of the preceding dynasty officially compiled by its successor. Before that time the dynastic histories had been private enterprises.

As in the case of the preceding chapter, useful general works in Western languages are de Mailla, *Histoire Générale de la Chine*, Wieger, *Textes Historiques*, Cordier, *Histoire Générale de la Chine*, Grousset, *Histoire de l'Asie*, Grousset, *Histoire de l'Extrême-Orient*, H. A. Giles, *A Chinese Biographical Dictionary*, R. Wilhelm, *A Short History of Chinese Civilization*, and A. Rosthorn, *Geschichte Chinas* (Stuttgart-Gotha, 1923, Vol. 10 of *Weltgeschichte in gemeinverständlicher Darstellung*, edited by L. M. Hartmann). L. C. Goodrich, *A Short History of the Chinese People* (New York, 1943), rich in cultural features, is peculiarly good on this period. See also a standard history, O. Franke, *Geschichte des Chinesischen Reiches* (Berlin, Vol. 2, 1936), and P. A. Boodberg, *Marginalia to the Histories of the Northern Dynasties* (*Harvard Journal of Asiatic Studies*, Vol. 2, pp. 223–253).

Special studies on the political history of foreign conquests are W. M. McGovern, *The Early Empires of Central Asia* (Chapel Hill, 1939), E. H. Parker, *A Thousand Years of the Tartars* (London, 1924); Ch. B. Maybon, *La Domination Chinoise en Annam (111 av. J. C.—939 ap. J. C.)* (*The New China Review*, Vol. 1, pp. 237–248, 340–355); Maspero, *Le Royaume de Champa* (*T'oung Pao*, 1910, pp. 125, 165, 319, 489, 547; 1911, pp. 53, 236–291, 451–589); a masterly work, replete with information about Central Asia, E. Chavannes, *Documents sur les Tou-kiue (Turcs) Occidentaux* (St. Petersburg, 1903); Ch. Piton, *China during the Tsin Dynasty* (*China Review*, Vol. 11, pp. 297–313, 366–378; Vol. 12, pp. 18–25, 154–162, 353–362, 390–402); A. Pfizmaier, *Aus der Geschichte des Hofes von Tsin* (*Sitzungsberichte der phil.-hist. Classe der Kaiserlichen Akademie der Wissenschaften, Vienna*, Band 81, 1875, pp. 543–616), translations from the *Chin Shu*; A. Pfizmaier, *Die Machthaber Hoan-wen und Hoan-hiuen* (*ibid.*, Band 85, 1877, pp. 601–676); also translations from the *Chin Shu*; A. Pfizmaier, *Ungewöhnliche Erscheinungen und Zufälle in China um die Zeiten der südlichen Sung* (*ibid.*, Band 79, 1875, pp. 361–440), from the *Sung Shu*; A. Pfizmaier, *Zur Geschichte der Aufstände gegen das Haus Sui* (*ibid.*, Band 88, 1877, pp. 729–806); A. Pfizmaier, *Die letzten Zeiten des Reiches der Tsch'in* (*ibid.*, Band 98, 1881, pp. 701–780), a translation of parts of the *Ch'ên Shu* with few critical or explanatory notes; Paul Pelliot, *Note sur les T'ou-yu-houen et les Sou-p'i* (*T'oung Pao*, 1920, pp. 323–331). The many translations by Pfizmaier, while admirable as pioneering efforts, are not now regarded very highly by sinologists.

On commerce and on cultural importations are B. Laufer, *Arabic and Chinese Trade in Walrus and Narwhal Ivory* (*T'oung Pao*, 1913, pp. 315–370); F. Hirth, *Ancient Porcelain, a Study in Medieval Industry and Trade* (Shanghai, 1888); F. Hirth, *China and the Roman Orient* (Shanghai, 1885); F. Hirth and W. W. Rockhill, *Chau Ju-kua* (St. Petersburg, 1912); B. Laufer, *Sino Iranica* (Chicago, 1919); Sylvain Lévi, *Le "Tokharien B," Langue de Koutcha* (*Journal Asiatique*, IIe serie, 2, 1913, pp. 311–380); K. Hara, *An Introduction to the History of Japan* (New York, 1920); and Sir Aurel Stein, *On Ancient*

Central-Asian Tracks: A Brief Narrative of Three Expeditions in Innermost Asia and Northwestern China (London, 1933).

On other cultural developments, aside from Buddhism, are J. K. Shryock, *The Study of Human Abilities. The Jen wu chih of Liu Shao* (New Haven, 1937); Paul Pelliot, *Les Classiques Gravés sur la Pierre sous les Wei en 240–248* (*T'oung Pao*, 1924, pp. 1–4); P. A. Boodberg, *The Language of the T'o-pa Wei* (*Harvard Journal of Asiatic Studies*, Vol. I, pp. 167–185); Edouard Biot, *Essai sur l'Histoire de l'Instruction Publique en Chine* (Paris, 1847); E. F. Fenollosa, *Epochs of Chinese and Japanese Art* (2 vols., London, 1912); Osvald Siren, *Histoire des Arts Anciens de la Chine* (6 vols., Paris, 1929–1932); Arthur Waley, *An Introduction to the Study of Chinese Painting* (London, 1923); Paul Pelliot, *Les Grottes Touen-houang* (Paris, 1914–1921); E. Chavannes, *Six Monuments de la Sculpture Chinoise* (Bruxelles et Paris, 1914); Osvald Siren, *Chinese Sculptures from the Fifth to the Fourteenth Century* (4 vols., London, 1925); C. Hentze, *Chinese Tomb Figures. A Study in the Beliefs and Folklore of Ancient China* (London, 1928); Mathias Tchang, *Tombeau des Liang Famille Siao, 1ère partie Siao Choen-tche* (Shanghai, 1912. *Variétés Sinologiques No. 33*); Victor Segalen, Gilbert de Voisins et Jean Lartique, *Mission Archéologique en Chine (1914–1917)* (2 vols., Paris, 1923, 1924); Anna Bernhardi, *Tao Yüan-ming* (*Mitteilungen des Seminars für Orientalische Sprachen*, Berlin, 1922, pp. 95–106); Arthur Waley (translator), *A Hundred and Seventy Chinese Poems* (New York, 1919); Chi Li, *The Formation of the Chinese People, an Anthropological Inquiry* (Cambridge, 1928); Hsieh Tin-yu, *Origin and Migrations of the Hakkas* (*Chinese Social and Political Science Review*, Vol. 13, pp. 202–227); and Paul Pelliot, *Notes sur Quelques Artistes des Six Dynasties et des T'ang* (*T'oung Pao*, 1923, pp. 215–291).

On the history of thought is A. Forke, *Geschichte der mittelalterlichen, chinesischen Philosophie* (Hamburg, 1934).

On the continued introduction and growth of Buddhism, the Buddhist pilgrims and literature, with the results in China, are Sir Charles Eliot, *Hinduism and Buddhism, an Historical Sketch* (3 vols., London, 1921), chaps. 42–45; H. Maspero, *Communautés et Moines Bouddhistes Chinois au IIe et IIIe Siècles* (*Bulletin de l'École Français d'Extrême-Orient*, 1910, pp. 222–232); Prabodh Chandra Bagchi, *Le Canon Bouddhique en Chine, Les Traducteurs et les Traductions* (Paris, 1927); Joseph Edkins, *Chinese Buddhism* (London, 1893); Samuel Beal, *Abstract of Four Lectures on Buddhist Literature in China Delivered at University College, London* (London, 1882); Samuel Beal, *Si-Yu-Ki, Buddhist Records of the Western World* (2 vols., London, 1906); James Legge, *A Record of Buddhistic Kingdoms, Being an Account by the Chinese Monk Fa Hien of His Travels in India and Ceylon (A.D. 399–414) in Search of the Buddhist Books of Discipline, Translated and Annotated with a Corean Recension of the Chinese Text* (Oxford, 1886); P. N. Bose, *The Indian Teachers in China* (Madras, 1923);

Friedrich Weller, *Kleine Beiträge zur Erklärung Fa Hsiens* (*Hirth Anniversary Volume*, London, 1923, pp. 560–574); L. Wieger, *Histoire des Croyances Religieuses et des Opinions Philosophiques en Chine* (1917); L. Wieger, *Bouddhisme Chinois* (1910); K. L. Reichelt, *Myth and Tradition in Chinese Buddhism: A Study in Chinese Mahayana Buddhism* (translated by K. van W. Bugge, Shanghai, 1927)—very uncritical but containing some useful material; P. Bose, *The Indian Teachers in China* (1923); C. H. Hamilton, *Buddhism in India, Ceylon, China and Japan. A Reading Guide* (Chicago, 1931) and Paul Pelliot, *Autour d'une Traduction Sanscrite du Tao Tö Ching* (*T'oung Pao*, 1912, pp. 351–430). On Bodhidharma, in addition to Eliot, *Hinduism and Buddhism,* mentioned above, see Paul Pelliot, in *T'oung Pao*, 1923, pp. 252–265. Pelliot believes that most of our accounts of him are purely legendary. A very important article, not only on Ch'an Buddhism but on general Buddhist history in T'ang and pre-T'ang times is Hu Shih, *Development of Zen Buddhism in China* (*Chinese Social and Political Science Review*, Jan. 1932, Vol. 15, pp. 475–505).

On Gandhara Buddhist art, see A. Foucher, *L'Art Gréco-Bouddhique du Gandhara. Étude sur les Origines de l'Influence Classique dans l'Art Bouddhique de l'Inde et de l'Extrême-Orient* (2 vols., Paris, 1905–1918). Also on Buddhist art see E. Chavannes, *Mission Archéologique dans la Chine Septentrionale* (Paris, 1909–1915), especially *Tome 1, Deuxieme partie, La Sculpture Bouddhique* (Paris, 1915).

CHAPTER V

REUNION AND RENEWED ADVANCE. THE SUI (A.D. 589–618) AND T'ANG (A.D. 618–907) DYNASTIES

INTRODUCTORY

THE prolonged disunion and internal and external weakness had at last come to an end. There now followed one of the most brilliant periods in the entire history of China. United politically, the Middle Kingdom entered upon renewed prosperity and expanded her borders farther even than under the Han. In the seventh and eighth centuries China was one of the most extensive and powerful states on the planet. Prosperous, her population increased and with it her commerce. Peoples all over the East of Asia were dazzled by her might and her culture and attempted to learn from her.

Under the Sui and the T'ang, moreover, China registered fresh advances in civilization. Originality in political thought, although by no means absent, was not so marked as in the later years of the Chou, and the dynasties produced no innovating administrative genius equal to those of the Ch'in and the Han. While in political theory and governmental organization the Sui and the T'ang were content to build upon foundations laid in the past, they showed skill in utilizing the principles and framework which they had inherited from the Chou, the Ch'in, and the Han. Never after the Sui and the T'ang was China to have such prolonged disunion and near-anarchy as preceded them, and it may well be— although it cannot certainly be demonstrated—that this was due to the effectiveness with which their statesmen did their work. In the realm of the æsthetic, moreover, especially in art and in poetry, the China of the T'ang displayed creativeness and attained a level previously never approached. In the last years of the period of disunion, under the Sui, and during the most prosperous years of the T'ang, Buddhism in China reached its acme and joined with other forces in stimulating a new outburst of the Chinese spirit—this time in an expression of the emotions in art and poetry. Buddhism also continued to stir the Chinese mind to grapple with problems of philosophy.

THE SUI DYNASTY

As the Ch'in preceded the Han but had, as compared with the latter, only a brief life, so the Sui enjoyed only a short tenure of power. The Sui, however, although responsible for many important developments, did not make so notable a contribution to the permanent heritage of the nation as had the Ch'in.

Yang Chien, the founder of the Sui, and known to posterity under the title of Kao Tsu or Wên Ti, appears to have been a better ruler than the average, lightening the taxes, codifying the laws, and setting an example of simple living—for a monarch. Under him the administration of the Empire was reorganized, modifications being made in the territorial divisions over which members of the bureaucracy were placed. He developed a succession of canals to connect the Yellow River with the Yangtze—advantageous in unifying the North and the South. Whether these were begun *de novo* or were a renovation and enlargement of a series which can be traced to Chou times is not clear. During his reign the Chinese reconquered what is now Tongking and part of Annam, which, on the southern edge of the Empire, had been in revolt since at least 590—in the years when Yang Chien was attempting to consolidate his rule. The Japanese, hearing of his fame, sent an embassy to him. Under Yang Chien, too, the Chinese once more took a hand in the politics of Central Asia. In the second half of the sixth century, the T'u Chüeh, or Turks, it will be recalled, had established a federation extending over a vast area in Mongolia and Central Asia. Like so many of these ephemeral empires, theirs soon broke apart, the Eastern (also called the Northern) Turks separating from those of the West (582). The Chinese sought to deepen the divisions among the Turks, as a preliminary to increasing their influence there and possibly also as a means of defense.

Yang Chien died suddenly in 604, perhaps assassinated by the orders of his son, the heir apparent, who succeeded him. This son,

Yang Kuang, better known to posterity as Yang Ti, is an enigma. It seems probable that he has fared badly at the hands of orthodox Chinese historians, for they have exaggerated his foibles and weaknesses. He was obviously a man of abounding energy, vaulting ambition, and creative imagination. He completed, by means of a vast army of laborers, the chain of canals developed by his father to connect the Yellow River with the Yangtze and extended it southward to Hangchow, in Chêkiang. He built, at heavy cost, two walls, portions of that bulwark of frontier fortifications which from at least the time of Ch'in Shih Huang Ti has intermittently played so large a part in the defense program of the Empire along its northern borders—a boundary which nature has left unusually vulnerable. He also erected vast palaces. He made changes in the administrative machinery of the Empire, restoring a type of territorial division which had been abolished earlier in the dynasty and creating a new set of officers—travelling inspectors whose charge it was to report on the conduct of other members of the bureaucracy, thus, presumably, to insure efficiency and prevent sedition. He encouraged schools. He also modified the examinations for the civil service. He is credited with the introduction of what became the examination in the capital leading to the degree of *Chin Shih*—which persisted into the twentieth century. The entire system of examinations, indeed, owed him much of the form which it was to have for over a thousand years. He augmented the imperial library, partly by adding to it existing works and partly by commanding scholars to come to court and each to write on his specialty.

Yang Ti continued the vigorous foreign policy of his father. In the South, in 605, a punitive expedition was dispatched against the Chams (in the present Indo-China) who had been raiding the Chinese domains. Chinese arms were possibly carried as far as the Gulf of Siam. Yang Ti further extended Chinese influence in what is now the New Dominion, aiding one Turkish prince against another and establishing Chinese sovereignty over some of the oases along the trade routes, among them Turfan. Yet the Turks remained strong.

Still, failures in foreign policy were the immediate cause of the dynasty's downfall. Yang Ti put forth great efforts, costly to his realm, in successive expeditions against a state in what is now the southern portion of Manchuria and the northern portion of Korea. The first met with disaster, a second with failure, and while, after a third, the Korean ruler offered a qualified submission, the Emperor had suffered greatly in prestige. These misfortunes were followed by a further loss of *kudos* when Yang Ti was trapped in a fortress (in Northern Shansi) by the Turks and was saved only through the strategy of a young officer, Li Shih-min—of whom more in a moment. These reverses fanned into flame the discontent which the vigorous measures and costly public works of the Emperor had fomented. Revolts broke out in several sections, Yang Ti shut himself up in one of his palaces in Yangchow, and, possibly because he saw that all was lost, gave himself over to pleasure. Some of the rebels forced their way in and killed him (618). Of the two puppets of the imperial family who were set up in the course of the revolt, one was killed and the other abdicated, both in 619.

THE FOUNDING OF THE T'ANG DYNASTY: KAO TSU (REIGNED A.D. 618–626) AND T'AI TSUNG (REIGNED A.D. 627–649)

Several of the rebels against the Sui attempted to set themselves up as its successor. One, however, Li Yüan, partly because of the ability of his second son, Li Shih-min, quickly eliminated the others. Li Yüan was of aristocratic lineage, a native of the North, and held a title of nobility from the Western Wei. His mother, it is well to note, was of non-Chinese extraction. The dynasty of which he was the first monarch, the T'ang, is dated from 618. The capital was established at Ch'angan (not far from the site of the Ch'angan of the Han), so that again, as so often before, the center of Chinese power was on the fertile plain of the Wei. The position was one from which commerce could be carried on across the overland trade routes and military expeditions be dispatched to the Northwest, that dangerous highway of invasions. It was a strategic location for the headquarters of empire—although such considerations did not necessarily enter into the T'ang's choice of the site. During most of his reign, Li Yüan, or, as he is better known to posterity, Kao Tsu, was largely engrossed in suppressing his rivals and in making his position secure. In 627, in his early sixties, he abdicated in favor of Li Shih-min.

Li Shih-min, or, to give him the title by which he is best known, T'ai Tsung (or, to make clear his dynasty, T'ang T'ai Tsung), was one of the ablest monarchs and had one of the most brilliant reigns in China's long history. Still only twenty-one years of age when his father ascended the throne (618), he contributed markedly to the latter's triumph, and, although he opened his own way to the succession by killing two of his brothers, he proved to be, for an autocrat, fairly magnanimous, frugal in his private life, usually affectionate to his family, and one who could attract and hold the loyalty of subordinates. During the nearly a quarter of a century of his reign (he died in 649) he succeeded in thoroughly unifying the country, in stimulating its culture and increasing its prosperity, and in placing it on a new pinnacle of power.

T'ang T'ai Tsung made no revolutionary innovations in administration. The districts inhabited by non-Chinese peoples were ruled through their own princes, who were given Chinese titles. For China proper, he and his father perpetuated most of the essential features of the governmental machinery of the Sui, as this dynasty, in turn, had received many of them from its predecessors, and these from the Han and the Ch'in. Over such of the Empire as was predominantly Chinese in population was a bureaucracy recruited largely—at least in theory—through civil service examinations. The Emperor could and did go outside the successful candidates at these examinations for some of his officials. Men who were reliably recommended to him as promising or whose ability he himself remarked, were appointed, even when they were not holders of literary degrees. The examination system helped in part to break the power of the old aristocratic families, but these still had prestige, and, naturally, could give their scions educational privileges which were of advantage in preparation for the tests. T'ai Tsung retained the distinction between military and civil officials which we have remarked during the centuries of disunion.

Some modifications of detail were made. The Empire was redivided into ten *tao*, or provinces, and these in turn into *chou*, or prefectures—of which in 639 there were 358—and the *chou* into *hsien*, or sub-prefectures. In addition to members of the official hierarchy assigned to each of these divisions, there were imperial commissioners who were sent directly by the Emperor to handle some emergency, such as a drought, a flood, or a rebellion.

All officials were appointed directly from the capital, so that centralization was characteristic of the system. The civil officials were charged—in true Confucian manner—with looking after the welfare and encouraging the morals of the people. Agriculture was fostered, a system of public granaries being reëstablished in which stores were accumulated in years of plenty to be distributed to the poor for food and for seed in times of dearth.

As a necessary foundation to this bureaucracy, T'ai Tsung maintained and reënforced the state schools and the public examinations. Although his family professed descent from Lao Tzŭ (for the latter's reputed patronymic was likewise Li) and so had Taoist leanings, he strengthened the Confucian cult by decreeing that in all the colleges of the Empire Confucius and Confucius' favorite disciple should be venerated. He discontinued the sacrifices which, in accord with earlier practice, his father had ordered made to Chou Kung jointly with those to Confucius. T'ai Tsung commanded a temple to be erected to Confucius in each of the *chou* and *hsien*, and later (647) honors were ordered paid in these not only to Confucius but to twenty-two noteworthy scholars, mostly of the Han.

It must be noted, however, that examinations and degrees were not confined to the Confucian Classics narrowly interpreted, nor even to the literature of the Confucian school. They were also given, among other subjects, in history, law, mathematics, poetry, calligraphy, and Taoist philosophy.

As a warrior, T'ai Tsung continued to deserve the reputation which he had earned in the campaigns which brought his family to the throne. He reorganized the army, placing it on a more regular and efficient basis, and improved its weapons. He laid emphasis on the cavalry—perhaps because of the example of his non-Chinese opponents on the north and west. He gave China a very good fighting machine.

It was not strange that under T'ai Tsung the Empire again entered on a career of foreign conquest. Especially in the West he extended its power, pushing the Chinese frontiers farther into Central Asia than they had been at any time since the Han. Toward the close of his father's and at the outset of his own reign, the Eastern Turks, taking advantage of the still imperfect pacification of the realm, made raids up to the very walls of Ch'angan and the city was saved largely by the personal bravery and energy of T'ai Tsung. Before long, however, T'ai Tsung was able to turn the tide. He was not content with building ramparts on the north against the invader—he is said, indeed, to have declined to repair the Great Wall—but insisted on carrying the war into the enemies' territory and rendering the marches safe from attack by subduing the would-be invaders in their native haunts. As Yang Chien had done before him, he sowed dissension among the Turkish peoples, and when this had done its work, his armies conquered the Eastern (or Northern) Turks (630) and brought their territories within his Empire. A little later the Western Turks, although then at the height of their power, were badly defeated, and the Uighurs, a Turkish tribe, were detached from them and became sturdy supporters of the T'ang in the Gobi. The Khitans, Mongols in Eastern Mongolia and Southern Manchuria, made their submission (630). In the Tarim basin and along the overland trade routes were several small states of Tochari and other peoples who seem to have been of Indo-European stock and whose language was certainly Indo-European. Some of these, including one in Turfan, were reduced to vassalage. Kashgar and Yarkand accepted Chinese garrisons, and across the mountains Samarkand and Bokhara acknowledged Chinese suzerainty. The vast Chinese domains in these regions were grouped into two administrative protectorates called Anhsi, "the peaceful West," with its capital first a little west of Turfan and later still farther west, and Peit'ing. At its greatest extent—after T'ai Tsung's death—they included much of what more recently have been called the New Dominion, Russian Turkestan, and Afghanistan—although on much of this Chinese rule sat fairly lightly. The great land routes were now more firmly under Chinese control than at any time since the Han. T'ai Tsung received and sent envoys from and into India and it is said that in 643 an embassy arrived from the ruler of Fulin—probably from somewhere in what we now call the Near East and identical with Ta Ch'in. The Tibetans, recently become a unified power, proved a formidable enemy, but T'ai Tsung, after his armies had beaten off an attack by them, gave to their prince a Chinese princess in marriage, and she is said to have had much to do with introducing among her new subjects Chinese customs and the Buddhist faith.

Having reduced the barbarians by force and diplomacy, T'ai Tsung was eager to assimilate them. Although they were usually placed under the administration of their own princes and governed according to their own customs, numbers of them were brought to Ch'angan in the military service of the Empire and many sons of barbarian princes were educated in the schools of the capital.

In only one of his major foreign enterprises did T'ai Tsung fail. He, like Yang Ti, attempted to reduce the kingdom in Northern Korea and, like Yang Ti, was unsuccessful. However, the reverse was not followed by any upheaval such as overthrew Yang Ti. T'ai Tsung passed on his power, unquestioned, to his son.

KAO TSUNG

So effectively had T'ai Tsung done his work that under his successor the boundaries and the prestige of China for a time continued to expand. This successor, known to posterity as Kao Tsung, was on the throne even longer than his father, from 649 until 683. Under him, two of the three states which made up Korea were at last conquered, together with part of Manchuria, and the third accepted the suzerainty of China. In the process a Japanese fleet was defeated and Japanese power in the peninsula was ended for the time being. For years T'ang control was vigorously maintained in the far West. By the aid of the Uighurs the Western Turks were crushed (657–659) and their territories were claimed by the Chinese, thus carrying Chinese authority into the valley of the Oxus and to the borders of India. Such centers as Tashkend, Samarkand, Bokhara, and Ferghana were included. The Arabs, recently started on their phenomenal career of conquest under the impulse of Islam, were now beginning to make themselves felt in Persia and Central Asia. The Sassanids, weakened by their struggle against the Byzantine Empire and the Turks, collapsed before them. A Sassanid aspirant to the throne of Persia is said to have sought the aid of China against them. Some of the Sassanian line, indeed, are reputed to have taken refuge in Ch'angan and there to have entered the imperial service. Due in part to dissensions among the Arabs which temporarily halted the onward march of the Moslem arms, the

Chinese retained for a time and even strengthened their influence in the valleys of the Oxus and the Jaxartes.

Kao Tsung, moreover, did what there had been much talk of doing during his father's reign, and renewed the sacrifices of *fêng* and *shan,* which had been inaugurated by Han Wu Ti. *Fêng,* it will be recalled, was a sacrifice to Heaven made from T'ai Shan. The revival seems to have been, in part, to show the glory of the imperial house and to secure for it something of the prestige and divine assistance that were supposed to have accrued to the Han. The ceremonies certainly involved elaborate preparation and great expense. Kao Tsung was a devout Buddhist and under him were erected many monasteries. He built, too, a famous palace at Ch'angan.

Kao Tsung was not the warrior that his father had been and disasters eventually overtook him. The Tibetans, now become more powerful, wrested from the Chinese some of the most important cities in the Tarim basin, it became impossible for the Chinese to intervene in Transoxiana, Turks in Ili and Mongolia took advantage of the situation to throw off the Chinese yoke, and most of Korea, so recently subdued, again slipped out of Chinese hands. It was during Kao Tsung's reign that, strengthened by an alliance with the T'ang, the Korean kingdom of Silla (or Shilla, Sin-ra—Japanese Shiragi) in Southern Korea conquered and united the peninsula—the first time that such a feat had been accomplished.

WU HOU

Kao Tsung, moreover, fell largely under the control of an able and ambitious woman, most frequently known to posterity as Wu Hou, or, at times, as Wu Tsê T'ien. She had been one of T'ai Tsung's concubines and on that monarch's death had retired to a Buddhist nunnery. Kao Tsung's Empress recalled her from seclusion to win the Emperor's affections from a concubine of whom the Empress was jealous. Wu Hou not only succeeded in displacing this concubine but supplanted the Empress herself and had her killed. She achieved such an ascendancy over Kao Tsung that during the later years of his life she was virtually the ruler. On his death, she quickly disposed of his successor when the latter showed too great independence and placed another puppet on the throne. Before long she deposed this next *roi fainéant* and openly assumed control of the government. She officiated at the imperial sacrifices, changed the dynastic name to Chou, and ruthlessly exiled or executed such members of the imperial family and their supporters as dared oppose her. She had her favorites, a Buddhist monk and later two handsome brothers, and scandalous stories were inevitably whispered about her relations with them. Whatever her private life may have been, she proved a competent and energetic monarch. She at least partly reëstablished the prestige of the Empire abroad (the Tarim basin, for example, was recovered in 692), and at home governed with an iron hand. She showed Buddhism great favor and it was probably under her that Buddhist sculpture reached the height of its beauty and artistic and religious inspiration. In Chinese political history only two women rank with her, the Empress Lü of the Han and the Empress Dowager Tz'ŭ Hsi of the Ch'ing (Manchu) dynasty. All three had much in common, especially in masterfulness. At length, in 705, when Wu Hou was about eighty years of age, and ill, a successful conspiracy deposed her and restored the first of the puppet Emperors whom she had dethroned.

This spineless creature continued to be a figurehead. He was dominated by his wife, a woman who had none of the ability of the great Wu Hou but was vicious enough and before many years had her husband poisoned. An insurrection soon made way with her and placed on the throne the second of the shadow Emperors whom Wu Hou had set up. After about two years he abdicated in favor of his third son, Li Lung-chi, who is best known as Hsüan Tsung or Ming Huang.

THE T'ANG REACHES ITS HEIGHT: HSÜAN TSUNG (MING HUANG)

Hsüan Tsung held the throne from 712 until 756, the longest reign of the dynasty. He began with great promise. It was largely because of his initiative that his father had been restored to the throne and he was successful in crushing court intrigues which threatened him. Under him the T'ang reached the pinnacle of its glory. Chinese authority again expanded in the West. The power of one of the most notable Turkish enemies of the Chinese collapsed and two Turkish peoples allied with the Chinese (one of them the Uighurs) controlled Mongolia and much of Turkestan. The Tibetans, formidable during much of the T'ang, after one outbreak were forced to agree to a truce, and a Turkish people in alliance with the Tibetans were reduced to submission. On the far West, the Chinese were feeling again the pressure of the young Moslem empire. About 670 the Arabs, having adjusted their differences of a few years before, were beginning to menace Tokharistan, on the middle Oxus, and between 705 and 715 the Moslem arms were carried into Sogdiana, between the Oxus and the Jaxartes, and even farther. Some of the little states west of and across the mountains from the Tarim basin, in Transoxiana, which during T'ai Tsung's reign had acknowledged Chinese suzerainty, now sought the protection of the Middle Kingdom against the renewed Arab advance. The princes of Samarkand, Bokhara, Tashkend, and Tokharistan repeatedly asked assistance. Armed aid was not accorded to the most distant of the vassals, but—after the death of a noted Arab general—Chinese diplomacy seems to have contributed somewhat to a temporary expulsion of the Arabs from a part of the region. The actual fighting was done by Turks and the local inhabitants. To the states in the Pamirs and in Kashmir, however, Hsüan Tsung gave more substantial support, and in 747 Kao Hsien-chih, a general of Korean extraction in the service of the Chinese and head of the garrisons in the four most important Western outposts, successfully led an expedition from Kashgar across the high and difficult passes in the Pamirs and the Hindukush to the upper Oxus and parts of the higher portions of the valley of the Indus with the object of breaking the junction which (about 741) the Tibetans had formed with the Arabs. Kao Hsien-chih's expedition was a most remarkable feat and greatly enhanced Chinese prestige in the West. Indian princes in the Indus Valley accepted Chinese suzerainty.

At home, moreover, Hsüan Tsung's reign was marked by a burst of cultural achievement. In Ch'angan the Emperor founded an institution known as the Hanlin Yüan. While under the T'ang it included court favorites, jugglers, and musicians as well as scholars, in later centuries membership in it became one of the most highly prized of literary honors. Hsüan Tsung founded a school for the teaching of music. He accorded Confucius additional honors. At his court were some of the most distinguished poets and painters whom China has known—Li Po and Tu Fu among the former, and Wu Tao-Tzŭ, Han Kan, and Wang Wei among the latter—all of them names to conjure with and of all of whom we shall have occasion to say more in a moment.

In spite of its brilliance, however, the glory of Hsüan Tsung's reign was partly illusory. Even before his accession, at the collapse of Wu Hou's régime, changes looking toward decentralization had been made in the bureaucracy. In place of direct control from Ch'angan over all members of the hierarchy, a resident commissioner or governor was appointed for each province with the duty of overseeing the officials within his jurisdiction. At the time the innovation probably seemed a wise method of supervising the Empire, but it proved a step toward disintegration, for it tended toward the reëstablishment of local states.

Hsüan Tsung, too, was to live to witness the decline of the prestige of Chinese arms abroad. In 751 Kao Hsien-chih—thanks in part to unrest among the subject peoples aroused by his own perfidy and cupidity—was badly defeated by the Arabs north of Ferghana. Its weakness thus vividly demonstrated, in much of the West Chinese rule crumbled like a house of cards and the region passed largely into the hands of two Turkish peoples, the Karluks in the West and the Uighurs in the North and East. To the Northeast the Khitans (Ch'i-tan) moved from the southern portion of Manchuria into the North China plain. In the Southwest the Chinese suffered disastrous reverses (751) in what is now Yünnan. Here a native principality called Nan Chao had submitted to the T'ang, and there had followed the most nearly effective control which the Chinese had yet exerted in the area. Now, with at least the moral support of the Tibetans, who gave to the king of Nan Chao the title of Tung Ti, or Emperor of the East, Chinese garrisons were expelled and Chinese armies defeated.

In China proper revolt arose against Hsüan Tsung. His wars and his court extravagances impoverished the people and complaint against him was widespread. Even in the days of his prosperity, his most influential minister, Li Lin-fu, had been a sinister influence and, among other acts, had encouraged him to slay the heir apparent without trial. The Emperor, too, fell largely under the control of one of the most famous of Chinese beauties, Yang Kuei-fei. Yang Kuei-fei had been the wife of one of the sons of Hsüan Tsung, but in 738 she was taken by the Emperor into his own household as his chief favorite. She encouraged her infatuated imperial master, now in his fifties, in a life of extravagance and gayety. Members of her family were given high rank, but neither she nor they appear to have had political ability to match her feminine charms. In his old age Hsüan Tsung was unable or unwilling to throw off her baleful influence and power began slipping from his weakening hands.

The rebellion which proved the final undoing of Hsüan Tsung was led by An Lu-shan, an able fellow of non-Chinese stock who had first acquired distinction in Chinese service by aiding in repressing some of the raids of the Khitans, had risen high in the favor of the Emperor and of Yang Kuei-fei, and had been given an important military command. In 755 An Lu-shan unfurled the standard of revolt in the Northeast, was soon master of most of the territory north of the Yellow River, and proclaimed himself Emperor. The aged Hsüan Tsung fled from Ch'angan to Szechwan. On the way, the imperial troops either themselves put to death or obtained the execution of Yang Kuei-fei and some of her family. Hsüan Tsung, now seventy years of age and thoroughly discredited, abdicated (756) in favor of one of his sons. He lived on, in seclusion, until 762, long enough to see the rebellion crushed. An Lu-shan was killed by his own son (757) and the murderer in his turn perished at the hands of another rebel of non-Chinese stock, Shih Ssŭ-ming. The T'ang forces retook Ch'angan (757), aided by contingents from Central Asia, including some Arabs. Shih Ssŭ-ming proclaimed himself Emperor, but within a few years was destroyed by his own eldest son and shortly afterward the latter was overthrown and put to death by the T'ang forces.

THE DECLINE AND FALL OF THE T'ANG DYNASTY

The rebellion of An Lu-shan marked the beginning of the end of the T'ang. The Li family held the throne for nearly a century and a half longer, and the brilliance of the era, although waning, displayed occasional temporary revivals. From the reign of Hsüan Tsung, however, the course of the house of Li Yüan was downward.

An Lu-shan's defection and the accompanying disorder unleashed other forces. From the northern and western frontiers came raiding barbarians, ever ready to pounce on the fertile and wealthy plains and valleys to the south. The Tibetans especially were persistent, and at one time took Ch'angan (763). In stemming invasions and reducing internal revolts the T'ang summoned non-Chinese peoples to their assistance. It will be recalled that the founder of the dynasty, Li Yüan, had a Turkish mother, and the vigor of his line may be attributed in part to non-Chinese blood. While the most competent of the imperial generals of the period, Kuo Tzŭ-i, who more than any other was responsible for the defense and perpetuation of the T'ang, was a Chinese, he was from Shansi and may possibly have had non-Chinese blood in his veins. The next greatest of the T'ang commanders of the time, Li Kuang-pi, was of Khitan stock. Even these were unable to defeat the Tibetans and reduce the rebellions with purely Chinese forces but called to their assistance the Uighurs, had Moslem Arabs in their armies, and brought in foreign troops even from Ferghana. It will be remembered, too, that the farthest extension of the T'ang power westward was under the direction of a general of Korean extraction. All this was quite different from the Han, when the commanders and the conquering armies appear to have been entirely or chiefly Chinese. Even with the support of aliens, the military achievements of the T'ang in its heyday were probably no more remarkable than those of the Han—although the T'ang Empire occupied a somewhat wider area—and in some respects were not so noteworthy.

Did this mean a decline in the vigor of the Chinese race? We do not know. The Chinese were certainly to increase in numbers and to occupy, as farmers and merchants, more territory, but it may be significant that during somewhat more than half the time that has elapsed from then to now at least part of the territory inhabited by the Chinese has been under foreign control, that during a third or a fourth of it all the Chinese have been subject to foreigners, and that never since the T'ang—except for the brief years of the Republic, when the Empire was maintained (and even that only partially) under the momentum acquired under the Manchus—has China under purely native rule attained to the total area in square miles that it reached under the T'ang. It is well to remember, however, that even in the nineteenth century there were notable Chinese generals and that the exploits of at least one of them, Tso Tsung-t'ang, rivalled the greatest of those of the Han and the T'ang. It must also be recalled that the Chinese have never, in historic times, been a pure race. It is one evidence of their strength that they have been willing to utilize and able to absorb peoples of many different stocks. The large numbers of men of prominence under the T'ang who were partly or entirely of foreign descent may mean in part that the assimilation was in process.

Whatever may have been the significance of the alien blood of some of the T'ang generals and forces, the power of the dynasty continued to decline. Internally, the administrative machinery did not fully recover from the disorders begun by An Lu-shan. The Empire had to be reconquered foot by foot, and largely by the assistance of military chieftains called in from the frontier. They, with their troops, dominated, in the name of the T'ang, whole sections of the realm. This *fait accompli* was later regularized by dividing the Empire into forty-seven districts governed by imperial commissioners who were also soldiers. The civil officials were continued, but—at least for most practical purposes—they were subordinate to and were usually appointed by the military. These satraps were, naturally, a menace to the supremacy of the Emperor. Disunion was further threatened when the hereditary principle began to be introduced into their commands. It is not surprising that some of them broke out into revolt.

The T'ang did not collapse all at once. When, in the middle of the ninth century, one of the princes of Nan Chao assumed the title of Emperor and invaded Annam (the "Peaceful South," a name which in 679 the Chinese first gave the extreme southern portions of their possessions—in the present Annam and Tongking—possibly to balance Anhsi—the "Peaceful West"—the designation of the administrative district that covered their holdings in the far West), a Chinese general, Kao P'ien, succeeded in driving him back into his own territory and later on expelled him from Szechwan. Chinese authority, too, was preserved on the western marches in the region of Tunhuang, and the northern portion of Korea was under Chinese control. Early in the ninth century the Tibetans, now weakened, made their peace with the Chinese and ceased to be a serious menace. Until nearly the middle of the ninth century, the Uighurs, long allies and supporters of the T'ang, dominated Mongolia and much of what is now the New Dominion. Even when they lost most of their territory to the Kirghiz, for a time they remained powerful in much of the Gobi and the Tarim basin. They were often called in to help the T'ang suppress internal rebellion and regarded themselves as at least the equals of the Chinese. Toward the close of the eighth century their khan obtained in marriage the daughter of a T'ang Emperor.

However, while outwardly the T'ang was still imposing, and Ch'angan, in spite of the damage it had suffered in civil wars and foreign invasions, was impressive and fairly prosperous, the family of Li was declining. In the luxurious life of the court, eunuchs were acquiring the control which so often presaged the end of a dynasty and spasmodic attempts at reform brought no lasting improvement.

Toward the end of the ninth century ineptitude and luxury at the capital and misgovernment in the provinces led to widespread discontent and revolt. Pirates ravaged the coasts. A popular uprising laid waste vast sections, including some of the port cities, and in the general disorder many of the foreign merchants living in the latter were massacred. A leader of the rebels, Huang Ch'ao by name, captured Ch'angan in 880 and proclaimed himself Emperor, giving to his dynasty the title of Ta Ch'i. The T'ang sent against him Li K'o-yung, a general of Turkish stock, with a force of Turks who had been in Chinese service, and the would-be Emperor was slain. Li K'o-yung was rewarded with a principality in Shansi and before many years was practically an independent monarch.

The end of the T'ang soon followed. Chu Wên, a lieutenant of Huang Ch'ao, transferred his allegiance to the T'ang and was rewarded with a principality in Honan. In 904 Chu Wên deposed and killed his imperial master and placed a boy on the throne. In 907 he compelled this puppet to abdicate in his favor and proclaimed himself the first of a new dynasty, the Later Liang. The T'ang had at last lost the mandate of Heaven.

CULTURAL DEVELOPMENTS UNDER THE T'ANG: COMMERCE

As we have several times said, the nearly three centuries of the T'ang were, with the exception of some of the later years of weakness, among the most prosperous and culturally brilliant in the history of China. During the years of disunion before the Sui and the T'ang, foundations were being laid for a new flowering of civilization. The Sui had encouraged the revival of culture. The internal order which characterized most of the first century and a quarter of T'ang rule made for prosperity. Although the census figures are probably highly inaccurate, the population seems to have been fairly large. A conjecture for 618, possibly excessive, speaks of a total of nearly one hundred and thirty millions. The census of 726 is said to have given the number of Chinese as about forty-one and a half millions, and an estimate for 733 put it at over forty-three millions. When every allowance is made for obvious errors, these figures disclose a state which must have been one of the most populous of its time. So large a body of people could not fail to attract merchants from other lands.

Foreign trade appears to have reached greater proportions under the T'ang than at any previous time. As in the earlier periods, it was due chiefly to the initiative of aliens. Foreign merchants in China seem to have been very much more numerous than were Chinese merchants and travellers abroad. This may have been because the Chinese were so engrossed in developing the vast resources of their own land that they were not tempted to go outside its borders.

Again, as in earlier dynasties, it was both by land and by sea that foreigners came to China. The routes through the basin of the Tarim to the Northwest were, of course, traversed, especially during the first century and a quarter or more of the T'ang when the authority of the Empire was usually strong in Central Asia. From the middle of the eighth century, when Chinese dominion in that region crumbled and when disorders in China itself increased, trade by these roads probably was not so prosperous. Even then, however, it continued, especially as long as the Uighur power gave a certain amount of unity to the Tarim Valley—in spite of tolls and exactions from local rulers which must have pressed heavily upon it and of raids and wars which must have interrupted it.

Ch'angan, the seat of empire and a sort of gateway to the populous regions of China, was naturally an important terminus of the trade, and its streets and inns must have presented a lively and cosmopolitan appearance, with merchants from many a city and land in the distant West.

The sea routes to the south coast grew in popularity, possibly in part because of the difficulty in the later years of the dynasty of traversing the overland roads. Even as early as the seventh century they were much employed. Canton won from the ports of Tongking the primacy in overseas trade. By the eighth century, Persians, Arabs, and merchants from India were coming to Canton in large vessels, and a special office was created in the city for the registry of ships, the control of exports, and the collection of duties. With the rise of their power under the first flush of Islam, Arabs began to have an important part in this seaborne traffic and continued to hold it for many years. Chinese goods were to be had in the bazaars of Bagdad, the capital of the Abbasid caliphate. In 758 Arabs and Persians were sufficiently strong in Canton to loot the city—perhaps in retaliation for Chinese exactions. In the ninth century we hear of Nestorian Christians, Jews, Moslems, and Persians in Canton—all of them obviously from the West. In the ninth century the Canton trade was still closely controlled by the state and, perhaps as an application of the Chinese principle of group responsibility, a Moslem was appointed to administer the law of Islam among his co-religionists and so to maintain order. This looks like extraterritoriality, but it must be noted that the head Moslem appears to have been named by and to have been responsible to the Chinese authorities and was not an official of his own government. By at least the ninth century others of the ports of South China, notably what is now Ch'üanchow, near the present Amoy, entered into competition with Canton. Yangchow also had foreign merchants and its share in sea-borne trade. Koreans controlled much of the coastwise shipping.

As under previous dynasties, the leading commodities of this commerce combined small bulk with large value. Silk was still a chief article of export, and spices and porcelain, some of the latter from Fukien, were also carried abroad. To China came such goods as ivory, incense, copper, tortoise shell, and rhinoceros horn. It seems probable, too, that negro slaves were brought by the Arabs to China and sold there.

Whether many Chinese merchants journeyed to foreign lands seems very doubtful. We know that for at least a time under T'ai Tsung an imperial rescript forbade Chinese going abroad—from which it may be fair to assume that some were in the habit of doing so. Chinese knowledge of the geography of neighboring lands was increasing, but, with the one exception to be noted in a moment, the accounts that have come down to us in any complete form appear not to have been derived through first-hand observation but from the kind of information which might seep through from aliens.

CULTURAL DEVELOPMENTS UNDER THE T'ANG: BUDDHIST PILGRIMS AND MISSIONARIES

This one exception is important. The journeys continued which, as we have seen, had been made to India by Chinese Buddhists from at least the close of the fourth century. Probably the most important and certainly the best known of the Buddhist pilgrims of the T'ang was he whose religious name was Hsüan-tsang. Hsüan-tsang was born in Honan in the first decade of the seventh century, the son of a learned official. Reared in the Confucian tradition, in his youth he was converted to Buddhism and became distinguished as a teacher of the faith. Dissatisfied with his knowledge, he wished to elucidate to his own satisfaction debated points of doctrine by inquiry and study in the land where Buddhism had had its birth. In spite of the imperial prohibition of foreign travel, in the year 629 he left for India, going by the overland route through the Tarim basin. In India he visited many of the sites made sacred by the life, teachings, and death of the Buddha, studied with experts, and collected sacred books. After an absence of about sixteen years, he returned to China, also overland, and spent the nearly twenty remaining years of his life in teaching and in translating some of the books which he had brought back with him. The amount of literature whose translation is ascribed to him is stupendous—about twenty-five times as voluminous as the Christian Bible. He gave a great impetus to the popularity and spread of Buddhism in China. In such esteem was he held that two of the Emperors wrote prefaces for his translations and at his death the state honored him with an official funeral. The record of his travels is so full and accurate that in our own day it has proved of invaluable assistance to archeologists in India and the New Dominion.

A few years after Hsüan-tsang's death, another Chinese, I-ching, left for India on a similar mission (about 671 or 672). He made the journey by sea, from South China, and, returning in 695, via Canton, he also brought books to be translated. We have, too, accounts of more than fifty other pilgrims of the second half of the seventh century, several of them from Korea and other countries bordering on China, and some from China. Some went by land and others by sea. Many of whom we have no record must have made the journey.

Although Buddhism was beginning to decay in India, missionaries still came to China—but apparently did not have quite so large a place in Chinese Buddhism as in the earlier centuries. Still, at least one sect, Chên-yen (Japanese Shingon) claims as its first patriarch an Indian who arrived in the first quarter of the eighth century.

Through Buddhism and its culture contacts, mathematics, astronomy, and medicine were stimulated.

There was an extraordinary amount of movement, then, throughout the Buddhist world, Chinese monks going to and from India, Indian monks arriving in China, and monks from countries adjoining China traversing the Middle Kingdom. Buddhism was helping to give a certain amount of cultural unity to Central, Eastern, and Southern Asia.

CULTURAL DEVELOPMENTS UNDER THE T'ANG: FOREIGN INFLUENCES, ESPECIALLY THE INTRODUCTION OF FOREIGN FAITHS

All of these contacts between the Chinese and other peoples brought foreign influences into the Middle Kingdom. The presence of so many Turks and others of non-Chinese stock in North China, commerce, with its foreign merchants and products in both North and South, and Buddhist pilgrims and missionaries could not fail to have their effect upon the life of the land. The natural obstacles between China and the other chief centers of civilization were formidable, but the isolation which they tended to produce was by no means complete. The empire of the Turks, followed by the westward expansion of Chinese power, helped to overcome the barriers and to facilitate trade and the exchange of ideas. Many of the currents of life in other parts of Asia made themselves felt in the T'ang dominions.

Many foreign influences are difficult or impossible to trace. Ideas, inventions, and institutions do not always bear the labels of their origin, and the dates of the introduction of plants and animals of alien antecedents are seldom easily determined. It was under the T'ang that the art of making wine from grapes seems first to have come to China, that something was learned— from India—of manufacturing sugar from the cane, and that spinach, one species of garlic, and one of the several kinds of mustard were brought in. The garden pea was cultivated in China at least as early as the T'ang. Chinese knowledge of optical lenses, seemingly derived from India, is first authentically reported from the T'ang.

The introduction of foreign religions is somewhat more easily traced, although even here exact dates often elude us. Usually the T'ang Emperors were tolerant of foreign faiths and at times even encouraged them. Occasionally, however, they proscribed and persecuted them.

It was apparently under the T'ang that Christianity first entered China. Certainly our earliest evidences of its existence there date from that time. The type which came was at least chiefly what is usually known as Nestorianism. This, the prevailing form of Christianity in Mesopotamia, was actively missionary and for hundreds of years—until, in the fourteenth century, the later Mongol invasions dealt it all but fatal blows—its representatives, both lay and clerical, were to be found in India and in Central Asia. It had numerous communities in India and in cities in Central Asia with which the Chinese were in touch under the T'ang. Herat and Samarkand, for example, were made episcopal sees in the sixth century. Balkh, too, was a strong center. It is not strange, therefore, that Nestorianism made its way to China. Our fullest account of it is engraved on a famous monument erected at Ch'angan in 781 and discovered in the first half of the seventeenth century. Other traces are in documents uncovered in the grottoes of Tunhuang in the far Northwest, in three imperial edicts of the T'ang, and in several other contemporary records. In the Ch'angan (Hsianfu) inscription, the introduction of the faith is ascribed to one A-lo-pên of Ta-ch'in (the name, it will be recalled, by which for several centuries the Chinese referred to the region which we, with equal inexactness, term the Near East). A-lo-pên is reported to have arrived in Ch'angan in 635, during the reign of T'ai Tsung, and to have been received with honor by the Emperor. T'ai Tsung is said to have ordered translations made of Nestorian sacred books and to have encouraged the dissemination of the faith. A monastery was built in the capital. The faith persisted in China proper until at least about the middle of the ninth century, and from time to time new missionaries came. A metropolitan for China was appointed sometime before 823 and churches were built in several cities. Occasionally Christianity was persecuted and sometimes Emperors encouraged it by favorable decrees and material subsidies. It seems never to have had many Chinese adherents but to have depended largely upon foreigners for initiative and leadership. About the middle of the ninth century a severe persecution seems practically to have wiped it out. After it disappeared from China proper it persisted and made important gains among some of the Turkish peoples on the edges of the Empire. Centuries later, as we shall see, it reappeared in the Middle Kingdom.

Some of the documentary remains of Christianity under the T'ang indicate at least the possibility of the presence not only of Nestorians, who stressed two natures, the divine and human, in Christ, but of Jacobite Christians, who were Monophysites, contending that there was in Christ only one nature, the divine. We know that there were thousands of Jacobites in the Sassanid Empire, and it is possible that some of them penetrated to China.

Another foreign faith under the T'ang was Manichæism. Originated by Mani in the third century and showing both Persian and Christian influences, by the time of the T'ang it had spread westward into Mesopotamia and the Mediterranean world and eastward into Persia and Transoxiana. Its first appearance in China seems to have been in the last decade of the seventh century, through Iranians. Early in the eighth century it benefited by the prestige of a Manichæan astronomer-astrologer. The use of the seven-day week in China appears to have accompanied this type of astrology. In the latter half of the eighth century, Manichæism was introduced among the Uighurs and won many adherents from them. Since the Uighurs were then predominant in Central Asia and often gave their support to the T'ang, it made some headway in China. Manichæan temples were erected in Ch'angan, in Lo-yang, and in several other centers. Manichæism was never very popular in the Middle Kingdom nor were its adherents numerous, and it suffered from the collapse of the Uighur power in the ninth century. Until the thirteenth century it persisted, greatly weakened, in what is now the New Dominion. In China it took the form of a sect with political-magical-religious activities —one of the many such in the history of the country—with certain outward resemblances to Taoism and Buddhism. For a time, indeed, two of its scriptures were included in the Taoist canon. Its survival was possibly assisted by the congeniality of its dualism with the *yin* and the *yang* that have played so large a part in Chinese thought. It lived on in Fukien, subject to persecutions, until at least the beginning of the seventeenth century.

Just when Islam entered China we do not know. Its early history there is shrouded in obscurity and uncertainty. We know that Moslems were in the Middle Kingdom during the T'ang, some of them as merchants in the ports on the south coast and some of them as soldiers of fortune—notably the Arabs who assisted in suppressing the rebellion of An Lu-shan. We know, too, that several embassies came to the T'ang court from Mohammedan Arab officials in Transoxiana. (It is probable, incidentally, that the embassies usually said to be from the Caliphs in Bagdad were really from these governors on the Arab frontier.) Whether these vistors made, or even attempted to make, any converts from among the Chinese we do not know. The accounts, traditions, and even some of the monuments of the present Moslem communities are practically undependable for T'ang times. For example, an inscription in Ch'angan (Hsianfu) professing to date from 742 has obvious anachronisms and is of much later origin. The story that a maternal uncle of Mohammed was sent to Canton and the claim that an ancient tomb still shown there is his are both undependable. Certainly it was not until several centuries later that large Moslem bodies appeared in China.

Mazdaism had entered China before the T'ang. We hear of it,

too, in T'ang times, but, like Islam, as the faith of foreign residents—Persian merchants and refugees from the Arab invasions. We know that there were Mazdean priests and that Mazdean temples existed in Ch'angan. We are not certain, however, that any converts were sought from among the Chinese.

Jews there were in China of the T'ang, but probably few in number and all merchants. The Jewish community in Honan which disintegrated only in our own day was probably of later origin.

CULTURAL DEVELOPMENTS UNDER THE T'ANG: BUDDHISM REACHES ITS APEX

From what has been repeatedly said in the preceding pages, it can readily be inferred that under the T'ang Buddhism prospered. It will be recalled that in the centuries immediately preceding the advent of the T'ang it had been increasing in influence. During the earlier years of the T'ang its growth continued —thanks in large part to the Buddhist pilgrims to India, particularly Hsüan-tsang—and throughout the T'ang it was very prominent. The T'ang may be called the Buddhist age of China.

This does not mean that Buddhism was not without enemies in high places. Scholars of the Confucian school often opposed it. To their mind it was superstitious, destructive to the family, derogatory to the authority of the Emperor, and in general antagonistic to that social and political structure which Confucianism cherished and upon which it depended. With the emphasis by the T'ang upon recruiting the civil bureaucracy from those trained in the Classics and with the granting of fresh honors to Confucius, Confucianism partly regained the prominence which it had won under the Han. From time to time one or another of its exponents denounced Buddhism to the Emperor. More than once, too, an Emperor took vigorous action against it. Under Kao Tsu a minister of state raised his voice in criticism of it. In 626 Buddhism and Taoism were ordered abolished. Early in the eighth century a vigorous anti-Buddhist memorial was presented. The most noted of the protests was that of the famous Han Yü, the outstanding exponent of Confucianism during the T'ang, who in 819 took the occasion of an official reception accorded to a bone of the Buddha to condemn that act and the Buddhist faith. His temerity cost him his position at court, but that was because he had chosen an unfortunate time for his tirade. Kao Tsung, T'ai Tsung, and Hsüan Tsung, the strongest monarchs of the dynasty, all sought to restrict the number of monks and nuns and to keep the religion under control. In 835 an imperial decree sought to prevent further ordinations of Buddhist monks. In 845 an Emperor who was a devoted Taoist issued an anti-Buddhist decree which is said to have led to the demolishing of more than forty thousand temples, the confiscation of temple lands, and the return to secular life of more than a quarter of a million monks and nuns. While these figures are quite probably an exaggeration, Buddhism undoubtedly was dealt a severe blow at a time when it had already entered on a slow decline.

On the other hand, none of these persecutions appears to have lasted any length of time, nor was any of them so severe as those which the early Christian church met in the Roman Empire or as some which Christians have inflicted on each other or Moslems on unbelievers. Probably the anti-Buddhist edicts were usually allowed quickly to become dead letters. Several rulers of the dynasty were ardent Buddhists, among them the great Wu Hou, who for a short time had been in a nunnery and under whose rule Buddhist monks were very influential. Hsüan Tsung in later years was more favorable to Buddhism than an earlier decree of his against the faith would indicate, and his successor was a devout believer.

Buddhist literature continued to be produced. Not only were foreign authors translated but original works were produced in Chinese. The larger proportion of the T'ang activity in the realm of philosophy was not in Confucianism or Taoism, but Buddhism. Whether in quality and originality Chinese Buddhist thought of the T'ang deserves to be ranked with the intellectual product of the Chou must be at present a matter of conjecture. Confucian scholars—to whom we of the West owe most of our knowledge of China's past—have usually had little understanding or appreciation of it. Modern scholarship is only beginning to delve into it. We may eventually discover that for profundity and acumen the best of Chinese Buddhist writers of the T'ang will bear comparison with the creators of the schools of the Chou.

Buddhism showed its vigor, too, by continuing to give birth to new sects. Ch'an was further developed late in the seventh century by Hui-nêng, who professed to hark back to Bodhidharma but really differed from him in experiencing and teaching sudden enlightenment as the way to salvation. In the latter half of the eighth century the Ch'an, in the form in which it had been developed by Hui-nêng and his successors, was made by an imperial commission the orthodox school of Buddhism. This preëminence it has held ever since. Hsüan-tsang is largely responsible for the Fa-hsiang, or Tz'ŭ-ên-tsung, also known as the Wei-shih-hsiang-chiao. Its founder was an Indian teacher, but to Hsüan-tsang are due the standard translations of its chief works. In the judgment of some experts, the Fa-hsiang school constitutes the highest point reached by Buddhist philosophy. It taught that the visible world is only an expression of thought. It was, therefore, highly idealistic. Its chief books were the product of profound reflection and careful, logical reasoning. It advocated Yoga practices as a way to religious realization. Closely related to the Fa-hsiang was the Hua-yen school. The Lü-tsung or Vinaya school frankly had a Chinese origin, being founded by Tao-hsüan in the seventh century. It was perhaps partly because of the Confucian background in China which emphasizes virtue that it stressed moral discipline and asceticism as the way to salvation.

The last Chinese Buddhist sect to appear was Chên-yen ("True Word," in Japanese Shin-gon) or Mi-chiao ("Secret Religion"), in the eighth century. Although, like so many of its predecessors, it claimed for itself an Indian origin and for its first head in China an Indian missionary, and although it was a development of Indian Tantrism, a late and somewhat degenerate form of Buddhism, like the others it could not have survived and prospered if it had not fitted into the Chinese environment. In its more intellectual forms pantheistic, rejoicing in symbolism, declaring that the one spirit manifests itself in many emanations and forms, and claiming that it has an esoteric—"true word"—doctrine revealed to initiates only after a long and gruelling novitiate, in practice it stressed magic formulæ and ceremonies and thus provided a short cut to salvation. From time immemorial the Chinese have made much of ritual as an important means of regulating and controlling the unseen forces of the universe. Hence, in its popular form, Chên-yen was eminently congenial to them. Moreover, it fitted in with Chinese ancestral rites and concern for the welfare of the dead, for it held that by funeral and post-funeral services performed by experts the soul of the departed could be rescued from the pool of blood and other unhappy states.

Thus Buddhism had become naturalized in China, its major sects, especially Ch'an, Ch'ing T'u, and Chên-yen being adaptations to the Chinese environment and Chinese needs. This, it must be remarked, was a notable intellectual and religious achievement. It is interesting to find, moreover, a Buddhist monk of the eighth and ninth centuries attempting to prove the accord of Buddhist and Confucian morality and of Taoist and Buddhist metaphysics.

In no dynasty after the T'ang did Buddhism develop a new sect. As we shall see in another chapter, down to our day it has contributed to the formation of numerous popular, lay cults. While these are additional evidence that Buddhism has become and is an integral part of Chinese life, so far as we know none of them has displayed any very original religious insight or has possessed high intellectual content. While Buddhism was to go on as an outstanding feature of Chinese culture, by the end of the T'ang its vitality had begun to ebb.

The cause of this decline must be a matter of conjecture. It may have been the decay of Buddhism in India and the consequent paucity of fresh currents flowing from there to China. It must probably also in part be assigned to the recruiting of so many members of the bureaucracy from those trained in the Confucian texts. With short interruptions, state examinations based upon non-Buddhist literature were to continue to our own day. Since through them lay the chief road to social and political distinction, they tended to absorb the best brains of the country. Buddhism was weak in that it was other-worldly and had no political program. Chinese rulers, seeking a system which would help them govern the Empire, found in Confucianism what Buddhism lacked. Whatever the cause, with the later years of the T'ang Buddhism began slowly to decay.

CULTURAL DEVELOPMENTS UNDER THE T'ANG: CONFUCIANISM AND TAOISM

As we have seen, Confucianism experienced a fairly marked growth under the T'ang. In their personal practices and beliefs, the majority of the Emperors were probably more inclined toward Taoism or Buddhism than toward this "cult of the learned." Taoism, indeed, seems to have reached the apex of its influence at court. Ming Huang (Hsüan Tsung) gave much attention to it. He even made an effort to grant degrees for excellency in the study of the faith—perhaps thus seeking to give the school something of the prestige that accrued to Confucianism through that means. We hear, too, of a later ruler of the dynasty who seriously impaired his health by taking potions supposed to be the elixir of life. With such advocacy in high quarters, Taoism was popular in the nation at large. One of the celebrated eight "immortals" (*hsien*) of Taoism, Lü Yen, lived in the eighth century and to him is traditionally attributed a famous Taoist treatise on ethics. Political expediency, however, demanded that the monarchs give official support to Confucianism. Here was a system on which government and society could be based far more effectively than upon Taoism or Buddhism. Taoism in its primitive documents would do away with much of government and social organization as the Chinese knew them, and in practice was individualistic and stressed the devotion of one's energies to the achievement of personal immortality through unsocial practices. Buddhism, otherworldly, with its eyes centered on life beyond the grave, demanded of those who followed it completely the renunciation of family and of participation in ordinary political and economic life. Confucianism, however, was essentially this-worldly, emphasized the family and practical yet idealistic political theories, and was in accord with the traditional structure of Chinese society. Upon it, too, was based a system of government and education which had worked well under the Han and which the Sui and the T'ang found ready to hand (although somewhat shaken by the disorder of previous centuries), the agency which, probably more than anything else, had been the means of perpetuating civilization through the years of invasion and civil strife. It is not strange, therefore, that the T'ang reënforced Confucianism and further developed the political and educational machinery which perpetuated it.

As we have seen, T'ang T'ai Tsung ordered (630) that in every *chou* and *hsien* a temple should be erected to Confucius. He also commanded that sacrifices be offered there by scholars and government officials. To the twenty-two names of distinguished exponents of the cult which he ordered placed in the temples, others were added later in the dynasty. The Confucian temple, indeed, became in time a kind of national literary hall of fame. Under the T'ang Confucius and his associated worthies were usually represented by statues—possibly as a result of the Buddhist example. These actions seem to have been innovations (although images of Confucius had been known before) and tended strongly to strengthen Confuciansm.

In the schools which the T'ang ordered maintained in the capital and the provinces, the subjects of study were the Confucian Classics of the Chou period, the histories of Ssŭ-ma Ch'ien and of the Han dynasties, and—for the legal experts—the law. We hear of the founding, at the capital, of a school for calligraphy, and, interestingly enough, of schools of medicine—although the students in these latter were probably not aspirants for the degrees which were the main road to office.

The tests by which admission was had to the bureaucracy were not of the kind to encourage any great originality of thought. The state examinations were greatly elaborated under the T'ang and included a large variety of degrees and something of a choice of topics. Those which admitted to the degree of *Chin Shih*, for instance, might be either in the Classics, law, calligraphy, or mathematics. One set of examinations was in Taoist studies, and for the army tests were given largely in skill in martial exercises. However, degrees taken in the Classics appear to have been the most highly esteemed. Any radical departure from established theories would scarcely commend itself to the bureaucrats who read the papers. Except in Buddhism, creative philosophic effort seems to have been largely lacking.

Still, the literary output was large. Due to the examination system and the training it presupposed, many an official was also an author. Essays, poetry, and the writing of histories of the preceding dynasties, all had their devotees. Tu Yu produced the

T'ung Tien, a treatise on the constitution, a masterly work which helped to set the precedent for a new type of history. Liu Chih-chi wrote the *Shih T'ung,* or Comprehensive Study of History, notable for its critical acumen. Some well-known dictionaries were compiled. Literary form was at a premium.

The greatest master of prose style of the dynasty was Han Yü (768–824)—later canonized as Han Wên Kung. A native of the North and an eager student from his boyhood, he rose to the presidency of the Board of Rites. His official career was somewhat checkered, especially since on at least two occasions he did not hesitate to incur imperial displeasure with frank-spoken memorials. He seems to have been—as may be inferred from these incidents—of an upright and courageous character. Han Yü's work is still considered a model—including an address to a crocodile by which he sought to drive that predatory beast out of a district over which he was the official. He began a new era in prose writing. His style was more supple than that of the Han and less ornate, simpler and more direct than that of most of the scholars of the period of disunion, of the Sui, and of the earlier years of the T'ang. In part it was modeled on the Classics of the Chou and was a reaction against the artificial "parallel" form of the centuries which immediately preceded him.

Han Yü, it will be noted, was a champion of Chinese conservatism—of what to-day might be called pure nationalism. Along with other Confucianists, he vigorously opposed those who would seek alliance with the Uighurs and who would admit Manichæism and tolerate Buddhism and other contributions from without. In the end, as we shall repeatedly see, it was this somewhat reactionary and rigidly nationalistic tendency which triumphed—although its victory was tempered with concessions to importations from without.

CULTURAL DEVELOPMENTS UNDER THE T'ANG: POETRY

The T'ang was the age of the greatest Chinese poetry and of some of the best painting. Such tides of the spirit are always difficult to account for. In this case they almost certainly had some connection with Taoism and Buddhism, for both these faiths encouraged the man of insight to look below surface appearances —held to be illusory—to the reality beneath, and to do so through the approach of the mystic. Buddhism, too, with its many Buddhas and Bodhisattvas, with its conceptions of heaven and hell, and with the art forms which came with it, both stimulated the imagination and provided it with subjects. Buddhism, moreover, was impressed with the impermanence of life—a note of sadness which runs through much of the T'ang poetry. On the other hand, the fact must be included that some of the greatest of the poets were of the orthodox Confucian school and were scornful of both Buddhism and Taoism. Unquestionably, also, the order and the prosperity which the T'ang gave the country afforded opportunity for the arts of civilization.

A technical discussion of Chinese verse would presuppose a knowledge of the Chinese language and would be both confusing and boring to the average Occidental reader. It need not, therefore, be entered upon here. This much must be said, however. To rhyme and length of line, which the older poetry had stressed, the T'ang added emphasis on tone, a practice begun in the centuries of disunion. As in prose, form and style were greatly prized, and it was in the originality and perfection of these that the T'ang poetic genius best expressed itself. In the ninth century, moreover, the songs of popular entertainers and of dancing girls led to a new type of verse which was to flourish for four centuries or so. The songs were written to go with popular tunes, had irregular lines, and so displayed more melody and greater variety than the older orthodox poetry. The subjects and sentiments of T'ang poems often harked back to those of preceding dynasties, but there was also a widening of the range of themes. Among the favorite topics were battle, a deserted concubine, the emotions aroused by a landscape, friendship, the meeting and parting of friends, a ruin, the song of birds, the moonlight, and wine. Translations of Buddhist poetry, moreover, exerted a marked influence.

The two most famous poets of the dynasty, and usually deemed the greatest in all Chinese literature, were Li Po and Tu Fu. Li Po was probably, although not certainly, born in the far West. The year seems to have been between 699 and 705. Most of his life he was a wanderer. In his youth he was something of a swashbuckler, and always he was fond of wine. At one period he retired to a mountain as a member of a gay group dubbed the "Six Idlers of the Bamboo Brook." His matrimonial ventures were many. He was never successful in attaining to high public office—the conventional road to distinction—nor was he long far removed from poverty. He was too much of a bohemian for that. For a time in early middle life he was in Ch'angan, a favorite with Hsüan Tsung (Ming Huang) and one of the brilliant and gay group who made the court of that Emperor famous. In company with others of the "Eight Immortals of the Wine-cup" he frequented the taverns of the city, and on at least one occasion is said to have been brought drunk into the imperial presence. After three years he fell into disgrace, why is not known, perhaps because he had incurred the displeasure of the reigning beauty, Yang Kuei-fei, whose charms he had celebrated in many a poem. Again he went on his travels. In his later years his wanderings were troubled by the confusion attending the uprising of An Lu-shan, and he narrowly escaped execution for having attached himself to the fortunes of another unsuccessful rebel of these stormy years. A popular tradition has it that he finally came to his end by drowning, when, drunk and out boating, he attempted to embrace the reflection of the moon in the water. Unfortunately for romance, he seems to have died, in most prosaic fashion, in 762, while living with a kinsman in the present Anhui. He was fond not only of the town and of gay and rather loose living, but of the mountain and the stream, and in him ran a strong Taoist strain. His poems appear to have been largely spontaneous, dashed off rapidly, not labored, and are noted for their lyric beauty, their mastery of the use of words, their originality of style, and both for their skill in handling the older poetic forms and for their successful variations of and departures from literary conventions. He knew anxiety and disappointment, but sought escape from them, and helped his readers to do so, into a dream world, lifted there in an ecstasy of form and rhythm.

Tu Fu (712–770), also for a time at the court of Hsüan Tsung and one of the "Eight Immortals of the Wine-cup," led a life marked by much suffering. Although precocious as a youth, he failed to attain distinction in the imperial examinations. After much waiting and disappointment, in early middle life he won favor, through his writing, with Ming Huang. He was separated from his family for long periods during the years of civil strife at the end of that reign and some of his children starved to death. Appointed in 759 to an official charge which irked him, he left it, thoroughly disillusioned. In the capacity of censor he ultimately fell into disgrace for dealing faithfully with Ming Huang's successor. In contrast with Li Po, he took great pains with his composition and his work lacks a certain daring and lyrical quality which are found in the other. The iron had entered deeply into his soul and he was a stark realist, portraying suffering in very moving fashion.

Later than Li Po and Tu Fu was Po Chü-i (772–846). The son of a minor official, he himself early passed the state examinations and entered upon an official career. Most of his life was spent in public office in the capital and the provinces, sometimes in and sometimes out of imperial favor, and, accordingly, occasionally in virtual banishment to an obscure and distant local post. Trained in the Confucian classics, he valued content above form and sought to make his verses the medium for moral instruction. In this he was not always successful, for the poet in him often broke the bonds of his Confucianism. It was the romantic lines which he composed while in this mood that were the most popular. He could use either the classical or the newer poetic forms and was careful to make his work simple, testing it, so we hear, by its intelligibility to an old peasant woman. For years many of his poems were enormously popular and were on the lips of high and low.

Many another poet of the T'ang might be mentioned—the soldier Ch'ên Tzŭ-ang, the military counsellor Sung Chih-wên, Wang Wei the painter, the Taoists Ch'ang Chien and T'ao Han, and Liu Tsung-yüan, the earnestly Buddhist friend of Han Yü. One collection includes nearly fifty thousand poems of the period, and many are still read and admired.

FICTION

It must also be noted that there was prose fiction, written in the vernacular and made up mostly of short stories and rudimentary novels. It arose from the story tellers who narrated their tales, sometimes in verse, sometimes in a mixture of verse and prose, and sometimes in prose. Beginning with about the eighth century, they began to put their tales into writing, much as they narrated them to their public. This helped to give rise to a vernacular literature.

CULTURAL DEVELOPMENTS UNDER THE T'ANG: ART

The T'ang is only a little less famous for its painters than for its poets. There was, indeed, a flowering of several kinds of art. In this Buddhism had a large part. The religious enthusiasm aroused by it stimulated the imagination, it was the vehicle for many new forms, and its temples were ornate with statues and paintings, most of them the work of Chinese. It will be recalled that in what is now the New Dominion many non-Chinese artistic influences were found—Greek as mediated through Gandhara, Sassanid, Græco-Roman, and Indian of the Gupta period (fourth and fifth centuries)—utilized by that great variety of races, Indo-European, Turk, and Mongol, who were found there. They could scarcely fail to have their effect on the Middle Kingdom. Their blending with older Chinese styles and ideals can be vividly seen in the Buddhist rock temples in the grottoes of Tunhuang, near the far western edge of Kansu.

In China itself many forms of sculpture were seen. Chinese sculpture, indeed, reached its apex in the first century of the T'ang. In some places the Han tradition survived, with its portrayals of animals and of scenes from human life. In Buddhist shrines the predominant *motifs* showed either the effects of Græco-Buddhist Gandhara or of the somewhat later Gupta period, with its more sinuous lines. Buddhist art of the T'ang possesses greater elegance than that of the Northern Wei, but probably less vigor. It was, however, of a very high order and some of the most beautiful statues ever produced by man were the work of this period—as may be seen from some of the surviving examples in China and Korea. In secular art much of the Han tradition, modified, was represented in huge monoliths and in wall carvings. The best of the sculpture had mostly been done before the downfall of Wu Hou. As the dynasty progressed, it tended to be less produced. In such as was created, secular influences increased at the expense of Buddhism (possibly an indication that Buddhism was waning), and there was more naturalism and less adherence to convention.

There have come down to us, too, many earthenware figurines

which display unusual vigor, grace, and lifelikeness—mounted horsemen, animals, men, and women—showing artistic freshness and marked skill.

It was probably in the sixth and seventh centuries, after a long preliminary development, that one of the most characteristic of Chinese artistic mediums, true white porcelain, first appeared. Not until later dynasties, however, was it to be put to its most extensive uses.

Painting now attained a high pinnacle—in the judgment of some, the highest in Chinese history. Buddhism and Taoism seem to have been chiefly responsible. The principles of calligraphy, a fine art in China, were also now fully applied to painting, with resulting improvement in skill and emphasis upon line. Probably the greatest painter of the T'ang—possibly of all Chinese history—was Wu Tao-hsüan (also known as Wu Tao Tzŭ and Wu Tao-yüan), who was one of the glories of the brilliant court of Ming Huang. A master of landscapes, in which field he was said to have initiated a new school, he was also, and especially, devoted to Buddhist and Taoist themes. It is about him that there grew up the interesting story of a landscape with which he had decorated a wall for the Emperor. As the two, the artist and the monarch, stood before it, the artist clapped his hands, a door opened, and he passed within it. Before his astonished patron could accept his invitation to follow, the door closed, and the painter was never again seen. Wu's greatest work, it is said, was on the walls of temples at Ch'angan and Loyang. He was an extreme realist but did not depart from the classical canons of his art. He also possessed both fertility of imagination and technical skill.

A friend of Wu Tao-hsüan was the poet, official, physician, and painter Wang Wei. An earnest Buddhist, he spent much time in quiet retirement in the country. His last years were greatly disturbed by the rebellion of An Lu-shan, for he accepted office under that upstart and was imprisoned for a time after the collapse of the revolt. His monochrome landscapes are especially famous, and later critics thought of him as belonging to the Southern as opposed to the Northern School. This distinction has no geographical significance but goes back to a classical allusion, the Southern School being supposed to be dreamy and to deal in subdued tones, and the Northern to use strong colors and to be characterized by force and precision. The classification is, however, artificial when applied to the T'ang.

A friend and protégé of Wang Wei was Han Kan, a noted painter of horses. His subjects were usually the steeds sent as tribute to the imperial court by the peoples of the North and West. A distinguished landscape painter and a leader in the so-called Northern School was Li Ssŭ-hsün, a great-grandson of the founder of the dynasty. He was followed and perhaps excelled by his son, Li Chao-tao. Yen Li-tê, of the seventh century, and his younger brother, Yen Li-pên, were both in high official position and both employed Taoist and Buddhist subjects and historical scenes. We hear, too, of painters of flowers and birds, of plants and insects—but to give the names of all the artists of distinction would be merely confusing.

It is possible that in many of the paintings were earlier Chinese influences—from the ceremonial processions seen on the bas-reliefs of the Han, and, possibly, from the formal observances in connection with the ancestral rites. Certainly there was more than one strain—Taoism, different schools of Buddhism, impulses and models from the semi-nomadic peoples with whom the Chinese were in touch on the northern frontiers and in the northern provinces, traditional Chinese forms, and the contributions from other lands and cultures which we have noted above. These were all present, acting either singly or in various mixtures on different men and localities.

Calligraphy, in the Chinese mind closely related to painting, had many devotees and the works of earlier masters were sought out and reproduced by imperial order. The dynasty could not, however, boast of as great calligraphers as could some others.

CULTURAL DEVELOPMENTS UNDER THE T'ANG: PRINTING

It is from T'ang times that we have our earliest examples of that revolutionary art, printing. From Japan, then recasting its life under Buddhist and Chinese influence, come charms of the latter part of the eighth century, in Sanscrit and Chinese, printed by wood blocks. From the grottoes of Tunhuang we have the earliest known extant printed book, a Buddhist sutra, struck off in 868, also from wooden blocks, for free distribution—presumably as an act of piety. How many years before these specimens the art originated we do not know—possibly as early as the Sui. Apparently it was an evolution, conceivably—although by no means certainly—from the use of seals. It was to have a noteworthy development in China, and as late as the close of the eighteenth century the Empire possibly contained more printed books than all the rest of the world put together.

ECONOMIC LIFE

One would like to know something of the life of the toiling masses of the T'ang—the way in which they made a livelihood, and their agricultural and industrial organization. Some fragments of information are accessible to us, but we still lack adequate monographs on the subject. We know that under the first Emperor of the dynasty a redistribution of land was ordered, with an attempt to equalize the holdings. We know, too, that efforts were made again and again to prevent the sale of these holdings, and so to forestall the growth of large landed estates. The system inevitably broke down and complaints were later repeatedly registered of landless poor against wealthy landowners. However, peasant proprietorship seems to have been fairly general. We hear of governmental promotion of irrigation canals. We read of movements to disband part of the army and to move the soldiers back to the land. We have records of many famines—even before the declining years of the dynasty—and often the government sought to give relief by distributing food and remitting taxes. Taxes were of many kinds, some of them based on the land and some on trade and commodities. At times they were very heavy. Standard forms long in use under the T'ang were a land tax, a levy in kind on each family (chiefly for town-dwellers), and required labor—which might be compounded by the payment of silk. Toward the close of the eighth century a statesman, Yang Yen, substituted for all these a single tax on the land, payable twice a year, a practice which was reverted to under later dynasties. Early in the eighth century a standing, mercenary army was substituted, at least for the time, for military conscription. There were currency troubles, with debased coinage and attempts to improve it. Gresham's Law operated—long before it was so named—the poorer money driving the better out of circulation.

Copper coins and silk were used as currency and negotiable certificates were tried out. Nowhere in T'ang times, however, do we have any such thoroughgoing radical social and economic experiments as under Wang Mang, or as were to be made under the Sung. Perhaps because of the preoccupation of so many of the best minds with other-worldly Buddhism, the T'ang saw no comparable revolutionary innovations either in governmental or in economic organization.

INFLUENCE OF CHINA ON SURROUNDING COUNTRIES

One last outstanding feature of the T'ang must be noted—the influence of China upon her neighbors. So extensive, so prosperous, and so brilliant an Empire could not fail to have a profound effect upon surrounding peoples. Even when they beat back the arms of the T'ang, they could not, or at least did not, resist her culture. Already under the Sui, Buddhism and with it Chinese civilization—which had been trickling in for centuries—were pouring into Japan and were working the revolution which so completely transformed the life of that vigorous people. Japanese came in numbers to China. Some of them were students and lived in the Middle Kingdom for many years before returning home. Others were official envoys. Chinese embassies were also sent to Japan, and intercourse between the governments of the two countries was maintained. The Japanese copied the plan of Ch'angan in their own capitals, first in Nara and then in Heian, and in art, literature, religion, and administrative organization, sought to imitate their great neighbor. The result was a sinicized Japan—although the islanders proved to be skillful adapters and not blind copyists. Korea, too, took over much of the culture of China, as, indeed, she had long been doing, even in those sections which had been politically independent. Much of what is now French Indo-China was within the circle of T'ang cultural influence. Tibet seems to have derived some of its Buddhism from China. In what is now the New Dominion the influence of Chinese art was felt, and Chinese Buddhism appears to have had some converts. It seems also to have been during the T'ang that the use of paper, in its origin a Chinese invention, spread to Samarkand —through Chinese captured by the Arabs after the defeat of Kao Hsien-chih in 751 and the consequent collapse of Chinese power in that region—and to Western Asia, whence, in due time, it made its way to Europe. A Chinese made prisoner at the time of the fall of the T'ang power in the far West journeyed to Mesopotamia and reported that at Kufa, one of the Abbasid capitals, some of his fellow-countrymen had inaugurated—a possible exaggeration—painting, the manufacture of silk, and work in gold and silver. China was a giver as well as a receiver of civilization.

SUMMARY

Under the T'ang, China was for centuries a unified, prosperous, and highly civilized Empire. During the first century and a half of the T'ang its territories surpassed in extent those of the Han, and even during the latter half of the dynasty it retained control of most of what is now China proper. If the T'ang rulers showed no striking originality in administrative devices, they had the good judgment to avail themselves of the machinery which had come down to them from earlier centuries and further to develop it. Their code of laws became basic for the codes of later dynasties.

Moreover, the culture of the Sui and the T'ang exhibited features markedly different from that of preceding dynasties. Contrasted with the Han, the Sui and the T'ang achieved a further and notable development of that examination system and bureaucracy which have been the most distinctive political achievement of the Chinese and which led to the firm establishment of the Confucian school. The art and poetry of the T'ang were in many respects dissimilar to those of the Han and even of the period of disunion. In poetry and sculpture, indeed, the T'ang was never to be surpassed. Buddhism reached its heyday and in its philosophy, partly imported but partly rethought by Chinese monks, it displayed profound and painstaking intellectual activity and religious insight. As against the dynasties of the centuries of division, the Sui and the T'ang reëstablished union and determined that China was not to be permanently divided nor to be always subject to aliens. Chinese civilization became more firmly established south of the Yangtze than ever before. It is significant that the Chinese of the far South have denominated themselves the "men of T'ang," much as those of the Yangtze Valley and the North have called themselves the "men of Han." The Sui and the T'ang gave a fresh impetus to Confucianism and did much to insure that that cult rather than Buddhism should be dominant. While they witnessed the years of the greatest prosperity of Chinese Buddhism, they were also largely responsible for its slow decline. The Confucianism of the T'ang and the literary style of the T'ang showed modifications in what had been handed down from preceding periods.

The Sui and the T'ang, then, were not only a brilliant age to which the Chinese rightly look back with pride. They witnessed distinctive changes and in some respects fresh advances over earlier eras.

BIBLIOGRAPHY

The *Pei Shih,* by Li Yen-shou of the seventh century, based in part on his father's notes, contains an account of the Sui. A longer account, in the *Sui Shu,* was compiled by an imperial commission under T'ang T'ai Tsung. For the T'ang there exist two officially recognized dynastic histories. The *Chiu T'ang Shu* is made up in large part of material compiled by at least three hands during the dynasty and was composed shortly after the fall of the house. It was severely criticized and in the eleventh century the *Hsin T'ang Shu* was compiled under imperial commission. It is based largely on the *Chiu T'ang Shu.* The *Tzŭ Chih T'ung Chien,* by Ssŭ-ma Kuang, of the eleventh century, with accompanying works by the same hand, begins in the fourth century B.C. and comes down through the five short dynasties which immediately succeeded the T'ang. The *T'ung Chien Kang Mu* is a reconstruction and condensation of this work, made under the direction of the famous Chu Hsi, of the twelfth century. Several times in succeeding centuries it was revised. It forms the basis of the largest history of China ever published in a European language, de Mailla's *Histoire Générale de la Chine* (13 vols., Paris, 1777–1785).

Among the general books in European languages useful for this period are the works mentioned in previous chapters—H. Cordier, *Histoire Générale de la Chine* (4 vols., Paris, 1920–1921), L. Wieger, *Textes Historiques* (2 vols., Hochienfu, 1903, 1904), René Grousset, *Histoire de L'Asie* (3 vols., Paris, 1922), René Grousset, *Histoire de L'Extrême-Orient* (2 vols., Paris, 1929), O. Franke, *Geschichte des Chinesischen Reiches* (Berlin, Vol. 2, 1936), and H. A. Giles, *A Chinese Biographical Dictionary* (London and Shanghai, 1898). Biographical sketches of a few of the great figures of the T'ang are in C. W. Allen, *The Makers of Cathay* (Shanghai, 1909)—a popularly written but highly uncritical book.

Special works and articles covering the political history and the foreign wars of the T'ang are C. P. Fitzgerald, *Son of Heaven. A Biog-*

raphy of *Li Shih-min, founder of the T'ang Dynasty* (Cambridge, 1933); W. Bingham, *The Founding of the T'ang Dynasty* (Baltimore, 1941); Gaubil, *Abrégé de l'Histoire de la Grand Dynastie Tang* (*Mém. Concernant les Chinois*, Paris, 1791 and 1814, Vols. 15, 16); E. H. Parker, *A Thousand Years of the Tartars* (second edition, London, 1924); Maspero, *Études d'Histoire d'Annam* (*Bulletin de l'École Française d'Extrême-Orient*, Vol. 16, 1916, pp. 27–45); Maspero, *Le Protectorat Général d'Annam sous les T'ang* (*ibid.*, Vol. 10, 1910, pp. 539–584, 665–694); M. Tchang, *Tableau des Souverains de Nan Tchao* (*ibid.*, Vol. 1, 1901, pp. 312–321); Goré, *Marches Tibétaines du Sseu-tch'ouan et du Yunnan* (*ibid.*, Vol. 23, 1923, pp. 318–398); C. Saison (translator), *Nan-Tchao Ye-che: Histoire Particulière du Nan-Tchao* (Paris, 1904); Albert von Le Coq, *Buried Treasures of Chinese Turkestan* (translated by Anna Barwell, London, 1928); A. Pfizmaier, *Zur Geschichte der Gründung des Hauses Thang* (*Sitzungsberichte der phil.-hist. Classe der kaiserlichen Ak. der Wissenschaften*, Vienna, Band 91, June, 1878, pp. 21–101)—largely a translation of Chinese material without critical notes; A. Pfizmaier, *Seltsamkeiten und Unglück aus den Zeiten der Thang* (*ibid.*, Band 94, May, 1879, pp. 7–86, Band 96, Apr. 1880, pp. 293–365); A. Pfizmaier, *Die Fremdländischen Reiche zu den Zeiten der Sui* (*ibid.*, Band 97, 1880, pp. 411–489); A. Pfizmaier, *Fortsetzungen aus der Geschichte des Hauses Sui* (*ibid.*, Band 101, 1882, pp. 187–266); A. Pfizmaier, *Darlegungen aus der Geschichte des Hauses Sui* (*ibid.*, Band 97, 1880, pp. 627–706) (Pfizmaier's work had the virtues and faults of a pioneering effort); W. Barthold, *Turkestan down to the Mongol Invasion* (2d edition, London, 1928); E. H. Parker, *The Old Thai or Shan Empire of Western Yünnan* (*China Review*, Vol. 20, pp. 337–346); E. Chavannes, *Documents sur les Tou-kiue (Turcs) Occidentaux* (St. Petersburg, 1903)—a masterly work shedding much light on Central Asia during the period, giving translations of Chinese documents, largely from the *Chiu T'ang Shu and Hsin T'ang Shu* and with copious critical footnotes; E. Chavannes, *Notes Additionelles sur les Tou-kiue (Turcs) Occidentaux* (*T'oung Pao*, 1904, pp. 1–10); Emile Rocher, *Histoire des Princes du Yunnan* (*T'oung Pao*, 1899, pp. 1–32, 115–154, 337–368, 437–458)—rather uncritical; E. H. Parker, *The Early Laos and China* (*China Review*, Vol. 19, pp. 67–106); Aurel Stein, *Serindia* (5 vols., Oxford, 1921); H. A. R. Gibb, *The Arab Conquests in Central Asia* (London, 1923); H. A. R. Gibb, *Chinese Records of the Arabs in Central Asia* (*Bulletin of London School of Oriental Studies*, Vol. 2, pp. 613–622); Aurel Stein, *A Chinese Expedition across the Pamirs and Hindukush, A.D. 747* (*The New China Review*, Vol. 4, pp. 161–183); Sir Percy Sykes, *A History of Persia* (2 vols., 2d edition, London, 1921); and Sir Aurel Stein, *On Ancient Central-Asian Tracks: A Brief Narrative of Three Expeditions in Innermost Asia and Northwestern China* (London, 1933).

On the administrative organization of the T'ang, see an excellent article by Robert des Rotours, *Les Grands Fonctionnaires des Provinces en Chine sous la Dynastie des T'ang* (*T'oung Pao*, 1928, pp. 219–332). The same author has a related study, *Le Traité des Examens Traduit de la Nouvelle Histoire des T'ang* (Paris, 1932).

On commerce, see F. Hirth, *China and the Roman Orient* (Shanghai, 1885); E. O. Reischauer, *Notes on T'ang Dynasty Sea Routes* (*Harvard Journal of Asiatic Studies*, Vol. 5, pp. 142–164); F. Hirth and W. W. Rockhill, *Chau Ju-kua* (St. Petersburg, 1912); M. Aurel Stein, *Innermost Asia* (Oxford, 1928); Henry Yule, *Cathay and the Way Thither*, edited by Henry Cordier, Vol. 1 (London, 1915); Gabriel Ferrand, *Relations de Voyages et Textes Géographiques Arabes, Persans et Turks relatifs à l'Extrême-Orient du VIIIe au XVIIIe siècles* (Paris, 1913); Chang Hsing-lang, *The Importation of Negro Slaves to China under the T'ang Dynasty* (A.D. 618–907) (*Bulletin No. 7, Catholic University of Peking*, Dec. 1930, pp. 37–59); Gabriel Ferrand, *Voyage du Marchand Arabe Sulaymân en Inde et en Chine Rédigé en 851 suivi de Remarques par Abû Zayd Hasan (vers 916)* (Paris, 1922); A. Sprenger, *Die Post- und Reise-routen des Orients* (erstes heft, pp. 79–91. Leipzig, 1864. *Abhandlungen der Deutschen Morgenländischen Gesellschaft*, III Band).

On the closely related topic of the Buddhist pilgrims, see Baron A. von Stael-Holstein, *Hsuan Tsang and Modern Research* (*Journal of the North China Branch of the Royal Asiatic Society*, 1923, pp. 16–24); Samuel Beal, *The Life of Hiuen-Tsiang by the Shaman Hwui Li* (London, 1911); Samuel Beal, *Si-Yu-Ki. Buddhist Records of the Western World. Translated from the Chinese of Hiuen Tsiang* (A.D. 629) (2 vols., London, 1906); René Grousset, *In the Footsteps of the Buddha*, translated from the French by Mariette Leon (London, 1932); Paul Pelliot, *Deux Itinéraires de Chine en Inde à la Fin du VIIIe Siècle* (*Bulletin de l'École Française d'Extrême-Orient*, Vol. 4, 1904, pp. 131–413); Paul Pelliot, *Autour d'une Traduction Sanscrite du Tao Tö King* (*T'oung Pao*, 1912, pp. 351–430); Thomas Watters (translator), *On Yuan Chwang's Travels to India, 629–645 A.D.* (2 vols., London, 1904–1905); E. Chavannes (translator), *Mémoire Composé à l'Époque de la Grande Dynastie T'ang sur les Religieux Éminents que Allèrent Chercher la Loi dans les Pays d'Occident, par I-tsing* (Paris, 1894); J. Takakusu (translator), *A Record of the Buddhist Religion as Practiced in India and the Malay Archipelago* (A.D. 671–695) by *I-tsing* (Oxford, 1896).

On miscellaneous cultural contributions from without, see B. Laufer, *Sino-Iranica* (Chicago, 1919).

On the history of thought see A. Forke, *Geschichte der Mittelalterlichen chinesischen Philosophie* (Hamburg, 1934).

On the various religions in China under the T'ang, see L. Wieger, *Histoire des Croyances Religieuses et des Opinions Philosophiques en Chine* (1919). On religion and philosophy, see Zenker, *Geschichte Chinesischen Philosophie* (Vol. 2, Reichenberg, 1927). On philosophy, see A. Pfizmaier, *Die philosophischen Werke China's in dem Zeitalter der Thang* (*Sitzungsberichte d.phil.-hist. Classe d.k. Ak.d.Wis. Vienna,* Bd. 89, Jan. 1878).

On Nestorian Christianity, see a summary in K. S. Latourette, *A History of Christian Missions in China* (New York, 1929). The best account of Christianity under the T'ang is A. C. Moule, *Christians in China before the year 1550* (London, 1930). Its footnotes contain references to most of the pertinent books. See also A. C. Moule, *Nestorians in China* (London, 1940). A very full account of the Hsianfu monument is Henri Havret, *La Stèle Chrétienne de Si-ngan-fou* (3 parts, Shanghai, 1895, 1897, 1902). The text of the monument presents many difficulties and there is no really satisfactory translation. A popular yet scholarly summary is J. Foster, *The Church of the T'ang Dynasty* (London, 1939). Less critical are P. Y. Saeki, *The Nestorian Monument in China* (London, 1916), and P. Y. Saeki, *The Nestorian Documents and Relics in China* (London, 1937). See also F. S. Drake, *Nestorian Monasteries of the T'ang Dynasty* (*Monumenta Serica,* Vol. 2, pp. 293–340).

The best account of Manichæism in China is E. Chavannes and P. Pelliot, *Un Traité Manichéen Retrouvé en Chine* (Paris, 1913). See also P. Pelliot, *Les Traditions Manichéennes au Foukien* (*T'oung Pao,* 1923, pp. 193–214), and P. Pelliot, *Mo-ni et Manichéens* (*Journal Asiatique,* 11e Série, Tome 3, 1914, pp. 461–470). See also H. A. Giles, *Confucianism and Its Rivals* (New York, 1915, pp. 190–195). An excellent summary in English is T. A. Bisson, *Some Chinese Records of Manichæism in China* (*Chinese Recorder,* July, 1929, pp. 413–428). A very scholarly work giving chiefly the translations of Manichæan and anti-Manichæan documents found at Turfan is A. V. Williams Jackson, *Researches in Manichæism* (New York, 1932).

On Buddhism under the T'ang, see E. H. Parker, *China and Religion* (New York, 1905); J. J. M. de Groot, *Sectarianism and Religious Persecution in China* (2 vols., Amsterdam, 1903); Sir Charles Eliot, *Hinduism and Buddhism, An Historical Sketch* (3 vols., London, 1921); Samuel Beal, Abstract of Four Lectures on *Buddhist Literature in China* (London, 1882); Joseph Edkins, *Chinese Buddhism* (London, 1893); K. L. Reichelt, *Truth and Tradition in Chinese Buddhism* (Shanghai, 1927); Hu Shih, *Development of Zen Buddhism in China* (*The Chinese Social and Political Science Review,* Jan. 1932, Vol. 15, pp. 475–505); and C. H. Hamilton, *Hsüan Chuang and the Wei Shih Philosophy* (*Journal of the American Oriental Society,* Dec. 1931, Vol. 51, pp. 291–308).

On Islam in China, see M. Broomhall, *Islam in China* (London, 1909) (faulty in some places), and Isaac Mason, *How Islam Entered China* (*The Moslem World,* Vol. 19, pp. 249–263).

On Confucianism under the T'ang, see J. K. Shryock, *The Origin and Development of the State Cult of Confucius* (New York, 1932).

On education, see E. Biot, *Essai sur l'Histoire de l'Instruction Publique en Chine* (Paris, 1847).

On literature, see E. D. Edwards, *Chinese Prose Literature* (London, 2 vols., dealing with T'ang times, 1937–8); Alexander Wylie, *Notes on Chinese Literature* (Shanghai, 1902), H. A. Giles, *A History of Chinese Literature* (New York, 1901) (a disappointing work), and Georges Margoulies, *Le Kou-wen Chinois. Recueil de Textes avec Introduction et Notes* (Paris, 1926).

On poetry, see Arthur Waley (translator), *A Hundred and Seventy Chinese Poems* (New York, 1909); A. Forke, *Dichtungen der T'ang- und Sung-Zeit* (German Text, Hamburg, 1929, Chinese Text, Hamburg, 1930); Shigeyoshi Obata, *The Works of Li Po, the Chinese Poet, Done into English Verse* (New York, 1922); C. Y. Sun, *English Translations of Li Po's Poems* (*Chinese Social and Political Science Review*, Vol. 11, pp. 463–476, 632–644); Florence Ayscough, *Tu Fu, The Autobiography of a Chinese Poet Arranged from his Poems and Translated* (Boston, 2 vols., 1929–1934); an excellent work by a thoroughly competent Chinese scholar and a Western poet, *The Jade Mountain, A Chinese Anthology. Being Three Hundred Poems of the T'ang Dynasty 618–906*, translated by W. Bynner from the texts of Kiang Kang-hu (New York, 1929); and Admiral Ts'ai T'ing-kan, *Chinese Poems in English Rhyme* (Chicago, 1932).

On art, see P. Pelliot, *Notes sur quelques Artistes des Six Dynasties et des T'ang* (*T'oung Pao*, 1923, pp. 215–291); E. F. Fenollosa, *Epochs of Chinese and Japanese Art* (2 vols., London, 1912); Alice Getty, *The Gods of Northern Buddhism* (Oxford, 1914); S. W. Bushell, *Chinese Art* (2 vols., London, 1910); Raphael Petrucci, *Chinese Painters: A Critical Study* (translated by Frances Seaver, New York, 1921; French edition, Paris, 1913); H. A. Giles, *An Introduction to the History of Chinese Pictorial Art* (London, 1918); Arthur Waley, *An Introduction to the Study of Chinese Painting* (London, 1923); Laurence Binyon, *Painting in the Far East* (London, 1908); P. Pelliot, *Les Grottes Touen-houang* (Paris, 1914–1921); E. Chavannes et Raphael Petrucci, *La Peinture Chinoise au Musée Cernuschi, Avril-Juin*, 1912 (Bruxelles et Paris, 1912); M. Aurel Stein, *The Thousand Buddhas. Ancient Buddhist Paintings from the Cave Temples of Tun-huang on the Western Frontier of China* (London, 1921); A. Waley, *A Catalogue of Paintings Recovered from Tun-huang by Sir Aurel Stein* (London, 1931); E. Chavannes, *Mission Archéologique dans la Chine Septentrionale* (Paris, 1909–1915), especially *Tome 1, Deuxième partie, La Sculpture Bouddhique* (Paris, 1915); Victor Segalen, Gilbert de Voisins, et Jean Lartique, *Mission Archéologique en Chine* (*1914–1917*) (2 vols., Paris, 1923, 1924); Osvald Sirén, *Chinese Sculptures from the Fifth to the Fourteenth Century* (4 vols., London, 1925); Osvald Sirén, *Histoire des Arts Anciens de la Chine* (6 vols., Paris, 1929–1932); R. L. Hobson and A. L. Hetherington, *The Art of the Chinese Potter from the Han Dynasty to the End of the Ming* (London, 1923); C. Hentze, *Chinese Tomb Figures. A Study in the Beliefs and Folklore of Ancient China* (London, 1928).

On porcelain, see B. Laufer, *The Beginnings of Porcelain in China* (Chicago, 1917).

On printing, see T. F. Carter, *The Invention of Printing in China and Its Spread Westward* (revised edition, New York, 1931), and a review of the first edition by B. Laufer in *Jour. Am. Oriental Soc.,* March, 1927.

On economic life, see Mabel Ping-hua Lee, *The Economic History of China, with Special Reference to Agriculture* (New York, 1921), and S. Belázs, *Beiträge zur Wirtschaftsgeschichte der Tang-Zeit* (618–906) (*Mitteilungen des Seminars für Orientalische Sprachen,* Vol. 34, pp. 1–92).

On T'ang influence on Japan, see K. Hara, *An Introduction to the History of Japan* (New York, 1920); F. Brinkley, *A History of the Japanese People* (New York and London, 1915); G. B. Sansom, *Japan. A Short Cultural History* (New York, 1943); M. Anesaki, *History of Japanese Religion* (London, 1930); J. Takakusu (translator), *Le Voyage de Kanshin en Orient, 742–754, par Aomi-no Mabito Genkai (799)* (*Bulletin de l'École Française d'Éxtrême-Orient,* 1928, Vol. 28, pp. 1–41, 1929, Vol. 29, pp. 47–62); and K. Asakawa, *The Early Institutional Life of Japan: A Study of the Reform of 645 A.D.* (Tokyo, 1903).

On the question of whether the famous Peking Gazette (*Ching Pao*) originated in the T'ang, as is sometimes claimed, see *China Review,* Vol. 3, pp. 13–18.

CHAPTER VI

POLITICAL WEAKNESS BUT CULTURAL BRILLIANCE: THE FIVE DYNASTIES (A.D. 907–960) AND THE SUNG DYNASTY (A.D. 960–1279)

INTRODUCTORY

THE collapse of the T'ang was followed by internal division and civil strife. For more than half a century the Empire was divided among many petty states, some of them dominated by rulers of alien extraction. When, in the latter half of the tenth century, a family of the older native stock once more united most of China proper, the political recovery was not complete: part of the Empire which had been traditionally Chinese and whose population was predominantly so remained in the hands of foreigners. Eventually most of the earlier seats of Chinese culture passed into the control of invaders from the North and only the Yangtze Valley and the South continued to be under Chinese princes. In the latter part of the thirteenth century all China became part of the great Mongol Empire. Not until the second half of the fourteenth century did a native dynasty succeed in effectively asserting its authority over all of the country which because of its population and culture could rightly be called Chinese. As before the Sui and the T'ang, so now after the T'ang, the Empire was again, and this time for nearly five centuries rather than a little less than four, partly or entirely under the heel of conquering outsiders.

This long period of partial or complete subjection to foreigners was not, however, marked by as much political weakness and extended anarchy as the earlier one had been. The Sung dynasty, which held the throne from 960 to 1279—or for over half the time—was stronger than any of the dynasties, Chinese or foreign, between the Han and the Sui. The years, moreover, registered much greater achievement in civilization than did those of the preceding long period of disunion. In this respect some of them rank among the most brilliant in the history of the Chinese. In political theory, in philosophy, and in literature and art, they were distinguished by great genius. Although governed in part by invaders, China made great strides toward regaining her cultural independence. The foreign faith, Buddhism, which had engrossed most of the best intellectual energy of the Chinese for the seven centuries between the downfall of the Han and the end of the T'ang, had now been largely assimilated to Chinese life. It remained an integral part of that life, but under the Sung vigorous thought of a very high order was once more to be found in that chief of the native schools, Confucianism. The forms in which orthodox Chinese intellectual life was to be set until the close of the nineteenth century were then molded.

THE FIVE DYNASTIES

The years between the final disappearance of the T'ang, in 907, and the inauguration, in 960, of the Sung, are conventionally designated by Chinese historians as the Five Dynasties. During these years five successive states arose in which the imperial succession is supposed to have been preserved. As a matter of fact, although the center of their power was in the region in which the imperial capitals had been through much of China's history and in the traditional home of Chinese culture, they usually controlled only parts of the present Shensi, Shansi, Honan, Hopei, and Shantung, and their authority was disputed by families who carved out domains in other sections of the Empire. Some of these latter states had their origin in the closing years of the T'ang, when the central power was too weak to prevent division, and had almost, if not quite, as much right to the imperial title as did those whom posterity has called legitimate.

On the north and northeast, moreover, was a newly emerging barbarian state, the latest successor to the many which had troubled the fertile valleys to the south. Toward the close of the ninth and the beginning of the tenth century, a people of Mongol tongue known to the Chinese as the Khitan or Ch'i-tan, a name which we have often run across in the last years of the T'ang, were establishing an empire in the present Mongolia and Manchuria. Their rulers later called their dynasty Liao. Until early in the twelfth century they menaced the northern frontiers and much of the time occupied part of China proper. It is from Khitan that Cathay is derived, the name by which medieval Europe knew North China, and it is from the same source that Khitai, the present Russian designation for China, has come. The Khitan rulers were cattle breeders and endeavored to preserve their culture uncontaminated by Chinese ways. Indeed, their nobles were punished if they studied Chinese or took the civil service examinations. The commoners kept their old ways and intermarried little with the Chinese. The Chinese in the Khitan realm south of the Great Wall were taxed heavily but otherwise retained their own customs.

Chu Wên, as we have seen, made an end to the enfeebled T'ang and set himself up (907) as the first monarch of the Hou Liang, or Later Liang. He was troubled both by external foes and by dissensions in his family and in 914 was murdered by his eldest son, who feared for his own succession to the throne.

In 923 the Later Liang was overthrown by Li Tsun-hsü, a general of Turkish stock, whose father, Li K'o-yung, had served under the T'ang and had been granted their family name, Li. On the downfall of the T'ang, Li K'o-yung set up a state in what is now Shansi and waged war on Chu Wên. The dynasty inaugurated by Li Tsun-hsü had its capital at Loyang and was, because of the imperial surname Li, called the Hou T'ang, or Later T'ang.

The Later T'ang was, in its turn, terminated, in 936, by one of its own generals, Shih Ching-t'ang, also of Turkish stock. Shih Ching-t'ang, although son-in-law of the next to the last Emperor of the Later T'ang, plotted against the line and called to his aid the Khitan. When, by their assistance, he overthrew his master and founded a new dynasty, the Hou Chin, or Later Chin, he paid them tribute and called their ruler the Father Emperor and himself the Child Emperor. Shih Ching-t'ang's son and successor attempted to throw off the suzerainty of the Khitan, but, instead, was carried into captivity.

The throne thus left vacant was occupied (947) by a general of the late dynasty, Liu Chih-yüan, also of Turkish descent, who forced the Khitan to retreat. His dynasty, the Hou Han, or Later Han, was even more short-lived than those of its three predecessors, for in 950 his son and successor was killed by the latter's own generals.

In 951 the commander of a victorious expedition against the Khitan was raised by his own soldiers to the throne and gave to his dynasty the name of Hou Chou, or Later Chou. An able general and administrator, he died (954) before he could bring peace to the distraught Empire. His successor, his adopted son, although an efficient ruler who added to the territory which he had inherited, did not conquer all China, and the minor who followed was powerless to do so.

Disorganized and anarchic though the first half of the tenth century was, the normal processes of peaceful life were by no means entirely suspended and some advance was registered. Much of the administrative machinery appears to have gone on but little disturbed by the rapid change of ruling houses. One statesman, for example, Fêng Tao, who described himself as the "ever gay old man," held high office under all but the first of the five dynasties. Printing by wooden blocks was further developed and gave a fresh impetus to scholarship. In the state of Shu, established in what is now Szechwan at the downfall of the T'ang by a general of that dynasty, the Classics were engraved in stone and set up in the capital, the present Chengtu, and at least part of them were printed by means of wooden blocks. In the East, under the ægis of several of the changing central dynasties, and under the inspiration of Fêng Tao, an imperial commission prepared a revised text of the Classics, and the completed edition, printed, was presented to the Emperor in 953. The way was further prepared for the remarkable painting of landscapes which so characterized the succeeding Sung dynasty.

THE FOUNDING OF THE SUNG DYNASTY

The welter of disorder was at last brought to an end by one Chao K'uang-yin. Chao K'uang-yin traced his descent through a line of T'ang officials and had risen to be the chief general of the Later Chou. He was proclaimed Emperor by his soldiers and proved able enough both to retain the title and, having pacified the Empire, to pass it on to his family. The dynasty was called Sung and Chao K'uang-yin was known to later generations as T'ai Tsu. With military skill T'ai Tsu combined magnanimity and political astuteness. Before his death, with the aid of some subordinates, he annexed several of the states into which China had been divided during the preceding short dynasties, including ones in Central China, Szechwan, South China, and around Nanking. Among these were Nan P'ing, in the present Hupeh, Ch'u, in the present Hunan, the Hou Shu, in the present Szechwan, Nan Han, in Kwangsi and Kwangtung, Wu Yüeh, in the present Chêkiang, Nan T'ang, with its center in what is now Nanking, and Min in Fukien. T'ai Tsu set up, as had other strong dynasties, a hierarchy of civil officials, substituting it for the military rule and semi-independent principalities which had been increasing since the rebellion of An Lu-shan under the T'ang. To bring about this change he induced his leading followers who had helped him obtain the throne to resign their military positions and compensated them with other rewards. Once more the Empire was highly centralized under an autocrat ruling through a bureaucracy. T'ai Tsu showed favors to Confucianism, the school through which the members of the civil service were trained. Education was fostered, presumably with something of the same purpose. Possibly to strengthen the imperial power—and perhaps as a gesture of clemency—T'ai Tsu decreed that all capital sentences were not to be left, as often heretofore, to the discretion of the provincial authorities, but must be passed on to the throne for review. A new criminal code was issued, based upon that of the T'ang, which, in its turn, had been influenced by that of the Sui. The country appears to have welcomed a hand strong enough to suppress the predatory armies and restore order.

Chao K'uang-yin's accomplishments during the thirteen years that he wore the imperial title were noteworthy, but when he died, in 976, the area which had owed allegiance to the T'ang, even within what is now China proper, did not all own his sway. In the Northeast the Khitan still held territory—in the present Hopei and Shansi—which was traditionally Chinese. In the present Shansi, with its capital at T'aiyüan, was a state called the Northern Han, set up by a half-brother of Liu Chih-yüan, the founder of the Hou Han. On the south coast Wu Yüeh, a principality with its capital at the present Hangchow, held out, and in the modern Yünnan Nan Chao maintained its autonomy. It became, therefore, the chief task of Chao K'uang-yin's successor, a younger brother, known to history as T'ai Tsung, to complete the unification of the Empire. This he only partially achieved. Wu Yüeh was annexed and the Northern Han eliminated. Attempts to oust the Khitan, however, failed. Some gains against them were registered, but reverses were also suffered. The two powers, the Sung and the Khitan, seemed about evenly matched. Nan Chao was not subdued, and a revolt for many years separated Annam from China.

THE EXTERNAL POLITICS OF THE SUNG TO 1127

The successors of T'ai Tsu and T'ai Tsung fell even farther short of clearing the Empire of alien rulers than had the founders of the dynasty. None of the line appears to have shown marked political ability. Several were dissipated weaklings and the best were amiable mediocrities, interested in literature and art, but not providing the type of leadership needed by an empire confronted with vigorous enemies. Divided counsels at court gave rise to vacillation in foreign policy. Sometimes offering effective military resistance under able generals, sometimes buying peace at humiliating terms, at others seeking to play off one enemy against another, the Sung Emperors often presented a sorry spectacle. Step by step their territories were wrested from them and eventually they lost their throne to foreign invaders.

For years the Khitan plagued them, especially as decline began to overtake the Sung. In the Northwest, moreover, a new menace arose. In the later years of the T'ang, a Tangut people, speaking a Tibeto-Burman language, had established a state called Hsi Hsia. They reached the acme of their power in the eleventh century, and one of the most vigorous of their rulers then assumed the title of Emperor. They were affected by Chinese culture, developing, among other things, a script which showed the influence of Chinese characters. Like the Khitan, they had no scruples against encroaching on the domains of the Sung, and their territories eventually included much of the Ordos country and of the present Kansu and some of the modern Shensi. Occasionally the Sung were aided against the Hsi Hsia by the Uighurs, still something of a power in the West, and at times, too, the Hsi Hsia and the Khitan were at war.

Although the fortunes of battle were not always against them, the Sung slowly lost ground. From time to time they were forced to sign agreements with the Khitan, promising them tribute and yielding them territory. The Sung capital, Pien Liang, the present K'aifêng, in Honan, was at least once in danger.

Early in the twelfth century relief seemed at hand. A Tungusic people, called by the Chinese Juchên (also Nüchên), first heard of in Manchuria, in the basin of the Sungari, and vassals of the Khitan, overthrew the latter, occupied their territory, including part of China proper, and their chief assumed the imperial title, calling his dynasty Chin, meaning Gold. At first the Sung welcomed the Juchên as allies and sent armies against the Khitan. They were speedily undeceived, however, for the new invaders proceeded to make humiliating demands of them. The Emperor Hui Tsung was a painter of note and a patron of the arts, but not a fit leader for his people in an emergency of this kind. Much of the control of the state and especially of the army centered in the hands of an ambitious eunuch, and eunuchs were ever a baleful influence. The nation was heavily taxed to maintain wars and an expensive and luxurious court. Discontent in the provinces and party struggles at court added to the general weakness.

Hui Tsung, discouraged by his impotence before the Juchên, abdicated in favor of a son (1125) and, on the approach of the Juchên, abandoned the capital and fled southward. The new Emperor bought off the invaders by a huge indemnity and the cession of territory. Soon, however, he violated the treaty, and the Juchên, returning to the attack, captured Pien Liang and, carrying into exile the reigning monarch and Hui Tsung and their families, appointed as Emperor one Chang Pang-ch'ang, a Chinese who had advocated submission to the invaders.

THE SOUTHERN SUNG DYNASTY (1127–1279)

The Chinese were not yet prepared to submit tamely to the dictates of foreigners and the House of Sung still retained the mandate of Heaven. A son of Hui Tsung, usually known to historians under his posthumous title Kao Tsung, escaped capture by the Juchên and was raised to the throne. This was done partly with the assistance of Chang Pang-ch'ang, who, deserting his Juchên masters, threw his support to the Sung and accepted office under the new régime. The Sung capital, after being moved from place to place, was eventually fixed at Lin-an, the present Hangchow. The dynasty after the break is known as the Southern Sung, in distinction from the Northern Sung, its designation before the southern migration. Lin-an was made over into a beautiful and wealthy metropolis. Marco Polo, who saw it after the fall of the Sung, described it as "beyond dispute, the finest and noblest [city] in the world."

The change of capitals did not mean peace with the Juchên. The Sung were unwilling to relinquish the territory north of the Yangtze and for a time the Juchên seemed bent on annexing the whole of the Empire. The result was prolonged war. Moreover, rebellion broke out in various parts of the Sung domains, and in the North, with the permission of the Juchên, one Liu Yü, who had been an official under the Sung, set himself up as Emperor.

Kao Tsung reigned for about thirty-five years, but he interested himself more in the pleasures of his court than in the camp. The struggle against the Juchên, however, was manfully carried on by his generals, the most famous of whom was the brave and loyal Yo Fei. Early in the reign of Kao Tsung the Juchên crossed the Yangtze and took several cities. They found it impossible to maintain themselves south of the great river and soon recrossed it. It may have been that they deemed the conquest of the South impracticable or undesirable. It is certain that they were pressed from two sides—by the Sung armies from the south and by enemies in their rear on the north. For a time they even lost part of the North China plain. Liu Yü, failing of support by the Juchên and badly defeated, was forced to abandon his imperial aspirations.

Even had the Sung pursued their apparent advantage, the North could probably not have been permanently rewon. The Chin were too strongly entrenched to be driven out and from the military standpoint usually had the superiority. It may have been from recognition of this fact that peace policies prevailed at the Sung court. The minister Ch'in Kuei—ever since regarded with scorn by patriotic Chinese—obtained the imprisonment and execution of Yo Fei, who had been markedly successful and would have pushed the battle against the invaders. Kao Tsung agreed to cede to the Juchên a large part of the former Sung domains in the North, making the Huai River the boundary between the two states, and promised the Juchên an annual tribute. Most of what is now Shensi and Honan, all of the modern Shansi, Hopei, and Shantung, and parts of the present Anhui and Kiangsu were, therefore, left in the possession of the Chin (Juchên).

The second quarter of the twelfth century saw the Chin at the pinnacle of their power. They were the acknowledged masters of North China and Manchuria, they had subdued the Hsi Hsia, and they had received the submission of the Uighurs. Their dominions stretched from the borders of the present Korea into and perhaps beyond what is now the western part of Kansu. About 1153 they moved their capital from the present Manchuria to Yenching (later Peking and now Peiping).

The peace between the Chin and the Sung proved unstable. In 1161, for example, the Chin attempted, although in vain, to force their way across the Yangtze, and in 1206 the Sung essayed, but also failed, to reduce the North. The two monarchies seemed about equally matched, and neither appeared likely to alter greatly the boundary between them. However, the Sung Emperors had to accept a kind of subordination to the Chin rulers, being as "nephews" to "uncles," and gave to the latter a large annual present.

Although the Sung abandoned the North, the Chinese people and their culture did not do so. Some infusion of non-Chinese blood in this region undoubtedly occurred, but again, as so often in the past, the vigorous but rude conquerors were being assimilated. The Chin rulers attempted to preserve the distinctive customs of their people, but they had the Chinese Classics translated into the Juchên language and maintained sacrifices to Confucius, and the Hsi Hsia rulers were also adopting Confucianism. The cultural reconquest of the North had quietly begun.

THE MONGOL INVASION AND THE END OF THE CHIN AND THE SUNG

About the time that relations between the Sung and the Chin had settled down to a kind of uneasy stalemate and the Juchên conquerors had begun, perhaps unconsciously, to face the likelihood of elimination by absorption, the scene was completely changed by a fresh invasion from the North. A new power suddenly arose which overthrew both the Chin and the Sung and set up what for a brief century or more was the most extensive empire yet created by man.

The authors of this new realm were the Mongols. The Mongols were related linguistically, and possibly racially, to the Turkish and the Tungusic peoples of whom we have seen so much in the preceding pages. At the beginning of the twelfth century most of them were living, divided into many tribes, to the south and east of Lake Baikal, on the borders of what are now Outer Mongolia, Siberia, and Manchuria. Originally of little consequence politically, they were welded into a formidable fighting force by Temuchin. Temuchin was born about 1155 or 1156, the son of a chief of a kind of confederation of some of the Mongol tribes. After his father's death, Temuchin had to fight his way to the headship of the confederation. This he did with ruthlessness and success. It was a rude age and region in which he lived and he who would survive in the struggle for existence must act vigorously and without too many scruples.

Under Temuchin's skillful and vigorous leadership, the confederation was extended to include more of the Mongol tribes. In his late forties, Temuchin felt himself strong enough to attack his overlords, the Keraïts, a Turkish people who had recently become Nestorian Christians and the outstanding power in Mongolia. The head of the Keraïts, it is interesting to note, was possibly the original of the Prester John who so appealed to the imagination of many Europeans of the Middle Ages. The conquest of the Naiman, in what at present is the northeastern part of Mongolia, followed the defeat of the Keraïts. Temuchin was now master of Mongolia and in 1206 was greeted by his people as Jenghiz Khan, the "Universal Emperor" of the Turco-Mongol peoples. He had, of course, to face some trouble from unsubmissive princes, but this he succeeded in suppressing. The capital of the new empire was at Karakorum, in the general region of the modern Urga. Jenghiz Khan's domains were soon augmented by the voluntary recognition of his suzerainty by the Uighurs and by the Karluks, both in what is now the New Dominion.

Having brought together the peoples of Mongolia and, in part, of the New Dominion, Jenghiz Khan now did as so many of the rulers of the preceding great, ephemeral empires of that region had done, and turned his attention to the populous and prosperous land to the south. He first attacked the Hsi Hsia, and after several campaigns (1205, 1207, and 1209) obtained their submission. The state was not immediately erased. It was not until 1227 that the last of its ruling princes was killed by the Mongols. The Chin, or Juchên, naturally were also attacked. The present Shansi and Hopei were invaded in 1211 and Yenching (now Peiping), the Chin capital, fell in 1215. The Chin offered stubborn resistance and moved their capital to the present K'aifêng. In 1219 Korea became vassal to the Mongols, and by 1223 the Chin had lost nearly all of their former domains except approximately those south of the Yellow River. Pressed on the one side by the Sung and on the other by the Mongols, they were in a sad plight.

The Chin gained a short and uneasy reprieve by the diversion of the conqueror's attention elsewhere. Through developments the details of which need not here concern us, even before 1223 Jenghiz Khan left the campaign against the Chin to be pressed by his lieutenants and directed his own energies against states in the West. Within a short time the remainder of what is now the New Dominion was annexed and the victorious Mongol arms were carried into the valleys of the Oxus and Jaxartes, to the banks of the Indus, into Persia, and even into the southeastern portions of Europe. Jenghiz Khan did not forget China, however, and died (1227) while directing the campaign which eventually wiped the Hsi Hsia from the map.

The onward sweep of the Mongol armies was not halted by the death of the "Universal Emperor." The vast domains of Jenghiz Khan were divided among his four heirs—the son of his deceased eldest son and his three other sons. This did not mean the break-up of the empire, however, for in 1229 an assemblage of Mongol chiefs chose Ogodai, Jenghiz Khan's third son, Grand Khan, for the head of the whole. Ogodai pressed the Mongol advance into China against the Chin. The Chin fought with desperation, but the Mongol armies closed in on them. The Sung, lured by the promise of some of the Chin territory, accepted the Mongol offer of an alliance and joined, probably not unwillingly, in the attack against their old enemies. What is now K'aifêng fell after a long siege (1233) and in 1234 the Chin line of rulers came to an end with the suicide of one and the killing of another.

The victorious Mongols could scarcely be expected to keep the peace with the effete Sung. The latter were not given all the portion of the former Chin possessions which they alleged had been promised them. They were naturally aggrieved and proceeded to seize some of the land which they claimed. This gave the Mongols the excuse for the inevitable attack. The Sung domains, however, were not easily taken. The Mongols made gains, especially in the present Szechwan, but the bulk of the Sung territory, south of the barrier offered by the Yangtze, long remained inviolate.

The Mongols meanwhile extended their power in other directions. Korea was further reduced to subjection, and the Mongol arms carried terror into the West, as far as Mesopotamia, Georgia, and Armenia in Southwestern Asia, and into Hungary and Poland in Europe.

Following the death of Ogodai (1241), for ten years a weak or divided leadership gave pause to the Mongol advance. With the accession of Mangu, a grandson of Jenghiz Khan, to the Grand Khanate (1251), the boundaries of the empire again expanded. In the West, Mangu's brother Hulagu captured Bagdad and administered the death blow to the Abbasid Caliphate, and Aleppo and Damascus were taken. In China, from the vantage point of Szechwan, for over ten years a part of the Mongol domains, an attack was launched by Mangu and another of his brothers, Khubilai, against the state of Nan Chao, in what is now Yünnan. Nan Chao was defeated and annexed (1253). From it a Mongol army penetrated to Tongking and thence northward into Kwangsi and Hunan. Its purpose was to join forces with another army, which, under Khubilai, had crossed the Yangtze and was besieging Wuchang. The death of Mangu, in Szechwan, in 1259, halted the campaign, and, confronted with the probability of a struggle for the succession to the Khanate, Khubilai hastily arranged a treaty with the Sung—by which the latter agreed to acknowledge the Mongols as their overlords and to pay them tribute—and repaired north to press his claims to the throne.

Khubilai was soon declared Grand Khan by his army in North China, but one of his brothers was also given the title by a faction, and at the old Mongol capital, Karakorum. Not until 1264 was this brother defeated and made captive, and not until some time later was Khubilai ready to resume with vigor the conquest of China.

Meanwhile the Sung authorities had treated with contumely the Mongol representative sent to announce the accession of Khubilai and so had given ample provocation for the renewal of hostilities. The Sung court was under the domination of the minister Chia Ssŭ-tao. He it was who had arranged the humiliating peace with the Mongols in 1259 and he was quite unable to meet the revived menace.

In spite of all the folly and feebleness of the Sung, the Mongol conquest was not quickly completed. The most famous episode was the five-year siege (1268–1273) of the cities of Hsiangyang and Fanch'êng, on opposite sides of the Han River, in the present Hupeh. Commanding the water approach to Central China, they occupied an important strategic site which at least once before had figured prominently in struggles for the mastery of China. After a gallant resistance the two cities were at last reduced, the Mongol forces penetrated to the Yangtze and, slowly making their victorious way eastward, closed in on the Sung capital, the present Hangchow. This was taken in 1276, and the infant Emperor was captured and sent north. Some of the Sung statesmen and generals, refusing to acknowledge the inevitable, declared Emperor another infant scion of the house of Sung, took refuge in the fleet, and, fleeing south, made Canton their headquarters. Canton fell in 1277 and the luckless boy ruler, a fugitive, died the following year. A remnant continued to hold out and, placing another child on the phantom throne, defended themselves in the fleet off the coast of Kwangtung. Here, in 1279, they were overwhelmed by the Mongols, and the Sung commander, bidding his wife and children throw themselves into the sea, took the young Emperor on his back and did likewise. The Sung had come to its end. For the first time in recorded history, all China was in the hands of non-Chinese conquerors. The Mongol Khubilai, from Cambaluc (Khanbaligh)—the present Peiping—which he had set up on and near the site of one of the late capitals of the Chin, was Emperor of a new dynasty, the Yüan.

The question naturally arises as to the reasons for the Mongol success. How did it happen that this people, at the outset barbarous and divided, conquered, in less than a hundred years, most of what is now China, much of Southwestern and Central Asia, and part of Europe, and established the most extensive empire that the world had yet seen?

One reason was the weakness of some of their opponents. In spite of the support of a few brave and able generals, the Sung Emperors were incompetent and could not give their people strong leadership. Both the Sung and the Chin had suffered from their long and indecisive wars with each other.

In the West the Abbasid Caliphs were a decaying power. The lack of vigor on the part of opponents does not account for it all, however, for some of the Mongols' victims put up a very able resistance. Thorough-going ruthlessness may also in part be responsible for the victories. The Mongols slaughtered almost the entire population of whole cities and provinces. This was not, apparently, simply from the lust of killing but from deliberate policy, perhaps to inspire terror, possibly as a simple but effective means of preventing insurrection. In the later stages of the conquest of China, the Mongols showed more clemency, perhaps because of a tendency to adopt civilized manners or because the attempt to exterminate any large proportion of the Chinese would have aroused such bitter opposition as to have defeated its own ends. Again the chief factor in the Mongol success does not seem to have lain here.

It appears, rather, to have been able leadership. Jenghiz Khan was an excellent tactician and a severe disciplinarian. He chose many of his generals from a comparatively small corps which underwent a most exacting training. He seems also to have been an excellent judge of men. Moreover, his armies were noted for their mobility and their quick blows. The Mongols owed much to their cavalry: they equipped their horsemen with plenty of mounts and were able to move swiftly and to strike with surprising quickness. Jenghiz Khan and his successors seem to have been eager to take advantage of all the latest technique and machinery in military operations, learning wherever and from whomever they could. For example, Moslems and even a German engineer were employed in constructing siege machinery in the beleaguerment of Hsiangyang.

Then, too, the Mongols appear to have shown some skill in

managing subject races. Religiously they were tolerant. They availed themselves of the services of other peoples and were willing to learn from them. Some of their foremost ministers were foreigners. For instance, Yeh-lü Ch'u-ts'ai, a sinicized Khitan, who had held offices under the Chin, served prominently under both Jenghiz Khan and Ogodai, and Uighurs were given high positions. Under the guidance of non-Mongol counsellors, the Mongols made advances in civilization and administration. They took over, with modifications, the Uighur alphabet. Some of their youth were put to school to study the Confucian classics, and the beginnings of a civil administrative system showed Chinese influence.

It was an enormously difficult, and, as it proved, an impossible task to hold together for long the vast empire which had been so quickly acquired, but in conquering it the Mongols displayed marked ability and energy, and the greatest of them were not without astuteness in governing it.

CULTURE UNDER THE SUNG: THE SOUTHWARD MIGRATION OF THE CHINESE

As was said at the outset of this chapter, in spite of its political divisions, and, as compared with the Han or the T'ang dynasties, its political weakness, the China of the Sung witnessed the geographic expansion of its culture, striking prosperity, and marked activity in thought and art.

The barbarian invasions of the North and the southward migration of the dynasty were far from meaning that either the Chinese people or their institutions were overwhelmed. Some infiltration of non-Chinese blood undoubtedly took place, for the conquerors, in addition to forming much of the ruling class, settled on the land, possibly in fairly large numbers, and the inevitable intermarriage modified the character of the population. How large the alien element was we do not know, but the older Chinese stock probably still predominated, and the newcomers tended to take on Chinese civilization.

The frequent fighting in the North between the Sung and the invaders also gave a decided impetus to the southward movement of the Chinese and made the Yangtze Valley and the south coast loom more prominently than heretofore in all phases of the Empire's activities. For example, of the many theories advanced to account for the origin of the Hakkas, that distinct group of Chinese in Kwangsi, Kwangtung, Kiangsi, and Fukien, one of the more credible declares that during this period they came from the region south of the Yellow River. Certainly other evidence points to population movements from north to south during the Sung and to an increase in the number of walled cities south of the Yangtze. It is significant that some of the greatest figures of the dynasty, notably Wang An-shih and Chu Hsi, were born south of the great river, the one in the present Kiangsi and the other in the present Fukien. Never before had so much of the leadership of the Empire come from natives of that region.

FOREIGN COMMERCE UNDER THE SUNG

With so much of the North in the hands of aliens and with the southward shift of the center of Chinese population and culture, it is not strange that there was much foreign commerce from the ports on the south coast. This had suffered, it will be recalled, in the disorders at the close of the T'ang. Under the Sung it revived and seems to have attained larger proportions than ever before. Navigation was aided by the employment of the compass for sailing and improvement in ship-building. The Chinese now, for the first time, controlled the sea routes to the southeast and India. What is now Ch'üanchow (known to Medieval Europe as Zaitun) in Fukien and Canton (known in some foreign writings of the time as Khanfu, although the identification of Khanfu with Canton is not universally accepted by sinologists) were usually the chief centers of this trade. Canton at first had most of it, but Ch'üanchow presently became a formidable rival and eventually was predominant. For a time the Sung continued the T'ang practice of placing the control of shipping and trade under one officer and his subordinates. Later special functionaries for this purpose were appointed. Commerce in some commodities was a government monopoly, open only to licensed vendors, who obtained their goods at state warehouses. The state derived a valuable revenue from an *ad valorem* tax on the trade. Early in the Sung an imperial embassy was sent abroad to encourage foreign merchants to come to China and special licenses were promised them.

The Sung was comparatively mild in its treatment of foreign

merchants in its ports. Not only did it continue the T'ang custom of allowing them to settle many of their disputes among themselves, but it permitted them to decide according to their own laws all but the more serious offenses of foreigners against Chinese. The foreign merchants seem mostly to have been Moslem Arabs. Many of them married Chinese women and at least one man of Arabic origin held high office under the Sung and at the close of the dynasty went over to the Mongols. A colony of Jews which has been finally absorbed into the surrounding population only in our own day built a synagogue at K'aifêng.

Trade with Japan flourished. Japanese Buddhist monks, principally of the Zen (Ch'an) sect, journeyed to China to visit the strongholds of their school. Chinese monks, coming to Japan, were often given high positions in monasteries and were transmitters, not only of Buddhism, but of Chinese civilization in general, including the Confucian Classics and secular literature. Sung Neo-Confucianism was to have a marked effect in the islands. Official intercourse between the two governments, however, appears not to have been established.

The Chinese records assert that tribute-bearing embassies arrived in the Sung court from Champa, in the present French Indo-China, from states in such distant regions as Java and Sumatra, and even from India. Whether these embassies indicate the recognition of China's suzerainty is highly doubtful, but they probably show that these principalities deemed commercial relations profitable. Before the dynasty was driven south, moreover, two embassies came from Fulin, or, as it will be recalled, what we now call the Near East.

The Chinese knowledge of geography was expanding, and a work of the time shows that some information concerning even such distant countries as Egypt and Sicily had reached the Middle Kingdom. This was brought not only by foreign merchants but also by Chinese who went abroad and returned with news of distant lands. Chinese sailing craft were improving: some of the vessels accommodated several hundred persons as passengers or crew.

The articles of trade included, as heretofore, only those which combined small bulk with large value—among them piece-goods, lead, gold, silver, porcelain-ware, incense and scented woods, drugs, ivory, coral, rhinoceros horns, amber, ebony, pearls, tortoise-shell, rare woods, and rock crystal.

The Sung faced an adverse balance of trade. Gold, silver, and especially Chinese copper coin were exported in such quantities that the government, although without success, tried to stop the precious metals from disappearing by forbidding the use of the luxuries to which the drainage was attributed. The extent of this outward flow of specie is shown by the fact that Sung coins have been unearthed in Java, Singapore, and even in Zanzibar and on the Somali coast in Africa, and that their circulation in Japan proved an embarrassment to the government of that country. To the resulting dearth of coin in China is ascribed, possibly in part correctly, the resort to paper money which was one of the outstanding features of the fiscal policy of the Sung. The evils attendant upon inflation were felt to the full, but the temptation to use the device proved too strong to be resisted.

Whether because of this contact with aliens or for other reasons, innovations were seen. The use of chairs became general. Tea was a common drink in both South and North. Sedan chairs were widely employed.

CULTURE UNDER THE SUNG: THE REFORMS OF WANG AN-SHIH

Marked though foreign commerce was, we have no indication that ideas coming from abroad through it profoundly influenced either Chinese thought or life. Nor did the occupation of so much of the North by non-Chinese peoples seem to work any great transformation in Chinese culture. Chinese Buddhist pilgrims still went to India by the overland routes and continued to do so until, about the middle of the eleventh century, the spread of Islam closed the roads to them. They seem, however, to have had no such effect on Chinese life as did their predecessors of pre-T'ang and T'ang times. Moreover, while the Mongol conquests were in progress, and before they finally overwhelmed the Sung, Chinese and more or less sinicized non-Chinese of North China travelled westward, sometimes as officials or envoys for the Mongols. They reached the valley of the Oxus and saw such cities as Samarkand and Balkh. At least one of them brought back reports of Bagdad and Egypt. It seems improbable, however, that the new ideas with which they came into contact made any very pronounced impression upon the Chinese at home. Such innovations as they brought probably affected chiefly the China of the North, and the North was so distinct from the Yangtze Valley, where centered so much of the cultural life under the Sung, that European travellers of the thirteenth and fourteenth centuries regarded it as a separate country.

However, the Sung period marks the opening of a new intellectual era. The general level of education was probably rising. The thought-forms to which most of the educated class assented down to the opening of the twentieth century were shaped. These patterns achieved their preeminence only out of controversy. The debates that marked the course of the dynasty, especially before the transfer of the Sung capital to Lin-an (Hangchow), probably stirred the thinking portion of the nation as profoundly as any that China had ever known, certainly more than at any time since the Chou.

The most acrimonious of the controversies, the one that influenced most of the others, centered around the political, economic, and educational program instituted by Wang An-shih. Wang was born in 1021 and died in 1086, and his lifetime therefore spanned some of the most vigorous years of the dynasty. His reforms contemplated a thorough-going reorganization of the fiscal and military policy of the state and were accompanied by important modifications in agriculture and internal commerce. The purpose back of them seems to have been to increase the prosperity of the masses and to strengthen the Empire in its struggle against the northern invaders.

Wang An-shih was born into the official-scholar class and passed successfully through the usual examination system prescribed for those who aspired to public office. He made no attempt to revolt against the authority of the Confucian Classics, but professed to find in these revered works the sanction for his proposals. The main features of his system included (1) the appointment of a commission to draft a budget for the state, a means of effecting a large annual saving in expenses; (2) a state monopoly of commerce, by which Wang would have the produce of each district used first for the payment of taxes and then for the needs of the district, the surplus to be purchased by the government and held either against future local needs, or to be transported elsewhere and sold, and depots to be set up for the exchange of goods and for advancing loans on merchandise and property (by this means Wang hoped to insure to the cultivators a more certain market for their produce and increase the revenue of the government); (3) loans by the state at two per cent. a month to farmers in the planting season on the security of growing crops, a device for promoting agriculture by enabling the farmer to plant and harvest his crop without falling into the clutches of the private money lender with his usurious rates of interest, but which incurred much criticism from the fact that as they were administered by some officials such loans were often compulsory on all, the rich as well as the poor; (4) the division of the land into equal sections and the annual reappraisal of it for purposes of taxation, thus to avoid the exemption of some of the cultivated soil from taxation and to insure a more equitable distribution of the land tax; (5) the taxation of all a man's property, both real estate and movable; (6) the abolition of the conscription of labor by the state (a long-used form of taxation which probably bore very heavily on the poor and which, because it might be levied at times which most interfered with the peasant's agricultural operations, was almost certainly a handicap to farming) and the substitution for it of a graduated tax based upon the division of property-holders into five groups according to their wealth; (7) military reorganization, by which unnecessary troops were to be returned to civilian and productive life, and external defense and internal order were to be maintained by a system of compulsory military service, families being organized into groups of tens and fifties and each family with more than one male providing one for the frontier forces and for the local police; (8) a method of supporting the cavalry needed in the wars against the northern invaders by requiring each family in certain areas to keep a horse, which, with its food, was to be supplied by the state; and (9) shifting the emphasis in the state examinations from literary style to the application of the principles of the Classics to current problems—a change designed to fit the successful competitors more directly for the fulfilment of official duties.

Few if any of these policies were entirely new. Whether Wang An-shih was aware of it or not, in part they were not unlike in principle the programs of the famous Legalists, Li K'uei and Wei

Yang—the latter of whom had done so much to give the state of Ch'in the organization which had enabled it to seize the Empire—and they bore some resemblance to suggestions of a Han dynasty statesman and to the reforms of Wang Mang and his assistants. For some of them precedent could have been claimed in long established practice. Wang An-shih professed to base his plan upon the principles of ancient sages honored by the Confucian school and prepared commentaries on some of the classical books which attempted to show that these latter sanctioned it. He made much of the *Chou Li*, that idealistic political program which dated from the late Chou or the Han.

However, Wang's schemes were revolutionary. They involved an enhanced paternalism on the part of the state, the assumption by the government of much larger responsibilities than under the earlier years of the Sung, and deprivations for the wealthy. They constituted what in the modern Occident would be called a kind of state socialism. They were, moreover, sufficiently radical to bring down on the heads of their proponents the vigorous denunciations of conservative scholars and statesmen. These contended for the earlier policies of the dynasty which favored more *laissez faire* and the Confucian theory of the rule of the prince by good example rather than by force.

In proposing his reforms Wang An-shih seems to have been entirely sincere and public-spirited. Frugal in his private life even to the neglect of care for his own person, having the welfare of the common people passionately at heart, serenely confident in the righteousness of his cause and in the wisdom of his program, and an ardent advocate by word and pen, he belongs to a type familiar in many ages and countries.

Wang rose to high office and for a time the Emperor gave him free rein. He had a few loyal and intelligent lieutenants, but the majority of the scholars of repute, among them many really distinguished names, notably an early patron who later turned against him—Ou-yang Hsiu (1007–1072)—would have none of him and vehemently argued against him. The opposition is generally known as the Yüan Yu party, but it did not enjoy internal harmony and in turn was divided into several factions. The debate continued through most of the last four reigns of the Northern Sung and echoes of it were heard after the southward migration of the dynasty. Emperors gave their support first to one and then to the other group: the program of Wang An-shih was adopted in whole or in part for a few months or years only to be abandoned and then, in turn, to be tried again. After the death of Wang, and toward the close of the Northern Sung, the most influential advocate of the reforms was Ts'ai Ching, a brother of Wang's son-in-law. Apparently Ts'ai Ching did not have the high-minded unselfishness of Wang An-shih, but used the latter's policies to further his own ambitions and when in power displayed a lamentable vindictiveness toward his enemies. For example, he pilloried the names of his opponents by engraving them on stone at the capital. Ts'ai Ching was chief minister when the Northern Sung came to its disastrous close and has been regarded as responsible for the sad fate of his imperial masters. It may be, however, that his reputation suffers unduly through histories written by his opponents.

Eventually Wang's program was abandoned, but some of its less novel features, in modified form, were adopted for longer or shorter periods down almost to our own day. The failure of the plan to win permanent acceptance was probably due to the absence of a sufficient body of intelligent, enthusiastic, and unselfish officials to make it effective, to the venality and self-seeking of some of its advocates, and to the opposition of many of the scholar class. This is another way of saying that the system involved too sudden and sweeping a change in the existing *mores*. The fact that it had been proposed and had been so seriously tried, however, is, when considered together with the many utopian schemes of the Chou dynasty and the suggestions of later reformers, especially of Wang Mang, significant evidence of the political and social mindedness of the Chinese and of a recurrent tendency—even though usually submerged by conservatism—toward radical experimentation in statecraft and economics. The dissension accompanying it contributed to the weakness of the Northern Sung, and to it must therefore be assigned a part of the responsibility for the misfortunes of the dynasty.

CULTURE UNDER THE SUNG: THE NEO-CONFUCIAN SCHOOL

Wang An-shih and the debate over his proposals formed only one feature of that marked intellectual ferment which gave to the

Sung one of its most distinctive characteristics and in which rests one of its chief claims to remembrance.

The other outstanding phase of this activity was a fresh interpretation of Confucianism which for more than six centuries constituted the orthodox philosophy of the scholar class and which during most of that time had the support of the state through the established system of education and examinations.

The examinations, it may be noted in passing, were further developed. Whereas even under the T'ang it had been possible to gain admission to the lower ranks of the bureaucracy without meeting the state literary tests, the Sung made the procedure more strict, increased the number of successful candidates, and rendered very difficult entrance to the civil service by any other route.

The Neo-Confucianism developed under the Sung claimed, like the reforms of Wang An-shih, to be based upon the Classics of the Confucian school but displayed some features which probably would not have been recognized by the authors of these documents. It was really a synthesis of Buddhism, Taoism, and Confucianism, in which Confucianism predominated. Buddhism as a separate cult was declining: there was not nearly such intellectual activity within its monasteries as in the T'ang and the centuries immediately before the T'ang. It was still sufficiently strong, however, to make itself felt in the reviving Confucianism. To put it in another way, Sung Neo-Confucianism was Confucianism thought through afresh under the influence of Buddhism and Taoism. It was an attempt to put into orderly form what the educated believed about the universe—to integrate into a consistent whole the philosophies of the age. As, not far from the same time, the schoolmen of Europe were building a cosmogony and a cosmology which claimed to be Christian but which were shaped by the Aristotelean tradition, and as out of them came the work of St. Thomas Aquinas which gave to the theology of the Roman Catholic Church what proved to be its official expression, so under the Sung Chinese thinkers, stimulated by Buddhist and Taoist thought, remolded Confucianism into the form which was long to remain standard, and the recognized master was to be Chu Hsi.

The stream of thought that culminated in Chu Hsi had its

springs at least as early as the T'ang. To it many Sung writers contributed. To give even the names of them all would burden this narrative overmuch with details. The most prominent, however, must be mentioned. Shao Yung (1011–1077) was a forerunner. He persistently declined to accept public office, preferring to live in poverty and have leisure for thought. However, many sought his counsel, among them some of the most prominent leaders of the anti-Wang An-shih group, and his writings had a marked influence. He made a special study of the *I Ching*. He was a mystic, much of whose thinking had a Taoist origin. Chou Tun-i (1017–1073), a native of the present Hunan, is the next of the chief contributors. Through most of his mature life he held office, and usually his literary pursuits had to be carried on in intervals snatched from administrative and judicial duties. Although reckoned as in the stream of Confucian tradition, he was influenced by both Taoism and Buddhism. Chou Tun-i was for a time the teacher of the next two important members of the school, Ch'êng Hao (whose years were 1032–1085 and who is also known as Ch'êng Ming-tao) and Ch'êng I (whose years were 1033–1107 and who is also known as Ch'êng I-ch'uan), and for him they had the greatest respect. The sons of an official of sturdy, independent character, an opponent of Wang An-shih, they shared their father's political views. Both also continued the family tradition by holding office, but the younger spent much of his time in retirement and study. They wrote voluminously, chiefly essays and letters, and Ch'êng I, with his longer life and greater freedom from official cares, thought through a philosophy more fully than did his brother. An uncle of the two Ch'êngs, Chang Tsai (1020–1076), by his teaching and writings aided the growth of the school.

Chu Hsi (1130–1200) was younger than any of the preceding, and, in consequence, was able to take advantage of their labors. The son of an official, the service of the state claimed most of his adult years and he seems to have performed his duties with fidelity and ability. By disposition, however, he was more the scholar than the administrator and had intervals of retirement, some of them voluntary and with sinecure positions which gave him leisure for study, but at least one of them due to the opposition of enemies at court. During one period of his life he was greatly impressed with Taoism and Buddhism, and while he later turned to what he deemed the classical Confucian tradition, he never escaped from the influence of these faiths. His was an intellect which delighted in synthesis and he was gifted both with clarity of thought and with an admirable literary style. Through his mind passed the ideas of the predecessors of the school to which he eventually gave himself, and adding to them and giving to the whole the interpretation and integration which were the fruits of his own genius he left behind him that system of thought which for centuries was to dominate the majority of the scholars of his race. In the entire history of mankind, few thinkers have been so influential as he.

To summarize accurately and in a few words the tenets to which Chu Hsi gave their standard form is a difficult undertaking, particularly since to the Occidental mind many of his concepts seem strange.

As we have said, the school was partly shaped by Buddhism, and especially by the Ch'an sect, which was so highly esteemed among the educated of the time. Ch'an declared that true insight and knowledge come through inner enlightenment. To be sure, Buddhism was declining. Its decay, which seems to have begun under the T'ang, may have been hastened by the policies of the financially embarrassed Sung. At least occasionally the state sold ranks and titles of temples and priests. Then, too, some of the rich entered the priesthood to escape the burdens of taxation and military duty. At times monks were accused of usury. All this contributed to the popular disdain of the faith. However, Buddhism was still a potent factor in the Empire and could not be disregarded by the educated.

Taoism, too, contributed markedly to Neo-Confucianism, and especially to Chu Hsi. Chu Hsi's writings contain a good deal of Neo-Taoist metaphysics.

Many of the Sung Confucianists showed the effects of their Buddhist environment by practising meditation. This they did from an ethical and spiritual motive—to cultivate the nobler and to eliminate the baser side of their natures. The better to succeed, they often retired to quiet and beautiful spots, sometimes alone, at other times collectively—pupils clustering about some revered teacher. These groups of students around their teachers, somewhat apart from the world, a kind of school, and somewhat akin to Buddhist monasteries (although they were not made up of celibates), apparently were fairly numerous and the stimulus given by them may in part account for the intellectual activity of the time. The Neo-Confucianists could, if they chose, plead precedent in the example of their Confucian predecessors, for one of the most important of the immediate disciples of Confucius had declared that he daily examined his actions and his thoughts to see whether they were correct and upright, and Confucius and some of his successors were surrounded by admiring pupils in a more or less informal fellowship. The emphasis on these features by the Sung philosophers, however, seems to have been due chiefly to Buddhism. It may also have been stimulated by the forcible retirement of members of the school from public office at the intervals when Wang An-shih's adherents were in power.

Negatively, many of the Sung thinkers revealed their Ch'an background by reacting against it. The Ch'an Buddhist held knowledge to be intuitive—derived by purely subjective processes. He offered no way of verifying the information obtained in this fashion and could not tell whether it corresponded with outward reality. He tended to believe that the only reality is mind. Neo-Confucianists opposed to this a Taoist conception of a universal reason, of which both external nature and ourselves are a part. This would exalt reason, and although numbers of Sung Neo-Confucianists held to the sudden enlightenment of the Ch'an, many had a philosophy arrived at by rational rather than intuitive processes. They believed that by looking within we understand the rest of the universe, and that we can correct the information so obtained by an investigation of the world outside ourselves. This investigation of the external world was justified in part by reference to a passage in the *Ta Hsüeh* ("Great—or Higher—Learning"), a small treatise of the Confucian school of the Chou dynasty which had been imbedded in the *Li Chi* and to which the Neo-Confucianists gave especial study and honor. This passage declared that the ancients had discovered that all ordered government, proper social organization, and ideal human conduct depend ultimately on the extension of knowledge, and that this, in turn, is to be achieved by the "investigation of things." Chu Hsi especially made much of the "investigation of things," and while he did not completely discard the sudden enlightenment of the Ch'an, he held that to be effective as the road to truth it must be preceded by long and profound study of all things under heaven. It should be noted that this "investigation of things," which on the surface seems closely akin to the modern scientific methods of the West, was in practice largely confined by the Sung scholars and their successors to things of the mind and to the ethics found in the Classics of the Confucian school. Neo-Confucian philosophy was largely subjective.

Associated with this process of arriving at knowledge were a cosmology and cosmogony. For their ultimate formulation, Chu Hsi, by temperament peculiarly fitted for synthesis and clarity of statement, was chiefly responsible.

Chu Hsi regarded the universe as a dualism—as having in it two elements or principles—but these, he believed, are so inseparably associated as to make a unity, a "universe." The two are *li* and *ch'i*, which can roughly, but by no means exactly, be translated as "law" and "matter." *Li* contains the ethical phases of the universe. *Ch'i* is also translated as ether: if it is to be regarded as matter, it must be more nearly in terms of matter conceived, as present-day Western physics tends to describe it, as force. In contrast with *li* it is the material element in all its myriad forms. Chronologically speaking, neither *li* nor *ch'i* is prior to the other, although, when pressed, Chu Hsi seemed, guardedly, to give to *li* a kind of precedence.

Chu Hsi was true to Confucius in that he made much of a high standard of morals. He held that morality in man is the expression of the *li* which is so basic in the universe—that it is of the very warp and woof of reality.

Chu Hsi also, like at least some others of his school, spoke of the *t'ai chi*, translated as the "great ultimate" or "great extreme," and also as the absolute, or the infinite. This term is found in one passage in the ancient *I Ching*, to which the school, as we have seen, probably following a Taoist suggestion, paid much attention. The *t'ai chi* was both *li* and *ch'i*. The *t'ai chi* in turn produced the *yin* and the *yang*, terms which since the Chou had been familiar to Chinese thinkers as expressing a kind of dualism—inertia and energy, darkness and light, female and male. Through the interaction of the *yin* and the *yang* sprang the five elements of which the Chinese believed the physical world to be composed —fire, water, earth, wood, and metal.

In spite of his power of synthesis and his beauty of literary style, Chu Hsi's conceptions present great difficulty to Western students, and marked differences of opinion exist as to their meaning. Western and Chinese categories differ so greatly that it is next to impossible to transfer the one into the other and easy-going parallelisms are misleading. Occidental scholars have been divided over the significance of Chu Hsi's philosophy for theistic belief. Some maintain that he tended toward materialism, or at least toward a depersonalizing of the ancient Chinese conception of *T'ien*. Others declare that Chu Hsi gave to *li* the moral values of personality and that, while eliminating all physical anthropomorphism from his portrayal of *T'ien*, he held views which leaned essentially toward theism. Whatever may have been Chu Hsi's personal beliefs, the effect of his teaching seems to have been to strengthen the agnostic tendencies in Confucianism. If he ascribed to *T'ien* personal qualities, it was in such abstract terms that for the great rank and file, even of the scholars, it became little better than impersonal law.

This Neo-Confucianism, it must be noted, was in several respects a departure from the views of the sage whose memory it professed to revere. Its withdrawal from the world for purposes of meditation, its views about sudden enlightenment, and its attempts to tell how the world came to be were all alien to the teachings of Confucius as found in the ancient records. At best they could legitimately claim only to be implicit in the sage's sayings. Yet members of the school seem sincerely to have believed that they were true to the spirit of Confucius and their emphasis upon the *Lun Yü* (Analects), the *Ta Hsüeh* (Great Learning), the *Chung Yung* (Doctrine of the Mean), and the Book of Mencius was not mere lip service or an attempt to win adherence to novel ideas by professing to find for them the sanctions of antiquity, but sprang from a conviction of the authority and permanent value of these documents.

The views of Chu Hsi did not immediately win the unqualified acceptance of the majority of the scholar class. The followers of Wang An-shih of course opposed them. Even among the conservatives who denounced Wang An-shih and who may be classed as Neo-Confucianists were many who could not agree with them. Chu Hsi, indeed, entered into controversy with several rival interpreters of Confucianism whom he deemed heterodox. One famous opponent was Lu Chiu-yüan (also known as Lu Hsiang-shan) who emphasized personal, subjective education and meditation and opposed any study beginning with the external world. His two elder brothers, less distinguished as scholars, joined in his opposition to Chu Hsi. An extended conference between the three and Chu Hsi only intensified the antagonism. Lu Chiu-yüan incorporated a marked strain of Ch'an Buddhism, while Chu Hsi emphasized study and speculation and carried the impress of Taoist metaphysics. There was also a utilitarian school which gave itself to the study of political, economic, and military problems. Still another was the so-called Shu school, whose greatest scholar was Su Shih (1036–1101), a decided liberal, seeking truth in Confucianism, Taoism, and Buddhism, and not committing himself to any one philosophy—although for many years his tablet was in the Confucian temple. His writings were long widely influential, even in Japan.

When, in later dynasties, Chu Hsi became dominant, there were still, as we shall see, dissenting thinkers, some of whom claimed that he had done violence to true Confucianism. In the main, however, for nearly seven centuries his interpretations were regarded as final and authoritative.

CULTURE UNDER THE SUNG: OTHER LITERARY DEVELOPMENTS

The literary energy of the Sung was not confined to the discussion of political science provoked by the proposals of Wang An-shih and to the philosophical works of the Neo-Confucianists and their rivals. It also expressed itself in poetry, essays, and history—particularly in history. Except possibly for Wang An-shih and his followers, the scholarship of the Sung seems primarily to have been historically minded. Why this should have been so is probably impossible to determine with accuracy. It may have been due in part to the strengthening of the examination system under the T'ang and the Sung and the consequent emphasis, in educational and intellectual circles, upon the Confucian tradition and the literature of the Confucian school. Then, too, the T'ang scholars included notable historians and in some respects the Sung historiographers adopted their methods and forms. Certainly Neo-Confucianism was, as compared with Buddhism, a reversion to China's past. Even Wang An-shih, as we have seen, had to reckon with this admiration for antiquity and sought justification for his schemes in the Classics. To obtain widespread acceptance, any view must make good its claim to be inherent in these records.

Under the Sung, historical-mindedness displayed itself in a number of ways. We have already mentioned Neo-Confucianism, by which the Confucian tradition was given a form acceptable to an intellectual class strongly influenced by Buddhism and Taoism, and so became more influential than it had been since the Han. Sung scholars also showed a greatly quickened interest in the writing of history itself. In addition to the compilation of dynastic histories of the T'ang and of the Five Dynasties, scholars showed an enthusiasm for preparing accounts covering the entire sweep of China's past. The most famous and widely used of these works was, fittingly (when one recalls the *Shih Chi* of Ssŭ-ma Ch'ien of the Han), by a scholar by the name of Ssŭ-ma—Ssŭ-ma Kuang (1019–1086). As already noted in the bibliography at the close of the last chapter, this was the *Tzŭ Chih T'ung Chien* and covered the period from near the end of the fifth century B.C. to the close of the Five Dynasties. The author was an outstanding leader in the opposition to Wang An-shih and part of the necessary leisure for his *magnum opus* was obtained during the long intervals when he and his party were out of power and Wang was in the ascendant. Ssŭ-ma Kuang supplemented his larger history with a number of smaller compilations—such as tables and the discussion of doubtful points. The *Tzŭ Chih T'ung Chien* became the basis of several other works, notably a reconstruction and condensation of it, the *T'ung Chien Kang Mu*, made under the direction of Chu Hsi. Another, prepared by one Yüan Ch'u, was a rearrangement by topics of the material in the *Tzŭ Chih T'ung Chien*. It was called the *T'ung Chien Chi Shih Pên Mo*, or "Root Causes and Effects of Affairs Recorded in the Universal Mirror," and served as a precedent for a new type of history. Judged by the standards of modern Occidental scholarship, Chêng Ch'iao probably deserves the first rank among Sung historians. His *T'ung Chih* covered Chinese history from Fu Hsi to the T'ang.

In addition to the general histories of China were many studies of special periods, persons, and phases of the past. Antiquarians and their collections and publications were numerous. There were compiled some of the earliest of the local topographies and histories, eventually a voluminous section of Chinese literature. Collections of extracts from the literature of the past were made, many critical essays written on the works of earlier authors, records prepared of the rites and customs of the court, and facts supplementary to the official historical records gathered. To the close of the Sung and the opening years of the Mongol dynasty belongs Ma Tuan-lin, who, taking as a basis a work of the T'ang dynasty, Tu Yu's *T'ung Tien,* collected the *Wên Hsien T'ung K'ao,* a compilation which contained a vast amount of information on government and related subjects. With true historic sense, Sung scholars also wrote many essays on contemporary events, valuable source material for later devotees of Clio.

The Sung dynasty witnessed, too, an expansion in the *lei shu*—collections of extracts from earlier works and often translated, although not with entire accuracy, as encyclopædias. Their beginnings date from hundreds of years before the Sung, but, with their penchant for the past, the Sung scholars compiled a number of them, some relatively short and on restricted groups of topics, and others of them longer than any which had yet appeared. Probably the most famous was the *T'ai P'ing Yü Lan,* prepared under imperial direction, comprising more than a thousand books and quoting from nearly seventeen hundred works.

To this zeal of Sung scholars for the past later generations have owed the preservation of much material which otherwise would have been lost. The Sung savants were not without serious defects and their inaccuracies often misled their successors in subsequent dynasties. Yet they were not uncritical of their historical source-material. Some doubted the authenticity of the *Chou Li,* others accepted only three of the Five Classics, another regarded the appendices to the *I Ching* as late interpolations, and Chu Hsi rejected the prefaces to the *Shih Ching* and threw doubt on the so-called "ancient text" of the *Shu Ching,* in later centuries conclusively proved to be a forgery.

Even poetry showed the effect of regard for the past and much of it was more closely bound to convention than that of the T'ang.

It did not, accordingly—at least in the judgment of many—rise quite to the heights attained during the T'ang. Some of it, however, displayed a freedom even from T'ang forms and was a relatively unhampered expression of the writer's inner emotions. As a rule it was not the work of professional poets, as had been so much of the best verse of the T'ang, but of scholars whose chief interest was elsewhere—in other literary pursuits, in the duties of public office, or in religion. Thus one of the most famous of the Sung poets, Su Shih, or Su Tung-p'o (1036–1101), was a brilliant scholar—already mentioned as a noted philosopher—who came up through the ordinary channels of the state examinations, spent much of his life in the employment of the government, was an art critic, the builder of a causeway in the West Lake by Lin-an, and wrote essays as well as poetry. Another was primarily a recluse who gave much time to Taoist studies, and still another finished his life as a Buddhist monk.

With all this interest in the past, under the Sung the Chinese mind was not so nearly closely bound by it as the preceding pages may have appeared to indicate. Works on astronomy, medicine, botany, and mathematics showed concern for other than humanistic and political studies. For example, several treatises on flowers and fruits have come down to us, among them what is probably the most ancient scientific account of the varieties of citrus fruits which is known in any language. Fiction, moreover, was written, and in the vernacular of the time. Chinese mechanical inventiveness, too, was displaying itself. It was probably under the Sung that gunpowder, previously employed for fireworks, was first applied to warfare—in explosive hand-grenades. Then, as we have seen, the compass now appears to have come into use as an aid to navigation. Near the close of the dynasty, moreover, occurs the earliest known reference to the abacus, that now familiar device for reckoning. Whether it was an importation or of native origin we do not know.

CULTURE UNDER THE SUNG: THE FURTHER DEVELOPMENT
OF PRINTING

Inventiveness and mechanical skill showed themselves especially in printing. That art which, as we have said, as far as our records show us, first developed under the T'ang, and, under the

Five Dynasties, had been employed, among other purposes, to print the Classics, now reached its flowering. The voluminous dynastic histories were published as a governmental enterprise, and private firms issued many works. The calligrapher, whose skill is so highly esteemed in China, could express himself through the block method of printing, the form chiefly in use, and his name, together with that of the author and printer, appeared on the finished works. Examples of the Sung editions still survive, and for quality of workmanship have never been surpassed. Leading modern editions frequently print in the Sung style or reproduce it by photographic processes. Movable type was invented, made first of earthenware and later, before the end of the Mongol dynasty, of metal and wood. This device, however, was not so extensively employed as was the carved wood-block, nor did it yield such artistic results.

It seems probable that the rapid development of printing had a close connection with the literary and intellectual activity of the dynasty—that it both stimulated it and was stimulated by it. The rapid multiplication of books made possible by printing must have encouraged authors to write and have augmented the number of libraries and the places where study could be pursued: it put the tools of literary work and of scholarship at the disposal of more people. The increased interest in thought and in books must also have spurred the printers to perfect their processes.

CULTURE UNDER THE SUNG: PORCELAIN AND PAINTING

It was not only in the realm of political science, philosophy, literature, and mechanical invention that the Sung genius expressed itself. It also appeared in art. For this the court was partly responsible. Hui Tsung, the unfortunate Emperor who shared in the collapse of the Northern Sung, was, as we have noted, a painter of some distinction and a devoted patron of the arts. He founded an institute of calligraphy and painting, and government examinations in painting were begun. The Emperors of the Southern Sung continued the tradition, greatly beautifying their capital, appointing official painters, and maintaining the institute of art. The very surroundings of Lin-an (Hangchow) provided incentive. The West Lake which the city seems eventually to have enclosed, the proximity of inspiring scenes of mountain, river, and sea, and the rich southern flora and fauna, all proved a stimulus to the æsthetic. Religiously, Buddhism, especially the Ch'an sect, remained strong, and Taoism was much studied and at times favored at court. Both faiths had fully as profound an influence upon art as upon the Neo-Confucian philosophy.

Porcelain now for the first time began to loom prominently as a medium for æsthetic expression. In beauty and craftsmanship, cups, bowls, and other objects made from it could bear comparison with the bronzes and jades of the ancients. It was covered with thick glazes. Often, although by no means always, only one color was used on one object. There were some figures, but the rich variety of painted patterns in which later manufacturers delighted was still in the future. Sung glazes were, however, in many colors, some of them delicate and rarely beautiful. Before the application of the glaze, figures were often placed on the clay, either by incision or in relief. Many objects, too, were covered by crackle-glaze. Porcelain was made at a number of centers, including the imperial factories located first at the present K'aifeng and Ching-tê-chên. The latter, to be long the most famous source of the ware, took its name from a Sung reign period (Ching Tê, 1004–1008). Later, with the southward migration of the dynasty, potteries were developed at the present Hangchow. The overseas commerce gave wide distribution to the ware and many highly prized examples survive.

Sculpture did not occupy the place under the Sung that it had under the T'ang, perhaps because of the decline of Buddhism. The sculpture was influenced by painting and tended to overrefinement, especially after the southward migration of the dynasty. Even the manufacture of earthenware figurines, so characteristic of the T'ang, fell largely into abeyance.

It may be that some connection existed on the one hand between the energetic military expansion and the vigorous, often massive statuary of the T'ang and on the other between the military ineffectiveness of the Sung and the dreamy, even though sometimes bold, landscapes of the artists of that dynasty. Certainly while the enemy was wasting the frontiers the Sung court was devoting itself largely to æsthetic and luxurious pursuits.

Certainly, too, landscape painting now came to the fore and reached heights of perfection never again attained in China. Probably no landscape painting equal to the Sung had ever appeared anywhere in the world, or was to appear, except possibly in a Japan inspired by it, and in recent times in Europe and America. Landscape was not the exclusive subject of the Sung painters. Flowers, birds, animals, and Buddhas and Bodhisattvas were portrayed. Even in painting, the love for the old, so powerful in philosophy and literature, asserted itself, and some of the artists spent much time in copying the masterpieces of the past. As in the æsthetic realm, poetry and sculpture reached their highest development in China under the T'ang, so the Sung is remembered for the greatness of its landscapes. Calligraphy, in Chinese practice so closely allied to painting that it profoundly modified it, received much attention and the dynasty saw some of the most famous masters of the art.

The prominence of landscape appears to have been due in part to Ch'an Buddhism. At least the spirit in which it was done owed much to it. Ch'an looked below the surface of nature and saw through it to another and ideal world, subjective in character. This vision the painters sought to portray. Taoism reënforced the tendency, for, as we have seen, in some respects, notably in its attitude toward the visible universe, it was closely akin to the Ch'an. The period may, indeed, be called one of romanticism, if this does not push too closely the parallel between it and the movements in Europe which bear that title.

In painting, one color rather than several was the rule: under the Sung monochrome reached its highest point. Both the Northern and the Southern School, mentioned in the last chapter, were represented.

Some of the outstanding painters are worthy of special mention, even in so abbreviated an account as this. Kuo Chung-shu, whose life spanned the latter part of the Five Dynasties and the earlier years of the Sung, held office, but was much of a wanderer and somewhat addicted to wine. He was noted for his pictures of buildings set among the hills. Kuo Hsi, born *ca.* 1020, and influenced by both Taoism and Buddhism, did much of his work on the walls of temples and palaces. He achieved fame as a painter of distances and of winter landscapes and as the writer of a treatise on painting. Li Lung-mien (born *ca*. 1040) belonged to the party of Wang An-shih but was also a friend of Ou-yang Hsiu and Su Tung-p'o and was affected by Taoism and Buddhism as well as by Confucianism. He was a versatile and brilliant genius, a poet and a prose-writer of parts, a master of calligraphy, and as a painter won distinction by his horses, his Buddhist subjects, and his landscapes. The memory of Mi Fei (1051–1107), an eccentric court painter who held both civil and military offices, has been preserved by his landscapes and figures of men and animals, his calligraphy, and his writing. He and his son initiated a school which enjoyed a great vogue in Korea. Hsia Kuei, possibly the greatest painter of landscapes in the history of China, loved, among other subjects, to portray the rugged seacoast and the tides. Attached to the court at the present Hangchow, he was much influenced by the scenery of the neighborhood. Another court painter of the Southern Sung was Ma Yüan, the greatest of a distinguished family of artists. His pictures include views of the West Lake and the villas of the great men of the capital. A school of Ch'an monks, not connected with the court or its imperial academy of painting but nevertheless delighting in landscapes and living in monasteries in beautiful natural surroundings, had as its leading name Mu Ch'i, about whom we know personally very little.

SUMMARY

The Five Dynasties constituted an important interlude between two great epochs in China's history. Behind them lay the T'ang with its territorial conquests, the golden age of Buddhism, and the best period of Chinese poetry. After them came the three centuries and more of the Sung. Although harassed on the north by enemies which it was never able to expel and before whom it finally succumbed, the Sung proved that from the cultural standpoint the creativeness of Chinese genius had by no means been exhausted. Some of its thinkers wrestled with political and economic theory with a boldness and originality not displayed in these fields since the Han and the Chou. Others worked through afresh the heritage of Confucianism in the light of the impulses which had come from Taoism and Buddhism and created a cosmogony and a cosmology which, with all their professed devotion to the past, show a breadth of conception and a profundity of thought that place them among the outstanding intellectual achievements of the race. Something of the same breadth of view and adherence to the past found expression in the writing of histories. Printing was perfected and widely used. Art—both ceramics and painting—registered memorable activity. Whatever may have been their failures in the political realm, the Chinese mind and spirit had never, in any one period, except in the philosophic schools of the Chou, broken out in as many fresh ways and with such lasting results. Just as the T'ang differed in culture from the Han, so the Sung was quite distinctive as compared with both the Han and the T'ang. Yet the Chinese spirit under the Sung was becoming ingrowing and was being confined to the national heritage. Not nearly so many new ideas were coming in from abroad as under the T'ang. It is doubtful, indeed, whether the Chinese would have welcomed them. China, on the defensive politically, tended to draw within itself culturally.

BIBLIOGRAPHY

Among the most important Chinese accounts of the Five Dynasties and the Sung are the *Chiu Wu Tai Shih,* or Old History of the Five Dynasties, compiled officially in the earlier years of the Sung, later fallen into disuse and almost lost, and of which our existing texts seem to be reorganized and imperfect reproductions; the *Hsin Wu Tai Shih,* or New History of the Five Dynasties, by Ou-yang Hsiu, who had first been a patron of Wang An-shih and then had opposed him; the *Sung Shih,* or History of the Sung, a chief author of which was T'o-t'o, a Mongol, and whose Annals section, by him, is not of very high quality; the *Liao Shih,* or History of the Liao (Khitan), by the same author, and which suffers from the loss of most of the records of the Khitan at the time of the overthrow of that people; the *Chin Shih,* or History of the Chin (Juchên), again by T'o-t'o, and of better quality than either the *Sung Shih* or the *Liao Shih;* the *Tzŭ Chih T'ung Chien* of Ssŭ-ma Kuang, which comes down to the end of the Five Dynasties, and the shorter *T'ung Chien Kang Mu* based upon it.

Among the general works in European languages useful for the period are de Mailla, *Histoire Générale de la Chine* (13 vols., Paris, 1777–1785); H. Cordier, *Histoire Générale de la Chine* (4 vols., Paris, 1920–1921); L. Wieger, *Textes Historiques* (2 vols., Hochienfu, 1903, 1904); René Grousset, *Histoire de l'Extrême-Orient* (2 vols., Paris, 1929); H. A. Giles, *A Chinese Biographical Dictionary* (London and

Shanghai, 1898); Vol. 1, chapters 8 and 9, of F. E. A. Krause, *Geschichte Ostasiens* (Göttingen, 1925); and Richard Wilhelm, *Geschichte der Chinesischen Kultur* (Munich, 1928: translated into English, New York, 1929).

Special works and articles, some of them highly unsatisfactory, covering the political history of the Five Dynasties and the Sung are E. H. Bowra, *The Liu Family, or Canton during the Period of the Five Dynasties* (*China Review*, Vol. 1, pp. 316–322); E. Chavannes, *Le Royaume de Wou et de Yue* (*T'oung Pao*, 1916, pp. 129–264); E. H. Parker, *A Thousand Years of the Tartars* (second edition, London, 1924); J. C. Ferguson, *Southern Migration of the Sung Dynasty* (*Journal of the North China Branch of the Royal Asiatic Society*, 1924, pp. 14–27); J. C. Ferguson, *Political Parties of the Northern Sung Dynasty* (*ibid.*, 1927, pp. 36–56); J. C. Ferguson, *The Emperor Hui Tsung, A.D. 1082–1135* (*China Journal of Arts and Sciences*, 1924, pp. 204–209); I. J. Schmidt (translator), *Geschichte der Ost-Mongolen und ihres Fürstenhauses verfasst von Ssanang Ssetsen Chungtaidschi der Ordus* (St. Petersburg, 1829); C. D'Ohsson, *Histoire des Mongols, depuis Tchinguiz-Khan jusqu'à Timour Bey ou Tamerlan* (4 vols., Amsterdam, 1852); E. Blochet, *Introduction à l'Histoire des Mongols de Fadl Allah Rashid-Eddin* (Leyden, 1910); J. Curtin, *The Mongols* (Boston, 1908), very poor; H. H. Howarth, *History of the Mongols from the Ninth to the Nineteenth Century* (3 parts, London, 1876–1888); B. Y. Vladimirstov, *The Life of Chingis-Khan* (translated from the Russian by D. S. Mirsky, Boston, 1930); V. V. Bartold, *Turkestan down to the Mongol Invasion* (translated from the Russian, second edition, London, 1928), especially the fourth chapter; E. Rocher, *Histoire des Princes du Yunnan* (*T'oung Pao*, 1899, pp. 132 *et seq.*, 115–154, 337–368, 437–458); Goré, *Marches Tibétaines du Sseutch'ouan et du Yunnan* (*Bulletin de l'École Française d'Extrême-Orient*, Vol. 23, pp. 318–398); G. Maspero, *Le Royaume de Champa* (*T'oung Pao*, 1910, pp. 125–165, 319, 489, 547; 1911, pp. 53, 236, 291, 451, 589); *History of the Southern Sung Dynasty, a Translation* (*Chinese Recorder*, Vol. 1, pp. 46–48, 103, 104, 137, 138, 160–162, 207, 208, 229, 230). Bearing on the Mongol conquest of Southwest China is E. Chavannes, *Inscriptions et Pièces de Chancellerie Chinoises de l'Époque Mongole* (*T'oung Pao*, 1904, pp. 357–447, 1905, pp. 1–42, 1908, pp. 297–428). See also E. L. Oxenham, *A Chip from Chinese History, or the Last Two Emperors of the Great Sung Dynasty, 1101–1126* (*China Review*, Vol. 7, pp. 167–176, 292–299, Vol. 9, pp. 100–107, 175–181, 481, 498, Vol. 13, pp. 90–101, 264–273, Vol. 14, pp. 151–163, Vol. 15, pp. 144–150, 197–206).

Extremely important is the first volume of a monumental work, K. A. Wittfogel and Fêng Chia-shêng, *History of Chinese Society. Liao (907–1125)* (Philadelphia, 1945). It includes texts and translations from the Dynastic Histories, with notes.

On the southward movement of the Chinese, see Chi Li, *The Forma-*

tion of the Chinese People, an Anthropological Inquiry (Cambridge, 1928).

On commerce and travel under the Sung, see F. Hirth and W. W. Rockhill, *Chau Ju-kua: His Work on the Chinese and Arab Trade in the twelfth and thirteenth centuries, entitled Chu-fan-chi* (St. Petersburg, 1912); J. Kuwabara, *On P'u Shou King, a Man of the Western Regions . . . together with a General Sketch of Trade with Arabs in China during the T'ang and Sung* (*Mem. of the Research Department of the Toyo Bunko*, II, 1928, pp. 1–79); E. Huber, *L'Itinéraire du Pelerin Ki Ye dans l'Inde* (*Bulletin de l'École Française d'Extrême-Orient*, 1902, pp. 256–259); E. Chavannes, *L'Itinéraire de Ki-ye* (*ibid.*, 1904, pp. 75–81); Gabriel Ferrand, *Relations de Voyages et Textes Géographiques Arabes, Persans et Turcs Relatifs à l'Extrême-Orient du VIIIe au XVIIIe siècles* (2 vols.; Paris, 1913, 1914); an account of a journey of an embassy from the Sung to the Chin court in 1177 in *Pei Yuan Lou. Récit d'un Voyage dans le Nord traduit par Ed. Chavannes* (*T'oung Pao*, 1904, pp. 163–192); and *The Travels of an Alchemist, the Journeys of the Taoist Ch'ang Ch'un from China to the Hindukush at the Summons of Chingiz Khan, Recorded by His Disciple, Li Chih-ch'ang*. Translated by A. Waley (1931).

On Chino-Japanese intercourse, see K. Hara, *An Introduction to the History of Japan* (New York, 1920).

On the reforms of Wang An-shih, see H. R. Williamson, *Wang An-shih* (London, 2 vols., 1935, 1937); J. C. Ferguson, *Wang An-shih* (*Journal of the North China Branch of the Royal Asiatic Society*, 1903, pp. 1 *et seq.*); J. C. Ferguson, *Political Parties of the Northern Sung Dynasty* (*ibid.*, 1927, pp. 36 *et seq.*); *Wang An-shih, the Innovator* (*China Review*, Vol. 2, pp. 29–33, 74–80); Tcheou Houan, *Le prêt sur récolte institué en Chine au XIe siècle par le ministre novateur Wang-ngan-che* (Paris, 1930), a doctoral dissertation; O. Franke, *Staatssocialistische Versuche im alten und mittelalterlichen China* (*Sitzungsberichte der Preussischen Akademie der Wissenschaften, Philosophisch-historische Klasse*, 1931, XIII, pp. 218–242); and O. Franke, *Der Bericht Wang Ngan-schis von 1058 über Reform der Beamtentums* (in *op. cit.*, 1932, pp. 264–312).

On the Sung Neo-Confucianism, see Fung Yu-lan, *The Philosophy of Chu Hsi*, translated with introduction and notes by D. Bodde (*Harvard Journal of Asiatic Studies*, Vol. 7, pp. 1–51); Fung Yu-lan, *The Rise of Neo-Confucianism and Its Borrowings from Buddhism and Taoism*, translated with notes by D. Bodde (*Harvard Journal of Asiatic Studies*, Vol. 7, pp. 1–51, 89–125); M. Freeman, *The Ch'ing Dynasty Criticism of the Sung Politico-Philosophy* (*Journal of the North China Branch of the Royal Asiatic Society*, 1928, pp. 79 *et seq.*); J. P. Bruce, *Chu Hsi and His Masters* (London, 1923); J. P. Bruce, *The Philosophy of Human Nature by Chu Hsi* (London, 1922); Stanislas Le Gall, *Le Philosophe Tchou Hi, Sa Doctrine, Son Influence* (*Variétés Sinologiques*, Shanghai, 1894); T. M'Clatchie, *Confucian Cosmogony* (Shanghai, 1874)—largely supeseded; L. Wieger, *A History of the Religious Beliefs and Philosophical Opinions in China*, translated by E. T. C. Werner (Hsien-hsien, 1927), Lesson 71; and some passages in A. Forké, *The World Conception of the Chinese* (London, 1925). Of these, Bruce's books are very good, although they are said to make Chu Hsi appear to approach more closely to theism than he really did and to have missed his emphasis upon "the investigation of things."

On a rival and critic of Chu Hsi, see Huang Siu-chi, *Lu Hsiang-shan* (New Haven, 1944).

On other literature, see A. Wylie, *Notes on Chinese Literature* (Shanghai, 1902); H. A. Giles, *A History of Chinese Literature* (New York, 1901); G. Margouliès, *Le Kou-Wen Chinois Recueil de Textes avec Introduction et Notes* (Paris, 1926); Vanhée, *Li-yé, Mathematicien Chinois au XIIIe siècle* (*T'oung Pao*, 1913, pp. 537 et seq.); Han Yen-chih's *Chü Lu* (*Monograph on the Oranges of Wên-chou, Chekiang*), translated by M. J. Hagerty with an introduction by P. Pelliot (*T'oung Pao*, Vol. 22, pp. 63–69); A. Forké *Dichtungen der T'ang- und Sung-Zeit* (German text, Hamburg, 1929, Chinese Text, Hamburg, 1930); C. D. LeGros Clark (with wood engraving, by A. LeGros Clark), *Selections from the Work of Su T'ung P'o* (London, 1932); and Admiral Ts'ai T'ing-kan, *Chinese Poems in English Rhyme* (Chicago, 1932).

On printing, see T. F. Carter, *The Invention of Printing in China and Its Spread Westward* (revised edition, New York, 1931).

On porcelain, painting, and sculpture see E. F. Fenollosa, *Epochs of Chinese and Japanese Art* (2 vols., London, 1912); S. W. Bushell, *Chinese Art* (2 vols., London, 1910); R. Petrucci, *Chinese Painters: A Critical Study* (translated by F. Seaver, New York, 1921; French edition, Paris, 1913); H. A. Giles, *An Introduction to the History of Chinese Pictorial Art* (London, 1918); Arthur Waley, *An Introduction to the Study of Chinese Painting* (London, 1923); Osvald Sirén, *Chinese Sculpture from the Fifth to the Fourteenth Century* (4 vols., London, 1925); Leigh Aston, *An Introduction to the Study of Chinese Sculpture* (London, 1924); B. Laufer, *T'ang, Sung and Yüan Paintings Belonging to Various Chinese Collectors* (Paris and Brussels, 1924); R. L. Hobson, *The Art of the Chinese Potter from the Han Dynasty to the End of the Ming* (London, 1923); R. Schmidt, *Chinesische Keramik von der Han-zeit bis zum XIX Jahrhundert* (Frankfurt am Main, 1924); Osvald Sirén, *Histoire des Arts Anciens de la Chine* (4 vols., Paris, 1929–1930); Sir Aurel Stein, *The Thousand Buddhas. Ancient Buddhist Paintings from the Cave Temples of Tunhuang on the Western Frontier of China* (London, 1921); W. C. White, *Chinese Temple Frescoes. A Study of Three Wall-Paintings of the Thirteenth Century* (Toronto, 1940. The dates of the paintings are uncertain, but are probably late Sung or early Yüan).

CHAPTER VII

CHINA UNDER THE RULE OF THE MONGOLS
(A.D. 1279–1368)

INTRODUCTORY

When the commander of the remnant of the Sung forces, in defiant despair, terminated the hopeless struggle against the Mongols by throwing himself and the boy Emperor into the sea, it was not only a dynasty but an era which had come to an end. China was now a part of the Mongol Empire and was ruled by foreigners. It was too huge to be absorbed into any alien civilization, and the Mongols, far from forcing their own crude culture on the Middle Kingdom, adopted much of that of their subjects. Gone, however, was the Sung court which, with all its political weaknesses and mistakes, had done so much to foster literature and art. Immigrants of many different races and cultures shared in the administration of the country. The rich flowering of culture under the Sung faded, and although here and there a few hardy survivors of its luxuriant blooming continued the older traditions, they were a dwindling remnant.

For some reason, contacts with foreigners under the Mongols did not stimulate the Chinese genius to any new life at all comparable with that which had followed the introduction of Buddhism. Some few significant and widely influential developments there were, as we shall see—in the drama and in the writing of novels, for instance—and Moslems now became a factor in Chinese life with which the realm had henceforth to reckon. However, very few new intellectual, social, or religious movements which profoundly affected the entire life of the people entered from the outside world, and none which equalled those of the centuries of disunion before the T'ang. When the Mongols were at last expelled and the Empire was once more under a native dynasty, culturally the Chinese tended to fall back upon the heritage of their pre-Mongol past, and, while in some respects elaborating it, to discourage departure from it. The Mongol conquest, in other words, was the beginning of that period of comparative cultural sterility, of sturdy and largely undeviating adherence to traditional models, from which the Chinese were not to be shaken until their revolutionary contacts with the Occident at the close of the nineteenth and in the early years of the twentieth century. To be sure, critics of this complacent orthodoxy were not wanting, but they were in the minority. Moreover, some significant innovations and noteworthy cultural achievements were registered. Compared with earlier periods, however, the tempo of change was slow.

Why this comparative stagnation should have prevailed is not clear. It is possible that the philosophical and artistic activity of the Sung had about reached the natural limits beyond which it could not pass without fresh stimulus from without. The very brilliance of the Sung genius resulted in an art, a philosophy, and a literature which later generations not unnaturally regarded as standard and sought to perpetuate. Sterility may have been due in part to the fact that the Mongol Empire broke down before China could be brought into prolonged intimate contact with foreign cultural contributions which could quicken the Chinese mind to such fresh endeavors as had Buddhism. Islam, the one spiritual importation of importance which under the Mongols was so strengthened as to win a permanent place in Chinese life, made less of an impression than had the Indian faith. Moreover, the type of Islam which reached China was not the bearer of a particularly varied or rich culture. The anti-foreign reaction which accompanied the expulsion of the Mongols sought to restore and conserve the national heritage and discouraged originality. To the triumph of the examination system must be assigned at least some of the responsibility for the unprogressive conservatism. Whatever the cause or causes, the Mongol conquest marks the end of a period of creativity and the beginning of a long era of relative lack of originality.

THE REIGN OF KHUBILAI: EXTERNAL POLITICS: MONGOL RULE AT ITS HEIGHT

The domination of the Mongols from which dates this transition in Chinese culture was of relatively brief duration. Less than a century after the extinction of the Sung it had come to an end. The reign of Khubilai, during which, as we have seen, the conquest of China was completed, saw the Mongol Empire at its apex. From the vantage of several centuries, it is to-day clear that in spite of the splendor of his reign Khubilai, probably quite unconsciously, saw the tide of Mongol conquest reach its flood and even begin to ebb.

Theoretically, Khubilai's rule extended over all the vast domains in Asia and Europe occupied by the members of his family. Practically, however, in the sections more remote from China that suzerainty was little better than nominal and in wide regions disputed. Khubilai was, to be sure, the Grand Khan, but distances in the huge Empire were so great that the subordinate khans who possessed the actual rule in distant sections, especially in Central and Western Asia, were in practice almost, if not entirely, autonomous. During much of the life of Khubilai, moreover, a relative, Kaidu, effectively disputed his rule in much of what is now the New Dominion and the southern part of Siberia, and for a time invaded Mongolia and threatened Karakorum. Another Mongol ruler, Nayan, a Nestorian Christian, whose domains were in Manchuria and Korea, joined Kaidu in defying Khubilai's power. Khubilai's forces defeated Nayan and put him to death, but Kaidu successfully continued his resistance until after Khubilai's death.

In several of his attempts to extend his domains, moreover, Khubilai notably failed. He succeeded in putting down revolts in Korea and in bringing that peninsula more effectively under the sway of the Mongols. When, however, he essayed to conquer Japan, he encountered signal defeat. Beginning with 1268 he sent several embassies to induce the Japanese to submit without fighting. These having failed, in 1274 he launched against them an expedition of Mongols and Koreans. This effected a landing on the island of Kyushu, but the Japanese, although unable to cope in the open field with Mongol tactics and equipment, put up a stubborn fight and the invaders withdrew. A storm coming up, the Mongol fleet suffered heavy losses. After Khubilai had conquered the Sung, he renewed the attack on Japan with a much larger force. The maritime resources of the southern part of China were now at his disposal. In the summer of 1281 a huge armada of Mongols, Chinese, and Koreans was dispatched against the recalcitrant islanders. Again a landing was made; again the Japanese offered stout opposition, this time by both land and sea; again the elements came to the rescue of the attacked and a storm destroyed a large proportion of the invading ships. The Chinese contingents were especially heavy sufferers. Khubilai did not at once give up hope of renewing the attempt, but the Mongols and the Koreans had no more stomach for the project, the heavy demands on the Chinese brought restlessness, and when the revolt of Nayan absorbed Khubilai's attention the idea of another invasion seems to have passed into oblivion.

It must be noted that trade appears to have revived after the war and that cultural influences, by the medium of Zen Buddhism and otherwise—including Chinese Buddhist missionaries—continued to flow from the Middle Kingdom into the island empire. Later in the Yüan amicable relations between the two governments were renewed.

In the South Khubilai's forces either encountered disaster or won relatively sterile victories. While the Sung rule was collapsing and the sweep of the Mongol arms seemed irresistible, the ruler of Champa, in Indo-China, accepted the suzerainty of Khubilai and dispatched envoys to the court of the Grand Khan. When, however, Khubilai demanded, as a more substantial recognition of his authority, a visit of the ruler in person to his court, he met with a refusal. To make his power effective, Khubilai thereupon sent an army (1282), by sea from Canton, to reduce Champa to a more obedient frame of mind. The expedition took the citadel of the Chams (1283), but the quarry escaped to the hills and there eluded capture.

The efforts of the Mongols to control Annam proved as futile as those in the neighboring Champa. Some of the adherents of the Sung fled to Annam to escape the Mongol advance. This helped to attract the attention of Khubilai to that state. Like the ruler of Champa, the Annamese monarch was willing to acknowledge the suzerainty of the Mongols through formal embassies to Khubilai's court, but persistently declined to come in person to make his submission. Khubilai sent army after army to bring the region to a more humble attitude and to place a creature of his own on the throne. In 1280, 1285, and 1287, Mongol armies penetrated Annam. On the open field they were usually victorious, but the tropical climate proved their undoing. Twice, shattered by disease, they were forced to retire, and the third time, enfeebled by the same enemy, they were overwhelmed by the Annamites with the loss of their fleet. Khubilai wished to continue the attack but had to be content with threats on his part and—to him—unsatisfactory present-bearing embassies from Annam.

Mongol experience in Burma was less disastrous but led to no more permanent conquest. Beginning with 1277 and ending in 1301, five separate expeditions sought to establish the rule of the Grand Khan. The invading armies were usually fairly successful in battle, three of them penetrating the valley of the Irrawaddy, at least two of them to the south of the present Mandalay, but they failed to establish any lasting foothold.

A Mongol-Chinese armada was sent to Java to punish a prince in the eastern part of the island who had treated with contumely an envoy sent by Khubilai to demand the recognition of Mongol suzerainty. With the aid of a local magnate, the force achieved initial successes, but after a few months the great distance from its base, heavy losses of life, and fresh difficulties from enemies, led the army to debark.

Tribute was received from a state in the present Siam, but no troops seem to have been ordered there.

An attempt to subdue the Liu Ch'iu (Ryu Kyu) Islands ended in failure, presumably because of the untimely death of the Chinese pilot of the invading fleet.

From the vantage of the centuries, it is evident, as has been said, that the miscarriage of these attempts to extend the Mongol possessions across the seas and to the south were an indication that the tide had reached its flood and was about to recede. Other factors than lack of vigor, however, entered into the failures of Khubilai's forces. The Mongols had been eminent as strategists on the land, but it is not strange that, coming from the desert and the steppes, they should not be at home on the sea. In the South, moreover, the tropical climate proved uncongenial and was a handicap which they could not fully overcome.

It must not be forgotten, also, that Khubilai greatly widened the Mongol borders. He completed the conquest of the Sung (no light task), and his generals permanently added Yünnan to the Chinese Empire, bringing to an end the independent, or semi-independent, state which had existed there for centuries—although the native line was continued for a time as Mongol officials.

Then, too, Khubilai's envoys went farther than had ever official envoys of China gone before. Embassies were dispatched to Ceylon and South India and even to Madagascar—or at least so Marco Polo declares—but these appear to have been for the purpose not of political conquest but of encouraging trade.

THE REIGN OF KHUBILAI: INTERNAL POLITICS

The spectacular and rapid rise of the Mongol Empire had been a tribute to the genius and energy of the men responsible for it. A greater test of capacity, however, was the task of welding together into some sort of permanent whole the vast area and the great diversity of races and cultures that had been conquered. If in this the Mongols signally failed, it was probably quite as much because of the difficulty of the problem as because of their own lack of ability.

How clearly Khubilai sensed the problem and how deliberate a policy he conceived and adopted for meeting it we do not know. He appears to have been too astute to believe that a great empire like China, even when it had been won by force, could long be held in subjection by that method alone. In practice his policy seems to have been in part one of conciliation of the conquered, in part an attempt at a cosmopolitan blending of races in the government, and in part the promotion of prosperity. He maintained travelling inspectors to report on the economic status of his subjects. He had public granaries—not a new device in China, as we have seen—in which the surplus grain of good seasons was stored for distribution in years of dearth. He made provision for the public care of aged scholars, orphans, and the infirm, and for the distribution of food among the poor. He encouraged education.

Religiously, Khubilai was tolerant. For himself, he seems to have held to some of the primitive shamanistic practices of his fathers and to have inclined toward Buddhism of the Tibetan type. He had a new Mongol alphabet devised on the basis of the Tibetan script—the old having been taken from that of the

Uighurs. Officially, however, he gave support, financial and otherwise, to several faiths. Like Ogodai and Mangu, he exempted Taoist and Buddhist monks, Nestorian priests, and Moslem teachers from taxation, with the condition that they offer prayers in his behalf. It was better to have the support of all these men of religion, with both their human and their spiritual constituencies, than to incur the enmity of the others by espousing the cause of some. Khubilai's only religious animosity appears to have been against the Taoists, and these seem to have been discouraged and their books ordered burned more because their violent antagonism to the Buddhists threatened the peace of the realm than from any dislike for their teachings. Under the Mongol rulers who preceded Khubilai, Buddhists and Taoists had carried on a bitter struggle in which, on the basis of official sanction, the Taoists claimed the advantage. Under Khubilai the tables were clearly turned in favor of the Buddhists. Even toward the Taoists, however, Khubilai was by no means implacable. He called into his presence the head of the cult and officially confirmed the title of *T'ien Shih,* or "Heavenly Teacher," which the latter had previously borne. Khubilai also honored Confucianism and summoned to court the representatives of the family of the sage. Confucianism, indeed, regained much of the ground which it had lost in the North under the Khitan and the Juchên.

In political administration, Khubilai enlisted Chinese scholars. Even under Jenghiz Chinese political ideas had begun to mold Mongol policy. Chinese scholars naturally favored an organization modeled on those of preceding dynasties. Khubilai became, indeed, a Chinese Emperor somewhat of the traditional type. He did not attempt to revolutionize the government of the country and employed Chinese in it. However, some modifications were introduced. Especially marked was the use of non-Chinese. Relatively few Chinese were placed in the higher offices. Foreign contingents were in the Mongol armies and garrisons and many aliens, including at least one Russian, were appointed to administrative posts—as governors of provinces and in leading positions in the cities. One outsider, Achmach or Ahmad, a chief minister, was assassinated by a plot of the Chinese, probably provoked by his tyrannical exactions. Khubilai discontinued the civil service examinations—possibly because the non-Chinese whom he wished to employ could not have obtained the education necessary to pass them. He also forbade the Chinese to carry arms and took away those which they already possessed.

Khubilai's capital, as we have seen, was at Cambaluc, the later Peking (Peiping), on and near the site on which had often been a capital of one of the states of China. Here he built an entirely new city, on a grand scale, and, as the administrative center of the Mongol Empire, it attracted a large population and was the marvel of European travellers. By moving his capital from the old Mongol headquarters, Karakorum, he was better able to govern that most populous and wealthy portion of his domains, the Middle Kingdom.

Probably also to improve communications and so to facilitate the administration of China, Khubilai reconstructed the Grand Canal, which connected the Yangtze Valley with the North. This waterway, as we have seen, had been begun many centuries before and at least once, under Yang Ti of the Sui dynasty, much labor had been expended on it to make it a means of through traffic between the North and the South. Khubilai put it again into good working order. He also improved some of the main highways and provided for rapid posts—as a means of holding his domains together.

THE SUCCESSORS OF KHUBILAI

Khubilai died in 1294, at the ripe age of eighty. None of his successors approached him in ability, but Mongols held the throne of China for nearly three-quarters of a century longer. The Yüan Emperors were still recognized as Grand Khans—the overlords of the vast Mongol domains—and when, after Khubilai's death, the revolt of Kaidu came to an end, there were no important areas in the Mongol Empire where nominally that suzerainty did not prevail.

As a matter of fact, however, the huge structure was falling apart. Distances, difficulties of communication, and cultural differences were proving too formidable to permit of permanent union once the initial wave of conquest had spent itself. The Mongols were taking over the customs of their subjects, and so were losing their own unity of culture. In Persia and Transoxiana, for example, they were becoming Moslems. In China they were more and more conforming to the ancient ways of the Middle Kingdom. Like Khubilai, they here favored Buddhism, particularly of the Tibetan type, and continued to exempt Buddhist, Taoist, Nestorian, and Moslem teachers and monks from taxation. Even more than he they supported Confucianism. In the fourteenth century the civil service examinations and the Hanlin Academy were restored and fresh honors were decreed for Confucius, for Mencius, and for Confucius's disciple Yen Hui. The temples to Confucius were maintained and never had the ceremonies in them been more ornate or elaborate.

Moreover, the ruling line at Cambaluc lost in vigor. In the forty years or so between the death of Khubilai and the accession of the last Mongol Emperor, in 1333, there were eight monarchs, none of them of outstanding merit, and the majority with too short a tenure of office to achieve distinction. Khubilai's grandson and successor, to be sure, ruled for about thirteen years and labored diligently to reform abuses, reduce corruption, achieve a more equitable system of taxation, and in other ways to improve the administration. Most of the others, however, were less energetic.

The last of the line to hold China came to the throne when he was little more than a boy and proved weak and pleasure-loving. During the thirty-five years that he reigned from Cambaluc the power of the Mongols almost steadily declined. Rebellious secret organizations flourished, among them the *Pai Lien Hui,* or White Lotus Society, which was to have a long and stormy career. Revolts broke out in several different parts of the country. Attempts of the Mongols to suppress sedition, such as the renewal of the interdiction of arms to the Chinese and the rumored proposal to slay all Chinese bearing certain common surnames, served only to increase the unrest. Famine in the North and trouble with the ever-treacherous Yellow River added to the problems of the alien rulers. The financial straits to which the Mongols were reduced led to an increase in the issue of paper money— a device which they had taken over from the Chinese even before their final conquest of the country—until the currency became worthless and the people were reduced to barter. Heavy taxation added to the dissatisfaction. The Mongols, too, were divided among themselves and could not present a united front to their enemies.

Had the leaders of the various revolts been able to agree among themselves, the Mongols would probably have been expelled more quickly than they were. As it was, each was ambitious for his own interests and some were almost as incompetent as the rulers against whom they rebelled. A little effort was made to restore the Sung (the descendants of Chao K'uang-yin), but victory finally rested with a man of humble birth, Chu Yüan-chang: in the rough-and-tumble struggles of the time, native ability and not hereditary position was the best guarantee of success.

Chu Yüan-chang was born in the present province of Anhui in the year 1328. His family was poor and in his middle teens his parents and elder brother died in one of the famines that scourged these unhappy years. For a while he sought support, as have so many of the poor of China throughout the centuries, by entering a Buddhist monastery. When, in the disorders of the time, his refuge was burned and the monks scattered, he entered military service under the leader of a force of rebels in the neighborhood. Here he displayed signal ability and rose rapidly. He made himself master of a large area in the lower part of the Yangtze Valley and in 1364 assumed the title of Prince of Wu. Chu's energy, discretion, and clemency quickly extended his domains in the South and in 1367 he felt strong enough to press northward. In 1368 Cambaluc fell before one of his generals (Hsü Ta) and in that year he was proclaimed Emperor of a new dynasty, the Ming. The incompetent Mongol ruler fled northward and died before two years were out. For decades thereafter the Mongols sought to reëstablish themselves south of the Great Wall and invasions by them were a fairly constant menace, but their day of power had passed. In China proper their dominion was only a memory.

FOREIGN CONTACTS UNDER THE MONGOLS: MIGRATIONS AND COMMERCE

One of the marked features of the Mongol period was extensive contacts with other peoples and cultures. As we have seen, it appears to have been a deliberate policy of the Yüan to appoint non-Chinese to a fairly large proportion of the official positions in China. Not only Mongols but members of other non-Chinese races were given office. Moreover, bodies of foreign troops were brought in. There were, of course, Mongol garrisons. We hear also of a contingent of Alans, Christians from the Caucasus, in Cambaluc.

Mongol rule made for a certain degree of security for travel in a vast area which had never before been brought together under one sway. China's foreign commerce flourished accordingly, possibly reaching dimensions never previously attained. Merchants from many countries frequented the chief marts. Arabs, Persians, and representatives of races of Central Asia entered in fairly large numbers. Ibn Batuta, from North Africa, left behind him a record of a visit to China in the latter part of the dynasty which gives a vivid picture of the extensive colonies of foreign merchants in the leading commercial centers. He describes the Arab groups as each being organized under a judge and a Sheikh-ul-Islam. Chinese merchants ventured abroad, and Chinese junks made their way to Java, India, and Ceylon. Chinese engineers were utilized on the irrigation of the Tigris-Euphrates Valley. There were Chinese colonies in Moscow, Novgorod, and Tabriz. The Yüan Emperors had commercial agreements with the princes of at least two of the states of South India.

Foreign trade was carried on both by sea and by the ancient overland tracks across the present New Dominion. Many of the cities of China, both on the coast and on the internal trade routes, shared in the prosperity which it brought, but the chief emporium was the present Ch'üanchow (known to European medieval travellers as Zaitun) not far from Amoy, in Fukien.

Commerce was not without its problems. The drain of copper coinage embarrassed the Mongol rulers as it had the Sung. Silver flowed out of the realm. The Mongols, too, found it difficult to maintain a state monopoly over foreign trade or to enforce the regulations which they desired.

As heretofore, commerce was chiefly in those commodities which combined small bulk and weight with large value. The leading export appears still to have been silk in various forms—several varieties of silken fabrics being mentioned in the lists of merchandise—but porcelains and other wares helped to swell the total. Imports included, among other items, spices, pearls, precious stones, and fine cloths.

From the standpoint of the nineteenth and twentieth centuries, one of the most interesting features of this foreign trade was the earliest known direct contact of China with the peoples of Western Europe. Mongol armies had, as we have seen, penetrated far into Europe and had brought alarm to the sovereigns of the western part of that continent. Travellers from the Mongol possessions must also have reached that region. We know, indeed, of a Uighur (or possibly an Ongut) Nestorian monk, Rabban Cauma (or Sauma) who had been born in Cambaluc and who in 1287 and 1288 visited Rome, Bordeaux, and Paris on a diplomatic mission from the Mongols. We do not know that any of the Chinese reached Western Europe, but, as we have said, we hear of them in Russia.

Compared with some of the states of the time, the kingdoms of Western Europe were then small in area and population and were by no means so important for their contemporaries as were several other realms—China, for example. Nor were they so populous or prosperous. A European traveller in China in the fourteenth century, for instance, declares that the former Sung domains contained "two hundred cities all greater than Venice." In the thirteenth century, however, Western Europe was already displaying some of the beginnings of that remarkable growth which was later to make it dominant in the world's life and which six and seven centuries later was to lead it to work the greatest revolution in China in that Empire's history. Even before the birth of Jenghiz Khan and the Mongol advance, the Crusades had carried the arms of Western European peoples into the Levant, and Italian cities had made commercial contacts there. The thirteenth century saw extensive trade between Italy and the Near East. It also witnessed the rise of the Franciscans and Dominicans and with it a new burst of Christian missionary endeavor, both inside and outside of Europe. Given the facility of travel in Asia which the Mongols had created, it would, therefore, have been strange if Europeans had not reached China.

Just how many merchants from Western Europe made the journey to China we do not know. Judging from those of whom our comparatively scanty records tell us, the number must have been considerable. We hear of Genoese and Venetians in China, and of many in Venice who had made the round trip. An Italian trade-guide of the fourteenth century describes one of the routes and gives instructions to those who would follow it. Travellers went either by the land roads—of which the most frequently traversed were one by way of the Black Sea, the Volga, Ili, and Kansu, and one through Persia, the Tarim River basin, and Kansu—or by sea via India to the ports on the south coast of China.

Due largely to the fact that he left behind him a record of his travels and observations, the most famous of these medieval adventurers was a Venetian, Marco Polo. Several years before the Mongols had made an end of the Sung rule in South China, Nicolo and Maffeo Polo—the father and uncle of Marco—had come to Cambaluc. Khubilai was much interested in them and dispatched them to the West with letters to the Pope asking for a hundred teachers of science and religion. Because of a papal interregnum the answer to the request was delayed. When at last the Polos started on their return journey, they were accompanied by only two of the hundred missionaries asked for, and these, frightened by the dangers in the way, turned back before going very far. The two brothers, however, were undeterred and in due course, together with Marco, whom they had taken with them, reached China. Their route was across Persia, the upper reaches of the Oxus, the Pamirs, and the valley of the Tarim. Khubilai received the Polos with cordiality (1275) and seems to have treated with especial kindness Marco, then about twenty-one years of age. Marco entered his employ, holding various positions, among them some which carried the young Venetian over much of China.

After a little more than a decade and a half in China, in 1292 the Polos left it as members of a large company appointed to escort a princess to Persia, where she was to become the wife of the reigning Mongol khan. The route this time was by sea—from Zaitun to Sumatra, India, and Persia—and the Polos, after seeing their charge safely to her destination, returned to Venice. It was probably while a prisoner of war in Genoa that Marco dictated an account of his travels and observations to a fellow captive. The result was a book which was to pass through many editions and which was to have a large influence upon European knowledge of geography and geographic discoveries. Few works of travel have had so wide a circulation or such far-reaching effects. Columbus, for example, owed much to it. Even to-day, it is one of our best sources of information about China and the countries of Central and Southern Asia in the days of the Mongols.

FOREIGN CONTACTS UNDER THE MONGOLS: FOREIGN RELIGIONS IN CHINA

Among the many influences from the outside which the presence of so many aliens brought to the Middle Kingdom, some of the most interesting were religious.

The timidity of the two Dominicans who began the journey with the Polos by no means characterized all their fellow friars. During the thirteenth and fourteenth centuries Dominicans and Franciscans, taking advantage of the comparative ease of travel under the Mongols, covered much of Central Asia and went to India and China. The new burst of religious zeal which these orders represented and aided spread the Christian message fully as widely as the Italian merchants extended European commerce.

Some friars were sent on political errands by European rulers: more of them went on purely religious missions. Notable among the diplomatic envoys were two Franciscans, John of Plano Carpini, who (1245-1247) accomplished the round trip to Karakorum, and William of Rubruck, who made the journey out to the same Mongol capital and back a few years later (1253-1255).

So far as we know, the first friar to reach China proper was one who went with a purely religious objective, a Franciscan, John of Montecorvino. John arrived in Cambaluc in 1294, having come by way of India, where a travelling companion, a Dominican, had died. He gained the favor of the Emperor and by 1305 had baptized about six thousand converts and had built a church. When, shortly after 1305, the news of his success reached Europe, the Pope appointed him Archbishop of Cambaluc and sent him reënforcements, three of whom, all Franciscans, reached China. Other Friars Minor went to China during the next few years, and we know of houses of the order at Zaitun (Ch'üanchow), the present Hangchow, and Yangchow—all three, it will be noted, important commercial cities—as well as at Cambaluc. So far as we know, the last Roman Catholic missionary to penetrate to China in the Middle Ages was a papal legate, John of Marignolli. Following the overland route, he reached Cambaluc in 1342, remained there three or four years, and, returning by the sea route, arrived at Avignon in 1353. Shortly thereafter the Mongols were expelled from China, their empire collapsed, and communications with Western Europe were cut off. Such Roman Catholic communities as existed—relatively small at best—disappeared, partly because they were either foreign in membership or were associated in the public mind with the now unpopular alien, and nothing remained of them but a few memories (mostly in Europe) and still fewer physical relics.

Nestorians, too, were in China under the Mongols. Nestorian Christianity was at that time widely spread in Central Asia and on the borders of China proper, and numbers of the foreigners who came from these regions into China under the Yüan were of that faith. A Turkish tribe, the Keraïts, which was closely affiliated with the Mongols, and from which many high officials and the mother of Mangu, Hulagu, and Khubilai were drawn, were Nestorians. So, too, were the Onguts, who lived near the northern bend of the Yellow River, and some of the Uighurs, whom the Mongols employed extensively. We hear of a Nestorian—probably from Syria—who under Khubilai was placed in charge of the astronomical bureau in Cambaluc and later became a member of the Hanlin Academy and a minister of state, of a Nestorian physician from Samarkand who was governor of Chinkiang, of a Nestorian archbishopric in Cambaluc (created some years before), of a Nestorian Uighur (or possibly an Ongut) born in North China, who went to Bagdad and in 1280 became patriarch of the entire Nestorian communion, of an office established by Khubilai to supervise the Christians, and of Nestorians in such widely separated cities and portions of China as Yangchow, Hangchow, Chinkiang, Kansu, Yünnan, and Hochienfu (in the present Hopei). The collapse of the Mongol rule was followed by the extinction of Nestorianism in China. Most of the foreigners who professed the faith probably either left the country or were killed. Moreover, on the edges of China and in Central Asia Nestorianism was superseded by Islam and Buddhism, and no sources remained from which missionaries might again propagate the faith in the Middle Kingdom.

We know that Armenian Christians resided in China under the Mongols, and the contingent of Alans who were a portion of the Mongol armed forces in Cathay belonged to one of the eastern

Christian communions before their conversion to Roman Catholicism by John of Montecorvino. These, of course, had no more permanent influence than did Roman Catholicism and Nestorianism.

Islam fared better than Christianity. Moslems from abroad appear to have been much more numerous in China under the Mongols than were Christians. As we have seen, merchant communities of Moslem Arabs were found in several of the chief commercial cities. Much of the present Yünnan was governed by a Moslem official who had rendered notable service during the conquest of China, his son succeeded to his power, and descendants, still Moslem by faith, were prominent in China after the expulsion of the Mongols. It is not surprising that a large Mohammedan community arose in that region, for not only is it probable that Moslem troops were serving there under the banner of their co-religionist, but many of the inhabitants would be likely, from motives of expediency, to accept the faith of their governors. Nor is it strange that in North China, and particularly in what is now Kansu, where the overland trade routes from the West debouch, many Moslem immigrants were found. Neither is it remarkable that Moslem communities survived the downfall of the Mongols. Not only were they probably more numerous than the Christians, but the growth of Islam in Central Asia maintained a constant Moslem influence in China's Northwest, and the Arab control of much of the sea-borne commerce between Western, Southern, and Eastern Asia in the fourteenth, fifteenth, and sixteenth centuries must have aided the persistence of Islam on the south coast. Moslems had been in China before the Yüan, but from this dynasty dates their prominence in Chinese life.

CULTURE UNDER THE MONGOLS

As we saw at the beginning of this chapter, contact with foreigners and foreign civilizations under the Mongols was not followed by any such burst of cultural creativity as succeeded the introduction of Buddhism. Some effect the extensive contacts with aliens had, however: the Mongol period is different from the Sung and marked developments took place.

In mathematics and medicine innovations were made, due chiefly, apparently, to foreign contacts.

Sorghum, eventually a major crop in the North, was introduced. Chaulmoogra oil became known and was used in the treatment of leprosy.

In painting, the Sung traditions, especially those which had arisen under the influence of Ch'an Buddhism, were continued in monasteries in the Yangtze Valley and the adjoining coast. Some secular artists among the scholars, too, in their disdain of things Mongol, attempted to maintain the Sung forms. There was also a reversion to T'ang styles. The Mongol conquest had a decided effect, however. Thanks to fairly close contact with the West, Persian art here and there left its mark. Due to their Buddhist proclivities, moreover, the Mongol rulers favored religious paintings of that faith. Especially noteworthy was the reintroduction of movement and color and the portrayal of scenes of everyday secular life. Horses provided favorite subjects, as did the festivities and diversions of the rich and the powerful. The so-called Northern School, with its more vigorous style, came to the fore. One of the greatest artists of the dynasty was Chao Mêng-fu, a descendant of the founder of the Sung. He held high office at court and was noted as a painter of landscapes and of horses, men, and historical scenes.

Not only in painting but in ceramics changes were registered. Persian influences made themselves felt in the forms of vases and in ornamentation. Moreover, cloisonné, of Byzantine origin, now seems to have appeared for the first time. New Indian impulses were present in Buddhist iconography.

In literature the outstanding developments were in the drama and the novel. Acting was not new in China but had a long history in connection with worship, in the pantomimes and historical recitals associated with the ancestral rites of antiquity, and in acrobatic performances stressing the use of weapons. There were jugglers, dancers, and simple plays as early as the Han, and the drama in several forms—comedies among them—was found in succeeding dynasties. The drama was also encouraged in the T'ang, notably under that great imperial patron of the arts, Ming Huang, and scores of titles of plays have come down from the Sung. Now, however, the stage came to sudden flowering, and henceforth occupied a prominent place in Chinese life. As a favorite method of diversion of both rich and poor it has had a profound influence upon the Chinese mind, and the historical plays that abound have been one of the chief methods of instructing the populace in the story of their nation's past. Many of the plays written during the Yüan have survived until our own day.

The novel, too, emerged suddenly into prominence. One of the most famous of the historical romances of China, the *San Kuo Chih Yen I*, or "Romance of the Three Kingdoms," portraying some of the stirring events of the period which succeeded the downfall of the Han, seems to date from the Yüan—although it is very probable that only the crude original was written in that period and that it underwent many revisions before, in the sixteenth century, it appeared in its finished form.

In popular songs there were also innovations.

Both the drama and the novel were usually written in a style which approached the vernacular and helped toward a popularization of literature.

Why they should now first have flourished is not entirely certain. One conjecture has it that it was because of outside influences; another surmise is that scholars, cut off from holding office, and, through the discontinuance of civil service examinations, denied the usual method of promotion, turned their energies into these channels. Whatever the causes, the fact is clear.

CHINESE INFLUENCE ON FOREIGN PEOPLES

While, thanks to the partial unity brought to so much of Asia by Mongol rule, foreigners were having an influence upon Chinese culture, China, in turn, was not without its effect upon other peoples. Commerce spread the use of Chinese silks and porcelains, and these left their stamp upon the fabrics and the designs of Central and Western Asia. The Chinese impress is seen, too, upon the painting of miniatures in Central Asia. It is just possible, moreover, that knowledge of that art of printing which had reached so high a stage of development in China under the Sung may have penetrated to the West in Mongol times and have had some share in the preparation for the revolutionary growth of the press in Europe a century or so after the downfall of the Yüan.

CONCLUSION

The Mongol period, then, was marked by distinct changes in Chinese life and was the break—or the transition—between the brilliant but over-refined culture of the Sung and the prosperous but somewhat commonplace and uninspired centuries which began with the Ming and were to continue nearly to our own day. It witnessed the coming of many aliens, but saw the introduction of very few foreign contributions which were long to have a prominent place. It is distinguished for the rapid development of the drama and the novel. By inducing a reaction from foreign control it contributed to the dominance of stereotyped and uncreative Confucianism in the dynasties which followed.

BIBLIOGRAPHY

The standard Chinese sources are the two dynastic histories, the *Yüan Shih,* composed hastily in the early years of the Ming dynasty, and with many imperfections, and the *Hsin Yüan Shih,* compiled recently, and recognized officially (1919) by President Hsü Shih-ch'ang. E. Haenisch has *Untersuchungen über das Yüan-chao Pi Shi* (*Die Geheime Geschichte der Mongolen*) (Leipzig, 1931), a study of a Mongol text which underlies part of the unofficial history of the Yüan dynasty.

As for earlier periods, general works in European languages useful for the Yüan are de Mailla, *Histoire Générale de la Chine* (13 vols., Paris, 1777–1785); H. Cordier, *Histoire Générale de la Chine* (4 vols., Paris, 1920–1921); L. Wieger, *Textes Historiques* (2 vols., Hochienfu, 1903, 1904); René Grousset, *Histoire de l'Extrême-Orient* (2 vols., Paris, 1929); H. A. Giles, *A Chinese Biographical Dictionary* (London and Shanghai, 1898); and F. E. A. Krause, *Geschichte Ostasiens* (Vol. 1, Göttingen, 1925). The first three suffer from lack of perspective and from defects in critical appraisal of the material. Giles's great work, moreover, is not always reliable.

Among the special books and articles on political history are C. D'Ohsson, *Histoire des Mongols, depuis Tchinguiz-Khan jusqu'à Timour Bey ou Tamerlan* (4 vols., Amsterdam, 1852); (on the invasion of Burma) Edouard Huber, *Études Indochinoises. V. La Fin de la Dynastie de Pagan* (*Bulletin de l'École Française de l'Extrême-Orient,* 1909, pp. 633–680); R. Groussset, *l'Empire des Steppes. Attila, Genghiz-Khan, Tamerlan* (Paris, 1939); A. C. Moule, *The Siege of Saianfu and the Murder of Achmach Bailo* (*Journal of the North China Branch of the Royal Asiatic Society,* 1927, pp. 1–35); A. C. Moule, *The Murder of Achmach Bailo* (*ibid.* 1928, pp. 256–258); A. C. Moule, *A Table of the Emperors of the Yüan Dynasty* (*ibid.* 1914, p. 124); and W. P. Groeneveldt, *The Expedition of the Mongols against Java in 1293 A.D.* (*China Review,* Vol. 4, pp. 246–254). See also H. H. Howarth, *History of the Mongols from the Ninth to the Nineteenth Century* (4 parts, London, 1876–1927). On the invasion of Japan, see J. Murdoch, *A History of Japan,* Vol. 1 (Yokohama, 1910); G. B. Sansom, *Japan. A Short Cultural History* (New York, 1943); K. Hara, *An Introduction to the*

History of Japan (New York, 1920); C. F. Brinkley, *A History of the Japanese People* (New York, 1915).

On other foreign contacts under the Mongols, see H. Yule, *Cathay and the Way Thither* (new edition by H. Cordier, 4 vols., London, 1913–1916); H. Yule, *The Book of Ser Marco Polo* (third edition, revised by H. Cordier, 2 vols., London, 1921); A. C. Moule and P. Pelliot, *Marco Polo, The Description of the World* (London, 2 vols., 1938); L. F. Benedetto, *Marco Polo Il Milione* (Florence, 1928); E. Bretschneider, *Medieval Researches from Eastern Asiatic Sources. Fragments towards the Knowledge of the Geography and History of Central and Western Asia from the 13th to the 17th Century* (2 vols., London, 1910 [Preface, 1887]); W. W. Rockhill, *The Journey of William of Rubruck to the Eastern Parts of the World, 1253–55, as Narrated by Himself, with Two Accounts of the Earlier Journey of John of Pian de Carpine* (London, 1900); W. W. Rockhill, *Notes on the Relations and Trade of China with the Eastern Archipelago and the Coasts of the Indian Ocean during the Fourteenth Century* (*T'oung Pao*, 1913, pp. 473–476, 1914, pp. 419–447, 1915, pp. 61–159, 236–271, 374–392, 435–467, 604–626); Gabriel Ferrand, *Relations de Voyages et Textes Geographiques Arabes, Persans et Turcs à l'Extrême-Orient du VIIIe au XVIIIe siècles* (2 vols., Paris, 1913–1914); H. Cordier, *Ser Marco Polo Notes and Addenda* (London, 1920); A. Ricci, *The Travels of Marco Polo* (London, 1931); George Phillips, *Two Medieval Fuhkien Trading Ports, Chüan-chow and Chang-chow* (*T'oung Pao*, 1895, pp. 449–463); and H. Cordier, *Les Voyages en Asie au XIVe Siècle du Bienheureux Frère Odoric de Pordenone, Religieux de Saint-François* (Paris, 1891).

On religion under the Mongols, see L. Wieger, *A History of Religious Beliefs and Philosophical Opinions in China*, translated from the French by E. T. C. Werner (Hsien-hsien, 1927) Lesson 72. Ed. Chavannes, *Inscriptions et Pièces de Chancellerie Chinoises de l'Epoque Mongole* (*T'oung Pao*, 1904, pp. 354–477, 1905, pp. 1–42, 1908, pp. 297–428) gives documents which bear upon Buddhism, Taoism, and Confucianism under the Mongols.

On Christianity in China under the Mongols, see a summary in K. S. Latourette, *A History of Christian Missions in China* (New York, 1929) and the works referred to in the footnotes in Chapter V of that book. The best account is one which has appeared since that book was published—A. C. Moule, *Christians in China before the Year 1550* (London, 1930).

On Islam in China, see M. Broomhall, *Islam in China* (London, 1919)—not altogether reliable—and D'Ollone, *Recherches sur les Musulmans Chinois* (Paris, 1911).

On art, see E. F. Fenollosa, *Epochs of Chinese and Japanese Art* (2 vols., London, 1912); B. Laufer, *T'ang, Sung, and Yüan Paintings Belonging to Various Chinese Collectors* (Paris and Brussels, 1924); Leigh Ashton, *An Introduction to the Study of Chinese Sculpture* (London, 1924); O. Sirén, *Chinese Sculpture from the Fifth to the Fourteenth Century* (4 vols., London, 1925); R. Petrucci, *Chinese Painters* (New York, 1921); R. L. Hobson, *The Art of the Chinese Potter from the Han Dynasty to the End of the Ming* (London, 1923); Osvald Sirén, *Histoire des Arts Anciens de la Chine* (4 vols., Paris, 1929–1930).

On literature, see A. Wylie, *Notes on Chinese Literature* (Shanghai, 1902); H. A. Giles, *A History of Chinese Literature* (New York, 1901); C. H. Brewitt-Taylor, *San Kuo, or the Romance of the Three Kingdoms* (2 vols., Shanghai, 1925); and A. E. Zucker, *The Chinese Theater* (London, 1925).

On the possible transfer of the art of printing from China to Europe, see T. F. Carter, *The Invention of Printing in China and Its Spread Westward* (revised edition, New York, 1931).

CHAPTER VIII

CHINA AGAIN UNDER CHINESE RULE: THE MING DYNASTY (A.D. 1368–1644)

INTRODUCTORY

The dynasty that Chu Yüan-chang founded was denominated Ming, which may best be translated "brilliant" or "glorious." To a certain degree it lived up to the implied promise. The genius of the period lay largely in being practical and efficient. From the military standpoint, the Ming was stronger than any native Chinese ruling house since the T'ang. It became the master of all of what we call China proper, as the Sung had never done. It interfered in Mongolian affairs and for a time held portions of what is now the New Dominion. It made its power felt as far south as Ceylon. Its form of government was, with slight changes, taken over by its successor, and was to last into the twentieth century. In culture leading achievements were in the applied arts. There was much building. The manufacture of cotton cloth greatly increased. In philosophy no radically new schools were developed, but there was vigorous loyalty to accepted ideals.

However, the Ming only partly deserved its title. It was never able to extend its boundaries to those occupied by the Han and the T'ang. In government it was content to perpetuate, with modifications, the machinery of its predecessors. Under it the Empire was elegant, wealthy, and populous, but only here and there displayed a tendency to break out creatively into new channels. Neither in intellectual nor in artistic achievement did the China of the Ming display the originality of the T'ang and the Sung. The very success with which the dynasty drove out the Mongol and reëstablished the cultural and administrative structure of China's past militated against innovations. Unity and internal peace seemed not to be consistent with experimentation.

POLITICAL HISTORY: HUNG WU

Chu Yüan-chang spent most of his reign in completing the conquest of China, in seeking to extend his power to neighboring lands, and in putting the machinery of government into good working order. He is usually best known as Hung Wu, the name (or *nien hao*) by which the period of his reign is designated.

The expulsion of the Mongols from Cambaluc and the proclamation of the new dynasty were soon followed by the acknowledgment of the authority of the Ming by the remainder of China. Hsü Ta, the general who had taken Cambaluc for Hung Wu, reduced Shansi, Shensi, and Kansu. Szechwan, where an independent principality had been set up by an adventurer, was brought under the control of the Ming. By the end of 1382 Yünnan had succumbed: Hung Wu finally suppressed the power of the family which for over four centuries had ruled there as independent princes or as governors under the Emperor.

Several outlying territories were also induced to recognize the Ming. The southern portion of what is now Manchuria made its submission. Under Hung Wu's successors, it may be added, most of Manchuria was for a time to a greater or less extent within the Chinese domains. Korea and the Liu Ch'iu (Ryu Kyu) islands recognized Hung Wu's suzerainty, and embassies were received from Burma and Nepal. Not content with expelling the Mongols from south of the Great Wall, Hung Wu carried the war into their own territory. Twice during his reign a Chinese army reached the ancient Mongol capital, Karakorum. He appears to have considered himself the legitimate successor of the Mongol Grand Khans who had ruled from Cambaluc, and as such sought to extend his sway over their former possessions in the West. His forces took at least one of the oases in that region, Hami, and his envoys obtained the acceptance of his suzerainty by several other centers in what is now the New Dominion.

When, however, Ming emissaries crossed the mountains to Samarkand, they met with a far different reception. In this region they found the truculent and energetic Tamerlane building a new empire out of some of the fragments of Mongol power and were imprisoned. In the course of time they were released, and Tamerlane and the Ming exchanged several embassies—the Chinese regarding those which came to them as bearers of tribute. Far from acknowledging the overlordship of the Ming, however, Tamerlane was planning the invasion of China when (1405) death terminated his career.

In another direction Hung Wu met with moderate success. Japanese pirates were ravaging the coasts of China, and the Ming dispatched an envoy to Japan to request that these be restrained. Japan was then nearing the end of a long period of civil war, during which there had been much anarchy, and some of the local magnates had become practically independent of the central authority. One of these latter, a scion of the Japanese imperial line, prevented the envoy from reaching Kyoto, the capital. A few years later, this same prince, possibly hoping for Chinese aid in the domestic strife, sent an embassy to the Ming court. The Chinese appear to have accepted it as coming from the Japanese Government, thus opening the way for an official intercourse between the two countries which continued intermittently for years —although not without friction. The pirates were never completely suppressed, partly, at least, because the Japanese authorities were unable to cope with them.

In internal administration Hung Wu showed no very pronounced originality, but, perhaps for the very reason that he was not an innovator but restored traditional Chinese institutions with skill, the country appears to have settled down fairly promptly to its ordinary pursuits. He was confronted with occasional revolts, as have been most Chinese Emperors, but none of them was of unusual consequence. His capital he established at Nanking, where he planned and began the construction of an enlarged city on magnificent lines. He promulgated a code of laws modeled on those of the T'ang. He adopted the traditional bureaucratic organization of the Empire. Although he modified this by dividing the country into principalities over each of which he put one of his sons as *Wang*, these were in addition to and not a substitute for the usual administrative subdivisions and the regular official hierarchy. However, Hung Wu abolished the premiership and replaced it with a Cabinet (*Nei Ko*), or Grand Secretariat, made up of several members—an innovation which possibly tended to accentuate the actual power of the sovereign. After some hesitation—first inaugurating them and then for a decade or so restricting them, reducing their power, and adopting the method employed for a time under the Han of having the governors of the provinces recommend to the throne men suitable for office—Hung Wu reëstablished firmly the civil service examinations and the principle of filling government offices from the successful candidates. Under the Ming, indeed, the examinations acquired an inflexibility—stressing a minute knowledge of the classical books and an artificial literary style—which may have had much to do with discouraging originality among the educated. The Sung dynasty had tended more than the T'ang to confine the state tests to the Confucian Classics. The Ming further regulated and stereotyped the system.

Mindful of his early background, Hung Wu showed some favor to the Buddhist monks, and had executed a high official who protested. He organized them nationally into a hierarchy, but this may well have been for the purpose of facilitating state control of the monasteries.

In spite of his friendliness to the Buddhists, Hung Wu strengthened Confucianism. He showed marked deference to Confucian scholarship; he ordered the establishment of an Empire-wide system of schools in which the basis of instruction was the Confucian Classics; he honored the Hanlin Academy; he preserved the traditional system of state religious observances which were so closely associated with Confucianism; he abolished all the state-awarded titles of the gods except those of Confucius. Under him the Chinese were reacting against the foreign importations and innovations of the Mongols, and were attempting to restore their traditional culture. It is not strange that in the process a conservatism was nourished which made later change difficult.

POLITICAL HISTORY: YUNG LO

Hung Wu was gathered to his fathers in 1398, at the ripe age of three-score years and ten. He had held the throne for thirty years and had established his family so firmly upon it that they retained it for another two and a half centuries.

Hung Wu's death was followed almost immediately by a struggle over the succession which for about four years plunged the country into civil war. Hung Wu had named as his heir a grandson, Chu Yün-wên—the son of his deceased oldest son. Only in his teens when the death of his grandfather placed him on the throne, Chu Yün-wên soon found himself in an impossible situation. He antagonized his uncles, including Chu Ti, the fourth son of Hung Wu. Chu Ti had been given by his father the control of a large district in the Northeast and came to be known as Prince of Yen. A man of marked energy and ability, he speedily found occasion to raise the standard of revolt. However, the young Emperor had many loyal supporters who fought valiantly for him, and it was not until 1403 that Chu Ti, after a war which laid waste much of the territory on the plain between the Yellow River and the Yangtze, succeeded in taking Nanking. In the fall of his capital Chu Yün-wên disappeared, and it is often asserted that he was not killed but escaped in the garb of a Buddhist monk, lived in hiding in a monastery, and had his identity disclosed many years later. Whatever his fate, he had permanently lost the Empire.

Chu Ti, in spite of the disloyalty and slaughter by which he had made his way to supreme power, proved an able monarch. While more correctly called by his dynastic title, Ch'êng Tsu, he is best known to us by the name of his reign period, Yung Lo (1403–1424). Under him the Ming dynasty reached the apex of its power. He vigorously maintained and extended Chinese prestige abroad and gave the Empire an energetic domestic administration.

In his foreign policy, Yung Lo was aggressive. He interfered actively in Mongolia, waging several campaigns there. He welcomed diplomatic relations with Yoshimitsu, the Shogun who controlled most of Japan. Yoshimitsu was eager for friendly intercourse with China, partly because it would further trade, and partly because the Zen (Ch'an) monks who were influential at his court desired it. Yoshimitsu promised to restrain the Japanese pirates who troubled the coasts of China and even acknowledged the Ming Emperor as his suzerain. In Annam Yung Lo took advantage of internal dissensions to occupy much of the land and to divide it into Chinese administrative districts. Under him the petty chiefs of Upper Burma acquiesced more or less in Chinese authority.

Yung Lo sent several naval expeditions to the lands to the south. These visited Cochin-China, Java, Sumatra, Cambodia,

Siam, India, and Ceylon. In Ceylon, a ruler who treated a Chinese envoy with contumely was taken prisoner and transported to China, and at least part of the island is said to have paid tribute to the Ming for the next half-century. In several others of the lands visited the local princes were induced, either peaceably or by force, to recognize Chinese overlordship. The leading commander in these southern exploits was a eunuch, Chêng-Ho, who had first distinguished himself in the suppression of a rebellion in Yünnan. Under his captaincy seven expeditions sailed to the southern seas, the last of them after Yüng Lo's death. He visited Annam, Cambodia, Malacca, Siam, Java, Sumatra, Borneo, Cochin, Ceylon, Bengal, Arabia, the Somali Coast (in Eastern Africa), and Ormuz (on the Persian Gulf). Tribute was received from Java, Yung Lo was sent presents from one or more rulers in South India and conferred the title of king upon one, and even from the distant Somali Coast four missions were dispatched to China before his death. During no other native dynasty has Chinese authority ever been so far extended overseas.

In domestic administration, the Yung Lo period saw notable achievements. The Emperor moved the seat of imperial government to the North, to what he called Peking, or the Northern Capital, in contrast to his father's choice, Nanking, or the Southern Capital. The reason for the change may have been that Peking, so much nearer the northern marches, held a better location for the defense of the Empire against its traditional enemies. It may also have been because the North had been the center of Yung Lo's power and was more friendly than the South. Peking, occupying part of the site of the Cambaluc of the Mongols, was largely rebuilt. The grandeur of the conception of the architects can be discerned in the present walls and imperial palaces and temples, for these, repaired and altered from time to time, in their main features date from the Yung Lo period. It is doubtful whether even to-day any capital in the world is more impressive. Certainly in Yung Lo's time Peking was unrivalled for the formal and stately expression in buildings of its position as the seat of administration of a vast empire. If one is tempted by the ornate painting and inferior sculpture of the dynasty to dismiss the æsthetic achievements of the Ming as degenerate, it is well to remember that the genius which could plan and carry out such structures as those in Peking was by no means decadent.

Yung Lo sought to promote the prosperity of his realm. He encouraged the migration of settlers into the regions laid waste in the wars which had brought him to the throne. For the purpose of facilitating the transportation of rice to Peking and of avoiding the dangerous sea passage around the Shantung promontory, he had the Grand Canal improved. Although his personal inclination was toward Buddhism, especially of the Tibetan type, officially he pursued his father's policy of strengthening the Confucian cult—by showing favor to the Hanlin Academy, by encouraging the study of the Confucian Classics, by honoring Confucius, and by maintaining the civil service examinations. He even endeavored to restrict the numbers of Buddhist monks by ordering some of them to return to secular life. It was under his orders that one of the most gigantic compilations ever made, the *Yung Lo Ta Tien,* was accomplished—a vast collection of excerpts and entire works from the mass of Chinese literature. So huge was it that the cost of printing appalled even the imperial treasury and, except for some excerpts, it remained in manuscript only.

POLITICAL HISTORY: THE SUCCESSORS OF YUNG LO

During the remaining years that it retained the mandate of Heaven, the family of Chu Yüan-chang produced no monarchs of the vigor and ability of Hung Wu and Yung Lo. Much of the time the Empire was fairly prosperous—although often we hear of agricultural distress and even famine—but for the more than two centuries which elapsed between the death of Yung Lo and the overthrow of the dynasty, no ruler emerged at all comparable with the chief rulers of preceding lines. No noteworthy effort was made to extend the frontiers: in area the Empire shrank rather than expanded. Before the fifteenth century was half gone, Annam had regained its independence. Tribute from the states across the seas gradually lapsed. Fighting with the Mongols was frequent, and the tide of battle did not always flow in favor of the Chinese. On one occasion, indeed, about the middle of the fifteenth century, a Mongol army defeated and captured the Ming Emperor, and in the ensuing peace the Chinese renounced all claim to intervention in Mongolian affairs. It seems to have been more because of the weakness of her neighbors than her own strength that in the last several decades of the dynasty China was not more frequently invaded.

Friction with the Japanese marked many of the later years of the Ming. In spite of the friendly relations earlier established with the Ashikaga Shoguns—the most powerful magnates in the Japan of the day—Japanese pirates persisted in ravaging the coasts of China, from Hainan northward, for the control of the Ashikaga was not effective over all the island realm. The raiders sacked even such important cities as Ningpo and Yangchow. Estrangement between China and Japan followed (*ca.* 1531) and commerce dwindled. The difficulties culminated in a determined Japanese attempt to invade and conquer China. The initiating and guiding mind in this venture was Hideyoshi, an able and vigorous soldier of lowly birth. In the period of internal turmoil which accompanied and followed the downfall of the Ashikaga, he had made himself master of the land. Japan pacified, he turned to the continent for further exploits. He asked the Koreans to allow his forces to pass through their territories, but was rebuffed. His armies thereupon invaded the peninsula (1592) and within a year had taken several of its principal centers. The Chinese dispatched troops to aid the Koreans. Their first contingent was small and was quickly repulsed, but a second, much larger, drove the Japanese southward, and Hideyoshi withdrew from the peninsula all but a few thousand men. Negotiations followed, but Hideyoshi abruptly and angrily terminated them when the Ming envoys, in what seemed to him an insultingly patronizing fashion, offered him investiture as a vassal prince. In 1597 he renewed the invasion of Korea. The following year a Chinese army in the peninsula was decisively defeated and the noses and ears of the slaughtered enemy were sent to Kyoto, where the tumulus over them is still shown. Hideyoshi's death (1598) led to the Japanese withdrawal from the Korean adventure and that particular threat to the Ming disappeared.

THE RISE OF THE MANCHUS AND THE END OF THE MING

The reign under which the Japanese invasion occurred—usually known by its year title, Wan Li (1573–1620)—was the longest of the dynasty. Thanks to the vigor of an able minister, its first days were auspicious, but when this leadership was removed by death the realm fell upon evil days. The monarch was incompetent (although sometimes in an emergency he acted with decision and dignity), the court was torn by factions, taxes were oppressive, agricultural distress was frequent, misgovernment was rife, great landed estates were assigned to imperial favorites and the politically powerful, and brigandage and insurrections multiplied. Scholar-statesmen there were who strove to stem the tide—some protesting against the misrule of the eunuchs, several of them at the cost of their lives, and others organizing political groups or parties to effect reform. These efforts, however, were unavailing, and conditions went from bad to worse.

At this juncture, a new power arose in the Northeast, and by the middle of the seventeenth century it had conquered the Empire. The latest of those invasions from the north which have been so frequent and important a factor in China's history, it proved to be the most successful of them all: the Manchus governed the whole of China—something which no foreign conqueror except the Mongols had ever done—and held it for more than two and a half centuries, approximately three times as long as had the Mongols.

The Manchus were a Tungusic people, related to the Juchên, or Chin, who had been such prominent opponents of the Sung. At the dawn of the sixteenth century they were dwelling in the valley of the Sungari, in parts of the present provinces of Kirin and Heilungchiang. About the beginning of the seventeenth century they were welded into a powerful organization by one Nurhachu (*ca.* 1559–1626). By the time of his death Nurhachu had extended his frontiers to the sea on the east and to the Amur on the north, and had moved his capital to Mukden, captured from the Ming. Under Nurhachu and his successor a large number of the Mongols were subdued and others voluntarily accepted the Manchu rule. The Manchus, too, obtained possession of the dynastic seal of the Yüan. Many Mongols were incorporated into the Manchu armies and acknowledged the house of Nurhachu as the imperial line of China. The name Ch'ing was assumed, the title by which the dynasty was to be known in Chinese history. The Manchus also launched repeated attacks against Korea and eventually succeeded in bringing it to acknowledge their suzerainty.

The Ch'ing often broke through the Great Wall and raided parts of the North China plain. However, they did not succeed in obtaining a permanent foothold south of the Wall until internal rebellion had fatally weakened their opponents. The last of the Ming to rule in Peking made desperate but vain efforts to retrieve the declining fortunes of his house. Resistance against the repeated attacks of the Manchus impoverished an already depleted treasury. The death blow was a rebellion led by Li Tzŭ-ch'êng, son of a village headman in Shensi. Famine and taxation had driven Li, as they have many another Chinese, to turn brigand. He proved an able general and disciplinarian, in 1642 captured K'aifêng and made himself master of Shensi, and in 1644 proclaimed himself Emperor of a new dynasty. In the latter year he marched upon Peking and took it, the Ming Emperor, in despair, hanging himself as the city fell.

On the northeastern frontier, holding it against the Manchus, was a Chinese general, Wu San-kuei. When Peking passed out of Ming hands, goaded on by the murder of his father by Li and by Li's seizure of a favorite concubine, he joined forces with the Ch'ing. The combined armies defeated Li in the open field and took the capital (1644). Li Tzŭ-ch'êng retreated westward and southward, his armies melted away, and he was soon eliminated—whether killed in Hupeh, as one report has it, or finding safety, incognito, in a Buddhist monastery and becoming a monk, as another account declares, is unimportant from the standpoint of the later history of the Empire.

The Manchus, although safely ensconced in Peking and supported by the powerful Wu San-kuei, found the conquest of the remainder of China no easy task. The adherents of the Ming made a determined resistance and might conceivably have held part of the country for an indefinite period had it not been for unfortunate weaknesses at the top. The Ming aspirants to the throne were inept and dissensions unnerved their supporters. The Ch'ing took Yangchow with great slaughter and not long thereafter Nanking fell to them (1645). One of the Ming claimants set up his headquarters in Chêkiang, but soon fled, took refuge in a fleet, lived a semi-piratical life, and died in 1662. Another, who had attempted to establish himself in Fukien, perished when the enemy carried their victorious arms through the province. Still another was put forward at Canton, but in 1647 that city passed into the possession of the Manchus. Serious resistance was encountered by the Ch'ing in Shensi and Shansi, and in Szechwan a Chinese who had taken the opportunity given by the fall of the Ming to proclaim himself ruler of a new dynasty was subdued only after much bloodshed.

The last of the descendants of Chu Yüan-chang to claim the throne, a prince who is usually known by his title, Kuei Wang, held out for some years in Kwangsi and Yünnan. In 1648, indeed, it looked as though he might regain the Empire. Chinese officers in Szechwan, Shansi, and south of the Yangtze, who had assisted the Manchus in the conquest, disgruntled with their new masters, turned to Kuei Wang. For a short time there was held in the name of that prince much of Kwangtung, Kiangsi, Hunan, Szechwan, Shensi, and Shansi, as well as Kwangsi, Kweichow, and Yünnan. By the end of 1650, however, the Manchus had regained most of the lost territory and only Kweichow and Yünnan remained to Kuei Wang. Although he then ceased to be a serious menace to the conquerors, Kuei Wang lived on in mountain fastnesses in the Southwest for a number of years and did not come to his end until 1662.

It was in 1662, moreover, that there died a picturesque and vigorous opponent of the Manchus, the pirate Chêng Ch'êng-kung, who is usually known to Europeans as Koxinga. The most distinguished son—by a Japanese mother—of a famous naval freebooter who had made loyalty to the Ming the excuse for ravaging the southern coasts, he was his father's chief lieutenant. Not only was his name a terror in the ports of China, but he took possession of part of the island of Formosa. When his father and two of his brothers were treacherously executed by the Manchus, he vowed to avenge their death. Through the control of commerce which the possession of Formosa gave him he gained the sinews of war. So serious a menace did he prove that the Manchus, to combat him and other Ming loyalists who were still strong on the sea, ordered the population removed from the coast from Shantung through Kwangtung. The measure was not fully carried out, but was most nearly completed in Fukien. Chêng Ch'êng-kung's possessions in Formosa passed to his son and only after the death of the latter were the Manchus able to annex the island and so bring opposition to an end. It was not until 1683 that an imperial order allowed the Chinese once more to dwell on the coasts of Fukien.

The relatively easy triumph of the Manchus—so much more quickly achieved than had been that of the Mongols nearly four centuries before—does not necessarily prove that the Chinese had become less valorous than their forefathers. Had they presented a united front, the path of the Ch'ing would have been more difficult. But for the internal rivalries and weakness of the Ming which made many prominent Chinese despair of any future for that house and look with hope to the Manchus as possible guarantors of order, and but for the active assistance of Wu San-kuei, of many another Chinese commander, and of Chinese troops the conquest would have been much slower and perhaps impossible. Moreover, even before their final victory, the Ch'ing were adopting Chinese civilization, and were posing as a legitimate Chinese dynasty. The conquest was not, strictly speaking, by foreigners, but by a people largely Chinese in culture and not unrelated to some of the Northern Chinese in blood. Although to the very end of their power—in 1912—they endeavored to keep themselves aloof from the Chinese as a race and to a certain extent in manners and customs, the Manchus zealously supported Chinese institutions. They were wiser than had been the Mongols. They perpetuated the administrative system and laws of the Ming with but little alteration. The fifteen provinces of the Ming were increased to eighteen by the subdivision of some of the larger ones. Manchu garrisons were placed in strategic cities in a number of the provinces and were supported at public expense. Manchus were appointed, along with Chinese, on the boards at Peking and were admitted to competition in the civil service examinations. The male Chinese were forced to shave part of their heads and wear the queue—the Manchu form of headdress—as a sign of loyalty to the dynasty. With these and a few other exceptions, however, government went on as it had under Chinese rule. The great majority of the positions in the bureaucracy, including some of the very highest, were held by Chinese, Confucius was honored, the civil service examinations were conducted with practically the same curriculum and machinery as under the Ming, and many of the Manchus became expert in Chinese lore.

FOREIGN INTERCOURSE: EXTENSIVE COMMERCE WITH VARIOUS
SECTIONS OF THE ASIATIC WORLD AND RENEWED
CONTACTS WITH EUROPEANS

It may be an indication of the practical-mindedness of the Ming age that during much of its history foreign trade flourished and that the Chinese often went actively forth to encourage it. This was particularly true in the early, vigorous years of the dynasty. We have seen how, under Yung Lo, naval expeditions were sent to lands to the south. Chinese carried on trade with Java, Sumatra, India, Siam, Ceylon, parts of what is now French Indo-China, and with lands even farther to the southwest. However, Chinese ships were later restricted, by imperial command, to coastal waters. With the Land of the Rising Sun, too, there was active trade. It was the means of bringing many Chinese products and much Chinese thought to Japan. For example, during part of the Ming the chief circulating medium in Japan was Chinese copper coins, and Chinese philosophy continued influential.

Before the dynasty had ended, moreover, those contacts with the Occident had begun which eventually were to work the greatest cultural revolution in China's history—infinitely greater than that wrought by the Mongols and Manchus and more thoroughgoing even than that which followed the coming of Buddhism. Commerce with Europe, it must be noted, was due to the initiative of Westerners and not to Chinese enterprise. At the time, this fresh touch with the Occident did not appear nearly so significant as did some other events, and the Manchu rule was more than two-thirds over before it had resulted in any very important changes in Chinese civilization. Because of its outcome in our own day, however, it must here be chronicled.

After the fall of the Mongols, no Europeans appear to have come to China, and the little Christian communities which might have perpetuated their influence seem entirely to have disappeared. However, in the latter part of the fifteenth century, the expansion of European peoples of which the merchants and missionaries of the thirteenth and fourteenth centuries were a foreshadowing began afresh and with increased energy and rapidity. It was in the last decade of that century that daring

European voyagers discovered a new world in the Western Hemisphere and an all-sea route around Africa to India. Only a few years later their successors were knocking at the doors of China. It was, indeed, the lure of the land which Marco Polo's famous story had portrayed to successive generations of Europeans which drew some of the explorers. This was notably true of Columbus, who sailed westward in the belief that the world was smaller than it proved to be and that the east coast of Asia was about where America was found: the search for Cathay was in no small degree responsible for the discovery of the New World.

The first Europeans to arrive in China in this new day were, naturally, the Portuguese, for it was they who first rounded the Cape of Good Hope and gained a foothold in India. Malacca fell to their arms in 1511, and there they found Chinese ships. A few years later, probably in 1514, they reached China and before long established themselves off the coast of Kwangtung and in ports in Fukien and Chêkiang. Their early career in China was stormy. The Moslem ruler of Malacca whom they had dispossessed complained of them to the Chinese authorities, and a Portuguese envoy, Pirès, who reached Peking in 1520 was treated as a spy, was conveyed, by imperial order, to Canton, was there confined with several of his companions, and died in prison. A settlement which the Portuguese established near Ningpo was wiped out by a massacre (1545) and a similar fate overtook a trading colony in Fukien (1549). For a time they retained a precarious tenure only on islands south of Canton.

For this ill fortune the Portuguese had chiefly themselves to thank. Truculent and lawless, regarding all Eastern peoples as legitimate prey, they were little if any better than the contemporary Japanese pirates who pillaged the Chinese coasts. The Ming authorities can scarcely be censured for treating them as freebooters.

Within a few years after these events—the exact date is not quite certain—the Portuguese succeeded in making a permanent settlement in China, at Macao, on a peninsula which commanded a harbor on an island south of Canton. Here they have remained to this day, although the harbor is too shallow for the great ocean-going steamers of recent years and the sleepy little town, a bit of

Portugal set down in the Far East, has subsisted largely on its dubious gains from gambling and opium.

While the Portuguese were journeying eastward, the Spaniards were coming westward. The Spanish expedition led by the Portuguese Magellan circumnavigated the globe in the first quarter of the sixteenth century, Magellan himself losing his life in the Philippines (1521). Before the century was out, the Spaniards had firmly established themselves in the islands with Manila (founded 1571) as their capital. For a few years in the first half of the seventeenth century the Spaniards also had posts in Formosa, but from these they were driven by the Dutch in 1642.

In their occupation of the Philippines the Spaniards found the Chinese a fairly constant problem. Soon after the beginning of their conquest they were attacked by a Chinese pirate, seconded by a Japanese. Chinese migrated to the islands and much of the business of Manila passed into their hands. The Spaniards, alarmed, met the problem by the simple but cruel expedient of wholesale massacres: in 1603 and again in 1639 insurrections of Chinese were suppressed by putting thousands to the sword. In spite of these disasters, the Chinese persisted in coming.

Before the downfall of the Ming the Dutch had arrived in China. In 1622 they made an unsuccessful attack on Macao, and then obtained a foothold in the Pescadores and a little later in Formosa. From this latter island they were driven by Koxinga.

Not far from the end of the Ming, moreover, a fourth European people, the English, destined two centuries later to have so important a part in the foreign affairs of the Empire, had made their first effort to open trade with the Middle Kingdom. In 1637 a squadron of five vessels arrived at Macao, proceeded to Canton—silencing the batteries which attempted to oppose their passage to that city—and disposed of their cargo. This troubled opening of relations was a grim augury of the future.

From the North, the Russians began to make their appearance. Adventurers who were pushing the frontiers of the Czar eastward crossed the borders of China, and before the Manchu conquest some had even visited Peking.

Under the Ming the merchants from Europe had no success in penetrating far inland. It was with great difficulty, indeed, that they obtained even a temporary entrance into the coast cities.

Before the Manchu conquest, however, European missionaries had not only travelled in the interior but had effected a settled residence in several of the most important centers, including Peking itself.

The great wave of European exploration and discovery of the fifteenth and sixteenth centuries was accompanied by a fresh burst of missionary enthusiasm in the Roman Catholic Church. In the sixteenth century the Church experienced a quickening of its entire life—the movement which Protestants call the Counter Reformation. The Society of Jesus came into existence and the older orders were stimulated into fresh activity. Wherever the Portuguese and Spanish explorers and conquerors made their way—and often in advance of them—went also the missionaries. In India, Africa, both Americas, the West Indies, Japan, and the Philippines were to be found the hardy and courageous representatives of the Roman Catholic faith.

So far as we know, the first missionary to seek to penetrate China in this new era was the great Jesuit, Francis Xavier. In 1552 he spent some weeks south of Canton, on the island of Shang-ch'uan, at that time the chief headquarters of Portuguese traders. Thence he made futile attempts to reach the mainland, and there, near the close of 1552, he died.

Xavier was followed shortly by other missionaries, some of his own Society, under Portuguese auspices, and some, of other orders, from the Philippines. In time Macao became the seat of a bishop and of several churches and religious houses and the center from which many missionaries sought to enter the regions beyond.

The first really successful mission outside Macao was established by the Jesuits, and its leading figure was an Italian, Matthew Ricci. Ricci arrived in China in 1582 and died in Peking in 1610. In the intervening twenty-eight years he did more than any other one man to win a hearing for his faith and to develop the methods which were to be employed by his colleagues and successors. He won the respect of many of the dominant scholar-officials by dressing as they did, by applying himself diligently to the study of the Classics which they held in esteem, by conforming to their practices so far as he conscientiously could, and especially by his knowledge of mathematics and astronomy, branches of learning in which Europe then markedly excelled China. He and his confreres saw that only through the friendship of members of the ruling class could they hope to gain access to the masses of China and to win the country to Christianity. It was by this means that Ricci made his way to Peking, and he had the satisfaction of seeing two of the Hanlin Academy and an imperial prince won to the faith.

Before the end of the Ming Jesuits were to be found in several centers, and Dominicans and Franciscans from the Philippines, after many persistent efforts, had entered Fukien. Occasionally persecutions had broken out, some of them fairly severe, but the faith was making headway. In Peking the Jesuits had gained further recognition by being assigned to the Imperial Bureau of Astronomy to reform the calendar.

The collapse of the Ming strengthened the position of the missionaries. In Peking, the Manchus gave Schall official rank and entrusted him with the preparation of the calendar. Jesuits, too, were to be found in the court of the last Ming aspirant, the unfortunate Kuei Wang. That prince's heir, his mother, and his heir's mother were baptized and his chief general and leading eunuch were also professing Christians.

CULTURE UNDER THE MING: FOREIGN INFLUENCES

Under the Ming, the contact with aliens, destined to be so revolutionary in the future, had little marked effect on Chinese culture. Through the Europeans came a few plants from the New World. Late in the sixteenth or early in the seventeenth century tobacco was introduced from the Philippines, and then or later were brought in the sweet potato (the batata, introduced into Fukien in 1594), maize, and the peanut—all of them of American origin, and all of them to become important agricultural products in China. The pineapple, also of American provenance, reached China at the beginning of the seventeenth century. Syphilis, originally from America, entered. The Spanish peso appeared. Through the missionaries there entered Christian influences, and new conceptions of mathematics, astronomy, geography, and mechanics. As yet, however, except possibly an increase in population through the new food plants, none of these importations worked any very great modification in Chinese life as a whole.

CULTURE UNDER THE MING: RELIGION AND PHILOSOPHY

In religion and philosophy, the nearly three centuries of the Ming, when compared with some preceding dynasties which had enjoyed a long tenure, were somewhat sterile. Buddhism and Taoism continued, but no new currents of life which eventuated in important sects disturbed them. They were, indeed, suffering from slow inward decay. To be sure, they seemed securely fixed as permanent features of Chinese life. We hear, for example, as though it were in the Ch'in or the Han, of imperial search for the elixir of life. However, most of such activity in philosophy as existed was to be found not in them, but in the Confucian school.

Confucianism was the dominant philosophy of that scholar-official class through which the Empire was ruled, and was kept so by the civil service examinations by which the members of the group were recruited. In official Confucianism the school of Chu Hsi was orthodox. With the distrust of speculation and the premium on action which so characterized the Ming, an eminent authority declared that "ever since the time of the philosopher Chu, the truth has been made manifest to the world: no more writing is necessary: what is left to us is practice." He who would openly challenge such complacent and accepted dogmatism must have no common courage. The Confucian cult was reorganized. In the sixteenth century tablets were ordered substituted in the Confucian temples for images, the designation of the temple was changed from *miao* ("temple") to *tien* ("hall")—alterations which tended to minimize the religious element—and some lesser modifications were made.

Why there should have been less originality than in some other dynasties must be a matter of conjecture. It may have been the absence of sufficient stimulus from the outside. No tides were flooding in from abroad so powerfully as had Buddhism in the centuries preceding and during the T'ang: neither Islam nor Christianity as yet attracted so great a following as had this other foreign faith. It may have been that, after freeing itself from its conquest by the Mongols, China was seeking to restore and preserve its cultural independence. It may have been the stereotyping of Chinese thought, through the agency of the civil service examinations, apparently now more fully developed than heretofore. Certainly a majority of the best minds appear to have sought official promotion and social recognition through the channels of these tests, and in so doing were shaped by the conventional mold. The extreme autocracy of the Emperors was intolerant of dangerous deviation from the established Confucianism. The very practicality of the period discouraged speculation.

There was, however, no little intellectual interest. Many societies existed for the discussion and study of philosophy and literature. These often engaged in debates and not infrequently were active in politics.

Some there were who became restive under orthodoxy and wished to think for themselves. The most distinguished, Wang Yang-ming (ca. 1472–1528), had the courage and originality to work out a philosophy which differed from that of his class. Coming from a family of scholars and officials, he passed through the normal routine of study and examinations and spent much of his life in the service of the state, holding important offices. He was unwilling, however, merely to work for degrees. He wished to arrive at knowledge for himself, and not to repeat, parrot-like, the findings of preceding thinkers. The quest led him into opposition to Chu Hsi and his followers. That school, it will be recalled, had professed to advocate the search for truth, moral and otherwise, through the "investigation of things"—the examination of the objective universe. Wang Yang-ming, on the other hand, by an experience of sudden illumination after a long period of attempting to arrive at knowledge through the method advocated by Chu Hsi, came to believe that truth must be sought by looking within—that his own nature was a sufficient source of wisdom. He emphasized intuition—conscience—as the channel of information concerning the moral law. As a logical corollary of this position, he opposed the dualism of Chu Hsi (although Chu Hsi was also a monist) and approached what the Western philosopher would call the position of monistic idealism. Also as a corollary, he discouraged labored thought and advocated self-discipline and action. In part Wang Yang-ming displayed a resemblance to both Taoism and Ch'an Buddhism. Probably, either consciously or unconsciously, he had been influenced by both. He was, however, neither Taoist nor Buddhist, but must be reckoned as in the Confucian line. His teachings proved not nearly so potent in China as in Japan. In the latter country (under the Japanese pronunciation of his name, Oyomei) he was to have a great vogue, the controversy between his followers and those of Chu Hsi often becoming acute. Even in China, he had many admirers.

In the latter part of the Ming at least one other heterodox school arose, stood persecution for its principles, and was active in politics.

The tendency of progressive and radical philosophers, including Wang Yang-ming, it may be noted, was more toward ethical living and saving society than abstract speculation. The practicality which was a dominant feature of the period found expression in them as in other more tangible directions.

CULTURE UNDER THE MING: LITERATURE

In literature the Ming displayed little marked originality. No new types of works of outstanding significance appeared. There was, however, much literary activity. In quantity the output was large and the quality by no means always mediocre. Great libraries were collected, both under imperial auspices and by private individuals.

Printing, now for many years a commonplace, made the circulation of books comparatively easy and inexpensive, and so continued to encourage authorship. Both wooden blocks and movable type were employed. Government presses at Nanking and Peking had a monopoly of the publication of the Classics and of other works issued by imperial authorization. Frequently books so printed were distributed among the various educational institutions. Private presses, some of them kept in the same families for generations, printed many other works, including those which fall within the classification of *belles lettres*.

The drama was popular and although the plays of former dynasties continued to be produced, at least one new type with the accompanying music was originated, simpler than the classical style.

The period appears to have made its chief intellectual contributions through the novel. This type of literature was, as we have seen, not an invention of Ming scholars, but had first risen into prominence under the Mongols. During the Ming, however, it was the vehicle for much literary expression, and, possibly because it was less stereotyped than some of the traditional forms of literature, at times gave indication of real genius. Most of the greatest fiction had probably circulated for centuries in the form of collections of incidents pieced together by popular professional story-tellers and handed down by word of mouth. Some of these cycles had wide popular currency, were familiar to a large proportion of the population, and were retold again and again with many variations. Then some of them were put into writing, at first crudely. Eventually authors of outstanding ability took a few of them in hand, often anonymously (for composition of such tales, and especially in the vernacular, was supposed to be beneath the dignity of a scholar), and lasting masterpieces came into existence.

It must be noted, moreover, that the greatest of Chinese travel diaries, that by Hsü Hsia-k'o, dates from the Ming. Hsü, who lived toward the close of the dynasty, travelled extensively through the Empire, apparently chiefly for the love of doing so, and wrote detailed and vivid descriptions of rivers, mountains, buildings, and local customs. Particularly did he explore the Southwest, determining the source of the West River, showing that the Mekong and Salween are separate streams, and demonstrating that the Chin Sha Kiang, or River of the Golden Sand, is the upper reaches of the Yangtze.

The activities of the Ming writers seem to have been molded in part by the dominance of the civil service examinations. Since, as we have said, through these lay the road to official preferment and social recognition, and since they emphasized a knowledge of the Classics and of the orthodox commentators, and form rather than content, their tendency was to restrict the minds subjected to them to pedestrian, laborious, and voluminous, but quite uninspired effort in the fields of history, government, and related subjects. Certainly the energies of Ming scholars were expended very largely on sober writings and compilations—among them being local geographies and histories, works of reference (although, interestingly enough, most of these were inferior to the compilations of T'ang and Sung scholars), collections of inscriptions, descriptions of government, biographies, a long study of Ssŭ-ma Ch'ien's *Shih Chi,* treatises on military training and strategy, a great work on agriculture by the most eminent Christian of the time, Hsü Kuang-ch'i, many treatises on law (which influenced Korea, Japan, and Annam), books on medicine, including a huge *materia medica* (the *Pên ts'ao kang mu*, by Li Shih-chên, and based in part on earlier works of the same kind), many encyclopædias, including the largest of its class, already mentioned, critiques of art, and collections of Buddhist and Taoist works. All these required diligence, but in imaginative power few if any rose above mediocrity. There were, to be sure, poets, some of whom became famous—such as Li Tung-yang—but none achieved the place in Chinese literature that those of the T'ang had won. Late in the Ming the beginning of a new scientific study of philology came into being. Moreover, in a work published in 1543, Mei Tzŭ questioned the "ancient text" of the *Shu Ching*—the portions of that venerable work which in the next dynasty were conclusively proved to be spurious. Ming thought, however, was largely confined to familiar channels. European missionaries brought in new ideas in mathematics, astronomy, and theology, and wrote extensively on them, but down to the close of the Ming these did little to stir the Chinese mind from its accustomed grooves.

CULTURE UNDER THE MING: ART

In art, the Ming period is sometimes described as decadent. For some forms the generalization holds true, but it is by no means entirely accurate.

Buddhist sculptured figures, while produced in large quantities, for vigor and religious feeling did not begin to approach those of earlier dynasties. It is in secular subjects from everyday life, and in the carving of jade, ivory, columns, and balustrades, that Ming sculpture is seen at its best.

In painting, too, it is questionable whether Ming artists attained the levels reached by their predecessors of the T'ang and the Sung. Hung Wu established at Nanking an Academy of Painting, probably in an attempt to emulate the Sung. For some years, indeed, the Sung traditions in style and subject matter were continued. The dynasty's roster of painters is a long one. The variety of subjects was fairly large—landscapes, birds, flowers, portraits of court ladies—and the elegance, delicacy, and careful finish of many of the products praiseworthy. On the whole, however, the work was inferior and appears to have become more so as the dynasty progressed, especially after the capital was moved to Peking. Ornateness was exaggerated, and in landscapes there was less intimacy with nature than under the Sung. Expert criticism of painting flourished and a well-known encyclopædia of painting was compiled—possibly an indication that painters were looking backward rather than giving themselves to original production. For this mediocrity the growing stagnation in Buddhism, that faith which had done so much to inspire the greatest of Chinese painting, may be responsible. Certainly, the attention to non-religious subjects indicates that this may have been the case.

However, in architecture, not only does the quantity produced appear to have been very large, but much of the quality was high. The Ming builders and engineers, indeed, displayed an ability which often rose to the level of genius. Many of the bridges, city walls, temples, and pagodas now in existence date from the Ming, and comparatively few ancient monuments of these types antedate it. The Great Wall was largely rebuilt: most of it as we see it to-day dates from the Ming. Numbers of the extant structures are from the Wan Li period, when politically the dynasty was staggering toward its fall, and when decay in skill might have been expected.

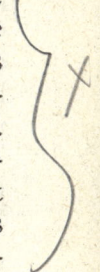

Moreover, in some other fields of art the Ming unquestionably registered marked advance. Magnificent pieces of cloisonné were produced. Rugs and carpets appear to have surpassed those of preceding centuries—perhaps because of contacts with that industry in Persia and the Near East. In the casting of bronze the Ming craftsmen attained great skill, particularly in the Hsüan Tê period (1426–1436).

It was especially in ceramics that the Ming excelled. The output was prodigious and both in form and style showed a marked and diversified departure from the Sung. Under the Sung, monochrome prevailed. Under the Ming, polychrome decoration was the rule, and monochrome products, while continuing, were in the minority. White porcelain was decorated with pictorial designs in colors—by glazes, enamels, and underglaze blues and reds. A beautiful cobalt blue came in, for this could stand the high temperature required to fuse the glaze. Later another blue, imported originally from Persia, became popular. In times still other colors appeared—green, yellow, purple, reds of various shades, black, and more blues—put on in varying combinations. Many, too, were the figures, scenes, and designs portrayed.

Production was at many centers. The chief place of manufacture was the imperial works at Ching-tê Chên, not far from the Poyang Lake, in Kiangsi. Here vast natural deposits of the minerals needed for the manufacture of porcelain facilitated the industry. The finest specimens are from the early reigns of the dynasty, before the best of the clays were exhausted. The Ching-tê Chên works either drove out of competition or overshadowed the other centers and were to retain their supremacy until the middle of the nineteenth century.

Porcelain wares were largely exported and reached not only the Near East but Europe, and eventually were thought of, with silk and tea, as the characteristic products of China.

SUMMARY

The Ming, while in political might inferior to the Han and the T'ang and in brilliance and originality not equal to the T'ang and the Sung, spanned one of the noteworthy periods of China's history. It ruled all of what we now think of as China proper, for a time it was master of Annam, and for shorter or longer periods Korea, Japan, and lands to the south as far distant as Ceylon acknowledged its suzerainty. In contrast to the earlier dynasties, instead of looking landward toward the north and west as the natural direction in which to extend its power, it faced seaward and southward. Increasingly commercial contacts were not by the overland trade routes but by the ocean. In this was a foreshadowing—although no one of the period could well have forecasted them—of those intimate contacts with the West which later were to work the greatest revolution that the Empire had known. The realm was prosperous. More abundant supplies of silver and copper became available and both metals were widely used as mediums of exchange. In culture the China of the Ming dynasty displayed practicality, elegance, diligence, and in a few directions originality, and influenced some of its neighbors, including especially Korea and Japan.

BIBLIOGRAPHY

The dynastic history which covers this period is the *Ming Shih*, compiled between 1679 and 1724 and revised under Ch'ien Lung.

General histories covering the period are H. Cordier, *Histoire Générale de la Chine* (4 vols., Paris, 1920–1921); de Mailla, *Histoire Générale de la Chine* (13 vols., Paris, 1777–1785); L. Wieger, *Textes Historiques* (2 vols., Hochienfu, 1903, 1904); René Grousset, *Histoire de l'Extrême-Orient* (2 vols., Paris, 1929); F. E. A. Krause, *Geschichte Ostasiens* (Vol. 1, Göttingen, 1925); and H. A. Giles, *A Chinese Biographical Dictionary* (London and Shanghai, 1898). Of these Grousset and Krause are the most trustworthy.

Works and articles covering special phases of the political history, including relations with Japan and the overseas expeditions to the South and West are Katsuro Hara, *An Introduction to the History of Japan* (New York, 1920); Y. Takekoshi, *The Economic Aspects of the History of the Civilization of Japan* (3 vols., London, 1930), especially Vol. 1, Chapters 17 and 18; G. B. Sansom, *Japan, A Short Cultural History* (New York, 1931); James Murdoch, *A History of Japan* (Vol. 1, 1542, Yokohama, etc., 1910, Vol. 2, 1542–1651, Kobe, 1903); Y. S. Kuno, *Japanese Expansion on the Asiatic Continent* (Vol. 1, Berkeley, 1937); L. C. Delamarre (translator), *Histoire de la Dynastie des Ming Composée par l'Empereur Khian-Loung. 1ᵉ partie, comprenant les dix premiers livres (1368–1505)* (Paris, 1865); E. Hauer (translator), *Huang-Ts'ing K'ai-kuo Fang-lüeh, die Gründung des Mandschurischen Kaiserreiches übersetzt und erklärt* (Berlin and Leipzig, 1926); F. Michael, *The Origin of Manchu Rule in China: Frontier and Bureaucracy as Interacting Forces in the Chinese Empire* (Baltimore, 1942), excellent on the pre-Ch'ing development of the Manchus; *Journal d'un Bourgeois de Yang-Tcheou (1645)*, translated by P. Aucourt in *Bulletin de l'École Française de l'Extrême-Orient*, a vivid description of the sack of Yangchow during the Manchu conquest; W. W. Rockhill, *China's Intercourse with Korea from the XVth Century to 1895* (London, 1905); W. W. Rockhill, *Notes on the Relations and the Trade of China with the Eastern Archipelago and the Courts of the Indian Ocean during the Fourteenth Century* (T'oung Pao, 1915, pp. 61, 236, 374, 435, 604); J. J. L. Duyvendak, *The True Dates of the Chinese Maritime Expedition in the Early Fifteenth Century* (T'oung Pao, Vol. 35, pp. 341–412); P. Pelliot, in *Bulletin de l'École Française d'Extrême-Orient*, 1904, p. 265; E. Huber, *Une Ambassade Chinoise en Birmanie en 1406* (*Bulletin de l'École Française d'Extrême-Orient*, 1904, pp. 428–432); J. Bouillard and Vandescal, *Les Sepultures Imperiales des Ming* (*ibid.*, 1920, No. 3, pp. 1–128); Gabriel Ferrand, *Relations de Voyages et Textes Geographiques Arabes, Persans et Turcs Relatifs à l'Extrême-Orient du VIIIe au XVIIIe siècles* (2 vols., Paris, 1913–1914); Hsieh Kuo Ching, *Removal of Coastal Population in Early Tsing Period* (*The*

Chinese Social and Political Science Review, Jan. 1932, Vol. 15, pp. 559–596); Feray, *Les Japonais à Hai-nan sous la Dynastie des Ming* (*T'oung Pao*, 1906, pp. 369–380); and E. H. Parker, *Mongolia after the Genghizides and before the Manchus* (*Journal of the North China Branch of the Royal Asiatic Society*, 1913, pp. 76–99).

On European contacts, see especially Cordier, *op. cit.*, Vol. 3, *passim*, Cordier, *L'Arrivée des Portugais en Chine* (*T'oung Pao*, 1911, pp. 483–543), and K. S. Latourette, *A History of Christian Missions in China* (New York, 1929).

On the importation of plants of American origin, see B. Laufer, *Sino-Iranica* (Chicago, 1919), B. Laufer, *Tobacco and Its Use in Asia* (Chicago, 1924), B. Laufer, *Plant Migration* (*Scientific Monthly*, Vol. 28, pp. 239–251, March, 1929).

On Wang Yang-ming, see Wang, *Wang Yang-ming* (*Variétés Sinologiques*, No. 63, Shanghai, 1936; F. G. Henke, *The Philosophy of Wang Yang-ming* (London, 1916), and a summary by the same author, *The Philosophy of Wang Yang Ming* (*Journal of the North China Branch of the Royal Asiatic Society*, 1913, pp. 46–64).

On literature, see L. C. Goodrich, *A Study of Literary Persecution under the Ming, by Ku Chieh-kang* (*Harvard Journal of Asiatic Studies*, Vol. 3, pp. 254–311); G. Margouliès, *Le Kou-Wen Chinois, Recueil de Textes avec Introduction et Notes* (Paris, 1926); P. Pelliot, *Notes de Bibliographie Chinoise. II. Le Droit Chinois* (*Bulletin de l'École Française d'Extrême-Orient*, 1909, pp. 123–152); and V. K. Ting, *On Hsü Hsia-ko (1586–1641) Explorer and Geographer* (*New China Review*, Vol. 3, No. 5, Oct. 1921, pp. 325–337). There are translations from a collection of Chinese stories, *Chin Ku Ch'i Kuan*, made toward the end of the Ming, in E. B. Howell, *The Inconstancy of Madam Chuang and Other Stories from the Chinese* (London, 1925), and E. B. Howell, *The Restitution of the Bride and Other Stories from the Chinese* (London, 1926). The reminiscences of a concubine by her husband are in Pan Tzeyen (translator), *The Reminiscences of Tung Hsiao-wan* (Shanghai, 1931).

On art, see E. F. Fenollosa, *Epochs of Chinese and Japanese Art* (2 vols., London, 1912); R. Petrucci, *Chinese Painters: A Critical Study* (translated by F. Seaver, New York, 1921); A. Waley, *An Introduction to the Study of Chinese Painting* (London, 1923); R. L. Hobson, *The Art of the Chinese Potter from the Han Dynasty to the End of the Ming* (London, 1923); R. L. Hobson, *The Wares of the Ming Dynasty* (London, 1923); R. Schmidt, *Chinesische Keramik von der Hanzeit bis zum XIX Jahrhundert;* Osvald Sirèn, *Histoire des Arts Anciens de la Chine*, Vols. 3 and 4 (4 vols., Paris, 1929–1930); Osvald Sirèn, *The Walls and Gates of Peking* (London, 1924); Osvald Sirèn, *The Imperial Palaces of Peking* (3 vols., Paris, 1926); A. Hubrecht, *Grandeur et Suprématie de Peking* (Peking, 1928); Ernest Boerschmann, *Chinesische Architektur* (2 vols., Berlin, 1925).

CHAPTER IX

THE CH'ING (MANCHU) DYNASTY: ITS HEYDAY AND THE BEGINNING OF ITS DECLINE
(A.D. 1644–1838)

INTRODUCTORY

THE Ta Ch'ing dynasty—usually called simply the Ch'ing (as a rule translated "pure" or "unsullied")—which the Manchus established was to be one of the longest-lived in the history of China. During the nearly three centuries of its rule (1644–1912) the Chinese experienced some of the most remarkable developments of their entire career. Under the Ch'ing the Empire reached its greatest territorial extent—not counting the Yüan period, for China was then only the chief unit of the Mongol domains. At its height the dynasty ruled over China proper, Manchuria, Mongolia, Sinkiang, and Tibet, and received tribute—in recognition of a more or less shadowy suzerainty—from Nepal, Burma, Laos, Siam, Annam, the Liu Ch'iu Islands, and Korea. Under the Ch'ing, too, the Chinese were more numerous than at any previous time. Moreover, during the heyday of the dynasty China attained a fresh level of material prosperity, probably higher than ever before. In the latter part of the seventeenth and through most of the eighteenth century, indeed, it was the most populous and possibly the most prosperous realm on the planet. In numbers of people it outstripped all the other great contemporary empires—the British, the Spanish, the French, the Russian, the Ottoman, and the Mogul. From the standpoint of order and justice it was probably as far advanced as any state of the time, for that was before the humanitarian movement had ameliorated the laws, the courts, and the prisons of the West. In total wealth, too, it very possibly surpassed every other nation of the period.

During these years, to be sure, culture underwent no especially great changes: the country was content to shape its life according to the patterns fixed in previous dynasties. This may have been in part because the Manchus, wishing, for reasons of political expediency, to prove themselves supporters of Chinese civilization, maintained orthodoxy with all the zeal of conscious converts. It may also have been because the Ch'ing Emperors, in their eagerness to prevent sedition and to root out any threat to their rule, endeavored to suppress cultural heterodoxy. Their emphasis, too, on the civil service examinations—through which lay the paths to social prestige, power, and wealth—induced most ambitious youths to confine themselves to the well-defined curriculum which led to the coveted degrees. The system first foreshadowed by the Han was being carried to its logical conclusion. Originality and experimentation were inconsistent with its perfect operation. Great prosperity was accompanied by adherence to past conventions. Even so, however, a few of the intellectuals were active in a movement of marked boldness and critical acumen which was to have important consequences.

In the last three-quarters of a century that the Manchus were on the throne, when their vigor was declining and the power slipping from their hands, came the greatest cultural revolution that the Chinese have ever known. It was then that the Occident at last surmounted the natural barriers which had prevented it from establishing intimate intercourse with the Middle Kingdom. Under the vigorous impact of the West the familiar structure of Chinese life crumbled. The traditional political, intellectual, and, to a certain extent, economic, social, and religious institutions disappeared or were profoundly modified. The changes into which the country was hurried proved more thorough-going even than after the collapse of the Chou, when the Ch'in and the Han rulers established the Empire, or than in the centuries after the Han, when Buddhism was being established. They seem, indeed, even yet only to have begun.

The dynasty, accordingly, naturally falls into two parts, one before the coming of the Westerner in force, and the other after that event. The dividing years are 1839–1842, when, in a successful war on China, Great Britain led what proved to be the vanguard of the great invasion. The first of these periods forms the subject of this chapter. More than half of it is included in the reigns of two of the ablest monarchs that China has ever had, most familiar to Westerners under the reign-names by which chronology is indicated, K'ang Hsi and Ch'ien Lung. The Emperor K'ang Hsi ascended the throne in 1661 and died in 1722. Then, after a comparatively brief reign, not especially noteworthy, of about thirteen years, came Ch'ien Lung, from 1736 to 1796. For nearly a century and a half, therefore, with a short interruption, China's government was in the hands successively of two extraordinarily strong men. It was probably due largely to this coincidence of longevity and competence that the dynasty became so firmly established and lasted so long.

K'ANG HSI

The first Manchu to rule in Peking, usually known by the name of his reign-period, Shun Chih, was placed on the throne as a boy of nine the year before his troops came into possession of the Ming capital. During his childhood under the tutelage of a very able uncle, he did not assume the full management of the government until 1651, after the regent's death. He himself died in his twenties, in 1661—although rumor declared that he was not dead, but had retired, incognito, to a monastery—and so scarcely had time to make a marked impression on the Empire.

Shun Chih was in turn succeeded by a minor son who is, as we have said, commonly known as K'ang Hsi. K'ang Hsi was not quite seven when his father's death elevated him to the throne, and he was to hold the imperial title for a little short of sixty-two years. In 1667, when he was thirteen, he took control, although it was not until 1669 that he was able completely to break the power of the regents. For more than half a century, therefore, he ruled the destinies of the Chinese. A contemporary of such notable monarchs as Louis XIV of France, Peter the Great of Russia, William III of England, and the fanatical warrior-conqueror Aurangzeb of the Mogul dynasty in India, in personal ability he was probably the equal and perhaps the superior of them all. He was characterized by great physical energy, an active and inquiring mind interested in a wide range of learning, an excellent memory, vivacity, and the will and the ability to lead and dominate men. Fond of vigorous outdoor life, he spent many of his days in the chase. He travelled extensively through his domains and gave much personal attention to his official duties, priding himself on his concern for the welfare of his subjects and his frugality in his personal and court expenses. Although originating nothing of great importance in governmental machinery, he gave to China as vigorous an administration as the Empire had ever known, and fostered not only order and material prosperity but cultural activity.

Very early after assuming full power, when he was still in his teens, K'ang Hsi faced successfully the most serious menace that had yet threatened his line. After their conquest of China, the Manchus had placed over much of the region south of the Yangtze four of the Chinese generals who had been of most assistance to them. One of these died without leaving male issue, but his son-in-law was given a position of trust in Kwangsi. Another was in Kwangtung and a third in Fukien. The most powerful was Wu San-kuei, who had had so large a part in introducing the Ch'ing to Peking. He had conquered for his new masters Shensi, Szechwan, and Yünnan, and had hounded the last of the Ming, the luckless Kuei Wang, to his death on the Yünnan border. He had been loaded with honors, one of his sons had been given in marriage a sister of the Emperor Shun Chih, and in Yünnanfu, his headquarters, he maintained a court which in splendor rivalled that of Peking. In the South as they were, remote from Peking, these Chinese dignitaries, with high titles and great authority, constituted a potential danger: it was the kind of division of the realm among feudatories which more than once had threatened the unity of the Empire.

There seems to be some uncertainty as to the exact steps by which the revolt came about. The occasion appears to have been the determination of the Emperor to bring to an end the anomalous power of these satraps. K'ang Hsi ordered Wu San-kuei to report to Peking to pay homage to the throne, but that worthy, warned by his son—a hostage in Peking—of a plot against him, twice refused. When one of the dignitaries, Shang K'o-hsi, in Canton, because of age and the desire to escape from the control of a son, asked leave to retire to Manchuria, K'ang Hsi promptly granted his request. Then when two others, as a matter of policy, or following the requirements of Chinese custom, made similar offers, K'ang Hsi brought to a head the entire issue by taking them at their word and ordering them to disband their troops.

The issue was now squarely joined, and Wu San-kuei revolted (1673). Kêng Ching-chung in Fukien, grandson of the original supporter of the Manchu power, and Shang Chih-hsin in Kwangtung, son of Shang K'o-hsi, also appealed to arms, the one fairly promptly, the other more tardily. Hence the rebellion is known as that of the *San Fan,* or the Three Feudatories.

The outlook for the Ch'ing was dark. Many Chinese joined in the uprising. On the coast, the son and successor of Koxinga, still strong on the sea and ensconced in Formosa, took the opportunity to attack his father's old enemies. Most of the South—Hunan, Kweichow, Yünnan, Kwangsi, Kwangtung, and Fukien—was in control of the rebels, and for a time Szechwan, Kansu, and much of Shensi seemed lost. It is not strange that Wu San-kuei proclaimed himself the first of a new dynasty. The Manchus, with only a boy at their head, and with more than half of the area of the eighteen provinces in the hands of their foes, were in desperate straits. It looked as though they might do wisely to accept the compromise suggested by Wu San-kuei and leave to him, as the price of peace, the territory south of the Yangtze.

However, the boy ruler showed himself fully equal to the emergency. He was aided by dissensions among his opponents. The rebels could agree only on enmity to the Manchus and some of them fell to quarrelling among themselves. Moreover, numbers of influential Chinese remained true to the Ch'ing. Before long the armies of K'ang Hsi began to regain the lost territories. The fate of the revolt was sealed by the death, in 1678, probably from natural causes, of the formidable Wu San-kuei. In the ensuing months others of the chief rebels were eliminated. So stubborn was the resistance, however, that not until 1681 did it come to an end—when the grandson of Wu San-kuei, besieged in his last stronghold, committed suicide.

Thanks largely to the ability of K'ang Hsi in suppressing it, the uprising resulted in establishing the Manchu rule more firmly than ever. The system of semi-autonomous feudatories was abolished, and the control of Peking over the provinces was strengthened by requiring officials to report to the capital at periodical intervals and by dividing functions among the head provincial officers and virtually setting them to watch each other. Moreover, in 1683, for the first time in the history of China, Formosa, after the death of the son of Koxinga (1682), was brought into the Empire.

Not only did K'ang Hsi succeed in confirming his family in their control of China: he extended his authority beyond his inherited frontiers. From time immemorial, as we have repeatedly seen, the fertile plains and valleys of North China had been subject to invasion from the less favored lands on the north, west, and northeast. Some of the rulers of China sought protection from the menace by constructing or maintaining the Great Wall. However, the greatest monarchs of the Han and the T'ang, it will be recalled, had not been content with remaining on the defensive, but had sought to dominate the regions from which the threats issued. It was this bold policy which K'ang Hsi adopted, and in it he was followed by his two immediate successors. As a consequence, by the end of the eighteenth century the territory controlled by the Ch'ing—as we have suggested—was more extensive than that which had acknowledged the suzerainty of any line which had reigned in China except that of Jenghiz Khan.

K'ang Hsi was led to embark upon a program of expansion by a threat to his frontiers. At the accession of the Ch'ing, the Mongols, as heretofore, were divided into many tribes. They were chiefly in two groups, the Eastern and the Western. The Eastern Mongols, in turn, were subdivided into the Northern, or Khalkhas, and the Southern, in what we now know as Inner Mongolia. We have seen that before the Manchu conquest of China proper many of the tribes of Inner Mongolia had submitted to the Ch'ing. One of the khans, or chiefs, of this region seized the opportunity given by the rebellion of Wu San-kuei to revolt. K'ang Hsi subdued him and followed up the victory by claiming suzerainty over the entire Mongol confederation. This presaged the extension of the power of the Ch'ing over the Khalkhas.

K'ang Hsi's authority over the Khalkhas did not become effective, however, until after a further development. The Western Mongols, or Kalmuks, had among them a tribe called the Eleuths (or Oelots). A leader of the Eleuths was then building one of those many more or less ephemeral states of Central Asia which have risen, flourished, and disappeared, usually all within a few decades. This chief not only became strong in the Gobi, but intervened in Tibet, posing as the protector of the Dalai Lama. His son, Galdan, was even more powerful. From his capital at Kuldja, he maintained the influence built up by his father in Tibet and Mongolia, and established his suzerainty over Kashgar, the rest of Eastern Turkestan, Turfan, and Hami. Before long Galdan found an occasion to interfere in the affairs of the Khalkhas and attempted to extend his sway over them. A new Mongol Empire appeared to be arising, with a threat to the Chinese frontiers. This K'ang Hsi would not tolerate. He gave the Khalkhas protection and in the last decade of the seventeenth century dispatched armies to clear their territories of Galdan and the Eleuths. Galdan was repeatedly defeated and his death (1697) was probably by his own hand. The Khalkhas, however, had only exchanged the threat of one master for the reality of another. K'ang Hsi had saved them from the Eleuths, but their chiefs now acknowledged the suzerainty of the Ch'ing, imperial residents were placed among them, and a garrison was installed in Urga. K'ang Hsi did not complete the conquest of the Eleuths' territory, but he did put contingents of troops in Hami and other strategic centers on the Western frontier.

After K'ang Hsi had ventured into the West, he was led, apparently by the logic of events, to extend his control over Tibet. At the close of the fourteenth and early in the fifteenth century a reform had been made—chiefly by a great religious leader, Tsung K'apa—in the prevailing corrupt Buddhist cult in that region, the "Red Sect," and a new type of Buddhism had arisen, called the "Yellow Sect" (from the color of its vestments) with insistence, among other things, upon the celibacy of the clergy and a more elaborate ritual. The heads of the new cult, and, consequently, of Tibet, in time came to be the Dalai Lama and the Panch'an Lama. The holder of each title was supposedly a reincarnation of his predecessor, and the successions theoretically traced back, respectively, to a great *bodhisattva* (Avalokita) and a *buddha* (Amitabha). By far the more powerful of the two politically was the Dalai Lama, with his capital at Lhasa. The Ming Emperors had shown him honor, the early Manchus had established relations with him, and a holder of the title visited Peking in 1652. It remained, however, for K'ang Hsi to extend the authority of the Empire over him and his realm.

Having embarked on a policy of controlling the Mongols, K'ang

Hsi was almost inevitably led to concern himself with Tibetan politics. Many of the Mongols had been followers of the Red Sect of Lamaism, and by the time of K'ang Hsi the Yellow Sect was gaining many converts among them. The Eleuths early adhered to the latter and sought to spread it—possibly as a means of extending their own control—while for years the Khalkhas remained loyal to the Red cult. Tibet, therefore, became a factor with which K'ang Hsi had to reckon in dealing with the situation on his northwestern frontiers.

In 1684, after many of the Khalkhas had become followers of the Yellow Sect, K'ang Hsi asked and obtained the coöperation of the Dalai Lama in bringing about peace among them. Galdan had been in communication with Lhasa and the ensuing friction with Peking was allayed only by his timely death. Then, too, the chief minister of the Dalai Lama had had some dealings with Wu San-kuei during the latter's sedition and had aroused K'ang Hsi's suspicions. About 1700 K'ang Hsi began strengthening his position in the great plateau. His troops occupied parts of the Tibetan-Szechwan border and he commissioned as regent of Tibet the friendly commander of the Eleuth forces which for a time dominated Lhasa. Before many years a disputed succession to the Dalai Lama-ship led K'ang Hsi to undertake the conquest of the country. One of the claimants was enthusiastically supported by some of the Mongols, Lhasa was taken, and the pro-Ch'ing group was put to the sword. The movement seemed to presage the rise of still another new Mongol Empire. In 1719, therefore, K'ang Hsi came out boldly on the side of one of the contestants, and in 1720 his forces entered Lhasa as victors. K'ang Hsi's protégé was successfully enthroned, Peking appointed two high commissioners to direct him and installed a garrison in the city, and troops were stationed at strategic points on the road to China proper. Tibet was now politically an appendage of China.

K'ang Hsi also dealt firmly with the Europeans who, following the contacts made under the Ming dynasty, continued to come to China. The authority of China over Macao, the one European settlement on the coast, was unequivocably asserted. Under K'ang Hsi's predecessor the Dutch had sent representatives to Peking who allowed themselves to be treated as envoys from a tributary state. They now dispatched ships to help in K'ang Hsi's conquest of Formosa. Since the sixteenth century the Russians had been moving into Siberia. Even under the Ming, Russians had reached Peking. During the reign of Shun Chih an embassy and merchants came to the capital, and in the early years of the K'ang Hsi period other emissaries and trading caravans arrived. Russian pressure on the west helped to weaken the Eleuths in the later stages of their contest with K'ang Hsi. K'ang Hsi's forces and the Russians came to blows in the valley of the Amur. The Russians were there establishing small colonies and fortified posts, to the great annoyance of the Manchus. In 1685 a Russian post, Albazin, was captured, and some of the garrison were taken to Peking, where they remained permanently. Neither side was especially eager for war, and, after other somewhat desultory encounters, in 1689 a treaty was signed at Nerchinsk, the first between China and a European state. Among other provisions, this defined the boundary, restored to China some of the territory claimed by the Russians, arranged for a limited commerce between the two countries, and stipulated that if Russians or Chinese committed crimes in the other's territory, they were to be sent across the border for punishment by the officials of their respective governments. It was not, as were so many treaties of the nineteenth century, dictated to a prostrate China by a victorious Western power.

Against Roman Catholic missionaries, too, K'ang Hsi asserted his absolute authority over his domains. As we have seen, Jesuits, notably Schall, attached themselves to the Manchus during the subjugation of China. About the time of the conquest, Spanish Franciscans and Dominicans from the Philippines succeeded in effecting a permanent foothold. Before the death of K'ang Hsi, Lazarists, French Jesuits, Spanish Augustinians, Italian Franciscans, and seculars, including representatives of the Société des Missions Étrangères of Paris, had entered the country. During most of his reign K'ang Hsi was tolerant of and even friendly to the missionaries, especially the Jesuits. During his minority, in 1664, there was a severe persecution, but when he assumed the reins of government he had it discontinued. He was greatly interested by the scholarly Jesuits in his capital, notably by Verbiest and some of the French members of the Society. Under them he studied European sciences, mathematics, and music, he employed them in astronomical and literary pursuits, he entrusted to them the mapping of the Empire, he used them in negotiations with the Russians, and he assisted them in erecting a church in Peking and in rebuilding one in Hangchow. In 1692 he issued what in effect was an edict of toleration, protecting existing church buildings and permitting freedom of worship. By 1705 there were probably more than two hundred thousand Chinese Christians, among them a few men of prominence.

Unfortunately, however, a prolonged dispute—the so-called Rites Controversy—arose among the missionaries. This had to do chiefly with the term to be used for the translation of the word God—whether the familiar *T'ien*, so frequent in Chinese literature, could be so employed—and with questions concerning the permissibility of participation by Christians in the customary Chinese rites in honor of ancestors and Confucius. If the word *T'ien* could be used, and if these rites could be tolerated by the Church, then Christianity could be made to seem less inimical to Chinese institutions. If, on the other hand, the Church conscientiously felt that they must be forbidden to Christians, the faith would appear an enemy to traditional Chinese beliefs and practices and destructive of such fundamental bases of society and the state as the family and the Confucian school. Most of the Jesuits favored toleration, but many members of other missionary organizations vigorously opposed it. The controversy lasted for a little over a century—from about 1628 until the final papal decision, in 1742. Much of the ecclesiastical Roman Catholic world entered into the discussion. Jealousies between orders, rivalries among European nations, the Portuguese claim of the right to control the Church in the Far East, and the rising tide of feeling in Europe against the Jesuits complicated the debate. The Pope finally decided against toleration and sent to China two different embassies (in 1704–1710 and 1719–1721), led respectively by Charles Maillard de Tournon and Jean Ambrose Charles Mezzabarba, in the attempt to gain the acquiescence not only of the Jesuits but of K'ang Hsi.

Before either legate arrived, K'ang Hsi had expressed his own conviction on the points at issue. This was for toleration and so was diametrically opposed to Rome. Both papal legates irritated him, especially the first. He felt that no foreigner, even though he be Pope, should attempt to enforce decrees counter to the imperial will, particularly when these would prove disturbing to basic Chinese customs. Accordingly, he gave missionaries the choice of abiding by his own decision in the controversy or leaving the country. Since Rome did not issue its final edict until 1742, long after the death of K'ang Hsi, some of the missionaries managed to reconcile their consciences to compliance with the Emperor. K'ang Hsi did not allow the controversy to terminate his friendship for the Jesuits, and instituted no drastic persecutions. He was, however, firm in insisting upon his jurisdiction over both foreign priests and Chinese Christians and in his later years displayed more animosity toward Christianity than in his prime.

K'ang Hsi was not only vigorous in maintaining his authority within China and in protecting and expanding his frontiers: he actively promoted the material welfare of his subjects and encouraged literature. He spent a good deal of his time on the road and saw for himself what was happening outside the walls of his palace. He attempted, unsuccessfully, to end the custom of binding the feet of Chinese women. He endeavored to lighten taxes and to encourage honesty and efficiency in the bureaucracy. He strove to insure a good currency. He instituted public works, especially for the control of "China's Sorrow," the Yellow River, whose floods for untold centuries had been a recurrent menace to the North China plain. He subsidized scholarship—not placing a premium upon originality (possibly fearing that it might bring sedition), but financing new editions of the Classics and of rare books and having great compilations produced and published. Among these latter were a famous dictionary, still very widely used, a huge classified collection of literary phrases, an encyclopædia, and a rhyming dictionary. He himself was a student of the Classics, collected a library, and had many Chinese works translated into the Manchu tongue. He was the author of sixteen short moral maxims, which in later reigns were expanded by commentaries, and with these, as the Sacred Edict (*Shêng Yü*), were officially taught to the populace. The great imperial porcelain works at Ching-tê Chên were devastated during the insurrection of Wu San-kuei, but K'ang Hsi had them restored, and their products during his reign are famous for beauty and prodigious in quantity. One observer estimated the population of the center in 1712 at about a million. When he died, December 20, 1722, in the sixty-ninth year of his age, K'ang Hsi had completed not only one of the longest, but one of the ablest reigns in the annals of the Empire.

YUNG CHÊNG (1723–1735)

In his last days K'ang Hsi had been disturbed by bitter rivalries over the succession, for he had many sons and no rule of primogeniture existed. The successful competitor is best known to posterity under the title of his reign-period, Yung Chêng. In his forties when his father's death placed him in power, he had only a little over twelve years more of life. He was by no means a genius, but he was ambitious and a hard worker. He reformed the finances and reduced corruption among officials. He was an interested student of religion, especially of Ch'an Buddhism. He wrote a number of books.

In internal administration Yung Chêng was more fearful of sedition than had been K'ang Hsi: at least he seems to have been at more pains to prevent it. He appears to have had a kind of secret service for ferreting out treason. He treated several of his brothers with great harshness, perhaps to prevent them from rebelling, but possibly to satisfy old grudges. These family quarrels, indeed, are a decidedly prominent and unlovely feature of the annals of the reign. While continuing to employ the Jesuits in Peking, Yung Chêng instituted a much more severe persecution of Christianity than had been known since his father's minority—perhaps because of the supposed support of the missionaries, during K'ang Hsi's lifetime, of other aspirants to the succession, and possibly out of dislike for that religion or from fear that it might lead to internal sedition. It was due to him that a new body, the *Chün Chi Ch'u,* usually called in English the Grand Council or Council of State was substituted for the *Nei Ko,* or Grand Secretariat of the Ming, as the inner group or cabinet with which the Emperor consulted on affairs of state—although the older institution continued to exist as an honorary body with much reduced functions. He centralized administration more and more in the crown.

In foreign affairs Yung Chêng had to face hostilities in the West. An uprising in the Kokonor region was followed by a fresh war with the Eleuths. These ancient enemies of his father were for a time successful and made threatening raids eastward. Eventually, however, Yung Chêng's forces inflicted defeats on them. The peace that was patched up left the Eleuths unsubdued, and their final reduction was not achieved until the next reign. Russian envoys continued to come to China, and in 1727 an additional treaty was signed, usually known by the name of Kiakhta, which further delimited the frontier between the two empires, regulated trade, and arranged for a kind of permanent semi-ecclesiastical, semi-diplomatic mission in Peking.

CH'IEN LUNG (1736–1796)

Yung Chêng died in his fifties and was succeeded by a son, then in his twenty-fifth year, who is usually denominated by the title of his reign-period, Ch'ien Lung. Ch'ien Lung was to live until an extreme old age, and while he abdicated in 1796, in his eighty-fifth year, after he had ruled for six decades, the Chinese cycle, he continued to dominate the government until his death, in 1799. Like his grandfather, K'ang Hsi, he displayed marked ability. He was hard-working and energetic, and was fond of the chase and outdoor life—although he seems to have practiced this with more pomp and luxury than had K'ang Hsi. He travelled extensively through his domains, and, ambitious and diligent as a scholar, poet, painter, and calligrapher, he was a patron of arts and literature. In personal ability he appears to have been fully the equal of the two most famous monarchs of the Europe of his day, Catherine of Russia and Frederick of Prussia, and in the wealth and population of his realm he surpassed all other contemporary rulers. In his reign the Manchu régime reached the pinnacle of its power and entered on its decline.

Under Ch'ien Lung the Chinese Empire was rounded out to its natural boundaries and attained the greatest extent in its history. First of all, the Eleuths (who were, it will be recalled, a branch of the Kalmuks, or Western Mongols) were finally eliminated. A dispute over the succession to the Eleuth throne gave Ch'ien Lung his opportunity. One of the worsted leaders, Amursana, sought refuge with Ch'ien Lung and was cordially received. In 1755 Amursana, aided by the Emperor's armies, was installed in Kuldja. He was not, however, allowed to rule in a fully independent fashion, for an imperial resident was placed in his capital to watch him and Ch'ien Lung proposed to reorganize the land in a way pleasing to himself. Amursana, ill content, soon revolted (1755), the Chinese garrison in Kuldja was massacred and the first forces dispatched by Ch'ien Lung to put down the outbreak were unsuccessful. Unrest developed among some of the Khalkhas (a branch of the Eastern Mongols), and for a time it looked as though much of Mongolia might throw off the Ch'ing yoke. However, a Manchu general, Chao-hui, soon turned the fortunes of battle, Amursana was driven into Siberia, and the Eleuth power was completely broken (1757). Thousands were killed, other thousands died of an epidemic of smallpox, and some of the remnant sought refuge in Russian territory. Their former home was largely repopulated by colonists, mainly from Manchuria, Kashgaria, and Kansu. In 1771, dissatisfied with Russian rule, a Western Mongol (Kalmuk) tribe, the Turguts, who had settled in the lower Volga, returned and were allowed by Ch'ien Lung to reside in their old haunts. However, the day had passed when any of the Kalmuks could hope to make a successful bid for power.

The conquest of the Eleuths was quickly followed by that of the Tarim basin. There, in Kashgar and Yarkand, two brothers, Moslems, scions of a princely family, set themselves up in opposition to the Ch'ing. Chao-hui boldly entered upon a campaign against them, but was surrounded and had to stand a desperate siege until reënforcements could reach him. When these arrived, Kashgar, Yarkand, and Khotan, the chief towns in the western part of the valley, fell to the Manchu arms (1759) and the defeated forces were pursued into the Pamir. While the suzerainty of the Empire was not carried so far westward as in the days of the Han and the T'ang, the area occupied to the north and west of China proper was much more extensive than under either. Manchu valor and vigor had revived the ancient martial glory of the realm. The recently conquered territory was organized into Sinkiang (the "New Dominion"). Into parts of it were moved, by imperial authority, to hold it for the Ch'ing, Manchu colonists and Chinese—mostly Moslems—from Kansu and Shensi.

Ch'ien Lung had also to meet difficulties in Tibet. In 1750 an uprising in Lhasa killed most of the Chinese and Manchu residents. Ch'ien Lung promptly (1751) dispatched an army which restored his rule, and then proceeded to strengthen his control. The Dalai Lama was confirmed in his title of temporal ruler of Tibet, but the two *ambans*—or representatives of Peking—were to supervise his political acts and were given the preponderance in determining the succession.

Before many years, a fresh power, that of the Gurkhas, began to arise in the Himalayas, in Nepal, on the southern borders of Tibet. The Gurkhas, bold in their new might, encroached on the frontier and in 1791 pillaged the seat of the Panch'an Lama. Ch'ien Lung thereupon sent an army, under a Manchu commander, which made the difficult march across the high Tibetan plateau, drove back the Gurkhas (1792), penetrated into Nepal, and forced it to recognize the suzerainty of Peking. It was a noteworthy military feat.

From his father Ch'ien Lung inherited a conflict with the non-Chinese peoples in the South and Southwest. Here, in Kwangsi, Hunan, Kweichow, Yünnan, and Szechwan, numerous aborigines lived under their own chieftains and observed their own customs. At the instance of a vigorous viceroy, Yung Chêng had inaugurated a policy of extending more fully over them the imperial administrative system—possibly in part as a protection for the Chinese settlers who were pushing into the lands occupied by the tribes—and had met with serious resistance. The opposition continued during much of Ch'ien Lung's reign. Fighting was especially severe and prolonged in the western part of Szechwan, where the rugged nature of the country greatly assisted defense. The imperial forces were eventually successful, but not until the reign was two-thirds over.

Given an aggressive administration in China, conflict with Burma was almost inevitable, for the boundary between the two states was somewhat indeterminate, and the regulation of the rude tribesmen on the frontier who were guilty of depredations on travellers and on their more civilized neighbors on both sides of the border might at any time become a source of friction. There was war between China and Burma from 1765 into December, 1769. The Burmese invaded Yünnan, and two Chinese expeditions into Burma followed. Neither side was overwhelmingly victorious, and Ch'ien Lung had to be content with the recognition of his suzerainty—decidedly vague—by the court at Ava and the periodical dispatch of presents (regarded at least by the Ch'ing as tribute) to Peking.

Ch'ien Lung also intervened in the affairs of Annam. That region, which ever since the time of Ch'in Shih Huang Ti had been now in and now out of the Empire, under the latter part of the Ming had enjoyed one of its periods of independence. On the final collapse of the last of the Ming, Kuei Wang, Annam had become slightly embroiled with the Manchus. Under Ch'ien Lung, civil strife in Annam gave the imperial forces an excuse for taking sides actively in the politics of the country. As a result, the rulers of Annam received investiture from Peking and paid what the Ch'ing held to be "tribute."

In his dealings with Europeans, Ch'ien Lung was fully as insistent upon his authority as his grandfather had been. An embassy from Great Britain, headed by the Earl of Macartney, arrived in Peking in 1793. The boats and carts assigned to convey it to the capital bore flags with the inscription: "Ambassador bearing tribute from the country of England," and while the Earl conducted himself with dignity he was unable to obtain the commercial concessions which had been hoped from the venture. A Dutch embassy in 1795 was treated with less consideration, and also as from a tributary state. It, too, was unsuccessful in achieving its objectives. Treaties were signed with Russia in 1768 and 1792 supplementary to the earlier ones, defining the procedure in extraditing and punishing criminals and further regulating trade, but no concessions of any importance were made to that power.

In his administration of the internal affairs of the Empire, Ch'ien Lung took vigorous measures to maintain his rule against sedition, real or potential. By a strict censorship he sought to discover and suppress all literature directed against the Ch'ing. Occasionally he had to face revolts. At least twice these were led by secret societies, once by the *Pai-lien Chiao*, or White Lotus Sect, and another time by the *Pa Kua*, or Eight Trigrams. We hear, too, of a Moslem uprising in the region of Kokonor, of a rebellion in Formosa, and of others in several of the more central portions of the Empire. It is significant that most of these occurred in the later years of the reign, when, with advancing age, the Emperor's vigor was beginning to abate.

In his treatment of Roman Catholic missionaries, moreover, Ch'ien Lung was no more lenient than his father and grandfather had been. He continued to employ them in his capital—among other things to assist in the astronomical bureau, to execute paintings in European style, and to erect structures of European design in his summer palace to the west of Peking. Missionaries, too, were scattered widely through the provinces. In theory, however, their religious activities were forbidden. While in practice these were often winked at, usually they had to be carried on without ostentation, and occasionally severe persecutions were instituted. Moreover, missions suffered from other causes. The Jesuits, the Roman Catholic body which had sent more missionaries to China than had any other, were being expelled by leading European states—driven out of Portuguese possessions in 1759, out of France in 1767 (they had been suppressed there in 1764), and out of Spain in 1767—and in 1773 the Pope dissolved the Society. Although the Jesuits already in China were at liberty to remain as seculars, and although, about ten years later, the Lazarists accepted the responsibility for carrying on the vacant work, the shock was severe. Moreover, the decline of missionary zeal in Europe due to the scepticism of the latter part of the eighteenth century, and the French Revolution and the ensuing wars which kept Europe in turmoil from 1789 to 1815 led to a diminution of support from the Occident. Under Ch'ien Lung, therefore, in spite of gains in some districts, taking the Empire as a whole the Church was slowly losing ground. The Christian communities probably decreased in numbers, and in morale they suffered severely.

Like his grandfather, Ch'ien Lung was interested in learning. He himself was a voluminous writer—of poetry, of notes on current topics, and of prefaces to books. He had new editions made of important works, and more "encyclopædias" were compiled and printed—what is usually translated as encyclopædia, it will be recalled, being composed not of articles especially written for it but of excerpts from existing books, and often being confined to a particular class of subjects rather than attempting to cover the entire range of human knowledge. Neither his court nor that of his grandfather equalled that of Ming Huang of the T'ang or that of some of the Sung Emperors in the brilliance of the men of art and letters attached to it. It displayed little of the sparkle of real genius. There was, however, much of laborious ability.

Thanks to the internal order of Ch'ien Lung's reign, and to the heritage of prosperity which had come down from K'ang Hsi and Yung Chêng, the eighteenth century witnessed a rapid increase in wealth and population. More land was brought under cultivation and Chinese pushed into Southern Manchuria and into Eastern Inner Mongolia, including especially Jehol and Chahar. Cities grew in size, and the total number of inhabitants rose rapidly— quite likely, although the census figures are not trustworthy, to heights never before approached either in China or in any other Empire. By the end of the reign it had probably well exceeded the three hundred million mark.

With all this prosperity and outward show of power, by the time of Ch'ien Lung's demise the Ch'ing had passed its zenith. Although, until a few months before his death, Ch'ien Lung's health continued to be remarkably good for a man of his advanced years, toward the end much of the real power was in the hands of a trusted favorite, Ho Shên, a Manchu of humble origin. Ho Shên became the Emperor's chief minister, he amassed a fortune which would be considered huge even in the present wealthy Occident, his son was married to an imperial princess, and his protégés held high office. It was a state of affairs which a K'ang Hsi would never have tolerated. Corruption began to be rampant in the bureaucracy. As we have already noted, rebellions broke out. When Ch'ien Lung retired, the Miaotsŭ—some of the non-Chinese tribes—were in fresh revolt on the Hunan-Kweichow border and a serious uprising of the White Lotus Society was brewing.

CHIA CH'ING (1796–1820)

No overwhelming disaster came immediately. Ch'ien Lung handed on his throne peacefully to a son, the title of whose reign was Chia Ch'ing. Soon after his father's death, Chia Ch'ing asserted himself against Ho Shên, confiscating the latter's fortune and permitting him to commit suicide (in commutation of sentence of death by execution). The revolts, too, which Chia Ch'ing inherited were suppressed. That of the White Lotus proved a prolonged affair and not until after 1800 was it finally crushed.

In ability Chia Ch'ing was far from being the equal of his father and great-grandfather. He attempted to reduce the inherited extravagance by economies at court and applied himself to the business of government with diligence and energy. Yet he was compromising and far from popular. The downfall of Ho Shên by no means ended the corruption in officialdom. Rebellions continued to break out—ominous indications that the government was neither so firm nor so efficient as formerly. A mutiny disturbed the army, for some years pirates infested the south coasts, an attempt to assassinate the Emperor barely failed of success, and another anti-dynastic secret society—this time called by the name of *T'ien Li,* or Heavenly Reason (or Eternal Principles)—engineered an uprising during which some of the plotters forced their way into the imperial palace during the Emperor's absence and were foiled in part through the courage of one of Chia Ch'ing's sons, the later Tao Kuang.

Chia Ch'ing, however, abated none of the attitude of his predecessors toward foreigners. He was, indeed, even more arrogant and unyielding. He vigorously persecuted the Roman Catholics, quite possibly because he feared that their efforts might lead to more sedition, and he began to terminate the employment of missionaries in the service of the government at Peking. A Russian embassy was turned back, in 1806, before it reached Peking, because the Czar's envoy refused to perform the *kotow* when he should be received by the Emperor. This *kotow*, or prostration, became to Europeans a symbol of that recognition of Chinese suzerainty to which they would not agree and long remained a bone of contention. A British embassy, led by Lord Amherst, arrived in 1816, seeking better trade conditions, but it was treated with much less courtesy than had been that led by Lord Macartney. After much disagreement over the method of reception it was dismissed without an audience, and with a haughty mandate which clearly indicated that the Emperor regarded the King of England as the prince of a tributary state.

THE BEGINNING OF THE REIGN OF TAO KUANG

In 1820 the death of Chia Ch'ing brought to the throne, under the reign title of Tao Kuang, the prince who had shown such courage when rebels invaded the palace. Tao Kuang proved to be little if any better a ruler than his father: luxury and the environment of the palace were softening the fibre of the once hardy Manchus. He is said to have sought to promote economy in the expenditures of his court, but he was restive under the criticisms of the official censors—one of the useful ways which the Chinese administrative system provided for bringing public opinion to bear on the throne—and found means of curbing them. He, too, suffered from rebellions—in Formosa and Sinkiang. None of these proved sufficiently serious to check the prosperity inherited from the first century and a half of the Ch'ing. Outwardly, in 1839, the Empire was still imposing. It was wealthy, and its population was probably increasing. It was unsound at the top, however, and disaster was imminent. When, in the first war with Great Britain, 1839-1842, China met the most significant crisis not only of the reign but of many centuries, it was in the hands of a ruling house whose best days were in the past. It is no wonder that the Chinese blundered and in the ensuing decades, by one misstep after another, stumbled, ill-prepared, into the greatest revolution of their history.

CULTURE UNDER THE GREAT CH'ING EMPERORS: ART

Chinese cultural achievements under K'ang Hsi and Ch'ien Lung were considerable. In art there was little departure from the traditions received from the Ming. The imposing palaces and temples in Peking were maintained with but few alterations or additions. Paintings continued to be produced in great abundance, and many of them showed technical skill, refinement, and taste. Few, if any, however, seem to have displayed outstanding genius. Flowers, birds, animals, and plants were exquisitely portrayed, but the landscapes were distinctly inferior to those of the Sung. There was much copying of old masterpieces. Beautiful works of lacquer appeared, and in carving wood, ivory, and the semi-precious stones the handicraftsmen showed elaborate diligence and cunning.

It was in porcelain that the period has its chief claim to artistic distinction. At the great potteries at Ching-tê Chên the technique and command of material were perfect, and the product is justly famous. Even in this field, however, there was very little of creative genius. The patterns and colors—both polychrome and monochrome—of preceding dynasties were extensively followed, and the innovations made do not arouse much admiration. Under Ch'ien Lung great ingenuity was exercised in imitating in porcelain natural objects, and in curious designs, including semi-transparent ones, made by deep incisions filled with glaze, but this was an indication of luxurious decadence rather than of vigor. Before Ch'ien Lung's reign was half over, decline was well on the way. In addition to the Ching-tê Chên potteries, many private ones were maintained, but with rare exceptions their products were inferior to those of the government works.

CULTURE UNDER THE GREAT CH'ING EMPERORS: LITERATURE

As we have seen, the literary output under the Ch'ing was enormous. Vast collections and works of reference were issued by imperial command. While, in the very nature of the case, even at their best these were the product of diligence and scholarly competence rather than of genius, they are not to be despised and are evidence of the high regard in which learning was held. The civil service examinations were firmly maintained as the chief road to official preferment and social distinction, and not only did they give prestige to scholarship, but the exacting preparation for them continued to recruit a numerous educated class which appreciated good literature.

A government can never call forth literary genius at will and most of the writing done under the Ch'ing was of mediocre or inferior quality. The output of the printers was voluminous, but much of it was paid for out of government funds by officials who in this way sought prestige. However, some of the literature produced was so distinctive that it is clear that originality was still to be found among the Chinese. Excellent poetry was composed. Novels continued to appear, among them what are probably the greatest and most original ever written in China. The best known and most popular of them all, the *Hung Lou Mêng*, usually translated as "The Dream of the Red Chamber," was the work of Ts'ao Hsüeh-ch'in (or Ts'ao Chan). In it the author seems to have described his own family environment, but to have left his book, incomplete, to be finished by other hands. Another novel, probably dating from about 1825, under the guise of travels in imaginary countries advocated far-reaching social reforms in the position of women—espousing the education of girls and denouncing foot-binding, the inequality of the sexes, and the determination of marriage by fortune-telling. There were, indeed, many novels attacking officialdom and accepted social usages.

Fresh developments also took place in the theatre, although these did not always make for improvement. Additional plays were composed, many of them based on popular novels, and new—and often more raucous—forms of music were popular.

In philosophy the first century or so of the dynasty was noteworthy. There was much more of inquiry and creative thought under the Ch'ing than under the other great foreign dynasty, the Yüan. The impulse that gave rise to it was the conquest of the country by the Manchus. Scholars were impelled to seek the reason for the weakness which had permitted so small a people to overrun the Empire. Among the pioneers were Huang Tsung-hsi and Wang Fu-chih. One of the most distinguished thinkers was Ku T'ing-lin, also known as Ku Yen-wu (1613–1681). Ku actively opposed the Manchu conquest and in later years, when he had become outstanding as a scholar and was repeatedly urged to accept public office, persisted in his resolution never to serve under the hated foreigner. He believed that part of the ineptitude of the Ming had been due to the absorption of the intellectuals in fruitless discussions of the quality of human nature and of Heaven's decree. He sought a cure for the nation's ills in turning from such debates to the cultivation of character. Another independent thinker was Yen Yüan (1635–1704). Stoical, despising mere book-learning, and given to practical activity, he published little and it was not until long afterward that his writings gained much recognition. He declared that the paralysis which had allowed his country to fall a prey to the Manchus arose from the concentration of the scholar on his books and on meditation, and that the remedy lay in hard labor at practical tasks, directed in part toward improving economic conditions. Both Ku and Yen, it will be noted, represented a reaction against the dominant philosophy of the school of Chu Hsi.

Another phase of the rebellion against the Sung philosophers was an attempt to get back of their commentaries to the original Classics. The protestants depended largely on the studies of the Classics made by the scholars of the Han dynasty, as being nearer in time to the revered books and hence presumably more accurate than were the Sung authors. Hence their movement is generally known as that of the *Han Hsüeh,* or Han Learning. Much energy was spent on philology, in the effort to reconstruct the ancient pronunciation of the characters of the Classics. Ku Yen-wu himself was the author of the book which laid the cornerstone of that science, and other scholars followed in his steps. The members of the school sought for early manuscripts, editions, and quotations, to determine what the original texts of the Classics had been. They studied epigraphy, philology, phonology, and historical geography. They developed a method of historical criticism which is clearly independent of but is surprisingly like that evolved in the Occident in recent times. Yen Jo-chü (1636–1704), for example, shook the scholarly world with a book *(Shang Shu Ku Wên Shu Chêng)* which demonstrated that the so-called "Ancient Text" (or "Ancient Script") of the Classic of History was a late forgery. A few in the Sung, Yüan, and Ming had suspected the spurious nature of this text, but none had gone so thoroughly into the subject as did Yen. Yen devoted a lifetime to the task and his arguments were conclusive—but his work was not published until 1745, nearly a generation after his death, and his findings were not accepted by the great majority of the scholars of the time. A younger contemporary of Yen, Yao Chi-hêng (1647–1715?) declared and attempted to prove that many books attributed to ancient times are unauthentic. Hu Wei (1633–1714) showed that the diagrams which some of the Sung philosophers used to illustrate and reënforce their arguments were not from remote antiquity, as the latter had claimed, but originated with a Taoist priest in the tenth century. Ts'ui Shu (1740–1816) put in the larger part of his life casting doubt on what were usually believed to be dependable facts and documents—such as the historicity of the Emperors whom Confucius and his school held up as models, the traditional authorship of the *Chou Li,* the concluding chapters of the *Lun Yü,* and the Bamboo Books. Many another name might be given of those who contributed to this school. Tai Chên (1724–1777), the outstanding philosopher of the Dynasty, marked the culmination of the intellectual renaissance. He rejected the dualism of the Sung for rationalistic, materialistic monism. Yet to the end of the eighteenth and into the nineteenth century there was much of able scholarship. With the loss of vigor which the dynasty suffered after 1800 and with the foreign wars and internal rebellions which shook the Empire in the middle of the nineteenth century, this activity declined. One of its greatest exponents and patrons, Yüan Yüan, who sought to organize research, died in 1849, the year after the outbreak of the most serious of these uprisings, that of the T'ai P'ings. The *Han Hsüeh* was not forgotten, however, and contributed to the intellectual revolution which came in the last years of the nineteenth and in the twentieth century.

The *Han Hsüeh* is significant not only for its combination of originality with reverence for the past, but for the evidence which it affords of the decline of Buddhism as an effective force in the intellectual life of the Empire. In the T'ang and the centuries immediately preceding the T'ang, most of the creative thought of China was absorbed in interpreting and developing Buddhist philosophy. Under the Sung, Buddhism, while producing few thinkers of any consequence, was still strong enough to mold Confucianism. Even under the Ming, Wang Yang-ming seems to show the effect of Buddhist environment. Now, under the Ch'ing, the *Han Hsüeh* was attempting to purge Confucianism of the Buddhist and Taoist elements which the Sung thinkers had brought into it. From one point of view, the *Han Hsüeh* was evidence of a further recession of the tide of Buddhism and the reëmergence above its waters of pre-Buddhist Confucianism. Buddhism was still powerful. Tens of thousands of monks and nuns were in its cloisters and it remained one of the most prominent factors in the folklore, the art, the customs, and the religious life of the Empire. Under Ch'ien Lung there was an attempt to reconcile Buddhism and Confucianism. Tibetan Buddhism was fairly prominent, through the Ch'ing rule of that land and the desire to keep the friendship of the Dalai Lama. On the whole, however, Buddhism was decaying.

There were other trends of thought, including that which kept up the tradition of Wang Yang-ming. The dominant Sung school was itself divided into at least three branches. The T'ung Ch'êng school fought the archaic and artificial literary style (*p'ien t'i*) by which sentences were composed in pairs, and strove to popularize the writings of T'ang and Sung masters and even older writers.

Confucianism as interpreted by the Sung thinkers remained the orthodox philosophy of the state and was enforced through the civil service examinations. The Confucian cult was maintained much as it had been under the later rulers of the Ming. Every imperial political subdivision had a temple in which were tablets to the sage and his distinguished followers and in which sacrifices were officially offered at stated intervals. New names, too, were added to this imperial hall of fame.

INTERCOURSE WITH THE OCCIDENT

Mention has repeatedly been made of the growing pressure from the Occident. Roman Catholic missionaries penetrated every province, bringing with them their religion, and the scholars among them residing in Peking introduced the court and the *literati* to the science and art of the West. In 1807 the first Protestant missionary, Robert Morrison, landed at Canton, and others followed. Portuguese, Dutch, French, English, a few representatives of other European states, and, last of all, Americans, made their way to Macao and Canton. The Russians maintained an overland trade. Upon all these the Ch'ing authorities kept a strict hand. Roman Catholic missionaries were closely watched: repeated persecutions prevented their flocks from increasing much beyond the two hundred thousand mark and were slowly stamping them out. Protestant missionaries were confined to Canton, to Macao, and to overseas Chinese in places like Batavia, Singapore, Malacca, and Bangkok. Commerce was closely regulated. While some smuggling was done, most of the maritime trade was carried on through one port, Canton, and there, during much of the period, it was conducted through an official guild of Chinese merchants, the *Co-hong*. Foreign merchants in Canton were restricted to a narrow strip on the river-bank, the famous "Factories," and might with Portuguese permission find more breathing space at the near-by Macao. The Occident, growing in wealth, power, and commercial activity, would not permanently brook such constraint and trouble loomed ahead. For the time being, however, Westerners had perforce to submit to the conditions imposed by the government in whose land they were guests.

In spite of all these restrictions, the impact of the Occident was already bearing fruit in China. The Christians included very few men of social or political prominence, especially in later years, but they were to be found in practically every province and usually numbered two hundred thousand or more. Western science, especially mathematics and astronomy, was being studied by Chinese scholars. Cannon of the more powerful kind then in use in the West—some of them cast by missionaries at the command of Manchus and Chinese—played a part in internal and external warfare. The Western style of painting was having its influence upon some of the Chinese artists. It is possible that the efforts of Chinese scholars to devise a phonetic system for writing the language—of which there were at least two—were due to contact with Western alphabets.

More marked than the influence of the Occident upon China was that of Chinese culture upon Europe. The Roman Catholic missionaries translated portions of Chinese literature and wrote extensively on the country. Their works were widely read. Since their reports, on the whole, were appreciative of Chinese culture, the result in Europe was an admiration for the Middle Kingdom. For a time in the eighteenth century things Chinese became a fad. Never before had China had so much effect upon lands so distant from her borders. Rococo art reflected a knowledge of Chinese forms. Chinese gardens, pagodas, and pavilions were built by the noble and the wealthy. Many plants were introduced from China, some of them later widely cultivated and extensively developed. Tea roses, azaleas, greenhouse primroses, chrysanthemums, mountain peonies, and China asters were among the flowers introduced into Europe from China in the seventeenth, the eighteenth, and the early part of the nineteenth century. Chinese sweet oranges were taken by the Portuguese to Europe and Brazil and spread throughout much of tropical and subtropical North and South America. Sedan chairs were fashionable, lacquer, incense, tea, Chinese colors, and the Chinese style of painting were popular, the earliest wall papers appeared in imitation of Chinese designs, and true porcelain was for the first time produced in Europe. The deism so widespread in intellectual circles was reënforced by the knowledge of Confucian philosophy which came to the West, for the two systems had much in common. Here, said the deists, was "natural religion" actually in operation. To the "liberals" who led in the "Enlightenment" in the Europe of the eighteenth century China was a kind of Utopia where their principles were practiced.

The admiration of Europeans for China was in marked contrast to the disdain with which that country and its culture were shortly to be viewed. The powerful Empire of K'ang Hsi and Ch'ien Lung compelled a respect which the feebleness of the later rulers could not retain. Moreover, in the nineteenth century information in the West about China came chiefly not from missionaries, in intimate contact with the best of Chinese society, as many of the early Roman Catholics had been. It was derived, rather, from merchants who were irritated beyond measure by the restrictions on their trade and who saw chiefly the seamy side of Chinese life. Then, too, the rapid increase of wealth and physical well-being in the Occident in the nineteenth century contributed to disdain for non-Europeans, including the Chinese. The revival of Classicism may also have had an effect.

The continued influence of China upon Japan must be noted. Several of the Ming scholars, unwilling to live under Manchu rule, with the coming of the Ch'ing dynasty took refuge in the Shogun's domains. Here they made a marked impression upon art and literature. For a time, too, Japan experienced a strengthening of the influence of the Confucian school. Although politically independent and making her own adaptations of what she received, she remained within the borders of China's cultural empire.

SUMMARY

The first hundred and fifty years of the Ch'ing dynasty, then, were among the most glorious in the history of China. With the exception of the Yüan, the area ruled from China had never before been so extensive. Internal order had never been better maintained over so long a period, and, as a result, prosperity was marked and the population multiplied far beyond all previous totals. China dealt firmly with the foreigners in its midst, and its culture was admired and copied in Europe. There was artistic and intellectual life.

With all this vigor and activity, however, in originality the China of the Ch'ing did not begin to equal that of the Chou, or even the Han, the T'ang, and the Sung. The best that the intellectual life of the K'ang Hsi and the Ch'ien Lung period had to show for itself was the Han Learning, and that was directing its energy not toward formulating institutions and giving birth to new ideas, but toward discovering what the forefathers had thought and done during the great creative centuries before the Han and the Ch'in. This comparative sterility of the Ch'ing was a prolongation of that of the Yüan and Ming. For nearly six centuries, then, China had been stirred by no great creative movement. Such innovating ability as was displayed affected merely the minority. It now seems probable that without some powerful shock from the outside the Chinese would have continued to repeat, with variations, the ideas of previous centuries. It is usually impossible to predict infallibly what would have happened under a different set of circumstances, but it seems likely that without such a stimulus Chinese culture had reached the end of its development. However, in the nineteenth and twentieth centuries the clash came. Under it the old institutional and thought forms crumbled and chaos resulted. It is still too early to predict with assurance whether the shock will not prove to have been too great—whether the Chinese genius will not be so overwhelmed that it can never again make fresh and outstanding contributions. In some such contact with other civilizations, however, appears to have lain the only hope of anything new from the Middle Kingdom.

BIBLIOGRAPHY

The dynastic history corresponding to those for the previous ruling houses is *Ch'ing Shih Kao,* or Draft History of the Ch'ing Dynasty, in one hundred and thirty-one volumes—the modest title being due to the fact that the work has not yet been officially approved by the national government. Its sale was for a time prohibited on the ground that it is not an adequate account of its period but in part from political motives. It is the product of a historiographical bureau established early in the Republic for the express purpose of compiling it and is the work of pundits trained under the old régime. The arrangement of material follows, with minor exceptions, that of the Ming history. The quality of the work is questioned, among other things because the authors have made little if any use of foreign sources in the account of the relations between China and Occidental peoples. Largely on account of financial difficulties and political unrest, some of the printing and even of the assembling of material has been badly done. The biographical material from the *Ch'ing Shih Kao* has been brought together in a separate work of eighty volumes. See also J. K. Fairbank and S. Y. Têng, *On the Transmission of Ch'ing Documents* (*Harvard Journal of Asiatic Studies*, Vol. 2, pp. 12–46) and J. K. Fairbank and S. Y. Têng, *On the Types and Uses of Ch'ing Documents* (*Harvard Journal of Asiatic Studies*, Vol. 5, pp. 1–71). E. Hauer has done an important piece of translating in *Huang-Ts'ing K'ai-kuo Fang-lüeh, die Gründung des Mandschurischen Kaiserreiches übersetzt und erklärt* (Berlin and Leipzig, 1926). The original work was compiled by official order in the latter part of the eighteenth century and deals with the beginnings of the dynasty.

Indispensable for the history of the Ch'ing era is A. Hummel, *Eminent Chinese of the Ch'ing Period* (Washington, 2 vols., 1943, 1944). It is made up of biographies prepared by a number of authors.

Of general histories of China covering the period, there are de Mailla, *Histoire Générale de la Chine* (13 vols., Paris, 1777–1785), which extends through the early portion of the dynasty and part of which has the value of being written by an eyewitness—for the author was a missionary in China; H. Cordier, *Histoire Générale de la Chine* (4 vols., Paris, 1920–1921), chiefly valuable here for its summary of relations with Westerners; René Grousset, *Histoire de l'Extrême Orient* (2 vols., Paris, 1929); L. Wieger, *Textes Historiques* (2 vols., Hochienfu, 1903, 1904); Li Ung Bing, *Outlines of Chinese History* (Shanghai, 1914); and H. A. Giles, *A Chinese Biographical Dictionary* (London and Shanghai, 1898). Of these Grousset is the most nearly trustworthy. Some of the others are often uncritical and are to be used only with caution. H. A. Giles, *A Chinese Biographical Dictionary*, represents an immense amount of diligent labor by one of the foremost British sinologists, but unfortunately contains no footnote references to the sources. A good deal on the great Ch'ing Emperors is contained in Sven Hedin, *Jehol, City of Emperors* (translated from the German. New York, 1932).

On the rebellion of Wu San-kuei, an important study is E. Haenisch, *Buckstücke aus der Geschichte Chinas unter der Mandschu-Dynastie. II. Der Aufstand des Wu San-kuei, aus dem Shêngwu-chi übersetzt* (*Toung Pao*, 1913, pp. 1–123).

On the form of government, see Pao Chao Hsieh, *The Government of China (1644–1911)* (Baltimore, 1925). The code of the dynasty, the *Ta Ch'ing Lü Li*, has been translated in part by Sir Thomas Staunton in *Ta Tsing Leu Lee*, etc. (London, 1810), and in full by G. Boulais in his *Manuel du Code Chinois* (*Variétés Sinologiques*, No. 55, Shanghai, 2 vols., 1923–1924). On law there is also E. Alabaster, *Notes and Commentaries on Chinese Criminal Law* (London, 1899). On the civil service examinations as maintained under the dynasty, see Etienne Zi, *Pratique des Examens Littéraires en Chine* (*Variétés Sinologiques*, No. 5, Shanghai, 1894).

On the foreign conquests of the period and relations between China and its Asiatic neighbors, there are J. K. Fairbank and S. Y. Têng, *On the Ch'ing Tributary System* (*Harvard Journal of Asiatic Studies*, Vol. 6, 135–246); W. W. Rockhill, *The Dalai Lamas of Lhasa and Their Relations with the Manchu Emperors of China, 1644–1908* (*T'oung Pao*, 1910, pp. 1–104); W. W. Rockhill, *China's Intercourse with Korea, from the XVth Century to 1895* (London, 1905); P. Pelliot, *Les Conquêtes de l'Empereur de la Chine* (*T'oung Pao*, 1920, pp. 183–274); C. Imbault-Huart, *Recueil de Documents sur l'Asie Centrale* (Paris, 1881); C. Imbault-Huart (translator), *Histoire de la Conquête de la Birmanie par les Chinois* (*Journal Asiatique*, 1878, 7th series, Vol. 11, pp. 135–178); C. Imbault-Huart (translator), *Histoire de la Conquête du Népal par les Chinois* (*Journal Asiatique*, 1878, 7th series, Vol. 12, pp. 348–377); Maurice Courant, *L'Asie Centrale aux XVIIe et XVIIIe siècles: Empire Kalmouk ou Empire Mantchou?* (Paris, 1912); E. Haenisch, *Der Chinesische Feldzug in Ili im Jahre 1755* (*mit zwei zeitgenossischen französischen Kupferstichen*) (*Ostasiat. Zeitschrift*, 1918, pp. 57–86); Lepage, *Soumission des Tribus Musulmanes du Turkestan par la Chine, 1757–1759* (*Mission d'Ollone, Recherches sur les Musulmanes Chinois*, Paris, 1911, pp. 321–355); J. F. Baddeley, *Russia, Mongolia, China* (2 vols., London, 1919).

On relations with the Occident, K. S. Latourette, *A History of Christian Missions in China* (New York, 1929), gives a summarized account of the Roman Catholic and Russian missions, and the footnotes contain references to the chief sources and secondary works. An excellent summary is A. H. Rowbotham, *Missionary and Mandarin. The Jesuits at the Court of China* (University of California Press, 1942). See also on one of the Jesuits, H. Josson and L. Willaert, *Correspondence de Ferdinand Verbiest* (Brussels, 1938). A good book on the intercourse of China with the Occident, chiefly in the nineteenth century, is H. B. Morse, *The International Relations of the Chinese Empire*. In the first volume, *The Period of Conflict, 1834–1860* (New York, 1910), pages 41–117 deal with the years covered by this chapter. A useful summary is found in G. F. Hudson, *Europe and China: a Survey of Their Relations from the Earliest Times to 1800* (London, 1931). On contacts with the Spaniards see W. L. Schurz, *The Manila Galleon* (New York, 1939). On intercourse with Great Britain, see H. B. Morse, *The Chronicles of the East India Company Trading to China, 1635–1834* (5 vols., Cambridge and Oxford, 1926, 1929); E. H. Pritchard, *The Kotow in the Macartney Embassy to China in 1793* (*The Far Eastern Quarterly*, Vol. 2, pp. 163–203); E. H. Pritchard, *The Crucial Years of Early Anglo-Chinese Relations* (Pullman, 1936); and G. Staunton, *An Authentic Account of an Embassy from the King of Great Britain to the Emperor of China* (2 vols., London, 1797). On intercourse with the United States, see K. S. Latourette, *The History of Early Relations between the United States and China, 1784–1844* (New Haven, 1917).

On relations with Russia, see J. F. Baddeley, *Russia, Mongolia*

China, being Some Record of the Relations between them from the Beginning of the XVIIth Century to the Death of the Tsar Alexei Mikhailovich, 1602–1676 (2 vols., London, 1919).

On the effect of China upon Europe, see A. Reichwein, *China and Europe: Intellectual and Artistic Contacts in the Eighteenth Century* (translated by J. C. Powell, New York, 1925); H. Cordier, *La Chine en France au XVIIIe Siècle* (Paris, 1910); P. Martino, *L'Orient dans la Littérature Française au XVIIe et au XVIIIe Siècles* (Paris, 1906); N. Söderblom, *Das Werden des Göttesglaubens,* pp. 324–360 (Leipzig, 1916); V. Pinot, *Documents Inédits Relatifs à la Connaissance de la Chine en France de 1685 à 1740* (1931); V. Pinot, *La Chine et la Formation de l'Esprit Philosophique en France (1640–1740)* (1932); E. Bretschneider, *Early European Researches into the Flora of China* (Shanghai, 1881); E. Bretschneider, *History of European Botanical Discoveries in China* (London, 1898).

On art, see E. F. Fenollosa, *Epochs of Chinese and Japanese Art* (2 vols., London, 1912); S. W. Bushell, *Chinese Art* (2 vols., London, 1910); R. L. Hobson, *The Later Ceramic Wares of China* (London, 1925); F. Hirth, *Scraps from a Collector's Notebook: Being Notes on Some Chinese Painters of the Present Dynasty* (T'oung Pao, 1905).

On the literature of the period, especially the Han Learning and the novels, see a monumental work in Chinese, *Ch'ing Ju Hsueh-an [The Lives and Works of Ch'ing Scholars]* (Peking, 208 vols., 1939); Hu Shih in *The China Year Book, 1924–5,* pp. 633–637 (Tientsin, 1924); A. W. Hummel (translator), *The Autobiography of a Chinese Historian* (Leyden, 1931); M. Freeman, *The Ch'ing Dynasty Criticism of Sung Politico-Philosophy (Journal of the North China Branch of the Royal Asiatic Society,* 1928, pp. 78–110); M. Freeman, *Yen Hsi Chai, a 17th Century Philosopher (ibid.,* 1926, pp. 70–91); R. Wilhelm, *Intellectual Movements in Modern China (The Chinese Social and Political Science Review,* Vol. 8, No. 2, Apr. 1924, pp. 110–124); Hu Shih, *A Chinese Declaration of the Rights of Women (ibid.,* Vol. 8, No. 2, Apr. 1924, pp. 100–109); Liang Ch'i-ch'ao, *An Outline of the Chinese Cultural History of the Last Three Centuries (ibid.,* Vol. 8, No. 3, July 1928, pp. 33–47); Tsao Hsüeh-chin and Kao Ngoh, *Dream of the Red Chamber Translated and Adapted from the Chinese by Chi-chen Wang* (London, 1929); H. A. Giles, *Strange Stories from a Chinese Studio* (2 vols., London, 1880), the translation of a collection *Liao Chai-chi I,* by P'u Sung-ling.

On censorship of literature, see the excellent study by L. C. Goodrich, *The Literary Inquisition of Ch'ien-Lung* (Baltimore, 1935).

An account which goes on into the nineteenth century is C. B. Malone, *History of the Peking Summer Palaces under the Ch'ing Dynasty* (Urbana, 1934).

CHAPTER X

THE TRANSFORMATION WROUGHT BY THE IMPACT OF THE OCCIDENT

The Empire Is Shaken by Wars with Western European Powers and the Resulting Treaties and by Internal Rebellion (a.d. 1839–1860)

INTRODUCTORY

As has been suggested several times, we now come to the period of the greatest revolution in Chinese institutions and culture of which we have record. What changes may have been wrought in the dim ages before the Chou dynasty we do not know. We do know, however, that not during the centuries whose main features we are able to reconstruct with some degree of assurance had there been such a thorough-going shattering of the structure of the nation's life. Eras of marked transition there had been. Of these, the chief were the chaos toward the end of the Chou, out of which emerged the imperial structure of the Ch'in and the Han, and the centuries of disorder and invasion, with the accompanying influx of Buddhism, which succeeded the downfall of the Han. In neither period, however, had the overturn of the inheritance from the past been so nearly complete as it has in these opening decades of the twentieth century. The end is not yet in sight and still further disintegration may be in store before there emerges a new structure with some promise of stability.

Up to the nineteenth century, the current of Chinese history had moved on without such marked disturbances as had punctuated that of the Occident. One dynasty succeeded another, each being founded by a successful warrior, and each, after a shorter or longer period, declining, its close marked by rebellions and civil chaos, and, frequently, invasions from the north. Then, after disunion of brief or prolonged duration, followed a new dynasty and a repetition of the story with comparatively unimportant modifications. After the Ch'in and the Han each dynasty perpetuated much of the administrative machinery of its predecessor; even Ch'in Shih Huang Ti did not effect a complete severance from the past, but strove to unify the country on the basis of the administrative organization which had worked well in the feudal state of his fathers and on one of the political theories inherited from the philosopher-statesmen of earlier generations. Under each major dynasty, too, Chinese civilization experienced alterations, often very marked. Chinese cultural history is by no means a dull repetition of a few themes, as was so much of political history between the Han and the end of the Ch'ing. However, there was no break so marked as that which occurred between the Persian and the Post-Alexandrian Hellenistic periods in Western Asia, or as that between the Roman Empire and Medieval Europe. No cultural or political invasion from without had so nearly overwhelmed the native inheritance as had several of those which the Occident had known.

The events of the nineteenth and twentieth centuries were, therefore, entirely without precedent in China's history. Heretofore the most dangerous invaders had come from the north, west, and northeast—by way of the land. Now they were arriving by the sea. The ocean had been spanned. On the north, too, a menace still loomed—Russia. The Empire was beset from both sides. Up to now, cultural invasion had not been a sequel of the political domination of aliens. Now both were combined. Former invaders and conquerors had adopted from China most of what civilization they possessed. Although they mastered all or part of the country, usually they ruled as Chinese monarchs and preserved native institutions. Many ideas had come in from abroad—more than have sometimes been recognized—but the structure of Chinese life was basically but very little altered. The major cultural importation had been Buddhism and that had entered chiefly through peaceful contacts with the outer world. Now came peoples possessed of a high civilization very different from that of China. Far from being disposed to adopt the latter, they regarded it as backward and semi-barbarous. The admiration for the Middle Kingdom which had been so strong in Europe in the eighteenth century was preserved only by a few savants, and by them chiefly for China's past. The attitude toward contemporary

China was almost entirely a compound of irritation, condescension, and contempt.

The conflict was one of civilizations as well as of governments and peoples. In each of the main phases of life, economic, political, intellectual, social, and religious, Chinese and Western culture displayed striking and in some cases fundamental differences. In the close interplay of modern life, one or the other system had to give way. In the eighteenth century it had seemed for a time that Europe might be partially sinicized rather than China Europeanized. As the nineteenth century progressed it became obvious that the opposite would take place. The effect on China was accentuated by the fact that the culture of the West was itself experiencing rapid changes which threatened its own traditional bases and even its existence. Here was an Occident being rapidly enriched by the new industrial processes which had begun to appear in the eighteenth century and which were to be extensively developed in the nineteenth and twentieth centuries. The West had discovered new ways of utilizing man's physical environment. In consequence, the structure of its own economic, social, moral, intellectual, and political life was being revolutionized. Moved by their desire for markets and raw materials and by the passion for power, and armed with the new appliances, Western peoples were rapidly mastering much of the globe. Wherever they went—whether to Africa, India, the South Seas, the Americas, Japan, or China—changes followed.

In China, in the clash of civilizations, the institutions of two thousand years were to be shaken to their foundations and many were to crumble. The political and economic organization which had proved fairly adequate for the old conditions was quite unfitted to cope with the invasion. The Chinese looked upon the intruders as barbarians and long resisted them. However, in time, defeated in war again and again, their independence compromised, their chief cities forced to house foreign communities, and their land traversed by merchants and missionaries conveying new ideas, the Chinese began adopting the culture of the alien. They did so partly in self-defense—in the attempt to defeat the conqueror with his own weapons—and partly because they were convinced of the superiority of much that the Westerner had to offer. Whatever the motive, the result was change affecting profoundly every phase of the nation's life.

The story of the period has been told again and again, often in much detail. Histories of China by Westerners have usually devoted half or more of their space to the years after 1839. It would be superfluous, therefore, to repeat extensively the narrative of the past ninety or a hundred years. If, however, this account of China's past is to be well-rounded, these momentous decades must be included, and because of their significance, especially for present-day China, we must go into them somewhat more fully than we have into any preceding era. It must always be remembered that we are still too near the events to view them in their true perspective. We must, however, make the effort so to see them, because upon the success with which we do so depends the accuracy of our understanding of the present situation. Time, too, may prove us to have been as competent judges as those who come after us.

The years after 1839 are divided by events into three main periods. First are slightly over two decades (1839–1860) during which in two wars (1839–1842 and 1856–1860) with Occidental powers China was defeated and forced to permit the Westerner to reside in several important cities and to travel freely elsewhere, and to grant him a certain degree of exemption from the jurisdiction of Chinese laws and courts. The treaties then exacted from Peking were the main framework of the legal basis for the Western penetration of China. During the uneasy truce (1842–1856) which separated the two wars a rebellion broke out (1848) which traced its history to contacts with the West and which devastated some of the Empire's fairest provinces and threatened to unseat the Manchus. The year 1860 ended with the dynasty in a parlous condition—the nation saddled with treaties which compromised its independence and rebellions rampant.

There followed, in the second place, slightly more than three decades (1861–1893) when the dynasty and the Empire appeared to have recovered. The rebellions were suppressed and internal order restored. In spite of recurring friction with Western governments and occasional further concessions to them, major humiliations were avoided and some show of dignity maintained. However, while outwardly the structure of Chinese life was little altered, influences from abroad were undermining it.

Then came, in the third place, beginning with 1894, a period, still unfinished, when the framework of Chinese civilization began to crumble. A disastrous war with Japan (1894–1895) was the signal, and was quickly succeeded by the threatened partition of the country among the powers (1895–1899). A vain attempt to oust the alien (1900) ended in humiliating prostration before him. In the revolutionary attempts at adjustment which followed, the Manchus were swept aside (1912) and a republic attempted. During the ensuing civil strife the nation declined more and more toward political chaos. At the same time startling changes came in every phase of the people's life—in the family and social structure, in religion, in intellectual activities, and in economic organization. After five decades (1894–1944), the process seems only to have begun. After 1931 and especially after 1937 events were complicated by the progressive conquest of much of the country by Japan.

THE FIRST WAR WITH GREAT BRITAIN (1839–1842)

As we have seen, the pressure of the West on China was due to the renewed expansion of European peoples, caused by what is usually termed the Industrial Revolution. We have also seen that Great Britain, the Occidental power in which that revolution originated, was the chief of the maritime commercial nations and, dissatisfied with the conditions under which the Chinese permitted trade, was the first in the new era to seek to coerce the Chinese into granting better terms. To the British, accustomed to intercourse between nations on the basis of equality, the Chinese procedure, grounded in the conviction that all other peoples were tributary to the Emperor, was intolerable. Chinese tonnage dues, taxes on imports and exports, other fees on commerce, and trade regulations seemed galling and arbitrary. Chinese judicial processes were regarded as high-handed and unjust: the legal procedures of the two nations differed, the Chinese theory of group responsibility clashed with the British concept of individual responsibility, the Chinese authorities employed torture as part of the judicial process, Chinese courts were corrupt, their penalties seemed excessive, and the innocent were often not given a fair hearing. Had the British been ready to abide by a basic principle of that international law by which they professed to be guided—the sovereignty of each nation—they might well have reminded themselves that they had no treaty rights in the country, were there on sufferance, and, if they did not like such terms as the Chinese gave them, had no option but to ask peaceably for modification or to withdraw. That, however, was not the temper of Europeans toward non-Europeans in the nineteenth century. Criticism of the ensuing war was not lacking in Great Britain and America, but it was on the ground that opium was being forced on China. Few challenged the right of an Occidental power to exact better conditions for what was deemed legitimate trade.

On both sides there was incredible ignorance of the other. High Chinese and Manchu officials believed the English to be "foreign devils," and therefore unable to bend their knees. British contempt and irritation were extreme. Each regarded the other as uncivilized.

As has just been said, the issue was complicated by the traffic in opium. Opium had long been in use in China. As a temporary escape from the monotony and tensions of life, it had much the same appeal as alcoholic beverages have made to some other peoples. Partly because of its deleterious moral and physical effects, and partly because its rapid increase reversed the favorable balance of trade and led to the export of silver, the Chinese court renewed long-standing prohibitions against the importation of the drug. These were violated—through the connivance and venality of Chinese officials—until late in 1838, when Peking, taking alarm, in a spasm for enforcement, appointed one Lin Tzê-hsü as imperial commissioner to stamp out the traffic. Lin arrived at his post in 1839 and acted with vigor. He ordered that all the contraband drug in foreign hands be surrendered and that foreign merchants give their formal promise no longer to import it. To win acceptance of his demands he virtually imprisoned the entire foreign community in Canton in its own quarters. Slightly more than twenty thousand chests of the drug were, accordingly, handed over and destroyed, and some of the foreigners gave the required bond. The British, aggrieved, withdrew—for a time to Macao, and soon, when ordered out by the Chinese, to the island of Hongkong, then almost uninhabited but commanding an excellent harbor not far from Canton. Further friction followed, and in November, 1839, an armed clash occurred between British and Chinese warships at Hongkong.

The war thus begun was interrupted from time to time by

negotiations, and was almost entirely confined to naval attacks by the British upon Chinese ports from Canton north to the Yangtze. Eventually, after the capture (July, 1842) of Chinkiang, where the Grand Canal crosses the Yangtze, had cut an important line of communication between Peking and the South, and an assault on Nanking had been ordered, the Chinese came to terms.

THE TREATIES OF 1842–1844

The resulting treaty of Nanking (August 29, 1842)—which the Emperor, Tao Kuang, very reluctantly allowed to be signed—had as its main provisions (1) the opening of five ports, Canton, Amoy, Foochow, Ningpo, and Shanghai, to the residence and trade of British subjects; (2) the cession of the island of Hongkong to Great Britain—for a naval and commercial base; (3) intercourse between British and Chinese officials on the footing of equality; (4) the establishment and publication by the Chinese of a "fair and regular" tariff on exports and imports, to take the place of the dues which the British claimed were subject to arbitrary change and the venality of Chinese officials; (5) the abolishment of the Co-hong; and (6) the payment by China of an indemnity as recompense for the opium destroyed by Lin, for the debts owed by the Co-hong to British merchants, and for British war expenses. This was followed (1843) by a supplementary treaty fixing a tariff schedule and further regulations for trade and containing a clause promising most-favored-nation treatment and granting the beginnings of extraterritoriality.

Other Western powers whose citizens had commerce with China watched with interest the war and its outcome and some of them soon requested concessions similar to those granted to the British. The British had asked no exclusive privileges for themselves, unless the cession of Hongkong be called such, and, although at first they were far from cordial to the idea, offered no very great opposition to the extension to other nations of the terms of commercial and official intercourse that had been won by them. The United States sent a diplomatic mission, headed by Caleb Cushing, which in 1844 obtained a treaty opening the same five ports to Americans, regulating trade, and elaborating extraterritoriality —defining it in criminal cases and extending it in part to civil ones. In October, 1844, the French obtained a similar treaty, in

December, 1844, brought about the issue of an imperial edict granting permission to erect Roman Catholic churches in the ports and to Chinese to accept Roman Catholicism, and in 1846 secured a second edict which confirmed the toleration of Roman Catholicism and promised the restoration to the Catholics of some of the churches built under K'ang Hsi which had been confiscated in the persecutions of the past century or more. A decree of 1845 extended to Protestants the privileges of the edict of 1844. In 1845 Belgians were given the right to trade and in 1847 Sweden and Norway obtained a treaty. In 1851 a convention with Russia further regulated trade between that country and China.

These treaties and edicts provided the legal basis of much of the foreign penetration which the next ninety years were to witness and their leading provisions formed the framework around which the intercourse of the next two generations was to be built. The opening of the five cities for the trade and residence of foreigners served as a precedent for designating others for the same purpose—"treaty ports," as they came to be called. Until 1929 the tariff continued to be fixed by agreement with foreign powers. It became customary to demand an indemnity of China after the latter had been defeated in war. Extraterritoriality was established and for three-quarters of a century was to be the general practice. By it, foreigners, when they were defendants in any criminal action against Chinese, were to be tried under their own laws and by their own authorities; in civil cases with Chinese they might invoke the aid of their consuls; and in controversies among themselves they were not to be subject either to Chinese laws or courts. When it was devised, the system probably helped to reduce the friction between foreigners and Chinese, but it was a decided infringement upon what in the Occident were considered the prerogatives of a sovereign state.

BETWEEN THE WARS (1842–1855)

Under the new treaties the pressure of the West upon China perceptibly increased. On Hongkong was developed a thriving city. Foreign merchants and missionaries settled there and in the five open ports. The Jesuits reëntered China (1840), several Roman Catholic and Protestant organizations sent representatives to begin work, and bodies. both Roman Catholic and Protestant, which had been in China before 1839 reënforced their staffs. Trade was stimulated by the growth of steam navigation. The settlement of the west coast of North America, especially California, from the older portions of the United States proceeded apace during the forties and fifties and led to more commerce across the Pacific. The emigration of Chinese laborers sprang up—to the mines of California, to Peru, and to the plantations of Cuba and British Guiana. Through these wanderers overseas alien influences were to flow back into China. In Shanghai, moreover, which rapidly became an important center of foreign trade, the Westerners acquired lands outside the city wall. There three settlements arose, French, British, and American (the last two later—1863—amalgamated as the International Settlement), and the foundations were laid of the status which in after years was to be one of nearly complete independence of Chinese control. The foreign commerce of Amoy, Ningpo, and Foochow did not become so important as that of Shanghai, and the foreign settlements at these ports did not reach the dimensions of those at the latter city. It should also be noted that Portugal in effect assumed full sovereignty over Macao, although China did not formally recognize the act until 1887.

The peace that was sealed by the treaties was little more than a truce. Neither side was satisfied. From the Chinese standpoint too much had been granted, and from the foreign standpoint not enough. Friction inevitably followed. Of the five treaty ports, Canton continued to have the largest number of foreign residents. These were still confined to the old narrow "Factory" district along the river front, and the Cantonese offered determined opposition to any extension of the area. British attempts to obtain better conditions were balked. Rioting, murders, and bitterness punctuate the annals of these years. Trouble, although not so marked, occurred at the other four ports. The smuggling of opium continued. Much of the emigration of Chinese took the form of "contract labor," and recruiting for it was often by violence and fraud. For a time foreign ships, especially Portuguese, undertook the "convoying" of Chinese merchant craft along the coast, ostensibly as a protection against pirates, but in reality a thinly veiled form of blackmail.

The American and French treaties of 1844 made provision for

their own revision at the end of twelve years. Great Britain, under the most-favored-nation clause of her supplementary treaty of 1843, claimed that the one of 1842 should come up for review in 1854 and enumerated to the Chinese added regulations for intercourse and fresh privileges to foreigners which she deemed desirable—among them access to more cities, the legalization of the opium trade, and the residence of Western envoys in Peking. These demands were supported by the United States and France. It may be noted, lest the alien seem entirely intent on his own gains, even at the price of debauching the Chinese, that some who favored provision for the importation of opium did so on the ground that, since the drug was coming into the country anyway, by smuggling, control could be exercised and a revenue derived for the Government if the traffic were recognized and regularized. In 1856 the American representative by independent action endeavored to gain a revision, then due, of the treaty of 1844. All these attempts for the moment ended in failure.

THE WAR OF 1856–1860

As is often the case in such strained situations, war broke out over a comparatively minor incident. In October, 1856, a craft, the lorcha *Arrow*, owned by Chinese, and with a Chinese crew, but registered at Hongkong, having a British captain, and flying the British flag, while at Canton was boarded by Chinese officers. Most of its crew were arrested—on the ground that they had been engaged in a recent act of piracy—and the British flag was hauled down. The British declared that British sovereignty had been violated and their flag insulted. The Chinese declined to give the satisfaction demanded.

This particular clash, apparently so trivial, might have been settled peaceably had it not been that by disposition and conviction the British Consul, Harry Parkes, and the Viceroy in Canton, Yeh Ming-shên, were both uncompromising. By the end of the month the British naval forces commenced hostilities, capturing the forts commanding the approaches to Canton and bombarding the Viceroy's yamen. The Chinese retaliated by what in effect was a declaration of war. The British ministry sustained the action of the British authorities in China, was defeated on the issue in the House of Commons, but, dissolving Parliament, appealed to the country, won an endorsement, and went on with hostilities.

France coöperated. France and Great Britain had been allied in the war which was just closing in the Crimea, and France had been given a *casus belli* in the execution (early in 1856), by the Chinese authorities in Kwangsi, in direct violation of the treaty of 1844, of a French priest, Chapdelaine. Great Britain suggested that the United States also join. This Washington declined to do—although late in 1856 an American force had obtained an apology for an indignity to the American flag by dismantling the offending forts (below Canton). The United States, however, had its representative on hand to ask for a revision of the treaty of 1844 when the French and British were forcing from the Chinese the revision of their corresponding documents. Russia, with the Crimean War so recently closed, could not collaborate, but was eager to take advantage of the situation to gain what she could.

Due to a war with Persia and to the Sepoy Mutiny in India (1857), Great Britain was delayed in pressing hostilities. Late in 1857, however, a sufficient British and French force had gathered in Chinese waters, Canton was taken, and the obdurate Viceroy, Yeh, was sent a prisoner to Calcutta. Great Britain, France, the United States, and Russia now dispatched demands to Peking. The reply proving unsatisfactory, the allied fleets proceeded north, where they could bring more direct pressure on the capital. The Taku forts, commanding the approach to Tientsin, were captured by the British and French. With Peking thus threatened, the Emperor yielded, and treaties (usually called the Treaties of Tientsin) were negotiated and signed (1858), not only with Great Britain and France but also with Russia and the United States.

Before these new agreements could become effective, they had to be ratified by their respective governments and the ratifications exchanged. The Russian, French, and British documents provided that ratifications should be exchanged at Peking. This the Russian minister accomplished without difficulty. When, however, in 1859 the British, French, and American ministers arrived off Tientsin for this purpose, more trouble ensued. The American minister went to Peking and effected the exchange, although not without some humiliation, but the British and French ministers insisted on going through Tientsin instead of by the route selected by the Chinese. They were opposed, attempted to force a passage, were repulsed (1859), and the war was renewed. In 1860 the British and French returned with reënforcements, captured the Taku forts and Tientsin, and moved toward their goal, Peking. In retaliation for the seizure of a party which had been sent forward under a flag of truce and the death of several of its members, when Peking was captured the Summer Palace was deliberately destroyed.

THE TREATIES OF TIENTSIN (1858) AND PEKING (1860)

The treaties of Tientsin and the supplementary conventions, including the ones signed at Peking in 1860, effected important modifications in the status of Westerners in China and made possible a much more extensive penetration of the Empire by the Occident than had those of 1842 and 1844. Many of the details need not concern us here, but some of the provisions are of great significance. (1) New ports were opened. Ten of these were designated by the treaties of Tientsin—Newchwang in Manchuria, Têngchow (for which Chefoo was substituted in 1862) in Shantung, four on the Yangtze, including Chinkiang and Hankow (not all were really opened at once, and one, Nanking, not until 1899), one on Hainan (actually not opened until 1876), two on Formosa, and Ch'ao-chow (actually its port, Swatow) on the south coast. Tientsin itself was added in 1860. These ports, particularly those in the North and on the Yangtze, put vast new sections in direct touch with Westerners. Several of these cities were already major centers of population. Some others, through the impulse given by foreign trade, rapidly rose in importance. Occidentals therefore were concentrated in entrepôts from which trade routes radiated into large areas of the country—with fateful consequences for existing Chinese ideas and institutions. (2) The merchantmen of the powers were given permission to use the Yangtze River. (3) Peking, although not technically made an open port, was to see the hated alien living within its walls, for the treaties specified that ministers or ambassadors, with their entourages, were to be allowed to reside there. They were, moreover, to be received as representatives of independent nations on a footing of equality with China. (4) Foreigners, when armed with proper passports, were to be permitted to travel anywhere in the interior. This accorded the Westerner the privilege of going wherever he wished and so furthered the extension of Occidental ideas beyond the limits of the ports. (5) To Christians, both aliens and Chinese, was given the privilege of propagating Christianity, and both were guaranteed toleration in the practice of their faith. In effect this provision in part removed Chinese Christians from the jurisdiction of Chinese officials, for any alleged persecution could be referred by the missionaries to a consul or minister for presentation to the imperial authorities. It led to abuses, because not infrequently Chinese professed conversion to obtain the assistance of the missionary and the consul in lawsuits. Even without such abuses, the "toleration clauses" made possible the percolation of Christianity through the Empire and so in part threatened the disintegration of existing Chinese institutions. (6) The French convention of 1860 gave further sanction to the promise made in the imperial edict of 1846 that the Chinese Government would restore to Roman Catholics the religious and benevolent establishments confiscated during the persecutions of the preceding century and a half. The Chinese text—which the Chinese have claimed was not authoritative—assured to French missionaries the privilege of renting and purchasing land in all the provinces and erecting buildings thereon. It was, therefore, long an especial source of irritation. The further (Berthemy) convention of 1865 continued its provisions, subject to restrictions which proved unsatisfactory to the Roman Catholics. An additional Franco-Chinese agreement of 1895 was designed to remove some of the causes of the missionaries' complaints. The net result of the mooted sections was to assist Roman Catholic missionaries in spreading their faith outside the treaty ports. The privilege of "renting and leasing in perpetuity" property outside the ports was not formally granted by treaty to Protestant missionaries until 1903, but in practice it was often conceded to them. A few other provisions can briefly be mentioned: (7) an elaboration of the regulations for extraterritoriality, (8) the cession to Great Britain of a bit of the mainland opposite Hongkong, (9) the payment of indemnities, and (10), in a new tariff drawn up in 1858 in pursuance of the treaties of Tientsin, the legalization of the opium traffic by the placing of a duty on the drug.

By force of arms, as in 1839–1842, Westerners had obtained additional privileges in China. Through the concessions granted them in the treaties which concluded these two wars, supported, when necessary, by the continued show of force, they were able to permeate a reluctant China with their commerce and ideas and so to bring about in Chinese culture a revolution much more thoroughgoing than any one at the time, either Chinese or foreign, dreamed possible.

TERRITORIAL AGGRESSIONS

As yet the aggressive Westerner had taken little of the territory of China. Here and there, however, he was nibbling at it. As we have seen, the island of Hongkong and a small bit of the adjacent mainland had been ceded to Great Britain, and Portugal had asserted an as yet unadmitted sovereignty over the peninsula of Macao, where she had so long been a tenant-at-will. China's manifest weakness and the growth of the activities of Occidentals in the Far East led to some other encroachments.

By the treaties between China and Russia in the seventeenth and eighteenth centuries, the boundary between the two empires was so fixed that China was recognized as owning much of the land north of the Amur (in Chinese, the Heilungchiang). Under the later Manchus, less vigorous than their predecessors, but little attention was paid to this distant and sparsely settled region. The Russians continued to push into Siberia and, shortly after the Anglo-Chinese war of 1839–1842, under the leadership of a vigorous governor, sent expeditions and colonists down the river. In 1858 China, defeated by the French and English and disturbed by internal rebellions, by the treaty of Aigun ceded to Russia everything that it owned north of the Amur and agreed to the joint occupancy by the two empires of the territory east of the Ussuri River. In 1860, by a new treaty, this joint occupancy was ended, and the land east of the Ussuri was ceded to Russia. Russia now possessed all the seacoast of Asia north of Korea.

At the time this loss probably did not appear to the Chinese as particularly important, for Manchuria had a comparatively small population and the settlement of the region by Chinese was very slight and in regions not directly affected by the cession. As a step in the Russian expansion toward the Pacific, however, and toward further encroachment on China, it was of great significance.

While Russia was taking territory from the Empire in the extreme North, in the extreme South France was pursuing a policy which was eventually to lead to the loss by China of its tributary territory in Indo-China. In response to the diplomacy of a missionary bishop, the French, in the latter part of the eighteenth century, had assisted in restoring a king of Cochin-China to his throne and in the conquest, by this same ruler, of Tongking. In the eighteen forties and fifties, France intervened on behalf of persecuted French Roman Catholic missionaries and their flocks. In 1858 Spain and France joined in further naval and military operations, the Spaniards finding a cause for war in the execution of a Spanish missionary bishop. In 1862 a treaty was signed which granted religious freedom to Roman Catholics, opened three ports to French and Spanish merchants, and ceded to France three provinces in Cochin-China.

INTERNAL DISORDER

The weakness of China against her foes from the Occident was both increased by and in turn facilitated the rise and progress of serious domestic rebellions.

The chief of these was due in part to the influx of new religious ideas through Christian missionaries from the West. The figure around whom it centered, Hung Hsiu-ch'üan, was a Hakka, a native of Kwangtung. In his twenties, while in Canton as a candidate for the civil service examinations, he appears—if we may trust the narrative of a cousin and intimate friend—to have been given some books which contained a summary of the teachings of Protestant missionaries. Some time afterward he was attacked by a severe illness in the course of which, in visions, he was taken to a large and luminous place where he was cleansed, given a new heart, and commissioned by an old man to exterminate the demons who were leading mankind away from his—the old man's—service. Several years later, in 1843, Hung seems to have had his attention again called to the books which had been given him in Canton. In perusing these he believed that he found the key to his visions—that the old man was God, the demons idols, and that he was under obligation to restore the worship of this true God. Thereupon he inaugurated a movement, at first entirely religious, which had in it many of the outward features of Protestant Christianity. Hung himself was later under the instruction of a somewhat eccentric Protestant missionary.

The sect which arose out of Hung's teaching, "The Worshippers of *Shang Ti*" (a Protestant term for God), became especially strong in Kwangsi, and developed at first without much direct leadership from Hung. Into it entered many elements of Chinese provenance: the cult was a bizarre syncretism of misunderstood Christianity and native beliefs. In time, by just what process is not entirely clear, but possibly under the guidance of one Chu Chiu-t'ao, who was soon eliminated, collaborating with an early convert of Hung, Fêng Yün-shan, who fell in battle in the summer of 1852, "The Worshippers of *Shang Ti*" became a political as well as a religious movement. In the early stages "Triads," members of a revolutionary society which sought to restore the Ming, joined with them. The rebels sought to overthrow the Manchus and establish in their place a new dynasty, to be called T'ai P'ing, or Great Peace, with Hung as its monarch. Hostilities began in 1848 but did not prove especially serious until 1850 and 1851. In 1852 the rebels moved northward into Hunan by the familiar route of the Hsiang River, taking several towns. Early in 1853 they captured Wuchang and in March of that year Nanking fell to their arms. At Nanking they established their capital.

In a certain sense the T'ai P'ings were a reforming group, the first wave, largely unintelligent, of that movement which sought to save China by reshaping it on lines learned from the West and which in the twentieth century was to work momentous changes. In their effects, however, they were almost entirely destructive.

From another angle the rebellion was a social and economic revolt—an uprising of peasants, the rural proletariat, hand workers, and poorer gentry against landlords, rich peasants, merchants, and wealthy gentry. Indeed, a recent Chinese student of the movement has seen in it chiefly an attempt of non-propertied groups to dispossess the privileged classes. Certainly the ultimate suppression of the T'ai P'ings was due to the support which the conservative elements of society gave to the imperial government.

Certainly, too, the influence of Christianity was only one factor, and probably a minor one, in bringing about the movement. Although to the last the leaders professed adherence to that faith which was so strange a compound of Christianity and Chinese beliefs and practices, what impelled the bulk of the rank and file of the T'ai P'ings was discontent with existing conditions, the love of adventure, and the desire for plunder. Religious fanaticism was only one of the ingredients. To understand the T'ai P'ings one must recall the economic pressure and the secret societies which are so constant a feature in Chinese society, and the oppression and incompetence which characterized so much of the local government in the years of the decay of the Ch'ing, the chronic jealousy of and hostility to the Manchus, and the traditional trend toward revolt whenever a dynasty showed signs of weakness. One must remember, too, the tendency of Chinese rebellions, since at least the last years of the Han, to take on the guise of religious sects.

Had Hung displayed any very great genius for organization or political leadership, the T'ai P'ings might well have overthrown the Manchus, for the latter, suffering from the humiliating defeat at the hands of Great Britain and harassed by smaller uprisings, were lamentably weak. However, he proved to be singularly lacking in the needed kind of ability, and after one raid which carried them almost to Tientsin, the T'ai P'ings never seriously threatened the Manchus' possession of the North. Moreover, their religious tenets and fanaticism and their wholesale destructiveness antagonized the influential classes and made impossible the winning of the assent of the nation to their rule. Still, the Ch'ing dynasty was so weak and so distraught by the attacks of the French and English, that the T'ai P'ings, aided by able generals who came to the fore in 1858 and by tapping new territory and hence new resources (*ca.* 1860), managed to hold Nanking for more than a decade and to devastate some of the fairest sections of the Yangtze Valley. Not until 1865, as we shall see in the next chapter, was Peking able to overthrow them and then only because of Chinese and foreign assistance.

The T'ai P'ings were not the only rebels who brought anxiety to the dynasty. Indeed, the foregoing paragraphs have probably given them proportionately too great attention. Because of their peculiar connection with Christianity and their contacts with foreigners in the lower reaches of the Yangtze, the T'ai P'ings have attracted more notice from Western historians of China than they deserve. They constituted only one of a number of revolts of these troubled years. About 1856 there broke out in Yünnan an uprising among the large Moslem population, due to a clash between themselves and their non-Moslem neighbors. The non-Chinese tribes of the region took the opportunity to harass the Chinese population, against whom they had many grievances. There were numerous other rebel bands in various parts of the country, among them the Nienfei, who were widely spread, particularly in the North. In the Northwest the Moslems were restless. What had happened many times before was happening again. As the ruling house became weak, revolt raised its head.

TAO KUANG AND HSIEN FENG

Had the Ch'ing dynasty possessed such leaders as K'ang Hsi or Ch'ien Lung, the disasters which the nation suffered at the hands of foreigners and rebels might never have overtaken it. To be sure, the growth of population and the consequent economic pressure which were so basic a cause of the internal unrest could not have been averted by a strong administration: in a very real sense they were a product of it. A K'ang Hsi or a Ch'ien Lung, indeed, by putting up a more stubborn resistance to Western powers than did Tao Kuang and Hsien Fêng, might conceivably have been ultimately defeated more overwhelmingly by the West, with greater immediate disaster to the country. It is certain, however, that K'ang Hsi or Ch'ien Lung would have handled the situation with more vigor than did their incompetent descendants, and it is not improbable that they would have dealt with it more wisely.

As it was, the Ch'ing was in that period of decline which appears to be the inevitable fate of all ruling families. Such was the Chinese system of government, where so much depended on the monarch, that both the dynasty and the Empire, with mediocrity or worse at the helm, stumbled into defeat and almost into disintegration. The Emperor whose reign period bore the name of the Tao Kuang had been unable to save his realm from defeat at the hands of Great Britain in 1839–1842 and was troubled by revolts. He died in 1850 and was succeeded by a son who is usually known by the title of his reign period, Hsien Fêng. Hsien Fêng proved even less competent than his predecessor and in his last days, disheartened, gave himself over to excesses. In 1860 he fled from Peking on the approach of the French and British armies and took refuge at Jehol, an imperial country seat north of Peking. Here, in 1861, he died, still a young man, leaving his throne to a five year old son. Defeated by foreign powers and menaced by internal rebellions, the Ch'ing seemed to be facing a dark future, and the Empire, under its nerveless leadership, to be threatened with chaos.

BIBLIOGRAPHY

The dynastic history—as yet not officially approved—is the *Ch'ing Shih Kao,* or Draft History of the Ch'ing, recently compiled.

H. Cordier, *Histoire Générale de la Chine,* Vol. 4 (Paris, 1921), is good, especially for foreign relations. Of greater value is A. Hummel, *Eminent Chinese of the Ch'ing Period* (Washington, 2 vols., 1943, 1944).

The best account of diplomatic relations and wars with Westerners during the period is H. B. Morse, *The International Relations of the Chinese Empire. The Period of Conflict, 1834–1860* (London, 1910). H. B. Morse and H. F. MacNair, *Far Eastern International Relations* (revised edition, Boston, 1931) contains much of the material in the larger work of Morse and in addition includes Japan, Korea, and Eastern Siberia in its scope and brings the narrative down into 1931. Another excellent account, by one who was an eyewitness of part of what he narrates, is in S. Wells Williams, *The Middle Kingdom,* Vol. 2 (New York, 1882). Brief summaries are in P. J. Treat, *The Far East* (New York, 1928) and H. M. Vinacke, *A History of the Far East in Modern Times* (New York, 1928). Useful also is H. F. MacNair, *Modern Chinese History—Selected Readings* (Shanghai, 1923). A view of a modern Western-educated Chinese is in M–C. J. Bau, *The Foreign Relations of China* (New York, 1921).

American relations through the first treaty of the United States with China are recounted in K. S. Latourette, *The History of Early Relations between the United States and China, 1784–1844* (New Haven, 1917), and American relations throughout the period are covered in T. Dennett, *Americans in Eastern Asia* (New York, 1922). Both works have extensive bibliographies and footnotes.

Descriptions of the status and the life of the foreigner in China shortly before the first Chino-British war are C. T. Downing, *The Stranger in China, or the Fan Qui's Visit to the Celestial Empire in 1836–7* (2 vols., Philadelphia, 1838), W. C. Hunter, *The Fan Kwae at*

Canton before Treaty Days 1825–1844 (London, 1882), W. C. Hunter, *Bits of Old China* (London, 1885), G. Nye, *The Morning of My Life in China* (Canton, 1873), and John Slade, *Narrative of the Late Proceedings and Events in China* (China, 1839).

Accounts of special phases of relations between China and the West are C. S. Leavenworth, *The Arrow War with China* (London, 1901); E. Griffin, *Clippers and Consuls, American Consular and Commercial Relations with Eastern Asia, 1845–1860* (Ann Arbor, 1938); C. L. Baron de Bazancourt, *Les Expéditions de Chine et de Cochin-Chine d'après les Documents Officiels* (2 vols., Paris, 1861–1862); what is largely an annotated translation of a diary, Ssŭ-yü Têng, *Changhsi and the Treaty of Nanking, 1842* (Chicago, 1944); G. Fox, *British Admirals and Chinese Pirates, 1832–1869* (London, 1940); H. Cordier, *L'Expédition de Chine du 1857–1858* (Paris, 1905); H. Cordier, *L'Expédition de Chine de 1860* (Paris, 1906); L. Oliphant, *The Mission of Lord Elgin to China and Japan* (2 vols., London, 1860); Huang Yen-yü, *Viceroy Yeh Ming-ch'ên and the Canton Episode (1856–1861)* (*Harvard Journal of Asiatic Studies*, Vol. 6, pp. 1–36); E. G. Ravenstein, *The Russians on the Amur* (London, 1861). On Russia in Manchuria, see also Shuhsi Hsü, *China and Her Political Entity* (New York, 1926). Treaties are in G. E. P. Hertslet, *China Treaties* (third edition, 2 vols., London, 1908), and in a briefer collection by W. F. Mayers, *Treaties between the Empire of China and Foreign Powers* (first edition, 1877; fifth edition, Shanghai, 1906).

On Christian missions see K. S. Latourette, *A History of Christian Missions in China* (New York, 1929) and the sources quoted in the footnotes of Chapters 14 and 15 of that work.

The best account of the T'ai P'ing Rebellion in a Western language is W. J. Hail, *Tsêng Kuo-fan and the Taiping Rebellion* (New Haven, 1927). Some features of it, however, are being challenged by Chinese writers. Excellent also is G. E. Taylor, *The Taiping Rebellion: Its Economic Background and Social Theory* (*The Chinese Social and Political Science Review*, Jan. 1933, Vol. 16, pp. 545–614). Among other accounts in Western languages are W. Oehler, *Die Taiping-Bewegung* (Gütersloh, 1923) and T. T. Meadows, *The Chinese and Their Rebellions* (London, 1856). The account of the visions of Hung Hsiu-ch'üan on which most later narratives are based is T. Hamberg, *The Visions of Hung-Siu-Tshuen* (Hongkong, 1854), which was derived from Hung Jên, a cousin and intimate friend of the rebel chief. Chinese scholars have lately been giving a good deal of attention to the T'ai P'ings.

On the history of the court and of Tao Kuang and Hsien Fêng, see E. Backhouse and J. O. P. Bland, *Annals and Memoirs of the Court of Peking* (Boston, 1914), and J. O. P. Bland and E. Backhouse, *China under the Empress Dowager* (Philadelphia, 1912).

Huc, *Recollections of a Journey Through Tartary, Thibet and China during the Years 1844, 1845, and 1846* (New York, 1852) contains a description of internal conditions in those years as this missionary traveller saw them.

CHAPTER XI

THE TRANSFORMATION WROUGHT BY THE IMPACT OF THE OCCIDENT

PARTIAL RECOVERY FROM THE SHOCKS OF THE PRECEDING TWO DECADES: THE RESTORATION OF INTERNAL ORDER BUT THE SLOW PERMEATION OF THE EMPIRE BY OCCIDENTAL TRADE AND IDEAS (A.D. 1861–1893)

IN 1861 it looked as though the Ch'ing dynasty might have but very little longer to live. A child was on the throne, there were dissensions at court, the Empire had just been defeated and its capital taken by foreign foes, and rebellions were wasting some of the fairest provinces. Not since the revolts in the early years of the reign of K'ang Hsi, and perhaps not even then, had the Manchus' tenure of power been so precarious. From this impending doom the dynasty was saved temporarily by an interesting combination of circumstances and its demise postponed for half a century.

THE EMPRESS DOWAGER, TZ'Ŭ HSI

First of all, new leadership emerging from the Manchus gave fresh vigor to the Ch'ing. The mother of Hsien Fêng's heir proved to be one of those remarkable women who at irregular intervals have forced themselves into the virtual rulership of the Empire. She is usually best known either as the Empress Dowager, by an official designation Tz'ŭ Hsi, or by a nickname popular among her entourage and in the North, the Old Buddha. A member of the Yehonala clan of the Manchus, and of an excellent family, she was chosen as a secondary wife to Hsien Fêng and had the good fortune to win his affection by her beauty and charm and by bearing him his heir. Upon Hsien Fêng's death, by vigorous action and the assistance of a lifelong friend and trusted adviser, Jung-lu, and of Prince Kung, a brother of Hsien Fêng, she got the better of a conspiracy and had herself and Hsien Fêng's Empress appointed co-regents. Much more able and aggressive than the other regent, she dominated the court. Her son, usually known by the title of his reign, T'ung Chih, proved active but dissolute, and died in 1875, not long after assuming the reigns of government. Thereupon his mother, in a decidedly high-handed manner, placed on the throne a child who is known by the title of his reign period, Kuang Hsü. Tz'ŭ Hsi not only held the reins while Kuang Hsü was a minor, but was the real power after he attained his majority. Upon Kuang Hsü's death, in 1908, by designation of this same masterful woman, now aged, another minor was installed on the throne, but the old Empress survived Kuang Hsü only a few hours. More vigorous as a ruler than any of the Emperors since Ch'ien Lung, Tz'ŭ Hsi was superstitious, was guilty of many major errors, was often subject to indecision, and never fully comprehended the significance of the new age into which the Middle Kingdom was being pushed by the Occident. Yet she was ambitious, loved power and money, possessed great physical vitality, had shrewd insight into the strength and the weaknesses of men in high places, and used tact and skill in attaining her ends. She knew a good deal about Chinese literature and was a calligrapher of more than average ability.

THE SUPPRESSION OF REBELLIONS BY THE AID OF CHINESE LEADERSHIP

The dynasty would have collapsed had it not been for loyal Chinese. It was to Chinese, chief among them a scholar-statesman from the province of Hunan, Tsêng Kuo-fan, that the Empire mainly owed the suppression of the T'ai P'ing Rebellion. Tsêng, although by training not a military man, and handicapped both by the jealousy of other officials and by an imperial administrative and military system which made it difficult to construct and finance an army strong enough to put down so formidable an outbreak, organized a force which, by what were often halting and blundering steps, crushed the revolt. Nanking, the T'ai P'ing citadel, was captured in 1864, and Hung Hsiu-ch'üan committed suicide a few weeks before its fall. The year 1865 saw the last effective forces dispersed.

Tsêng was assisted by able lieutenants, among them one who

became the leading Chinese statesman of the close of the century, Li Hung-chang. Foreigners also had a part. Many Westerners were at first disposed to view the rebels hopefully, partly because the profession of a religion which seemed a form of Christianity appeared to promise more tolerance of Occidentals than that shown by the Manchus. As time passed, the T'ai P'ings were seen to be more fanatical than the Ch'ing and fully as haughty, and their depredations in the lower part of the Yangtze Valley threatened the safety and trade of Westerners. After peace had been made with the Ch'ing (1860), the powers became decidedly unfriendly to the uprising, and foreign forces helped to free the region around Shanghai from the rebels. Under Frederick T. Ward, an adventurer born at Salem, Mass., at the outset against the opposition of the American and British authorities but eventually with their tacit approval, a contingent was organized, at first foreign and later Chinese with foreign officers, which won the sobriquet, "the Ever Victorious Army." After Ward's death—in action—and after several experiments in commanders, a British officer, Charles George Gordon, was placed in charge, and the force gave able assistance to the Ch'ing armies until the end of the rebellion was in sight.

One of the many unfortunate results of the T'ai P'ing Rebellion was the severe blow which it gave to learning. The Yangtze delta, long a center of wealth and culture, was laid waste. Most of the best libraries, including three imperial ones, were burned, and many *Shu Yüan*, retreats for scholarly pursuits, were destroyed.

Still another result may have been a delay in reforming the Empire. In a certain sense, as we have said, the T'ai P'ings were a premature effort to use Western ideas to reshape China. Naturally, because of the excesses of the rebels, intelligent and influential Chinese tended to abhor all alterations in the established order and conservatism was reënforced.

When the radical movement gained control in the twentieth century, it owed much to the efforts of Chinese who had gone overseas. Some of the zeal of the emigrants is traceable to T'ai P'ings who, escaping after the collapse of their cause, kept alive abroad the desire for change. Sun Yat-sen, the arch-revolutionist of the twentieth century, seems in his youth to have had close contact with groups of T'ai P'ing origin.

It was due chiefly to Tsêng Kuo-fan, Li Hung-chang, and other Chinese that the Nienfei, who remained formidable after the T'ai P'ings had been suppressed, were dispersed (1867).

The Moslem, or Panthay, Rebellion, in Yünnan, had its stronghold at Talifu and as its head Tu Wên-hsiu. For years it held out, but in 1873 it, too, was crushed, and chiefly by forces under Chinese rather than Manchu leadership.

It was also principally due to Chinese generalship that the Northwest and the far West were restored to the Ch'ing. In the widespread unrest in the Empire, many of the Moslems in Shensi and Kansu had rebelled, and about 1864 much of the New Dominion had become virtually independent—under a number of different leaders. One of the more prominent of the latter was Yakub Beg, who became master of Kashgar and much of the western portion of the Tarim River Basin. It looked as though the work of the great Ch'ing Emperors in this vast region was to be undone.

The reconquest of the West was almost entirely the work of Tso Tsung-t'ang, a fellow provincial and former lieutenant of Tsêng Kuo-fan. He had had a prominent part in the suppression of the T'ai P'ings and of the Nienfei. Before 1870 he had pacified Shensi. Slowly but fairly steadily he fought his way westward. Suchow in Kansu fell in 1873 after a siege of almost three years. Far from the central provinces and forced to find his own supplies, in more than one season Tso set his army to planting and reaping a crop for its subsistence. In 1877 Yakub Beg, his chief opponent, was removed by death—whether by violence or disease seems uncertain—and by the early part of 1878 Kashgar, Yarkand, and Khotan had surrendered. Tso's achievements are comparable to those of the great commanders who carried the Chinese arms into that region under the Han and the T'ang.

Just as the last of the great rebellions was being suppressed, flood and drought brought distress—floods in five of the southern provinces in 1876, and drought in 1877 and 1878 in the North, especially in Shansi and Shensi. Millions died of the ensuing famine, but, fortunately, by this time the dynasty had so far regained its strength that the load placed on the treasury by relief funds and loss of taxes did not prove more than a temporary embarrassment.

FOREIGN RELATIONS

The life of the Ch'ing dynasty was prolonged not only by the opportune suppression of internal rebellion, but also by the absence of crises in the Empire's relations with Occidental powers so grave as those of 1839–1842 and 1856–1860. While not entirely satisfactory to Westerners, the treaties which came as the result of these wars at least promised the removal of most of the chief complaints which the aliens had against their former status in China. Neither the officials nor the populace of the Empire were yet prepared to be cordial to foreigners, and friction was often acute over the attempt of Westerners to obtain what had been pledged them. The Westerner, too, was still aggressive. He often wished greater privileges than those already his and on more than one occasion encroached on the territory of the Empire. However, for several years after 1860 Western powers, and especially Great Britain and the United States, conducted their relations with China on the basis of the belief that their interests would be best served by supporting the dignity and authority of the imperial government to strengthen it in the suppression of internal disorder. Now that China had granted terms which made possible the growth and fairly peaceable conduct of foreign trade, those powers whose primary concern was commerce, notably Great Britain, decided that this would be best conserved through a united and orderly China, and that the most promising outlook was under the Ch'ing dynasty. Between 1861 and 1895 China suffered no such humiliation at the hands of the Occident as she experienced just before and after these years.

Had the court and the leading statesmen been aware of the significance of the pressure from the West and set out wholeheartedly to reorganize the Empire and its culture, learning all that they could from the alien, as the Japanese were doing during these very years, the distresses of the next generation might conceivably have been avoided. Given the cultural pride of the ruling scholar-official class, however, and the decadent ineptitude of most of the Manchus, this was too much to expect. Only a very few, and those usually with but little if any influence, were aware that the Empire was being hurried into a new world to which it must make revolutionary adjustments or suffer overwhelming disaster. Moreover, as we have seen, the foreign wars and the T'ai P'ing Rebellion led to a reaction against the foreigner and his ways. These had threatened the existence of the Empire. It seemed to intelligent men to be the part of prudence to hold to the old ways as the only sure safeguard against more of the anarchy of which the nation had had so unfortunate a taste. Hence scholar-statesmen like Tsêng Kuo-fan and Tso Tsung-tang sought to strengthen the cultural heritage of the Empire and identified this in part with the neo-Confucianism of the Sung. The Sung philosophy, moreover, with its subjective qualities, offered a refuge and a consolation in face of the uncertainties and threatened upheaval of the times. The precious years of reprieve, therefore, instead of being used for thorough-going reorganization, became only a breathing space before the *descensus Averni*.

The main events of these years in the relations with Western governments can be rather briefly sketched.

One early development was the collection of the customs duties under the supervision of foreigners. In 1853, during the T'ai P'ing Rebellion, a group of rebels (not T'ai P'ings) took advantage of the general disorder to occupy the walled city of Shanghai and the imperial machinery for the collection of duties on foreign imports and exports broke down. After brief and unsatisfactory attempts to find a substitute, by an arrangement between the consuls and the local *taotai* the Chinese appointed (1854) foreign nominees of the consuls to supervise the payment of the customs. The system worked well, and by an Anglo-Chinese agreement of November, 1858, its extension to other ports was made possible. When the conventions of Peking (1860) charged against the customs the indemnities then assessed on China, a further organization of the service became necessary and a foreign Inspector General was appointed by Peking. In 1863 there came into this office a remarkable Irishman, Robert Hart. Under his direction the Imperial Maritime Customs, as it came to be called, had an extraordinary growth. Its chief posts were held by foreigners of several nationalities, the British outnumbering those of any other citizenship. In a government honeycombed with corruption, the service was honest. Under it not only were the duties collected, but the coast and some of the main navigable rivers were provided with lighthouses and buoys and an imperial post of a

Western type was begun. The service was national in scope and controlled from Peking. This centralization rendered it largely independent of the provincial organization and so ran contrary to the existing practice of committing to the provincial officials all the tasks possible.

The treaties of 1858 provided for the residence of foreign ministers in Peking. To deal with them and with foreign affairs, a new central body was created (1861), the *Tsungli Yamen*. The necessity forced upon the government by the powers of handling foreign affairs directly through the capital rather than indirectly through the local authorities, as in many instances had formerly been the case, tended, as did the customs service, to alter the principle on which the administration had been conducted.

For many years the problem of the reception of the representatives of the powers by the Emperor remained troublesome. The treaties of Tientsin specified that foreign envoys should, when accorded audience with the Emperor, be treated as coming from nations independent of and of equal dignity with China. This in practice the Chinese found a bitter pill. While T'ung Chih remained a minor the question was not urgent, but when, in 1872, he attained his majority, the envoys demanded an audience. After much hesitation and long negotiation this was granted, but the ceremony was carried out with a subtle suggestion that the Empire still thought of itself as outranking other nations. Not until 1894, after Kuang Hsü had reached his majority, was an audience given which satisfied the diplomatic body.

The Empire was very slow to send representatives to Western capitals. The first attempt of the kind was somewhat anomalous. In 1861 there arrived in China as American minister Anson Burlingame. By his affability and sympathy and his policy of supporting the imperial government rather than causing it embarrassment, he won the confidence of the Tsungli Yamen. When, in 1867, he was on the eve of resigning, the Chinese authorities suggested to him that he serve as the envoy of Peking to the treaty powers of the West. In this capacity, with an extensive retinue, he visited the United States (1868), representing China in public addresses in glowing, optimistic terms. There he negotiated a treaty on the basis of equality, providing, among others things, for the territorial integrity of China, for the free immigration of

Chinese laborers into the United States, for reciprocal rights of residence and travel, and for freedom from interference in the development of China. In London he obtained from the British Government a declaration that it would not apply unfriendly pressure inconsistent with the independence and safety of China and that it desired to deal directly with the central rather than with the local authorities. The American and British Governments, it will be noted, were simply giving further form to a policy which was already theirs. The mission was well received in Paris and Berlin, but in neither capital obtained either treaty or declaration. In St. Petersburg Burlingame contracted pneumonia and died. Deprived of its moving spirit, the mission returned to China by way of Brussels and Rome, but without additional achievement.

The Burlingame Mission paved the way for resident legations in the capitals of the West. The first of these was opened in London, in 1877, and in that and the following two years others were established on the Continent of Europe and at Washington.

It would have been hoping too much to ask that the decades between 1860 and 1894 should be entirely without friction between China and the West. Of this there was always an undercurrent, and occasionally it broke out into serious disturbance.

The British treaty of Tientsin provided that either party might demand a revision at the end of ten years. In the late sixties, accordingly, there was much discussion, in both British and Chinese circles, of possible changes in the earlier document. While the only immediate outcome was a convention (1869) which was never ratified, what was in effect a partial revision was made by the Chefoo Convention, in 1876. This latter was precipitated by an attack, on the borders between Burma and Yünnan, upon a British exploring expedition and the murder there of Mr. Margery, of the British consular service. The British held the Chinese authorities responsible for the unfortunate incident and made of it the occasion not only for the demand of an indemnity and the safeguarding of the trade across the Burmese-Yünnan frontier, but also for the settlement of some of the outstanding differences between the two governments and for gaining concessions, such as the opening of new ports to trade, which had no connection with the original episode.

Chinese emigration was a source of friction. The Chinese were utilizing the new facilities for trade and navigation to spread beyond the borders of the Empire. Some of the emigration was in the form of a contract labor which was little better than slavery, but by 1880 most of the abuses had been prohibited by agreements between China and the powers or by unilateral action of the powers. The emigration to the United States aroused much opposition in the Pacific coast states, particularly in California, where Chinese came into competition with native American white labor. After much unpleasantness, including anti-Chinese riots, the United States, partially with the consent of China, suspended the further admission of Chinese laborers. Eventually, after 1900, without the consent of China, she prohibited it entirely.

Here and there some of the powers encroached on China's territory and on her vassal states. In the South, France extended her protectorate over Cambodia (1863), annexed three more provinces of Annam (1867), and (1874) obtained from Annam extraterritoriality for all Europeans, the opening of the Red River to navigation, and of more ports to commerce. In 1883 and 1884, due to a renewal of French pressure, Annam recognized the protectorate of France. China, disturbed by these attacks on a vassal state and by an arrangement that would end her suzerainty, protested. Hostilities followed, although of a somewhat desultory nature and with China helpless before the high-handed French. In 1885 the difficulty was ended by Chinese recognition of the French protectorate of Annam and freedom of trade between Tongking and the adjoining Chinese provinces, but without the indemnity which the French had demanded.

In 1886 Great Britain annexed that part of Burma which she had not previously seized. In that same year China formally recognized the change, but with the provision that the decennial Burmese "tribute" mission was still to be sent to Peking.

In 1887 China agreed to what was really an accomplished fact and ceded Macao to Portugal, but with the provision that it should never be alienated without her consent.

During the rebellions in the far West of the Empire, Russia, to safeguard her trade across that region, occupied much of Ili, with the promise that she would restore it to China when the latter was able to maintain order there. When Tso Tsung-t'ang had suppressed the insurgents, and China asked Russia to withdraw, a treaty was negotiated which gave to Russia the better part of Ili, a large indemnity, and extensive trading privileges in the West. This agreement Peking would not ratify and war seemed imminent. However, a compromise was effected by which most of Ili was returned to China and a somewhat larger indemnity was promised Russia.

CHRISTIAN MISSIONARIES

One of the most persistent sources of irritation between China and the powers was the Christian missionary. The treaties of Tientsin, which opened up the interior of China to foreign travel and guaranteed protection to the foreigner and his converts, synchronized with a rapid growth of missionary interest and activity among both Roman Catholics and Protestants of the Occident. The wealth brought by the industrialization of the West and the attendant commerce furnished the means, and the revival in Roman Catholicism after the Napoleonic wars and in Protestantism by the movements following the Evangelical Awakening of the eighteenth century provided the religious incentive for a pronounced expansion in the efforts of these two great groups of Christians to spread their faith throughout the world. It is not strange, therefore, that the years after 1860 saw the penetration of every province of China by both Roman Catholic and Protestant missionaries.

New Roman Catholic orders and congregations entered the country and those already represented added to their staffs. By 1897 there were a little over half a million Roman Catholics in the country, as against about two hundred thousand at the beginning of the century, and the missionaries numbered a little more than seven hundred and fifty.

Protestants, who before 1860 were confined almost entirely to the five open ports and Hongkong, had an even more phenomenal growth. Many societies now for the first time sent representatives to China, one of them, the China Inland Mission, which was organized by J. Hudson Taylor for the purpose of taking the Christian message to parts of the Empire unreached by Protestants, having over six hundred missionaries at work in 1895. In 1893 there were about fifty-five thousand Chinese communicants in Protestant churches, most of them in the coast provinces, and in 1889 missionaries numbered nearly thirteen hundred, not quite half of them men, representing forty-one different societies. These figures were an increase from about fifty-seven hundred communicants in 1869 and from about one hundred and eighty-nine missionaries in 1864.

In addition to spreading a knowledge of the Christian Gospel by the printed and the oral word, Protestant missions were chiefly responsible for introducing Western medicine to China. They also had a large part in inaugurating education of an Occidental type, and in preparing and circulating literature which familiarized Chinese with Western ideas.

With merchants and diplomats, and often in advance of them, missionaries were pioneers of the infiltration of China with Western ideas. Although some of them were unpleasantly aggressive, and a few of them bigoted and intolerant, they had sincerely at heart what they believed to be the best interests of the Chinese, usually worked with a high and selfless devotion, and helped to put the Chinese in touch with the spiritual, moral, and intellectual forces of the Occident much more than did merchants or diplomats. Many thousands of Chinese were profoundly improved morally and spiritually by the contact.

When all is said for the missionary that can be said—and it is much more than is usually realized—it must also be acknowledged that, especially during the three and a half decades after 1860, he was often the source of great annoyance to the Chinese populace and to officialdom. His teaching, intolerant of the customary honors to ancestors, seemed to threaten the Chinese family. Religious practices which formed an integral part of guild, community, and political life were anathema to him. Christians, therefore, seemed to their neighbors recreant to moral, social, economic, and political obligations and to be attacking the foundations of society and civilization. Few, if any, foresaw that these were to crumble, anyway, within the next few decades and that the missionary would prove of great help in the work of replacing them. Moreover, the missionaries' activities were often misunderstood and the most absurd rumors about them were circulated and widely believed—for example, that in Christian orphanages and hospitals the eyes and other organs of children were extracted for medicinal and photographic purposes. Missionaries, too, in their efforts to rent or buy property in the interior frequently aroused opposition. Some Chinese of the baser sort professed conversion to obtain the protection of the toleration clauses, and others made a similar profession to win the assistance of the missionary or his Chinese colleagues in lawsuits and feuds. Most Roman Catholic missionaries were from the Continent of Europe and for years the majority of them were French. Over all of them France exercised a protectorate until toward the close of the century and used it as a means of heightening her influence in China. The great majority of Protestant missionaries were either British or Americans. Neither Great Britain nor the United States used them for ulterior purposes and the British Government was sometimes reluctant to enforce their treaty rights—for fear that trade would be injured. Both governments, however, often felt that they must act to uphold the obvious treaty rights of their missionary citizens, and in doing so repeatedly clashed with the Chinese authorities.

The persecutions, riots, and disturbances which arose out of the work of the missionary are too numerous to catalogue here. Probably the most serious between 1860 and 1894 were the so-called Tientsin massacre (1870) in which a mob destroyed an orphanage and the adjoining church and killed the French consul and several other French men and women including ten sisters and one priest, and widespread riots in the Yangtze Valley in 1890 and 1891 in which Protestants were the chief sufferers. Foreign governments had repeatedly to take up the cause of their nationals.

Not unnaturally, Chinese officialdom sought to obtain new agreements which would limit the activity of the missionary and establish a more effective control over Chinese Christians. To this the powers would not agree, and the status of missionaries and Chinese Christians remained as it had been fixed by the Treaties of Tientsin and the French Convention of Peking (1860), with a slight modification of the latter by the Berthemy Convention (1865).

FOREIGN TRADE

During these years of the restoration of the domestic authority of the Ch'ing and of comparative quiet in China's international relations, the infiltration of the Empire by the culture of the

Occident was proceeding not only through the activities of Christian missionaries but through a growth in commerce. The opening of the Suez Canal in 1870, with its more direct route to Europe, and the increased use of steam in navigation augmented the commercial pressure on China. In nearly two decades the customs multiplied over fourfold, and foreign vessels developed a profitable carrying trade on the coast and the Yangtze. On the other hand, the total value of imports and exports rose with surprising slowness. Between 1865, when the close of the T'ai P'ing Rebellion allowed trade to come back toward normal, and 1885, it increased only about a fifth. After 1885 it grew more rapidly, nearly doubling by 1894. Cotton led as the major article of import, with opium second. Tea and silk remained the chief exports, but by 1893 were suffering from competition with other Eastern lands—in the case of tea chiefly India, Ceylon, and Java, and in the case of silk Japan and the Levant. The American share in the carrying trade, which had been very large, sharply declined in the seventies. The British were still predominant in the ocean-borne commerce and therefore also in the foreign communities in the treaty ports.

In those of the treaty ports which loomed most prominently in foreign trade, the merchants and some of the missionaries generally resided in special "concessions"—British at Newchwang, Tientsin, Hankow, Kiukiang, Chinkiang, and Canton, and French in Tientsin and Canton—in which the usual arrangement was that the ground was leased in perpetuity to the foreign government, and then sublet to individuals. These resembled but were not identical in form with the older Settlements in Shanghai. In all of them foreigners lived a life largely apart from the Chinese. Most merchants did not know the Chinese language—although to this there were notable exceptions. They were protected by extraterritoriality—for this privilege had been accorded to citizens of other Western powers as their governments made treaties with China. Only in business did those in commercial pursuits have contacts with the Chinese, and then more often than not through an interpreter and pidgin English. Of the foreigners, the missionaries were the ones who usually touched Chinese life intimately at the most angles. Under these circumstances, the permeation of the Empire by foreign culture was slower than it might otherwise have been.

BEGINNINGS OF MODIFICATIONS IN CHINESE CULTURE

In spite of the presence of the foreigner, until the late nineties the institutions and thought of China were almost entirely unaffected by contact with the Occident. When compared with the total of the domestic trade, foreign commerce was very small and of little importance. Economically, the Empire was still practically self-sufficing. Of the imports, only opium made a perceptible impression on any large proportion of the population. Most of the Westerners were concentrated in a few treaty ports and numbered merely a few thousands. Christians were too few and too scattered to alter the *mores* of their fellow-countrymen. With minor exceptions, the economic, social, intellectual, and political structure of the nation was as it had been a century before.

Some exceptions there were, however—foreshadowings of change. The T'ai P'ing Rebellion had shaken orthodox scholarship by devastating its chief stronghold, the Yangtze Valley. Chinese organized (1873) the China Merchants Steam Navigation Company, which came to have a large share in coastal and river transportation. The first railway in China—running out of Shanghai—was built by foreigners, then bought by the Chinese, and its rails and rolling stock shipped to Formosa and allowed to rust. It is only fair to add that this apparently reactionary procedure seems to have been adopted chiefly because the Chinese objected to the extension of foreign-owned property outside the ports. By 1894 the beginnings of quite a system of railroads had been constructed by the Chinese in the North. In the early eighties a telegraph line was built, under contract from the government, between Shanghai, Tientsin, and Peking. There was a slight development of coal mines by modern methods. Introduction of Western appliances might have proceeded more rapidly had the Chinese not been fearful, because of the probable international complications, of admitting foreign capital, either directly or by loans.

Some attempts were made to arm the country against the West with Occidental devices—arsenals, a few modern war craft, and troops drilled and equipped after the European fashion.

In Peking and Canton the government established schools for the training of men for the diplomatic service. Yung Wing, who had received his initial education in things Western in a school maintained by Protestant missionaries and had had a college course in the United States, not only promoted the introduction of Western machinery but was responsible for inducing the government to send to the United States, in the seventies, over one hundred youths to study in the schools there. The government abruptly terminated the mission before all of the group had completed their training, but the experiment was an interesting precedent for the great student exodus which was to take place a generation later.

SUMMARY

For nearly a generation after the first armed conflicts with the Occident, then, most Chinese who thought about the matter at all—as the vast majority did not—probably believed that the Empire was to be able to hold the foreigner at arm's length and go on without altering its life. Certainly internal order was restored and the country resumed its ordinary pursuits almost exactly as it had before the interruption of foreign wars and internal rebellions. However, the seeming security was illusory. The cumulative effects of Western influences would sometime become apparent. Christian missionaries and their converts, foreign ships and sailors, Western merchants with their Chinese connections, buildings in the ports in Occidental style, imports of machinery and machine-made goods, returning Chinese travellers, of whom there were a few, letters from Chinese overseas, telegraphs, foreign banks, and translations of Western books—all were making impressions with which conservatism would sometime have to reckon. Within a few years a small neighbor that had heeded the writing on the wall delivered a blow that was to lead to the collapse of exclusiveness and to be followed by a change which was the more overwhelming because it had so long been resisted.

BIBLIOGRAPHY

As for the preceding chapter, the dynastic history for the period is the *Ch'ing Shih Kao*.

On the domestic history of the period, and especially of the court, see J. O. P. Bland and E. Backhouse, *China under the Empress Dowager* (Philadelphia, 1912) and the Princess Der Ling, *Old Buddha* (New York, 1928), the latter by a Manchu lady who was an attendant of

Tz'ŭ Hsi. See also W. L. Bales, *Tso Tsung-t'ang* (Shanghai, 1937). On the T'ai P'ing Rebellion, see W. J. Hail, *Tsêng Kuo-fan and the Taiping Rebellion* (New Haven, 1927) and G. E. Taylor, *The Taiping Rebellion: Its Economic Background and Social Theory* (*The Chinese Social and Political Science Review*, Vol. XVI, pp. 545–614).

On foreign relations, the standard longer general works are H. B. Morse, *International Relations of the Chinese Empire. The Period of Submission, 1861–1893* (London, 1913), and H. Cordier, *Histoire des Relations de la Chine avec les Puissances Occidentales, 1860–1900* (3 vols., Paris, 1901, 1902). H. F. MacNair, *Modern Chinese History—Selected Readings* (Shanghai, 1923) is useful. See also S. T. Wang, *The Margary Affair and the Chefoo Agreement* (New York, 1940), T. Dennett, *Americans in Eastern Asia* (New York, 1922), F. W. Williams, *Anson Burlingame and the First Chinese Mission to Foreign Powers* (New York, 1912), E. V. G. Kiernan, *British Diplomacy in China, 1880–1885* (New York, 1939), H. F. MacNair, *The Chinese Abroad. Their Position and Protection* (Shanghai, 1924), and M. F. Coolidge, *Chinese Immigration* (New York, 1909). Foreign treaties are in G. E. P. Hertslet, *China Treaties* (third edition, 2 vols., London, 1908) and in the shorter collection by W. F. Mayers, *Treaties between the Empire of China and Foreign Powers* (fifth edition, Shanghai, 1906).

On Christian missions, see K. S. Latourette, *A History of Christian Missions in China* (New York, 1929). The extensive footnotes in that work give information about other material.

On Yung Wing, see Yung Wing, *My Life in China and America* (New York, 1909). On the students whom he brought to America, see T. E. La Fargue, *China's First Hundred* (Pullman, Wash., 1942).

On foreign trade, see C. F. Remer, *The Foreign Trade of China* (Shanghai, 1926) and the Quarterly, Annual, Decennial, and Special reports of the Chinese Maritime Customs.

See also, R. S. Britton, *The Chinese Periodical Press, 1800–1912* (Shanghai, 1933).

CHAPTER XII

THE TRANSFORMATION WROUGHT BY THE IMPACT OF THE OCCIDENT

The Crumbling of the Structure of the Old Chinese Culture and Foreshadowings of the New (A.D. 1894–1933)

RELATIONS WITH JAPAN, 1871–1893

The decades of comparative quiet and security which followed the foreign wars and rebellions of the middle of the century were rudely terminated by a contest with a near neighbor, Japan. The defeat which the Empire then suffered was followed by the renewed aggression of Western powers and by internal changes which proved momentous.

During the seventeenth, the eighteenth, and the early part of the twentieth century, Japan had been even more nearly closed against intercourse with the Occident than had China. In 1853, shortly after the first war between China and Great Britain, the famous American expedition led by Commodore Perry entered the Bay of Yedo, and the opening of Japan to more extensive contact with the Occident followed. Much more quickly than the Chinese, the Japanese saw the necessity of adjusting themselves to intercourse with the Occident. By 1894 they had taken remarkable strides toward the reorganization of the entire structure of their life. Among those who rapidly rose to leadership were men who early sensed the fact that the entire world was being dominated by the Occident and that, whether a nation liked it or not, if it were to retain its political independence it must adopt the appliances which had given the West its power. Politically, the dual form of government and feudalism were abolished, a constitution modeled partly after that of Prussia was adopted, and an army and a navy of Western type were built. Intellectually, a school system like that of Europe and America was constructed and much of the literature of the West put into Japanese. In economic life, the beginning was made of that amazing industrialization which latterly has proceeded apace, with factories, railroads, and a merchant marine of steam craft. More quickly than any other non-Occidental people, the Japanese adapted themselves to the new day and achieved admission to the family of Western nations.

The greater success with which the Japanese accepted the Occident does not prove them superior in ability to the Chinese. China is so much larger that her task is much more difficult. The Japanese, too, had the tradition of learning from foreigners: they had adopted and adapted Chinese civilization, and most important movements in thought and culture in China had had repercussions in Japan. On the other hand, except for Buddhism, the Chinese had consciously learned little from any one: they regarded themselves as teachers, not pupils. Japan, regimented under the Tokugawa Shoguns, was more easily directed by those in favor of Westernization once they had obtained control than was China, for the latter was not by tradition so closely coördinated. In Japan, moreover, there was a tradition that the Emperor reigned but did not govern and that the imperial house was too sacrosant to be disturbed. The institution of the Emperor formed a center of unity and the government could be altered without abolishing it. In China much more in practice depended on the Emperor, and if he proved incompetent rebellion against him might be justified. Dynasties had changed many times. When, in 1912, in conformity to this tradition the Ch'ing passed the way of its predecessors, the unity and peace of the nation were shaken to their foundations.

Long before 1894 the new Japan had begun to clash with China. In 1871 a treaty between the two countries was signed on a reciprocal basis, without some of the concessions, so galling to the Chinese, contained in the current treaties with Western powers. About the same time, however, trouble arose over the Liu Ch'iu (Ryu Kyu) Islands—which paid tribute to China and were also claimed by the Japanese. In 1871 some inhabitants of the islands were killed by aborigines on Formosa (Taiwan). The Japanese raised the question of China's responsibility, and upon a disclaimer by that country, in 1874 sent a punitive force which occupied part of Formosa. This act endangered peace, but the matter was amicably adjusted by the withdrawal of the Japanese forces and the payment by China of compensation to Japan for lives lost and roads and buildings constructed. In the process China tacitly renounced suzerainty over the Liu Ch'ius.

More serious friction arose over Korea. Here China claimed suzerainty, acknowledged by annual tribute-bearing embassies from Seoul to Peking and by the Chinese investiture of each new Korean ruler. The relationship was of that somewhat nebulous kind subsisting between China and several of her neighbors, but was rather stronger in the case of Korea than of some others. For centuries Japan also had been interested in Korea. Repeatedly Japanese armies had operated in the peninsula, and from 1671 to 1811 occasional missions were sent by Korea to Japan.

Korea was slower than either China or Japan to open her doors to the West. The Japanese obtained a treaty with Seoul in 1876 (on the explicit basis of the independence of Korea), and this was followed, in the 1880's, by treaties between Korea and several Occidental powers. In Seoul struggles between the court cliques were complicated by the opposition of anti-foreign, conservative elements to the new intercourse with the outside world. In one of these the Japanese Legation was attacked (1882) and both Japan and China sent forces to restore order. In the ensuing settlement Japan declined to accept Chinese mediation. In the main, the conservatives among the Koreans looked to China for support and the liberals to Japan. In 1884, in a palace upheaval, the king sought refuge with the Japanese guard, the latter occupied the palace, and an attack was made on the Japanese, in which Chinese troops stationed in Seoul joined. In the negotiations which followed, China and Japan each agreed (1885) to withdraw its troops from Korea, not to send them again into the country to suppress disorder without notifying the other, and to remove them, if so dispatched, as soon as quiet was reëstablished.

Peking, urged on by Li Hung-chang, was determined not to renounce its suzerainty over the peninsula. A customs service was organized for Korea theoretically independent of but practically partially subordinate to the similar service in China. Yüan Shih-k'ai, later President of China but then a protégé of Li Hung-chang and in Korea on military duty since 1880, was for a number of years kept at Seoul as Chinese Resident.

WAR WITH JAPAN, 1894-1895

Interference of Japan and China in Korean affairs at last brought on war between the two countries. A rebellion of a secret society, the Tong Haks, led the Korean monarch, on the advice of Yüan Shih-k'ai, to ask for Chinese assistance. This was sent, and the Japanese, not to be checkmated, also dispatched troops. In the meantime the Korean forces had dispersed the rebels, but the Chinese and Japanese remained, watching each other. Tokyo proposed that Japan and China join in promoting reforms in the decadent and inept Korean Government. This Peking declined to do. In the negotiations it continued to claim suzerainty over Korea, a relationship which Japan refused to recognize. The Japanese took forcible possession of the palace and the monarch's person, and a decree was issued abrogating the Korean treaty with China and calling upon the Japanese to expel the Chinese troops. This was soon followed by the outbreak of war between China and Japan. The struggle was brief and full of humiliation for China. Although its forces often put up a courageous resistance, largely because of corruption in the administration and inefficiency in the use of even such modern naval and military equipment as it possessed, China was defeated on sea and land, and the fortified posts of Port Arthur in Manchuria and Weihaiwei in Shantung, although armed after the European manner, were captured.

The treaty—of Shimonoseki (1895)—which terminated the war was also humiliating. China was constrained to acknowledge the independence of Korea (thereby renouncing the traditional suzerainty), to cede to Japan Formosa, the Pescadores Islands, and the Liaotung Peninsula (on which Port Arthur was situated), to pay an indemnity, to open four more ports, and to give to Japan the privileges of the most favored nation pending the negotiation of a new commercial treaty between the two countries. This treaty of commerce, when drafted, gave Japanese extraterritorial privileges in China and continued the most-favored-nation status. Japan had thus driven China from Korea, annexed important territory, and acquired for its nationals in China the privileges enjoyed by Westerners—at the time when it was seeking to be rid itself of the extraterritoriality granted to Westerners in its own domains. To protect its interests Japan was to be led to a more and more active part in the affairs of its huge neighbor.

RENEWAL OF EUROPEAN AGGRESSION IN CHINA

The defeat of China at the hands of Japan was the signal for a renewal of European aggression in China. The closing decades of the nineteenth century found European powers engaged in a scramble for such of the world as had not already been parceled out among Western peoples. They were being more and more industrialized, were increasing in wealth, and wished to control "backward" peoples, both as a matter of prestige and for markets, raw materials, and an outlet for surplus capital. They partitioned most of Africa and extended their possessions in Asia. They now proceeded to encroach upon a palpably impotent China in a manner which threatened the speedy dismemberment of that Empire. To recount all the intricacies and details of the negotiations and even of the resulting treaties and conventions would unduly prolong these pages. However, the main outlines of what was done must be sketched.

First of all, Japan was made to disgorge part of the territory ceded by China. The ink was scarcely dry on the treaty of Shimonoseki when France, Russia, and Germany lodged protests with Tokyo against its possession of the Liaotung Peninsula, alleging that it would be a menace to the capital of China, render illusory the independence of Korea, and make precarious the peace of the Far East. The powers were, of course, moved by no regard for China: their interests in both Europe and the Far East were involved. Japan was in no position to defy the powers. Tokyo renounced its claim to the Liaotung Peninsula in return for an additional indemnity from China.

To pay the indemnity to Japan, China had to have recourse to foreign financiers. The privilege of advancing the first portion of the loan—made on the security of the maritime customs and with the possibility of demanding additional guarantees in the form of political or other concessions—was won by Russia, who was to have the assistance of French bankers. To offset the Franco-

Russian combination, Great Britain and Germany insisted that China also borrow from the Hongkong and Shanghai Banking Corporation—a British institution—and the Deutsche-Asiatische Bank. This China did in 1896 and 1898, giving as security not only the customs revenue but also the salt tax and likin in part of the Yangtze Valley.

In June, 1895, Franco-Chinese conventions were signed in which China consented to a modification of the frontier between itself and Annam. Territory was thus given to the latter—in effect to France—some of it land which the year before China had earmarked for France by promising not to cede it to any other nation. By these conventions China also opened three new treaty ports on the Sino-Annamese frontier, agreed that in the event of the exploitation of mines in Yünnan, Kwangsi, and Kwangtung, French manufacturers and engineers would be given prior rights of assisting, and made provision for some railway building in the region.

This was a threat to British interests in Burma, Southwest China, and the Yangtze Valley. Great Britain sought safeguards in an understanding with France in January, 1896. By an agreement with China in February, 1897, she obtained a "rectification" of the frontier between China and the British possessions on the South, the opening of the West River and ports on it to commerce, the promise not to cede certain portions of the frontier without British consent, the assurance that railways in Yünnan when built would connect with British roads in Burma, and additional trading privileges.

Worse for China was to follow. In 1895 Germany asked Peking for a coaling station, but was refused. Berlin did not give up the project, and in 1896 fixed its eyes on Kiaochow Bay, an excellent harbor on the southern coast of Shantung—on which Russia also had designs. The opportune murder in Shantung of two German Roman Catholic missionaries (November, 1897) gave the desired pretext. Kiaochow was seized by German ships, a heavy indemnity was exacted, and in March, 1898, Germany obtained a ninety-nine year lease to Kiaochow Bay with about two hundred square miles of the adjacent territory, the right to build fortifications, the privilege of constructing two railways in the province, and the promise that if China ever needed foreign assistance in Shantung, in capital, persons, or material, it would be asked first of Germans.

A few days later Russia obtained a twenty-five years lease on Talienwan (more commonly known to foreigners as Dalny and, later, as Dairen) and Port Arthur—on the tip of that Liaotung Peninsula so recently retrieved from Japan—with the privilege of erecting fortifications and naval depots and building a railway to connect the territory with the main line across Manchuria (the Russo-Chinese road, the Chinese Eastern Railway, to be mentioned in a moment). A glance at the map will show that this gave Russia a strangle hold on Manchuria and put her in a position to control the sea approaches to the North.

Great Britain was opposed to any alienation of Chinese territory, for that threatened to close the open door to its trade—its chief interest in China. The Russian lease of Port Arthur, however, made the British eager for a counter-weight to a naval station dominating so much of the North. With the consent of Japan, whose troops were still occupying it pending the payment of the last of the indemnity promised in 1895, and with formal assurance to Berlin that they would not build a railway into the interior and so compete with German interests, the British acquired (1898) a lease to Weihaiwei "for as long a period as Port Arthur shall remain in the possession of Russia." In the same year Great Britain obtained a ninety-nine year lease to such of the peninsula of Kowloon, opposite Hongkong, as had not been ceded it in 1860.

In the spring of 1898, France was given a ninety-nine year lease to the bay of Kwangchow, in Southwestern Kwangtung.

Thus within a few weeks the leading European powers had acquired leaseholds on the coast of China which might be followed by partition.

Other steps were taken which looked in the same direction. In 1897 France had gotten from China a promise that the latter would never cede the Island of Hainan to any third power. In February, 1898, Great Britain obtained assurance from China that the latter would not alienate to any other power any territory in the provinces adjoining the Yangtze, and in April of that year France was given a similar assurance for the provinces bordering on her possessions in Indo-China. When, also in April, 1898, Japan asked for such a promise for Fukien, she was told that

China would not alienate any part of that province to any power.

Still another form which foreign aggression and competition assumed was the demand for concessions to build railways. Such concessions, of course, would make a convenient basis for a claim to the territory they traversed, in case, as seemed very possible, China were to go the way of so much of the non-Occidental earth and be partitioned. Late in 1896, Russia obtained a secret alliance with China against Japan with the provision for the construction of a railroad across Manchuria. This line, to be known as the Chinese Eastern, was to be a subsidiary of the Russo-Chinese Bank and was, in effect, a continuation of the Trans-Siberian Railway. It would not only save distance as against the all-Russian route on the north bank of the Amur, but would give Russia a grip on Manchuria. Special privileges were accorded the road which increased this hold. China also promised to seek only from Russian banks the loans it might require for the construction of certain trunk lines which it contemplated building north of the Great Wall. Li Hung-chang, who negotiated the agreement, was hoping to play Russia off against Japan and so to save something for China.

In addition to the concessions granted the Russians in Manchuria and the Germans in Shantung, the British obtained the predominant financial position in the Peking-Mukden line. In June, 1898, a contract was signed with the Belgians for a loan on the proposed road from Peking to Hankow. The Belgians had French and Russian support and the backing of French capital. The line was originally planned by the Viceroy Chang Chih-tung as a Chinese undertaking and later had almost been entrusted to an American company. In 1899 a concession was made to British and German interests for a railway—which Americans thought had been secured to them the preceding year—between Tientsin and the Yangtze, the Germans to finance and build the northern and the British the southern portion. In 1896, 1897, 1898, and 1899, France obtained concessions for railways in the South, the most important of which was for one from Tongking into Yünnan. Americans acquired, in 1898, the concession for the Hankow-Canton line, but some years later, after the Belgians had bought a controlling interest in the American company, the grant was repurchased by the Chinese. In 1898 the British secured concessions, or signed preliminary agreements for them, for roads from Shanghai to Nanking and from Shanghai to Hangchow. In 1898 and 1899 agreements were also made with an Anglo-Italian company for mines and railways in Shansi and Honan, with the Russo-Chinese Bank—and later transferred to a French syndicate—for a railway to connect the capital of Shansi with the Peking-Hankow line, and with a Franco-Belgian syndicate for a road paralleling the Yellow River. Great Britain attempted to keep the Yangtze Valley clear for her own railway projects by an agreement with Germany (1898) for reciprocal respect for each other's spheres, and with Russia (1899), whereby Great Britain was not to encroach with railways north of the Great Wall or Russia in the Yangtze Valley.

There were also grants of concessions similar to those that Great Britain had enjoyed in several of the ports. Most of those made at this time were in Hankow, which appeared about to become a great railway center.

The British attempted to assure the continuation of their predominance in the administration of the customs by a promise from Peking (1898) that so long as their trade remained greater than that of any other nation, the Inspector General should be of British nationality. The French endeavored, with scant success, to obtain the confirmation of a similar control over the postal service.

AMERICA AND THE OPEN DOOR POLICY

In 1898 and 1899, then, the scramble for portions of what seemed to be a disintegrating empire was both active and sordid. The Chinese Government, unable to defend itself by force, found its chief recourse in delay. Occasionally it scored a victory—as when, in 1899, it declined outright to give Italy a naval station on the coast of Chêkiang. Too often, however, it was helpless. Russia appeared to be about to seize full control of Manchuria and Mongolia, Germany that of Shantung, France that of much of the South and Southwest, and, possibly, Great Britain that of the Yangtze Valley.

Within the next few years, three major efforts were made to save the Empire from its impending doom. One of these was by foreigners, the other two by Chinese.

The one by foreigners was what is usually known as the "open door policy." Its purpose was to keep all of China accessible to the trade, and, so far as possible, to the other economic activities of citizens of all nations—to insure equality of treatment to all in all the Empire. It was not especially altruistic, for the powers who were its leading advocates had their own interests chiefly in mind. However, it had as an obvious corollary the preservation of the territorial integrity of China. In its broadest sense the policy was not new. Great Britain had not attempted to restrict to itself the privileges accorded it in 1842. The most-favored-nation clauses which were in several of the treaties between China and Western powers were a distinct attempt in that direction. Repeatedly in their intercourse with China—as in 1858—several of the major powers had acted coöperatively.

As we have suggested, the British had viewed with alarm the leasing of territories and the creation of spheres of influence, for these threatened to obstruct the free course of their commerce—their chief interest in China. They reluctantly entered the struggle to get what special privileges they could, but repeatedly their spokesmen declared themselves for the open door and their government made several attempts to preserve it.

The best-remembered action of this time in favor of the open door was by the United States. Americans were as yet too engrossed in the development of the resources of their own broad land to take so active an interest in economic openings in China as did some other peoples. They had, however, a little commerce and, as we have seen, had taken part in the struggle for railway concessions. In 1898, moreover, the United States acquired the Philippines and Hawaii. Now, in 1899, Secretary of State John Hay attempted to safeguard the open door by obtaining the assent of the powers to certain specific promises—that there should be no interference with any vested interest in any "sphere of interest" or leased territory, that the Chinese tariff should apply to all merchandise in such regions and be collected by the Chinese Government, and that harbor dues and railroad charges in these "spheres" should be equal to all. Notes embodying these proposals were sent to Great Britain, Germany, Russia, Italy, France, and Japan, and a favorable reply was given by all, although evasively by Russia. The Hay notes were in part a surrender of full equality of opportunity, for they admitted the existence of spheres of interest. It is probable, however, that they helped to avert the partition of China.

THE REFORM MOVEMENT

One of the two major efforts by Chinese to save the Empire from disintegration was by those who wished to effect changes in China, largely after Western patterns. The reformers were numerous and of varying degrees of radicalism. After the war with Japan, many Chinese became convinced that they must adopt some of the Western devices which had enabled their enemy, whom they had thought of as much less strong than they, so easily to defeat them. Reform societies were organized, some with influential members. The great Viceroy, Chang Chih-tung, for a time sponsored one of them and in a book called *Learn* (largely a compilation of essays by various authors), while stressing loyalty to Confucianism and the dynasty, advocated adopting some of the new methods from the West, lest the Empire lose its independence as some other states had done. The writings and personal counsel of Protestant missionaries, notably Timothy Richard, stimulated and helped guide the movement.

More radical by far than Chang Chih-tung was a young man best known later as Sun Yat-sen or Sun Wên. Born in the year 1866, in a village about forty miles from Canton, the son of a tenant-farmer, when about thirteen years of age, at the suggestion and expense of an older brother who had migrated to Hawaii, he was sent to Honolulu, to receive a Western education. In Honolulu, in 1879, he was placed by his brother in a school conducted by an Anglican bishop, and was there for about three years. He became convinced of the truth of Christianity, and his brother, alarmed, had him recalled to China. Sun, returning to his native village, was by no means cured of his new convictions, but disfigured the images in the local temple. For this sacrilege he had to flee to Canton. There he was befriended by an American Protestant missionary physician. Before long he again began studying—this time in Hongkong, and also chiefly, although not entirely, with Protestant missionaries. Here he was baptized and here, in 1892, he received a medical diploma. He began practicing in Macao, and there organized a reform society most of whose membership was made up of men trained in mission schools. The Portuguese Government soon ordered him out, probably because he was competing with Portuguese physicians. He went to Canton and petitioned Peking to start agricultural schools. This request was not granted, and he joined in organizing a revolt against the Manchus. The plot was discovered, some of Sun's friends were captured and executed, but he himself escaped to Hongkong (1895) and then to Japan. Sun now became a wanderer among the Chinese overseas, seeking to enlist their support in the overthrow of the dynasty and the foundation of a republic. Once, in 1896, in London, the Chinese Legation apprehended him and would probably have sent him to China for execution had not the British Government, at the instance of a former missionary teacher, ordered his release. He continued his agitation against the Manchus, with results which, as we shall see, were to be startling.

A reformer, rather than a revolutionist as was Sun Yat-sen, and more immediately prominent than the latter, was K'ang Yu-wei. K'ang, also a native of Kwang-tung, was born in 1858. His training was purely Chinese. He had, however, imbibed the traditions of the Han Learning and criticized vigorously the historicity of the older classical writings. He maintained that many of the Classics venerated by the orthodox scholars were forgeries made (about the time of Christ) by Wang Mang and his chief minister to sanction their social and political program. He would thus attack the conservatism of his times and prove that Confucius, far from being a conserver of the values of the past, was a creative ethical leader and statesman, to whom reformers could turn for inspiration and guidance. He thereby sought to show that in Confucius support could be found for his own radical views. He made of Confucius, too, a religious reformer and helped to inspire a later attempt at a new Confucian cult. He worked out a radical social and political philosophy which was largely his own. His program included the eventual erasing of national boundaries, the popular election of officials, and the abolition of the family, with the rearing of children and the care of the aged in public institutions. He professed to base his philosophy upon a passage in the *Li Chi*, and he would have the ancient books read as guides to solving present problems. It must be added that K'ang did not seek to carry out at once all his program. As immediate steps he advocated much less drastic measures.

Under pressure from the reformers—of whom the three mentioned above were only among the more prominent—between the peace of Shimonoseki and the summer of 1898 a number of innovations were undertaken or projected by the provincial and national governments and by private initiative. Schools teaching Western subjects were founded and railways planned.

The reformers found a champion in the Emperor, Kuang Hsü. Not physically robust or forceful, brought up in the seclusion of the palace, with the masterful Tz'ŭ Hsi always keeping a vigilant eye upon him, Kuang Hsü had neither the vigor of personality nor the direct contact with the outside world to enable him to be the kind of leader which the dynasty and the Empire needed. However, he was intelligent, studious, felt that something must be done, and read eagerly some of the literature of the time, including the books of K'ang Yu-wei. In the summer of 1898, with K'ang as a confidant and adviser, he instituted what were later known as the hundred days of reform. During June, July, August, and September of that year, edict after edict was issued introducing changes.

Compared with the sweeping innovations of a few years later, none of the decrees advocated anything especially radical. Contrasted with the official conservatism of the time, however, they were amazing. Among them were ones ordering a modification of the civil service and military examinations, the establishment of a system of schools, including an imperial university for the study of the new as well as the old learning, the founding of an official bureau of translation, the encouragement of railway building, military and naval reform, the opening to Manchus of professions other than office-holding, and the abolition of many sinecure posts.

The decrees inevitably aroused a storm of opposition from those who by conviction or interest were wedded to the old order and from some who, while willing to see change, believed the Emperor to be acting too precipitately. The situation was complicated by the rivalries of two factions at court, one of them, with its leadership from Kiangsu, disposed to countenance alterations to discomfit its rivals, and the other, largely from the North. taking the conservative side.

THE ATTEMPT AT SALVATION BY REACTION: THE COUP D'ÉTAT OF 1898 AND THE BOXER UPRISING

The reactionary elements looked to the Empress Dowager for support and leadership. In September, 1898, Tz'ŭ Hsi took charge of the government. She had kept closely in touch with the developing situation and at first had allowed Kuang Hsü to go his own way. However, she distrusted his measures and became both alarmed and annoyed by the rapidity and—to her—lack of wisdom with which he was veering toward the left.

Conflict between the two was inevitable, for heretofore the Old Buddha had kept Kuang Hsü in leading strings, and independence of action on his part must lead to a trial of strength. The Emperor moved first, secretly ordering the death of Jung-lu, her loyal supporter and trusted adviser. Yüan Shih-k'ai, to whom Kuang Hsü committed the execution, revealed the plan to Jung-lu and the latter at once went to see the Empress Dowager. Tz'ŭ Hsi acted promptly and vigorously. She had Kuang Hsü seized (September 22, 1898), and, although she permitted him to live and to retain the title of Emperor, she kept him a prisoner in a portion of his own palace and in his name once more assumed the regency. Several of the reformers were arrested and executed, and others, including K'ang Yu-wei, escaped a like fate only by fleeing the country. Many of the edicts of the hundred days were countermanded, although a few were allowed to stand. A second Chinese attempt to save the country—by conservatism—was in full swing.

The reaction culminated in an outbreak, usually known as the Boxer Rebellion, which, ultimately with the sanction of the Empress Dowager, sought to oust the alien and his ways from the Empire.

That an anti-foreign upheaval of some kind came was not surprising. Irritation against the alien was widespread. The defeat by Japan, the seizure of ports by European powers, the granting of railway concessions and the beginning of railway construction, fear of the partition of the Empire, bitter feeling against missionaries and their converts—due partly to absurd rumors of cruel and immoral practices and to interference in lawsuits and disturbance of cherished customs and institutions—all contributed to it. Famine added to the unrest. After 1897 sporadic outbreaks against the foreigner were frequent.

The Northeast was the scene of most of the violence. Here was the court, now given over to reaction. Here were some particularly anti-foreign officials, notably Yü Hsien, who was first Governor in Shantung and then in Shansi. Here, too, the Empress Dowager ordered the local trainbands to be in readiness to defend the country. These units of the militia, sometimes known as the I Ho T'uan, were also termed the I Ho Ch'üan, or "Righteous Harmony Fists." From this latter designation and from the gymnastic exercises which were practiced came the Western name Boxers. The groups early adopted such slogans as "Protect the country, destroy the foreigner," and "Protect the Ch'ing (dynasty), destroy the foreigner." Into their membership pressed many of the rowdies who, in China, as elsewhere, are to be found in every community. They were also associated with some of the secret societies which abound in China. As had long been customary in such popular military organizations, charms and occult practices were employed which the users believed would render them invulnerable to enemy weapons.

It was in 1899 that the Boxers began seriously to annoy Westerners. In Shantung, where the anti-foreign Yü Hsien was Governor, they persecuted Christians and killed an English missionary. Yü Hsien, under pressure from the powers replaced by Yüan Shih-k'ai, was welcomed at court as a hero and was appointed Governor of Shansi. By June, 1900, the situation in Chihli (Hopei) had become acute. Christians were being massacred and aliens were in danger. To safeguard the latter, and especially the legations in Peking, on June 10th an international body of troops left Tientsin. It was attacked, however, and with difficulty made its way back. To protect the foreign community in Tientsin, now in danger, the Taku forts, commanding the river approach from the sea, were stormed by parties made up of six nationalities (June 17th).

Not unnaturally, this last act was interpreted by the Boxers and the court as tantamount to a declaration of war. In retaliation, the Tientsin concessions were attacked and the diplomatic body ordered to leave Peking within twenty-four hours. It has been claimed that on June 24th the Empress Dowager, goaded by a forged note from the foreign ministers demanding her abdication, ordered the extermination of all aliens in an edict sent broadcast throughout the Empire—thus in effect declaring war against the world. The evidence for the existence of this document, however, has been seriously called into question.

For several days Westerners and Japanese in Peking had been in a virtual state of siege. On the morning of June 20th, the German Minister was killed while on his way to the Tsungli Yamen, and that afternoon foreigners and Chinese Christians were placed in a real state of siege in their refuges—the Roman Catholic cathedral and the legation quarter. The powers assembled at Tientsin an allied relief expedition, but not until the middle of August did it fight its way through to Peking and effect the release of the beleaguered.

In the meantime, the storm brought great distress outside as well as inside the capital. Throughout the Empire aliens were in danger, especially missionaries, for by the nature of their calling the latter were more frequently beyond the shelter of the treaty ports than were merchants. Most foreigners in the interior found it necessary either to go to the ports or to leave the country entirely. Except in the Northeast very little loss of life occurred. In Chihli (Hopei), Shansi, Manchuria, and Mongolia, however, the toll was heavy. Here more than two hundred foreign missionaries and several thousand Chinese Christians were killed. In Shansi the truculent Yü Hsien was particularly rabid against the strangers and their converts, and personally assisted in the execution of one of the Roman Catholic bishops.

That the loss of life was no greater was due in large part to the Chinese and Manchus themselves. At the court were those, among them Jung-lu, who recognized the folly of the war, and their moderating counsels were not without effect—even during the siege of the legations. In local communities many Chinese, both private citizens and officials, risked their lives to save foreigners. On June 20th the admirals off Tientsin declared that they were using force merely against the Boxers and those who opposed them in their attempt to rescue their fellow-countrymen in Peking. This meant that the powers did not consider themselves at war with China but as merely helping to suppress an internal upheaval which threatened the lives of their nationals. The Viceroys at Nanking and Wuchang and several of the Governors took steps to preserve order within their jurisdictions. Li Hung-chang, now Viceroy at Canton, attempted, not without some success, to obtain the assurance of the powers that they did not consider a state of war to exist. When the inevitable diplomatic settlement should be made, it would be of advantage to China if she could claim that as a nation she had not fought. Certainly the loss of life and the consequent penalties were very much less than if all Chinese officialdom had supported the war party.

Even though only a small minority actively attempted to oust the alien, in the autumn of 1900 the situation for China was desperate and humiliating enough. Peking was in the hands of the powers and had been plundered by their troops. The court had fled precipitately and ignominiously to Hsianfu. Contingents of foreign soldiers went through much of Chihli (Hopei), relieving a few missionaries who had been standing siege at isolated points and wreaking vengeance for the indignities shown to their nationals during the preceding months. The Russians had taken possession of much of Manchuria.

THE POST-BOXER SETTLEMENT

The diplomatic settlement which officially adjusted the Boxer outbreak was arrived at in 1901 after prolonged negotiations and much wrangling among the powers. The terms were drastic, but not so much so as some of the powers had wished. The American Government exercised a moderating influence on the side of the territorial integrity of the Empire and of an indemnity within China's capacity to pay, and an Anglo-German agreement, to which France, the United States, Italy, Austria, and Japan acceded in whole or in part, attempted to prevent the acquisition of territory or the violation of the open door.

The terms of the Protocol, as it is called, can be briefly summarized as follows: (1) an apology for the murder of the German Minister and the erection of a memorial monument; (2) the punishment (by the Chinese Government rather than the powers—a device which helped to save some prestige to China) of some of the officials chiefly responsible for the attacks on foreigners; (3) the suspension for five years of the official examinations in towns where foreigners had been mistreated; (4) an apology for the murder of the Chancellor of the Japanese Legation; (5) the erection by the Chinese Government of expiatory monuments in desecrated foreign cemeteries; (6) the prohibition by China for two years or more of the importation of arms and ammunition; (7) the payment by China of an indemnity of 450,000,000 haikuan taels—in United States currency $333,000,000—with interest at four per cent., in thirty-nine annual installments, ending with 1940, to be secured by the maritime customs, the salt tax, and the native customs, and to be distributed among thirteen of the powers, Russia receiving the largest share, and Germany, France, Great Britain, Japan, the United States, Italy, Belgium, Austria-Hungary, the Netherlands, Spain, Portugal, and Sweden following with amounts progressively smaller in the order named; (8) the reservation to foreigners and the defense by the powers of the legation quarter in Peking; (9) the razing of the Taku forts, thus to permit free communication between Peking and the sea; (10) the maintenance of free communication between Peking and the sea by right of occupation by the powers of certain specified points; (11) the publication of edicts designed to discourage further anti-foreign outbreaks; (12) the amendment of existing treaties of commerce and navigation (a provision carried out in 1902 and 1903 with the United States, Great Britain, and Japan, but without revolutionary additions to earlier documents); (13) the improvement of the river channels leading to Tientsin and Shanghai; and (14) the reconstruction of the Tsungli Yamen into a Ministry of Foreign Affairs (*Wai Wu Pu*) which should be accorded precedence over all the other ministries of state, thus giving added dignity to intercourse with foreign powers.

The Boxer outbreak marked another stage in the collapse of the old China. Partly because of the folly of its court and partly because of policies of the powers which had goaded some of its leaders to fury, China had been brought further under the heel of the foreigner.

By the Protocol, as the price of the mad action of Tz'ŭ Hsi and some of her officials, China was saddled with a large addition to her debt, the legations in Peking took on the guise of armed fortresses, and other humiliations were endured. For more than two decades thereafter, many aliens consciously or unconsciously took the arrogant attitude of those living in a conquered country, and the Chinese seldom dared openly show resentment. Any anti-foreign movements were promptly and vigorously dealt with. Moreover, the Ch'ing dynasty was now badly shaken. It had shown itself incompetent to lead in the necessary reorganization, either when headed by the reforming Kuang Hsü or by the reactionary Tz'ŭ Hsi. It was to go on for a few years longer, thanks partly to the inertia of tradition and the lack of organized resistance and partly to the vigor of Tz'ŭ Hsi. The Empire, however, lacked the intelligent leadership at the top which the times so urgently demanded.

Still, China retained the semblance of independence and territorial integrity. The partition which had been threatened in 1898 and for which the events of 1900 might have been given as a pretext was not accomplished and its possibility became more remote. China emerged from the Boxer year less weakened than some observers would have deemed possible.

THE RUSSO-JAPANESE WAR (1904–1905) AND ITS IMMEDIATE AFTERMATH IN FOREIGN AFFAIRS (1905–1910)

Although China emerged from the Boxer madness with its territory nominally intact, its possession of one great region, Manchuria, was seriously threatened. A war between Russia and Japan soon followed in which Manchuria was the chief battlefield and which ended with Japan as well as Russia firmly entrenched in that land of virgin resources.

Russia, while professing friendship for China, was reluctant to withdraw from the occupation of the Three Eastern Provinces which it had effected during the Boxer uprising. Again and again it delayed the evacuation of the region beyond the time promised and seemed bent on permanent possession.

To these Russian ambitions Great Britain, Japan, and the United States offered opposition. The United States was unwilling to go to war to enforce its policy, and Great Britain, embarrassed by the struggle with the Boers in South Africa, could scarcely do so. It was left to Japan to act. Reënforced by an alliance with Great Britain (1902) in which each party undertook to come to the other's aid in case more than one power were to attack the other in defense of its interests in the Far East, and after repeated attempts to reach a settlement by negotiation, Japan struck (February, 1904). Its primary concern was for Korea, where Russia was also aggressive, but most of the fighting was in Manchuria. China declared its neutrality. The major neutral Western powers suggested to the belligerents that they localize the area of warfare. This they agreed to do, although Russia maintained that all Manchuria must be included in the zone. As the war progressed, the United States, fearing that in the negotiations of peace between Japan and Russia neutral powers might make demands for Chinese territory, obtained from the chief of them the assurance of their adherence to the policy of the integrity of China and the open door.

In the war, Japan was successful and Russia was badly defeated. In the peace treaty (of Portsmouth, September 5, 1905), the terms which vitally concerned China were the recognition by Russia of Japan's paramount political, military, and economic interests in Korea; the transfer to Japan of the Russian rights in the Liaotung Peninsula and in the railways of South Manchuria; the withdrawal by Russia and Japan of their troops from Manchuria, but the retention there of guards for the railways; the promise of Japan and Russia that they would not obstruct any general measures common to all countries which China might take for the development of the commerce and industry of Manchuria, and that the railways in Manchuria would be used purely for commercial and industrial, and—except in the Liaotung Peninsula—not for strategic purposes; and the declaration by Russia that it did not possess in Manchuria "any territorial advantages or preferential or exclusive concessions in impairment of Chinese sovereignty or inconsistent with the principle of equal opportunity." China soon signed a treaty with Japan assenting to such terms of the Treaty of Portsmouth as dealt with matters within her territory, and in a secret agreement granted to Japan additional advantages in Manchuria.

The Russo-Japanese War, then, greatly increased Japan's tangible interests in China. Not only did the Island Empire succeed to Russia's holdings in South Manchuria, but its augmented influence in Korea, followed shortly, in 1910, by the annexation of that country, brought it to the very borders of China. Increasingly Japan was a major factor in Chinese affairs.

Moreover, instead of settling the Manchurian question, the war complicated it. The Three Eastern Provinces continued to be a storm center in China's international relations. Japan, having obtained a foothold there at great cost in blood and treasure, was fully as jealous of its position as Russia had been. It rapidly developed its holdings and complaints were not long in forthcoming that the principle of the open door was being violated. British and Americans were especially outspoken in their criticisms. Moreover, Japanese blocked all the various projects by British and Americans for the construction of railways in Manchuria. The British Government did little, at least partly because of the Anglo-Japanese Alliance, which was revised and renewed in 1905 and again in 1911. The United States, which after 1905 was moving away from its earlier policy of warm friendship for Japan, was left as the chief hope of official opposition from the West to the extension of Japanese control. The Root-Takahira notes of 1908 seemed for a time amicably to settle Japanese-American differences over Manchuria, but these were revived in 1909 by the proposal of the American Secretary of State, Knox, that the Russian and Japanese railways in Manchuria be neutralized through their purchase, by China, by means of an international loan. The effect of the Knox plan was to drive the Russians and Japanese to an agreement (1910) to maintain the *status quo*.

China, too, attempted by various measures to retain and strengthen her hold in Manchuria. Peking reorganized the administration of the three provinces, planned railways, and attempted to enlist foreign capital.

International friction over Manchuria, as we shall see, remained a prominent feature of China's international relations. The region was a chronic storm center.

REVOLUTIONARY POLITICAL CHANGES: INTERNAL POLITICS, 1901–1931

The humiliating failure of the policy of reaction in the Boxer uprising, and the helplessness of China while Russia and a Westernized Japan fought on her soil at last convinced even the most conservative that the only way to avoid national ruin was reorganization and the adoption of at least some of the processes of the Occident. Some entered upon these changes with reluctance. Others were enthusiastic. After 1900, however, the structure of China's older culture crumbled and no very important effort was made at resistance. The changes affected every realm of the nation's life—political, economic, intellectual, religious, and social. They have been going on at the same time in each of these realms and any attempt to classify them must be simply for the purpose of clarifying what is at best a confused story. To be true to fact, the record cannot but be bewildering.

To most observers in the Occident, particularly the more casual, the most important changes have appeared to be in domestic politics and in international relations. These have certainly been spectacular, even though eventually they may prove not to have been the most significant of the movements of these decades.

In domestic politics the opening decades of the twentieth century, and particularly the years after 1911, presented a kaleidoscopic picture. In general, until 1926 the record was one of the progressive collapse of central and local government and an increase in civil strife, banditry, and anarchy. The *descensus Averni* was not constant: at times it appeared to have been halted and recovery even seemed to have begun. Until the year 1926, however, each attempt at stabilization proved abortive and was followed by renewed and often intensified disorder.

In general, the causes for the disastrous record were six—the pressure of the Occident and Japan, the collapse of the Ch'ing dynasty, the necessity of making radical alterations in the political structure of the country, corruption, economic distress, and internal dissensions.

The pressure of the Occident and Japan took many forms, but it always increased rather than abated. It made inevitable profound changes in all phases of China's culture, including, of course, government.

The collapse of the Ch'ing dynasty deprived China of its best chance of going through the inescapable transformation without chaos. Although the structure of the Chinese state left a great deal to local initiative, much depended on the Emperor. We have seen that again and again through the centuries, when that office was incompetently filled rebellions wasted the land. When weakness at the top was too marked, the dynasty was overthrown and a period of civil strife followed. This strife usually lasted for several decades and once, after the downfall of the Han, for several centuries. Military chieftains fought each other for the control of the Empire, often taking dynastic names and establishing ephemeral states, until one conquered all the others and succeeded in uniting the Empire under his sway and in passing the throne on to other members of his family. Had the Ch'ing survived, this rivalry might have been avoided or controlled. With the downfall of the Ch'ing, the traditional struggle between military leaders began again.

This time, however, the civil strife which had always been the interlude between dynasties was complicated by attempts at basic innovations in the form of government. Heretofore, after Ch'in Shih Huang Ti and the Han had devised machinery for ruling the Empire, each dynasty had been content to adopt, with modifications, the framework inherited from its predecessor. Even foreign conquerors had done this. When the Ch'ing fell, this was no longer possible. The new problems thrust upon the state by the coming of the West and the new ideas from abroad made imperative a reconstruction more revolutionary even than that of Ch'in Shih Huang Ti. No people has the political genius to work out a new system of government without experimentation and the attendant mistakes. Certainly new political machinery cannot be evolved for so large a mass as four hundred millions, most of whom are quite unprepared for the change, without costly failures. When, as in China, the attempt to devise a new type of government was complicated by strife between self-seeking military chieftains, the result could not but be temporary chaos.

The breakdown of government was furthered by widespread corruption. Much of this existed under the Ch'ing, notably in the declining years of the dynasty. It bred a popular distrust of officialdom. When traditional controls were removed, the selfish use of political power for private profit was accentuated. This fostered rebellion and still greater lack of confidence in government.

Anarchy was accentuated by economic factors. Under the excellent government of the great Emperors of the Ch'ing, prosperity was marked and population multiplied. The disorders of the nineteenth century brought about no widespread economic breakdown

—except temporarily in the third quarter of the century. The civil strife of the twentieth century, however, so consumed the scanty surplus of food in many regions and so disrupted economic life over wide areas that millions were brought into dire poverty. To this was added, after 1931 and especially after 1937, the miseries of foreign invasion. Many, deprived of their ordinary livelihood, took to banditry or swelled the ill-disciplined cohorts of the warlords. The armies and the hordes of bandits increased the distress, still others were driven to depredations on their neighbors, and a vicious circle was created which made the establishment of order increasingly more difficult.

Moreover, China's troubles were complicated by the ever-changing combinations, intrigues, and clashes between the many social, economic, and political groups which were part of the structure which the new China inherited, in more or less modified form, from the old. Guilds, clans, secret societies, and political cliques were involved. Secret societies, indeed, played a much larger part than all but a few well-informed foreigners realized. Many of the political and military leaders belonged to them and their affiliations often determined or modified political events. Chinese politics were exceedingly complex, with many currents and cross-currents, and were confusing in the extreme.

Only the main outline of the story need here be given. As we have repeatedly seen, the Ch'ing dynasty had been in decline since the close of the eighteenth century, and its demise had probably been postponed only by the loyalty of some able Chinese. By 1901 its sands had nearly run out. The Boxer fiasco discredited it. The Emperor, Kuang Hsü, was virtually a prisoner. The father of the heir apparent was one of the most ardent supporters of the Boxers, and the heir apparent himself an uncouth roué. The new heir apparent appointed after 1900 was an infant. Tz'ŭ Hsi, while able and vigorous, was unfitted to give adequate leadership.

After 1900 the Ch'ing attempted to reorganize the government to meet the demands of the new day. Important changes were effected in the administrative system, from the central boards in Peking to the bureaucracy in the provinces. A beginning was made of a new code of laws. The old civil service examinations were discontinued, and a system of tests introduced for aspirants for public office, based upon Western as well as Chinese subjects. Fiscal reform was projected. Army reorganization was planned, and a part of it was carried out, especially by Yüan Shih-k'ai, in the North. A commission sent to the United States and Europe studied the forms of government in use there, a constitution was promised, and steps were taken looking toward the introduction of representation based upon popular election. Provincial assemblies and a National Assembly were convoked, the former in 1909 and the latter in 1910.

Given more competent leadership, the dynasty might have made the needed adjustments. As it was, the new wine proved too potent for the old wineskins. November 15, 1908, the Empress Dowager died, presumably preceded by only a few hours by the Emperor Kuang Hsü. With the passing of Tz'ŭ Hsi went the last outstanding figure in the imperial house. The infant heir apparent came to the throne (under the reign name of Hsüan T'ung) and the regent did not have the force of character required by the times. Under these circumstances, the dynasty was easily upset.

The revolution which overthrew the Ch'ing broke out in Hankow and Wuchang in October, 1911, the 10th being the day that is celebrated. There had been unrest in the Yangtze Valley, particularly in Szechwan, over a foreign loan to finance railways in South, Central, and West China and an accompanying greater centralization of railway administration under Peking. By the end of September, 1911, an active revolt had arisen in Szechwan. A fortuitous incident in Hankow brought about the premature inception of a more widespread outbreak. Troops in Wuchang, mutinying, forced their commander, Li Yüan-hung, to lead them in the new movement, a republic was declared, and the strategic cities Wuchang, Hanyang, and Hankow quickly fell to the rebels. So unexpected had been the uprising in the Wuhan center that it surprised even the most ardent anti-imperialists.

Peking called to its assistance Yüan Shih-k'ai. Yüan had been dismissed soon after the beginning of the new reign, probably because of his betrayal of the regent's brother, the late Emperor Kuang Hsü, in 1898. As the creator of the strongest army in the country, he appeared indispensable. He responded somewhat deliberately to the frantic summons for help and came only on his own terms. Had he acted promptly, he might possibly have suppressed the revolt. As it was, he dallied, and, although Hankow was retaken by the end of October, the interval had been sufficiently long to enable the revolution to gain headway. In October and November, city after city and province after province threw off the Manchu yoke and in them independent governments were set up. The only fighting of any importance was in the Wuhan cities (Wuchang, Hankow, and Hanyang) and Nanking. In several places Manchu garrisons, helpless, were massacred. Concessions by Peking availed nothing. Before the end of the year, a national council representing the revolutionists assembled at Nanking and (December 28) elected as President of the Republic Sun Yat-sen. Sun had been in Europe at the inception of the outbreak, but recently, amid great acclaim, had returned to China.

Before Sun's arrival, negotiations had been begun between Yüan and the revolutionists. Wise heads on both sides strove to save the country from further debilitating civil strife. Yüan succeeded, partly by threats, in convincing the court of the import of the writing on the wall, and on February 12, 1912, edicts were issued from Peking, in the name of the young Emperor, by which the Ch'ing accepted its fate. Hsüan T'ung abdicated and Yüan was instructed to organize a republic. The Emperor, so the republicans agreed, was to retain his title for life, was to receive a large annuity, and was to keep his private property and the use of a palace. The tomb of Kuang Hsü was to be completed at public expense. Manchus, Moslems, Mongols, and Tibetans were promised equality with the Chinese and were secured in their titles and their property. Within a few days, further to insure peace, Sun withdrew from the Presidency and the republican body at Nanking elected Yüan in his stead. Li Yüan-hung, who had become something of a popular hero by his part in the outbreak of the revolution, was elected Vice-President. The Ch'ing dynasty, with a minimum of bloodshed, had passed the way of its predecessors. The nation, outwardly united, had embarked on a perilous experiment with republican forms.

So perished, with scarcely a struggle, a monarchical institution which had its beginnings in prehistoric times, which had been reinstituted and remodeled by Ch'in Shih Huang Ti, and which had been modified by the Emperors of the Han. With it inevitably went much of that elaborate bureaucracy and of those political theories which were among the greatest achievements of the Chinese. Disorders could scarcely be avoided. It is still an unanswered question whether the Chinese can construct a type of government which will meet the new conditions as successfully as did the old—whether China, having lost the political structure which through the centuries brought it unity, will be able to preserve that unity by other means.

At first sight, the abandonment of the monarchy and the attempt to transform China into a republic seemed the height of folly. With almost no preparation, the Chinese were scrapping political institutions with whose operation they were familiar and were adopting from the West a form of government with which they were quite inexperienced. On second thought, however, it is clear that this offered some, perhaps the best, hope of avoiding prolonged civil war and possible foreign intervention. The Ch'ing dynasty could, at best, have been kept alive but little longer. Yüan Shih-k'ai, the most powerful military figure in the country, and hence possessed of the best chance of founding a new dynasty, would probably not have been peacefully accepted as Emperor by the nation and certainly not by the revolutionists. There was a bare possibility that under the name of a republic the nation might work out in an orderly fashion the political institutions required by the new day.

At first it looked as though this hope might be realized. Gradually, however, the machinery inherited from the old régime disintegrated. The new was slow in being constructed. Within a decade and a half only the barest shadow of a national government remained and the country was racked by fighting.

The administration of Yüan Shih-k'ai began fairly auspiciously. Yüan controlled the strongest army, and outwardly had the support of the republicans and the former adherents of the Manchus. He succeeded in keeping the capital at Peking, near the center of his strength. The foreign powers accepted him.

Almost immediately, however, Yüan's troubles began. The provisional constitution which the body at Nanking adopted in March, 1912, and to which he was supposed to conform, placed the President under the control of Parliament and gave him little independence. He was to have about the functions of the President of France under the Third Republic. Parliament, when elected, was dominated by the radicals who had brought about the revolution and who had been organized into the Kuomintang. A decisive clash between Yüan and the radicals came in the spring and summer of 1913. Against the opposition of the Kuomintang, Yüan completed a large loan made by banking groups of five countries—Great Britain, France, Russia, Germany, and Japan. This both gave him the sinews of war and assured him the moral support of these powers. When he replaced with his own men several of the military commanders in the Yangtze Valley and the South, his critics, with the endorsement of Sun Yat-sen, broke out into open rebellion, declaring a "punitive expedition" against him. Yüan easily suppressed the outbreak and Sun fled to Japan. Yüan followed up his advantage by obtaining the adoption of the sections of the "permanent" constitution which had to do with the selection of President. He secured his own election to that office, unseated, soon afterward (November, 1913), the Kuomintang members of Parliament, and then (January, 1914) dismissed the remnant of Parliament.

Thus rid of the elements which had inaugurated the revolution of 1911, for more than a year Yüan preserved the outward form of a republic, but with changes in its structure which made it clearly submissive to himself. In 1915, after going through the motions of a carefully directed "referendum," he declared the monarchy restored with himself as Emperor. Opposition proved stronger than he had anticipated. Japan, supported by Great Britain, Russia, and France, counseled delay. In December, 1915, rebellion broke out in distant Yünnan and quickly spread to adjoining provinces. Yüan first postponed his formal enthronement, and then, as the rebellion spread, canceled the monarchy. The insurgents, however, were not content to leave him in power on any terms. Broken by chagrin and ill-health and with his prestige gone, Yüan died of disease (June 6, 1916) before his enemies could remove him.

The Vice-President, Li Yüan-hung, had never consented to Yüan's restoration of the monarchy and had been elected President of the opposition government which Yüan's opponents had set up in Canton. With Yüan gone, the entire country recognized him as President. Although well-intentioned, Li was not strong enough for the difficult post, and the calm which followed his accession was deceptive. He pleased the radicals by restoring the constitution of 1912 and recalling the Parliament which Yüan had dismissed. Fêng Kuo-chang, a prominent military figure in the Yangtze Valley, was elected Vice-President. Tuan Ch'i-jui, a henchman and appointee of Yüan Shih-k'ai, and commanding the support of the military machine which the latter had built, continued as Premier. The major factions were thus represented in the government, but it required a leader with more than Li's ability to keep them working harmoniously.

In the spring of 1917 the inevitable dissension broke out—over the question, as it chanced, of China's entry into the World War. In March China broke off relations with Germany. Tuan wished her to take the next logical step, but Parliament refused to join in a declaration of war while he was Premier. The President acceded and dismissed Tuan (May 23). Tuan withdrew to Tientsin and here a group of military leaders representing the faction which had formerly backed Yüan Shih-k'ai declared the independence of several provinces—most of them in the North. Li Yüan-hung, faced with this opposition and without adequate military support, called in as mediator Chang Hsün, a picturesque chieftain who had adhered to the Manchus in the revolution of 1911 and was now military governor of Anhui and in command of a force astride the Tientsin-Pukow railway. Following the counsel of Chang Hsün, the President dismissed Parliament (June 13th). On July first, after bringing his troops to Peking, Chang Hsün electrified the world by declaring the restoration of the Ch'ing dynasty—an act probably due to his sense of the traditional Confucian obligation owed by a minister to his prince. The generals assembled at Tientsin, however, were not minded to tolerate any such turn of events and marched on Peking. Before the middle of July Peking had been taken, Chang Hsün had sought sanctuary in the Dutch Legation, the boy Emperor had again retired, and the Republic had been officially restored.

Li Yüan-hung refused to resume the Presidency, for he had lost enormously in prestige and had no powerful friends at hand to support him. Fêng Kuo-chang, as Vice-President, automatically came into the Presidency, and Tuan Ch'i-jui resumed the Premiership. Having won in the arbitrament of arms, the northern military group was now in control. The following year (August, 1918) a body assembled by it, and known, because it was dominated by the military chiefs, or Tuchüns, as the "Tuchüns' Parliament," passed over Fêng for the Presidency—because he was from another clique than that of Tuan—and elected to the office a scholar and ex-official of the old régime, Hsü Shih-ch'ang. Tuan's group, now organized into what was called the Anfu Club, was supreme.

In the meantime, members of the radical Parliament of 1913, once dismissed by Yüan Shih-k'ai and now again by Li Yüan-hung, assembled in Shanghai and Canton, and set up, with Canton as the usual headquarters, a government which they declared to be the only legitimate one—for they held the constitution of 1912, under which they had been elected, still to be binding. The Canton régime did not have nearly the power of its rival at Peking and often its hold on life was very tenuous. However, much of the South acquiesced in a nominal allegiance to it. The country, accordingly, was divided. In 1921 Sun Yat-sen was elected President of the southern government and maintained himself precariously at Canton.

The government at Peking became progressively weaker. In the summer of 1920, Chang Tso-lin, the master of Manchuria, and two other generals, Ts'ao Kun and Ts'ao's most powerful lieutenant, Wu P'ei-fu, joined in a successful effort to drive Tuan Ch'i-jui and the Anfu clique out of Peking. Hsü Shih-ch'ang, a somewhat pathetic figure, was left with only the shadow of power. In 1922 Wu P'ei-fu and Chang Tso-lin went to war with each other. Chang was defeated and withdrew his troops to Manchuria. Wu, victorious, sought to bring the nation together by ousting Hsü from the Presidency and calling back into power Li Yüan-hung and the Parliament of 1913—under whom the country had last been united. The effort proved disappointing. From the outset both Sun Yat-sen and Chang Tso-lin were hostile, and other powerful commanders were unreconciled. The following year (1923) a rising military figure and subordinate of Wu P'ei-fu, Fêng Yü-hsiang, who had already gained distinction by his conversion to Protestant Christianity and his earnest attempts to propagate his new faith among his troops, helped to make Li

Yüan-hung regard his position as untenable. Li, disheartened, once more withdrew to the quiet security of his home in a foreign concession in Tientsin. Soon afterward (September, 1923), Wu's technical superior, Ts'ao Kun, by the brazen use of heavy bribes, was elected to the Presidency by what remained of the Parliament of 1913. The twelfth anniversary of the Revolution of 1911 was celebrated by the promulgation of what was optimistically called the "permanent" constitution.

By this time the recurrence of civil war had become almost as regular an annual event as the return of spring, and in 1924 the major generals were once more moving against each other. This year Chang Tso-lin was victorious, due chiefly to the sudden defection of Fêng Yü-hsiang from Wu P'ei-fu. Ts'ao Kun was deprived of his office and imprisoned, and Fêng and Chang placed Tuan Ch'i-jui at the head of the Peking Government. Tuan, however, did not have the title of President, but was denominated what may be translated as Provisional Chief Executive. Moreover, he had under him only the skeleton of a national government. In 1925 the inevitable falling-out between Fêng and Chang resulted in the withdrawal of the latter, thanks to the disloyalty of some subordinates. The following year (1926), however, Wu P'ei-fu and Chang Tso-lin ignored their differences for the moment and joined in driving Fêng Yü-hsiang's forces out of Peking and into the Northwest. A few weeks afterward, Tuan Ch'i-jui retired to the convenient haven of Tientsin. Not even a "Provisional Chief Executive" was left in the capital. A rapidly shifting cabinet kept up, with the consent of the warlords, the form of a government with which the powers, in default of anything better, were willing to deal under the fiction that it was the legal representative of China.

While what remained of a government at Peking went through the motions of speaking for the country, all semblance of actual national political unity was rapidly disappearing. In fact the country was divided among many warring chieftains, most of whom rose to power rapidly and as quickly disappeared, and the boundaries of whose spheres of influence were constantly shifting.

Throughout the country, however, the continuous strife was producing increasing war weariness. Moreover, the spirit of nationalism, reënforced by the impetus given it almost everywhere in the world by the Great War of 1914–1918, was abroad and growing, particularly among the younger intellectuals. As we shall see in a moment, this nationalistic sentiment was directed in part against the special privileges of foreigners. It also wished to unify China internally. Now, in the spring and summer of 1926, there came rapidly into prominence a movement which seemed to offer hope to these aspirations and which soon attracted to itself, either actively or passively, most of the progressive and radical elements in the country and was looked to expectantly by all who longed for an early end of China's woes.

Sun Yat-sen was very successful as a propagandist. He also possessed idealism—in striking contrast to the crass self-seeking of most of the military chiefs of the day. An omnivorous reader in both Western and Chinese literature, he was a student of society—a social philosopher—and dreamed of a new utopia. Of his many interesting suggestions for the reorganization of the country, some were bizarre and impracticable, but others had in them a hint of genius. Sun had a gift of attracting others to himself and no one else quite so much caught the imagination of the younger elements in China. As an inspirer and organizer of revolution he was extraordinarily able. As an administrator, however, he was a distinct failure. Under his leadership, therefore, the Kuomintang and the government of which he was the head made little progress toward mastering the country. Some of the time he was even driven out of his capital, Canton. March 12, 1925, he died in Peking while on a mission to the North to confer with Fêng Yü-hsiang and Chang Tso-lin.

Sun's death was of almost as much service to his cause and his party as his life had been. Not long before his end, in 1923, he called to his assistance as advisers Russians of the Communist school—because, so he declared, he had sought in vain help from the United States, Great Britain, and Japan, in his struggle to overthrow the Peking Government. The chief of these Russians was Michael Borodin, a vigorous and astute revolutionary who had been educated in the United States, who had had experience in Chicago, Mexico, and Turkey, and whom some one has called the most influential foreigner who so far in the twentieth century has come to China. Under the tutelage of these counselors the Kuomintang began to take over some of the main features of the program which had won for the Bolshevists their success in Russia. The organization of the Kuomintang was made to conform in large degree to that of the Russian Communist Party. Sun Yat-sen (*à la Lenin*) was canonized as the national hero and weekly memorial services before his picture were encouraged. He left behind him a last will and testament directed to the nation and several books outlining his program. These were now adopted as infallible guides for the party and the nation. The will was regularly read in public with great solemnity, and one of the books, the *San Min Chu I,* or the Three People's Principles, became the party's manual. These three principles—government by the people and for the people, a sufficient livelihood for all, and freedom from the control of foreign nations—were broadcasted as popular slogans. Propaganda was highly developed and very skillfully employed. The attempt was made to adapt Communism to Chinese conditions. Unions of laborers and peasants were organized against the propertied classes. Since the industrialization of China had not proceeded very far and the *bourgeosie*—in the Marxian sense of that term—was not prominent, agitation was directed in large part against the "capitalistic" and "imperialistic" powers of the Occident. Moreover, Sun Yat-sen had come to oppose Russian Communism and had rejected the orthodox Marxian theory of the class war. The Kuomintang had more than one element and more than a single attitude toward the method and goal of revolution. In a military academy at Whampoa, near Canton, officers for the army were trained both in military tactics and in the party program.

In the summer of 1926 the armies of the Kuomintang—or Nationalist Party, as the title is often loosely translated—began a northward advance. Their young general, Chiang Kai-shek (or Chiang Chieh-shih), proved an able leader, and unusually effective propaganda helped to smooth their way. Here at last seemed to be salvation from the interminable civil wars, the heartless selfishness of the militarists, and the economic distress of the past few years. Little well-organized opposition existed short of the North. The progress of the Nationalist armies was almost an uninterrupted triumph. By the early spring of 1927 the Yangtze had been reached, Wu P'ei-fu and the general in command in the Shanghai area (Sun Ch'üan-fang) had been eliminated, and such centers as Wuchang, Hankow, and Shanghai had come into the possession of the Nationalists. It was freely predicted that the autumn would see Chiang in Peking.

Victory, however, was delayed by dissensions within the party. The Communist wing of the Kuomintang gained in power as the tide of victory mounted. In Central China, and especially in Hunan, radicalism was in the saddle. Through the party organization and the newly formed unions of laborers and peasants great excesses were committed. "Capitalists" and "imperialists" were denounced, many of the wealthy were dispossessed, particularly of their lands, and some of them were murdered. The headquarters of the government, established at Hankow, were dominated by the left wing. Communism was strengthened by returned Chinese students from Russia. The Soviet Government had set up in Moscow especially for them (1925) a university named after Sun Yat-sen, which by the end of 1927 had an enrollment of about six hundred—mostly from Hunan and Kwangtung. Radicalism, moreover, appealed to the youth of the nation, especially to the students, and many of these latter became its ardent apostles. The more moderate elements in the party, led by Chiang Kai-shek, looked with alarm upon the growing left wing, realizing that before long it would alienate the more substantial portions of the population. The Communists were out not only to destroy religion, including Christianity, but Confucian morality, and much of the nation was scandalized. Then, too, many believed that the Russians were interested in China merely as a cat's-paw against the capitalistic powers of the West.

The issue began to come to a head after the capture of Nanking, in March, 1927, when radicals roughly handled foreigners and killed some of them. The right and left wings were soon openly at outs with each other and the progress northward came to a pause. The moderates organized a government at Nanking, in opposition to the one at Hankow. Before the end of 1927 public opinion had turned overwhelmingly against Communism, the moderates, led by Chiang Kai-shek, were in control, the non-Communist members of the left wing had broken with the Communists, the government in the Wuhan cities had come to an end, the Soviet advisers were on their way to Russia, many of the radicals had been executed and others, among them the widow of

Sun Yat-sen, were in exile, and the Nationalists had closed the Russian consulates. The government which the right wing set up at Nanking was distinctly anti-Communistic in tone and depended for its finances upon the bankers of Shanghai.

At the head of the Nanking Government was Chiang Kai-shek. In 1927 his position was strengthened by his marriage to Miss Soong, a sister of Madame Sun Yat-sen. Since T. V. Soong, a brother of Madame Chiang, was Minister of Finance and another sister was the wife of H. H. K'ung, the Minister of Industry, Labor, and Commerce, people began to speak of the "Soong dynasty."

The Kuomintang was now outwardly largely reunited and the Communist elements had been outlawed or were no longer vocal in the national councils of the party. In the spring and summer of 1928, therefore, the Nationalist advance once more began. In coöperation with the forces of Fêng Yü-hsiang, now called the Kuominchun, or "Nationalist Army," and of Yen Hsi-shan—the latter the "model Governor" of Shansi, where he had held office since 1912—Chiang Kai-shek's forces moved northward. In June the Nationalist armies entered Peking. While retreating to his capital, Mukden, their most formidable opponent, Chang Tso-lin, was killed by a bomb. His son and successor, Chang Hsüeh-liang, made his peace with the Nationalists and nominally accepted a prominent place in their organization.

Theoretically the country was now united. Certainly the main military figures gave outward support to the Nationalists. At Nanking an administration had been set up on the outline suggested by Sun Yat-sen, with Chiang Kai-shek as its ranking officer. It was still a one party government, dominated by the Kuomintang, but more than any other of the many attempts under the Republic it sought to combine the machinery of the Occident with the best of the devices of the older China. It proposed, for example, to institute civil service examinations and a body of censors—although nothing very effective was done in these directions. In several of the chief posts were able men, most of them formerly students in the Occident. The modern, Western-trained leader had come to the fore. The outlook appeared more hopeful than for many years. Nanking throbbed with life as it had not since the times of the T'ai P'ings, new government buildings were erected, and on Purple Mountain, overlooking the city, was built an imposing tomb, to which, with great pomp, were brought the remains of Sun Yat-sen. Moreover, Nanking as a capital proved an advantage to the Nationalist Government. It had historic associations and it was removed from the galling presence of the armed legation quarter in Peking (now renamed Peiping). More important still, it was in the most populous and prosperous region of China. A government with headquarters there had a better chance of controlling the nation than if it had been off on the periphery, at Canton or Peiping.

In itself the Kuomintang helped to give unity to the country. Its organization was almost nation-wide. Its many units, the *Tangpu* (the name usually given to the executive committee of the local precinct or sub-precinct organization) had much influence in local affairs and headed up in the National Congress of the party. This was represented, in the long interims between meetings, by the Central Executive Committee. The Central Executive Committee, in turn, controlled the national government.

In many respects the political situation at the beginning of 1929 was more encouraging than at any time since the revolution of 1911. However, the nation's troubles were far from an end. Much of the country was overrun with bandits, some of whom were made more ruthless by the profession of Communist principles. Famine was taking a toll of millions of lives in the Northwest. In only a few provinces was Nanking's authority effective enough to bring taxes into the national treasury. In 1929 a serious rift appeared in the Kuomintang. The major military figures could not long live in harmony. In the spring and summer of 1930 Yen Hsi-shan and Fêng Yü-hsiang joined in opposing Chiang Kai-shek. By the autumn of 1930 the latter had won and the Nationalist Government at Nanking had gained a breathing space. Fêng Yü-hsiang was in semi-retirement, Yen Hsi-shan had withdrawn first to the security of mountainous Shansi and then had sought sanctuary in Tientsin, and Chang Hsüeh-liang, although he had advanced his forces south of the Great Wall and had occupied much of Hopei (as the province of Chihli had been renamed by the Nationalists), professed to be on friendly terms with Nanking.

However, in vast sections life and property were insecure. Armed bands, often of former soldiers, unpaid and lawless, roamed over large areas, bringing terror, bandits possessed large regions, and local organizations for mutual protection of peasants added to the confusion. In at least one region, Manchuria, bandits formed a kind of second government. On the eve of the death of Chang Tso-lin they had an organization which covered much of the Three Eastern Provinces, with a head, with a division of territory, and with an espionage system and methods of discovering and levying on wealth which bore similarities to the contemporary "racketeers" of the United States. In spite of official disapproval by Nanking and Mukden, and of vigorous anti-Communist reactions in many places, Communism remained strong. Russian agents were still at work and numbers of the students were becoming Communists. In 1930–1933, indeed, large sections of the country, especially in Kiangsi, Anhui, Northern Fukien, and Hupeh, were in the hands of those who called themselves Communists. In the summer of 1930 Communists captured the capital of Hunan and held it for a few days. Some of the so-called Communists were led by men who knew a good deal of the Russian system and believed in it. Others knew very little of Western Communism but used the slogan as an excuse for murder and robbery. The majority of "Communists," indeed, were really bandits or locally independent military groups. To most of them Communism, whether comprehended or not, was a philosophy of despair, a possible way out of the personal and collective suffering into which the Chinese had been thrown. The movement, too, was in large part one of land-hungry peasants to appropriate the holdings of their neighbors and the well-to-do. Campaigns waged against Communists by Chiang Kai-shek and his associates in 1930 and 1931 were interrupted by dissensions within government ranks and by the Sino-Japanese crisis of 1931.

The most serious rift in the ranks of the Nationalist Party in 1931 was the protest against the rule of Chiang Kai-shek by a number of leaders of varied political background. In the spring, these malcontents gathered at Canton and there set up a government which claimed to represent the Kuomintang but which repudiated Chiang Kai-shek. The Manchurian crisis of the autumn tended to encourage negotiations. The collapse of Chang Hsüeh-liang before the Japanese in the autumn of 1931 weakened Chiang, for the former had been a strong supporter of the latter's government. In December, 1931, to pacify his opponents and the many vociferous students who had flocked to Nanking and were clamoring against him for his failure to take more vigorous action against Japan, Chiang Kai-shek resigned the titular headship of the civil régime. However, he remained the dominant military figure in the Nanking Government and as such was still the most powerful man in the nation.

RELATIONS WITH FOREIGN POWERS, 1911–1919:
FURTHER HUMILIATION

While the downfall of the Manchus, the subsequent struggles between rival aspirants for power, and the attempts to devise new governmental machinery were distracting the country, momentous changes were taking place in China's relations with other nations. For about eight years China descended still farther into the valley of humiliation. Then began one of the strangest spectacles of the time. China, although distraught by civil strife and utterly impotent to obtain her will by armed force, began to make headway against the powers and to cancel the privileges which, for more than three-quarters of a century, she had been progressively conceding to aliens. This was halted only by the events in Manchuria which began in 1931.

First came the further humiliation. The outbreak of the revolution of 1911, it will be recalled, had been hastened by the conclusion of a loan with a four-power syndicate for the centralization of railway administration due to the proposed construction of lines in Central, South, and West China. This loan, while designed in part to allay international friction, increased foreign financial interests, and, accordingly, foreign control.

The first years after the revolution witnessed further encroachments by foreigners. China was weaker and the powers were still rapacious and strong.

Both Great Britain and Russia took advantage of the situation to extend their spheres of influence—the former into Tibet and the latter into Mongolia. In 1904, the British, alarmed by Russian machinations in Tibet and moved by a desire for commerce, dispatched an armed expedition which fought its way to Lhasa and obtained a convention which provided for trade and forbade the Tibetans to grant concessions without the consent of Britain. In 1906, China, as Tibet's overlord, confirmed the agreement, with safeguards against further aggression by the British, and in 1907 an Anglo-Russian agreement recognized Chinese suzerainty in Tibet and promised that neither power would seek concessions in the country. China had begun by force to strengthen its position in Tibet. After the establishment of the Republic it still attempted to do so and insisted upon regarding Tibet as an integral part of its domains. By the end of 1912, however, Chinese troops were driven out of all but the edges of the land and Tibet became practically independent. Efforts were made, at British instance, to settle Anglo-Sino-Tibetan relations by negotiations, but with results to which the Chinese would not consent. In 1914 Great Britain and Tibet reached an agreement whereby, among other provisions, Inner Tibet—that portion of the country which adjoins India—was to be autonomous, although nominally still under Chinese suzerainty.

In the last years of the Ch'ing China had pursued an aggressive policy in Mongolia. For years Chinese settlers had been pushing the frontier of cultivated land ever northward of the Great Wall into Inner Mongolia. Just before their downfall, much to the annoyance of the natives, the Manchus were seeking to increase their authority in Outer Mongolia. The revolution of 1911, accordingly, was welcomed by the Mongols as an opportunity to throw off the Chinese yoke. Late in 1911, Outer Mongolia declared its independence and the Hutukhtu of Urga, the ranking ecclesiastic of the Lamaistic sect of Buddhism of that region, was invested with the headship of the state. In 1912 Russia recognized the autonomy of Outer Mongolia in return for an extension of Russian privileges in the region. The following year China, in an agreement with Russia, assented to the new status in return for the Russian acknowledgment of Chinese suzerainty in the area, and in 1915 a tripartite agreement between the interested parties confirmed this relationship. The Russian claim to a voice in Mongolian affairs was, therefore, acknowledged by Peking. Although China was reluctant to admit it, some of the distant portions of the Empire won by the great Ch'ing Emperors, Outer Tibet and Outer Mongolia, were slipping from its grasp.

The loan made to Yüan Shih-k'ai in 1913 by an international group of bankers, which had so much to do with the break between the radicals and himself, increased the grip of foreign financiers on the country—chiefly by pledging the salt tax to pay the debt and placing the collection of the tax under foreign administration. The coöperative feature of the loan helped to allay friction among the powers, but so strongly did President Wilson feel China's independence to be compromised that he withdrew the support of his government from the American participants, and the latter did not join in the final arrangements.

The outbreak of the European war in 1914 brought fresh difficulties to the harassed young Republic: with so much of the world in turmoil it could not hope to remain unaffected. The first really serious complications came early. August 15, 1914, Japan presented an ultimatum to Germany advising the latter government to withdraw all its armed vessels from Japanese and Chinese waters and to turn over to Japan the leased territory of Kiaochow "with a view to the eventual restoration of the same to China." No reply was vouchsafed by Berlin and on August 23d Japan declared war.

This action of Japan was natural in view of the Anglo-Japanese Alliance, a Franco-Japanese *entente* dating from 1907, and an *entente* and treaties with Russia. Events proved, however, that it was not entirely, and perhaps not even chiefly, out of loyalty to treaty commitments that Japan entered the war. Its interest in China was growing. Japan's population was rapidly increasing, and, since the preëmption by the white races of the best of the unoccupied sections of the world denied it the possibility of relief by extensive emigration, the one recourse for a livelihood for the added millions was the continued development of industry and commerce. If these were to prosper, Japan must have both markets and a convenient source of raw materials, including iron and coal—for nature had endowed it with but little of the one and insufficient supplies of the other. China was at once both an adjacent undeveloped market of great possibilities and an available storehouse of raw materials. It is not surprising, therefore, that Japan regarded the maintenance of easy access to China as essential to its very life and was fearful of the closing of the door to China by greedy Western powers. Now, with most of the Occident engrossed in deadly struggle, was its great opportunity to make secure its position in its huge neighbor. This it attempted to do.

The Japanese promptly followed their declaration of war on Germany by an attack on Kiaochow, the leasehold of the latter power in Shantung. In this their forces were assisted by a small British contingent, but the enterprise was primarily theirs. The campaign was conducted with scant regard for China's neutrality. Territory, railways, and telegraph lines outside the leased area were seized, and individual Chinese were treated cavalierly. When, in November, 1914, Tsingtao, the city which dominated the Kiaochow region, surrendered, Japan appeared to have every intention of remaining in possession, not only of that port, but also of much of Shantung.

In January, 1915, Japan followed up its activities in Shantung by what soon became famous as the Twenty-one Demands. At the outset made secretly, they soon became known to the world. They were in five groups. The first had to do with Shantung. Here China was to assent to any agreement which Japan might make with Germany for the disposition of the latter's possessions in the province, to promise not to alienate any part of the coast to a third power, to open additional cities to foreign trade, and to grant to Japan certain railway privileges. The second group stipulated that in South Manchuria the Japanese leaseholds—on Port Arthur and Dairen (Dalny) and the railways—were to be extended to ninety-nine years, that anywhere in South Manchuria and Eastern Inner Mongolia Japanese might reside, travel, engage in business, lease and own land, and open mines, and that in these regions no official advisers were to be employed without the consent of Japan. The third provided that the Hanyehp'ing Company, the great iron-mining and smelting concern in Central China, was to become a Sino-Japanese enterprise and that it could not be sold without Japan's consent. The fourth group wished to bind China not to cede or lease to a third power any harbor, bay, or island along its coast. The fifth, the most far-reaching of all, demanded that China employ Japanese as advisers, share with Japanese the administration of the police departments in important places, purchase from Japan half or more of its munitions or establish a Sino-Japanese arsenal, grant certain railway concessions in the Yangtze Valley, give to Japanese the privileges of religious propaganda and of buying land in the interior for schools, hospitals, and churches, and that Japan be consulted before foreign loans were contracted for mines, railways, and harbor works in Fukien.

When these demands became known, a storm of protest swept over China. In the United States, too, criticism was freely expressed, and shortly after China had yielded to Japan's ultimatum and agreed to comply with Japan's modified requests, the American Government notified both Tokyo and Peking that it could not recognize any agreement impairing American rights in China or the political or territorial integrity of China or the open door. However, China could not hope to support its position by armed force, the United States would not do so, and possible opposition from Great Britain, France, and Russia was estopped by the necessity of retaining Japan's support in the European war. China did demur, however, and it was only after months of negotiation and a sharp ultimatum that Japan was able to obtain a settlement. Even then Tokyo had to be content with only part of what it had asked. China acceded to the first three groups with important modifications in its favor; group four was met by a presidential mandate which directed that no portion of China's coast should be leased or ceded to any power; and the fifth group was reserved for further consideration, except that Peking stated that it had not permitted foreign nations to establish on the coast of Fukien dockyards, coaling stations for military use, or naval bases, and that it had no intention of borrowing foreign capital to set up such establishments. Japan had won only a partial victory, and even that at the price of the bitter hatred of the Chinese.

Although it had obviously bungled, Japan did not give up its purpose to strengthen its hold on China. In 1916 Tokyo took the occasion of a clash between Chinese and Japanese on the Mongolian-Manchurian frontier to make fresh demands—from which, however, it subsequently largely receded. In February and March, 1917, it obtained secret assurances from Great Britain, France, Russia, and Italy that at the peace conference these powers would support its claims to the former German holdings in Shantung.

In 1917, China entered the war against the Central powers. It broke off relations with Germany in March, and in August, after the internal dissensions which have been recounted above, declared war. Because of its domestic weakness, China could take no active part in the struggle. It seized the German and Austrian vessels interned in its ports and chartered some of them for the service of the Allies. It permitted what had already begun—the recruiting of Chinese laborers for non-combatant service in England, France, Africa, and Mesopotamia.

To China formal entry into the war brought both advantages and disadvantages. It canceled the portions of the Boxer indemnity due its enemies and obtained the suspension for five years of payments on that indemnity due the Allies—with the exception of most of those owed to Russia and some portions required for supporting educational projects initiated by the return of the indemnity due the United States. It took over the German concessions in Tientsin and Hankow and the Austro-Hungarian concession in Tientsin. This weakening of the privileges enjoyed by some of the Western powers proved later to be no inconsiderable advantage in the campaign against the "unequal treaties." China also obtained a seat at the peace conference, with the hearing of its grievances which that assured. On the other hand, Japan's influence in China was augmented. Although American authorities sought to minimize their significance, by the Lansing-Ishii notes (November, 1917), the one great foreign opponent of Japan's aggressions in China, the United States, by recognizing that Japan, because of "territorial propinquity," had "special interests in China," appeared to have acceded to Japan's claims. A "war participation board" with a Japanese adviser, an "arms contract," and extensive loans by Japan to Peking on the security of railways, mines, forests, telegraphs, taxes, and bonds seemed ominous. In 1918, the two countries entered into agreements for military and naval coöperation, chiefly against a possible menace from the North. Such "coöperation," of course, would mean more Japanese control.

For a time, too, it looked as though Japan might substitute herself for Russia in Northern Manchuria. With the Russian revolution of 1917 and the temporary chaos before the new Socialist Soviet Republic eliminated opposing elements, Eastern Siberia fell into disorder. There was intervention (1918) in

Eastern Siberia by Japan, the United States, and some of the European Allies. Japan, with the largest body of troops, sought control of the Chinese Eastern Railway and might have obtained it had it not been for the appointment in 1919, largely at the insistence of the United States, of an inter-allied railway commission (in which Japan, Great Britain, France, Italy, China, and the United States were represented) to operate the road. This inter-allied control lasted into 1922. In 1920, before it was withdrawn, China asserted itself and for a time had the upper hand in administering the line.

The end of the war and the peace conference at Paris gave China an opportunity to state its case to the world. This it did through an able delegation representing not only Peking but also the government at Canton. The conference listened, but in the Treaty of Versailles confirmed Japan in the possession of the former German properties in Shantung. China declined to sign and concluded a separate treaty with Germany. The peace settlements, however, marked some gains. China's late enemies lost their extraterritorial privileges, their special concessions, and their share in the unpaid portion of the Boxer indemnity. By signing the general treaty with Austria—in which the objectionable clauses about Shantung were not included—China acquired membership in the League of Nations, a channel for the further presentation of its position. Japan, moreover, promised eventually to restore Chinese sovereignty in Shantung.

RELATIONS WITH FOREIGN POWERS, 1920–1931: CHINA PARTLY WINS EMANCIPATION

In retrospect it is clear that the World War of 1914–1918 marked a significant turning point in China's relations with foreign powers. From now until the autumn of 1931 China made progress toward regaining the privileges which for nearly three-quarters of a century it had been conceding to aliens. The West was too weakened and divided to impose its will on non-European peoples as forcefully as formerly. Occidental writers were soon talking about "the rising tide of color," "the revolt of Asia," and "the twilight of the white races," and instanced movements in Negro Africa, Egypt, Turkey, India, and China, in support of their contention. Liberals in Europe and America talked approvingly of the "self-determination" of subject peoples and objected to the use of arms to restrain "national" desires. A war-weary Occident was now inclined to prefer peaceful adjustments to gunboat diplomacy. The wave of European political aggression seemed to be receding. The fact that some Western powers had been deprived of their special privileges in China furnished a precedent for demands that the others surrender theirs. Chinese, too, watched with eagerness the success of Turkey in freeing itself from the unique status which foreigners had enjoyed within its borders, and found there encouragement and precedent for similar action. The war, moreover, had greatly stimulated nationalism the world over, and China proved one of the most fertile soils for its growth.

Chinese nationalism employed with great effect an old Chinese weapon, the boycott. Often used by Chinese in local disputes among themselves and from time to time against foreigners, it was now organized on a nation-wide scale. The telegraph and postal service, covering all China like a network, and the rapid growth of daily newspapers helped to make concurrent action possible. Students were eager agitators. The populace was appealed to by slogans, vivid posters, and fiery speeches. The boycott, to be sure, was not unadulterated patriotism. Those responsible for its enforcement often made many a pretty penny from toll levied on goods which they allowed to pass. The boycott, too, was a double-edged weapon, which injured those who wielded it as well as the enemy. Chinese merchants frequently suffered from it as much as the foreigner and secretly were often far from enthusiastic in its support. Moreover, it was hard to sustain over a long period. However, in spite of abuses and defects, the Chinese, powerless in armed conflict with Japan and the West, had developed in it an instrument which proved as potent in attaining their ends as have been some successful wars.

The rising Chinese nationalism had displayed itself in the protest against the Twenty-one Demands and in the delegation at Paris. It now fulminated against the Shantung award of the Treaty of Versailles. Students led in the denunciation. Two cabinet officers regarded as particularly pro-Japanese were forced to resign, and a nation-wide boycott against Japanese goods attacked the enemy at a peculiarly vulnerable point—its commerce.

It was the spirit of nationalism, moreover, which helped to make ineffective a new consortium of bankers of several of the powers, finally agreed upon in 1920 for the financing of loans to China— after Japan, because of American opposition, had given up the attempt to obtain an economic monopoly in parts of Manchuria and Mongolia.

Insistent nationalism was chiefly responsible for the transfer to China by Japan of the former disputed property in Shantung and for simultaneous progress toward the abolition of foreign control in China. In the winter of 1921–1922, at the invitation of the United States, a conference was held in Washington on the limitation of armaments and on Pacific and Far Eastern questions. Competition in the construction of navies and naval bases and friction in the Pacific seemed to threaten another war, and this the conference forestalled. Great Britain, France, Japan, China, Italy, the United States, Belgium, the Netherlands, and Portugal were represented. Once more China urged its claims on the nations. Most of the treaties and agreements which emerged from the gathering affected it, some of them profoundly. Several of them marked another step in the relaxation of foreign domination. The "Four Power Treaty" between Great Britain, the United States, France, and Japan, reënforcing for ten years the *status quo* in the Pacific, tended to stabilize conditions in that area and to insure China an opportunity to work out its salvation untroubled by a general war in that region. In a "Nine Power Treaty" all participants in the Conference agreed to respect the sovereignty, the independence, and the territorial and administrative integrity of China, to give China free opportunity to develop and maintain a stable and effective government, to use their influence to preserve the open door (described as "the principle of equal opportunity for the commerce and industry of all nations throughout the territory of China"), to refrain from taking advantage of conditions in China to seek special privileges which would abridge the rights of subjects or citizens of friendly states, and to respect China's rights as a neutral in any war to which it was not a party. The nine powers agreed to a revision, by a commission, of the duties on imports into China. They also promised to appoint a commission to study extraterritoriality with a view to assisting China in effecting legislative and judicial reforms which would make possible its relinquishment. Those having postal agencies in China agreed to discontinue them not later than January 1st, 1923. The powers declared it to be their purpose to withdraw their armed forces from China as soon as it assured the protection of the lives and property of foreigners within its borders. Resolutions were adopted concerning foreign radio stations in China, the unification of Chinese railways, the reduction of Chinese military forces, the Chinese Eastern Railway, and the notification of all of the powers of the treaties and agreements which each had with China. Finally, the conference gave Japan and China the opportunity to come to an understanding about Shantung. Japan proved conciliatory and promised to return the former German holdings in the province. However, it retained a share in some of the mines and large commercial interests and landholdings in Tsingtao and insisted upon lending to China the sum needed for the redemption of the railways with the provision that during the term of the loan the roads were to have a Japanese traffic manager. The Twenty-one Demands and the treaties of 1915 still rankled in Chinese breasts, and Japan, while refusing to reëxamine them, declared, although not by formal agreement, that it would abandon all claims to preference in loans for railway building in South Manchuria and Inner Mongolia, to priority in the appointment of advisers and instructors in South Manchuria, and the reservation made in 1915 that the fifth group of the demands should be postponed for further discussion. At the conference, moreover, Great Britain promised to restore Weihaiwei to China, and did so, although after a considerable delay for which it was by no means entirely responsible, in October, 1930. China did not obtain all that it asked of the conference, but made marked headway toward doing so.

In still another direction—in its relations with Russia—China registered some gains, although often incomplete and much qualified, in its struggle to free itself from partial foreign domination. The Russian revolution of 1917, which overthrew the Czarist régime and by the end of the year replaced it with Communist control, could not but alter Sino-Russian relations. For a time collapse and civil strife in Siberia made impossible any aggressive Russian action. In 1919 the Peking authorities took advantage of the situation to renew Chinese control in Outer Mongolia. For more than a year Chinese troops and diplomacy succeeded in reëstablishing Chinese authority at Urga. Early in 1921, however, Baron Ungern, a picturesque anti-Communist Russian, captured the city and brought Chinese rule to an end. In the summer of 1921, he in turn was driven out by Soviet troops, and a government was set up which was friendly to Moscow and which, for most practical purposes, became one of the Union of Socialist Soviet Republics. While, by the treaty of May 31st, 1924, Soviet Russia recognized Outer Mongolia as "an integral part of the Republic of China," it regarded Outer Mongolia as autonomous, entitled to freedom from Chinese interference in its foreign affairs, and opened direct relations with it. The influence of China became negligible and that of Soviet Russia dominant.

In some other phases of its relations with Russia China had better success. For a time after the Russian revolution, the Czarist diplomatic and consular staffs continued to function in China, supported by the Boxer indemnity. Many adherents of the old régime—"White Russians"—took refuge in China. In August, 1920, China suspended Boxer indemnity payments to Russians, the following month it withdrew its recognition of the Czarist officials within its borders, and before long the Russian post offices in China were closed. While, theoretically, the old treaties with Russia were intact, in practice Russians were deprived of their extraterritorial privileges. In 1919 the Soviets issued a manifesto offering to negotiate with China on the basis of the renunciation of all special privileges of Russia and Russians in China, the cancellation of further payments on the Boxer indemnity, the restoration to China, without compensation, of the Chinese Eastern Railway and the mines and forests acquired by the Czar's government from China, and the return of territory seized by the former régime. This action of Moscow was not from such disinterested generosity as might at first appear. It was good policy. Russia hoped for the spread of the Communist revolution into the Far East. Much of what Moscow proposed to give up it no longer possessed, and its surrender of extraterritoriality would injure chiefly the Russian "Whites"—on whom the Soviets were quite happy to inflict suffering.

When it came to actual negotiations, Soviet Russia proved unwilling to fulfill some of its promises, particularly those concerning the Chinese Eastern Railway. Russian activity in Mongolia, too, was a bone of contention. May 31st, 1924, however, an agreement was signed which annulled all treaties between the Czarist government and China and relinquished Russian extraterritoriality and consular jurisdiction, the Russian portion of the Boxer indemnity, and special Russian concessions in China. But, while consenting to the principle of the eventual restoration of the Chinese Eastern Railway to China, the agreement provided that the Chinese must buy back the line, that the amount and conditions of repurchase and of the provisional management should be determined by conference between the two governments, and that in the meantime the road should be operated under the terms of the original contract of 1896. In the case of the Boxer indemnity, the Russian share was not to be canceled unconditionally but was to be set aside for education among the Chinese and was to be administered by a commission of three—two appointed by China and one by Russia—no action of which could be taken without a unanimous vote. Russia, therefore, held a veto in the use of the funds.

China had gained much, but Mongolia and the Chinese Eastern Railway—especially the latter—remained causes of friction. In Outer Mongolia China had lost all but the name of suzerainty. While in the case of the Chinese Eastern Railway it was specifically declared that the road was a purely commercial enterprise, the recognition of the reëntry of Russia as an effective force in its control, after it had been all but eliminated during the period of chaos and civil strife in Siberia following the revolution, might well prove a renewal of its threat to the territorial integrity of Northern Manchuria. September 20th, 1924, Russia entered into an agreement with "The Autonomous Government of the Three Eastern Provinces"—meaning, of course, Chang Tso-lin—which attempted a settlement of the question of the Chinese Eastern Railway. It was much like that of May, although it differed in some important respects. The Russia of the Soviets was no more minded to relinquish its control over the road than had been the Russia of the Czars.

Joint management by Russians and Chinese inevitably led to repeated friction. This was increased by the anti-Communist, anti-Russian reaction in China in 1927, especially since Chang Tso-lin was particularly bitter against Communism. In July, 1929, the dissension culminated in the seizure of the road by the Chinese and the dismissal and arrest of the Soviet officials. For several months a virtual state of war between China and Russia existed along the Siberian-Manchurian frontier. Before January, 1930, a Russian invasion forced the Chinese to restore the *status quo* in the operation of the railway, but negotiations looking toward a permanent settlement dragged on for months, unsatisfactorily and inconclusively. Russia had strengthened its hold on the railway, for it demanded greater loyalty than before from the Russian employees. Moreover, it was pouring into the Manchurian market many of the manufactured products which had come out of the Five Year Program.

In Sinkiang, too, Soviet Russia was a threat to China. This region, never securely Chinese, was more and more cut off from China proper by the internal disorders in the Republic. On the other hand, by 1932 improved rail communication between Moscow and the Russian territory west of Sinkiang, combined with the automobile, facilitated the Russian commercial penetration of the region. This was followed by Russian political influence, but that did not become predominant.

Toward the end of 1932, Russian relations with China, strained and sometimes broken off after the conservative reaction in Nationalist ranks in 1927, became more friendly. China, looking for support against Japan in Manchuria and impatient with the failure of the League of Nations to restrain the Nipponese, was willing to bid for Russian support. Accordingly Nanking and Moscow resumed cordial diplomatic relations.

Against the other privileges of Westerners China made continued gains. Several more of the major powers remitted the unpaid portions of the Boxer indemnity due them—the United States in 1924 (a part had been previously remitted, in 1908), France in 1922 and 1923, Japan in 1923, Great Britain in 1925, Belgium in 1925 and 1927, and Italy in 1925. Never was the remission unconditional. In the case of France, the funds were in part to be used for the satisfaction of the Far Eastern creditors of the (French) Banque Industrielle de Chine, which had recently failed. Of the amount due Italy, a sum was set aside for the redemption of a loan made to China by the Banca Italiana per la Cina. In some instances the returned portions were to be allocated to educating Chinese—with the assumption, either tacit or expressed, that the education would be of the type calculated to spread the culture of the remitting power. Parts of the funds, too, were to be assigned to the construction of works of public utility, such as railways, with the provision that the materials used should be purchased in the remitting country. It must be added, however, that China willingly entered upon these arrangements and bent the administration of most of them to its own ends. The continuation of the allocation of so large a part of the customs revenues to the "indemnity services," moreover, helped to preserve the unity of the Customs Administration in the face of perils of disintegration.

Rather noteworthy progress was made by the Chinese in regaining control of the portions of their cities administered by aliens. The German concessions at Hankow and Tientsin and the Austro-Hungarian concession at Tientsin were restored to China as a result of the World War. The Russian concessions fell into her hands some time after the collapse of the Czarist régime. Persistent pressure, by boycott, agitation, and force, brought about increased Chinese participation in some more and the return of still others. This pressure first became spectacular after an incident on May 30th, 1925. A strike in Shanghai led to a demonstration in the International Settlement by students and other sympathizers with the workers. The police arrested some of the agitators and in the disturbances which ensued, goaded to desperate self-defense by the attacks of Communists who wished to provoke them to violence, fired into the crowd. Resentment against foreign privileges under the "unequal treaties"—as the Chinese called them—was already acute and the shooting of May 30th precipitated an anti-foreign, and especially an anti-British explosion. The direction of the agitation against the British seems to have been the deliberate policy of certain left-wing Communist elements. A boycott was organized which lasted for months and cost British merchants millions of dollars. On June 23d, 1925, an armed clash occurred between the Chinese and the defenders of Shameen, the foreign settlement in Canton. In August and September, 1926, a fight between British and

Chinese forces over an attack on British shipping, at Wanhsien, on the upper Yangtze, further strained the relations between the two countries. When, in 1926 and 1927, the Nationalists moved northward into the Yangtze Valley, there was widespread propaganda against "imperialism," particularly as represented by the British. Foreigners, especially British and Americans, were harassed, in some instances by the armed seizure of their properties and often by persecutions inflicted on their Chinese associates, by local boycotts and the cutting off of their supplies, and by threatened mob action. These conditions and the urgent advice or actual orders of their consuls and the pleas of their Chinese friends led many to come out of the interior and either to seek refuge in the port cities or to go abroad. The British concessions at Hankow and Kiukiang were seized by the Nationalists, and only large forces of foreign marines kept the radicals from annexing the settlements at Shanghai. Under the circumstances, foreigners felt it necessary to yield to some of the demands—especially since several years before 1925 Great Britain, against whom much of the agitation was now directed, had embarked on a policy of relaxing her special privileges in China. The Shanghai Mixed Court, by which Chinese defendants were tried, and which had been taken over by the consular body in 1911, was restored to Chinese control on January 1st, 1927. Chinese were admitted to membership on the councils of the French Concession and the International Settlement in Shanghai, of the British concession in Tientsin, and of the International Settlement (Kulangsu) at Amoy. The British concessions at Hankow, Kiukiang, Chinkiang, and Amoy were returned to the Chinese, the first two in 1927, the third in 1929, and the fourth (not Kulangsu but a small area in the city) in 1930. In 1929 Belgium agreed to return her concession in Tientsin. Several concessions remained in the hands of the powers, however, and in 1930 Japan declined to accede to China's suggestion that she restore the one held by her in Hankow.

The Chinese, moreover, regained the right to fix their own import and export duties. For some time they had been working toward this end, and a prolonged international conference on the question was held at Peking in 1925 and 1926. In 1928 and early in 1929, practically all the powers, with the exception of Japan, entered into agreements with China consenting to tariff autonomy. Japan signed such an agreement in May, 1930, and ratifications of a similar Sino-Dutch treaty were exchanged in November of that year. On February 1st, 1929, China resumed tariff autonomy by putting into effect a schedule of duties fixed by itself, but practically the same as those determined at the Peking conference. This was raised rather markedly in 1931. The Customs Administration, moreover, while still largely under the direction of foreigners—as it had been for two generations—and maintained much on the old lines, was more and more under direct Chinese control. Its policy was determined by the Ministry of Finance, Chinese were rapidly promoted into higher ranks, no new foreigners were taken onto the staff, and the tendency was to use the aliens already employed not as administrators but as technicians.

In the abolition of extraterritoriality China, while making considerable progress, was not so completely successful. The commission promised by the Washington Conference was appointed and visited China, reporting in 1926. It believed that the time was not yet ripe for the extinction of extraterritoriality, but offered suggestions looking toward the gradual attainment of the goal. China made various attempts to hasten the desired end. New treaties based on "equality" and specifically providing for tariff autonomy and the jurisdiction of local courts and laws over their respective nationals were signed with Bolivia (1919), Persia (1920), Germany (1921 and 1928), Russia (1924), Austria (1925), Finland (1926), Greece (1928), Poland (1929), Czechoslovakia (1930), and Turkey. Several of the treaties by which extraterritoriality had been granted provided for their termination in whole or in part at fixed dates or after certain periods of notice. In 1926 the Chinese Government took advantage of these clauses to declare the treaties at an end at the specified dates, and to say that new treaties would be negotiated only on the basis of equality and reciprocity. Such notes were sent to Belgium and Spain in 1926, to Portugal and Japan in 1928, and to Mexico in 1929. In July, 1928, the Chinese Ministry of Foreign Affairs issued a declaration to the effect that all "unequal treaties . . . which have already expired shall *ipso facto* be abrogated and new treaties shall be concluded" and that the Nationalist Government would immediately take steps to terminate those "unequal treaties which have not yet expired and conclude new treaties."

Most of the powers against whom specific steps had been taken protested the legality of the action, denying that the wording of the treaties gave China the right which it claimed. Mexico alone acceded. With the others prolonged negotiations followed. Belgium brought its case before the Court of International Justice but later withdrew it and negotiated a new agreement. With Belgium, Spain, and Portugal treaties were made which provided not only for China's resumption of tariff autonomy but for the end of extraterritoriality. Similar treaties were negotiated with Italy and Denmark. In each instance, however, China agreed, through an exchange of notes, that in the event that by January 1st, 1930, detailed arrangements had not been made between China and the power concerned for the assumption by China of jurisdiction over the subjects of that power, the abolition of extraterritoriality was not to go into effect until all the powers signatory to the treaties arising from the Washington Conference of 1921–1922 (in the case of Belgium, until a majority of the powers "now" possessing extraterritorial privileges) should have assented to it. Switzerland agreed to relinquish extraterritoriality only when all the other treaty powers had done so. What had been obtained, therefore, was merely a promise. By 1928, however, of the approximately 130,000 foreigners (excluding Koreans) living in China, 75,000, or over half, were without extraterritorial status.

Against Great Britain, Japan, France, and the United States—who, after all, controlled China's relations by way of the sea—China made little progress. These powers were, to be sure, conciliatory, and Great Britain especially offered (January 27th, 1927) to make important modifications in the privileges of its subjects in China. They persisted, however, in conserving the main structure of extraterritoriality. New treaties with the Netherlands, Norway, and Sweden, moreover, while assenting to the resumption by China of tariff autonomy, contained no provision for the end of the obnoxious status of aliens. Brazil and Peru also retained their extraterritorial privileges, although a new treaty with Peru was in process of negotiation. To a Chinese note of April, 1929, to the powers, stating that before January 1st, 1930, the new civil and commercial codes would be ready for promulgation and that China desired to have restrictions on its jurisdictional sovereignty removed at the earliest possible moment, Great Britain, France, and the United States replied that the time was not ripe—that China had not sufficiently reëstablished order and reorganized its courts and laws to be able to insure protection and justice to foreigners. An American note suggested the gradual abolition of extraterritoriality but not the immediate complete relinquishment which China desired. Earlier notes and declarations by China in 1928 and 1929 and its invocation of Article XIX of the Covenant of the League of Nations proved equally fruitless. In December, 1929, Nanking announced, by unilateral action, the termination of extraterritoriality, to take effect on January 1st, 1930, but by ordering the appropriate branches of the Government to frame regulations to make this operative it postponed the actual assumption of jurisdiction over the foreigners involved. May 4th, 1931, Nanking issued a mandate announcing the completion of these regulations and declaring that they would go into effect on January 1st, 1932. The regulations stipulated that special chambers should be set up in certain courts for the trial of cases in which foreigners were involved and provided for legal counselors for these, of whom some might be foreigners. The Japanese attack on China in the autumn of 1931 and domestic political troubles prevented the Chinese from carrying out their purpose at the announced time.

The powers concerned did not consider that these declarations had terminated their rights. They were, however, yielding, even if slowly. The British and American Governments were in close consultation and were disposed to submit to the inevitable, but many thorny questions remained to be settled—among them that of the status of the foreign settlements in Shanghai.

The powers were less inclined than formerly to impose their will on China by gunboats and marines. A decade and a half before, such violence against foreigners by Chinese as that at Nanking in March, 1927, would almost undoubtedly have been followed promptly by vigorous reprisals and the imposition of heavy indemnities. As it was, no force was used—except a barrage which was laid down by the gunboats to bring to an end violence against aliens and permit them to escape—and the settlement, reached more than a year later, was surprisingly lenient.

It must be added that existing conditions often reënforced the arguments of those who sought to delay the end of extraterritoriality. In the chaotic state of much of the country, the course of even-handed justice was repeatedly disturbed by military and political interference. Foreign merchants and property interests frequently encountered serious legal difficulties. Well-informed Chinese often lamented the Government's failure to register substantial improvement in the actual operation of laws and courts. The "unequal treaties" were passing, but rather because of Chinese propaganda and of foreign reluctance to back them by arms than because of added security to foreign life and property.

Even Japan, with so much at stake, for several years was very much less unyielding than in 1915. In May, 1928, when the Nationalists moved northward through Shantung, a serious clash occurred at Tsinan between the Kuomintang armies and the troops which had been sent by Tokyo to defend Japanese subjects against possible violence (not unlikely in view of what had happened at Nanking the preceding year). The Nanking Government appealed to the League of Nations, but since it was not yet recognized by the powers the League did not accept its plea. The controversy was ultimately settled by direct negotiations between the two governments. Tokyo accepted China's guarantee of protection to Japanese life and property and in May, 1929, withdrew its troops from Shantung.

In South Manchuria, where it was more strongly intrenched, Japan at first was not unconciliatory. It permitted the Chinese to construct railway lines. Some of these, to be sure, were financed by Japanese funds and were feeders to the (Japanese) South Manchuria Railway. Others of them, it believed, offered competition to Japanese roads and contravened an agreement of 1905 (not contained in any formal treaty) which Tokyo held forbade such construction. China did not have the mailed fist shaken under its nose so much as formerly.

By 1931, Manchuria seemed to have become clearly Chinese, at least in population. To be sure, Russia still had an effective voice in the management of the Chinese Eastern Railway, and Japan retained the South Manchuria Railway, with its railway zone and with important mines. In Dairen (Dalny) on the leased territory on the Liaotung Peninsula, Japan had developed a great modern city as the chief port of the Three Eastern Provinces. It had huge and increasing investments in the region which it could not willingly allow to be jeopardized. Koreans, now Japanese subjects, were moving by hundreds of thousands into Manchuria from their overpopulated homeland. All Manchuria remained a potential seat of grave international friction. In actual occupancy, however, the Chinese were more and more claiming it as their own. Until the twentieth century, Manchuria had remained largely undeveloped, although Chinese were settling extensively in the southernmost of the three provinces. The Manchus long tried to keep the northern and larger portions for their exclusive use. Yet the Chinese pressed into it and by the beginning of the century were more than three-fourths of its population. However, compared with the provinces south of the Great Wall, in 1900 Manchuria was still sparsely settled. During the twentieth century the Chinese poured in by the millions. Especially under the Republic, when so much of North China was troubled by civil war and famine and Manchuria was relatively prosperous and orderly, the migration swelled. By 1930, the greatest movement of population on the planet was that into the Three Eastern Provinces. Whatever Russia or Japan might do, it was clear that the region would long remain Chinese in population and culture. Under these circumstances, the demands of a nationalistic China for increased control were greatly strengthened. By 1931, as has been suggested, the Chinese had built or were building or projecting numerous railways which would render them in part independent of the Japanese and Russian lines. They were making some of these debouch at Hulutao, on the Gulf of Liaotung, so that they might have a port to rival the Japanese Dairen.

The Chinese attitude toward aliens was changing. For many years, and especially after 1900, foreigners had acted as though they were living in a conquered and subject country, many of them with open contempt for the Chinese. The Chinese had writhed under an attitude so galling to a people who traditionally regarded outsiders as barbarians, but they had had, perforce, to tolerate it. They now discovered that the powers had become only half-hearted in defending the treaty rights of their citizens. Particularly in the interior, therefore, the foreigner did not enjoy the prestige and security which once were his. Moreover, the

Chinese authorities were often powerless to protect aliens against bandits and "Communists." As a result, in the 1920's, not since the treaties of 1858 authorized travel in the interior had foreign life and property been so unsafe. Scores—particularly those whose calling took them most outside the main centers, the missionaries—were captured by bandits and held for ransom.

In spite of the gain which the Chinese had made toward abolishing special foreign privileges, by 1931 these were far from having disappeared. Several of the powers, among them the majority of those having the chief commercial and territorial stakes in China—Great Britain, the United States, Japan, and France— retained most of what they had once possessed. Many alien residents still viewed the Chinese with disdain. Foreign gunboats continued to patrol the coast and the Yangtze River and did not hesitate to fire on those attacking the persons or shipping of their nationals. The legations, reluctant to move to Nanking, were ensconced in their semi-fortress in Peking. China had made amazing inroads on the structure of alien control and privilege, but much of it remained.

RELATIONS WITH FOREIGN POWERS: RENEWED JAPANESE AGGRESSION: INITIAL STAGES, 1931–1937

In 1931 new and startling developments occurred which altered the entire situation in the Far East. Indeed, they were the preliminary stages of what culminated in the second world war of the twentieth century. So far as China was concerned, the slightly less than six years from September, 1931, to July, 1937, embraced the initial section of the renewed struggle with Japan. The second portion was from July, 1937, to December, 1941, and the third section, which began in the last-named month, is not yet (1945), completed.

In September, 1931, Japan, for several years conciliatory and friendly, suddenly reversed its policy and began waging what in effect was an undeclared war on China. The Japanese had become increasingly restive over the Chinese encroachments on what they believed to be their rights in Manchuria. Japan was crowded and its population was rapidly growing with no chance of an outlet through emigration. The country had never recovered from the readjustment which followed the World War and suffered acutely in the world-wide depression which began in 1929. To many Japanese Manchuria seemed their "life line" and their control of that region the one hope of escaping a national collapse. From the military standpoint, Manchuria appeared necessary as a strategic position against a possible war with Russia. Moreover, in case of a naval war with the United States or some other power, it would prove invaluable as a source of raw materials and perhaps of manufactures. A growing group of military men and super-patriots were impatient with the half-way measures of the politicians and diplomats. Chinese nationalists, on the other hand, were more and more resentful of Japan's special position in Manchuria. Chang Hsüeh-liang's government was not always considerate of Japanese interests and was frequently extremely annoying to the Japanese authorities.

As is so often the case when a tense situation exists, the immediate incidents which provoked the crisis were comparatively trivial. In the summer of 1931 a conflict occurred between Chinese and Koreans over an irrigation ditch, but with no casualties. Koreans, overcrowded at home, had moved into the adjacent portions of Manchuria by the hundreds of thousands. For the most part they remained Japanese subjects. In Korea, by the disorders in Manchuria, public opinion was inflamed and anti-Chinese riots broke out with heavy losses of Chinese life and property. In June, moreover, a Japanese army officer and several companions were shot by Chinese soldiers in an interior station in Manchuria, and the Japanese maintained that the Chinese authorities were not sufficiently active in punishing the offenders.

On the night of September 18–19th Japanese troops seized Mukden, alleging that Chinese had blown up a part of the track of the South Manchurian Railway near the city. This Japanese action was followed, in the next few weeks, by the occupation of other strategic centers in Manchuria, including several in North Manchuria, in what had been regarded as the Russian sphere of interest. Chang Hsüeh-liang, most of whose forces were south of the Great Wall, had headquarters in Peking but with manifestly waning prestige. With the collapse of Chang's régime in the Three Eastern Provinces, temporary local governing committees of Chinese were set up, with assistance and often under pressure from the Japanese. Early in 1932 a Manchuria-wide government, known as Manchoukuo, was organized, ostensibly by Chinese and Mongols, but manifestly with Japanese assistance and reenforced by Japanese troops and many Japanese advisers. On February 18th, 1932, Manchoukuo declared its independence of China. P'u-i, the last Emperor of the Ch'ing dynasty, who, it will be recalled, had ruled from 1908 to 1912 under the reign title of Hsüan T'ung, was asked to be the head or Regent. He accepted and was inaugurated in his new capital, Changchun (soon renamed Hsinching, the "new capital"), on March 9th, 1932. Later in the year Japan officially recognized the new régime and negotiated with it a defensive alliance. Obviously Manchoukuo could not exist without outside support and neutral observers believed it to be a puppet created and controlled by the Japanese.

The new government, upheld by Japanese bayonets, had an uneasy course. Much of Manchuria was overrun by irregular troops, by bandits, and by volunteer corps which received aid from the Chinese south of the Great Wall. The Japanese found the ensuing guerrilla warfare disappointingly expensive and prolonged.

By 1933 Japan seemed to have pacified Manchuria fairly thoroughly. Early in January, 1933, Manchoukuoan-Japanese forces began the invasion of the province of Jehol, which Japan claimed to be part of Manchoukuo. Within a few weeks the Chinese defense crumbled and the occupation was completed. Chang Hsüeh-liang, discredited once more by his failure to defend the North, resigned and left Peking, though later taking high office under Nanking. In April, 1933, the Japanese, alleging the necessity of protecting the recently won boundaries against Chinese aggression, moved south of the Great Wall.

In the meantime in China proper a vigorous boycott was organized which seriously cut into Japanese trade. Friction occurred, notably in Shanghai, stirred up by lawless elements on both sides. The Japanese believed the Chinese Government to be at least partly responsible for the agitation against them and peremptorily demanded the dissolution of the Shanghai boycott associations. Although the Chinese municipal authorities eventually expressed a willingness to comply, Japanese marines, supported by the fleet, occupied by force Chapei, a densely populated section of the city (beginning January 28th, 1932). In the fighting which followed, Chinese civilians suffered severely and a large section of the city was laid waste. Chinese troops offered an unexpectedly stout resistance and were dislodged only after a month of heavy fighting and when the Japanese had received large reenforcements. Hostilities ceased early in March, 1932, and partly through the machinery of the League of Nations a working peace was restored and the Japanese began to evacuate the occupied areas.

Not unnaturally, the rest of the world was deeply concerned over the Sino-Japanese controversy. Although officially war was not declared between China and Japan, diplomatic relations were maintained, and technically the two nations were at peace, in actual fact war was in progress. Both governments were members of the League of Nations, both had signed the Pact of Paris renouncing war "as an instrument of national policy," and Japan had bound herself by the Nine Power Treaty of 1922 "to respect the sovereignty, the independence, and the territorial and administrative integrity of China." The situation gave the peace machinery of the world its most severe test since the close of the war of 1914–1918.

Promptly after the incident of September 18th, 1931, China appealed to the League of Nations. The American Government also early expressed to Japan and China the hope that both would refrain from further hostilities. Space forbids a recounting of all the diplomatic steps taken in and out of the League of Nations to bring about a peaceful settlement. Japan at first insisted on direct negotiations with China. China refused to enter upon them while Japanese troops were in Chinese territory. Tokyo declared that it had no territorial aspirations in Manchuria but gave the impression of being very reluctant to allow the League to act. As a rule, the United States and the League worked in fairly close conjunction. Moscow, absorbed in its Five Year Plan, was not disposed to enter into active opposition to Tokyo, even though the resumption of Russo-Chinese diplomatic relations, at the end of 1932, made the Japanese uneasy. January 8th, 1932, the United States notified both China and Japan that it could not recognize any agreements between Japan and China which would "impair the treaty rights of the United States or its citizens in

China, including those which relate to the sovereignty, independence, territorial and administrative integrity of the Republic of China" or "any situation, treaty, or agreement which may be brought about contrary to the covenants and obligations of the Pact of Paris." This note, while directed in diplomatically correct language to both Japan and China, was in reality a notice to Tokyo that the latter's actions in Manchuria would not be approved by Washington. From the name of the American Secretary of State who devised and sent it, the policy thus expressed became known as the Stimson Doctrine. It was in the direct tradition of American Far Eastern policy and marked a step toward the more active participation of the United States in the effort to save China from Japan.

The League of Nations found the problem extremely knotty. The smaller member nations vigorously denounced Japanese action, for if it were allowed to go unrebuked and unchecked, their own safety was threatened. The larger member powers were more guarded. Both Japan and China agreed to the appointment by the League of an international commission of inquiry. This commission, headed by the Earl of Lytton, proceeded to the Far East and made a study extending over several months. In the autumn of 1932 it reported to the League, giving an account of events and suggesting a method of settlement which it felt would safeguard the interests of both contestants. The report satisfied neither China nor Japan, but the Japanese were the more outspoken in their disapproval.

On February 24th, 1933, the Assembly of the League, acting under Article XV of its Covenant, adopted findings which condemned Japan, and recommended a method of settlement by negotiation between Japan and China in close coöperation with a committee on which the League, the United States, and Russia were to be represented. Japan dissented and March 27th, 1933, served notice on Geneva of its intention to withdraw from membership. The issue was now squarely joined and the honor and perhaps the very life of both the League and Japan were at stake.

By the summer of 1933, however, it was clear that at least for the time being Japan was the victor. May 31st, 1933, China and Japan signed a truce by which Chinese troops were to be withdrawn from an area between Peking and the Great Wall, and the Japanese were to retire north of that barrier. This truce was in effect a treaty of peace by which Nanking tacitly acquiesced in Japan's position in Manchuria. In Manchuria Japanese were building railways which would greatly diminish the importance of the Chinese Eastern and were negotiating with the Russians for the purchase of that line. Except for bandits, armed opposition to the new régime of Manchoukuo had been crushed.

The year 1933 did not mark any sharp dividing line in Sino-Japanese relations. The Japanese army was clearly intent on using its enhanced control of Manchuria as a preliminary to further advances both southward and westward.

In this Japan was actuated in part by distrust of Russia. Russia was deemed the most probable menace to Japanese plans. Russian Communism was feared. It was, presumably, with the purpose of checkmating Russia that the Japanese army pressed westward into Inner Mongolia, and thus sought to outflank a possible Russian attack through Outer Mongolia. In December, 1932, diplomatic relations between China and Russia, which had suffered from the conflicts of 1927 and 1929, were reëstablished, and this Japan viewed with suspicion as incipient combination against her. To be sure, the Chinese Eastern Railway was removed as a bone of contention. In March, 1935, after long negotiations, Russia sold to Japan her holdings in the line and thus surrendered the sphere of interest in the northern part of Manchuria which she had held since the 1890's. Yet friction was frequent on the borders between Japanese-controlled Manchuria on the one hand and the Russian Far Eastern provinces and Russian-aligned Outer Mongolia on the other. Russia made it clear that any encroachment on Outer Mongolia would not be tolerated. Armed clashes were frequent in the second half of the 1930's and in 1938 serious fighting occurred near the corner where Manchuria, Siberia, and Korea met. In November, 1936, Japan and Germany entered into an anti-comintern pact, clearly aimed at Russia, and in August, 1937, China and Russia signed a non-aggression pact, quite obviously as a warning to Japan. However, neither Russia nor any other of the powers was as yet willing to undertake war with Japan on behalf of China.

After 1933 Japan continued to strengthen its hold on Manchuria and to develop the resources of the region in its own interest. It further reduced the armed resistance to its rule. It gave the area a unified and fairly stable currency, tied to the yen. It greatly curtailed the use of opium, long a severe scourge. It gave to Manchoukuo a monarchical form of government. On March 1, 1934, P'u-i, hitherto the Regent of the new state, became officially Emperor under the reign title of Kang Tê. The new order was to be based upon Confucianism. Yet the resounding designation of the ostensible ruler and the nominal independence of Manchoukuo were not permitted to shake Japanese domination. Japanese were in key official positions either openly or as "advisers." Extraterritorial privileges were abolished, but this was a gesture which deceived no one. If anything, it brought more fully under the Japanese such non-Japanese aliens as were still in the region. Japanese rapidly extended the railway system, partly for strategic reasons in case of war with Russia and partly to open to exploitation the resources of the puppet state. The endeavor was made to knit Manchuria into the economic fabric of the Japanese Empire. In general, to Manchuria was allocated the role of supplying raw materials for the industries of Japan and of providing foreign exchange for the Japanese bloc. Coal, oil shale, iron ore, and timber were to be contributions to Japan and the sale of the soya bean and its derivatives, oil and bean cake, for which the chief market had been in Germany, was to aid in enhancing the imperial supply of foreign exchange. Iron works were developed, notably at Anshan. Japanese poured in, chiefly as business men, officials, and soldiers. The attempt of the authorities to stimulate the settlement of Japanese farmers on the land met with scant success, for the latter had to compete with Chinese and Koreans who had a lower standard of living and had already taken up most of the best soil. After a pause, the immigration of Chinese from the south of the wall was resumed. In 1936 Manchoukuo was said to have a population of nearly thirty-four millions which was being augmented at the rate of over eight hundred thousand a year. In foreign circles there was some question as to whether Manchuria was proving profitable to Japan as a whole, but there could be no doubt that the hold of Japan on the region was tightening. The articulate Chinese south of the Great Wall still regarded the area as an integral part of the Republic. If possible, they were even more insistent that the Japanese occupation was aggression and could never be legalized, but for the time being there seemed not the slightest chance that Japan would be dislodged.

After 1933 the Japanese army continued to edge forward in Inner Mongolia and in the northeastern provinces of China proper. In Inner Mongolia the Japanese endeavored to take advantage of the long struggle between Chinese and Mongols. The Chinese were chiefly farmers, seeking to push farther the cultivated land at the expense of the grazing grounds of the pastoral Mongols. Climatically the region was marginal. Not always was the rainfall sufficient to mature planted crops. Yet the Chinese pressure of population was so great that many were willing to take the risks. The Mongols were, quite naturally, antagonistic. The Japanese professed to side with the latter. However, the Mongol leaders found that Japanese occupation meant the substitution of annoying competitors by dominating masters and did not always willingly coöperate. By 1937 the Japanese were in control of most of Chahar, the province whch lay immediately to the west of Jehol. Presumably they would press on westward into Suiyüan. In 1933, as we hinted a few paragraphs above, by an arrangement known as the Tangku truce, the Chinese and Japanese agreed to withdraw their troops from an area in the northeast of the province of Hopei, thus demilitarizing a zone next to Manchuria. This would prevent effective Chinese efforts to regain Manchuria and marked a Japanese step southward of the Great Wall. In 1935 the Japanese constrained the Chinese entirely to remove one of their armies from Hopei, to dissolve units of the Kuomintang in the region, and to undertake to suppress anti-Japanese activities. In 1935 there were rumors that Japan was planning the organization of an "autonomous" government, independent of Nanking and presumably under Japanese control, which would embrace Hopei, Shansi, Shantung, Chahar, and Suiyüan. Nanking sought to forestall the move by setting up a regime in the eastern part of Hopei which, while still affiliated with it, would be less objectionable to the Japanese.

Japan was serving warning on the rest of the world that it would not brook outside interference in its designs in China. In 1933 it proposed the close political and economic collaboration, through formal protocol, of itself, China, and Manchoukuo, but, since this meant in practice Japanese control, Nanking would not give its consent. In 1934 a spokesman for Tokyo's foreign office declared that Japanese would oppose "any attempt on the part of China to avail herself of the influence of any other country in order to resist Japan" and would include in this category "detailing military and naval instructors or military advisers to China" and loans "to provide funds for political uses." Part of this protest arose from efforts of the League of Nations, now anathema to Japan, to assist China in her economic reconstruction. In 1935 a project for the reform of China's currency, believed by the Japanese to have been inspired by a British expert, brought down a blast of condemnation from Tokyo. In other words, Japan was seeking to make China a protectorate.

Leading Chinese were striving to put the country in readiness for the heightened struggle which must come with Japan. Chinese students, in their youthful ardor, sought to organize against Japanese encroachments. Older heads in the government, apprehensive of provoking the extremists in Japan, sought to restrain the hot-heads but labored assiduously to make such preparations as they could for a war which might be postponed but which, short of a miracle, could not be avoided without abject submission. The building of roads for automobiles was pushed. Most of the highways so constructed were without rock surface but they were better than nothing. The railroad from Wuchang to Canton was completed, thus giving through rail communication between Peking and Canton except for the unbridged Yangtze. Several other railways were built. Industrialization proceeded. The beginnings of an airforce were made.

In 1936 a peace was patched up between the Kuomintang and the Communists. This came in the course of a long and exhausting struggle which obviously was weakening the country in its resistance to Japan. Chiang Kai-shek, the most powerful figure in the Kuomintang, was pushing for the unification of the country. His most obdurate opponents were the Communists. These, expelled from the Kuomintang in 1927, had kept up their resistance. For some time their chief center was in Kiangsi. There they sought to establish a separate administration. The armies of Chiang Kai-shek pressed them so hard that late in 1934 the Reds evacuated their strongholds in that part of the country. By a series of forced marches they made their way, at a heavy cost in life, over a route of possibly six thousand miles, much of it across incredibly difficult mountain terrain, to the Northwest. Here some Communists were already to be found. Subsequently, in territory in Shensi and in the northeastern portion of Kansu, a strong Communist enclave was developed. The capital was eventually at Yenan, west of the Yellow River, about a hundred miles south of the Great Wall. Chiang Kai-shek endeavored to have his troops attack them there and eliminate them. He entrusted the task to Chang Hsüeh-liang, who had headquarters at Hsianfu. Some of the Communists began fraternizing with Chang's troops and urged that the weakening civil strife be suspended and a common front presented against Japan. When Chiang Kai-shek went to Hsianfu to inspect the progress of the anti-Communist campaign, he was taken captive by Chang Hsüeh-liang (December, 1936). His life was in imminent danger, but late in the month he was released. Apparently he made no formal commitments to his captors, but the war against the Communists was called off and, in theory, harmony was established and coöperation against the Japanese menace undertaken. Yet suspicion persisted on both sides and the ostensible peace was little better than an armed truce. The Communists still maintained what in effect was a distinct government with its own armies and administration.

RELATIONS WITH FOREIGN POWERS: RENEWED JAPANESE AGGRESSION: THE JAPANESE OCCUPATION IS ACTIVELY PUSHED IN CHINA PROPER, 1937–1941

While the Chinese were moving, somewhat haltingly, toward unity and were making progress toward the defense of their country, events in Japan were leading toward a more active extension of Japanese arms in China. Many Japanese, especially among the middle-aged and young, were discontented with conditions in their home land. They were feeling the pinch of economic pressure and were impatient with parliament, the political parties, and the capitalists, for to these they attributed the nation's woes. They wished more control by the military and more vigorous action on the continent. Through a series of assassinations of high officials, the most spectacular of which were in February, 1936, they strove to purge the government of the elements to which they were opposed. Increasingly the control of the army and navy was passing into the hands of extremists, fanatical militarists who dreamed of the expansion of the empire, the expulsion of Western influence from China and, indeed, from all the Far East, and the knitting of East Asia, later enlarged to "Greater East Asia," into a "Co-prosperity Sphere" in whose benefits all its members would share—but in which Japan would hold the hegemony. The chauvinists did not immediately gain full control, but more and more they became the dominant force.

In July, 1937, the Japanese army, presumably emboldened by its increasing power at home and determined on positive action which would commit the nation and press forward the borders of the Japanese sphere before the mounting Chinese resistance could become more formidable, took a further step which precipitated a momentous and titanic struggle. Now, as in September, 1931, what on its face was a minor incident was utilized as the occasion for a decisive move. On the night of July 7, a clash occurred on the edge of Peking between Chinese troops and Japanese who were executing training maneuvers in a section where they had no treaty right to be. Although locally the Chinese were disposed to be conciliatory and to withdraw their troops, punish the responsible officers, and suppress anti-Japanese activities, the Japanese army rushed reënforcements into Hopei. Possibly it had hoped that hostilities could be confined to the North and that it could employ the opportunity to make effective its ambitions in the northeast of China proper and Inner Mongolia. Late in the month the Japanese took Peking. They expanded their operations in Hopei, Chahar, Suiyüan, and Shansi. In the last named province they encountered formidable resistance from the Communists, now (August, 1937) in theory incorporated into the national forces as the Eighth Route Army. Yet, apart from the Communist obstacle, they appeared to be having their own way.

However, the war could not be confined to the North. Apparently the Japanese had underestimated the degree to which the spirit of nationalism had permeated the country. No longer, as during the Anglo-Chinese wars of the preceding century or even as recently as the suppression of the Boxers, could foreign troops operate in one section while the rest of the land kept peaceably about its normal pursuits. Chinese mobs attacked Japanese in several parts of the country. Fighting broke out in and near Shanghai. The central government was clear that the hour for final decision had struck and that the Japanese must be resisted to the full extent of the nation's strength. The best troops and the air force, pitifully small, were thrown into the defense of Shanghai and its neighborhood. The immediate outcome was not long in doubt. The Japanese, with much better and more extensive mechanical equipment, the full command of the sea, and the industrial basis at home for a long struggle, poured in such forces as were required. The Chinese lacked the industries requisite for a modern war, had few well-trained officers, and possessed only a weak air force and no navy. However, they had almost unlimited man-power. In November, 1937, the Chinese retreat from Shanghai began. Early in December of that year Nanking, evacuated by the national government, fell a victim to the advancing Japanese troops amid scenes of wholesale rape and the slaughter of helpless prisoners and civilians which shocked the civilized world. The Chinese moved their capital to Hankow and then, after a few months, to Chungking. Chungking, at the upper end of the difficult gorges of the Yangtze, was comparatively secure from attack except from the air.

Within a very few months after July, 1937, the Japanese were in command of most of the railways, of a large proportion of the lower reaches of the chief navigable rivers, and of several of the main riverine and coastal ports. They were in a position to begin the slow strangulation of China should the latter not acquiesce in their program.

Yet Chinese resistance continued. Thousands of Chinese, including a very large proportion of the student and more substantial classes, moved west to "free" China. There refugee universities set up temporary plants and continued. With striking resolution and with no little skill, machinery was taken west to continue the manufacture of equipment for the maintenance of the struggle. Industrial coöperatives were organized to further both democracy and the production of needed goods. Behind the Japanese lines in "occupied" China guerillas harassed the enemy. Neither the Nationalist government, controlled by the Kuomintang and with Chiang Kai-shek as its leading figure, nor the Communists showed signs of yielding. They were unable to drive the Japanese out. By tradition and temperament the Chinese were better at defensive than offensive warfare. Yet, to their surprise, the Japanese found themselves confronted with a long war.

In pursuance of their plan to win the "coöperation" of the Chinese, the Japanese set up a regime which they hoped would comply with their wishes. They professed to be fighting to liberate the Chinese from Communism and those associated with Chiang Kai-shek. In December, 1937, they set up at Peking what was termed the Provisional Government of the Republic of China with elderly, anti-Kuomintang Chinese in charge. Eventually they induced a former intimate of Sun Yat-sen, Wang Ch'ing-wei, to head a government which they trusted would be something more than provisional. March 30, 1940, the "return" of the "national government" to Nanking was staged amid great pomp. Wang had held high office at Chungking but had broken with that régime. The government of which he was now the titular chief executive was hailed by the Japanese as the legitimate one for the entire country and as representing the real Kuomintang and the heir of the Sun Yat-sen tradition. With it Tokyo entered into treaty relations with a promise for reciprocal respect for each other's territories and sovereignty and for coöperation against Communism and in economic, political, and cultural measures. The new Nanking government gave formal recognition to Manchoukuo and was in turn recognized by the then associates of Japan, Germany and Italy, and their satellites. It was obviously as much a puppet as was Manchoukuo. Wang Ch'ing-wei never possessed real power and died in 1944.

Japan went about the organization of the portions of China proper which it occupied in such fashion as to take advantage of their resources. Mines, railways, telephones, telegraphs, factories, banks, dockyards, and shipping were taken over by Japanese companies or, if the Chinese shared the ownership, the control was in Japanese hands. Japan also reconstituted the schools of "occupied" China in such a way that they would support its aims. Japanese was substituted for English as the second language taught and textbooks were revised to make them friendly to Japan.

Among the dark phases of the Japanese occupation were the rapid extension of the sale and use of narcotics, the dissensions and corruption among Japanese officialdom, and the ruthless treatment of the Chinese.

The Japanese slowly tightened the noose of blockade around the unoccupied portions of China. They had full command of the sea and of most of the main ports. Supplies still reached "free" China through the blockade. They also went in by way of Hongkong, for that was in British hands, and by the railway from French Indo-China to Kunming, formerly Yünnanfu, the leading city of the province of Yünnan. Moreover, with a prodigal expenditure of human labor a track traversible by automobiles was built from the China side of the border to connect with roads and railways in Burma. This was what became famous as the "Burma Road." It was more a symbol and an aid to morale than in goods transported, for it was narrow, in places tortuous, and traversed high divides and deep canyons. Yet it gave connection with Rangoon and so with the outer world, and some freight began to move over it. The Japanese made progress in plugging these holes. In the summer of 1940 the fall of France before German arms, the memorable defeat of the British at Dunkerque, and the threatened German invasion of the British Isles gave Japan the opportunity to bring pressure on these two powers. Through agreement with the Vichy régime in France, Japan sent troops into Indo-China and ended the shipment of supplies into "free" China by road and railway from the convenient ports in that region. In July, 1940, the British authorities, most reluctantly, felt constrained to suspend for three months the shipment of goods to China by way of the Burma Road.

Moreover, for the time being Japan had nothing to fear from Russia. In a pact of April, 1941, framed at a time when Moscow was coöperating with the Axis powers, the two governments entered into a non-aggression agreement. The German invasion of Russia in the summer of 1941 engrossed all the energies of the Soviets on their European front. This meant that Russia was unwilling to enter into a war with Japan and thus to face foes on two fronts. Japan, accordingly, had nothing to fear from that quarter. Moreover, Russia, while maintaining correct diplomatic relations with Chungking, could not be expected to give the latter much help in the form of munitions. Distances for transport across Sinkiang were great and, even had they been shorter, Russia had need for all the war supplies which she could muster and, in addition, would not risk antagonizing Japan to the point of hostilities.

RELATIONS WITH FOREIGN POWERS: RENEWED JAPANESE AGGRESSION: THE ENTRANCE OF THE BRITISH EMPIRE, THE UNITED STATES, AND THE NETHERLANDS INTO THE FAR EASTERN STRUGGLE, DECEMBER, 1941, AND AFTER

On December 7, 1941 (December 8, by Chinese time), by dramatic and sudden Japanese moves, the Sino-Japanese conflict was broadened and became a more integral part of the vast world struggle then in progress. The British Empire, the Netherlands, and the United States became involved in war with Japan and, therefore, were actively on the side of China. This brought to the assistance of China the resources of these powers, in the aggregate enormous, and boded ill for Japan.

The events of December 7–8, 1941, while bursting like a bomb upon a startled world, were a climax, not altogether illogical, of a long development. The League of Nations and the United States had been critical of Japan's adventure in China since its inception in September, 1931. Indeed, American opposition to Japan's advance at the expense of China dated from not long after the Russo-Japanese War of 1904–1905. Commencing with the momentous Hay note of 1899, the Open Door in China had increasingly become one of the major concerns of the foreign policy of the United States. Since its victory over Russia in 1905 Japan had been the chief and growing threat to the realization of that policy. By various means, some of which have been noted in the preceding pages of this chapter, the United States had endeavored to check Japan. Among these were the proposed neutralization of the Manchurian railways (1909), financial consortiums, criticism of the Twenty-one Demands, the blocking soon after the end of the World War of 1914–1918 of Japan's attempts to seize Eastern Siberia and the Chinese Eastern Railway, and the Washington Conference with its Nine Power Treaty and the promise, to which both the United States and Japan were signatories, to respect the sovereignty, the independence, and the territorial and administrative integrity of China. In 1931-1932 the United States had bolstered the courage of the League of Nations in its vain attempt to check Japan in Manchuria and through its Stimson Doctrine had effectively discouraged recognition of Manchoukuo by most of the nations of the earth. On the renewed advance of Japan into China in 1937 the League of Nations and the United States had made clear their disfavor and the United States joined in a conference held in Brussels in pursuance of the terms of the Nine Power Treaty which sought, futilely, to solve the problem presented by Japan's new violation of that agreement. Japanese quite obviously regarded Great Britain as an obstacle to their program in China and wished to eliminate from that land remaining British enclaves and influence. After 1937 and especially after the outbreak of the European war in September, 1939, preoccupied the British and rendered them all but impotent in the Far East, the Japanese inflicted many indignities upon British subjects, both private individuals and officials. Public and governmental opinion in the United States progressively hardened against Japan. Washington long exercised much restraint and contented itself with lodging protests against Japanese violations of American property and persons in China. Even a Japanese attack upon the American gunboat *Panay* in December, 1937, did not bring the United States into the war. However, by successive steps short of war the United States strove to restrain Japan. It strengthened its fleet and its Hawaiian defenses. In July, 1939, it denounced its commercial treaty with Japan and, within the next two years, took measures to restrict exports to Japan of iron, steel scrap, and petroleum products, commodities essential to Japan's armed forces. In July, 1941, by command of the President both Chinese and Japanese assets in the United States were "frozen." The United States also gave financial aid to China. Negotiations between Japan and the United States made it increasingly clear that neither power would accede to the other's proposals for adjusting the difficulties. The United States was unalterably opposed to Japan's program in China and Japan was adamant. Japan, in a formal note, terminated the discussion on the very day that its forces assailed Pearl Harbor, seized the International Settlement in Shanghai, and bombed Singapore and centers in the Philippines.

The early effect of the Japanese attack upon the United States, the British Empire, and the Netherlands Indies was to render the position of China more rather than less perilous. The British were fighting in Europe with their backs to the wall and could not even successfully defend their own possessions in the Far East. Clearly they had little or no resources to spare for China. Moreover, the Chinese leaders had not forgotten that Great Britain had led in forcing open the doors of their country in the preceding century and had been the leader and to them the symbol of the Western imperialism which surging nationalism had led them, especially since 1911, to struggle to throw off. The huge resources of the United States could not be immediately mobilized and made effective in prosecuting the war. For the United States, too, the winning of the fight against Germany and Italy was given priority over the Pacific. In the Pacific distances were vast and Japan had the advantage of the command of most of the littoral of the east coast of Asia. Japan, prepared for some such eventuality as it precipitated in December, 1941, promptly followed up the advantage acquired by its initial moves. On Christmas Day, 1941, Hongkong capitulated and thus another important hole in the cordon which was being tightened around China was stopped. Before the middle of the summer of 1942 Japan had taken the Philippines and Guam, thus cutting off American outposts in the Western Pacific, had captured Singapore, had overwhelmed the Dutch power in the East Indies, and had expelled the British rule from Burma. By the conquest of Burma Japan closed ingress to "free" China by the Burma Road, thereby locking another of the few remaining doors of communication between the fighting Chinese and their friends in the outer world. Japan had all but succeeded in expelling the Westerner from China. Of the Occidental enclaves of a few years earlier, only Portuguese Macao remained, and that on sufferance.

"Free" China showed the effects of the long strain. On the land front a stalemate seemed to have set in. From 1940 to the middle of 1944 the Japanese made few important gains in the interior, but the Chinese could not muster enough power to expel them from positions already acquired. Inflation appeared, both in "free" and "occupied" China. By the middle of 1945 prices were more than fifteen hundred times what they had been five years earlier. Dissensions within the Chinese ranks were not healed. In moving west the national government found itself in part dependent on the landed gentry in Szechwan, as it had earlier been on the bankers, merchants, and manufacturers in the Shanghai area. This tended to make it conservative and to deepen the rift between itself and the Communists, for the latter wished to dispossess the wealthy landowners. Some of the warlords survived and had to be pacified by subsidies. Chiang Kai-shek was compelled, if even a semblance of national unity were to be preserved, to attempt to hold together very diverse groups. Within officialdom corruption and inefficiency were rife. The salaried and professional classes suffered, as is usually the case in marked inflation. The rift between the Kuomintang and the Communists was unhealed. Each maintained its own government and armies, the one centering at Chungking and the other at Yenan. Although the Communists had a representative at Chungking and the latter had the recognition of all the powers but those in the Axis and the adhesion of more of "free" China than did Yenan, no love was lost between the two regimes and Chungking was said to be keeping some of its best troops on the border to watch its rival. While in general in 1944 "free" China was more nearly united under Chungking than it had ever been under Nanking, transportation by automobile was breaking down and with its weakening internal ties were being threatened. This loss of automobiles was partly because of the hard use given the existing cars, partly because of bad roads, partly through the lack of proper fuel, and also because new cars could not be brought in and none could be manufactured in China. Nor did "free" China have the kind of industry essential for the waging of mechanized war.

Slowly their associates in the struggle, chiefly the United States, began to bring in aid through the siege to the beleaguered Chinese. Air communication was developed with India. The route was one of the most difficult in the world, over the high and tangled mountains between Assam and Yünnan, and chronically imperilled by Japanese air attacks. Yet before three years had elapsed after Pearl Harbor freight was being brought in by the air in larger amounts than had ever been transported over the

Burma Road. Before the end of 1944 American air forces in "free" China were mounting, bases for them were built and in operation, and not only were Japanese ships, troops, and installations in China proper being bombed, but Japanese war plants in Manchuria and the Japanese islands were also being hit. Chinese planes, provided by the United States, were in action against the Japanese. British, Chinese, and American forces based on India forced the Japanese out of the north of Burma. Early in 1945 they were so far successful that road communications between China and Assam were opened through a new highway, the Ledo Road, built over difficult terrain and connecting in Yünnan with the Chinese roads. A pipe line, for the conveying of petroleum and petroleum products, was also under construction from Assam to China. Moreover, in the Pacific the Americans were pushing back the Japanese. In May and June, 1942, the American navy inflicted severe defeats upon the Japanese fleet in the Battle of the Coral Sea and the Battle of Midway. That summer American forces won a foothold on Guadalcanal, in the Solomon Islands. By the end of 1944 they had acquired springboards in the Gilbert, Marshall, and Mariana groups, they had recaptured Guam, and they had effected landings in the Philippines and in the process had dealt severe blows to the Japanese navy. In February, 1945, they retook Manila. Before the end of 1944 the Japanese were expelled from the Aleutians. By the middle of 1945 American island-based and carrier-based planes had bombed important centers in Japan, the Kuriles, the Bonin and Volcano groups, and Formosa. Important footholds had been acquired on Iwo Jima (in the Volcano Islands) and on Okinawa (one of the Liu Ch'iu Islands). Moreover, American and British submarines took heavy toll on Japanese shipping, thus making more difficult the utilization by Japan of its overseas empire and the maintenance of its armies of occupation.

Yet, as the Allied and especially the American tide advanced against them, the Japanese strove persistently and with considerable success to push farther into "free" China. In 1944 and the fore part of 1945 they took most of such of the railways as had remained in Chinese hands. In doing so they all but established through rail communication between Manchuria and Canton, largely cutting off from Chungking the parts of China east of that line. They also captured some of the air bases from which American and Chinese planes had been operating. They seized Foochow, one of the few seaports remaining in Chinese hands. The outcome of the titanic struggle seemed to be resolving itself into a race between China's associates, chiefly British and Americans on the one hand, pressing in through the ring of Japan's defenses and bringing succor to the "free" China which had been bearing the long strain of war, and, on the other hand, the drive of the Japanese army to move on into China, dispersing the Chinese armies, and entrenching itself ever more deeply.

In spite of the advance of Japan on its soil, the exhaustion of prolonged war, the dissensions within its borders, and the rapidly mounting inflation, even after 1937 China was making progress in a number of directions. The outside world had difficulty in learning what was taking place in the areas controlled by the Communists, but from such information as seeped through the censorship it seemed probable that under direction of these elements important changes were effected in the north and northeast of China proper. Local administration containing some popular features was being developed and rents and interest rates were being lowered. The leaders were trained in Communist ideology, but thoroughgoing Communism or even the socialism of the Russian type was not being enforced. Elaborate and, in general, effective resistance to the Japanese was organized and maintained. The movement had in it much that was akin to peasant uprisings or of reforms on behalf of the peasants in earlier periods in China's history. In the areas, much larger in extent and population, which were controlled by the Kuomintang through the Chungking regime, progress was also being achieved. Much criticism was directed against the Kuomintang and the party itself contained factions. Some of the latter had what were commonly but rather loosely called Fascist tendencies. Secret societies and dissident groups existed, more or less openly flaunting the authority of the government. Yet Chiang Kai-shek retained his leadership. If anything, it was strengthened. He visited India. He shared in a conference in Cairo, in 1943, with Prime Minister Churchill of Great Britain and President Roosevelt of the United States. Concentration camps were maintained for those deemed dangerous politically, yet through the People's Political Council (first constituted in 1938) an organ was provided for an untrammeled expression of public opinion. In the earlier days of the removal of the center of government to Szechwan, before inflation and war weariness had become acute, something of the thrill of adventure was apparent in the West. Migrants from the coast brought to the interior Western influences and the permeation of Occidental culture in that region was stimulated. Improvements were made in local governments, the enrolment in schools mounted, the opium poppy was suppressed, industrial co-operatives were organized, natural resources were surveyed, efforts were put forth to bring into the Chinese cultural circle the non-Chinese peoples on the Tibetan borders, and the influence of the central government in Sinkiang was strengthened.

Moreover, advance was registered in freeing the land from the restrictions and inequalities imposed by the treaties and conventions of the nineteenth and the fore part of the twentieth century. In "occupied" China Japan went through the motions of turning over to Chinese administration several of the foreign concessions in the ports. These included Japanese concessions in five cities, the International Settlement at Amoy, British concessions in Canton and Tientsin, and the famous and wealthy International Settlement in Shanghai. Steps were taken to restore Chinese authority in the several French concessions and the Italian concession in Tientsin. In 1943 Japan accorded to Nanking the right to tax its subjects and their property. All these measures were transfers of nominal authority to a puppet government which was controlled by Japanese and so were more apparent than real. However, when Japan had been expelled, Occidental powers would find difficulty in reëstablishing their special privileges in the areas affected. In 1943 Great Britain and the United States negotiated new treaties with China in which they surrendered the extraterritorial privileges which had long been a source of friction. That same year the United States repealed the exclusion acts against the Chinese, placed that people on the same quota basis with European immigrants, and permitted the naturalization of Chinese. For China the war was far from being without compensating features.

CHANGES OTHER THAN POLITICAL, 1894–1944: INTRODUCTORY

The developments in China's internal politics and international relations after 1894 were startling and momentous. At the same time, as though these were not enough for any one people to face, a revolution was being wrought in other phases of the nation's life. Under the impact of the Occident all the main features of the structure of Chinese culture were being altered, some of them drastically. The pace was accelerated by the struggle with Japan in the 1930's and 1940's. In less than a generation the Chinese had moved into a different world—economic, religious, intellectual, and social. To ignore the changes would be to miss parts of the picture which may prove the most significant. Since we are to recur to them in later chapters, at this point they can be summarized much more succinctly than have the political events.

The revolution was accentuated by the fact that during these years, especially after 1914, Occidental culture was suffering from profound disturbances. It was contact with a West which itself was being basically modified and much of whose life was in process of disintegration which was transforming Chinese civilization.

CHANGES IN ECONOMIC LIFE, 1894–1944

The West was most aggressive in the realms of politics, economics, and religion. Naturally, therefore, not only in government but also in the economic and religious phases of China's life these nearly four decades witnessed striking innovations.

It was chiefly for better facilities for commerce that the Occident had forced on China the treaties of 1842–1844 and 1858–1860. Commerce was the chief interest of the power which long held the leading place in China's maritime relations—Great Britain. In its broadest sense, commerce was also the main concern of Japan. Moreover, China, with its huge population—the largest of any nation—and its traditions of hard work and canny trading was presumably the greatest potential market in the world.

However, in spite of all these factors leading one to expect a startling development in foreign commerce, the increase, while marked, was not phenomenal. China's total foreign trade for 1913 was more than twice the value of that of 1899, and that of 1899 had been a record, being two-thirds greater than that of 1894 and nearly three times that of 1884. The years of the First World War—1914–1918—saw a decline followed by a slight growth, the figures for 1918 being about six per cent. greater than those for 1913. After the war came a sharp increase: the totals for 1921 were almost fifty per cent. larger than those for 1918, and for 1929 more than twice those for 1921.[1] The totals for 1929 were more than seven times those for 1894. With the world-wide financial depression which began in 1929, the increase practically ceased, and in 1932, as might have been expected, particularly in view of political and Sino-Japanese developments, a decline of about one-third was registered. After 1937 the increasing Japanese blockade worked further diminution until imports to "free" China dwindled almost to the vanishing point. A very little went by air. Some trade was carried on across the borders between the "free" and the "occupied" sections. Japan all but monopolized the commerce of the territories which she held.

Even the pre-1929 gains were not so large as might first appear. The totals compared are in a currency subject to wide fluctuations. The actual growth in goods exported and imported was not so marked. In terms of gold dollars the peak of foreign trade was reached just after the World War of 1914–1918, in 1920. Since then there was no rapid advance, although in terms of Chinese prices, which did not reflect so quickly the value of silver in terms of gold, the increase was probably considerable. Moreover, these years were ones of rapid growth in international trade the world over. Consequently, while in 1896–1898 China's foreign trade was 1.5 per cent. of that of the world, in 1911–1913 it had risen only to 1.7 per cent. and in 1921 only to 1.9 per cent. of that total. Japan, with a sixth or a seventh of the population of China, had about the same proportion of the world's commerce, and India, with a population probably about a fourth smaller and with a per capita wealth possibly no greater and perhaps less, had twice as large a proportion. Economically, China was still self-contained. Her time-honored self-sufficiency, her defective

---

[1] In figures, the average annual total foreign trade for 1911–1915 was 923,900 haikuan taels, for 1916–1920 1,182,501 haikuan taels, for 1921–1925 1,707,595 haikuan taels, and for 1926–1930 2,154,522 haikuan taels.

systems of transportation, and her civil strife combined to make her resistant to external commercial pressure. Her poverty and the chaotic state of her currency were additional obstacles to the realization of her commercial possibilities. As a market for other nations she was comparatively undeveloped.

The nature of China's exports and imports and the proportions of her trade shared by foreign countries had altered considerably during the past third of a century. In 1894, it will be recalled, cotton led the list of imports in value, with opium second. Tea and silk, although suffering from the competition of other countries, were the chief exports. In China's overseas trade the British still predominated.

Throughout the period from 1894 to 1930, imports exceeded exports in total value, although during the World War the latter nearly caught up with the former. The difference was accounted for largely by the remittances of Chinese overseas emigrants, expenditures by tourists and by foreign naval, military, and diplomatic staffs, the large sums sent to China for the work of Christian foreign missions, and loans. The most important item is probably the first one mentioned.

Among the registered imports, opium disappeared. A phenomenally successful campaign carried on against it toward the close of the Ch'ing and the consent of Great Britain eliminated it from lawful trade. However, under the disorder which eventually came in under the Republic the domestic production rose markedly, for military chieftains found it a convenient source of revenue and some of them practically compelled the cultivation of the poppy. Opium was imported, in large quantities, but surreptitiously and partly in the form of concentrated derivatives, such as morphine and heroin. In sections controlled by the Japanese after 1937 the sale of opium products mounted in striking fashion. Cotton remained an important item but its relative prominence decreased. With the rise of cotton mills in China, moreover, cotton yarn and cloth declined among the imports. In 1913 cotton goods formed almost a third of the imports and in 1931 and 1932 less than ten per cent. More and more the list of imports became varied, and included hundreds of items, many of which, in total value, were significant. Among the products which loomed large were kerosene (almost trebled in quantity between

1900 and 1929, used extensively for lighting purposes, and sold through a nation-wide network of agencies by such huge foreign concerns as the Standard Oil Company and the Asiatic Petroleum Company), foodstuffs, tobacco (much of it cigarettes, the consumption of which had become nation-wide under an efficient and persistent campaign of advertising), and metal goods, including especially machinery. The civil wars of later years led to the importation of large quantities of arms and ammunition.

In the main, imports were made up of manufactured goods, products of the factories of Japan and the Occident. The growing prominence of machinery on the list, however, was evidence that factories were being built and that China was beginning to produce goods by the new methods. Raw cotton, principally of long staple varieties, was being imported for use in the mills. Significant, too, was the prominence of flour and wheat, for it showed that China was depending on other countries to help it meet the ever-present problem of the pressure of population upon subsistence. Sugar and even rice were also among the imports. Some plants of foreign origin were introduced, among them new kinds of cotton and of drought-resistant grains. By 1937, indeed, China was arriving at the position of being an importer instead of an exporter of food and raw cotton and an exporter rather than an importer of manufactured goods.

Tea did not disappear from among the exports, but by 1927 it was only about three per cent. of the total. Silk remained the largest single item, but it was only about a fifth or a sixth of the total. It suffered greatly in competition with Japan. In both America and Europe, however, the best quality of Chinese silk was in demand for the finest fabrics. Such items came to the fore as vegetable oils (from the soy bean, the peanut, sesamum seed, a tree whose oil was used in varnishes, and the castor bean—an export which grew rapidly before and during the First World War and which waned afterward), bean cake, dried vegetables, eggs (in great quantities), furs, hair, coal, raw cotton, cotton goods and thread, timber, antimony, and some cereals. The exports were still chiefly of raw materials, the product of field and mine, but here and there were manufactures, an indication that the industrial age had arrived. Very significant was the decline in the imports and the increase in the exports of cotton goods. The marked decline of the imports has been noted. Cotton goods increased from less than one per cent. of China's total exports in 1913 to about ten per cent. in 1932. This seemed to mean that China was less and less a market for the products of the mills of Lancashire and Japan and more and more a competitor in foreign markets. Some of the exports, too, showed the effect of the rapid development of Manchuria, with its soy beans, its coal, and its timber. One form of export which in total market value did not bulk largely but from which large economic (and æsthetic) consequences might follow, was seeds and plants. One American botanist, for example, introduced from China to the gardens of Europe and America over a thousand new plants and sent abroad seeds of more than fifteen hundred different species. A French missionary is said to have sent home specimens of at least four thousand species from Yünnan alone. The Department of Agriculture of the United States Government had agents in China searching for plants which might prove of value in America.

The machinery by which foreign trade was handled was altered. The old style compradore who served as an intermediary between Chinese and foreigners was disappearing. More and more foreign manufacturers had their own agents who dealt directly with the Chinese merchant. More Chinese firms were appearing in the importing trade and tended to deal directly with foreign countries without the aid of intermediaries. Chinese banks, too, were entering into competition with foreign banks. The marked decline in the proportion of trade which passed through Hongkong—from 28.7 per cent. in 1913 to 16.8 per cent. in 1929, 15.6 per cent. in 1931, and 8.7 per cent. in 1932—seemed to indicate that this British-controlled port of middlemen was being supplanted by direct dealing between Chinese merchants and foreign lands.

Great Britain continued to lead European countries in the total amount of its trade with China. As late as 1927 it had more than twice that of any other nation of Europe. In direct commerce with China Japan surpassed it. However, the anti-Japanese boycott which began in 1931 as the result of Tokyo's Manchurian adventure, in 1932 gave the British Empire a larger proportion. Before 1930 the United States passed Great Britain and in 1932 surpassed Japan. In 1913 the British Empire had 18.7 per cent.

of China's foreign trade, Japan 19.4 per cent., and the United States 7.5 per cent. In 1929 the percentages were 15.1, 26.8, and 16.8 respectively. In 1932 they were 20.6, 18.4, and 21.6 respectively. The British percentages, however, included all the Empire, comprising not only the United Kingdom, but Canada, Australia, India, and the Straits Settlements. Those for the British Isles were much less—in 1913 17 and in 1929 only 8.5. In many ways the British retained their old position of leadership in China's sea-borne commerce. Until the spread of Sino-Japanese hostilities in the 1930's, they had more tonnage entering and clearing from Chinese ports—approximately a third of the whole —than any other people, although by 1930 the Japanese almost equalled them. In 1930 they probably still had as much capital invested in China as did any other nation. In that year, as nearly as could be determined—although the figures are very doubtful— the investments in China of the major foreign countries were, in round numbers, Great Britain about one and a quarter billion gold dollars (if Hongkong was included), Japan about the same (of which about a billion dollars was in Manchuria), Russia between two hundred and four hundred millions (largely in the Chinese Eastern Railway and subsequently sold to Japan), the United States probably between two hundred and two hundred and fifty millions (of which between fifty and eighty millions were in philanthropic enterprises, such as missions), France two hundred millions, and Germany one hundred millions. Of Western nations, the United States, next to Great Britain, had the largest financial stake in China. Moreover, in spite of the keen competition of Canton and the declining importance of the foreign middleman, Hongkong, a British possession, continued a great distributing center for the China trade. In the later years of the period, it will be recalled, except during and after 1932, about a sixth of the exports and imports of China were listed as passing through it. The trade of China with all parts of the British Empire, including Hongkong, was, therefore, decidedly in excess of that of Japan. Until 1942, outside of Manchuria, the Hongkong and Shanghai Banking Corporation remained the leading foreign bank, and British influence, although badly shaken, continued to be strong in the administration of the customs service. Shanghai, too, where until the 1940's the British remained more prominent than any other foreign people, continued to be the chief port of entry for foreign goods. However, in the total commerce of Great Britain, China was not so important as in that of Japan or the United States. In 1929 China accounted for more than a fourth of Japan's foreign trade, for about three and a half per cent. of that of the United States, and for only about one and a half per cent. of that of the United Kingdom.

Even before its conquests in the 1930's and 1940's, Japan loomed prominently in China's economic life and China was similarly very important to Japan. Japan's domination of South Manchuria has repeatedly been noted. In 1927, 91 per cent. of the iron ore produced in China was from properties under Sino-Japanese control and most of it was consumed in Japan—which, as we have seen, lacked extensive iron deposits of its own. In January, 1930, Japanese owned and operated in China cotton mills having 39 per cent. of the spindles of the entire country.

The years between 1894 and 1937 witnessed great changes in the internal transportation system of China. The twenty years after 1894 were ones of railway building, for they saw the construction of two roads connecting Peking with the Yangtze Valley, of trunk lines in Manchuria, and of several shorter roads in various parts of the country. However, before the entire country could be equipped with railways, the World War of 1914–1918 and increasing civil strife in China intervened. Foreign capital was reluctant to enter and little domestic capital could be obtained. The major part of the country, therefore, and even most of China proper remained entirely unequipped. Sinkiang, Mongolia, and Tibet were without a single mile, vast Szechwan was equally free from the iron horse, and south of the Yangtze only a few hundred miles had been constructed. After 1914, most of the new railway construction was in Manchuria. By 1930 over a third of the total mileage was there.[2] With the increase of civil war, especially after 1925, existing lines, except in Manchuria, fell into alarming disrepair. Their use by rival armies all but ruined the rolling stock and jeopardized the maintenance of the roadbeds. Their receipts were often appropriated for military or other non-railway purposes, frequently their equipment was not paid for, and interest on bonds was repeatedly allowed to become overdue.

[2] 6.987 kilometers out of a total for all China of 17.488 kilometers.

However, after the Kuomintang came into control, railway building was resumed in China proper. By the year 1942 the line between Canton and Wuchang had been completed and various other roads, notably in Hunan, Kiangsi, Anhui, Kwangsi, and Chekiang, had been built.

What the railway failed to provide was supplied in part by the automobile. Especially in the decade before 1937, this new type of conveyance came into widespread use. Thousands of miles of road were built, hundreds of them being even in such relatively backward provinces as Kwangsi, Kansu, and Kweichow. After the retreat to the West in 1938 the construction of roads was pushed in Yünnan and Szechwan. Much of the construction was by military leaders for the operations of their armies, but a large proportion was for peaceful purposes. Motor omnibuses plied between many of the leading cities. Moreover, in numbers of cities new, broad streets were constructed, even through congested districts, and here and there city walls were torn down and replaced by broad thoroughfares. These made possible the use of automobiles in centers where the old narrow streets would have prevented it. However, most of the automobiles were in the ports, especially Shanghai, and the vast majority of the city streets were left as before, impassable or inconvenient for motor cars. Moreover, most of the new highways had dirt surfaces. Very few would support traffic in heavy trucks. The automobile was still employed almost exclusively for passengers and not for freight. Except for the infrequent railways, the latter was, perforce, transported as formerly by boat, on the backs of men and animals, or by cumbersome carts. Late in the 1930's and in the 1940's the exigencies of war increased the use of trucks for freight. Between 1941 and 1945, because of the Japanese blockade, new cars could not be brought in and other fuels had increasingly to be substituted for gasoline.

Marked development was registered in steam navigation, most of it on the coastal waters and the Yangtze and its tributaries. Though Chinese companies were growing, most of the larger steamers were foreign-owned. Long before 1937 the "fire wheel boat" had penetrated even into Szechwan, craft with especially powerful engines plying the dangerous gorges which were the main outlet from that great inland province. Bicycles were introduced and in some sections became very numerous. By the 1930's the airplane, too, had become an established feature of Chinese transportation. Regular air service was maintained for mail and passengers between some of the principal cities. Airplanes even penetrated some of the more remote provinces. After 1937 the conflict with Japan speeded up the use of planes.

In production, the factory and Western machinery were being introduced. Long before 1937, in such cities as Shanghai, Canton, Hankow, and Tientsin, and in numbers of smaller centers factories were in operation. The chief output of this new power-driven machinery was cotton goods. China ranked third among the cotton-growing countries of the world, being surpassed only by the United States and India. With the vast supply of cheap labor, and with coal available, the manufacture of cotton by modern Western processes multiplied. By 1928 about a quarter of a million Chinese were employed in cotton mills. In 1929 there were one hundred and twenty cotton mills in all China, nearly two-thirds of them the property of Chinese, forty-four of Japanese, and three of British citizens. Measured by numbers of spindles, the Japanese owned about two-thirds as much of the enterprise as the Chinese and the British a little less than a tenth as much. Approximately half of the cotton manufacturing was in Shanghai, and it was freely predicted that eventually the lower part of the Yangtze Valley would be one of the world's largest centers of the cotton industry.

Although cotton yarn and cloth were the chief products of the new processes, factories were erected for a variety of other goods. Steam filatures, for silk, appeared in a number of cities. Flour mills, mills for pressing oil from the soy bean, match factories, saw mills, and sugar refineries were among the kinds of plants equipped with modern machinery.

However, the industrial revolution had only barely begun in China. By 1930 only about one per cent. of the population was connected with large-scale industry. This was not due to the dearth of the essential minerals. These, although probably insufficient for any such extensive manufacturing by modern methods as in Europe and the United States, were ample for a far greater development than had yet occurred. The causes for the retardation must be sought elsewhere. Internal unrest made foreign capital, usually timid, reluctant to enter the country, and the Chinese themselves did not yet possess the quantities of fluid capital or the type of banking system essential for the financing of an extensive industrialization. The returns elsewhere for the meagre supply of such capital as existed were so great that such long term investments as factories were not favored. Technical skill was scanty, transportation facilities usually inadequate, and taxes and official interference often disastrous. Nor had the Chinese yet succeeded in operating many of the stock companies by which the industrialization of the Occident had been made possible. Time-honored loyalties required that, regardless of the interests of stockholders, directors create posts for members of their families. This militated against the efficiency of the Western device. The bulk of the manufactures of China were, therefore, still produced by the customary handicraft methods organized in small units by guilds. After 1937 the Japanese invasion led to a migration of modern industry to the West. Machinery was moved and set up in new sites in "free" China.

Rifts in the old organization of the industrial life of the country began to appear. In many places, especially in the chief cities, the guilds were weakening, particularly in occupations in which the new methods had been introduced. Labor unions were formed, notably among workers on the railways and in the new industries. Before 1926 they had begun to be important, and the Kuomintang in its northward movement of that and the following year actively encouraged their organization. Unions of peasants were also initiated by the Kuomintang. These were facilitated by the Chinese habit of association through occupational guilds, a tradition which easily carried over into the new types of grouping. They were, however, primarily political organizations. The unionizing of workmen and peasants was due chiefly to the radical, Russian-advised elements in the Kuomintang. When, in 1927, these latter were discredited and suppressed, the unions formed by them suffered reverses and many of them disappeared. By 1937 they were, on the whole, few and weak. Not only laborers but also employers organized. Long before 1937, chambers of commerce became familiar features of the business structure of many of the cities. They were an easy evolution from the guild system or were formed by a federation of existing guilds.

The currency became worse confounded. To the copper cash, the many kinds of taels, and the foreign-coined dollars of the monetary system in existence before 1894 were added Chinese-minted dollars of several varieties, a subsidiary coinage of silver and copper (much debased), and floods of paper issued by banks, governments, and generals. Plans for improvement were elaborated, but while the Nanking Government showed marked self-constraint in the issue of paper currency, on the whole attempts at reform proved illusory. The situation was complicated by the use of silver as a medium in large transactions in a world where the normal standard was gold. Foreign exchange fluctuated widely and foreign and domestic commerce suffered. However, Chinese founded many banks on Western models and competed with the foreign banks which played so large a part in the finances of the country.

Prices were mounting. This was due partly to the general rise, before 1929, the world over, and partly to the fact that, having entered into the economic life of the world, China could not preserve permanently a scale decidedly lower than that of other nations. The prolonged civil strife operated in the same direction. Wages also rose, and as a rule probably about kept pace with the heightening cost of living—although accurate figures for the nation as a whole are lacking. In the larger centers, and especially in the newer industries, the tendency appears to have been to shorten the hours of labor rather than to increase the standard of living. Late in the 1930's and in the 1940's the Japanese invasion was followed by skyrocketing inflation and in both "free" and "occupied" China prices rose to fantastic heights. This applied both to commodities and to labor.

Severe famines occurred in portions of the country, especially the North. Famines were no novel phenomenon. Drought or flood and a lack of adequate means of conveyance to transport food to the afflicted sections were nothing new. Civil strife, however, aggravated the dearth, for fighting used up surpluses of grain and the breakdown of government weakened some of the usual agencies for administrating relief. It must be noted, however, that by 1937 Chinese organizations, both state and private, showed an increased willingness and ability to cope with such domestic distress.

In the main, in spite of many gains, the economic life of China seemed thus far to have suffered rather than benefited by contact with the Occident. It had been disorganized and millions had died of famine. Much of the famine, it is true, arose from natural causes for which foreigners were not in any way responsible. Many foreigners, indeed, had worked heroically and sacrificially to relieve it. A great deal of the distress, however, was due to the prolonged civil strife which had come partly (although by no means entirely) as a result of the foreign impact upon the political structure of the country. Moreover, in the 1930's and 1940's war with Japan, especially in the wide areas devastated by the armies, was accompanied by famine on a gigantic scale. If and when domestic and foreign war should subside, it was probable—given the industry and commercial ability of the Chinese—that economic recovery would be rapid.

Evidences of what alterations might be expected in the physical environment of the nation were to be seen in some of the cities. For example, in Amoy, once called the dirtiest port in China, by the 1930's broad, concrete-paved, electric-lighted streets took the place of the narrow, crooked, rough ones of other years, four- and five-story ferro-concrete buildings were erected, a modern sewage system and a supply of running water were installed, parks and recreation centers replaced slums, and the surrounding hillsides were cleared of graves to be terraced for future residences for the living.

CHANGES IN RELIGIOUS LIFE, 1894–1944

The years after 1895 witnessed marked changes in the religious life of the country. These were in part due to the total impact of the Occident—political, economic, and intellectual— and in part to the labors of Christian missionaries.

To the first cause must be ascribed the weakening of Confucianism. Even before the fall of the Ch'ing dynasty, the abolishment of the traditional system of civil service examinations (1905) shook to its foundations the form of education which had done so much to perpetuate Confucianism. Other innovations in education brought in new subjects of study and ended the concentration on the old learning. The substitution, in 1912, of the Republic for the Empire, dealt Confucianism another blow. The form of government was swept aside with which, since the Han dynasty, Confucianism had been almost inextricably associated. Some of the religious ceremonies maintained by the state disappeared, notably those which had been performed by the Emperor, and many others gradually lapsed. Confucius himself was unacceptable to numbers of the new student class, for he had supported monarchical institutions and his name was identified with the now discredited conservatism and the discarded system of education. With the growth in popularity of Western science and other studies from the Occident, interest in the Classics waned. Experts in the older literary pursuits were respected, but few were willing to pay the price of emulating them.

Confucianism did not succumb without a struggle. Attempts were made to show that it was not incompatible with the new order and to have the Republic adopt it as the official cult. Here and there officials and associations of scholars maintained the customary rites in honor of Confucius and his disciples. Study of the Classics was embodied in the new curricula. Moreover, a philosophy which had become part of the very bone and sinew of the nation could not at once disappear. In the China of the 1940's Confucianism was still an important influence. It had, however, suffered greatly.

To the general impact of the Occident, moreover, were to be ascribed a widespread loss of interest in and an antagonism to religion. The twentieth century witnessed in many countries a decline in religion. To thousands the great increase of knowledge of his physical environment which man had achieved through scientific methods had made religion intellectually untenable. To even larger numbers, absorption in the pursuit of physical comforts made possible by this new knowledge rendered religion unimportant and irrelevant—or even an enemy. This scepticism and preoccupation with material concerns found in China peculiarly fertile ground, for much of the traditional philosophy tended to make China's scholars agnostic: one of the most prominent of the younger thinkers declared that China's educated class had outgrown religion earlier than any other large group in the history of mankind. The militant anti-religious convictions of Russian Communism were especially influential. In 1922 an organized anti-religious movement came to birth, and the radical elements in the Kuomintang were vigorous in their anti-religious activities, especially during the days of their power in 1926 and 1927. Most of the agitation was focused against Christianity, for the latter was palpably foreign in its origin and in much of its leadership, and it was associated with the "capitalistic" nations for which Communism had so strong an aversion. Some of it, however, was directed against other forms of religion. More than one temple was converted into a school, and even the Taoist "Pope" was forced to flee from his accustomed residence.

The religious spirit here and there showed signs of a fresh awakening. In some sections a reform movement galvanized the somnolent Buddhism into new activity. For a time, especially before 1922, new and usually ephemeral syncretic sects, such as the Tao Yüan, interested small minorities. For a few years, too, after 1926, it looked as though Sun Yat-sen would become the center of a new state cult. A weekly ceremony in his honor was required in all schools and his tomb near Nanking became a kind of shrine. Yet by the 1940's enthusiasm for this innovation had decidedly waned.

Most of the earnest and aggressive new life entered through Christianity. After 1895 and until about 1925, Christianity had a phenomenal expansion. The persecutions of the Boxer year proved only a temporary check: in the long run, through the added zest which came to the Church from the heroism of the martyrs, they probably stimulated the spread of the faith.

The reasons for this growth were to be found partly in China and partly in the Occident. Conditions in China were favorable. The old structure of Chinese life was crumbling, and with it went much of the resistance which it offered to Christianity. Things Western were popular. In many places the Christian missionary was the only resident Westerner. As a representative of the Occident, therefore, he was given a hearing and was often influential. Repeatedly the altruistic services of the missionary won respect for the Christian message. Moreover, numbers of thoughtful Chinese, eagerly seeking means of extricating the nation from its confusion and weakness, and taught by their Confucian rearing that the salvation of the state and society depended ultimately upon the moral character of the individual, wondered whether the needed dynamic might not be found in the Christian

Gospel. Never since the period of disunion between the Han and the T'ang had conditions in China been so favorable for the acceptance of a foreign faith, and at no time in the more than twelve centuries since it first reached China had Christianity there been confronted with so great an opportunity. As, between the Han and the T'ang, Buddhism won a lasting place in China, so Christianity might now establish itself as an integral part of Chinese life.

Moreover, the situation in the Occident was propitious. Europe and America, the regions from which missionaries came, were increasing rapidly in wealth and so had the means for expanding their religious enterprises. In Protestantism the years were ones of growing enthusiasm for foreign missions. The magnitude of the opportunity in China stirred the churches and there was great optimism for the outlook both for China in general and for missions in particular. Even the World War of 1914-1918, accompanied and followed though it was by momentous changes, did not at once work a reduction in the total support from the Occident. To be sure, Protestants in Great Britain had difficulty in maintaining their missions at their pre-war level, and German Protestant mission societies were impoverished. Support from Protestants in the United States, however, more than made up for the deficiency. The War was followed by huge campaigns in the American Protestant churches for added funds and personnel for foreign missions in the attempt to make permanently effective the idealism with which much of America had entered that struggle. The result was extensive reënforcements for the staffs of American missions.

The interest of American Protestants in China, both before and after the War, led to an increase in their proportionate share in missions in that country. In 1889 the numbers of British and American Protestant missionaries in China were about equal, and together they accounted for more than nine-tenths of the missionary body. In 1929 Americans made up approximately three-fifths of the total foreign staff of Protestant missions in China.

Roman Catholics, too, augmented their efforts in China, both before and after the War. French missions declined relatively in the predominance which they once held, particularly after the separation of Church and State in France in 1905 and the actions of the French Government against Catholic schools. However, the increase from other nationalities more than compensated for the difference. In Roman Catholic circles the War was followed by an enhanced interest in foreign missions. Especially among American Catholics concern for foreign missions, once negligible, rapidly mounted, and much of it centered in China.

The figures of this growth of Christian missions are impressive. In 1889 the roll of Protestant missionaries in China contained about thirteen hundred names. In 1905 the number had risen to almost thirty-five hundred, in 1910 to more than five thousand, and in 1936 to slightly more than six thousand. Because of furloughs and health leaves, the number actually at work in China at any one time was probably about one-fifth or one-sixth less than each of these figures. In 1890 not quite six hundred and fifty foreign Roman Catholic priests were in China. In 1896 or 1897 the number was a little more than seven hundred and fifty, in 1901 more than a thousand, in 1912 nearly fifteen hundred, and in 1926 over seventeen hundred. In 1926 the total foreign staff—bishops, priests, lay brothers, and sisters—was slightly over three thousand, and in 1933 about forty-four hundred.

The number of Chinese Christians rose even more markedly. In 1889 Protestant communicants numbered about thirty-seven thousand, in 1898 about eighty thousand, in 1904 about one hundred and thirty thousand, in 1914 a little over a quarter of a million, in 1922 slightly over four hundred thousand, and in 1932 about four hundred and fifty thousand. In 1936 the total Protestant community, reckoning baptized Christians and those under instruction, was over seven hundred thousand. In 1896 there were about a half a million (baptized) Roman Catholics in China, in 1901 the number was estimated as being over seven hundred thousand, in 1907 about nine hundred thousand, in 1912 a little short of a million and a half, in 1918 a little under two millions, in 1924 a little under two and a quarter millions, in 1929 a little less than two and a half millions, and in 1941 slightly above three and a quarter millions. In no other non-Occidental country—with the exception of the Philippines and India—were there so many Roman Catholics. There were as well, in the 1930's, over one hundred thousand Russian Orthodox, most of them non-Chinese.

The activities of the missionaries, particularly of Protestant missionaries, were multifarious. Protestants, seeing the Chinese hunger for a Western type of education, opened many schools, stressing especially secondary and higher education. They founded and maintained some of the best educational institutions in the country. They gave much attention to hospitals and to education in Western medicine. The modern medical and nursing professions owed to them their inception and most of their development. They organized Young Men's and Young Women's Christian Associations, schools for the blind, and leper asylums. They promoted education in public health, helped in relieving famine, and aided the study of agricultural problems and methods. From the impulses derived from Protestants came a valiant Chinese effort to teach the masses to read. Protestants prepared and distributed an extensive religious literature: in 1924, for instance, they circulated nearly ten million copies of portions of the Bible. They presented the Christian message to millions, partly through the printed page, partly in personal conversations, and partly by means of public meetings. Although divided, as is the nature of Protestantism, into scores of denominations, they made extensive progress toward coöperation and union.

Protestant missions and the Protestant Christian community were having an influence quite out of proportion to their numerical strength. Some of the nation's leading educators either were Protestant Christians or had studied in Protestant schools. The Commercial Press, the largest publishing house in the country and an influential purveyor of the new knowledge, was founded by men trained in a Protestant mission press. Several of the nation's outstanding political leaders were baptized Protestant Christians —among them Sun Yat-sen, Fêng Yü-hsiang, Chiang Kai-shek, and some of the heads of ministries of the Nanking Government.

Roman Catholics were not so diverse in their activities. Compared with Protestants, they had little medical work, nor did they place such emphasis upon schools for educating the general public. They did not attempt to influence from so many angles the life of the country as a whole. They concentrated, rather, upon building Christian communities. To this end they brought thousands into catechetical schools, often paying the expenses of those in attendance. They expended much energy upon baptizing infants in danger of death, and, as a corollary, maintained scores of orphanages for the care of destitute children and for rearing in the Catholic faith those waifs who survived infancy. Most of the education provided by Roman Catholics was of a religious nature—giving to the laity the rudiments of the faith and preparing a Chinese clergy. Prospective priests were required to undergo a prolonged and exacting training.

Largely as a result of these methods, Roman Catholics continued to be much more numerous than the Protestants—although until 1925 the proportionate rate of increase of the latter was greater—but Roman Catholicism made decidedly less impression upon the life of the country at large.

Upon the masses of the nation the direct effect of Christianity, whether Protestant or Roman Catholic, was still negligible. Professing Christians totaled less than one per cent. of the population and the great majority of the Chinese were probably only barely aware, if at all, of the existence of the faith.

Beginning with about 1925, Christianity, and especially Protestantism, suffered grave reverses. The anti-religious movement, which became largely and often explicitly anti-Christian, began in 1922, was revived in 1924, and was intensified as a result of the Shanghai incident of May 30th, 1925. In 1926 and 1927 the left wing of the Kuomintang, encouraged by Russian Communists, was vigorously anti-Christian. Christianity was accused, among other things, of being "imperialistic" and "capitalistic," and since the rage of the Nationalists was just then directed chiefly against Great Britain and a considerable number of Protestant missionaries were British, Protestantism suffered more than Roman Catholicism. In 1926 and especially in 1927, at the height of the activity of the left wing of the Kuomintang, a great exodus of Protestant missionaries occurred. When, in the summer of 1927, the conservative reaction set in, missionaries began to return.

Christian schools, moreover, became the target of many Nationalists, on the ground that they existed for religious propaganda rather than education, and that they were part of the cultural invasion of the imperialistic powers. Since Protestants had devoted a larger proportion of their efforts toward maintaining schools than had Roman Catholics, they suffered more from this phase of the attack.

Added to the specifically anti-Christian agitation was the danger from the widespread banditry. Missionaries, being foreign and supposedly rich, were believed to be valuable for ransom. Scores of them were captured and many lost their lives.

Then, too, while in the Occident support for Roman Catholic missions was increasing, that in the United States for Protestant missions fell off. For a variety of reasons, beginning about 1924 a marked decline in giving cut the incomes of most of the major American Protestant mission boards. The incomes of Protestant missionary societies in the rest of the world remained about stationary, and so did not make up for the loss in American contributions. The world-wide financial depression which began in 1929 brought further losses in gifts. This meant that while Protestant missions were under heavy fire in China, their support from the Occident was suffering. The combination proved serious. Accurate figures are lacking, but it is certain that the growth of Protestantism in numbers of communicants decidedly slowed down after 1924 and in many places experienced an actual decline. Nor did the Roman Catholic community show so large a rate of increase as in the immediately preceding years.

In some respects, however, the persecutions and trials of the years after 1924 stimulated Christianity to throw out deeper roots into Chinese soil. It became unmistakably obvious that if the faith were to survive in the intensely nationalistic China of the day it must become more Chinese in sympathy and leadership. Rome took pains to show itself friendly to Chinese patriotism. After May 30th, 1925, group after group of Protestant missionaries and board after board came out in favor of removing from the treaties the clauses guaranteeing toleration for missionaries and Christianity, and some expressed themselves as opposed to extraterritoriality and foreign control of the tariff. Moreover, partly because of the nationalistic wave, Protestants rapidly pushed Chinese into positions of leadership, electing several Chinese bishops, placing Chinese at the head of their colleges and universities, and in many other ways seeking to transfer control to them. Roman Catholics redoubled their efforts to train a Chinese clergy, and in 1926, at Rome, the Pope consecrated six Chinese priests to the episcopate—the first since the sole previous appointment in the seventeenth century. Within the next four years five more Chinese were raised to the episcopate, and by 1940 at least nineteen ecclesiastical divisions were administered by Chinese. In its financial support and in its liturgy and creeds the Church was still largely foreign, but it was less exotic than it had been a decade before.

The Japanese invasion had mixed effects upon Christianity. In Manchuria after 1931 some check was placed on the activities of missionaries and churches. After 1937, as the Japanese moved farther into China, many missionaries were forced to leave. After 1941 British and Americans in "occupied" China were interned. Thousands of Chinese Christians joined in the exodus to the West. There, especially among Protestants, they strengthened the Christian cause. Moreover, Christians, both Chinese and foreign, by their ministry to the sufferers from war, won much respect from the non-Christians. By the mid-1940's China was said to be more open to the Christian message than at any earlier time. Yet missionary staffs were suffering depletion. World War II and transportation difficulties put obstacles in the way of reënforcements. From some countries funds were cut off. Christianity was under a new handicap.

CHANGES IN INTELLECTUAL LIFE, 1894–1944

Fully as great as the changes in government and in the economic and religious life of the country were those in education, literature, and language. In some respects, between 1895 and 1945 the mental life of China moved farther from its old moorings than that of the West had done between the thirteenth and the twentieth century. It was in greater turmoil than at any time since the Chou.

In 1895, in spite of a few foreshadowings of change, China's intellectual life was still shaped almost entirely by the civil service examinations. Through these led the road to power, wealth, and social recognition, and all formal education was determined by their requirements. As we shall see in a later chapter, the system had its virtues as well as its defects. Success in it demanded, however, so exclusive a devotion to Chinese classical studies and to the acquisition of skill in writing in a highly artificial literary style that few of those passing through it had leisure and scarcely more of its products had interest for venturing into other fields of learning. China's *literati* were all but impervious to what their fellows in the West were thinking and achieving.

After 1895, and particularly after 1900, conditions rapidly altered. Schools with curricula combining Western and Chinese subjects were established in increasing numbers. The abolition, in 1905, of the old civil service examinations brought to an end the structure by which much of Chinese thought had been molded since the Han. The government planned a school system in which the old and the new learning should be combined. It had as its ideal compulsory primary education for all, with higher primary and secondary schools and universities. Through the years various modifications of this were projected.

Enormous difficulties confronted the realization of such a plan—among them the training of the thousands of teachers required, political influence in appointments to faculties and corruption in administration, the cost of equipment, and the expense for maintenance and salaries in a country heavily burdened by the exactions of military leaders. It is not strange that at times progress was slow. Promising universities arose and attracted students, only to disintegrate after a few years with a change in leadership and the fluctuations of politics. The disorganization was particularly great in the years 1926–1928 when the Nationalist Government was fighting to establish itself. In 1923 about six and a half million pupils enrolled in government schools of all grades (a substantial increase over any preceding year for which figures are available), about half a million were in schools maintained by Christian missions, Protestant and Roman Catholic, and an unknown number, perhaps three or three and a half million, in private schools of the old type. Figures for 1931 showed thirty-four universities and colleges with 17,285 students, sixteen technical institutions with 2,168 students, and about thirteen hundred secondary schools with 234,811 students. Many cities extended their primary schools, especially after 1928. In 1929–1930 primary schools enrolled over eight million eight hundred thousand children. True to their traditions, the Chinese had a passion for education and showed an almost pathetic confidence in it as a means of national salvation. Private initiative supplemented that of the government, not only in maintaining schools of the old type and assisting Christian institutions, but in establishing and supporting schools of the newer sort. Private aid was especially marked in secondary and higher education.

The quality of the new education often left much to be desired. Many teachers were badly prepared and owed their positions to family or political influence. In numbers of instances the physical equipment of the schools was inadequate. Students were restive under discipline, whether moral or intellectual, often insisted upon a deciding voice in the management of the institution, and at times demanded that all be given credit for the work of a course, regardless of their competence. The faculty, for fear of losing their positions, usually yielded. Fortunately there were exceptions. Some schools consistently maintained high standards.

Many Chinese sought the new learning either in Japan or in its sources in the West. After 1900 their numbers swelled to one of the greatest student migrations in history. Most ambitious youths were dissatisfied until they had studied abroad. For some years they flocked to Japan by the thousands. A large proportion of the prominent military men were trained there. From time to time the stream to that country dwindled somewhat, partly because of the recurrent strong feeling against Japan after 1915. America was the host to other thousands, hundreds of whom were financed by the remitted portions of the Boxer indemnity due the United States. This fund, moreover, was drawn upon to establish just outside of Peiping a higher school, Tsing Hua, largely after American models. For years the United States had more Chinese students than did any European country. English was by far the most widely used of the European languages and was much sought after. This was probably both a cause and a result of the America-ward movement. Then, after the World War of 1914–1918, France made a strong bid for Chinese students, offering them many inducements, and for a time the number there exceeded that in America. In 1930, of the 1,484 applying to the Ministry of Education for passports to study abroad, 55.6 per cent. were expecting to go to Japan, 18 per cent. to the United States, and 11.6 per cent. to France. Hundreds were to be found in other European countries, notably Great Britain and Germany, and, for a short time before the anti-Communist reaction of 1927, in Russia.

The "returned students" played a notable part in the new

China and more and more came into control, especially in politics and education. In 1929, for example, of the employees of the National Government at Nanking, nearly six per cent. had studied in the United States, nearly four per cent. in Europe, and nearly seven per cent. in Japan. A still larger proportion of the higher offices at Nanking were filled by them.

The "Mass Education Movement," an attempt to teach great groups of illiterates to read, was begun after the World War of 1914–1918, under the auspices of the Young Men's Christian Association, by a returned student from America, James Y. C. Yen. Yen worked out a list of the most used characters, approximately a thousand in number, and devised methods of teaching these efficiently and quickly to large numbers. The Movement soon formed an independent organization and became very popular. Its results were often disappointing, for many taught by it dropped back into illiteracy, and only a few went on to read anything really useful. Vast areas knew little or nothing of it. Yet it had at least an indirect effect in stimulating the emergence of popular schools and the simplification of elementary reading classes. In time Yen, with his staff of expert assistants, settled down in one rural area in the North, there to make effective his ideals of education in the transformation of a single community.

The Japanese invasion of the 1930's and 1940's worked marked changes. In Manchuria it discouraged higher education and made the schools subserve the new régime. Many universities in China proper moved to new sites in the West, beyond the Japanese zone. In "occupied" China Japan reorganized the curricula of the schools to suit her purposes. In "free" China the numbers of students in all grades rapidly mounted. Yet inflation, undernourishment for teachers and students, and lack of proper buildings, libraries, and laboratories wrought grave hardship.

Chinese students, both those trained abroad and those whose education had been entirely in China, were inclined to take an active interest in public affairs. In this they perpetuated the tradition of the older education, for that had been designed to prepare men for the service of society through the state. Particularly after 1911, students gave much attention to political agitation. The "Student Movement," at times organized on more than a local scale, was often a factor to be reckoned with. For example, students were prominent in effecting the various boycotts against Japan and Great Britain. The Student Movement was particularly strong in middle (secondary) schools. The youths of that immature age were susceptible to mob psychology and were easily swayed by older leaders, often from the outside, who found it to their advantage to organize them. Students were engrossed in the campaign of the Kuomintang in 1926 and 1927, and, as is the nature of impetuous youth, gravitated toward the left. Many became zealous propagandists of Communism. When, in 1927, the anti-Communist reaction set in, numbers were executed for their radicalism. The authorities now frowned on student activities, admonishing the youth to concentrate on their books. For a time the Student Movement subsided. In 1931 it had an active part in agitating for direct action against Japan and in bringing about a change of government in Nanking. In "free" China in the 1930's and 1940's it largely ceased. The Kuomintang was unfriendly and, indeed, organized a "Youth Corps" to reënforce its own power. Many students were so pressed by the physical struggle for existence that they were apathetic. In Communist China youth was even more strongly indoctrinated with the ideals of the dominant party.

Inefficiency there was in much of the new education, and energy was often diverted from intellectual pursuits to political agitation. Yet there was activity in scholarship. Western and Chinese philosophers were examined, some having their advocates and all being freely criticized. Ancient Chinese thinkers, such as Mo Ti, long looked at askance by the orthodox, were enthusiastically rediscovered. Reprints were issued of many books proscribed by the Ch'ing. China's history came in for fearless restudy. Both the critical procedure developed in the Ch'ing dynasty by the scholars connected with the movement known as the Han Learning and the methods of Western historians were applied to the records of China's past—to the discrediting of much that had been currently accepted, particularly concerning the pre-Confucian period.

Books multiplied, and new publishing houses arose as their purveyors. One company sold in one year $800,000 worth (Chinese currency) of books in Western languages. Translations of hundreds of Western works were printed. Experiments were made in fresh types of literature. New journals appeared, many of them quite inconsequential and most of them ephemeral, but some of them influential and all of them symptomatic of the variety and freedom of thought and the desire for literary self-expression which characterized the young educated class. One of the most famous of the journals was the *Hsin Ch'ing Nien Tsa Chih* ("The New Youth Magazine"), begun in 1916 and first edited by one of the outstanding writers of the period, Ch'ên Tu-hsiu.

Other printed channels of the new ideas were the textbooks for the schools, the newspapers which sprang up like mushrooms and which were mostly of very poor quality and used largely for political, personal, and partisan propaganda, and the placard, with vivid pictures and telling phrases, likewise developed largely for propaganda.

Moving pictures from the Occident (especially the United States) invaded the land and achieved popularity. Although looked upon primarily as a form of amusement, they depicted (even if usually in distorted and bizarre fashion) the life of the West and could not fail to be a potent means of education. As a rule their quality, both morally and æsthetically, was atrocious. The Western ones were often discards and the increasing numbers of Chinese films were usually fully as bad.

Among the most influential scholars of the time was Liang Ch'i-ch'ao, who first came into prominence in the reform movement of 1898 as a pupil of K'ang Yu-wei. Although he was more of a popularizer than an exact and careful thinker, his writings were widely read. Younger than he but also having an enormous effect upon the thoughtful youth of his time was Hu Shih. Born in 1891, of a scholarly family and trained in the older learning, he had a brilliant career as a student in the United States, and, returning to China, wrote and lectured voluminously and ably.

In the general disintegration and modification of the intellectual containers of the past, the language itself could scarcely hope to escape. Hundreds of fresh terms described the new objects and ideas. Some of them were imported from Japan, where for more than a generation Chinese characters in new combinations had been used to express the fresh concepts entering from the West. Others were coined in China. Various attempts were made to substitute for the cumbersome though beautiful and expressive written characters a simpler and purely phonetic system, but none achieved wide success. Quite otherwise was the fate of a movement to adopt as a medium for scholarship and serious writing a dignified form of the *Mandarin*—the vernacular most widely spoken—rather than the old literary style so remote from the tongue of every day. The vernacular had often been employed in centuries past for such purposes as the writing of novels, but the new movement to utilize the *pai hua*, or "plain speech" of the people for literary purposes is usually dated from a manifesto of Hu Shih, on January 1st, 1917. Hu Shih had the courage of his convictions and employed the *pai hua* in his own writing. Others followed, and, in spite of some criticism from the conservatives, the *pai hua* quickly became the medium of expression of the younger and some of the older writers and was polished into a worthy literary vehicle. The revolution was fully as great as the substitution in Europe, some centuries before of the vernaculars for Latin as the language of scholarship. Along with the use of the *pai hua* went the effort to have all the country adopt one dialect of the spoken language, a form of the *Mandarin*, as the *kuo yü*, or national speech. This was taught in the schools, even in some non-*Mandarin* districts (it was made compulsory in 1920), and gained rapid headway. Especially in the provinces along the southern coast, where *Mandarin* had once been as little understood as though it were a foreign tongue, by 1937 student audiences were easily able to follow addresses in it.

Much of this fresh intellectual life was styled the "New Tide," "Renaissance," "New Thought," or "New Culture" movement. The "New Tide" had many angles. It included the use of the *pai hua*, experiments in novel types of literature, the examination of China's past, discussions of philosophy, and, in general, the many intellectual currents which joined in the stream which was the new China and which, it was fondly hoped, would issue in the birth of a civilization. It strongly emphasized what it believed to be the value of science and the scientific approach and made much of social science, psychology, and education. It also had a political aspect, the reënforcement of nationalism. In general it was individualistic and incorporated a revolt against the past. It was given impetus by the prolonged visits to China, for extensive lecture tours, of outstanding Western thinkers, notably John Dewey and Bertrand Russell.

The "New Tide" had no headquarters. For some years, under its Chancellor (1917–1923), Ts'ai Yüan-p'ei—a *Hanlin* under the old régime and later a student in Germany and France—the National University at Peking was its most active center. A number of brilliant men, such as Ch'ên Tu-hsiu and Hu Shih, served on the faculty and intellectually the University was the most stimulating institution in the country. Misfortune overtook it, however, the more prominent members of its staff resigned, and the leadership of the Movement scattered.

The "New Tide," technically so called, is said to have begun in 1916 and to have reached its height between 1920 and 1923. It was essentially the proclamation of new ideas. When, as was soon the case, these found wide acceptance and controversy died down, the reason for its existence passed. As a phase of the coming of fresh currents of thought it ceased to be. However, much of the general intellectual activity of which it was an expression continued.

What the outcome of all this intellectual ferment would be no one could accurately predict. For the time, scholars of the new type, both young and old, were chiefly animated question marks. Much of their scepticism was purely destructive. The old Confucian orthodoxy had passed and with it the intellectual unity and uniformity of the educated class. Many schools of thought, as in the Chou, were competing for the mastery. In the realm of mind as in that of politics chaos was the order of the day. Some there were, however, who were groping toward the building of a substitute for what had been swept aside: they might well be laying the foundations for a structure of thought and society which would equal or excel the old.

At the moment, in the 1930's and 1940's science and scientific subjects were popular. Here, in the application of science, was supposed to lie the salvation of the country. Whether this trend would persist no man could say.

CHANGES IN SOCIAL LIFE, MORALS, AND CUSTOMS, 1894–1944

The revolution in political forms and ideals, the innovations in economics and religion, and the intellectual unrest could not fail to be accompanied by great changes in social organization, morals, and customs. The telephone, the moving picture, the widespread use of electric lights in cities (which made another type of night life possible), the factory, the railway, the automobile, the newspaper, all joined, as in the Occident, to revolutionize society. To be sure, the innovations were chiefly in the ports and here were by no means universal. Even as late as 1944 vast areas were but slightly affected. Yet the changes had begun and were prominent in the centers from which they would be most likely to spread to the rest of the nation.

Many of the old forms of etiquette were passing and were being succeeded by others, often less elaborate and more brusque. Sometimes, in the transition, a lamentable lack was shown of any of those manners which ease the intercourse between individuals and groups, and in which the Chinese have been traditionally skilled.

Old styles of dress were also going. Even before the revolution of 1911, the queue, the form of wearing the hair imposed by the Manchus, had begun to disappear—somewhat furtively. With the revolution came a wholesale cutting of queues—although that appendage persisted and in the 1930's was even seen in such a modern city as Shanghai. By the 1930's the coiffure of bobbed hair had been widely adopted among women and girls. Many abandoned Chinese garb for Western costumes—a surrender which always involved a loss in picturesqueness and often in dignity and good taste. While, with the increase of nationalism, especially after 1925, for a time a decided reaction occurred in favor of the traditional garb, Occidental styles were in part retained and later increased again in use. This was particularly true in the uniforms of soldiers and of school children and older students and in the dress of those who had frequent intercourse with the foreigner in business and diplomacy.

The relations between the sexes were shifting. Freedom of social intercourse between boys and girls and men and women, once looked upon with abhorrence after childhood years and tolerated only with women of doubtful morals, now became frequent and respectable. Women were given more liberty. Sometimes they participated in politics and were employed in government posts. In the radical movement of 1926–1927 even Amazon corps were heard of.

Youth paid less deference to age. More and more young people insisted upon making their choice of their life mates without the interference or even the advice of parents.

Former distinctions between classes were also passing. Members of occupations once despised, such as that of the soldier, were coming into power.

Here and there, too, notably in the cities, the large family was breaking up. Instead of members of several generations living in patriarchal groups in one compound, as had often been the custom, in the case of such new groups as laborers in the factories and graduates of secondary and high schools it was not unusual for each married couple to have its individual home. In some circles concubinage was regarded with less tolerance than formerly.

What the effect of all these changes would be no one could foresee. Especially were the alterations in marriage customs and family life fraught with unpredictable consequences. More than among most peoples, the family had formed the basic social unit, an extremely important agency for education and social control. The weakening of its traditional ties could not fail of significant results.

Never before in the recorded history of China had the gap in customs and outlook between generations been so wide and deep. In breaking with the constraints of the past, many of the youth came to moral and physical shipwreck, and others were seriously injured. On the other hand, the old customs were not without deleterious consequences and something could be said in praise of the new freedom.

These changes, like so many of the others, did not come simultaneously throughout the length and breadth of the nation, nor were they to be found everywhere in equal degree. They were more in evidence in the cities, particularly along the coast and where the largest numbers of foreigners were found. The westward movement of population to "free" China in the 1930's and

1940's spread them in hitherto remote and slightly altered areas. In the 1940's the presence of thousands of American troops accelerated them. Rural districts were the least affected, and in many places life was but little modified. Practically everywhere, however, some departure from the past was seen, and it increased as the years passed. The old China was going, seemingly never to return.

SUMMARY

The years following 1894 witnessed the most startling and revolutionary changes in China's history. Foreigners threatened the nation's independence. Although it was not subjugated to an alien political yoke nearly so fully as it had repeatedly been in earlier centuries, and by the 1930's had made decided progress toward the recovery of such portions of its independence as had been sacrificed, in almost every other phase of its life the country yielded to the Occident. It was frequently said that China was experiencing in one generation a transition as varied and momentous as that through which Europe had passed in the Renaissance, the Protestant Reformation, the French Revolution, and the Industrial Revolution.

There was swept aside the political framework under which the nation had been living for more than two thousand years—a structure to which it owed its unity—and experiments were being made with Western types of government. Nothing which could confidently be called stable had yet emerged. Administratively the land was divided and repeated civil strife and banditry were impoverishing it.

On the other hand, in some respects the country was more nearly a conscious unit than ever before. Nationalism, reënforced by the new educational system, the telegraph, the Customs Service, the post office, and, to a less extent, by the railway, the steamship, the automobile, and the airplane, was welding China together and was as effective in producing cultural uniformity as was the old administrative system.

These new institutions and appliances, with others, bade fair also to transform the economic life of the people.

Religiously the practices and beliefs of the masses were little altered, but the observances maintained by the state were discontinued or fell into neglect, and the Confucian theory by which social relationships had long been ordered was either discredited or on the way toward desuetude. Christianity made notable gains, and Buddhism experienced something of a revival, but the majority of the educated were moving toward a religious scepticism which at times became militant.

Intellectually the younger educated men had passed almost completely out of one world into another and were dominated by an enthusiasm for science—of a Western type.

Socially old customs were going, here and there the family was showing signs of disintegration, the relations between the sexes were being revolutionized, and former moral standards were actively challenged. The nation had struck its tents and was on the march—but whither no one could foresee.

On the other hand, while China was being so altered by contact with the Occident, she was having but little influence upon the West—far less than in the eighteenth century. Chinese art was eagerly collected by Western museums, courses on China's history and culture appeared in the curricula of universities of Europe and America, but the culture of the Occident was, apparently, unaffected. The old civilization of China was being shattered by the West, but as a rule Westerners had almost no knowledge or appreciation of China. Only a few savants and here and there a far-seeing individual were aware of the greatness of the civilization which was so rapidly disappearing. Even some of these questioned whether China had anything to teach the Occident. There was no reciprocal fertilization of Western culture.

BIBLIOGRAPHY

Books and articles on one or another phase of events, movements, and problems of the China of these years are numbered by the thousands. The attempt to select the most useful and significant of them is both necessary and fallible.

With the *Ch'ing Shih Kao,* or draft history of the Ch'ing, recently compiled, the long line of dynastic histories comes to an end, and no single work in Chinese carries, in so authoritative a manner, the story beyond the beginning of 1912.

Of general accounts in foreign languages, H. Cordier, *Histoire Générale de la Chine* (4 vols., Paris, 1920, 1921) brings the narrative only to the end of the Ch'ing, and this also is true of the monumental work by H. B. Morse, *The International Relations of the Chinese Empire* (3 vols., London, 1910–1918). H. B. Morse and H. F. MacNair, *Far Eastern Relations* (Shanghai, 1928; second edition, Boston, 1931) carries the story into 1927 and is very good, but lacks the extensive footnotes which are part of the value of the larger work by Morse. An enormous amount of material on practically all phases of current life and events is contained in the successive issues of *The China Year Book* (edited by H. T. Montague Bell and H. G. W. Woodhead, 1912–1921, and by H. G. W. Woodhead, 1922 *et seq.*; published London 1912–1920, Tientsin 1921–1930, Shanghai 1931–1939). Semi-official is *The Chinese Year Book*, 1935–36 (Shanghai, 1935). Fully official is *China Handbook, 1937–1943* (New York, 1943).

Brief accounts, in the nature of textbooks, are S. K. Hornbeck, *Contemporary Politics in the Far East* (New York, 1916), which deals almost entirely with events between 1911 and 1916, P. J. Treat, *The Far East* (New York, 1928), and H. M. Vinacke, *A History of the Far East in Modern Times* (New York, 1928).

A periodical useful for its news and giving a strongly British point of view is *The North China Daily News* (in its weekly form *The North China Herald*) (Shanghai, 1850–1941).

Pertinent documents for diplomatic history are in Chinese Maritime Customs, *Treaties, Conventions, etc., between China and Foreign States* (second edition, 2 vols., Shanghai, 1917), J. V. A. MacMurray's great work, *Treaties and Agreements with and concerning China, 1894–1919* (2 vols., New York, 1921), and a continuation of the latter, *Treaties and Agreements with and concerning China, 1919–1929* (Washington, 1929), compiled by the Carnegie Endowment for International Peace. An account of extraterritoriality is in G. W. Keeton, *The Development of Extraterritoriality in China* (London, 1928). W. W. Willoughby, *Foreign Rights and Interests in China* (revised edition, 2 vols., Baltimore, 1927) is the standard treatise in its field. Georges Soulie de Morant, *Exterritoralité et Interêts Étrangers en Chine* (Paris and Shanghai, 1925), is also worth noting.

On events through the death of the Empress Dowager, see J. O. P. Bland and E. Backhouse, *China under the Empress Dowager* (Philadelphia and London, 1912), E. Backhouse and J. O. P. Bland, *Annals and Memoirs of the Court of Peking* (London, 1914), the Princess Der Ling, *Old Buddha* (New York, 1928), and the Princess Der Ling, *Two Years in the Forbidden City* (New York, 1914). On attempts at reform preceding the fall of the Manchus, there is a book by M. E. Cameron, *The Reform Movement in China, 1898–1912* (Stanford University Press, 1931).

On foreign aggression between 1894 and 1900, probably the best specialized study, based upon careful research, and arguing that Great Britain, rather than the United States, was chiefly responsible for the maintenance of the open door during these years, is P. Joseph, *Foreign Diplomacy in China, 1894–1900* (London, 1928). Covering practically the same ground, also very carefully done and based upon an examination of the printed documents, is R. S. McCordock, *British Far Eastern Policy, 1894–1900* (New York, 1931). Other accounts are Lord Beresford, *The Break-up of China* (New York and London, 1899) and A. R. Colquhoun, *China in Transformation* (New York, 1912). Good accounts of the share of the United States in these events are in T. Dennett, *Americans in Eastern Asia* (New York, 1922), and A. L. P. Dennis, *Adventures in American Diplomacy, 1896–1906* (New York, 1928). See also *The Memoirs of Count Witte* (translated and edited by A. Yarmolinsky, Garden City, 1921).

On the Boxer outbreak, some of the best works, amid the great flood of books on the events of that year, are A. H. Smith, *China in Convulsion* (2 vols., New York, 1901), W. A. P. Martin, *The Siege in Peking. China against the World* (New York, 1900), Putnam Weale (B. Lenox Simpson), *Indiscreet Letters from Peking* (London, 1906) (all three by eye-witnesses of much that they narrate), G. N. Steiger, *China and the Occident: the Origin and Development of the Boxer Movement* (New Haven, 1927), J. J. L. Duyvendak (translator), *The Diary of His Excellency Ching-shan. Being a Chinese Account of the Boxer Troubles* (Leyden, 1924), J. J. L. Duyvendak, *Ching-shan's Diary—A Mystification* (*T'oung Pao*, Vol. 33, pp. 268 et seq.), W. Lewisohn, *Some Critical Notes on the so-called "Diary of His Excellency Ching-shan* (*Monumenta Serica*, Vol. II, fasc. 1, pp. 191–202), *Report of William W. Rockhill, Late Commissioner to China, with Accompanying Documents* (57th Congress, Senate Doc. 67, Washington, 1901), and Wu Yung, *The Flight of An Empress,* translated by Ida Pruitt (New Haven, 1936).

On the Russo-Japanese War are K. Asakawa, *The Russo-Japanese Conflict* (Boston, 1904), scholarly, but emphasizing the Japanese side of the struggle; T. Dennett, *Roosevelt and the Russo-Japanese War* (Garden City, 1925), very well done; E. J. Dillon, *The Eclipse of Russia* (New York, 1918), giving something of the views of Count Witte, a leading Russian statesman; A. M. Pooley (editor), *The Secret Memoirs of Count Tadasu Hayashi* (New York, 1915), by a leading Japanese statesman, especially important on the events centering around the formation of the Anglo-Japanese Alliance.

An unusually stimulating description of conditions in China, chiefly social, on the eve of the revolution of 1911, is in E. A. Ross, *The Changing Chinese* (New York, 1911). The author, a noted American sociologist, gives here his impressions from several months of travel in China.

On all phases of China's history since 1911 an unusually valuable publication is *The China Year Book,* noted above. It contains many documents, tables of statistics, and articles of varying importance. *The China Mission Year Book,* published annually, with occasional gaps, in Shanghai, beginning with 1910, and beginning with 1926 known as *The China Christian Year Book,* covers the life of the nation from the standpoint of Protestant missionaries and is particularly good for social, religious, and educational matters." *Pacific Affairs* (Honolulu, 1928 et seq.), published monthly by the Institute of Pacific Relations, and *Asia* (New York, 1911 et seq.), a popular magazine of high grade, often contain important articles on China. *Pacific Affairs* also has book reviews and summaries of articles. Another excellent periodical, valuable particularly for documents on foreign and domestic politics, is *The Chinese Social and Political Science Review* (Peking, 1917–1939). *The Annals of the American Academy of Political and Social Science* for November, 1931 (Philadelphia), is devoted entirely to China and contains papers on recent movements in most phases of China's life. See also an excellent general treatment in E. R. Hughes, *The Invasion of China by the Western World* (New York, 1938).

On internal history, chiefly political, since the beginning of the Republic, the best accounts are probably Paul Monroe, *China: A Nation in Evolution* (New York, 1928), covering all phases of China's life, by an American educator who had repeatedly visited China and who had known many of her leading men; A. N. Holcombe, *The Chinese Revolution* (Cambridge, Mass., 1930), by a professor of government at Harvard, who spent several months in China and who writes chiefly but not entirely on developments since 1925; and S. K. Hornbeck, *China To-day: Political* (Boston, 1927), a succinct summary by a competent scholar. Particularly valuable is the series by L. Wieger, *Chine Moderne*, published by the Jesuit Mission Press at Hsien Hsien (Hopei) at somewhat irregular intervals, beginning with 1921. It contains French translations and summaries of an immense variety of Chinese writings. It provides the best source in a Western language for Chinese opinion and Chinese analysis of public questions and events. See also an excellent sketch, G. Clark, *The Great Wall Crumbles* (New York, 1935).

Also useful, in varying degrees, on China's internal history are George E. Sokolsky, *The Tinder Box of Asia* (Garden City, 1932), by a journalist, and covering the Manchurian affair of 1931–1932 as well as China's internal affairs; R. F. Johnston, *Twilight in the Forbidden City* (New York, 1934), an intimate but biased account by an English tutor of P'u-i; H. F. MacNair, *China in Revolution. An Analysis of Politics and Militarism under the Republic* (Chicago, 1931), which covers in brief survey the story from 1911 to 1931; E. V. Dingle, *China's Revolution: 1911–1912* (Shanghai, 1912), by one who was in China at the time; P. H. B. Kent, *The Passing of the Manchus* (London, 1912); Putnam Weale (B. L. Simpson), *The Fight for the Republic in China* (New York, 1917), by an expert but marred by an anti-Japanese bias; H. G. W. Woodhead, *The Truth about the Chinese Republic* (London, 1926), by a journalist long resident in China; L. M. King, *China in Turmoil. Studies in Personality* (Boston, 1927), a description of some Chinese whom the author had known, largely in West China, who vividly illustrate currents in the Chinese situation; Bertrand Russell, *The Problem of China* (New York, 1922), by a well-known radical, after his sojourn in China, and decidedly tinged with his bias; M. S. Bates and F. W. Price, *Kuomintang* (*Encyclopædia of the Social Sciences*, Vol. 8); Anna Louise Strong, *China's Millions* (New York, 1928), an account, by a sympathetic eye-witness, of the radical Kuomintang activities in Central China in 1927; H. A. Van Dorn, *Twenty Years of the Chinese Republic* (New York, 1932), very sympathetic with the Chinese and covering intellectual, religious, social, and economic, as well as political developments; three books giving the viewpoint of the left wing of the Kuomintang, the first of them a history of the party—T'ang Leang-li, *Wang Ching-wei, A Political Biography* (Tientsin, 1931), Wang Ching-wei, *The Chinese Revolution, Essays and Documents* (Tientsin, 1931), and Hu Shih and Lin Yu-tang, *China's Own Critics, A Selection of Essays* (Tientsin, 1931); Sun Yat-sen, *San Min Chu I. The Three Principles of the People*, translated by F. W. Price, edited by L. T. Chen (Shanghai, 1927), the standard translation into English of the most widely influential of Dr. Sun's books; a translation of the same into French, P. M. d'Elia, *Le Triple Démisme de Suen Wên* (Shanghai, 1930), which has also been put into English; a very interesting volume showing how Sun's ideas in the latter part of the *San Min Chu I* were radically modified—to the extent of repudiating the orthodox Marxian theory of the class war—by reading Maurice William's *The Social Interpretation of History*, in Maurice William, *Sun Yat-sen versus Communism* (Baltimore, 1932); Sun Yat-sen, *The International Development of China* (New York, 1922), a quite impracticable program; on the early life of Sun Yat-sen, with a brief sketch of his later years, H. B. Restarick, *Sun Yat-sen, Liberator of China* (New Haven, 1931); a competent summary of well-known material, B. Martin, *Strange Vigour. A Biography of Sun Yat-sen* (London, 1944); the best biography of the revolutionist, L. Sharman, *Sun Yat-sen, His Life and Its Meaning, a Critical Biography* (New York, 1934); H. M. Vinacke, *Modern Constitutional Development in China* (Princeton, 1920), only fairly good; R. Gilbert, *What's Wrong with China* (London, 1926), by a newspaper correspondent of several years' residence in China, taking an extremely pessimistic and highly controversial view of the ability of the Chinese to govern themselves; M. T. Z. Tyau, *Two Years of Nationalistic China* (Shanghai, 1930), largely an account, sympathetic, of the organization of the Kuomintang and the Nationalist Government at Nanking, in 1930; N. Peffer, *China, The Collapse of a Civilization* (New York, 1930), by a journalist of a good deal of experience in China, well written, and decidedly pessimistic; a novel portraying social and political changes, Lin Yutang, *Moment in Peking* (New York, 1939); Hallett Abend, *Tortured China* (New York, 1930), also a pessimistic account by a journalist, but not so well written as the last; A. M. Kotenev, *New Lamps for Old* (Shanghai, 1931), a history mostly of recent events, of irregular value and reliability; T'ang Leang-li, *The Inner History of the Chinese Revolution* (London, 1930), by a Chinese non-Communist radical; T. A. Bisson, *The Nanking Government* (Foreign Policy Association, Information Service, Oct. 30, 1929, Vol. 5, No. 17); *Communism in China* (*Foreign Affairs*, Jan., 1931, pp. 310–316); E. Snow, *Red Star Over China* (New York, 1938).

On the internal political history of China after 1937 see three excellent studies, each approaching the scene from somewhat different angles: P. M. Linebarger, *The China of Chiang Kai-shek: a Political Study* (Boston, 1941); L. K. Rosinger, *China's Wartime Politics, 1937–1944* (Princeton, 1944); and D. H. Rowe, *China among the Powers* (New York, 1945).

No really good biography of Chiang Kai-shek has yet been written. A somewhat conventional one, favorable to him, is H. H. Chang, *Chiang Kai-shek, Asia's Man of Destiny* (Garden City, 1944). Somewhat more objective is R. Berkov, *Strong Man of China* (Boston, 1938). Translations of some of his writings are Chiang Kai-shek, *All We Are and All We Have* (New York, 1943?) and Chiang Kai-shek, *Resistance and Reconstruction* (New York, 1943). Selections from the writings of his colorful wife are in May-ling Soong Chiang, *This Is Our China* (New York, 1940). See also F. W. Price, editor, *Wartime China as Seen by Westerners* (Chungking, 1942).

The son of Sun Yat-sen, influential, but not fully in accord with his brother-in-law, Chiang Kai-shek, set forth some of his views in Sun Fo, *China Looks Forward* (New York, 1944).

On the foreign settlements in Shanghai there are C. B. Maybon and J. Fredet, *Histoire de la Concession Française de Changhai* (Paris, 1929); G. Lanning and L. Couling, *The History of Shanghai* (Shanghai, 1902); F. L. H. Pott, *A Short History of Shanghai* (Shanghai, 1928); R. H. Barnett, *Economic Shanghai: Hostage to Politics, 1937–1941* (New York, 1943); and A. M. Kotenev, *Shanghai. Its mixed Court and Council* (Shanghai, 1925). The report of Mr. Justice Feetham to the Shanghai Municipal Council made in 1931 is a notable document. A summary, by Feetham, of Vol. 1 is in *The China Year Book, 1931–2*, pp. 45–86.

On the foreign relations of China after 1905, the following are among the most useful: T. E. La Fargue, *China and the World War* (Stanford, 1937); J. G. Reid, *The Manchu Abdication and the Powers, 1908–1912* (Berkeley, 1935); F. V. Field, *American Participation in the China Consortiums* (Chicago, 1931); H. Croly, *Willard Straight* (New York, 1924), the biography of a young American who attempted to maintain the open door in Manchuria and had much to do with negotiating international loans for China; P. S. Reinsch, *An American Diplomat in China* (Garden City, 1922), a narrative of events by the American Minister to China during the World War; G. Z. Wood, *The Shantung Question, A Study in Diplomacy and World Politics* (New York, 1922), an *ex parte* statement of the Chinese position; C. F. Chang, *The Anglo-Japanese Alliance* (Baltimore, 1931); R. L. Buell, *The Washington Conference* (New York, 1922), the best general report of that gathering; W. W. Willoughby, *China at the Conference*

(Baltimore, 1922), a fuller account of the actions of the Washington Conference which affected China; *Report of Commission on Extraterritoriality in China* (Washington, 1926), the official findings of the international commission promised at the Washington Conference; H. K. Norton, *China and the Powers* (New York, 1927), excellent; V. A. Yakhontoff, *Russia and the Soviet Union in the Far East* (New York, 1931), a history of the international situation in the Far East with a bias in favor of Soviet Russia; Louis Fischer, *The Soviets in World Affairs. A History of Relations between the Soviet Union and the Rest of the World* (New York, 1930), informed and moderately favorable to Russia; Wong Ching-wai, *China and the Nations* (New York, 1927), setting forth the foreign policies of the radicals of the Kuomintang; T. F. Millard, *The End of Extraterritoriality in China* (Shanghai, 1931), siding with the Chinese and valuable for its many documents and appendices; *Problems of the Pacific* (Chicago, 1928, 1930, 1932), three volumes comprising the papers and discussions of the biennial meetings of the Institute of Pacific Relations, one at Honolulu in 1927, another at Kyoto in 1929, and a third in Shanghai in 1931, and all containing important material on China's foreign affairs. Some phases of American policy are discussed in a monograph prepared for the Institute of Pacific Relations, P. G. Wright, *The American Tariff and Oriental Trade* (Chicago, 1931). Lionel Curtis, *The Capital Question of China* (London, 1932) offers a program by which he believes Western powers can help China. Robert T. Pollard, *China's Foreign Relations 1917–1931* (New York, 1933) is a carefully written survey of these interesting years. See also the important book, A. W. Griswold, *The Far Eastern Policy of the United States* (New York, 1938), H. L. Stimson, *The Far Eastern Crisis* (New York, 1936), P. H. Clyde, *United States Policy Toward China. Diplomatic and Public Documents, 1839–1939* (Durham, 1940), R. T. Pollard, *China's Foreign Relations, 1917–1931* (New York, 1933), G. E. Taylor, *The Struggle for North China* (New York, 1940), H. S. Quigley, *Far Eastern War, 1937–1941* (Boston, 1942), E. Snow, *The Battle for Asia* (New York, 1941), W. C. Johnstone, *The United States and Japan's New Order* (New York, 1941), and I. S. Friedman, *British Relations with China, 1931–1939* (New York, 1940).

On Manchuria, among others, there are C. W. Young, *The International Relations of Manchuria* (Chicago, 1929), a study prepared for the Institute of Pacific Relations; C. W. Young, *Japan's Jurisdiction and International Legal Position in Manchuria* (3 vols., Baltimore, 1931), a much fuller study than the last; P. H. Clyde, *International Rivalries in Manchuria* (Columbus, 1926), an historical survey; Shuhsi Hsu, *China and Her Political Entity* (New York, 1926), a scholarly study with a pro-Chinese bias of China's foreign relations with reference to Korea, Manchuria, and Mongolia; Owen Lattimore, *Manchuria, Cradle of Conflict* (New York, 1932), a thoughtful and independent description and analysis by one who has travelled extensively in Manchuria; Chih Meng, *China Speaks on the Conflict between China and Japan* (New York, 1932), an *ex parte* statement; K. K. Kawakami, *Japan Speaks on the Sino-Japanese Conflict* (New York, 1932), likewise *ex parte* and much less careful with its facts than the one by Meng; and K. K. Kawakami, *Manchoukuo, Child of Conflict* (New York, 1933), also propagandist and pro-Japanese. The report of the so-called Lytton Commission appointed by the League of Nations is singularly fair. It is in *League of Nations. Appeal by the Chinese Government. Report of the Commission of Inquiry* (*Series of League of Nations Publications, VII. Political. 1932. VII, 12*). The story of the League of Nations' relation to the Sino-Japanese dispute into the spring of 1932 is in Felix Morley, *The Society of Nations* (Washington, 1932). The Japanese case is officially presented in two large volumes, *The Present Condition of China. Document A* (July, 1932) and *Relations of Japan with Manchuria and Mongolia. Document B* (July, 1932). The Chinese case is in V. K. Wellington Koo, *Memoranda Presented to the Lytton Commission* (2 vols., New York, 1932). Some Chinese fiction portraying the resistance to the Japanese is translated in T'ien Chün, *Village in August* (New York, 1942).

On economic history and conditions, some excellent books are W. H. Mallory, *China, Land of Famine* (New York, 1927); C. F. Remer, *The Foreign Trade of China* (Shanghai, 1926), a careful historical survey of China's foreign commerce in the nineteenth and twentieth centuries; J. L. Buck, *Chinese Farm Economy* (Shanghai and Chicago, 1930); Julean Arnold, *China, A Commercial and Industrial Handbook* (Washington, 1926), by the well-known commercial attaché of the American legation in China; R. H. Tawney, *Land and Labour in China* (1932), by a distinguished British expert; T. P. Meng and S. D. Gamble, *Prices, Wages and the Standard of Living at Peking, 1900–1924* (*Special Supplement to the Chinese Social and Political Science Review*, July, 1926). Two excellent books dealing with recent economic conditions, especially in foreign trade, are Edith E. Ware, *Business and Politics in the Far East* (New Haven, 1932) and Grover Clark, *Economic Rivalries in China* (New Haven, 1932). An even more inclusive book is J. B. Condliffe, *China To-day. Economic* (Boston, 1932). See fuller bibliography at end of Chapter XV. See also G. H. Blakeslee, *The Foreign Stake in China* (*Foreign Affairs*, Oct. 1931, Vol. 10, pp. 81–91), C. F. Remer, *Foreign Investments in China* (New York, 1933), Chang Kia-ngau, *China's Struggle for Railway Development* (New York, 1943), H. Freyn, *Free China's New Deal* (New York, 1943), Kuo-heng Shih, *China Enters the Machine Age. A Study of Chinese War Industry* (Harvard University Press, 1944), and E. M. Hinder, *Life and Labour in Shanghai* (New York, 1944).

Some of the new religious movements in China are described by L. Hodous in *The Christian Occupation of China* (Shanghai, 1922), pp. 27–31. K. S. Latourette, *A History of Christian Missions in China* (New York, 1929), the standard book on its subject, brings the story down into 1927. See also J. Richter, *Das Werden der christlichen Kirche in China* (Gütersloh, 1928). Important reference books and periodicals for Protestant missions are *The Christian Occupation of China*, edited by M. T. Stauffer (Shanghai, 1922); *The Chinese Recorder* (a monthly, covering all Protestant missions, and published at Foochow, 1867-1872, and at Shanghai, 1874 *et seq.*); *The China Mission Year Book* (with occasional gaps, published yearly at Shanghai, 1910 *et seq.* and beginning with 1926 called *The China Christian Year Book*). On Roman Catholic missions see J. M. Planchet, *Les Missions de Chine et du Japon* (published about every other year at Peking, the second issue being in 1917). See fuller bibliography at end of Chapter XVI.

On intellectual movements, including the Renaissance, see *Bulletins on Chinese Education* (various authors, Shanghai, 1923); *China Today Through Chinese Eyes* (various authors; first series, London, 1922, second series, London, 1927), by younger Chinese; Paul Monroe, *A Report on Education in China* (New York, 1922); R. S. Britton, *The Chinese Periodical Press, 1800-1912* (Shanghai, 1933); Hu Shih, *The Chinese Renaissance* (Chicago, 1934); P. W. Kuo, *The Chinese System of Public Education* (New York, 1914); T. C. Wang, *The Youth Movement of China* (New York, 1928); C. H. Peake, *Nationalism and Education in Modern China* (New York, 1932); T'ang Leang-li, *China in Revolt* (London, 1927); F. R. Millican, *Philosophical and Religious Thought in China* (*China Christian Year Book*, 1926, pp. 423-469); Ph. de Vargas, *Some Elements in the Chinese Renaissance* (*New China Review*, April and June, 1922). The autobiography of a modern scholar, Ku Chieh-kang, who bridges the transition between the old and the new, and a very intimate and revealing document showing the forces playing on men of his kind and his reaction to them, has been translated by A. W. Hummel in *The Autobiography of a Chinese Historian, Being the Preface to a Symposium in Ancient Chinese History* (*Ku Shih Pien*) (Leyden, 1931). See also the bibliography at the end of Chapter XIX.

On social changes, see Lady Hosie, *Portrait of a Chinese Lady and Certain of Her Contemporaries* (New York, 1930); William Hung (editor), *As It Looks to Young China* (New York, 1932); and many articles in *The China Mission Year Book* and the *China Christian Year Book*. See also the bibliography at the end of Chapter XVII.

THE CHINESE
THEIR HISTORY AND CULTURE
VOLUME II

CHAPTER XIII

THE CHINESE PEOPLE

RACIAL COMPOSITION

RACIALLY the Chinese are a mixed people. That much we know. We have definite records of many invasions of the fertile valleys and plains of North China by non-Chinese stocks from the less favored regions on the north, northeast, and west. Whenever one of these incursions led to a prolonged or extensive occupation of territory—as numbers of them did—it must have been followed by an infiltration of the blood of the conquerors into that of the conquered. Knowing as we do the names of at least the chief of these invaders, we can be aware in a general way of some of the more potent strains which in the past two thousand or twenty-five hundred years have mingled with whatever may have been the Chinese stock or stocks at the dawn of recorded history. Hsiung Nu, Turks of various kinds, several branches of the Mongols, Tanguts, and Tungusic peoples, including the Juchên and the Manchus—to mention only some of the more prominent—each occupied part or all of North China. Each must have made a more or less permanent contribution to the population of the region. It is also a commonplace that the Chinese are bordered to-day as they have been for centuries by non-Chinese of many kinds—such as the Koreans, the Mongols, the Tibetans, the Miao, the Lo-lo, and the Mo-so—with almost inevitable intermixture.

We do not know, however, all the racial strains which have entered to form the Chinese of to-day, nor are we sure of the relationships among many of the stocks of whose names we are aware. That is chiefly because we are not certain of all the components of the population of what is now China at the dawn of the historic period. It is not yet clear, for example, whether the earliest civilized Chinese were a mixture—even though, from analogy with other early inhabitants of fertile valleys, we may guess that they were. We can only conjecture that the sharp division between commoners and aristocrats in ancient times represented also a racial difference. It appears to be probable that the skeletal remains associated with the chalcolithic culture discovered in North China in recent years indicate a continuity that is almost an identity between the peoples of that remote civilization and the inhabitants of the same region to-day. If that should prove to be true, later infiltrations of other stocks can have wrought no very profound modifications. It is clear that the civilized Chinese of the Shang and the Chou were surrounded by peoples whom they regarded as barbarians and who appear to have been divided into many tribes. What the precise ethnology of all these barbarians was, however, is by no means established. Nor are we at all sure of the racial affiliations of these early Chinese themselves. South China was quite probably once peopled, at least in part, by negritos of types similar to those still found in some of the islands southeast of Asia. Linguistic groups represented, which probably to some extent were identical with racial stocks, were the Mon-Khmer, the Tibeto-Burman, and the Sino-T'ai. The T'ai, now strong in the extreme South and Southwest, and represented by the modern Siamese, very likely once reached much farther northward than at present. Possibly, too, there were other strains.

Similarly, it is certain that through the centuries there has been a southward migration of Chinese from the North into and south of the Yangtze Valley. The northern Chinese there encountered other peoples whom they probably partly drove back and partly absorbed. Again, however, we do not yet know whether the Chinese were originally related to these stocks, and, if so, to what extent. It is obvious to the most casual observer that the Chinese of the North are somewhat different from the Chinese of the South—for instance, that as a rule the former tend to be taller by an average of two or more inches, heavier, less dark of complexion, with less broad noses, more conservative, more stable, and more phlegmatic than the latter. The people of Central China are intermediate between the two extremes. How much these differences are the result of varying racial admixtures and how much they are due to contrasts in climate, food, and physical environment is not, however, at all clear.

Even more difficult than the determination of the racial stocks which have formed the Chinese is the discovery of the proportion in which the different known strains have entered into the present population. The process of amalgamation by which the Chinese of to-day have come into being is by no means complete. Chinese are usually black of hair, yet many, especially among the children, have dark and light-brown hair, and a reddish tinge is not unknown. The Chinese are usually scant of beard, yet heavily bearded individuals are by no means lacking. Chinese, moreover, are popularly called members of the "Yellow Race," yet, although the skin of most Chinese is, when compared with that of the peoples of Northern Europe, "yellow," some, particularly among the classes where bathing is customary and the body is protected by clothing from the sun and wind, have a skin as white as that of Europeans. Chinese are usually spoken of as "slant-eyed," yet great numbers entirely lack that kind of physiognomy. Some variations are, of course, individual and occupational. Others, however, appear to be survivals of racial differences.

Among peoples obviously Chinese some marked groupings occur which verge on the racial and are evidence of imperfect amalgamation. One of the most notable examples is the Hakkas. The word itself means "guest people" or "stranger people." The Hakkas dwell mostly in the hilly regions of Kiangsi, Fukien, Kwangtung, and Kwangsi, speak a distinctive dialect, and possess some customs which set them apart from their neighbors— as, for example, the refusal to bind the feet of their women. They appear to be the descendants of immigrants from the North who came south at several different times and were never fully absorbed, but preserved, among other characteristics, a tongue more nearly like that of the North than the other Chinese around them. Moslems, too, while most of them are Chinese in language and a large proportion of them are of older Chinese stock, often have differences in accent, dress, and appearance which reveal traces of immigrant blood, and some are distinctly non-Chinese in race and language. The immigrant Moslem stock is itself not uniform, but has in it at least Turkish, Mongol, and Arab strains, each of which predominates in certain sections.

In the South and the Southwest, moreover, are numerous peoples who are not Chinese in speech or customs. Intermarriage has often taken place, and in many places the process of assimilation to the Chinese—which has undoubtedly been in progress for many centuries—can still be observed. In parts of Szechwan, in Hunan, Kweichow, Yünnan, Kwangsi, and Kwangtung, including Hainan, are hundreds of thousands of these non-Chinese peoples. As a rule they tend to inhabit the hills and mountains, apparently because the Chinese have driven them out of the more fertile valleys and plains. They are divided into numerous tribes, such as the Chung Chia, the Miao, Miao Tzŭ, or Miao Chia (made up of several groups, among whom are the Hei Miao, or "Black Miao," apparently so called because of their dark-colored clothes, and the Hua or "Flowery" Miao), the Kachins, the Keh-lao, the Loi (on Hainan), the Lo-lo, the Yao, the Mo-so, and the Man Tzŭ or Man Chia. The ethnological classification of these peoples is highly debatable. There may well be among them some remnants of negrito stock. One linguistic analysis divides them into three groups—Lo-lo, Shan, and Miao—and another into Mon-Khmer, Shan, and Tibeto-Burmans. As we have seen, it is probable that some of them are unassimilated remnants of peoples who were once more widespread in China than at present and have been in part absorbed by and so have entered into the racial composition of the people whom we now call the Chinese. Usually they are much inferior to the Chinese in civilization (although representatives in Indo-China and Siam have reached high cultural levels) and are regarded by the latter much as folk of primitive manners are nearly everywhere viewed by peoples of more advanced cultures. The Chinese have exploited them, have driven them out of desirable lands, and have held them in contempt.

In the North and Northwest live other peoples whom the Chinese have not absorbed. In regions such as the New Dominion and Outer Mongolia the non-Chinese form the majority and the Chinese are obviously still immigrants. In Inner Mongolia the Chinese seem to be making a fairly effective bid for supremacy wherever sufficient moisture exists for settled agriculture. In Manchuria the Chinese, as a race, are in the ascendancy, although in some sections the Koreans, seeking escape from intolerable economic conditions at home, are serious competitors. In the northernmost tier of the old Eighteen Provinces, especially in Kansu, reside many unassimilated descendants of immigrants. Numbers of these are Moslems, and religious differences slow down amalgamation.

In spite of all the surviving variations in race, the great mass of the Chinese people is remarkably homogeneous in physical appearance and culture. The differences are neither so marked nor so numerous as are those in Western Europe, in the Near East, or in India.

The approach to uniformity is probably due chiefly to the type of government and culture under which the Chinese have lived. The political structure of the Empire, made up largely of a bureaucracy educated in the orthodox philosophy of the state, and inculcating conformity to this philosophy, welded people into a cultural whole. Political unity favored movements of peoples within the Empire. Some of these were engineered by the state—as, for example, the extensive colonization and forced migration under the Ch'in and the Han. Others were entirely voluntary and often took place on a large scale in times of famine, when thousands of refugees fled from their old homes in search of food. The absence of marked differences of caste and the principle of recruiting the powerful official class on the basis of worth as disclosed in the civil service examinations and not on that of birth helped to produce a more or less fluid society in which wide intermarriage was comparatively easy. The long-established custom that no man could marry a bride of his own family name operated in the same direction. Conquerors were usually assimilated fairly promptly. This was in striking contrast with India, where caste lines tended to keep races apart and to preserve blood distinctions between the successive waves of invasion. The political unity of China during a large part of its history and the consequent absence of internal political barriers to migration within the Empire also made for uniformity—in contrast, for example, with Europe. As a result, no other group of mankind anywhere nearly equal to the Chinese in numerical strength approximates it in homogeneity.

NUMERICAL STRENGTH

The usual figure quoted for the population of China is four hundred millions. All totals are, however, a source of sharp disagreement among experts. Census methods comparable in accuracy with those employed in the modern West and Japan and even in India have never been applied to China as a whole. The best estimates possible are approximations which may ultimately prove to be in error by tens of millions. For example, a census was taken by the government in 1910, in which the returns were by households. Serious uncertainty exists as to the average number of individuals in a household, and attempts to translate the figures from households to individuals result in such variant totals for all China as 342.6 millions and 329.6 millions. Even the accuracy of the number of households is highly debatable. A careful estimate made in 1918–1919 by the Protestant missionary forces gave a total of individuals in all China of 452.6 millions (for China proper and Manchuria of 440.9 millions), but the compiler regarded the figures as only approximations and declared that the then population of Chinese Republic was between 350 and 400 millions. An estimate made in 1920 by the Post Office placed the population of China proper and Manchuria at 427.6 millions, and another one made in 1926 by the same agency gave for China proper and Manchuria a total of 485.5 millions. At least one other calculation is still higher than this last. Another estimate—for 1930—put the population in that year at 445 millions, official figures of the Nanking Government released in 1931 give it as 474.4 millions, and the total announced by the Nanking Government in 1932 was 474.78 millions. One of the greatest of Occidental authorities on population statistics, after some years of study and evaluation of available returns, estimated all China to have had 342 millions in 1930, but recognized "that no one knows what the population of China is within many millions." His figure, however, has been vigorously contested as far too low.

The population is very unevenly distributed. The areas of greatest density are in the fertile alluvial plains in the southeastern part of Kiangsu and the northeastern part of Chêkiang, on the North China plain, particularly where Shantung, Honan, and Hopei (Chihli) corner on one another, in the extraordinarily productive Red Basin in the center of Szechwan, and around Canton, where favorable harbors and rich bottom lands encourage trade and agriculture. Other congested centers are along the coast of Fukien and Chêkiang and in and around the Wuhan cities in Hupeh. In some of the most thickly settled regions the number of farmers eking out an existence on a square mile of land rivals that of any other section of the world.

The necessary inaccuracy which is the despair of all who wish exact figures for to-day bedevils all attempts to estimate the numbers of Chinese in existence in earlier centuries. The Chinese Government has taken enumerations many times. This was an almost inevitable accompaniment of the levying of taxation and of the recruiting of armies. As a rule, however, the returns gave only the totals by households or adults. Even in these the percentage of error was probably high, if for no other reason than because of the desire of individuals to avoid taxation or military service and of officials to juggle the figures for their own benefit. Even if the summaries were accurate, the problem of determining from them the total population would remain. Moreover, the areas included are not always the same. The results of the several attempts which have been made to estimate what the population of the Empire was at various periods must, then, be regarded as conjectures which may be very far removed from the truth.

Ma Tuan-lin, a distinguished scholar who flourished in the thirteenth century A.D., is responsible for the statement that in the ninth century B.C. a census gave 13.7 million persons between the ages of fifteen and sixty-five as living north of the Yangtze River, and an estimate based upon his report declares that the total population of this area was then 21.7 millions. Ma Tuan-lin gives the results of ten enumerations of the population taken between A.D. 2 and 155. The average of the ten, reduced to individuals (on a conjectural scale which may be greatly in error), is 63.5 millions, varying from 83.6 millions, the first, to 29.1 millions, the fifth, the great differences being ascribed to civil war and to incomplete returns. Probably, too, the areas measured were not exactly the same. In A.D. 280, after long strife, the population is put at 23.1 millions, and in 606 at 46 millions.

An estimate for A.D. 618, much higher than some others, places the total at 129.45 millions. A return from 652 gives 3.8 million households, or, on the basis of 5.5 persons per household—at best a rough estimate—24.9 million individuals. One for 733 gives 7.86 million households, or, on the same basis, 43.2 million individuals, and another, for 755, 9.6 million households, or, again on the basis of 5.5 persons per unit, 52.8 million individuals. These four, all from the T'ang dynasty, reflect something of the prosperity of that period. In 1097, under the Sung, before the provinces in the North had been lost to invaders, the total population, based on households (19.4 millions) is estimated at 101.2 million persons. In Mongol times the figures indicate a population of between 55 and 60 millions. Ming figures point to a population of about the same total as under the Mongols. Under the Ch'ing, especially in the eighteenth and the early part of the nineteenth century, when the Empire was enjoying great material prosperity, the totals seem to have mounted very rapidly. Many estimates have been made, based in part upon census returns. What appears to be a fairly conservative set of figures, arising out of the studies made by Western scholars, gives the following totals:

1650	70 millions
1710	140 "
1850	342 "
1910	342 "
1930	342 "

Another set of figures, less conservative, gives the following:

1741	143,410,559
1771	214,600,356
1793	313,281,795
1800	295,237,361
1821	355,540,258
1840	412,814,828
1849	412,986,643

Government figures, giving only partial returns, have been interpreted as showing an increase of about 7.8 per cent. between 1910 and about 1929. Estimates most carefully made by one of the universities in about 1931 and based on a variety of data, including buildings, occupied land, and the like, indicate an increase of twenty per cent. since the close of the T'ai P'ing Rebellion (1864) and of ten per cent. since 1900.

THE EXPANSION OF THE CHINESE PEOPLE

All the figures for the past two hundred and fifty years which have any claim to credibility indicate a phenomenal growth in the population of China—an increase, it may be noted, which is paralleled by that of the rest of the world, so that the Chinese probably now constitute only a slightly larger proportion of the total bulk of mankind than in 1650.

The Chinese have been not only multiplying but geographically expanding. We have seen how, in early historic times confined chiefly to the North China plain and the valley of the Wei, they gradually spread, amalgamating with and absorbing many of the other cultural and racial groups with whom they came in contact. For many centuries that expansion was largely but by no means exclusively southward. Particularly were there southward movements in the centuries when the North was in the hands of invaders—between the Han and the Sui, and during the Sung. Migration also brought the Chinese into the highlands of Shansi, Shensi, and Inner Mongolia, into the valleys of Kansu, into Szechwan, into Yünnan, into Manchuria (long only in inconsiderable numbers and in the southern districts), and, to a limited extent, into the oases of what is now Sinkiang. After all of this expansion, however, at the beginning of the Ch'ing dynasty, nearly three centuries ago, the Chinese were chiefly confined to China proper.

In the nineteenth and twentieth centuries (and probably, although less markedly, in the seventeenth and eighteenth centuries) the Chinese spread widely beyond these boundaries. This was due to several causes—the great multiplication of population under the beneficent rule of the strong Ch'ing Emperors, the improved transportation facilities and the economic development of lands in the Pacific basin, and, latterly, political disorders in China. The Chinese have proved to be physically adaptable to many different climates. They have thrived in the cold of Manchuria and in the heat of tropical lands. To be sure, those who have moved into Manchuria have been from northern China, where the winters are frigid, and those who have gone to the tropics have been from the provinces on the south coast, so that in neither case has the change in climatic environment been revolutionary. Even with this qualification the Chinese have proved adaptable—much more so than have the Japanese. As manual laborers they have been industrious, frugal, and capable of withstanding great hardships. As merchants and artisans they have been enterprising and persistent. As a race, they have displayed great capacity for survival and multiplication, qualities which have given them an advantage in competition with other peoples.

In the past three centuries the Chinese have spread into many and widely scattered regions. They have pushed into Inner Mongolia and lately their settlement in that area has been recognized by the creation of the new provinces of Jehol, Chahar, Suiyüan, and Ninghsia. The Mongols, as we said in the last chapter, often resent this Chinese settlement.

Chinese have poured into Manchuria by the million. During most of the years of the greatest strength of the Ch'ing dynasty, the Manchu rulers attempted to reserve the larger part of their ancestral home for their own race. They long tried to keep the Chinese out entirely, and, when that proved futile, to restrict the immigration to certain sections, chiefly in the province of Fengtien. Yet considerable numbers of Chinese filtered past the barriers set up by the Manchus into some of the most fertile portions of the forbidden districts. For years, although there were many permanent settlers, much of the migration into Manchuria was seasonal—made up of laborers, chiefly from Hopei (Chihli) and Shantung, who went north for the months when they could find work on the farms and in the winter returned to their homes. By 1900 there were probably only between ten and fifteen million people in all Manchuria (and perhaps much less), although of these the majority seem to have been Chinese. In the twentieth century the population has greatly increased. One estimate placed it at twenty-two and a half millions in 1920 and in 1927 at more than twenty-six millions. In 1932 it was estimated as being thirty millions. Of the thirty millions all but about two millions were Chinese or assimilated Manchus. This growth was due partly to the improved transportation afforded by the railways and steamships, partly to labor recruiting agents from Manchuria, including representatives of the Japanese mines, partly to the opening of new lands, and partly to the disorder south of the Great Wall and the comparative peace in Manchuria before 1931. Particularly did the immigration increase after 1924, mounting in 1926 to not far from a million. Of this a larger proportion than in earlier years seems to have been made up of permanent settlers. The changing character of the settlement is evidenced further by what appears to have been an increasing proportion of women and children in the immigration. Immediately before 1931 the movement to Manchuria, moreover, was stimulated by Chinese officials. In parts of Manchuria settlers were offered free lands. Chinese Government railways gave them reduced rates, and at least one Governor of Shantung encouraged his people to go. Both the Chinese Eastern Railway and the Japanese lines gave reduced fares to Chinese immigrants. Numbers migrated north of the Amur and east of the Ussuri and hence constituted a factor in the population of the eastern part of Siberia. The rate of migration into Manchuria and the regions north of it slowed down somewhat immediately after September, 1931, but later seems again to have increased.

The Chinese have settled Formosa. At the outset of the Ch'ing dynasty that island appears to have had comparatively few of them. However, Formosa became a haven for many partisans of the Ming and for a time was controlled by Koxinga. After annexation by the Manchus it remained part of the Empire until, in 1895, it was ceded to Japan. It was peopled largely from Kwangtung and Fukien and the movement to its shores continued even after the Japanese occupation. To-day the bulk of the population is of Chinese stock, either pure or mixed with other elements.

There have been a few thousand Chinese in Japan and Korea, chiefly merchants and skilled workmen.

A fairly extensive migration has moved towards the lands immediately to the south of China. Indeed, the Chinese have here won an economic empire, even though the political control remains in other hands. Most of the emigrants have found occupation as merchants or skilled laborers. They have come chiefly from Kwangtung and Fukien. A large proportion of them have not remained abroad permanently, but have thought of China as their home, and their remittances to their families and the contributions, both economic and in ideas, which the returning wanderers have made to their native communities have been important factors in the development of the two southern coast provinces.

In the days of the Spanish occupation Chinese held an important place in the economic life of the Philippines. From time to time their number was reduced by massacres, but they persisted in coming. After the cession of the islands to the United States, the Chinese exclusion acts of that government were extended to the Philippines, but even to-day probably about one hundred and twenty thousand Chinese have their homes in the archipelago. The major part of the retail business and much of the wholesale trade has been in their hands.

Several scores of thousands (perhaps half a million) Chinese are to be found in French Indo-China. They have a large share in the retail trade of the country. Until recently, they controlled much of the rice market and held many of the peasants in a kind of economic bondage, but in the past few years that monopoly has been shaken—partly by the French and through the introduction of Western methods of administering large plantations.

Chinese have long been prominent in Siam (Thailand), especially in Bangkok, and have intermarried extensively with the Siamese. The Chinese of pure race in the kingdom probably number not far from three millions. A Chinese Government estimate of about 1920 asserts that they total a million and a half, but this is probably greatly below the facts. They have been prominent in business, the trades, and the professions, and in their hands has been much of the mining, the refining of sugar, and the rice milling.

Chinese are very important in the trade and industry of Burma. Perhaps four hundred thousand of them were there before the Japanese invasion. They have come both by sea and overland by way of Yünnan. Nearly every village has its Chinese moneylenders.

In what in 1941 was British Malaya—the British-controlled portions of the Malay peninsula and its adjoining islands—the number of Chinese was about equal to the native Malay stock. They began arriving centuries before the British occupation, but under British rule greatly multiplied and formed the major part of the population of Singapore. As laborers, artisans, merchants, miners, contractors, planters, and professional men, they have been largely responsible for the economic development of the region. The British were in possession politically and controlled no small part of the economic life, but the Chinese profited enormously from the peace and prosperity which were the fruitage of British rule. The Chinese have been so important a factor in the population of British Malaya that in more ways than one they have constituted a special problem: for example, it has been a moot question as to how large a share they should be given in the government.

For centuries the East Indies have known the Chinese. Fairly large migrations took place under the Ming and again after the downfall of the Ming. For some years after the beginning of their power in the East Indies, the Dutch encouraged the Chinese to come, for the presence of the latter aided the development of the islands. When, in later years, the Chinese seemed to have become a menace, the Dutch instituted restrictions and oppressive measures, and in 1740 these culminated in a massacre, centering at Batavia, in which several thousand Chinese were killed. The Chinese continued to arrive, however, particularly after the middle of the nineteenth century, and by 1917 their number in the Dutch East Indies was estimated at seven hundred and seventy thousand, of whom nearly half were in Java. A census of 1930 gave the total as 1,233,856 (749,530 men and 484,326 women) and that of 1940 placed the total at 1,430,680. Thousands were manual laborers in mines and on plantations, but other thousands were skilled mechanics and traders and many became large landowners and wealthy merchants. To Borneo likewise the Chinese have been going for hundreds of years, and the island now contains an undetermined number of them—possibly between four and five hundred thousand. As elsewhere in the lands immediately to the south and southeast of China, much of the mining and trade is in their hands.

In Australia and New Zealand the chief attraction which first drew numbers of Chinese was gold-mining—although a few had arrived earlier for other purposes. The initial large immigration was in the eighteen fifties. Before long opposition developed, for the Chinese proved competitors to some of the dominant white stock. Restrictions were placed on Chinese immigration, and the total number of Chinese in the two dominions is small—not far from twenty-five thousand. Groups of Chinese, none of them—except in Hawaii—numerically very considerable, are to be found in several others of the Pacific islands.

Early in the twentieth century an experiment with Chinese contract labor was made in the gold mines of South Africa, but it was not long continued and the laborers were sent home. Only a few hundred Chinese are now to be found in that dominion.

We have already seen (Chapter XI) that Chinese first began coming in large numbers to the United States in the eighteen fifties in connection with the gold rush to California. They supplied much of the unskilled labor and later many were employed in building and maintaining railroads. We have seen that agitation against them began early, the basic reasons being that, with their low standard of living, the Chinese competed successfully with white laborers, and that they were not easily assimilated. We have seen, too, that, except for the temporary residence of such groups as merchants and students, immigration was prohibited, earlier for periods of years and later (1902 and 1904) indefinitely. In 1943 this exclusion was repealed. The largest number of Chinese reported in the continental portion of the United States was by the census of 1890, when the total had mounted to 107,448. From then on it dwindled. Except for the large number of students, most of the Chinese in the United States are engaged in such specialized occupations as domestic service, market gardening, labor in canneries, laundrying, and restaurant-keeping.

At the time of their annexation to the United States the Hawaiian Islands contained about twenty-five thousand Chinese residents, and that in spite of measures which had been taken in the eighteen eighties and nineties to reduce the number of new arrivals. After annexation, the exclusion acts of the United States were applied, and Chinese laborers who were not American citizens were forbidden to go to the mainland. Chinese still constitute one of the largest racial elements of the extremely mixed population of the islands.

In Canada the story is similar. Chinese began coming in numbers in the eighteen sixties to engage in mining and to do much of the rough work in building the Canadian Pacific railway. Opposition later developed because of competition with white labor, and restrictions on further immigration were enacted, chiefly in the form of a head tax on each arrival. The tax was increased until it became almost prohibitive.

There are Chinese contingents in Mexico, in several of the countries of Central and South America, and in some of the islands of the West Indies. The largest numbers are in Mexico, Cuba, Trinidad, British Guiana, Panama, Brazil, and Peru, the two last-named countries having more than any of the others. In 1931 a vigorous anti-Chinese movement broke out in Mexico which led to the exodus of several thousands, and some anti-Chinese agitation occurred in Peru.

Except for the laborers employed in the World War and for students, very few Chinese have been resident in Europe.

From this necessarily brief and somewhat statistical survey, it is clear that widespread migrations of Chinese have been in progress, especially during the second half of the nineteenth and in the twentieth century. Outside the political boundaries of China (or at least the territories occupied by the Ch'ing dynasty), however, the total number of Chinese, when compared to that of those who have remained at home, is inconsiderable—with Manchuria, Hongkong, and Formosa counted out, probably eight millions, or about two per cent. of the whole. Emigration, then, has afforded but little relief to the congestion of population in China.

The small size of this movement overseas has been due in part to the reluctance of the Chinese to expatriate themselves and in part to the restrictions placed on them in most of the lands to which they would care to go. Unpopularity has been the result partly of the clannishness of the Chinese—for in spite of extensive intermarriage with natives they have tended to keep apart—but probably has been due chiefly to economic factors. In lands immediately south of China the Chinese trader and moneylender are often more aggressive and thrifty than the natives and even hold some of that stock in a kind of economic servitude. They are frequently, therefore, both feared and hated. In lands like Australia and North America, which have been preëmpted by the white race and which are suitable to extensive settlement by them, the Chinese laborer, with his industry and his lower standard of living, is feared as a competitor and is either completely or all but completely excluded. It seems probable that so long as the white race remains in control of the more salubrious of the comparatively thinly settled sections of the world, there will be no very large migration of the Chinese beyond their own borders. Wherever he has gone, however, especially in British Malaya and the Dutch East Indies, the Chinese has contributed substantially to the prosperity of his adopted country.

The effect upon China of this rather limited overseas migration has been very considerable. Economically, the sums brought or remitted home by the emigrant have made for the prosperity of the regions from which he has come—chiefly the provinces of Fukien and Kwangtung. In the realm of ideas the results have been little short of startling. It was an emigrant, Sun Yat-sen, who more than any other one man was responsible for the radical political revolution in China, and his initial impulse came from his residence, as a boy, in Hawaii. For years in his propaganda for renovating China he sought and obtained support from his fellow-countrymen abroad. These, indeed, have again and again aided in financing changes in many realms of Chinese life—political, economic, intellectual, and religious. Thousands of other emigrants, some of them nationally and even internationally known, but most of them obscure, have returned to the land of their ancestors seeking to bring it into partial conformity to the ways of the Occident. The transformation in China during the past few decades might not have been so thorough-going and certainly in many instances would have taken a different course had it not been for these emigrants.

BIBLIOGRAPHY

On the racial composition of the Chinese see O. Franke, *Geschichte des chinesischen Reiches* (Berlin, 1930), Vol. 1, ch. 2; S. M. Shirokogoroff, *Anthropology of Northern China* (Shanghai, 1923); S. M. Shirokogoroff, *Anthropology of Eastern China and Kwangtung Province* (Shanghai, 1925); S. M. Shirokogoroff, *Who are the Northern Chinese?* (*Journal of the North China Branch of the Royal Asiatic Society*, 1924, pp. 1–13); S. M. Shirokogoroff, *Northern Tungus Migrations in the*

Far East (*ibid.*, 1926, pp. 123–183); Chi Li, *The Formation of the Chinese People* (Cambridge, 1928); T. Y. Hsieh, *Origin and Migrations of the Hakkas* (*The Chinese Social and Political Science Review*, Vol. 13, pp. 202–227); L. H. D. Buxton, *The Peoples of Asia* (New York, 1925); L. H. D. Buxton, *China, The Land and the People* (Oxford, 1929).

On non-Chinese peoples within the borders of China, see S. Couling, *The Encyclopædia Sinica* (London, 1917), pp. 1–5 (the article includes a fairly extensive bibliography); J. H. Edgar, *The Country and Some Customs of the Szechwan Mantze* (*Journal of the North China Branch of the Royal Asiatic Society*, 1917, pp. 42–56); Miss M. M. Moninger, *The Hainanese Miao* (*ibid.*, 1921, pp. 40–50); W. C. Dodd, *The Relation of Chinese and Siamese* (*ibid.*, 1920, pp. 1–13); J. H. Edgar, *Notes on Names of Non-Chinese Tribes in Western Szechwan* (*ibid.*, 1922, pp. 61–69); F. M. Savina, *Histoire des Miao* (Hongkong, 1930); P. Vial, *Les Lolos* (Shanghai, 1898); S. M. Shirokogoroff, *Social Organization of the Manchus* (Shanghai, 1924); *Ethnographie des No-so, Leurs Religions, Leur Langue et Leur Ecriture. Avec Documents Historiques et Géographiques Relatifs à Li-kiang* par Éd. Chavannes (Leyden, 1913); C. P. Fitzgerald, *The Tower of Five Glories* (London, 1941).

On the population of China, see R. S. Britton, *Census in Ancient China* (Population, Vol. I, pp. 83–94); C. P. Fitzgerald, *A New Estimate of the Chinese Population under the T'ang Dynasty for 618 A.D.* (*The China Journal*, Vol. 16, pp. 5–14, 62–72); M. T. Stauffer, *The Christian Occupation of China* (Shanghai, 1922), pp. 11–14; E. H. Parker, *China, Her History, Diplomacy and Commerce* (New York, 1917), pp. 191–204; S. W. Williams, *The Middle Kingdom* (New York, 1907), Vol. 1, pp. 258–288; S. Couling, *The Encyclopædia Sinica*, pp. 446–448; and especially, because they are by a recognized expert who has taken advantage of earlier studies, W. F. Willcox, *The Population of China in 1910* (*Journal of the American Statistical Association*, March, 1928, pp. 18–30), W. F. Willcox, *A Westerner's Effort to Estimate the Population of China, and Its Increase since 1650* (*ibid.*, September, 1930, pp. 255–268), and W. F. Willcox, *Increase of the Population of the Earth and of the Continents* (preprinted from *International Migrations*, Vol. 2, New York, 1930). Willcox's conclusions are vigorously contested.

On the migrations of Chinese, see F. L. Ho, *Population Movement to the Northeastern Frontier of China* (*The Chinese Social and Political Science Review*, Oct. 1931, pp. 346–401); Chi Li, *The Formation of the Chinese People* (Cambridge, 1928); E. Biot, *Mémoire sur les Colonies Militaires et Agricoles des Chinois* (*Journal Asiatique*, 4e sér. XV, 1850, pp. 338–370, 529–595); F. W. Williams, *The Problem of Chinese Immigration in Further Asia* (*American Historical Association*, 1899, Vol. 1); W. H. Mallory, *The Northward Migration of the Chinese* (*Foreign Affairs*, Vol. 7, pp. 72–82); H. F. MacNair,

The Chinese Abroad (Shanghai, 1924); P. C. Campbell, *Chinese Coolie Emigration to Countries within the British Empire* (London, 1923); C. Walter Young, *Chinese Labor Migration to Manchuria* (*Chinese Economic Journal,* July, 1927); R. Adams, *The Peoples of Hawaii* (Honolulu, 1925); E. Dennery, *Foules d'Asie* (Paris, 1930); Ta Chen, *Chinese Migrations* (U. S. Bureau of Labor Statistics No. 340, 1923); Amry Vandenbosch, *A Problem in Java. The Chinese in the Dutch East Indies* (*Pacific Affairs,* Vol. 3, November, 1930, pp. 1001–1017); C. C. Wu, *Chinese Immigration in the Pacific Area* (*The Chinese Social and Political Science Review,* Vol. 12, October, 1928, pp. 543–560); T. Y. Hsieh, *The Chinese in Hawaii* (*ibid.,* Vol. 14, January, 1930, pp. 13–40); and G. B. Cressey, *Chinese Colonization in Mongolia* (*Pioneer Settlement, American Geographical Society Special Publication,* No. 14, New York, 1932). W. Campbell, *Formosa under the Dutch* (London, 1903), a translation of seventeenth century Dutch records, gives some idea of the extent of Chinese settlement on Formosa at that time. The most recent comprehensive treatment is H. Mosolf, *Die Chinesische Auswanderung* (Rostock, 1932). See also Ta Chen, *Emigrant Communities in South China. A Study of Overseas Migration and Its Influence on Standards of Living and Social Change* (New York, 1940). Important on the internal and external movements of population in the 1930's and 1940's is B. Lasker, *Asia on the Move* (New York, 1945).

CHAPTER XIV

GOVERNMENT

INTRODUCTORY

One of the most noteworthy achievements of the Chinese has been in the realm of government. Here they have been among the most successful of all the peoples of the globe. To those who know only the China of to-day, with its prolonged political weakness and near approach to chaos, this may seem a strange and unwarranted assertion. Yet it can easily be justified. Judged by the area and the number of people which it controlled, the length of time it endured, and its record in promoting the unity of an empire and maintaining order and insuring justice, the governmental structure which disappeared in the twentieth century compares favorably with that of any other ever devised by man.

Under such dynasties as the Han, the T'ang, and the Ch'ing the area governed by the Chinese through their political machinery has been surpassed only by such empires as the Mongol (which, though ephemeral, was huge), the British, and the Russian, and, possibly, the Persian, the Macedonian, the Roman, the Arab, the Spanish, and the Portuguese. Even under such dynasties as the Sung and the Ming, China was larger than Western Europe. With the exception of the British Empire, the population held together by China's political structure at the beginning of the twentieth century was greater than that ever under one government.

The Chinese state which has been so revolutionized in the past generation has had a longer duration than any other of which we know. Its roots go back into the Chou dynasty. Its essential outlines, as it was to be seen at the close of the nineteenth century, took form in the Ch'ien Han, in the second century B.C.

This government of China was by no means faultless. In

spite of and sometimes because of it, civil strife and foreign invasion often devastated the land. Under it injustice and inhumanity were to a certain extent fairly chronic and at times widespread. Occasionally it broke down almost completely. The Chinese seem never to have been so successful in ruling subject peoples or peoples of very diverse racial stocks and cultures as were the Romans or as have been the British, the French, and the Dutch.

When all of this has been said, however, the fact remains that seldom has any large group of mankind been so prosperous and so nearly contented as were the Chinese under this governmental machinery when it was dominated by the ablest of the monarchs of the Han, the T'ang, the Sung, the Ming, and the Ch'ing. It was due largely to their government, moreover, that the Chinese achieved and maintained so remarkable a cultural unity and displayed such skill—all the more notable because they were partly unconscious of it—in assimilating invaders. When one recalls how Western Europe, no larger than China proper and with no more serious internal barriers of geography, failed, both to its great profit and infinite distress, to win either political or cultural unity, the achievement of the Chinese becomes little short of phenomenal. It was, indeed, a success which ultimately defeated itself. Political and cultural unity, with the concomitant lack of the stimulus which comes from variety, tended dangerously toward self-satisfaction and stagnation, and so, ultimately, toward weakness and decay.

Why were the Chinese so successful in their government? A completely accurate answer is probably unattainable, for it would have to take into account such elusive factors as inherited racial characteristics and the as yet unknown prehistory. A few contributing elements, however, seem fairly clear. Of these, one was certainly the political- and social-mindedness of the educated classes. When, in the throbbing intellectual life of the Chou, the Chinese first began to put down in writing anything like an adequate record of themselves, the articulate were largely absorbed with political and social themes. The chief concern of most of the outstanding thinkers of the Chou was the present well-being of man—the creation of a society which would make for the good life. Theories as to what constituted the good life differed, and still greater lack of agreement existed as to the means by which it was to be attained. Eventually, as we have seen, after experiments with Legalism and Taoism, one of the schools of thought, usually called Confucianism, was adopted—by the Han and in a modified form—as the orthodox philosophy on which the state was to be built.

In Confucianism was a second reason for China's success with government. Any attempt to sum up in a few words the political theory which goes under that name is probably foredoomed to be unsatisfactory. This is partly because, in spite of its professed allegiance to Confucius, a good many other influences molded it, and the proportions of these changed from time to time. Taoism has been a fairly constant factor in Chinese life and since it was often popular at court and much studied by many of the educated, its influence on political ideals was not inconsiderable. Taoism probably made for quietism, a minimum of governmental machinery, and a distrust of force. Other philosophies of the Chou which as separate schools had disappeared before the close of the Han also left their impress. In general, Confucianism believed that human society could prosper only as men preserved right relations to each other and to the universe about them. Ethics was stressed. The education of all the nation in moral character was regarded as one of the chief purposes of the state. This was to be by the example of the ruling classes rather than by force. Hence much emphasis was placed on discovering and training officials who would measure up to the ideal. Happiness, moreover, so Confucianism declared, depended in no small degree upon the maintenance of right relations between men and the universe about them. This was to be achieved partly by righteousness of life and partly by the regular and correct observance of ritual, particularly of the sacrifices and prayers to the spirits of many kinds by which man was believed to be environed. Even those who, like Hsün Tzǔ, were entirely sceptical as to the existence of these spirits, contended that the ritual should be perpetuated—for purposes of social control.

In the third place, the success of China's government was due to the means by which the Confucian ideal was inculcated. The beginnings of the system of state education, especially for the ruling classes, are said to be traceable in the Chou or even earlier. Whether or not this is true, the device of a bureaucracy recruited through civil service examinations was one of the most noteworthy inventions of the Chinese. We know that some of the principles back of it are to be found in writings of the thinkers of the Chou. We know, too, that in its essential features it was, in embryo, in operation under the Former Han, and that it was elaborated by later dynasties. The bureaucracy, membership in which in theory and usually in practice was based upon merit, attracted to itself much of the ability of the nation. Through it lay the chief road to what ambitious men most crave—power, social recognition, and financial independence. Admission to it was by way of the civil service examinations. These, in turn, were designed to test the applicant's competence in remembering and expounding the tenets of Confucianism as contained in its standard texts. Since education in the schools was mainly for the purpose of preparing candidates for the examinations, that, too, was based upon Confucianism. As a result the governing class and all who aspired to belong to it were given a uniform training in Confucianism. The prestige, influence, conviction, and self-interest of this class joined in inducing in the masses a similar although perhaps not nearly so thorough-going a uniformity. As a consequence China was fully as much a cultural as a political unit. Indeed, by its acquired momentum, cultural integrity persisted when, at intervals, the structure of the state was temporarily disrupted, and proved an aid to reunion.

THE STRUCTURE OF THE IMPERIAL GOVERNMENT AS IT WAS BEFORE THE MODIFICATIONS WROUGHT BY THE COMING OF THE EUROPEAN

To the Western specialist in political science the history of government in China should prove fascinating. Here is a vast body of political thought, experimentation, and experience reaching back over hundreds of years. An extensive literature provides a mine of information. Education was so much for the purpose of preparing recruits for the service of the state and had to do so largely with the underlying Confucian principles, and so many of the intelligentsia actually held official positions, that for a large proportion of those who produced and read literature government was a major interest. In consequence, Chinese histories, including the voluminous dynastic records, have a good deal to say of government and the functions performed by it, and treatises of varying degrees of antiquity, some of them very extensive, deal more specifically with it.

Only a very small proportion of this literature, and most of that in fragmentary form, has been translated into European languages. Even in Chinese the task is still undone of going through the huge mass of material and compiling a history of the Chinese state in categories and according to a framework familiar to the student of Occidental governments. A fabulously rich and almost untilled field awaits modern scholarship.

It must be added that it is very difficult to parallel all of the Chinese political structure with Occidental examples. Some Western observers, indeed, especially of late years, have insisted that the Chinese state was always so different from any we have known in the West that in our sense of the term it can scarcely be called a government. This, it must be emphatically said, is not true. However, enough difference has existed between Chinese and Western political forms to give some ground for the assertion. In pre-twentieth century China unity was dependent not upon a feeling of nationality, as in the modern world, or primarily upon force (although that entered into the plan) but upon cultural ideals, in part social, in part moral, and in part political, which were inculcated through the imperial organization.

Occasionally in the preceding chapters hints have been given of some of the main developments in political machinery: an early Chinese state centering around a monarch and occupying only a small territory; the feudalism of the Chou with the progressive increase of territory occupied by the Chinese and the decline in the power of the central authority; the conquest by the Ch'in of the whole Chinese cultural area and the establishment of a highly autocratic state ruling through a hierarchical bureaucracy and according to the principles of the Legalist school; the collapse of the Ch'in with the partial revival of feudalism under the Han, and then, also under the Han, the strengthening of the power of the monarch operating through a modified form of the hierarchical bureaucracy of the Ch'in recruited partly through civil service examinations and based upon Confucianism; the interesting experiments of Wang Mang; the interruptions in the operation of the government during the years of invasions and civil strife between the Han and the T'ang, with the many attempts at reëstablishing it under the various states of that period; the strong centralization under the early Emperors of the T'ang utilizing and developing the structure inherited from the Ch'in and the Han, followed by partial decentralization and the weakening of the effective authority of the monarch; and the perpetuation, with modifications and amplifications, of the machinery of the Ch'in, the Han, and the T'ang by the Sung and the Ming, and even by foreign conquerors, including the Manchus. Since the Han no basic revolution had been made in the form of government. Changes in detail there were, and many of them, and occasional interruptions in the operation of the machinery. Territorial subdivisions varied in titles, names, numbers, and boundaries; the relations of officials to each other and to the crown were repeatedly modified. Even a Wang An-shih, however, with all his radicalism, did not venture to interfere with the essential features of the administrative system. The Manchus certainly did not do so. Bent chiefly on enjoying the fruits of a structure already in existence, the modifications wrought by them were comparatively minor. Not until the twentieth century did there come fundamentally important departures from the past.

This is not the place to go into the history of Chinese political institutions. To do so would require much more space than is here available. Moreover, as has been suggested, the specialized studies necessary for such an account are still lacking. It is, therefore, best to content ourselves with a description of the main outlines of the government in the first part of the nineteenth century, just before the beginnings of the changes brought by the irruption of the Occident. It was in this form that the state continued, with important modifications, until shortly after 1900.

As has repeatedly been said, since the Han the state had usually been based upon Confucian principles modified to meet the exigencies of changing situations. According to these, all civilized mankind was held ideally to be included under one ruler. Human society was thought of as integrated into an all-embracing world empire rather than made up, as in the West in modern times, of mutually independent sovereign states. Governments there were, like those in Burma and Indo-China, not closely supervised by the Emperor, but all were held to be subordinate to him and were expected to recognize his overlordship by periodical tribute-bearing embassies.

Up to the beginning of the twentieth century this theory of universalism was cherished and constituted one of the reasons for the difficulty of intercourse between the Chinese and the Occident. To Westerners the assumption seemed preposterous and bigoted. It had, however, something sublime about it, resembling the dream back of the Roman Empire and the Papacy. In China, indeed, the state combined religious and political functions. All civilized mankind was conceived as having but one organization and fellowship. In principle such religious and political divisions as have drenched the rest of the world in blood were not to be tolerated. More nearly than any other large group of mankind, moreover, the Chinese approximated to this ideal. In the great periods of their power they controlled most of the civilized world with which they were in close contact.

The state was regarded as an enlarged family and the attitudes of a patriarchal society permeated the whole. The people were to be reasoned with and educated quite as much as commanded. So, under the Ch'ing, the famous *Sacred Edict* became a means of popular education. Originally sixteen sententious moral maxims from the pen of K'ang Hsi but eventually expanded into easy colloquial, it contained instructions in the duty of Chinese to each other and the government and was supposed to be read to the public twice a month in every city and town.

THE EMPEROR

At the head of the state stood the Emperor, regarded as a kind of father of his people. He was declared to hold his office through a mandate of Heaven. His subjects, and especially his ministers, owed him loyalty. He in turn was believed to be able to retain this mandate only through his own virtue. In theory he was represented as ruling fully as much by the influence of his character as by force. If he persistently proved himself unworthy, Heaven might transfer its decree to some one else. A flood, a drought, or some other natural disaster might be interpreted as a sign of Heaven's displeasure. Or persistent tyranny and oppression might be regarded as an offense against the sacred trust. Thus revolt could seek to justify itself: a rebel who succeeded in supplanting the reigning monarch and placing himself on the throne might be regarded, if he had not employed too obviously unethical methods, as having in turn received the divine commission. It is doubtful whether in practice any family had ever acquired the throne solely because of its "virtue"—as Confucian theory required it to do. Once on the throne, however, it professed adherence to Confucianism to maintain its power. Within a given dynasty the rulers came from the same family. Under the Ch'ing, the succession was determined according to the special rules of the Manchus. With the exception of the last two Emperors, where the preceding monarch had left no male issue, it was in direct descent in the male line. In only one instance, that of the Emperor T'ung Chih, who was an only son, did the throne come to the eldest. Until the Emperor Kuang Hsü each of the Ch'ing had been designated by his predecessor. Kuang Hsü and Hsüan T'ung had, as we have seen, been the choice of the Empress Dowager—although made through a council of the notables of the imperial family and the realm.

The Emperor had many designations, some of them official, some popular. Among them were *Huang Ti* (a title adopted, it will be recalled, by the famous First Emperor of the Ch'in dynasty), *Huang Shang, T'ien Tzŭ* (Son of Heaven), and *Wan Sui Yeh* (Lord of Ten Thousand Years). The personal name of the reigning monarch was never to be mentioned. On his death, the Emperor received a temple name, by which he is usually designated in histories. There was also a *nien hao,* literally "year designation," usually called "reign name" or "reign title," by which dates were reckoned. The custom of employing a *nien hao* dated from early in the Han. Until the Ming the *nien hao* might be changed, occasionally several times, during the reign of a monarch. Under the Ming, with one exception, and after the Manchus came into power, the same *nien hao* was employed throughout a reign. In Western histories, then, the Emperors of the Ming and Ch'ing are almost invariably known by their *nien hao*. Thus the Emperor whose temple name is Shêng Tsu Jên is best known in the Occident by his *nien hao*, K'ang Hsi.

In theory, the Emperor was supreme over all civilized human society. He was the administrative director of the state and officials derived their authority and titles from him. In him resided the power of legislation, and he was the supreme judge. The religious head of society, he not only performed many ceremonies, either in person or by proxy, as the high priest of mankind, but appointed or confirmed the chief dignitaries of various cults, such as the Dalai Lama and the Taoist "Pope." He presided over the intellectual world, and certain of the highest of civil service examinations were supposedly conducted by him in person.

In practice, of course, the power of the Emperor was curtailed in many ways. Most of the imperial powers had to be delegated. Precedent, public opinion, customs, the inertia of the vast body of officialdom, particularly of the local authorities, the distances, great if measured by the time required for travel, the elaborate formalities and ceremonial which governed the court and by which even a strong monarch found himself restrained, the moral law as expressed in the Classics of the Confucian school, legal codes inherited from the past, councilors, the official censors, the impossibility, even for the ablest, of fulfilling in person all the exacting duties of the office, and, in the case of the Ch'ing, the racial incompatibility between the Manchus and the Chinese—all acted as a check on the Emperor. A man of extraordinary energy and ability, such as a K'ang Hsi or a Ch'ien Lung in his younger days, could dominate the entire machinery of state. A monarch of lesser ability could not make his will so effective—as when Kuang Hsü failed to carry through the reforms of 1898.

The Emperor had an Empress Consort, secondary wives, and concubines of several ranks. None of these, however, was supposed to have a voice in the government. As we have seen, an Empress Dowager might have immense influence. If the Emperor were a minor, a regent acted for him, and the power of an Empress Dowager was greatly enhanced if she held that office.

The administration of the palace necessitated a vast array of functionaries and servants. The heads of the organization of the imperial household were usually of high rank. Much of the work of the palace was performed by eunuchs, and in the last years of the Ch'ing—as on several occasions under preceding ruling lines—a few of these unfortunates acquired a good deal of power.

THE CENTRAL MACHINERY

Below the Emperor, in the capital, and acting for him, were numerous bodies through which much of the supervision of the realm was exercised. In practice the highest was the *Chün Chi Ch'u,* usually translated (very freely) as the Grand Council or Council of State. Originated by the Manchus, it dated, at least in the form in which it became the Grand Council, from 1730. It usually met daily—in the very early morning. The number of its members was undetermined, but for many years was four or five, about half Chinese and half Manchu. In it most of the more important affairs of state were discussed.

In theory the highest body was not the *Chün Chi Ch'u* but the *Nei Ko*—literally Inner Cabinet or Hall, but usually denominated in English the Grand Secretariat. This had been created under the Ming, taking the rank but not the power of the ancient premiership. Even after it had been superseded by the *Chün Chi Ch'u* as the active Council of State, admission to one of its ranking posts (there were four Grand Secretaries and two Assistant Grand Secretaries, half being Manchus and half Chinese) was the highest honor which could come to a Chinese official. Its functions had, however, become almost nominal, and its members usually had other duties which took them away from the capital most of the time.

In addition to these two councils numbers of bureaus and boards existed to which were delegated specific portions of the business of state. The chief of these were the "Six Boards"—the *Li Pu,* or Board of Civil Office, the *Hu Pu,* or Board of Revenue, the *Li Pu,* or Board of Ceremonies (in Chinese this *Li* is a different character from that for the Board of Civil Office), the *Ping Pu,* or Board of War, the *Hsing Pu,* or Board of Punishments (probably, if its duties are taken into account, more accurately named the Board of Law), and *Kung Pu,* or Board of Works. The functions of these boards were, in general, those indicated by the titles and, in a work of this length, require little further elaboration.

Probably the only boards whose designations—in English—sound especially strange to the ears of modern Westerners were those of Civil Office and of Ceremonies. The Board of Civil Office was charged with the direction of the bureaucracy through which the Empire was administered. Appointments, promotions, degradations, retirements, and honors—both to the living and the dead—in that body of officialdom were made on its recommendation. In a state ordered on the Confucian theory a Board of Ceremonies had an important place. From the standpoint of that school it was essential to the welfare of society that the ritual, both secular and religious, maintained by the government be correctly and regularly performed. Upon it depended the smooth coördination of mankind with the spiritual and material universe which was deemed so essential to the happiness and prosperity of men. By it, too, men were held to be educated and regulated. *Li,* then, is only imperfectly translated as ceremonies. It possessed an ethical meaning. The outward ritual was supposed to be both an expression of and an incentive to morality. The system was not unlike that support of religion by the state which has been a familiar phenomenon in the West. Hence it is not strange that a special and major board in charge of the *Li* was regarded as necessary.

Each of the Six Boards had two presidents, one Manchu and one Chinese, and two Manchu and two Chinese vice-presidents. Each, too, had its staff or secretaries and clerks. Moreover, each was subdivided into several departments, and attached to some were subordinate bodies, such as the Board of Music, to which was entrusted the music of state functions, especially of religious services, and which was under the *Li Pu.*

In addition to the Six Boards there were three other major bodies. One of these—uniquely characteristic of China—was the *Tu Ch'a Yüan,* or Censorate. This institution had its origins at least as far back as the Ch'in, but, as was natural, its form and detailed duties changed from time to time. In general, its function was, as its name suggests, to criticize the government. This, as it was made specific, included such duties as keeping a watch on officials and reporting to the Emperor any delinquencies, taking exception to the acts of the Emperor himself, checking over important state documents for mistakes, assisting in the examination of officials, investigating reports of financial corruption in governmental accounts, keeping watch over state property and the construction of public buildings, supervising the ceremonies on formal occasions to be sure that they were properly conducted, and joining with two others of the central bodies as a high court of review for a large range of cases. Naturally, there was a subdivision of duties among its members.

The censors expressed their criticisms in the form of memorials to the throne. Theoretically, they were given great liberty of speech. In practice, too, they were often fearless. However, censors did not rank very high in the official scale. Moreover, a censor might be punished for his pains. Yet during the Ch'ing dynasty only about half a hundred such penalties are recorded. Timid censors might fear to speak, or occasionally one might use his position to bring embarrassment to an enemy. On the whole, public opinion, as voiced by the articulate classes (usually scholars and officials), rallied to the support of a censor whose strictures were well founded.

Another body was the *T'ung Chêng Ssŭ*, or Office of Transmission, whose function it was to open, record, and transmit memorials on routine business. Still another was the *Ta Li Ssŭ*, or Grand Court of Revision, which exercised a general supervision over the administration of the criminal law. It, the Board of Punishments, and the Censorate were known as the "Three Supreme Tribunals." They met together as a court of appeal, to which all verdicts of capital punishment were sent up for review.

These nine bodies, sometimes called the Nine Chief Ministries of State, by no means exhausted the central bureaus in Peking. There was the *Li Fan Yüan*, sometimes inaccurately called, in English, the Colonial Office, which had charge of most of Mongolia, Tibet, and Sinkiang. There was the famous *Hanlin Yüan*, rather freely translated as the Imperial Academy. Admission to it was reserved to those who had stood high in the civil service examinations, and so was esteemed a great honor. It also served to provide posts for some who had not yet been appointed to other offices in the bureaucracy and formed a kind of springboard to desirable posts. Its functions were literary, such as the expounding of the Classics, the preparation of official documents, and the composition and preservation of elaborate records, especially of the words and actions of the Emperor, from which the history of the dynasty would eventually be compiled. Then there was a department charged with the instruction of the heir apparent. During most of the Ch'ing, however, positions in it were purely honorary sinecures, since very infrequently was the public appointment of a successor to the throne made until the death bed of the Emperor. The list of relatively minor bureaus included one on sacrificial worship (for the dead), one on state ceremonies (for the living), another in charge of formal official banquets, an imperial college (whose students were in preparation for the civil service), and the Imperial Board of Astronomy (connected with the Board of Rites).

The government issued an official publication, the *Ching Pao* —usually called by foreigners the Peking Gazette—in which such documents as decrees and memorials were reproduced. The *Ching Pao* circulated among high officials throughout the Empire and was widely reprinted, in full or abridged form, on private initiative, for more popular distribution.

This structure at the imperial capital had strong similarities, in its general subdivision of functions among specialized boards and its central councils of state, to monarchical states in the Occident. However, some striking and significant differences must be noted. Among these were the absence of any provision for a voice in the government by elected delegates of the more influential classes, and the complete lack of any foreign office for the conduct of intercourse with nations of equal rank. At least one recognized means existed by which members of the most powerful group, that of the scholar-officials, could bring pressure to bear—memorializing the throne. Often it was very effective. Yet it differed decidedly from the device which had been evolved in Western Europe during the course of centuries—that of a body such as Parliament or the Estates General, representing the weightiest and most vocal groups in the realm, and recruited in part or in whole by election. The absence of a ministry of foreign affairs coördinate in dignity with the other major central boards was, as has been suggested, but one evidence of a basic conviction concerning the nature of the Chinese state. Mankind was conceived of as forming a political as well as a cultural unit. It was known that some civilized as well as some barbarous peoples had not acknowledged that ideal. However, in spite of experience which we noted under the Chou, the recognition that governments existed which were permanently entitled to deal with the Emperor on the basis of equality and that there was a body of international law by which such intercourse was to be guided, involved nothing short of a revolution in the existing Chinese theory of society.

THE OFFICIAL HIERARCHY OUTSIDE THE CAPITAL

The major territorial administrative divisions of China proper were the provinces (*shêng*). The number had been altered from time to time and remnants of pre-Ch'ing units lingered in popular and literary parlance. Under the latter part of the Ch'ing, however, the provinces of China proper totalled eighteen—the ones named in the initial chapter of this work. In 1884 Sinkiang was made a province. Manchuria was divided into three additional provinces, but the machinery and control of these varied from those of the eighteen of China proper. The administration of the outlying dependencies of the Empire was still different.

The eighteen provinces were in turn subdivided into *fu*, or prefectures, *t'ing*, sub-prefectures independent of a *fu*, *chou* not governed through a *fu*, *chou* subject to a *fu*, and *hsien*, usually translated as districts, and also subject either to a *fu* or to one of the *chou* which was not under a *fu*. The *hsien* were much more numerous than either the *t'ing* or the *chou*.

The chief officers of the province were usually rather loosely designated in English as the Viceroy or Governor-general (*Tsung Tu, Chih Chün,* or *Chih T'ai*), the Governor (*Hsün Fu, Fu Yüan,* or *Fu T'ai*), the Lieutenant Governor or Treasurer (colloquially called the *Fan T'ai*), the Provincial Judge (colloquially called the *Nieh T'ai*), the Salt Comptroller, and the Grain Intendant. The officers of the subdivisions most frequently mentioned were the Intendant of a circuit (colloquially, the *Tao T'ai*), the Prefect, or head of a *fu* (*Chih Fu*), the Sub-prefect (*T'ung Chih*), the Magistrate of an independent *chou* (*Chih Chou*), and the District Magistrate (*Chih Hsien*). There were, of course, other officials who did not figure so frequently or so prominently in the administration. Ranks in the hierarchy were indicated by colored buttons on the official caps and by insignia on the front and back of robes of state.

The Viceroys outranked all the others. Under most of the

Ch'ing there were eight of them. Usually a Viceroy was placed over two provinces (Fukien-Chêkiang, Hupeh-Hunan, Shensi-Kansu, Kwangtung-Kwangsi, and Yünnan-Kweichow). In one instance he was placed over three, Kiangsu-Anhui-Kiangsi. Chihli and Szechwan each had a Viceroy but no Governor. Each of the other provinces had a Governor. Shantung, Honan, and Shansi each had a Governor but were not under a Viceroy. In general, the Viceroys were supposed to have the powers of a monarch within their jurisdictions—subject always, of course, to the crown. In theory the Governor had much the same functions, but subject to the Viceroy, except of course, in the three provinces over which there was no Viceroy. In practice the two often conflicted and exercised a check over each other. The functions of the other provincial officers are, for our purposes here, sufficiently described by their titles.

The members of the hierarchy who came most directly in touch with the masses were the heads of the *fu,* the *chou,* the *t'ing,* and the *hsien,* especially the last. They were judges and had charge of the police, of the performance of certain religious rites, and of the collection of taxes, and were charged with other administrative functions which touched the ordinary man. In accordance with patriarchal ideals, they stood *in loco parentis* to the populace and were called "fathers and mothers" of the people within their jurisdictions.

Along with its obvious virtues, the system had many defects. Among the chief was financial corruption. Salaries were small and expenses large, especially as every official had many dependents to support—including relatives and a throng of secretaries and other functionaries necessary to the conduct of his office. He had, moreover, to pay sums more or less substantial (theoretically as gifts) to various officials to obtain appointment and had to be prepared to part with additional sums when he came up for reappointment. To be sure, offices carried with them many emoluments which were regarded as legitimate, but the temptation to gain money in every possible way was very strong.

It will be seen that in effect the country was divided into huge semi-autonomous states whose heads were entrusted by the Emperor with almost independent powers. With certain exceptions, each Governor and Viceroy was supposed to handle the affairs of his own jurisdiction with as little reference to Peking as possible —and in turn was held responsible by Peking for whatever went amiss in his realm. This independence of action of the heads of provinces was repeatedly seen in the nineteenth century, and never more vividly than when, in 1900, the Viceroys and Governors outside of the Northeast chose to disregard the apparent declaration of war on the powers by Peking and remained on friendly terms with the invaders. Local semi-autonomy was, of course, necessary in a land the size of China in a day when no railways, telegraphs, automobiles, or airplanes bound the country together. If so large an area were to be successfully governed from one capital, it had to be by some such device of granting discretionary power to the highest officers in each major administrative unit.

The danger was that strong officials in the provinces would set themselves up as fully independent monarchs and even make a bid for the control of the Empire. This was heightened by strong local loyalties and prejudices. The menace was fairly chronic through the entire history of China. Early in the course of the Ch'ing, it will be recalled, the dynasty was almost wrecked by the rebellion of Wu San-kuei and other territorial magnates in the South. Throughout the centuries strong monarchs had tried various safeguards against it. Since the Han, government through a hierarchy recruited through civil service examinations had been the most nearly constant and successful. In addition, a number of ingenious devices were employed by the Ch'ing in much of the eighteenth and nineteenth centuries. By no means all of them originated with the Manchus, however, nor is it clear that each was adopted with this specific purpose in mind. The larger proportion of all officials in the hierarchy, even the most humble district magistrates, were appointed from the capital. Their specific local assignments might come from the provincial authorities, and a powerful official might and often did exert pressure to bring about the appointment of a protégé, but Peking did not risk the possibility of any Governor or Viceroy building up a regional machine. Moreover, no official was permitted to hold a post in his native province. Seeming exceptions were sometimes made when a man was designated as a *locum tenens* to a position in the province of his birth—but he appears seldom if ever to have been more than a *locum tenens* and repeatedly a deviation from the usual course of promotion was made to avoid breaking the rule. Obviously such a procedure rendered it difficult for any official plotting rebellion to appeal to provincial loyalties. Appointments to office were, moreover, only for the term of three years, and while the assignment was often renewed, it seems only infrequently to have been for more than an additional *triennium*. Then, too, both Peking and the provincial authorities sent out messengers from time to time on special errands. Some of the imperial commissioners might even outrank a Viceroy. The censors might impeach provincial officials, and the right of officials of certain ranks to memorialize the throne gave a recognized channel for voicing criticisms. An elaborate system of checks and balances existed—of Viceroy and Governor against each other, and of the other high provincial officials on one another and on the Governor and the Viceroy. Moreover, while there were hereditary titles, especially among the Manchus, a post in the civil service did not go automatically with them, and members of the imperial family could not hold office in the provinces. Then, in spite of all the authority given them, Peking held the high provincial officials strictly accountable for whatever happened in their jurisdictions. Certain decisions, such as final action on many cases involving capital punishment, were reserved to the capital. These safeguards did not prevent rebellion, but they must have done much to minimize its frequency and to hold together, with a nice balance between needed local initiative and responsibility to a central authority, the large area that was China proper.

THE CIVIL SERVICE EXAMINATIONS

In theory and to a large extent in practice, the members of this impressive hierarchy of civil officials were recruited through an elaborate and gruelling system of examinations. Three main sets of tests led to what roughly correspond to the degrees awarded by Western universities. The three "degrees" were *hsiu ts'ai, chü jên,* and *chin shih,* and are sometimes, but far from accurately, said to be equivalent to the bachelor's, master's, and doctor's degrees of the Occident. In addition to these three, as variations from them or as subdivisions of them, were other stages, each designated by a distinct title.

In every *hsien* and roughly every two years in each *fu*, under the proper official, there were conducted the first of the examinations. Those who passed them were given the title of *hsiu ts'ai*. This had the effect of recognizing its possessor as qualified to prepare further and to compete in the next stage of the system. The *hsiu ts'ai* had certain privileges. Some of them received a subsidy from the government to enable them to continue their studies; they were exempt from liability to corporal punishment by the magistrates; they were considered members of the local gentry and could be invited to share in the discussion of local affairs; and they were accorded other rights and immunities. Within the ranks of the *hsiu ts'ai* were subdivisions and titles of honor. In general the *hsiu ts'ai* constituted a privileged class to which accrued a good deal of social prestige. Now and then a minor officer was appointed directly from among their number, but they were not eligible to such posts as that of a *hsien* magistrate. To hold their titles, they had to continue their studies and to stand a reexamination every three years.

The next major set of examinations led to the title of *chü jên*. This was held in the provincial capitals, as a rule in the early autumn, and at intervals of three years (actually, on the average, somewhat more frequently). In each of these cities was a plot of ground on which hundreds of permanent stalls were erected for this purpose. The tests were more formidable than those leading to the *hsiu ts'ai*. They were under the direction of a supervisor and an associate appointed directly from Peking, and much ceremony attached to them. Every examination was divided into three sessions, each with its separate topics. The night before the session the aspirants were led to their cells and sealed in them, and did not emerge until the third day. The mere physical strain was by no means slight, and it was not uncommon for a candidate to die under it. The successful in the ordeal were marked and honored men, especially those who passed at or near the head of the list.

Even the "degree" of *chü jên* did not usually entitle its recipient to hold office. As a rule a man was eligible only after having passed a third set of examinations, held at Peking. These also were usually at triennial intervals, and in the spring following the examinations leading to the *chü jên*. Only *chü jên* were admitted. Again there were three grilling sessions. The successful examinees were rewarded with the title of *chin shih*. Those emerging with the highest credit were honored by additional designations. Still another examination was held, theoretically in the presence of the Emperor and on a theme set by him, which resulted in further grading the *chin shih*.

Chin shih who passed with the greatest distinction were usually given posts in the *Hanlin Yüan*, in itself no mean honor, and all were either awarded official posts or were placed on the list of "expectant officials" from which appointments were to be made. *Chü jên* who had been unsuccessful in their efforts to enter the ranks of the *chin shih* might either attempt the examination again or be appointed to office after meeting tests which were presumably somewhat less exacting.

The subject matter of the examinations was largely Chinese literature, chiefly that of the Confucian school. Most of them consisted of composing essays and poems on topics selected from this literature. The essays and poems were required to conform to decidedly artificial standards and were judged by the criteria of style rather than of originality of thought. Yet questions of a practical kind were also among those asked, at least at the end of the Ming.

The competition was much more keen than any to which we are accustomed in educational tests in the Occident. Only a small percentage of the contestants at each of the successive examinations achieved the coveted degrees. Of those who presented themselves for the *chü jên* at any one time, only one out of fifteen or more was successful, and of those who sat for the *chin shih* usually much fewer than one in ten. The number admitted to the degree of *chin shih* in any one year was seldom more than three hundred and fifty and as a rule much less. Candidates often tried again and again, and occasionally a grandfather, father, and son came together. While in many instances younger men attained the rank of *chin shih*, the median age was somewhere in the thirties.

The defects of the system were obvious—the absorption in purely verbal matters, the premium upon memory and upon ability to write according to the standards of an arbitrary literary style, rather than upon originality or vigor of thought and promise in administrative skill. In many scholars, too, there were fostered an intellectual arrogance, a narrowness of outlook, and a stereotyping of thought which discouraged all progress. Other weaknesses not necessarily inherent in the procedure frequently accompanied it. In spite of elaborately devised safeguards, some men cheated, undetected, or bribed the readers of the papers. From the Sui through the Ch'ing, sons of high officials could enter the bureaucracy either without meeting the ordeal of the examinations or by passing tests which were much easier than those required of others. The right to use the title of the lower degrees was sold by the government, especially in the years of the decadence of the Ch'ing.

Yet over and beyond the weaknesses were values which the foreign observer might easily miss. Even in the worst years of the dynasty only a small minority of the degrees were obtained fraudulently. Titles which had been bought were popularly not regarded so highly as those acquired by merit. The competition was so exacting that as a rule success went only to men of more than average mental ability and capacity for concentrated application. Possession of the degrees and of a position in the hierarchy was the most coveted honor in the Empire. The examinations, then, probably brought into the service of society through the state many of the really able men of the country. Even more important was the promotion of cultural unity. All civil officials had passed through the same training in the literature which set forth the ideals of the Confucian school. Not only officials but the thousands of disappointed aspirants, many times as numerous as the successful, had been subjected to the same regimen. Since the entire formal education of the country was dominated by the purpose of preparing men for the civil service tests and drew its teachers from the ranks of those who had been in training for them, many thousands who had never proceeded far enough with their studies to compete in the examinations had at least a smattering of the standard learning. The educated class trained in this uniform fashion enjoyed a prestige probably greater than that accorded to scholars in any other nation: they dominated society. Their ideals and manners were, accordingly, largely taken over by the masses and tended to permeate the entire nation. The Confucian dream of a society molded by the example of an educated ruling class had to no small extent become an actuality.

Under the Ch'ing, moreover, this popular education in the principles of Confucian morality was furthered by the widespread circulation and the public reading of the famous Sacred Edict.

In spite of its great geographic extent, therefore, China proper was essentially one in civilization and government. Political division was seldom more than temporary and never permanent.

With all its defects, the culture upon which this unity was built was rich and worthy. It inculcated high ideals in the relations of men to one another, so essential to an ordered and prosperous society; it possessed and fostered an extensive and varied literature; and it set high store by good taste and by an appreciation of certain phases of the æsthetic side of life.

The hierarchy and the civil service examinations, then, were among the most notable devices ever originated by any branch of the human race.

LOCAL GOVERNMENT

Underneath the official hierarchy recruited through the civil service examinations was the local government. Most of it was by units which were largely self-governing—such as the village, the family (including its enlarged form, the clan), and the guild. In a certain sense China was a vast congeries of these all but autonomous units, and the hierarchy intervened only when they failed to function or fell out with one another, or when some crime was committed of which it could not but take cognizance. The picture, too, was complicated by the presence of secret societies, some of them very powerful.

The imperial government acted chiefly as an umpire between interests which at any time might come into conflict. It provided, too, for the supervision of certain large economic enterprises, such as extensive public works, and for the common defense against external invasion and internal disorder.

The local units were controlled in part on a principle of which much was made in Chinese administration—that of group responsibility. All the members of a family or a village could be held accountable for the deeds of each of their fellows. Pressure was usually brought from above upon the recognized headman or headmen, but might be exerted upon all the individuals in the unit.

Nothing more need be said at this point concerning the family, the guild, and the secret societies, for these are to be described in later chapters. It must be noted, however, that they were very important factors in local and—at times—in provincial and national administration. The village government had as its chief organs a council of elders or managers and a headman, the latter usually termed the *ti pao*. The council of elders was often made up of the leaders of the more important families and of the men who were generally recognized as having the most influence in the village—scholars, and those who had won esteem by their force of character, experience, and administrative ability. In some localities and times, however, these positions went to rich schemers or to men who used corrupt measures to attain them. As a rule no formal election seems to have been held, although in theory the elders were nominated by their fellow villagers and confirmed by the responsible magistrate, usually the *chih hsien*. Membership appears rather to have come through tacit recognition by public opinion. In theory the *ti pao* was chosen by the magistrate and was the one through whom the village had its communication with the official hierarchy. In at least some villages in the South, the village council was associated with the village temple. To the council of elders and the *ti pao* went such tasks as lighting the streets, maintaining the watchmen, building and repairing dikes, constructing and maintaining the wall (if there was one), supervising markets, approving of all transfers of land, erecting and repairing temples, sinking and cleaning community wells, collecting the taxes and contributions levied by the state, and adjusting disputes between fellow villagers or with other villages. Controversies which could not be settled in this manner might be taken to the magistrate, but such litigation was usually costly and prolonged and was entered upon only as a last resort. In some sections, it may be noted, tax collectors constituted an hereditary group, distinct from the *ti pao* and elders.

This organization of local government was to be found not only in the villages but in the larger towns and cities. These were usually divided into wards, each with its council of elders and its *ti pao* who functioned much as did those of the villages.

It must be added that local institutions varied markedly in the different areas of China. Few descriptions can be written which prove valid for the entire country.

Then, too, the "local gentry," as foreigners sometimes called them, were very influential. Scholars, retired officials, men of wealth, the elders of the leading clans, were much listened to in local affairs and exercised a good deal of initiative in matters affecting the welfare of the community.

In addition to the family, the guild, the secret society, the village, and the local gentry, there were many other local organizations that took over some of the functions which in some countries in the Occident are performed by the government. Among these were volunteer fire companies, benevolent societies, groups for watching the crops, and associations for mutual aid. The Chinese have a great capacity and zeal for organization. This has been displayed in scores of ways and has helped to render them, in their local affairs, self-managing with the minimum of interference from above. It must be added, however, that repeatedly they were and are hampered by reciprocal distrust and by incapacity for administration. Often individuals, groups, and classes display a distressing lack of ability or willingness to coöperate.

LAWS AND COURTS

What in the West is called law was much of it in China a matter of tradition and custom. Thanks largely to the common basis of culture insured by the civil service examinations, certain ethical principles were recognized as authoritative throughout the land. This, indeed, was in accordance with the dominant Confucian theory. Life and conduct were supposed to be governed by universally valid principles. These were included, in general, under what the Chinese denominated *li* (not the same character as that employed for ceremonies). Originally quite possibly employed to designate the manners and customs of the aristocracy, in the course of the centuries *li* came to be regarded as binding on all civilized mankind. It was conceived of as conforming to the will of Heaven and was akin to although not identical with the concept of natural law which was present in the Græco-Roman world and has been transmitted to the modern Occident. In addition, each local unit had its customs. Enforcement of *li* and local customs was chiefly through public opinion, which was very powerful, and by the various local organizations.

There was, as well, a body of statutory law issued in the form of a code. Although much narrower than *li*, it was supposed to conform to it. In a sense the introduction of written law was a departure from strict Confucian theory and, whether consciously or unconsciously, resembled, rather, the concepts of the Legalists of the Chou and the Han. Statutory law was perpetuated by dynasty after dynasty, like the form of the official hierarchy. For example, the Ch'ing adopted, with modifications, the code in use under the Ming. It was, of course, altered from time to time by imperial decree and showed marks of a distinct development.

The code was made up largely of what in the Occident would be called criminal and administrative law. Some items of civil law (proportionately not very numerous) were included in it. The code of the Ch'ing was called the *Ta Ch'ing Lü Li* and was composed, as the name indicates, of *lü* and *li*. The *lü* were fundamental laws based largely upon the Ming code. Promulgated early in the dynasty, in theory they remained unchanged. The *li* seem to have been introduced first by Hung Wu, of the Ming, and were an attempt to incorporate the results of judicial decisions in actual cases. They were also in the nature of supplementary statutes modifying and extending the *lü* and subject to periodical revision. The *lü* were divided into seven main heads—general, civil, fiscal, ritual, military, and criminal laws, and laws concerning public works. The general section included principles applying to the whole; the civil dealt with the system of government and the conduct of magistrates and regulated the succession to hereditary titles; the fiscal related to such matters as inheritance and the census; the section on ritual had to do with state sacrifices and ceremonies; the military included the protection of the palace, the guarding of the frontier, and the equipping and provisioning of the army; and the section on public works provided for such undertakings as dikes and the examination and repair of public buildings.

Several features of the criminal law—the bulkiest portion of the *lü*—impress the modern Anglo-Saxon reader as different from the legal system under which he has lived. There was the principle of joint responsibility, by which, for a particularly heinous crime, an entire family might be exterminated, with the mitigation that sons below the age of puberty were merely to be emasculated. Then, too, although no liability attached for an accidental death, the judgment as to what was accidental at times differed radically from that of the West. Persons were often held culpable for deaths for which in the Occident they could have been adjudged free from blame. Even in the case of some fatalities which were decided to have been accidental those persons who had been the innocent cause were fined or required to make a payment to the deceased relatives. Moreover, the rules of evidence were dissimilar to those in most lands in the modern West, and torture might be used to extract confession from the prisoner—although all but certain forms of it were illegal. From the standpoint of the modern Occident, certain punishments were barbarous, such as beating with a bamboo until the victim's back was badly mangled, and death by slicing the culprit into fragments (prescribed, apparently, not so much for the present suffering it caused as for the erasure, so far as possible, of the criminal from the spirit world by the complete dismemberment of his body). Those condemned to death were sometimes, as an act of clemency, allowed to commit suicide.

Such differences as these were among the causes of friction between foreigners and Chinese officials in pre-treaty days and were urged as reasons for extraterritoriality. It should be remembered, however, that the law provided regular schedules by which penalties might be reduced or commuted, that Chinese punishments and torture were not a whit more extreme than those once employed in Europe, and that as late as the eighteenth century Chinese criminal procedure was probably more humane than that of some of the most powerful of the governments of the Occident. Only with the reform of the laws and prisons of the Occident in the nineteenth century—under the influence of the humanitarian movement—did China fall behind.

Precedent played a large part in legal cases, and, although perhaps not so extensively as in the Occident, there were voluminous compilations of court decisions. An extensive legal literature existed, and magistrates, along with their other duties, were supposed to be sufficiently acquainted with the law to act as judges. However, litigants and prisoners did not employ counsel as in the

West, and (at least under the Ming and Ch'ing), although the magistrates had jurisconsults, Chinese society partly lacked that learned professional, the lawyer, who has loomed so large in the Occident. Perhaps because of the difference in tradition, the educated Chinese thinks less legalistically than does the educated man of Europe and America. This also has been a cause of friction. Especially in intergovernmental relations between China and the Occident, the latter, accustomed to its own categories, has both misunderstood and been misunderstood.

Much corruption was found in the courts, perhaps in part because of the absence of a legal profession. The many underlings attached to the magistrates' offices derived their income largely from litigation and criminal cases. The magistrate, even when he himself was honest, was a stranger in his district and so was largely dependent upon his subordinates for a knowledge of the local situation. The function of judge was, moreover, only one of that official's many duties and suffered from divided attention. As a result, entry into the courts usually proved costly in the extreme and the verdict often went to the longest purse.

TAXATION

The revenue to support the hierarchy of officials and the machinery of district, provincial, and imperial governments came chiefly from four sources—the land tax, tribute, customs duties, and the salt monopoly. The land tax was supposedly fixed according to an assessment made in 1713, but in practice, since the charges for collection were in addition to it and constituted a source of income for some of the officials, it was as much more as the collector could get. Usually the addition seems to have been from ten to fifty per cent. The tax could be increased in other ways, quite legal and regular, so that in practice the actual sums paid might be twice or more as large as those authorized in 1713. As assessed under the Manchus, or at least the later Manchus, in most sections the land tax was a combination of several levies of more or less ancient origin—a poll tax, a tax as commutation for forced labor, and another as a substitute for assistance in transmitting official communications.

In addition to a land tax, paid in cash, was a tribute collected in produce—such as silk, copper from mines, and especially grain.

The tax in grain, levied on the land, and often compounded by a cash payment, in effect was usually an addition to the land tax. There were many government granaries and much of the grain was transmitted to Peking.

In the days before the treaties and augmented foreign trade and before collection by the foreign-dominated maritime customs service, the customs duties did not loom as prominently as the land tax. They were, however, a fairly considerable source of revenue and were derived both from imposts on foreign trade and domestic commerce.

Salt was, as it had been for centuries, an important source of income. The manufacture, distribution, and sale of salt constituted a state monopoly, although they might be conducted through individuals or firms to whom the government had farmed them.

Several other sources of revenue were regularly tapped, although most of them yielded comparatively minor sums. The sale of office sometimes brought in fairly considerable amounts. Taxes on tea, on fish, and on reeds used for fuel and thatching, mining royalties, fees on the transfer of land and houses, licenses to pawnbrokers and to other financial and mercantile enterprises, a consumption and production tax, and what corresponded to the octroi of Europe—a levy on produce as it entered a town—all swelled the total.

Contrasted with the revenues of governments of the modern West, those of the old China were not large. Compared with the total income of the people the tax load seems to have been much less than that of most of the major countries of the present-day Occident. This was very possibly true even when the expenses of local governments and the more or less extra-legal "squeeze" of officials were added. Moreover, in times of disaster, such as drought or flood, the government often remitted or reduced the taxes of the afflicted districts. The relative lightness of the imposts was due partly to the comparatively limited functions of the older Chinese state. Many of the tasks undertaken by Western governments of to-day were left to the initiative of local units or entirely non-political organizations. The members of the civil hierarchy amounted to only a small fraction of the population. The holders of degrees in the service of the state probably seldom if ever exceeded ten or fifteen thousand. Even when the large number of non-degree holders attached to most offices was added, the percentage of the population deriving its income from the public purse was probably not nearly so high as that in many Western states of to-day. Then, too, no huge public debt existed, with heavy charges for interest and sinking funds. Moreover, while the military forces took a large proportion of the revenues of the government, the burden was not nearly so crushing as is that of the armies and navies of many modern states. The China of the Ch'ing dynasty was by no means a fiscal paradise. It displayed much corruption and inefficiency. However, the financial burden placed upon the realm by the Emperor and the hierarchy, judged by modern standards, appears not to have been particularly onerous.

THE MILITARY ESTABLISHMENT

After the great revolt during the early part of the reign of K'ang Hsi and before the foreign wars and rebellions of the middle of the nineteenth century, the military organization of the China of the Ch'ing was, in its main outlines, about as follows. First of all, there were the descendants of those who had conquered China, now become, in theory, an army of occupation. The original army of conquest, it will be recalled, had been made up of Manchus, Mongols, and Chinese. This was grouped into what were called "Banners"—of varying colors. Eventually these numbered twenty-four, although often they were called the "Eight Banners," each of the latter being divided into three groups—of Manchus, Chinese, and Mongols. Incidentally, the Banners and the civil service provided posts for most of the Manchus resident in the Eighteen Provinces. At the time of the conquest, the Bannermen amounted possibly to two hundred thousand, a total later raised to about two hundred and fifty thousand. Membership was inherited, and eventually the Banners possessed an enrollment of not far from three hundred thousand. About half were stationed in Chihli (Hopei), where they could defend the capital. A large number were in Manchuria, the home of the dynasty, and good-sized contingents were placed in Sinkiang, to hold that turbulent possession, and in Kansu, Shensi, and Shansi, to defend the northern frontier. There were garrisons, but totalling only a small minority of the whole, in other strategic centers of the Eighteen Provinces, notably in a city in Hupeh, in Nanking, and in Canton. The heads of the major divisions of the Banners—commonly known as Tartar Generals—outranked the Viceroys, and nominally served as a check on them—part of that elaborate system in which the Ch'ing sought safety against revolt. As time wore on, the members of the Banners became parasitic pensionaries, totally incompetent as a military force. They proved entirely useless, for example, at the time of the T'ai P'ing Rebellion and in the uprising which ushered in the Republic.

In addition to the Banners was the Army of the Green Standard, made up of Chinese, organized by provinces, and subdivided into land and naval forces. About the middle of the nineteenth century this numbered, in theory, somewhat more than six hundred thousand. The body in actual service, however, was probably very much smaller, for officials padded the rolls to draw pay for as many as possible and increased their own incomes by reducing to the lowest possible point the numbers of those in the ranks. The units of the Green Standard were so divided under various commands that only with difficulty could they be welded into an effective force on a large scale—an insurance against serious rebellion, but also a severe handicap when a major revolt or foreign invasion had to be faced. Each province had a commander of the Green Standard, but in practice heads of subordinate units were accorded much latitude, and some of the civil officials, such as the Viceroys, had contingents directly under their control.

For admission to official position in the army, a system of military examinations existed which corresponded fairly closely in its main stages and degrees to that for the civil service. There were tests in the *hsien* and the *fu* for entrance to the first degree, others, usually every three years, in the provincial capital, for the second degree, and for the third degree examinations, only at Peking, and usually also about every three years. As in the case of the tests for the civil service, successful aspirants became expectant officials, and appointment to office generally depended even more upon family connection and discreet gifts to those who could bring about promotion than upon high rank in the competition. The subject matter of the examinations was in part tests in military pursuits, such as archery and gymnastics, and in part essays on military subjects. The profession of a soldier was socially vastly inferior to that of a civil official. Military degrees, therefore, were not nearly so highly regarded as those admitting to the civil service.

It will easily be seen that the military organization of China under the Ch'ing was far from being as efficient as the civil hierarchy. It was too weak ever seriously to threaten to dominate the state or overthrow the dynasty, but at times it proved useful in maintaining local order and curbing minor revolts.

THE GOVERNMENT OF OUTLYING DEPENDENCIES

During the years of vigor of the Ch'ing, before the foreign wars and rebellions of the middle of the nineteenth century, the portions of the Empire outside the Eighteen Provinces were kept, so far as possible, directly under the Manchus. Chinese were seldom appointed to official position in them. Efforts were put forth to exclude Chinese settlers from sections next to China proper, notably Inner Mongolia and Manchuria, and when, as was almost inevitable, these restrictions broke down, attempts were made to prevent Chinese from intermarrying with the natives. The Manchus looked upon all of their empire as a conquest. If they were to continue to hold China proper, they had, perforce, to associate Chinese with themselves in its administration. However, they jealously guarded their other possessions as their own and as not to be regarded in any sense as belonging to the Chinese. Only in their years of decay did they find it necessary to share them with the latter.

Manchuria was divided into three provinces organized somewhat after the fashion of China south of the Great Wall. Much of the officialdom was military, but the southernmost of the provinces, Shengking, which, because of its proximity to China proper, had increasingly a large settled Chinese population, was given more of a civil administration. In the days of the dynasty's strength, both civil and military officials were Manchus, and a large proportion of them belonged to the imperial clan. Apparently the Manchus wished to keep their hold unshaken on their ancestral home.

Through the rest of the outlying dependencies, the Ch'ing governed on the principle of disturbing as little as possible the political institutions which had existed before the conquest—much as in China proper they ruled their new subjects through the machinery to which the latter were accustomed—but exercised a fairly close oversight by planting Manchu officials supported by garrisons at strategic centers, by keeping up communication with these, and by insisting upon the right to appoint, or at least to confirm, all heads of important local units. Most of the peoples of Mongolia and Sinkiang were allowed to maintain something of their old tribal and family organization, although the Manchus often sought to group them in such a manner as to bring about a coalescence between some of the tribes and so to weaken old tribal loyalties. Colonists were brought into some regions, moreover, as a rule from Manchuria or the western portion of China proper, in the attempt to strengthen Manchu control. The local unit was usually the Banner, each Banner being composed of about fifty or more adult males capable of bearing arms. In the majority of instances the Banner had at its head a chieftain or *dzassak*. The *dzassak* held his post by virtue of imperial appointment, but generally in practice also by heredity. In turn the Banners were often grouped by tribes. In Inner Mongolia, where the control of Peking was more minutely exercised and the organization had some resemblance to that of China proper, the tribes were organized into leagues. Outer Mongolia was divided into four large regions. At important towns and cities, such as Urga, Yarkand, and Turfan, Manchu officials of varying grades were placed, for the most part supported by troops. The quality of the holders of these positions often suffered from the practice of using many of them as posts to which to exile officials who for some reason, possibly for serious moral delinquency, had incurred the imperial displeasure. Over the administration of the peoples of Mongolia and of much of Sinkiang was the *Li Fan Yüan* at Peking.

Connecting Peking with the most important centers in these outlying dependencies were post routes, diligently maintained. The submission of the peoples of these regions was further sought by the practice of according titles to influential individuals and by requiring periodical visits to Peking of important natives, either in person or by proxy.

In Tibet the organization was somewhat different. Here was a vast region governed by a political-ecclesiastical machine, the Lama hierarchy. None of the leaders of the hierarchy, either at the capital or at the largest monasteries, could be chosen without the consent of a representative of Peking. At the head of the Manchu administration in Tibet, at Lhasa, was an imperial resident. Major subordinates were stationed at three centers, including Lhasa. All were under the *Li Fan Yüan*.

The system by which the Ch'ing administered the non-Chinese sections of their Empire succeeded fairly well so long as the imperial line remained vigorous. It was, however, foredoomed to ultimate failure, for it was designed to do the impossible—to maintain the *status quo*. No attempt was made to amalgamate the Empire by the extension of Chinese culture outside the Eighteen Provinces. Each major section of the realm was encouraged in maintaining its own institutions in so far as these did not immediately threaten revolt.

SUMMARY OF THE OLD SYSTEM OF GOVERNMENT

This, then, was the system of government under the Ch'ing before it was affected by the coming of the Westerner. Like all human institutions, it had its weaknesses. It suffered from corruption and inefficiency, especially from the latter part of the eighteenth century. The large degree of local autonomy in both the civil and the military organization and the many checks and balances devised to prevent rebellion hindered quick, effective action on a large scale against a foreign foe or a serious revolt. But for these defects, China might not have proved so helpless a victim in her wars with Western powers and the rebellions of the middle of the nineteenth century might not have gained such headway. The civil service examinations, with their concentration on verbal matters and a memoriter training in the literature of a particular school of philosophy, nourished a pride of culture which made it difficult for the Chinese to be willing to learn from another civilization. This greatly delayed adjustment to the new conditions brought by the coming of the West and thus heightened the debacle when the pressure of Occidental culture could no longer be resisted. Cultural uniformity through the civil service examinations was a brake on change and possible progress. The lack of honor in which military service was popularly held became a decided handicap in dealing with an Occident armed to the teeth and from which only force could hope to win freedom and respect.

Serious, too, was the dependence upon an hereditary imperial line. In the Chinese system of government the monarch formed the keystone of the arch. The structure had been erected by great autocrats such as Ch'in Shih Huang Ti and Han Wu Ti. The hierarchy was simply hands and feet to the Emperor. Except for a regency in the case of a minor, no method had been devised and legalized, either by custom or formal enactment, for carrying on the government in the name of the prince. When a ruler or a ruling line proved hopelessly incompetent, the remedy to which resort was most frequently had was revolt. This in part accounts for the repeated change in dynasties and the much more frequent rebellions. Rebellion, indeed, was the chief means by which discontent could become vocal. It was usually either a protest or an instrument of the ambitious. Loyalty of a minister to his prince was one of the cardinal Confucian virtues, but, as we have seen, accepted political theory also had a place for popular revolt against a dissolute or unjust ruler and recognized in the *fait accompli* of a change in the reigning family the transfer of the mandate of Heaven. This was in marked contrast to Japan, where loyalty to the throne has been even more a cardinal virtue, where history records only one imperial line, and where at a very early time the tradition was established of having the rule carried on by the most competent, but in the name of the legitimate house. In China, whenever an able and vigorous monarch was on the throne, the system worked well. When, however, as is inevitable under the principle of hereditary succession, a vicious or incompetent heir came into power, the machinery creaked and not infrequently broke down. As we have so often noted, it was this defect which largely accounted for the undoing of China in the nineteenth and twentieth centuries. The Empire was headed by a decadent family at the time when it faced the greatest crisis of its history.

Probably the basic weakness lay in the fact that as the theory on which the government rested was carried to its logical conclusion stagnation was unavoidable and decay probable. As the

T'ang, the Sung, the Ming, and the Ch'ing perfected that system on which the Ch'in and the Han had begun to organize the state—a bureaucracy dependent on the Emperor and drilled in a particular social philosophy—ossification set in. A system relentlessly applied threatened to ruin a great people.

The failings must not be allowed to obscure the achievements of the Chinese imperial system. These have been mentioned repeatedly in the preceding pages and do not require reiteration. In spite of its defects the political structure which so largely disappeared in the first three decades of the twentieth century was among the most remarkable and successful ever devised by man.

THE CHANGES IN THE GOVERNMENT WROUGHT BY CONTACT WITH THE OCCIDENT

Space is lacking to record, even in its main outlines, the history of the changes in the structure of the government of China due to contact with the Occident. Some of the most important have been mentioned in previous chapters. Their course has been kaleidoscopic and confusing in the extreme. The end is not yet. In fact, China may be only at the beginning of her political revolution. Any description of the current form of government may be out of date before it can be printed.

Although an historical narrative is here out of place, certain prominent features and trends must be noted. One of these was the attempt of the Ch'ing to guide China through the transition by introducing new institutions and making adjustments while preserving the essentials of the old—such as the monarchy and the hierarchical bureaucracy. Given a dynasty in its prime under such a monarch as a K'ang Hsi, this, while extremely difficult, would have had a fair chance of success. As it was we now know that failure was practically certain. At the time of the T'ai P'ing Rebellion, instead of renovating from the ground up or else abolishing the Banners and the Green Standard, these were allowed to go on their somnolent way and a new military force was created. Later came attempts to create an army of the Occidental type, but the most noteworthy result was the forging of a weapon by which the commander of the best units, Yüan Shih-k'ai, was eventually able to dominate the country and for about four years to maintain a certain degree of internal order. A few new central bureaus, such as the Tsungli Yamen, were added to the old ones at Peking. New nation-wide services, principally the post office and the maritime customs, were created. A direct handling by Peking of many affairs formerly delegated to provincial and local officials was brought about by pressure from the highly centralized governments of the West. New taxes were levied, especially *likin*—the latter originally devised to help meet the cost of suppressing the T'ai P'ings. Late in the dynasty beginnings were made at bringing the laws and courts of the country more nearly into conformity with those of the West. After the Russo-Japanese War the administration of Manchuria was reorganized and Chinese were given a much larger share in it. The reform of the civil service was attempted and eventually (1905) the old system of examinations was abolished. Representative, elective provincial assemblies and a national assembly were instituted, and a parliament promised. The expenses of government increased, partly because of indemnities to the powers, partly because of the greater cost of the new military establishment, and partly because the state was compelled to undertake additional functions. Moreover, the financial stability of the government was threatened by the pledging of some of the major revenues, notably the customs duties, for the payment of sums due foreigners. None of these changes would necessarily have proved fatal to the fundamental features of the old government. It was ineptitude in high places which made impossible the orderly assimilation of innovations from the West.

As we have seen, the old has been progressively swept aside amid repeated Empire-wide disorder and civil strife. Only remnants survive, and many of these are threatened. The passing of the examination system dealt the death blow to the prestige and dominance of Confucianism, which had been the means of national cultural coherence. In the new educational system, Confucianism retreated more and more into the background. The abolition of the monarchy cut off the head of the official hierarchy. This did not necessarily mean the end of a bureaucracy, for a somewhat similar institution has existed in republican France. The demise of the monarchy and of the old system of examinations, however, made essential radical readjustments in the methods of recruiting and choosing the members of the civil service, and the institution was greatly weakened and threatened to disintegrate. The many abortive attempts at national and provincial constitutions modeled at least in part on those of the West were a further cause of disorganization. Of national constitutions at least four were adopted in twenty years, some of them confessedly temporary, but at least one hopefully denominated "permanent." Several provinces formed constitutions, usually only to allow them soon to fall into desuetude. Financial solvency was threatened by the pledging of additional sources of revenue to secure foreign loans. New organizations, such as local and national educational associations and chambers of commerce, arose and often had an important voice in political affairs.

The disappearance of the old was hastened by the attempts at introducing the institutions of Communist Russia. For example, the *tangpu*, local committees of the Kuomintang which had Russian prototypes, for a time supplanted in part the village elders and even the magistrate. From 1927 on the country was ruled by the Kuomintang. This party, organized by Sun Yat-sen and his colleagues long before the Russian Revolution, later was modified under Russian influence. Eventually it attained a nation-wide organization, in an ascending scale from the *tangpu* through intermediary regional committees and offices to the National Party Congress. In theory the Congress, made up of delegates from subordinate units, met once a year, in practice not so frequently. In the interim it was represented by a Central Executive Committee. The program under which the party operated called for three stages—a period of military operations to crush opposition, one of political tutelage during which the nation, under the control of the party, was to be prepared for self-government, and one of constitutional government in which the dictatorship of the party shall have ended and popular democratic institutions come into being. The first period was officially fixed as ending in 1929, and in 1945 the country was still regarded as in the second. In the 1930's progress was made in the formulation of a constitution. What purported to be a final draft was published in 1936. In the 1940's a fairly representative People's Political Council became a recognized voice for criticism and constructive proposals.

The Nationalist Government, established at Nanking in 1927,

was in theory organized (1928) on an outline inherited from Sun Yat-sen and had in it many Russian features. It was under the Kuomintang and derived its mandate from the Central Executive Committee and the Central Supervisory Committee elected by the National Congress of that party. In direct control of the government was a Central Political Council of the Kuomintang made up of the membership of these two committees and presided over by a standing committee of the three. This was succeeded, in 1937, by a Supreme National Defense Conference, later the Supreme National Defense Council. The central government had five bodies, executive, legislative, judicial, examining, and controlling (something like the old censorate, for impeaching and auditing), each called a *yüan*. Subordinate to the Executive *Yüan* were the usual ministries and commissions (of interior, foreign affairs, military affairs, navy, finance, communications, industry, justice, education, opium suppression, railways, Mongolian and Tibetan affairs, and famine relief).

Marked progress was made in framing codes in accord with the ideals of the Occident, so that there might be no longer any excuse for extraterritoriality. The coming of the new laws, however, meant the passing of another feature of the old order. For the time being, an independent judiciary could scarcely be said to exist. The dominance of the military precluded it.

The civil strife and the rule of the military were corrosive forces. Early in the history of the Republic, for instance, the Military Governor overshadowed and eventually usually entirely displaced the Civil Governor. The country was largely carved up among military men, often of very humble origin and poorly educated, who rose to power out of the general disorder. Such provincial and local government as survived generally existed on their sufferance. At the head of each province was a kind of committee with a chairman. In practice many of the provinces were controlled by military leaders who were largely independent of the national government. After 1926 these war lords were mostly eliminated. Only the Communists remained persistently independent.

Yet remnants of the old organization persisted and it was to these that the country largely owed such order as existed. The old provinces continued, and six additional ones were created (usually from existing divisions) on the borders of the original twenty-two inherited from the Ch'ing. The *hsien* survived as a characteristic local administrative unit, and villages, families, and guilds kept up their functions, although often much modified and weakened. There were many irregular tax levies, but the land and salt taxes and the customs duties (sadly diminished after 1937 by the Japanese blockade) continued to be basic sources of revenue. Guilds, clans, and secret societies still played an important part in government. Secret societies, indeed, may even have become more influential under the Republic. A large proportion of the educated belonged to them. Seldom did a man join more than one. While their membership and proceedings were not public and their activities were seldom heralded in the public press, they formed extremely important factors in politics. The Control and the Examining *Yüan* of the Nationalist Government were attempts at reviving two of the characteristic features of the imperial system, the censorate and the civil service examinations. To be sure, they were rather futile, for the Examining *Yüan* had for years a large salaried staff and only after 1930 were a few feeble attempts made at holding examinations. Still, they were the result of an effort to carry over into the new some of the best elements of the old.

Prophecy is always dangerous and never more so than in present-day China. What the government of China will be, if and when it becomes fairly stabilized, it is impossible to predict. That the old can never return seems fairly clear. For better or for worse, the Chinese have broken with the system inherited from the Chou, the Ch'in and the Han. Some of the spirit of the old may well persist. For example, an educational system under the close control of the government and inculcating a uniform culture as a means of national unity has been stressed. Since it is in accord with the tendency in the Occident and finds strength and incentive in the rising tide of nationalism, it will probably grow, and achieve in a somewhat different manner what was accomplished by the former civil service examinations. Two conflicting tendencies common to most governments and long visible in China are present—the desire for local autonomy and the urge to national unity through some kind of hierarchical bureaucracy. It seems safe—and something of a banality—to guess that, as heretofore, a working compromise between the two will be arrived at, presumably, since this is the trend of modern states, with greater centralization than under the Ch'ing. Western influences and the spirit of nationalism are so strong that it appears probable, and this is also platitudinous, that whatever form or forms of government develop will not be reproductions of the old but will be something new—will possess many features derived from the Occident, and yet will be attempts at adjustment to China's needs and to the genius of the past. It seems clear, moreover, that the nationalism which has been rising so rapidly and which shows no signs of abatement will not permit the Chinese to rest satisfied short of the complete union of all territory traditionally Chinese and of full independence from all foreign control. This will mean one government for at least the old Eighteen Provinces, Inner Mongolia, and Manchuria. If the country is to be permanently unified, the acceptance by the nation, whether consciously or unconsciously, of some sort of fundamental philosophy, doing for the new what Confucianism did for the old, would seem to be necessary. It is possible that nationalism will supply the needed bond—and that in spite of its many obvious shortcomings both for individuals and for groups.

It will be fascinating to watch the progress toward the evolution of the new. Certainly, unless the Chinese have lost their remarkable capacity for government—and this seems entirely unproved—in time they will erect once more a reasonably stable and efficient structure.

BIBLIOGRAPHY

The materials in Chinese on government are extremely voluminous—documents of many kinds, compilations, and treatises. The following may be mentioned as prominent examples. Tu Yu of the T'ang wrote the *T'ung Tien,* which contains sections on political economy, examinations and degrees, government offices, rites, music, military discipline, geography, and national defense, and traces its subject historically, beginning at the earliest times. Ma Tuan-lin, of the thirteenth century, compiled, on the basis of the *T'ung Tien,* his *Wên Hsien T'ung K'ao,* larger than the latter, including a somewhat wider range of material, and coming down from the beginning of history almost to his own time. A supplement was added in the sixteenth century and a revision of this latter, made by imperial order, was completed about 1772. An extension was published in the eighteenth century. An official description of the government under the Ch'ing is the *Ta Ch'ing Hui Tien,* modeled after a similar one under the Ming, compiled in 1694, revised in 1727 and 1771, and rearranged in 1818.

The theories underlying the older government are dealt with in Liang Ch'i-ch'ao, *History of Chinese Political Thought during the Early Tsin Period* (New York, 1930), in W. S. A. Pott, *Chinese Political Philosophy* (New York, 1925), and in Leonard Shihlien Hsü, *The Political Philosophy of Confucianism* (New York, 1932).

Useful books dealing entirely or in part with the government of China under the Ch'ing before the changes brought by contact with the Occident are H. B. Morse, *The Trade and Administration of China* (revised edition, London, 1913); S. W. Williams, *The Middle Kingdom* (New York, 1883); Pao Chao Hsieh, *The Government of China (1644-1911)* (Baltimore, 1925), using in part Chinese sources, especially the *Ta Ch'ing Hui Tien;* W. D. Mayers, *The Chinese Government. A Manual of Chinese Titles, Categorically Arranged and Explained* (Shanghai, 1878), very useful, especially for the names and descriptions of various boards and officials; the even fuller N. S. Brunnert and V. V. Hagelstrom, *Present Day Political Organization of China* (Shanghai, 1912); and Pierre Hoang, *Mélanges sur l'Administration* (*Variétés Sinologiques* No. 21, Shanghai, 1902).

The civil service examinations are described in Etienne Zi, *Pratique des Examens Littéraires en Chine* (*Variétés Sinologiques* No. 5, Shanghai, 1894), in W. F. Mayers, *op. cit.*, in S. W. Williams, *op. cit.*, Vol. 1, chapter 9, and P. C. Hsieh, *op. cit.*, chapter 6. Some material on the history of these examinations is in E. Biot, *Essai sur l'Histoire de l'Instruction Publique en Chine* (Paris, 1847).

On the older local government of China there is an interesting account in Y. K. Leong and L. K. Tao, *Village and Town Life in China* (London, 1915), rather too idealized and too inclined to dodge the defects and abuses. Another, more realistic, but tending to be pessimistic and limited chiefly to the sections, in the North, of which the author had intimate knowledge, is in A. H. Smith, *Village Life in China* (New York, 1899). Still another, describing more recent conditions but in which are many survivals of the past, is in D. H. Kulp II, *Country Life in South China. The Sociology of Familism. Vol. I, Phenix Village, Kwantung, China* (New York, 1925).

On laws and the administration of justice in China before the changes wrought by the coming of the Westerner, the *Ta Ch'ing Lü Li* has been translated in part by Sir Thomas Staunton in *Ta Tsing Leu Lee*, etc. (London, 1810) and more fully by G. Boulais in *Manuel du Code Chinois* (*Variétés Sinologiques*, No. 55, Shanghai, 2 vols., 1923–1924). Another standard work is E. Alabaster, *Notes and Commentaries on Chinese Criminal Law* (London, 1899). T. R. Jernigan, *China in Law and Commerce* (New York, 1905) contains an interesting summary, based largely on Staunton. R. T. Bryan, *An Outline of Chinese Civil*

Law (Shanghai, 1925) is a brief synopsis of current laws, principles, and procedure, which combines the old and the new. A longer study of ancient and especially modern law is J. Escarra, *Le Droit Chinois* (Peking, 1936).

On government finances, and especially on taxation, there is Han Liang Huang, *The Land Tax in China* (New York, 1918)—a doctoral dissertation; another doctoral dissertation, Chuan Shih Li, *Central and Local Finance in China* (New York, 1922); still another of the same origin, Kinn Wei Shaw, *Democracy and Finance in China* (New York, 1926)—largely historical and carrying the story into republican times; E. H. Parker, *China* (New York, 1917), chapters 10, 11, 12; Morse, *op. cit.*, chapter 4; and Hsieh, *op. cit.*, chapter 7. On the salt tax, see an excellent article by E. M. Gale, *Public Administration of Salt in China: A Historical Survey* (*The Annals of the American Academy of Political and Social Science*, Nov. 1930, pp. 241–251).

A summary and criticism of the older military system is in W. J. Hail, *Tsêng Kuo-fan* (New Haven, 1927), pp. 1–16. The organization of the army is also described in Mayers, *op. cit.*, chapters 6 and 7. On the examinations leading to office in the army, there is Etienne Zi, *Pratique des Examens Militaires en Chine* (*Variétés Sinologiques* No. 9, Shanghai, 1896).

On the government of the dependencies, see Mayers, *op. cit.*, pp. 80–114, and Hsieh, *op. cit.*, chapter 12.

There is a wealth of treatises and material on the changes in government in the past generation. An excellent account, somewhat optimistic and dwelling especially on the changes since 1926, is A. N. Holcombe, *The Chinese Revolution* (Cambridge, 1930). Morse, *op. cit.*, chapter 3, contains a brief description of government under the first years of the Republic. J. C-h. Lynn, *Political Parties in China* (Peking, 1930) is a somewhat sketchy account of the major parties and cliques, chiefly since the establishment of the Republic. A fairly short summary is H. M. Vinacke, *Modern Constitutional Development in China* (Princeton, 1920). One set of documents is *Constitution and Supplementary Laws and Documents of the Republic of China* (translated and published by the Commission on Extraterritoriality, Peking, 1924). See also P. M. A. Linebarger, *Government in Republican China* (New York, 1938). Translations of important documents and periodical descriptions of the current government are to be found in the various issues of the *China Year Book* (London, 1912–1919, Tientsin, 1921–1930, Shanghai, 1931 *et seq.*). Some of the new laws are contained in T. Chen and N. F. Allman, *The Modern Commercial Legislation of China, Translated and Compiled* (Shanghai, 1926), and *The Civil Code of the Republic of China*, translated by C. L. Hsia and others (Shanghai, 1930). Some documents and articles of value are also to be found in *The Chinese Social and Political Science Review* (Peking, 1916 *et seq.*). Min-Ch'ien T. Z. Tyau, *Two Years of Nationalist China* (Shanghai, 1930), has much excellent material. There are several doctoral dissertations in French—subject to the usual limitations of such works—which have useful material and interesting points of view—among them Sié-ying-chou, *Le Federalisme en Chine: Étude sur quelques Constitutions Provinciales* (Paris, 1924), Tsien Tai, *Le Pouvoir Législatif en Chine* (Paris, 1914), and T. T. Ouang, *Le Gouvernement de la Chine Moderne* (Paris, 1923). A brief *ex parte* description of the Nationalist Government at Nanking by an able Chinese Minister to the United States is C. C. Wu, *The Nationalist Program for China* (New Haven, 1929). The basis on which the Nationalist Government at Nanking is organized, *The San Min Chu I*, is translated by F. W. Price and L. T. Chen in *San Min Chu I. The Three Principles of the People. By Dr. Sun Yat-sen* (Shanghai, 1927). A brief but comprehensive description of the Nanking government is in M. S. Bates, *The National Government* (*China Christian Year Book*, 1931, pp. 13–21), and of the Kuomintang in M. S. Bates and F. W. Price, *Kuomintang* (*Encyclopædia of the Social Sciences*, Vol. 8, 1932, pp. 610–614).

A treatise on some phases of the legal aspects of China's relations with foreigners is L. Tung, *China and Some Phases of International Law* (London, 1940).

See also the bibliography at the end of Chapter XII.

CHAPTER XV

ECONOMIC LIFE AND ORGANIZATION

FOOD, clothing, and shelter have loomed large in the objectives of the Chinese. This, of course, is of necessity true in any society. Rather more than most peoples, however, the Chinese have been this-worldly in their ideals. In a certain sense they can be characterized as materialistically minded. Certainly interest in the physical basis of life has been prominent in the philosophies on which the state has acted. As far back as we can trace Chinese culture, it was consciously dependent upon agriculture and sought to further it. Most of the great schools of thought of the Chou endeavored to promote man's bodily welfare as an essential condition of all gains in morals and the arts. The Legalists, on whose theories Ch'in Shih Huang Ti unified the Empire, stressed the economic organization of society. Confucianism recognized the fact that if there were to be civilization the masses must not be allowed to go unclad and hungry. Of the native philosophies accorded a prolonged place of honor in Chinese life, only Taoism belittled the striving for bodily comforts and sought to make man independent of the trammels of the flesh.

In this respect, it may be noted, China differed fundamentally from India. However much in practice the great majority of the Hindus have been engrossed in the struggle to maintain their physical existence, usually in theory they have sought to free themselves from it, have honored the ascetic, and have tended to regard this present, visible world as an illusion. It may also be remarked that for this reason the Chinese have fitted more easily into the climate of opinion of the modern Occident than have the Indians. The difference is seen in the two men who in the twentieth century have most aroused the enthusiastic loyalty of their respective peoples. On the one hand has been Gandhi, ascetic and wishing to save his people from Western industrialism. On the other has been Sun Yat-sen, simple in his tastes but by no means ascetic, and who, far from wishing to keep Occidental mechanical appliances out of China, emphasized "the people's livelihood," at one time assumed the task of developing the railroads of China, and at another set forth a scheme for the economic development of the nation with vast funds from the capitalistic West. Even more striking is the contrast between a Tagore who denounced the West for its "materialism" and a Hu Shih who wished his nation to emulate the Occident in its scientific knowledge and utilization of man's physical environment.

It is not surprising that, with this background, the Chinese state should have concerned itself with the economic life of the country, and that it should continue to do so. Nor is it remarkable that more than once so thorough-going a direction of the production and distribution of the country has been essayed by the state that Westerners and modern Chinese have dubbed the attempt socialism. A Wang Mang and a Wang An-shih were simply carrying out in an exaggerated form the principle of the possibility of governmental control which seems usually to have been acknowledged as valid by the Confucianists as well as the ancient Legalists.

While something akin to socialism was by no means alien to Chinese thought, under the Ch'ing and many earlier dynasties the imperial policy was very largely that of *laissez faire*. Here and there the government stepped in. Coinage was in the hands of the state. The salt trade was an official monopoly—although as a source of revenue rather than as a means of reducing the price and improving the quality for the consumer. Close supervision was exercised over foreign trade. State granaries in which was stored the rice collected as one form of taxation could in times of scarcity be used to equalize prices and relieve distress. Officialdom usually determined the disposition of waste land, and no title to any real estate was secure without its imprimatur. In the main, however, the imperial and provincial governments exerted almost no authority over the agriculture, business, and industry of the country.

Comparative freedom from bureaucratic interference did not mean that individualism was rampant in the Empire's economic life. On the contrary, the regulation which the hierarchy did not impose was exercised by local and extra-political agencies, such as the family and the guild. The actual situation was almost the opposite of *laissez faire*. Far from being free to do as he liked, the individual was closely bound by custom and a network of coöperative agencies.

This organization differed markedly from the capitalistic system of the modern Occident. The old China had no huge accumulations of mobile wealth. Great riches were in the form of lands, pawnshops, rich clothing in vast quantities, jewels, and bullion. No stock companies existed, with their facilities for centering in one enterprise the investments of hundreds or thousands of individuals. The partnership, the guild, the secret society, and the family were the characteristic forms of economic combination. Moreover, in contrast with most peoples of the modern Occident, economically China was almost entirely self-contained. Foreign trade never bulked large in the total business of the realm. Even to-day were China to be cut off suddenly from the rest of the world, in terms of food and clothing it would be only slightly inconvenienced.

An economic history of China should prove most illuminating. A record of the experience of a people which has devoted so much attention to both the theory and the practice of supplying man's physical needs would have much of interest. Unfortunately the story has yet to be written. The available material is enormous, but only the most tentative beginnings have been made toward collecting and interpreting it.

We do know that in the main the Chinese were fairly successful in solving their economic problems. Their organization made possible a livelihood for a great number of people. Under such dynasties as the Han, the T'ang, the Sung, the Yüan, the Ming, and the Ch'ing they constituted one of the most numerous and prosperous masses of mankind. In the latter part of the eighteenth and in the nineteenth century, indeed, the Chinese were the largest fairly homogeneous group of the human race. The standard of living which they had achieved probably compared favorably with that of any people before the sixteenth century. It will be recalled with what enthusiastic superlatives Marco Polo, who had travelled in most of the highly civilized sections of the world of his day, described the populous cities and the wealth of Cathay.

It was not until the modern age that the Occident, enriched by its geographic discoveries and its industrial revolution, forged ahead of China and set a new standard of comfort for the race.

On the other hand, it must not be forgotten that the majority of the Chinese have lived and continue to live at an economic level which to the modern Occident seems grinding poverty, that even in good times there have been thousands of professional beggars, that again and again throughout China's history famines have devastated great sections (one estimate shows an average for two thousand years of nearly one famine a year which was important enough to find a place in the records), and that at several periods gigantic declines in population seem to have occurred and must have been accompanied by intense physical suffering. Much of this distress, to be sure, has been due primarily to other factors than economic. Floods and drought, the collapse of dynasties with the attendant civil strife, invasions, high mortality in youth, wasting disease, religious beliefs, and a family system which makes for the rapid multiplication of population, each has had a part. But for defects in the economic structure, however, there would probably have been fewer rebellions, for many of these were in large part induced by the pinch of poverty, and a better organization or a greater control of man's physical environment would have prevented or mitigated the distress due to disasters of nature. It is significant that the mechanical inventions which have made possible the increases both in population and in standards of living in so much of the world during the past century and a half originated not in China but in the Occident. The reasons must be a matter of debate, but the fact is indisputable. The Chinese, with all their devotion to the material well-being of man, fell behind the West in achieving it.

AGRICULTURE

From time immemorial agriculture has been the major occupation of the Chinese. It is estimated that eighty-five per cent. of the population are now engaged in it. This figure is far from exact, and if it is put that high it must be made to include allied occupations—such as merchants, traders, artisans, blacksmiths, restaurant-keepers, and the like in the villages and market towns, and the many who help to transport farm produce from the fields to the cities. Certainly, however, most of the Chinese have been and are supported directly by farming and by the occupations immediately connected with it. The devotion to agriculture has been furthered, as was suggested in the first chapter, by natural environment. Much of China's soil is very fertile, especially in the great deltas of the Yangtze and Huang Ho, and in some of the smaller river valleys. Moreover, agriculture has been held in honor. The farmer has ranked high in the social scale. The Emperor officially opened the spring by ceremonial ploughing, and magistrates throughout the Empire were supposed to perform a similar rite.

The absorption of so large a proportion of the population in the task of raising food and the raw materials for clothing is an indication of the nature of agricultural methods. These are marked by the intensive application of human labor and a paucity of machinery. Agriculture is more akin to gardening than to farming. Machinery there is—from the standpoint of the modern West simple and some of it crude—and the use of draught animals. By far the major part of the work, however, is performed by human beings. Even on larger farms, where animals can be and are employed more extensively than on smaller ones, as a rule more than half the labor is by human hands.

Along with intensive cultivation by man-power are some other characteristics. Most of the units are small. In at least many sections the majority of these are farmed by their owners, and although there are renters—in some regions heavily burdened—practically all the laborers are free. Under the Manchus there was very little of slavery or of binding the peasant to the soil in semi-free serfdom.

Some of these generalizations require elaboration. The units of cultivation were usually small. No accurate survey has been made for all China, and holdings naturally vary in size with the character of the soil, the kind of crops raised, the water supply, and the human factor which in places amasses large estates. One survey of the last decade of portions of six provinces in North and East Central China gives the average size of nearly twenty-four hundred farms as a little over five acres, varying from an average of slightly over ten acres in two *hsien* in Anhui to about two and a half acres in one *hsien* in Fukien. Another survey made about the same time seems to show that in the places examined two-thirds of the farmers in Kiangsu and slightly more than half in Hopei (Chihli) were attempting to make a living off one acre or less of land. It found the average of the holdings in Kiangsu to be about three and a quarter acres, and in Hopei about four acres. An earlier and probably less accurate estimate gave the average holding in Hopei as a fraction over twelve acres, and one, also earlier, gave that in Kiangsu as about three and a half acres. As is to be expected, in the North, with its smaller rainfall, the average farm is larger than in the Yangtze Valley or on the south coast, where the precipitation is heavier and the growing season longer, where more rice can be raised, and where more than one crop a year is usually possible.

While the above figures indicate that the great majority of farms are small, there are numerous exceptions. China has had and still has many large landed estates, some of them family possessions and others held as endowments of temples or of various philanthropic enterprises. Some are hundreds of acres in extent. These great domains, however, are not necessarily cultivated as units. Most of them appear to be rented out to tenants in plots but little if any larger than those worked by their owners. Many of the proprietors reside on their land and so form in places a kind of country gentry. Title to a considerable proportion of the rented land, however, has been and is held by absentees. This makes for a very different kind of rural society than where the owners live on their estates. When paid in cash, the rent yields the landlord about eight and a half or even eleven per cent. on his investment. When rent is a share of the crop, it takes about half of what the tenant produces. The proportion of the agricultural land included in the larger holdings varies from section to section. The percentage of peasant proprietors appears to be highest in the older provinces of the North, and lowest in Fukien, Kwangtung, and the Yangtze Valley. Conditions have been modified in some sections by Communism, for this has promoted peasant proprietorship at the expense of the landlords.

The exact percentage of farmers the country over who own the land they till is not known. Certainly, however, it is fairly high. One set of figures seems to show that somewhat more than half the farmers cultivate their own land, that about a fourth lease part and own part, and that only about a fourth are entirely tenants. Many of the tenants, moreover, rent their fields from the communal holdings of the clan to which they belong. Peasant proprietors have acquired their land chiefly through inheritance, although transfer by sale or mortgage is not unusual. The division of ancestral acres through successive generations of heirs has made for the smallness of the tracts farmed. Inherited ownership, it may be noted, promotes a stable rural population. Probably much less than half of the work on the farms—on the average—is done by hired labor, and most of this appears to be of local origin and not migratory. The rural population, staying by its ancestral acres unless uprooted by some such catastrophe as a famine or a war, has had and continues to have a profound effect on Chinese society. Conservatism and stability in outlook and customs are of its essence.

Not only are the total holdings of any one farmer small, but in turn they are usually made up of still smaller tracts scattered in several places about the village and separated from the farmhouse, on the average, by a distance of from a third to half a mile. As inevitable corollaries, such farms cannot be cultivated as units, it becomes difficult if not impossible for one peasant to fight plant and animal diseases without the coöperation of his neighbors (often not easily obtained), time and energy are lost in going from one plot to another, and labor-saving machinery cannot be employed to advantage. It is an inefficient form of rural organization. Moreover, a large proportion of the farms prove too small for economical cultivation. It is the larger farms which are most profitable.

With these small holdings and the intensive application of human labor, the density of population in some portions of China is almost unbelievable. The survey which shows that farms average a little over five acres also discloses the fact that the average family supported by each is 5.7 persons. The most crowded rural sections have more inhabitants per square mile than Bengal, the most thickly settled part of India, or than rural Japan.

A standard of living inevitably follows which, from the Western standpoint, is appallingly low. To this contributes the fact that, especially in the North, where the growing season is shorter, there are some months when labor cannot be applied to the land.

Supplementary industries occupy part of the spare time, but by no means all. A survey, made before the inflation of the 1940's with their skyrocketing prices, indicated that the average yearly income of a farmer's family, excluding any allowance for house rent but including produce raised on the ground and consumed by the family, was only $147 (American currency), or only about $2.30 a month per capita. Half even of this distressingly slight sum was taken up by the costs of farming, so that only about $73 were left for the subsistence of the average family. In North China, where the poverty is greater, an investigation showed that the rural population had only about $5 American currency per capita a year for food, fuel, shelter, and clothing, whereas a minimum living wage was three times that sum. Only by rigid economy can the masses eke out the barest existence. For most of them the money required for even elementary education is all but out of the question. The rate of illiteracy is correspondingly high and the problem of achieving a democratic national or provincial government is consequently augmented.

Yet in fairly normal times chronic semi-starvation is by no means universal. Infant mortality is excessive, but it seems probable from statistics taken from several widely separated areas that a larger proportion of the population attains old age than in rural India—although decidedly less than in France and slightly less than in Germany. Moreover, many farmers make an annual profit on their operations. No one who has travelled in China, especially in the Yangtze Valley and the South, can forget the comfortable farmsteads he has seen, with their air of dignity and peace. Many a well-to-do rural family has nourished for generations a tradition of culture and self-respect. As has been suggested, both incomes and profits average much less in the North, with its smaller rainfall, than in the Yangtze Valley. In the North, therefore, the average standard of living is lower than in the South.

Given the method of cultivation by the lavish application of human labor, it follows that a considerable proportion of the land remains untilled. Only the more fertile soils can be made to yield a sufficient return to justify the investment of labor required by the traditional methods. Much of the unploughed land, to be sure, is not utterly waste. Some of it is utilized for pasturage—usually of a scanty type. Hilly land especially is employed for sheep grazing—although neighbors' dogs often become a problem. It is also largely cut over for fuel—of dried grass, brush, or wood. Some observers have suggested that much of the wild land could be brought under profitable cultivation by the more extensive use of machinery, fertilizers, and seed selection. Certainly in many sections the customary practice is more than wasteful. Cutting off the wood, brush, and grass from the hills, even to digging up the roots (as is often done under the pressure for fuel), hastens erosion. Any humus and most of the tillable top soil are washed away, and the land impoverished. Often much of the remaining sand and gravel is carried to the plains by heavy rains and there impedes cultivation.

Even in the fertile plots some of the space, possibly five per cent. or more on the average, is taken up by paths and the ever-present graves.

In spite of its dense rural population, therefore, China proper has by no means extended its farm land to the ultimate possible limits. In Manchuria, too, many thousand acres remain relatively unoccupied, and, in spite of its scanty rainfall, Inner Mongolia still contains probably other thousands of acres which wise tillage and selection of crops and seeds could render productive.

Agricultural experts from the Occident have more than once remarked on the skill of the Chinese farmer in taking advantage of the materials at his hand. Even to the amateur observer the application of practical agricultural lore is apparent. The most obvious testimony to it is the huge population which China has been made to support, a considerable minority of it in comparative comfort. In this, to be sure, the Chinese have been favored by soil and climate, but natural advantages alone would not account for their success. In utilizing their environment they have accumulated much experience and have displayed no small degree of intelligence. Some of their knowledge has been arrived at empirically and some has doubtless been stumbled upon accidentally. Probably most of the Chinese farmers are simply following with little if any understanding methods inherited from the past. In this, however, they are not unlike the peoples of other lands. Moreover, superstition rather than intelligence often dictates procedures—as also in many other sections of the earth. Modern scientific research in agriculture has much to contribute and, if its results are utilized, marked improvement will undoubtedly be registered. Yet after all the qualifying deficiencies have been taken into account, the fact remains that the traditional Chinese agriculture has much to commend it.

First of all, the Chinese have cultivated a very wide range of plants. This variety has been favored by the size of the country and the ensuing differences in climate and soil. Much of it, however, is due to the eagerness of the Chinese to appropriate whatever useful plant has come to their attention. To native varieties have been added, through the years, many from foreign lands. Some of the most prevalent of the food plants, indeed, have certainly and others have possibly been importations. The average Westerner thinks of the Chinese as eating chiefly rice. For large portions of the country this impression is not entirely untrue. For most of China proper south of the valley of the Yellow River, and particularly for the lower part of the Yangtze Valley and the provinces on the south coast, rice—of many varieties—is a major article of diet and the crop most extensively grown. However, scores of millions of Chinese, especially in the North, have never tasted rice. Probably for more than one hundred and fifty millions it does not count as an article of diet. Many other grains are raised. Wheat is cultivated in Manchuria and over most of China proper and is a major crop on the North China plain, in Shantung, Kansu, Shensi, and the northern portions of Anhui and Hupeh. Millet is extensively raised in the North, and particularly in the semi-arid portions of Kansu, Shensi, Shansi, and Inner Mongolia. Kaoliang, a kind of sorghum, is widely planted in the northeast of China proper, and forms the staple crop in much of Manchuria. Kaoliang supplies not only food in the form of grain, but its stalks and leaves are used for thatching, matting, packing, bridges, and fuel. Rice, wheat, millet, and kaoliang constitute the chief grains, but others, such as buckwheat, barley, and oats, are to be found in some sections.

Some sugar is produced, but its consumption is scanty and a good deal is imported from Java and Formosa.

Many legumes are raised. Peas, alfalfa, clover, and beans of several kinds, including the soy bean, are among them and are valuable not only as food but for maintaining the fertility of the soil. The soy bean especially is notable (particularly the yellow variety) for the total of its production and its extensive use as a source for oil, sauce, bean curd, soup, and other forms of food, and for oil cake for fertilizer and for fattening hogs. Root crops, such as peanuts and sweet potatoes, are very common. Sesamum seed is cultivated chiefly for its oil. Rape, which ripens before the planting of rice and cotton, is widely grown, and its seeds supply oil, its new shoots greens, its dried stems fuel, and the refuse cake fertilizer.

Many vegetables are raised. Note should be made of the edible water chestnut and lotus roots which are widely grown. Numerous kinds of fruit, too, are cultivated, although some foreign observers believe that the Chinese could, with benefit, give greater attention to them. The very name of tea is of Chinese origin, and while the export of the leaf has sharply declined of late years, it remains, as it has been for many centuries, a staple crop and the source of the universal Chinese drink. Our first reference to the drinking of tea is from the second half of the third century after Christ. Tea drinking was first confined to the South but under the T'ang it became widespread. By the eighth century even the poor were using tea, and the growth and preparation of the tea leaf had become an important occupation. Melons of various kinds, including especially the watermelon, are characteristic. Pumelos, oranges, bananas, pineapples, papaws, and lichees are raised in the tropical and sub-tropical South, and such fruits and nuts as oranges, pears, cherries, peaches, apricots, walnuts, chestnuts, grapes, plums, and apples in some other parts of the country. The bamboo is grown over much of China, in many varieties, and has almost innumerable uses. Its young shoots provide food, its foliage clothing, and its stalks material for building and for many kinds of furniture and implements.

The raw materials for clothing are also raised by the farmer. From time immemorial the silkworm and its associated mulberry tree have been a chief care of the Chinese. A wild silk, from larvæ fed on oaks, is also produced, especially in Shantung, Hopei, and Manchuria. Cotton is the material of the larger proportion of Chinese clothing and has been and is grown in North, in Central, and in South China. It forms a major crop of the lower part of the Yangtze Valley, and some have predicted that in time this region will become one of the chief sources of the world's supply. Ramie provides most of the material for China's "grass cloth." A number of other plants are cultivated for their fibre, among them hemp and jute.

It must also be noted that a great deal of tobacco is grown, in which, whatever its solace, there is no food value, and that of late years much land has been given over to the raising of the opium poppy—a serious economic waste, with disastrous moral and physical concomitants.

In addition to producing a wide variety of plants, the Chinese are noted for their slight dependence upon meat and animal products for food. They appear never to have cared for butter or cheese, and have made almost no use of cow's or goat's milk. In North China the amount of meat consumed per capita seems to be only about a sixth of that in France, a tenth of that in the United States, and even only about half of that in Japan, where much the same economy exists. In the main this is a saving. Whether it was entered upon intentionally as a matter of principle, gradually arrived at through more or less unconsciously recognized experience, or purely by accident, need not here concern us. To use the products of the field directly for human food without the waste of first passing them through the digestive processes of an intermediary animal obviously effects an economy in the area needed to support a given number of human beings. The Chinese diet has not been entirely lacking in meat. Most of it, however, has been derived from fish, which take up no land, and from pigs and chickens, which are in part scavengers and hence not a full charge upon food otherwise available for man. In at least one region thrifty farmers effect a further saving by planting their irrigation pools to fish and gathering their harvest in the autumn after the water is no longer needed on the fields. Ducks and geese are also widely raised. Mutton and beef are used, but in relatively small quantities. Some animals, we have seen, are utilized to assist man in his work—the water buffalo in the Yangtze Valley and the South, the donkey, the horse, the mule, and the ox in the North. All these, however, seem to average less than one to a farm.

Yet in spite of their independence of flesh and animal products, the Chinese have achieved a fairly well balanced diet. This again has probably not been through scientific method but by chance experience and instinctive taste. Proteins not acquired through meat are supplied by vegetable products, such as bean curd. Fats are obtained in the form of vegetable oils. Roughage and some of the needed salts and vitamins come through vegetables, a large proportion of them served green and not cooked long enough to destroy their beneficial elements. A laborer with his bowl of rice, his greens, and his bean curd, and perhaps with some tidbit cooked in oil, is not far from a well balanced ration. The brewing of his tea necessitates boiling the water, and since a large proportion of his liquid is taken in this manner he has a partial safeguard against the infections which lurk in most of the streams and wells.

Defects this diet doubtless has. To obtain the requisite amount of protein the Chinese must often eat a large quantity of grain. The practice of polishing the rice and the semi-white condition of much of the wheat flour deprive him of some of the salts and the vitamins in the outer covering of the grain. Often the food has too little variety. The insistence on rice as the only grain eaten in wide regions means semi-starvation for some who could procure wheat or sweet potatoes at a lower cost per unit of food value. Much land better suited to other crops is devoted to rice culture. In the North too few vegetables are grown. It seems probable that the average diet suffers from a calcium content too low for maximum growth. For these reasons and because of the narrow margin by which even in normal times a large proportion of the population is removed from the starvation level, the bulk of the Chinese appear to be dangerously underfed. The diet permits of no emergency reserve. It is significant that when students overwork the collapse tends to take the form of tuberculosis rather than nervous exhaustion. This is due in part to several other factors than diet, but a deficiency in food is probably in a measure responsible for it.

Not only does the Chinese farmer raise a wide variety of plants and economize on flesh, but he is noted for the pains with which he seeks to keep up the productivity of the land. No natural fertility, even as great as that of some of China's alluvial plains, could have yielded, unassisted, such continuous returns over so long a period as has that of China. The fact that to-day China maintains so large a population is due in no small degree to the persistence and the skill with which the farmer has kept his fields supplied with the needed plant food. A chief source of fertilizer has been what the Westerner euphemistically and somewhat squeamishly denominates "night soil." This, which in the sewage disposal systems of the modern Occident is completely wasted, and often does positive harm by polluting the rivers, is carefully collected and returned to the fields. The laborer carrying pails of night soil from the cities to the country is one of the most familiar sights—and smells—of China. Legumes, which add nitrogen to the soil, are extensively grown. In some instances they are turned under, before ripe, as green manure. Compost piles are frequent sights. Droppings from animals are carefully collected and used either for fuel or for manure. Ashes are scattered on the cultivated land, with, of course, their potassium and phosphorus. Soil from the canals, probably rich in needed minerals, is also placed on the fields, and sun-dried earthen bricks, when past their usefulness in buildings, may be pulverized and made once more to serve plant life. Rotation of crops is practiced. In many ways the Chinese peasant could give the average Western farmer lessons in conservation.

Some wastefulness there is. In parts of Fukien, for instance, the rice straw is burned to get it out of the way. Elsewhere, because of dearth of fuel, straw which otherwise might be put back on the land is consumed for domestic heating and cooking. The fields must usually provide both fuel and food. Moreover, the comparatively small number of animals make for a shortage in manure and so for a certain handicap in maintaining fertility. Much of the soil is, then, partly impoverished.

The Chinese farmer has acquired great skill in handling water. From the dawn of recorded history he has been draining swamp lands, controlling streams, and building canals for irrigation. Today the plains of China proper are usually traversed by a network of canals. Millions of acres of hillside and rolling ground have been carefully terraced, often at great expenditure of labor, both to retain water when flooded for wet rice culture and to prevent washing. Water is usually conveyed to the fields from the canal or pond in buckets carried by men or by pumps operated either by man power or by animals. Hundreds of miles of dikes have been constructed and maintained to keep lowlands from being flooded. Canals, too, are frequently not only an aid to irrigation out to drainage. The Chinese have learned to keep the surface soil stirred to conserve moisture. This has been of especial advantage in the semi-arid regions of the North, and particularly in Inner Mongolia, where "dry farming" extends the area of cultivation beyond what would otherwise be possible.

The Chinese have discovered means of fighting some of the pests which attack their crops. Thus in the South they have for centuries introduced colonies of ants to their orchards to feed on insects which infest the trees.

Force of circumstances and his own intelligence have made the Chinese farmer an expert in economy. Not only does he raise several crops a year on the same field wherever the season is long enough to permit it, but he often has more than one crop growing on the same land at the same time. For example, while wheat, sown in drills, is maturing, cotton seed is scattered broadcast, and its young plants have made a good start by the time the grain is cut. As many as three crops ripening at different times may be seen at once on the same plot. The Chinese is an adept at conserving fuel. Although through much of the country the winters are chilly and in some sections very cold, rooms are generally heated, if at all, only by a charcoal brazier or, in the North, by a *k'ang*—a bed of brick or earth with flues running through it horizontally. Instead of spending fuel in warming the air of an entire house, the Chinese puts on heavier clothing. For most of the populace this is in the form of garments between the two layers of which loose cotton is inserted as winter comes on. In some instances the cotton is quilted. The well-to-do may use fur. The *k'ang,* often warmed by the flue from the kitchen fire, may, from the Western standpoint, leave much to be desired in the way of comfort and may be plentifully infested with vermin, but it has at least the virtue of getting a good deal out of a given amount of fuel. Much building material comes directly from the farmer's own field. Sun-dried brick and tamped earthen walls, bamboo and kaoliang are common and relatively inexpensive materials for the house.

While Chinese farm tools are usually very crude and have many defects, often they display excellent features. Then, too, in a land where labor is cheap, and the farms small and the fields still smaller, the expensive power-driven agricultural machinery of the

United States and Canada would be far from economical. The Chinese have shown no little ingenuity in contriving or utilizing helpful devices. They hatch eggs by simple but effective methods of artificial incubation. In fishing they have many types of nets and also employ cormorants. Their methods of pumping water and of pressing bean cakes for oil are worthy of comment.

Coöperation is obviously desirable, especially since most of the farms are so small. This the Chinese have not been altogether successful in achieving, but by no means have they entirely failed. In protecting crops, in irrigation, in guarding dikes, to a certain extent in saving or borrowing capital and making loans, and in their villages and family and clan systems and secret societies, Chinese farmers have developed organizations for mutual aid and protection.

Deforestation is regarded as one of the great defects of China's economy. Much of the country once was adequately and in places densely wooded. The richness and variety of the native flora can be seen even to-day both in the North and the South, where a temple, the remnants of an imperial hunting preserve, or some other protection, artificial or natural, has allowed a grove to survive. In many a bare area, where nature is given a chance, young growth quickly springs up, often of many kinds of plants. Yet centuries of human occupation have denuded the major part of the country. In the earlier days much of the forest was probably cut simply for the purpose of fitting the land for tillage or to destroy the coverts of wild beasts. In later centuries the need for fuel and building material has kept the hillsides stripped. One result has been the carrying away of the soil to the plains. Disastrous floods have often occurred because a rain has quickly run off from denuded watersheds. Here is to be found one of the causes of the recurrent famines, especially in North China.

Yet even in the management of their timber resources the Chinese have often displayed much skill. Many of the groves of marketable trees are owned by temples and monasteries, and in some an approximation to a scientific procedure of forest management has been developed which has produced a constant supply of wood for revenue and for the use of the religious community. In at least one section of China private owners have had a traditional system of cutting trees for the market and replanting for future crops. The culture of bamboo, in itself a kind of forestry, has been very highly and skilfully developed.

Even from this brief description some of the effects of Chinese agricultural economy upon the life of the nation must be fairly apparent. The lack of machinery, the relatively small utilization of draft animals, and the extensive use of human labor mean that in order to produce for the nation the requisite food and materials for clothing and shelter the great majority of the population must be engaged in agriculture. After the needs of those who till the soil have been met, only a small surplus of farm products remains for exchange with the towns. The predominantly rural character of the nation has made for conservatism, for old social institutions ever persist longest in farming districts. The presence of so large a proportion of peasant proprietors has encouraged sturdy self-reliance and self-respect. It is probably also an insurance against the sort of Communism that is known in Russia and favors a certain kind of democracy.

In spite of all its virtues, the Chinese use of the soil has many and obvious defects, some of which could be remedied by the application of methods and knowledge now available in the Occident. The usual means of borrowing capital is costly in the extreme. Interest rates are high—twenty and thirty and even eighty and one hundred per cent. a year. As a result of the small size of the farms, the average peasant has little capital against lean years or unusual expenses, such as a wedding or a funeral—both often costly. This and the demands of normal farming operations mean that many of the peasants are in debt and burdened by a ruinous weight of interest. Great areas now periodically flooded could be completely reclaimed by modern methods. For instance, some years ago Western engineers worked out a project for draining hundreds of square miles of fertile land in the valley of the Huai River. The necessary capital could have been obtained from abroad if civil strife had not so seriously threatened the investment. In some regions in North China the driving of deeper wells would provide needed water for semi-arid lands. Less shallow plowing would frequently result in increased yields. As we shall see a little later, roads have been atrocious and land transportation costly—a defect which the automobile and the railway could largely remove and in some places are beginning to remedy. In spite of the immense amount of labor expended, the grain harvest per acre is not much if any greater than that in the less intensively cultivated farms of the United States. For example, the average yield of wheat per acre is about that in the United States, and of rice only about fifty per cent. more. Much of this can be accounted for by differences in climate and other physical surroundings. However, better seed selection and scientific methods of fighting plant and animal diseases would work improvement. Poor methods of production and marketing have been largely responsible for the loss of foreign markets for silk and especially for tea. Better agricultural implements within the reach of the Chinese farmer's purse are also possible. More propagation of better varieties would improve the quality and quantity of fruit. There are many days of seasonal unemployment, for both man and beast, and while the profitable utilization of idle time presents a serious difficulty, progress could probably be achieved toward meeting it by a better organization of the work of the farmer and by domestic industries.

Underlying the pressure of population upon subsistence are certain social and religious customs and institutions which encourage early marriage and a high birth rate. These are to be treated more at length in a later chapter, but no picture of the supply of the physical necessities of life in China is complete without the notice that they exist. Their alteration presents one of the most perplexing and fundamental of China's economic problems. Unless some reduction in the birth rate can be effected, all attempts to relieve poverty become mere palliatives.

CHANGES IN AGRICULTURE WROUGHT BY CONTACT WITH THE WEST

The Occidentalizing of China in the past three or four decades has affected the farmers less than some other sections of the population. The West has made itself felt chiefly in the cities. Except for a few details, the life of the great majority of the cultivators of the soil goes on much as it did a century ago. Even in rural areas, however, changes are beginning to appear. The railway has brought modifications in the transportation system in the regions it traverses—although fully two-thirds of China proper is as yet unaffected by it. To regions bordering the coast and the Yangtze and its tributaries the steamboat has made some difference. Of late years the automobile is having more widespread effect than either the railway or the steamboat. Thousands of miles of highways are being constructed for it. Many of these have been built by foreign famine relief agencies, and others for military purposes, but most of them by Chinese for civilian use. Judged by the standards of the United States or Western Europe, they leave much to be desired. Usually they are without any other surface than that of the native earth, and carts, wheelbarrows, and bad weather often work havoc with them. On many roads, however, efforts are made to reserve either the whole or one track for the exclusive use of automobiles, and a few have received a rock dressing. Moreover, bad though many of the new highways are, they are traversed by motor busses, and each year sees hundreds of miles more of such lines in operation. It is said that by 1931 over six thousand busses were in operation and that twenty thousand miles of road were available for them. Since then the mileage has been largely increased. Busses are usually crowded. Hamlets and villages formerly a day or more apart by the old methods of travel are now removed from each other by only a few hours. Even though road surfaces do not yet permit of much transportation of freight by automobile, the increased mobility of the population cannot but have far-reaching consequences in rural life.

A few products from the West have been widely spread, notably kerosene, the kerosene lamp, cotton goods, matches, and the cigarette. Imports of grain from abroad have affected domestic markets in some regions accessible by steamship or railway. For instance, occasionally American wheat can be purchased at a lower price than the home grown product.

As serious a dislocation of agriculture as any has been the devotion of a great deal of land to the opium poppy. As we have seen, in the 1920's numbers of military leaders compelled farmers to raise the poppy, for opium provided a convenient source of revenue. In this way thousands of acres were withdrawn from the production of foodstuffs and raw materials for clothing, and dire want was still further accentuated. Opium not only directly diminishes the vitality of those who use it but indirectly further impoverishes the nation. Chiang Kai-shek fought it but under the Japanese it flourished.

In some districts the demands of foreign trade have worked

changes. There has been a good deal of exporting of wood and vegetable oil, of timber from Fukien and Manchuria, of meat and poultry from the Yangtze Valley, Tsingtao, and Tientsin, of the soy bean and its products from Manchuria, and of eggs from the Yangtze Valley. Vegetable tallow, pig's bristles, hides, furs, bones, vegetable fibre (hemp, ramie, and jute), silk, nuts, straw braid, and diminished amounts of tea have been among the exports. The foreign demand for them has had some effect upon agriculture, in places marked.

We have repeatedly seen that in the course of the centuries many useful plants have been introduced. The last few years are no exception. Among those imported have been a cotton with a longer staple than of that of the native fibre grown in the cotton producing areas near the mouth of the Yangtze.

Foreign famine relief agencies and Christian missionaries have made beginnings at various improvements in agricultural methods. Some Roman Catholic communities are in advance of their non-Christian neighbors in irrigation and utilization of the soil. Several Protestant colleges, universities, and missions have agricultural experts on their staffs. One especially, Nanking University, has had an important school of agriculture and forestry. The (Protestant) National Christian Council has had secretaries devoting themselves to rural welfare. New techniques for fighting the diseases of plants and animals and better methods of seed selection have been introduced or devised and attempts have been made to disseminate them. In Kiaochow the Germans had an agricultural school. Central and provincial governments have paid increasing attention to agricultural education by schools and extension courses and to establishing and developing experiment stations. Rural coöperatives have been organized to provide better credit facilities. For instance, within the two decades or so in the North the China International Famine Relief Commission helped to bring about the formation of approximately a thousand credit coöperatives. Foreign famine relief funds have also built irrigation works and sunk wells in the semi-arid North and Northwest.

Some efforts have been made to bring in Western methods of forestry, especially for reclaiming waste areas. During their occupation of Kiaochow the Germans by planting bare hills to trees demonstrated what could be done in a few years by proper methods. Other agencies have made beginnings—although taking the country as a whole the problem is as unsolved as it was a half-century ago.

Recently many thoughtful Chinese have come to a profound conviction that the farmer must be helped to a richer life and a higher standard of living if the nation is really to make progress. Toward this end a good many experiments have been made and are being made by individuals and groups. The movement has probably been hastened by the attention which the Communists have paid to the farmer. In some sections the Reds have broken up the large estates and have brought about a considerable redistribution of the land.

What results these efforts at improvement will have ought not yet to be confidently predicted. Agriculture and the status of the farmer will inevitably, however, remain a determining factor not only in the economic life of the country but in social, political, and religious development.

INDUSTRY

One of the interesting features of agriculture in China is the considerable percentage of his produce which the farmer exchanges for cash. This means that with all their simplicity and monotony of life and low standards of living farms are not entirely self-sufficient. It also means considerable specialization in industry, no small amount of domestic commerce, and marked development of towns and cities.

Towns seem to have begun in very early historic times. As far back as the Chou dynasty an urban life was appearing. In a certain sense primitive Taoism was a protest against the resulting complexity of civilization. Certainly under the Ch'ing there were great cities and hundreds of smaller towns and villages. It is not at all improbable that until the modern methods of transportation and agriculture of the nineteenth and twentieth centuries had given rise to the huge growth in the metropolitan populations of the world, the chief cities of China were as large as those anywhere on the planet. This indicates a diversified economic life.

As in practically all the rest of the world before the nineteenth century, industry in China on the eve of the changes wrought by the Occident was in the handicraft stage. Some machinery there was, but it was generally of the simplest and relatively little application was made of other power than that of men's muscles. In industry as in agriculture one of the outstanding features was the lavish expenditure of human labor.

As in much of the rest of the world, too, a tendency existed to specialization by localities. Thus the makers of furniture, the manufacturers of the mock money used in ceremonies for the dead, and the silversmiths have tended to group themselves along particular streets of a city. In Peiping several hundreds of families engaged in making artificial flowers have lived and worked not far from the market where these are sold. Certain cities, too, have been noted for particular products. Thus the manufacture of one type of rug was and is centered mostly in Peiping and Tientsin, the carving of ivory in Canton, the production of a particularly fine type of lacquer ware in Foochow, and the manufacture of porcelain at Ching-tê Chên. In Shansi each village engaged in smelting iron concentrated on one type of article. Either the proximity of the essential raw materials or the creation of a reputation and the acquisition of experience in a famous shop or shops, or possibly a combination of factors, tended to give a particular city or district a natural monopoly of a certain product. In Ching-tê Chên this monopoly was furthered by the state.

To attempt any enumeration of the products of industry in China would prolong this chapter unduly and have but little more interest than would a catalogue of ships. It need only be said that the very length of the list would indicate not only the complexity and variety of Chinese life but the high standard of living of many of the Chinese. Poor the great majority of the population undoubtedly have been and are, with little or no means of acquiring more than the necessities for the barest kind of existence. A small house, most of the materials for which come from the farmer's own acres, a few tools, a little furniture, cotton clothing, sandals or shoes and not always these, a simple and not too varied diet, tea as a drink and sometimes that only as a luxury, have been and are as much as the masses can expect. However, the production and exchange of even these would have given rise to a certain amount of specialized industry and commerce. A minority, moreover, and a fairly numerous one, has utilized the economic, social, and political organization of the land to rise above this level. There have been and are many in comfortable circumstances and still others who are wealthy. These have provided a market for more than the necessities and their demands have increased and diversified manufactures. Silk has been extensively spun and woven and in many kinds of fabrics. Furniture has often been of rare woods elaborately carved and inlaid. The homes of the powerful and wealthy are large and into them have usually gone a great deal of labor, both skilled and unskilled. In a land which has held literature in such esteem and which so early invented both paper and printing, the manufacture of paper and the occupation of the printer have engrossed the time of some of the urban population. Barbers, shoemakers, dye makers, fur dealers, tailors, hat makers, paperhangers, manufacturers of effigies burned for the sake of the dead, and makers of incense and of toilet articles are all to be found. In a land which has numbered, in the aggregate, so many of the well-to-do, the manufacturers of luxuries have found support—goldsmiths, silversmiths, carvers of semi-precious stones, workers in ivory, producers of the more costly types of pottery, weavers of rugs, and the like. Manufacturers of drugs have done a thriving business. The list might be continued at great length. To the visitor from the West many Chinese cities still present a fascinating picture of what, *mutatis mutandis,* the industries of Western Europe must have been like before the advent of power-driven and labor-saving machinery.

As in medieval Europe, moreover, industry has been organized by guilds. China did not invent the stock company with its provision for combining the savings of many individuals into one huge and powerful unit of production. Until the coming of the West, capitalism as we know it in the modern Occident had not appeared. Industrial units have been small, owned and operated by individuals or families or in the form of partnerships. These have needed protection against ruinous competition and the aggression or oppression of officials or powerful groups. Accordingly they have formed guilds.

How far back in Chinese history guilds originated we do not know. Certainly for centuries they have been a prominent feature of economic and social life. The Chinese display great capacity for extra-political organization. The individual who attempts to stand alone has found and finds himself at a great disadvantage. Families, secret societies, villages, and guilds of many kinds have long been characteristic. The guilds have been largely confined to walled towns and cities—the larger population centers. As we shall see more in detail later, guilds have been of many kinds and have been formed not only by handicraftsmen but by merchants, by various occupations and interests, such as the barbers, the beggars, the blind, the masons, the carpenters, the cooks, the story-tellers, the actors, and the waiters. Those that for the moment concern us may be called craft guilds, although that classification would probably not be made by the Chinese.

The craft guilds have usually not been so elaborate or so wealthy as the merchants' guilds. As a rule they have been purely local organizations and not provincial or national—although there may be affiliations which exercise wider than local influence. Membership has been practically compulsory to all those of a particular craft. If an individual refuses to join, ways can be found to induce him to change his mind. He may even be visited with personal violence, and government officials know better than to interfere. It has been exceptional, however, for an eligible man to decline to apply. The advantages are so obvious that usually no persuasion is required. The guild, indeed, has had as one of its functions the maintenance within its vicinity of a monopoly for its members. It seeks to restrain competition within its ranks. To that end it fixes both the minimum prices of the products and the wages of employees. For the same reason it regulates the hours of labor and the rest periods. A member who refuses to conform or who violates the rules is subject to punishment, ranging all the way from fines to death. The guilds have performed many services for their members. They have helped them collect debts and have afforded protection against thieves. They also often assume some of the functions of a benevolent society. Some of them have their own cemeteries, and many provide coffins and funeral expenses for the burial of their poor. Numbers arrange for medical care for ill members. Each has a patron divinity or divinities to whom it pays communal worship. For example, in at least one place the tailors have had the mythical Emperor

Huang Ti as their god. The guilds are also a means of social intercourse. They hold periodical meetings, and the guild hall, when such exists, forms a kind of club house.

The guild has included both employers and employees, although, even before the modern labor union appeared, at times the latter temporarily formed a separate organization to enforce demands about wages. Boys come up into guild membership through an apprenticeship and after completing the latter are admitted, sometimes with quite a little ceremony, and at others merely upon payment of an initiation fee. Often the guild has regulated the number of apprentices which a member may have—and thus has kept down future competition. A trained worker on moving to another city may, if local feeling is not too strong, become affiliated with the corresponding guild in his new home upon the presentation of a card from the guild from which he comes.

The income of the guilds has been derived from initiation fees, periodical dues, fines, special assessments, and taxes on sales. The budgets of some guilds have needed to be fairly large, for the wealthier organizations own and maintain guild halls and have secretarial staffs. The head secretaries are often men of some importance, and in the old days a few in the larger centers possessed a degree from the civil service examinations—an advantage in dealing with officials. Other guilds are much more modest and meet in the shop of one of the members, rent a room, perhaps in some temple, or obtain the temporary use of a temple for worship and the annual meeting. The secretarial staff, too, may be very small or even be dispensed with.

The forms of organization have differed widely. There have usually been at least a president and a board of directors who generally are elected, although in at least one instance they are chosen by lot. Regular meetings are held, more frequently for the officers, but at least annually for all the members. A guild may employ inspectors to see that its rules limiting competition are obeyed: members have found it advisable to keep watch of each other. A guild court may be held to deal with infractions.

In a land in which the struggle for existence is of necessity as fierce as in China, and the individual is so greatly in need of protection against the government and various economic and social groups, the guilds have played a useful function. They have regulated competition and have been an agency for concerted action. It has been quite customary for a guild to institute a strike or a boycott to obtain its wishes or to enforce its objection to some governmental order. Those who carry away the night soil, for example, may cease work in protest against a police ruling, until the inconvenienced community forces an accommodation to their demand. Butchers have united against taxes, and sometimes all the merchants of a community have banded against badly controlled troops. The nation-wide boycotts by which more than once in the last few years the Chinese have expressed their indignation against the Japanese and the British have taken their rise in an old tradition of group resistance to obnoxious persons and measures. To the Chinese they are a perfectly natural way for public opinion to express itself.

Yet the guild system has also had its disadvantages. By restraining free competition it has been a brake on improvement both in machinery and in efficiency and so has prevented progress. It may in part account for the slowness of the changes in Chinese industrial life.

CHANGES IN INDUSTRY PRODUCED BY CONTACT WITH THE OCCIDENT

Whether the presence of the guild in China can be held in any degree responsible for the fact that the Industrial Revolution did not originate there but entered from the Occident must be a matter of conjecture. Whatever the reason, it was from the West, as we have seen in earlier chapters, that the innovations came. These have affected industry much more than they have agriculture. What some of them are have already been briefly recounted. Steam-driven machinery and the factory have been introduced. As has been noted above, the manufacture of cotton has been most affected. By 1930 the amount of capital invested in cotton mills was about $300,000,000 (Chinese currency) and the number of hands employed about a quarter of a million. Cotton mills have been particularly numerous in East Central China, especially in Shanghai, where in 1928 about half the cotton spinning and weaving of China (by modern machinery) was located. In 1930 the province of Kiangsu, including Shanghai, had approximately two-thirds of the cotton spindles of China. Hupeh ranked next. In the North, notably in Shantung and Hopei (Chihli), cotton mills are to be found. Cheap labor has even developed the industry beyond the supply of local cotton, and the raw fibre has been imported, especially the long staple in which China is deficient.

While cotton mills outstrip all other forms of the industrialization of China by the new machine methods of the West, steam silk filatures have also been introduced, and for them, too, Shanghai has been the chief center. Some of the other industries in which modern Western appliances have entered are the milling of flour, the manufacture of matches, the smelting of iron, and the manufacture of steel. Among modern factories have been listed some for the preparation of albumen from eggs, canneries, bakeries for biscuits, cement works, chemical and dye works, breweries, distilleries, plants for bottling aërated waters, shipyards, electric light and power works (in rapidly increasing number), glass works, ice plants, leather factories, plants for expressing oil, rubber works manufacturing shoes, soles, overshoes, and hot water bags, paper mills, rice-hulling and cleaning mills, saw mills, soap and candle works, sugar refineries, and woollen and knitting mills. Few of the larger cities have been completely untouched by the new processes. The Japanese invasion in the 1930's and 1940's led, after 1937, to the transfer of factories to the West and to the development of new industries in that region. Industrial coöperatives, too, developed under war conditions. In Communist-controlled areas modern industries began to emerge but in small units and under very difficult conditions.

The traditional forms of industrial organization have of necessity suffered from the entrance of the factory and from competition with products from the West. The guilds have by no means disappeared. In many places, however, they have been greatly weakened, and some have gone out of existence. The passing of the guild has been hastened by the advent of the labor union. In March, 1927, one hundred and eighty such unions were reported in the city of Canton, of which at least seventy grew out of guilds. Labor unions began to appear several years before the spectacular advance of the Kuomintang in 1926 and 1927. Indeed, over twelve hundred strikes were recorded between 1918 and 1926, of which about two-thirds were successful. Of the factories and companies in Shanghai affected by strikes in 1927, more than ninety-five per cent. were Chinese and less than five per cent. foreign in ownership. A national labor party was formed in Shanghai in 1913. An all-China labor congress was held in Canton in May, 1922, and in the preceding months Hongkong had been paralyzed by strikes of seamen and sympathetic workers. It will be recalled that, as the Kuomintang moved northward, the radical wing organized unions of laborers and that these made demands, often preposterous, upon their employers. It is significant of the changes in progress in China, that some of the new unions were composed exclusively of women, and that women also joined some of the trade unions of which the members were chiefly men. With the reaction of the moderates and conservatives within the Kuomintang against the radicals, and the vigorous action taken against Communists, many labor unions disappeared and others became less vocal. By no means all of them died, however. The strongholds of the labor union have been in Canton, where the radical movement first centered, and Shanghai, which has led the nation in the new types of industries. So schooled in the tradition of combination have Chinese workers been by the guild that the organization of Chinese workers and operators into new types of groupings demanded by the changing situation probably has been greatly hastened. So far, however, the labor union has been employed chiefly for purposes of compulsion and for pressure in politics.

It must be said that the labor unions have often had ground for legitimate protest. Judged by standards now prevailing in the West, the working day is inordinately long, the hygienic and safety conditions in factories often shockingly bad, and wages low. Usually no effective rules exist against child labor. There are a few humane employers, the more advanced of whom have devices for profit-sharing with employees and provide ample light and ventilation in their factories. In 1929 the National Government promulgated a factory law with some enlightened provisions. The Ministry of Industry, Commerce, and Labor has had among its functions the regulation of labor. Some of the Protestant Christian groups have the welfare of the worker at heart and even the conservative wing of the Kuomintang has not dared to go counter to the emphatic endorsement of the cause of labor in Sun Yat-sen's *San Min Chu I.* Several local governments and war lords have issued regulations for the protection of labor. Although thus far none of these efforts has obtained more than comparatively slight results, it is probable that conditions in modern factories, in both hours and sanitation, have averaged somewhat better than those under the handicraft system. Appalling abuses, for example, were disclosed a few years ago in the rug industry in Peking, where the old order persisted. When all that can be brought forward for conditions in the modern factories in China has been said, however, the fact remains that on the average the workers have cause for complaint.

How rapidly the introduction of Western machinery will proceed must be a matter of conjecture. It is not without serious obstacles. Domestic capital is comparatively scarce and foreign capital is usually reluctant to enter because of the risk entailed by unsettled political conditions and the uncertainty of the future legal status of the foreigner. Laws and the administration of justice are highly undependable. The chronic civil war has discouraged the development of factories by either foreigners or Chinese. The Chinese do not yet produce much of the new machinery. Although, judged by Western standards, wages are ridiculously low, inefficiency is also marked. Even were a higher standard of living achieved by the laborer, it would probably be several generations before sufficient experience in operating the new type of machine could be attained to make the Chinese factory hands equal in skill and output to those of the West. It is, moreover, quite apparent that as yet comparatively few Chinese are operating successfully the stock company, through which the industrialization of the West has been achieved. Family loyalty is traditionally so strong that many a Chinese sees no turpitude in making sinecure positions for kinsmen in the company of which he is president or director—or in other ways doing what in the West would be regarded as defrauding the stockholders. Therefore, in spite of notable and probably increasing exceptions, in Chinese hands, unless it is in reality a family affair, the stock company is for some time to come likely to prove a failure. As yet, moreover, the deficiencies in the transportation system and the currency of the country—to be elaborated a few pages farther on—make impossible any such widespread industrialization as in the United States and Western Europe. Then, too, raw materials are often of uneven or poor quality—notably silk and cotton, which are so extensively utilized by the new factories. These handicaps are all removable, and it is conceivable that a few decades hence they will be much less in evidence than to-day. It is probable, however, that the more fundamental lack in natural resources can never be fully remedied. We have earlier seen that the coal and iron reserves of China do not begin to equal those of the United States or of Western Europe. They are, to be sure, much larger than those of any other region on the Pacific rim, and the potential hydroelectric power is enormous. Still it is doubtful whether any such thorough-going industrialization can be achieved by appliances now known as has taken place in Great Britain or in the northeastern portions of the United States.

Perhaps it is just as well that the industrialization of China by the new methods from the West is proceeding no more rapidly. Were it to come on apace it might bring with it problems much more quickly than China could solve them. The urbanization of life with the resulting disintegration of the family and the other old forms of social control, the exploitation of labor, and the violent clashes of employers and employees are only some of the conditions which the country would face. They might prove even more disastrous than the recent political upheavals. The gradual arrival of the factory system may give the country time to work out the necessary safeguards.

MINING

The Chinese have long been making use of the mineral resources of their land. From very early days they have known iron, copper, bronze, zinc, gold, silver, and lead. In mining coal they antedated Western Europe. Coal was probably utilized at least as early as the fifth century A.D. and as far back as the T'ang was employed in smelting iron. Shansi was the center of iron manufacture for the North, for here are large deposits of coal as well as some iron ore. In Szechwan salt was produced from brine which was pumped from wells, some of them two or three thousand feet deep, notable engineering feats bored by a primitive but effective type of the percussion process now so widely used in the

West. The brine was evaporated either by natural gas obtained from borings in the same region, or by coal or straw. Native supplies of the precious metals are not particularly plentiful in China proper, but gold ornaments have been popular, and silver and copper have formed the basis of the Empire's currency. Copper seems to have come chiefly from Szechwan and Yünnan, and that in relatively recent times. The Chinese probably took more advantage of the available mineral resources than did any other people before the last three or four hundred years.

Yet mining in the old China faced handicaps. At times officials taxed it heavily. *Fêng shui,* that strange system of pseudo-scientific superstition which has had so marked a hold on the Chinese mind, often discouraged it and even forbade it. It is only in comparison with the small use made of other than the precious metals by the rest of the world before the modern era that the Chinese appear to have learned to take advantage of their mineral deposits.

With the penetration of China by the Westerner have come further drafts on China's reserves. Raw materials in the form of minerals are among the valued prizes sought by the Occidental in his exploitation of the world. In a number of provinces Western methods of smelting iron have been introduced, by Chinese as well as by foreigners. For many years the largest output was by the Hanyehp'ing Company, long a Chinese enterprise, in Hupeh. Lately some has been coming from Anhui, the chief producer there being a Chinese company assisted by Japanese capital. All of this, however, when compared with the great plants in the West, is very slight. Quite a little iron is derived from South Manchuria, through Japanese concerns. The extraction of coal has more than doubled in the past thirty years. There are large mines operated by modern machinery in several provinces, notably in Fengtien where, at Fushun, the Japanese have what is called the largest open pit coal mine of the world, and in Hopei, by the Kailan Mining Administration. Most of the world's supply of antimony now issues from China, chiefly from Hunan, and more than half the tungsten. In her total output of minerals, however, except in these two rare metals, China ranks low, especially in proportion to her population. Moreover, much of her coal and iron has been consumed not in China but in Japan, to whose industry they have been of great importance. Petroleum, which has recently become so prominent in the world's life, is produced almost not at all. It is very questionable, indeed, as we have said, whether considerable deposits of it will be found.

COMMERCE

We have repeatedly seen that from the economic standpoint China has been and even still is almost entirely self-sufficient. To this has contributed her geographic isolation and her own vast area with its variety of products. Foreign trade there was, and from early times, but until very recently it was largely in luxuries. Even with the overpassing of natural barriers and the marked increase in foreign commerce in the past few decades, in proportion to her population China's foreign commerce, as we have noted, is smaller than that of any other major group of civilized mankind.

This small participation in international trade does not mean the absence of internal commerce. One of the features of Chinese civilization, indeed, has been the merchant. The scholar might affect to despise him and rate him low on the social scale, but he flourished nevertheless. To this testify the many towns and large cities, for they would have been impossible but for his presence. One of the outstanding characteristics of the Chinese, indeed, is their keenness as traders. Not only at home, but, it will be recalled, in foreign countries, especially in the lands immediately to the South, Chinese have proved and continue to prove their skill in business.

Commerce, like industry, has been by small units organized in guilds. Firms are family or partnership affairs, and the need of organization for protection against each other and outsiders has forced those of the same trade together into guilds which in their essential features resemble those formed by craftsmen. They have their officers, their membership, their regular meetings, and their rules. Through them are negotiated many of the transactions with merchants of other cities. They fix the minimum prices which their members can charge and exact penalties for infringement of these or of other regulations. They serve as benevolent societies to assist impecunious members. They tend to be wealthier than the craft guilds and many of them own sumptuous halls which are not only places of business but centers of social life. Merchant guilds have often been very powerful and have even coerced officials or the general community.

In addition to the guilds organized by particular crafts, professions, or types of business there have been what are usually called in English provincial guilds. Uniting the natives of a province or city who reside in another city, they are evidence of the strong local loyalties found in China, as elsewhere, and of community discrimination in favor of natives and against outsiders. The provincial guilds provide social and business *rendezvous,* give aid to indigent fellow-provincials, and at times assist in promoting the business interests of their members.

So strong has been the habit of working through guilds that in some cities an organization like a guild and including most of the merchants of the locality has become the governing body of the entire community. Notable instances have been seen in Swatow and Newchwang.

Moreover, secret societies, so prominent a factor in Chinese life, have entered into commerce. Organizations of that character of more than local extent sometimes bring together members of related businesses and occupations in an entire region—boatmen on the Yangtze, for example, and some of the shippers.

These societies and the guilds have often been a force in politics and even in international affairs. For instance, the guilds were largely responsible for the boycott on American trade in 1907 which was induced by the ill treatment of Chinese immigrants to the United States by American officials.

Thousands of villages are too small for guilds, or, indeed, to keep alive even one merchant. In many villages and towns a market is held every day and special fairs annually or a few times a year. To them come buyers and sellers—most of them from the immediate neighborhood, but sometimes from greater distances. Often a fair has been held under the auspices of a temple, as a means of income. In the larger villages, as well as in the towns and cities, there are, of course, many shops, each usually specializing in a particular commodity or group of commodities. Peddlers have been and are very numerous. Food shops, too, are multitudinous, perhaps partly because, living so close to the margin of subsistence as do so many of the Chinese, very little surplus is accumulated in the homes.

Much commerce has been by means of a "middleman." The

"middleman," indeed, was and is of even more importance in China than in the West. The purchase and sale of land and the negotiation of betrothals are regularly transacted and the transfer of goods of many descriptions is often accomplished through him. This has not meant, however, the development of wholesale houses or of the commission merchant on any such scale as in the modern West, nor is any close similarity implied to the jobbers, small dealers, and distributors of the Occident.

Weights and measures have been almost as confused and confusing as in medieval Europe. Theoretically the decimal system has prevailed—a great aid in reckoning. In practice, however, it has often been departed from. Thus while in theory one hundred catties (the foreign name for the Chinese *chin*) made one picul (the foreign name for the Chinese *tan*) in practice the number of catties to a picul has varied from commodity to commodity and from city to city. Moreover, the catty also has fluctuated in weight from locality to locality and according to the commodity and the trade. So, too, measures of length have differed with the occupation and the trade. A unit with the same name might be one length for the carpenter, another for the mason, and still another for the tailor. Similarly in areas: the *mou*, which is usually roughly reckoned as a sixth of an English acre, in some regions is only about one-twelfth and in other nearly a third of an acre. This, not unnaturally, has been something of a hindrance to business on anything more than a local scale.

Uncertainty in commerce has been heightened by the absence of fixed prices. As in so much of the rest of the world, each transaction is a trial of wits between purchaser and seller, the one offering much less than he expects to pay, the latter asking much more than he hopes to get, and the ultimate transaction involving a compromise. The "one price stores" seen of late years in Chinese cities appear to be a Western innovation—although long before the coming of the Westerner some of the larger shops probably had fixed prices (often subject to adjustment by bargaining).

As an aid in computation the Chinese have employed the abacus. The origin and history of this device in China seem uncertain, but apparently it has been known there for centuries.

In some manner the impression has gotten abroad among Westerners that in business the Chinese merchant of the old school has been a model of honesty. This undoubtedly has been true of some individuals, and particularly of importers who have found a reputation for probity advantageous in dealing with foreigners. A manager of the largest foreign bank in China is said to have declared that he had never known a Chinese defaulter. Chinese, however, have labored under no delusion as to one another's complete trustworthiness, but have devised elaborate safeguards to protect themselves against the deceitful. As we have seen, guilds have means of detecting and punishing those who take unfair advantage of their fellow-members by disobeying rules designed to give an equal chance to all. The family may be held responsible for the misdeeds of one of its number. The Shansi bankers, to be described in a moment, are said to have held as hostages the families of employees, especially those entrusted with business in other provinces, and not to have released them until the employee, having discharged his errand, made a satisfactory accounting. Then, too, the plan has been adopted of guarantors for the fulfilment of obligations, or for the good behavior of an individual. Moreover, what the Westerner denominates "squeeze" has been regarded as normal—a percentage made on purchases by a servant for his master, or exacted by officials. While in theory a tacitly recognized form of commission and, since it is allowed by all parties, being not, strictly speaking, dishonest, in actual operation it has often been the means of peculations, from very small to very large sums. A great deal of adulteration of goods has been practiced, weights and measures juggled, and tricks played on the customer with bad money. All this does not mean that the Chinese have been so very much less upright than other peoples. It does, however, indicate that the current assertion that they were and are extraordinarily trustworthy must be qualified.

MONEY AND BANKING

From the standpoint of the Occident of the present—and even of earlier days—the currency system of the older China was crude and sometimes chaotic. In very early times various mediums of exchange were in use, including cowries—those shells widely employed as money not only in China but in many other parts of the world. Cowries, indeed, were in circulation in China as late as the fourteenth century. Coinage began as far back as the Chou dynasty and seems to have been continuous from that time to the present. It will be recalled that Han Wu Ti made it an imperial prerogative, forbidding the existing method of the issue of money by various local dignitaries. Some of the early coins were in the form of cowries, and others had the shape of swords, knives, or spades. Even until a comparatively late date, salt and pieces of silk served as money in at least one province, and their use for this purpose was widely spread and over long periods. For more than two thousand years, however, the prevailing coin was of copper or of copper alloy and had the outline of the "cash" familiar into our own day—round, with a square hole through the center. A generation or less ago among the cash in daily circulation could be found those issued in the T'ang and the Sung.

The cash were reckoned by strings, or *tiao*, of a thousand each. The number was largely theoretical, for the string was practically always several short of that number. Money-changers charged twenty or thirty cash for their labor and for the cost of the string and by common consent deducted them from the *tiao*. In some districts the *tiao* had only five hundred cash. Cash, too, varied in size and value. The debasing of coinage has been by no means unknown in Chinese history.

Individually the copper cash were of small value. At the rates of exchange common during the fore part of the twentieth century an American dollar would buy from two thousand to three thousand of them—and even more. Manifestly they were a convenience only in a land where, compared with the modern Occident, the price level was very low, and where the struggle for existence was so severe that a coin the value of a cash was worth haggling over.

Until the present century, with occasional exceptions the only metal minted in China was copper. Iron was sometimes employed. Silver and gold were practically never coined. This may have been due in part to the comparative scarcity of these metals. The paucity of natural deposits of gold and silver ore within China proper must greatly have limited the supply.

As we have seen, the Chinese have had paper money in more than one dynasty, beginning at least as early as the T'ang, and have had sorrowful experience with inflation by the unwise overissue of it.

Obviously, even in a country with a low price level, units of exchange larger than a cash were needed. The demand was not met by coins. Under some dynasties paper money made partial provision for it. Gold was seldom used as a medium of exchange but only for jewelry and in the arts, or in ingots or gold leaf for hoarding. The customary device was silver ingots. These were not minted by the government, but were issued by private initiative. The unit was the *tael* (the foreign name for the Chinese *liang*). Theoretically a *tael* was worth a thousand cash, but in practice the actual weight and fineness varied from locality to locality and from agency to agency. There were at least seventy-seven distinct kinds of *taels*—and probably more than twice that number. Thus the Shanghai *tael* differed from the Hankow *tael* and that of the imperial Board of Revenue from that of the Maritime Customs. By Western standards, the *tael* was usually somewhere between five hundred and six hundred grains, Troy measure, of pure silver. (It will be recalled that the American dollar is 412.5 grains in weight, and of .900 fineness.) The Chinese lump silver of commerce was called sycee (*hsi ssŭ*) and was made up into ingots of varying fineness and shape, called by foreigners "shoes"—a term whose derivation is uncertain. The weight of a shoe also was not fixed, but was usually slightly above or below fifty *taels*. The Chinese divided the *tael* according to a decimal system. The foreigner called the tenth of a *tael* a *mace* and the hundredth part of a *tael* a *candareen*. In practice, in making payments which required silver of a fractional part of a shoe, a portion of the ingot was cut off. Weighing pieces of silver and testing them for fineness formed a regular part of business transactions and necessitated the assistance of experts.

Naturally all this variation in the currency was a handicap to business, not only within the Empire as a whole but within individual cities and communities.

Given this development of commerce and this complexity of the currency, banking almost inevitably came into existence. Apparently it began at least as early as the T'ang. Its chief functions were domestic exchange. Banks dealt in drafts which made possible the buying and selling of goods between towns and cities of the Empire with the minimum shipment of silver. They assisted in the transfer of government funds. They facilitated change. They issued bills which circulated locally as money.

They received deposits from customers, allowed overdrafts, and made loans—although to a smaller extent than do banks in the modern Occident.

On the eve of the modifications wrought by the impact of the West at least four different kinds of institutions conducted a business which may be classed as banking. Many merchants who regularly bought and sold in more than one city dealt in bills of exchange payable in the cities in which they did business. Incidentally they might, as a matter of accommodation, accept deposits from their regular customers, make advances to them, and allow overdrafts. Then there were "cash shops," whose primary function it was to make change from cash into *taels* or vice versa, or from one kind of *tael* to another. These too might make small loans or allow overdrafts to shopkeepers who were their regular customers. There were pawnshops, the better of them licensed by the government and often powerful. A large proportion of them were eminently respectable and not only loaned money on security of clothing, jewelry, and similar chattels, but acted as places for the storage of valuables. Then there were institutions more nearly corresponding to banks of Western types whose function it was to receive deposits, make loans, and buy and sell drafts. They were usually small, rarely having as large a capital as 100,000 *taels*. They were never stock companies, but were organized by families, by individuals, or as partnerships. Every city of importance had its bankers' guild, but this did not serve as a clearing house.

The most influential of the bankers were usually from the province of Shansi. The Shansi bankers, indeed, constituted one of the most prominent features of the business and financial structure of the Empire. Just how far back in Chinese history they go it is difficult to say. The best Chinese authorities seem to agree that they arose in the seventeenth century. The necessary capital may have been originally derived from the coal and iron of the province. Shansi is especially rich in coal, and for centuries some of it was shipped to adjacent valleys and plains. In Shansi coal was used to smelt iron, and the province was long the source of much of the North's supply of that metal. The system, too, may have arisen out of other forms of trading. Whatever the origin of the business, in the nineteenth century, just before the revolutionary changes induced by the impact of the West, Shansi bankers were a recognized part of the economic life of the Empire and were found in the principal towns and cities. They did not constitute a corporation, for no such device existed, but they coöperated as a close association of the prominent banking families of Shansi, and the agents and employees seem usually to have been from that province. It was through them that the government transmitted much of its funds, they assisted the state in other ways, and in turn were accorded official patronage.

In spite of this banking system, credit played a less prominent part in the commercial life of China than of the West. Loans there were, and merchants were often deeply in debt. The New Year's season was famous, among other reasons, as the time by which debts must be met. To a less extent, the fifth and the eighth month festivals were a time for paying bills. When loans were needed, they were often obtained through a coöperative effort. Several people clubbed together and contributed equal sums to a common fund. The use of the fund went to each member for a given length of time. When all had had their turn, the organization was dissolved. However, a large proportion of the business of the country was conducted on the basis of cash transactions. Farmers sold to townspeople for cash, and merchants usually demanded cash. The actual exchange of commodities, without money as an intermediary, seems to have been much more frequent than in the modern West. There was much less advancing of credit by one merchant to another than in the present-day Occident. Interest rates were high, and mobile capital comparatively scarce. Much of the country's wealth was in land, and the majority of the Empire's richest men seem not to have been merchants but officials. The characteristic form of endowment for a temple, or for any other purpose, was not stocks and bonds, as in the modern Occident, but lands.

TRANSPORTATION

The internal commerce of China has inevitably been dependent on transportation. Here the achievement has been decidedly a mixture of success and failure. The Chinese have displayed great skill in utilizing their waterways. Practically every stream that can be considered at all navigable has its boat traffic. For centuries, too, the Chinese have made extensive use of the canal, not only for irrigation but for transportation. Locks were devised to transfer boats from one level to another. Hundreds of miles of canals were and are in use. They are particularly numerous on the great alluvial plains on the lower reaches of the Yangtze River, especially in East Central China.

The craft range all the way from great ocean-going junks to sampans which, to use an Americanism, can "float on a heavy dew." On the upper reaches of the Yellow River rafts of inflated skins are not uncommon. Wherever a boat can go, the Chinese have employed it. They have even laboriously pulled them up through the rapids and gorges of the Yangtze and so have made that passage the main route in and out of Szechwan. Many boatmen have acquired extraordinary skill in handling craft which, to the inexperienced foreigner, seem clumsy. When oars are employed, as is often, they are manipulated chiefly by sculling rather than by rowing. It will be recalled that boat traffic, especially when the propelling power is wind or current, is a relatively inexpensive, even though leisurely, form of conveying freight.

In land transportation the Chinese have been much less successful. To be sure, bridges are a familiar feature of almost every Chinese landscape and are of many types—such as massive ones of stone in or near some of the chief cities, gracefully arched smaller stone structures, and ingenious suspension bridges which span the torrents of West China. Great Emperors, notable among them Ch'in Shih Huang Ti and Han Wu Ti, made lavish use of wealth and labor to construct highways throughout their domains. Many of these were paved with huge stones. Officials, too, were supposed to be charged with the care of roads. Great virtue was held to attach to building roads and they were often undertaken at private initiative. However, once constructed, they were usually allowed to fall into disrepair, and the tillers of adjacent fields encroached on them. Through much of China's history they seem to have been very poor. Certainly those which the foreign traveller of the nineteenth and twentieth centuries encountered could seldom be called good.

In the North, land transportation has been partly by crude carts, partly by wheelbarrows (sometimes helped by a sail), partly by donkeys, and partly on the shoulders of men. Camel trains are common in Mongolia and Sinkiang and to a certain extent in the northern part of China proper. In the South, wheelbarrows and men have predominated. Donkeys are utilized somewhat, especially in hilly districts. From the Yangtze Valley southward roads have generally been narrow. If paved, it has usually been with blocks of stone laid end to end and affording a track broad enough only for the wheelbarrow. No foreign resident of China where these older methods of transportation prevail will soon forget the lavish use of human labor, or the shrill complaint of the ungreased wheelbarrow. Sedan chairs often have served for the conveyance of passengers, donkey, mule, and horse litters have been known, and travel by horseback has not been uncommon, particularly in the North.

Inns are frequent on the main roads, and even on the by-ways are to be found in many of the villages. Judged by the standards of the present-day West they are decidedly uncomfortable, but probably they compare not unfavorably with those of the rest of the older Orient or of medieval Europe.

Manifestly, where a district can be reached only overland, commerce in commodities which combine large bulk and weight with comparatively small value proves unprofitable. It is obvious, too, in the light of these handicaps, why so often famine has wasted one part of the Empire when a surplus of food was to be found in another. Measured by days of travel, even China proper is a huge area.

Judged by modern standards, the postal service of the old régime was inadequate. A government post took charge of official dispatches. Many private agencies transmitted letters, parcels, drafts, and specie by couriers and post boats. Few if any of the private agencies, however, extended over more than one or two provinces. Time distances, too, were great.

Given the many handicaps to internal commerce—the varieties of weights, measures, and monetary values, the lack of capital and of stock companies, and the poor transportation facilities—the wonder is that so extensive a domestic trade has existed. Obviously anything resembling the standardization of products and the huge corporations of the present-day United States has been quite out of the question. The economic organization of China is, too, manifestly in a much earlier stage of development than that of Western Europe of the nineteenth and twentieth centuries. It is not strange that the impact of the West is producing startling changes.

CHANGES IN COMMERCE, MONEY, BANKING, AND TRANSPORTATION PRODUCED BY CONTACT WITH THE OCCIDENT

Many of the alterations wrought in recent years in commerce, money, banking, and transportation have been noted in earlier pages and chapters (especially in Chapter XII), and need not here be repeated. We have seen the growth in foreign trade, together with the fact that the per capita volume is so small that China is still largely self-supporting. We have mentioned some of the innovations in transportation—the railway, the automobile, bicycles, the airplane, and steam craft, the latter ranging all the way from ocean liners down through the comfortable foreign and Chinese boats which have plied the lower reaches of the Yangtze, the smaller steamers with especially powerful engines that have made the dangerous trip through those gorges of the Yangtze which are the chief channel of communication between the inland empire of Szechwan and the outside world, to the steam launches, often very dingy, which compete with sailing craft even on some of the canals and the smaller rivers. We have noted the rise in prices, in general paralleling that in the rest of the world, and the inflation of the 1940's. We have hinted at innovations in commercial organization and in currency. However, some of these changes require slightly further elaboration.

In the organization of the country for commerce the presence of the foreigner has initiated modifications, some of them marked. Foreign trade, while probably only in its infancy, has already had profound effects. The alien has brought some of his own mercantile institutions and customs or has worked out others adapted to the Chinese situation, and these have made their impression on native practices. For instance, the Chinese have become familiar with the stock company, partly because many of the largest foreign concerns operating in the country are organized after that manner. They have, accordingly, formed stock companies of their own, and while many of these have had only indifferent success or have failed, some have made money for their owners.

Of late years the influence of Western types of organization has rapidly increased. This is partly due to the growth in foreign trade, to the more extensive penetration of China by foreign goods, and to the changes occurring in every phase of Chinese life. It is probably also due to alterations in the old structure for the conduct of foreign commerce. For many years the usual channel between alien and native merchants was a Chinese middleman, called in Western parlance a compradore. This in itself was a concession to local conditions. The compradore was salaried by the foreigner and, in addition, as his chief source of income, was allowed commissions on transactions made through him. He engaged and discharged the members of his employer's Chinese staff and made all the contacts with Chinese merchants. While his reign endured, direct intercourse between Chinese and foreign merchants was at a minimum. The compradore owed his position, indeed, to his knowledge of the Chinese language and of Chinese business methods. It was to his interest to see that no change took place in the latter. In recent years, however, the compradore has been declining in importance. Less and less of a foreign firm's business has been conducted through him. The merchant from abroad has dealt directly with Chinese without his mediation, and the Chinese merchant has tended to establish immediate contacts with foreign countries. The removal of this barrier may be both a result and a cause of the modification of Chinese business institutions.

The characteristic unit of Chinese mercantile enterprise is still an individual, a family, or a partnership. Stock companies, while some of them are very important, are in the minority. Merchants continue to be organized by guilds. The chambers of commerce appearing in almost every important city (they multiplied rapidly after 1900 and as long ago as 1914 there were about thirteen hundred of them) seem to have owed much to their Occidental prototypes, but it is probable that the Chinese experience with guilds facilitated their formation. To some of them only representatives of guilds have been admitted, and they have provided a means—largely lacking under the old régime—whereby guilds can cooperate.

The chambers of commerce have been recognized intermediaries between the merchants and the government, and from time to time they have been subjected to official regulation and control. It was through them, too, that a conquering general usually made his demand on a city for a financial contribution. Some years ago, apparently as a result of the visit of representatives of the Affiliated Chambers of Commerce of the Pacific Coast, a national organization of chambers of commerce was formed and for a time its annual meetings were of considerable importance. However, although their influence on the government has grown, the merchants and bankers of China still have no predominating part in shaping the political destinies of the nation. Sometimes through their chambers of commerce merchants have had an important rôle in local politics, and now and then have been a factor to be reckoned with nationally. Their financial contributions have been essential to the success of many of the generals and warring factions, notably the present Nationalist Government, and more than once have been granted with conditions attached. Probably more often than not, however, the contributions have been forced, a kind of irregular tribute for which the only return has been a temporary reprieve from additional exactions or from torture and death.

Western example is largely responsible for a new banking structure. Huge foreign institutions, the chief of which has been the (British) Hongkong and Shanghai Banking Corporation, have played so important a part in financing loans of the government and in overseas commerce that it would have been strange had the Chinese not organized banks of the Occidental type. The Bank of China and the Bank of Communications have come into being, both of them originally state institutions and coming down from the last few years of the Ch'ing dynasty. Both have branches in many cities, both have had decidedly checkered careers, due in part to their political connections, and they have been rivals, at times bitterly so. In each the government now appoints only a minority of the directors, and both are very prominent in the financial world. In 1928 the Nationalist Government brought into existence a new Central Bank designed to be more fully a state institution than either of the others. A good many banks have been founded by provincial governments. All too often these were the tools of war lords, who through them issued floods of paper money, much of it worthless but for a time kept in circulation by force. In addition, a large number of banks of a modern Western type have been organized by private individuals. Each of several of these has a paid up capital stock running into the millions. Some are fairly substantial, and several have offices in more than one city. They indicate a rapid change in the financial organization of the country and probably are evidence of an increasing amount of fluid capital.

Old style banking houses still exist, but in greatly diminished importance. Many of them succumbed under the financial crisis brought by the passing of the Manchus. The end of the Ch'ing dynasty was a particularly severe blow to the Shansi bankers, who had been used to transmit government funds and whose fortunes were accordingly fairly closely identified with those of the old régime. Some of the Shansi banks, however, managed to weather the storm.

The currency of China, it will be recalled, has become even more intricate and jumbled under the influence of the alien. Although partly superseded by dollars and in 1933 officially demonetized, *taels* continued as a unit of reckoning and in as confusing a number as ever. Cash persisted, but of late years, especially during the World War of 1914–1918, when copper was greatly in demand, many were melted down and other forms of currency took their place. Indeed, cash have almost entirely passed out of circulation. Coined silver first entered in the form of Spanish dollars, brought by Western traders. To them were later added Mexican dollars, and these became so common that prices were frequently quoted in "Mex."—although a native Chinese term, *yüan,* eventually supplanted it. Hongkong, Straits Settlements, and many other kinds of dollars of alien origin were imported. In time the government began to mint silver, also in the form of dollars (or *yüan*), and these coins were issued by various national and provincial administrations. In the 1930's, following the trend in other countries, silver was nationalized and largely passed out of circulation. A subsidiary currency in silver and copper was minted in quantities. Added to this was the paper money of governments and of native and foreign banks. These mediums of exchange fluctuated in value with reference to one another, and often very markedly and rapidly. The number of subsidiary coins which could be bought for a dollar changed with the locality, the sort of dollar, and the kind of minor coin. Often, too, the coin or bill standard in one city was at a discount in the next. However, notes of some of the larger and more stable institutions, such as the Bank of Communications and the Bank of China, were widely circulated and passed at face value or at only a small discount. To add to the bedlam, China has been in effect on the silver basis and foreign exchange has been subject to the fluctuations in the price of that metal in the markets of the world. These rapid shifts in foreign exchange did not affect so greatly the prices of domestic products, but since goods purchased abroad must be paid for in gold the repercussion upon foreign trade was serious. In the 1940's the runaway inflation which accompanied the war with Japan was the outstanding feature of the monetary situation. It prevailed in both "free" and "occupied" China and upset earlier standards.

In the course of the past several decades many suggestions have been offered for reforming the currency, and now and again a more or less half-hearted attempt has actually been made to put one or another of these into effect. So far, however, they have been comparatively fruitless. Some of them may even, indeed, have made the situation worse.

After what has been said previously about the innovations in the transportation system, little more need be added. Obviously marked improvements have been registered. Quite as obviously, however, communication continues to be one of the nation's major problems. Until better means of transportation, particularly of freight, can be more widely extended, local famines can devastate inland provinces, trade in foreign goods and domestic commerce will be retarded, and the general government will find it difficult to enforce its authority against recurring rebellions. The development of transportation is hindered by official exactions and interference. In a land where a railway or a line of steamers could be made to support an army, the temptation to divert the revenue of such agencies to the purposes of some militarist often proved too great to be resisted. Railways, too, have been commandeered by armies, and even in time of peace soldiers have been accustomed to demand passage free of charge and to misuse the rolling stock. Under such conditions, the normal growth of railroads and steamship lines could not but be retarded. After 1937 the Japanese advance and the accompanying fighting disrupted the railways or monopolized them for war.

We have previously noted how much the post office and telegraph have done to tie the nation together. The government postal service of to-day first arose through foreign initiative under the Customs. In 1896 it was formally established by imperial decree. Although the control is in Chinese hands, a few foreigners were long associated with its supervision. It has had a remarkable record in maintaining its service throughout the country in the face of the civil disorder of the past two decades. Its agents have frequently been known to get the mails through bandit lines into a beleaguered town. By money orders and parcel post as well as the transmission of letters it has contributed to the unification of the nation. By association with the postal system of the world it helps to keep China in touch with other lands. In 1908 the telegraphs of the country passed into the hands of the state. To-day a network of lines connects the chief cities and many of the towns of the Republic. The radio, too, has been developed most remarkably, both for internal and for international communications.

SUMMARY

Obviously the fate of China is inextricably bound up with economics. No nation in which great areas are overpopulated, in some of whose districts famine is recurrent, and in which millions are underclothed and undernourished can hope easily to maintain a stable government. Under such conditions, always there will be discontented spirits who prefer rebellion to starvation. As we have noted before, China is caught in a vicious circle. Under the great Manchu Emperors population increased rapidly. For more than a century these rulers had so maintained internal peace and order that the margin of subsistence expanded. With the collapse of the Ch'ing dynasty and of the old form of government, and with the ensuing political disorder, the margin shrank rapidly. As a result, millions were left stranded. Thousands of these entered the armies and other thousands became bandits. The result has been the still further restriction of the margin of existence, more distress, and more fighting and banditry. The political and the economic problem go hand in hand. Both must be solved together.

Yet the Chinese have by no means entirely failed in their economic life. Even to keep alive so huge a population has been and is no mean achievement, and millions, though a minority, have been and are maintained in comparative comfort.

So huge a mass of mankind on a low standard of living must be a problem not only for itself but for the rest of the world. The world cannot but be interested in watching the outcome of the phase of the present revolution which affects the economic life of China. If the Chinese succeed in regulating their birth rate and in adapting Western machinery and agricultural and commercial methods in such a manner as to raise the average level of existence, the rest of the human race cannot fail to be benefited. If the standard of living for the masses should fall still lower, not only China but also the rest of mankind will be the loser.

BIBLIOGRAPHY

Much information on economic life in China, chiefly on recent developments, is contained in *The Chinese Economic Bulletin,* issued by the Chinese Government, the *Chinese Economic Monthly,* issued by the Chinese Government (1923–1926), and the *Chinese Economic Journal,* also issued by the government.

General books are L. D. Stamp, *Asia: An Economic and Regional Geography* (New York, 1929), and L. D. Buxton, *China, the Land and the People* (Oxford, 1929). Partly general are K. A. Wittfogel in *Zeitschrift für Sozialforschung,* Vol. 4, 1935, Heft 1; Ch'ao-ting Chi, *Key Economic Areas in Chinese History as Revealed in the Development of Public Works for Water-Control* (London, 1936); and R. P. Hommel, *China at Work. An Illustrated Record of the Primitive Industries of China's Masses* (New York, 1937).

An occupation so important to the Chinese as agriculture almost inevitably has given rise to a fairly extensive literature. We know of a book on this subject as early as the fifth century of the Christian era. At least one fragment of a T'ang dynasty treatise, on the construction of ploughs, has come down to us. A work of the Sung dynasty containing pictures of various phases of agricultural operations and of weaving has survived. There is another one of the same dynasty which treats of farming, the breeding of cattle, and the rearing of silkworms. Still another, drawn up by imperial order, appeared in the Yüan dynasty. There are others from the Ming and the Ch'ing, either compiled or published by imperial decree. One of these Chinese treatises on agriculture has been translated by O. Franke in *Kêng Tschi T'u, Ackerbau und Seidengewinnung in China* (Hamburg, 1913).

Of books on Chinese agriculture in Western languages the following may be mentioned: Mabel Ping-hua Lee, *The Economic History of China, with Especial Reference to Agriculture* (New York, 1921), a somewhat ill-digested doctoral dissertation whose value lies almost entirely in its excerpts from various Chinese works; F. H. King, *Farmers of Forty Centuries, or Permanent Agriculture in China, Korea, and Japan* (Madison, Wisconsin, 1911), by a prominent American expert on agriculture on the basis of observations during a visit to the Far East; *Agrarian China. Selected Source Materials from Chinese Authors* (Chicago, preface, 1938); J. L. Buck, *Chinese Farm Economy, a study of 2866 farms in seventeen localities and seven provinces in China* (Shanghai and Chicago, 1930), using careful scientific methods, and covering certain sections in Fukien, Chêkiang, Kiangsu, Anhui, Honan, Hopei, and Shansi; J. L. Buck, *Land Utilization in China. A study of 16,786 farms in 168 localities, and 38,256 farm families in twenty-two provinces in China, 1929–1933* (Chicago, 3 vols., preface, 1937); K. A. Wittfogel, *Wirtschaft und Gesellschaft Chinas. Erster Teil, Produktivkräfte, Produktions- und Zirkulationsprozess* (Leipzig, 1931), based upon extensive research in the literature available in Western languages; Wilhelm Wagner, *Die Chinesische Landwirtschaft* (Berlin, 1926), an encyclopædic treatment by an expert, based upon observation during several years of residence in China and on examination of a large amount of material in European languages; W. H. Mallory, *China: Land of Famine* (New York, 1926), by a former secretary of the China International Famine Relief Commission; F. W. Otte, *China: wirtschaftspolitische Landeskunde* (Gotha, 1927, Vol. 42 of Petermans *Mitteilungen*); and J. D. H. Lamb, *Development of the Agrarian Movement and Agrarian Legislation in China (1912–1930)* (Peiping, 1931).

The following articles are among those having interest and value: P. C. Hsü, *Rural Coöperatives in China* (*Pacific Affairs*, October, 1929, pp. 611–624); W. H. Mallory, *Rural Coöperative Credit in China* (*The Quarterly Journal of Economics*, Vol. 45, May, 1931); W. H. Adolph, *Aspects of Nutrition and Metabolism in China* (*The Scientific Monthly*, July, 1929, pp. 39–44); J. B. Tayler, *The Study of Chinese Rural Economy* (*The Chinese Social and Political Science Review*, January and April, 1924); W. C. Lowdermilk, *Forestry in Denuded China* (*The Annals of the American Academy of Political and Social Science*, November, 1930, pp. 127–141); J. L. Buck, *Agriculture and the Future of China* (*ibid.*, pp. 109–115); on milk economy in China, B. Laufer, *Some Fundamental Ideas of Chinese Culture* (*Journal of Race Development*, 1914–1915, Vol. 5, pp. 160–174); C. C. Chang, *A Statistical Study of Farm Tenancy in China* (*The China Critic*, Sept. 25, 1930, Vol. 3, pp. 917–922); and C. C. Chang, *Farm Crops in 1930* (*ibid.*, April 30, 1931, Vol. 4, pp. 417–430). See also the bulletins of the College of Agriculture and Forestry of the University of Nanking. Pearl S. Buck, *The Good Earth* (New York, 1931) is, in fiction form, an excellent description of rural life in a particular section.

On the general subjects of industry, foreign and domestic commerce, and transportation, the following are useful as works of reference: H. B. Morse, *The Trade and Administration of China* (revised edition,

London, 1913); Julean Arnold (the distinguished Commercial Attaché of the American Legation in China) et alii, *China, A Commercial and Industrial Handbook* (Washington, Government Printing Office, 1926); Julean Arnold, *China through the American Window* (Shanghai, 1932), describing Chinese-American trade in most graphic and readable fashion; *The China Year Book* (London, 1912–1919, Tientsin, 1921–1930, Shanghai, 1931 *et seq.*), unusually rich in information; and S. Couling, *The Encyclopædia Sinica* (London, 1917), in which the articles are mostly brief but excellent and are often appended by a brief bibliography. See, too, Fung Yu-lan, *Why China Has No Science* (*International Journal of Ethics*, April, 1922). The reports and other published documents of the Maritime Customs are a mine of information. T. R. Jernigan, *China in Law and Commerce* (New York, 1905), has some good summaries. As a short special study see H. Feis, *The International Trade of Manchuria* (*International Conciliation*, New York, April, 1931). Still more recent studies are J. B. Condliffe, *China To-day: Economic* (Boston, 1932), E. E. Ware, *Business and Politics in the Far East* (New Haven, 1932), and Grover Clark, *Economic Rivalries in China* (New Haven, 1932).

On villages in a part of North China as they were at the close of the last century there is a very readable but somewhat pessimistic account by a resident in that region, A. H. Smith, *Village Life in China, A Study in Sociology* (New York, 1899). On a village in South China an account by a trained sociologist is D. H. Kulp, *Country Life in South China. The Sociology of Familism. Vol. 1. Phenix Village, Kwantung, China* (New York, 1925). See also the excellent study, Fei Hsiao-tung, *Peasant Life in China. A Field Study of Country Life in the Yangtze Valley* (London, 1939). On twentieth century conditions in Fukien, see Lin Yueh-hua, *The Golden Wing, A Family Chronicle* (New York, 1944).

On conditions in a big city, see S. D. Gamble, *How Chinese Families Live in Peiping. A Study of the Income and Expenditure of 283 Chinese Families Receiving from $8 to $550 Silver per Month* (New York, 1933).

On the guilds of China there is a little book by H. B. Morse, *The Gilds of China* (London, 1909), the information being drawn largely from *Chinese Guilds, or Chambers of Commerce and Trades Unions*, by D. J. Macgowan in the *Journal of the North China Branch of the Royal Asiatic Society*, 1888–1889, pp. 133–192, and the *Decennial Reports of the Chinese Imperial Maritime Customs*. Descriptions of several guilds, together with translations of documents, are in S. D. Gamble, assisted by J. S. Burgess, *Peking, A Social Survey* (New York, 1921). J. S. Burgess, *The Guilds of Peking* (New York, 1928), depends partly upon his earlier study with Gamble, but contains much additional information.

On conditions of labor and labor legislation and the modern labor movement, see Ta Chen, *The Labor Movement in China* (Honolulu,

1927); S. H. Lin, *Factory Workers in Tangku* (Peking, 1928); J. D. H. Lamb, *The Origin and Development of Social Legislation in China* (Yenching University, Peiping, 1930), formal and "official" in the extreme; Adelaide Mary Anderson, *Humanity and Labour in China, An Industrial Visit and Its Sequel (1923 to 1926)* (London, 1928); Fang Fu-an, *Chinese Labour* (Shanghai, 1931); R. H. Tawney, *Land and Labour in China* (1932); C. C. Chu and T. C. Blaisdell, *Peking Rugs and Peking Boys. A Study of the Rug Industry in Peking* (Special Supplement to the *Chinese Social and Political Science Review*, April, 1924); Monpeng Mou, *L'Evolution des Corporations Ouvrières et Commerciales dans la Chine Contemporaire* (1931); Nym Wales, *The Chinese Labor Movement* (New York, 1945); and Shih Kuo-cheng, *China Enters the Machine Age. A Study of Labor in Chinese War Industry* (Cambridge, 1944).

On modern industry in China, among many articles and books are H. D. Fong, *Industrialization and Labor in Hopei* (*The Chinese Social and Political Science Review*, April, 1931, pp. 1–28); H. D. Fong, *Cotton Industry and Trade in China* (*ibid.*, Oct. 1932, pp. 347–424); D. K. Lieu, *China's Industry and Finance* (Peking and Shanghai, *ca.*, 1927); E. M. Hinder, *Life and Labour in Shanghai* (New York, 1944); J. W. Frey, *Economic Significance of the Mineral Wealth of China* (*The Annals of the American Academy of Political and Social Science*, Nov. 1930, pp. 116–126); E. B. Alderfer, *The Textile Industry of China* (*ibid.*, pp. 184–190); W. Voskuil, *The Iron and Steel Industry of China* (*ibid.*, pp. 191–95); Ta Chen, *Fundamentals of the Chinese Labor Movement* (*ibid.*, pp. 196–205); Franklin L. Ho, *Industries* (*Symposium on Chinese Culture*, Shanghai, 1931, pp. 278–329).

On railways see Chang Kia-ngau, *China's Struggle for Railway Development* (New York, 1943).

On money and banking, see D. H. Leavens, *Chinese Money and Banking* (*The Annals of the American Academy of Political and Social Science*, Nov. 1930, pp. 206–213); F. M. Tamagna, *Banking and Finance in China* (New York, 1942); T. W. Overlach, *Foreign Financial Control in China* (New York, 1929); S. R. Wagel, *Finance in China* (Shanghai, 1914); S. R. Wagel, *Chinese Currency and Banking* (Shanghai, 1915); W. P. Wei, *The Currency Problem in China* (New York, 1914); F. E. Lee, *Currency, Banking, and Finance in China* (Washington, 1926); J. Edkins, *Chinese Currency* (Shanghai, 1901); E. Kann, *The Currencies of China* (second edition, Shanghai, 1927), probably the best book on the subject; W. Vissering, *On Chinese Currency, Coin and Paper Money* (Leiden, 1877), valuable because it is drawn chiefly from the encyclopædia of Ma Tuan-lin and consisting largely of a history of money in China into the Sung dynasty; and G. Vissering, *On Chinese Currency. Preliminary Remarks about the Monetary Reform in China* (Batavia, *ca.* 1912), dealing chiefly with current problems.

On prices and wages, see *Prices, Wages, and Standards of Living in*

Peking, 1900–1924 (*Special Supplement to the Chinese Social and Political Science Review,* July, 1926); S. D. Gamble, *Peking Wages* (Yenching University, Peiping, 1929); F. L. Ho, *Prices and Price Fluctuations in North China, 1913–1929* (*The Chinese Social and Political Science Review,* Oct. 1929, pp. 349–358); S. D. Gamble, *The Household Accounts of Two Chinese Families* (New York, 1931); S. D. Gamble, *Daily Wages of Unskilled Chinese Laborers, 1807–1902* (*The Far Eastern Quarterly,* Vol. 3, pp. 41–73); and L. K. Tao, *Livelihood in Peking* (Peking, 1928).

CHAPTER XVI

RELIGION

HISTORICAL SUMMARY

In connection with the chapters on history we have already rehearsed the main outlines of the development of religion in China. We have seen that the nature of the earliest religion of the Chinese is in dispute. There are those who contend that it was monotheism and that it was later corrupted by polytheism and by the worship of ancestors and of spirits residing in various natural objects. Others—and this is the present tendency—believe that the theistic elements in some of the ancient literary remains were late accretions and that the primitive faith was probably a mixture of animism, including the worship of ancestors, and of reverence for forces and objects of nature, such as Heaven and Earth and some of the heavenly bodies, whose coöperation was regarded as necessary to the well-being of man.

Whatever Chinese religion may have been in its primitive stages, its main outlines in the latter part of the Chou are fairly discernible. There were ceremonies in honor of ancestors. Spirits of varying degrees of potency were believed to reside in many natural objects—such as mountains and rivers—and to demand reverence. Some of the stars, notably those in Ursa Major, were highly esteemed. Heaven and Earth, particularly the former, were held in great veneration and sacrifices were offered to them. One Power was regarded with such awe and to it were ascribed such attributes of personality that a type of theism may be said to have existed. This Power was denominated either *T'ien* (Heaven) or *Shang Ti* (the Supreme Ruler or the Ruler Above). The two terms probably had separate origins and at one time different meanings, but by the latter part of the Chou they had all but coalesced and were declared by some to be identical in the object designated. This theism, of course, was not monotheism in the sense that no spiritual beings other than *T'ien* or *Shang Ti* could be worshiped. Moreover, varying conceptions existed of the Supreme Power. By some, probably the majority, it was held to be personal, but at least a few conceived it as entirely impersonal.

The duty owed to the spiritual beings was believed to be largely ceremonial. Ritual correctly performed was regarded as extremely important. Music and posturing, along with sacrifices of food and even, on occasion, of human beings, had their place. At least before the close of the Chou dynasty—whether as a late development or as a heritage from the past is in dispute—an ethical element entered and Heaven was believed to be displeased with violations of the moral code.

The correct performance of the ceremonies and other duties owed to spiritual beings was declared essential to the welfare of man. All nature was thought of as an orderly whole, a universe. If this universe were to be kept functioning properly man must do his part—a part in which both ritual and loyalty to moral obligations were important. If man failed to perform his duty the machinery of the universe would be disarranged and natural disasters of various kinds would ensue, such as floods, drought, and the failure of crops.

Ceremonies were of many kinds and grades. Each class or group in society had those appropriate to it. No one must infringe upon those of another or the harmony of nature would be disturbed. The head of the state, the various territorial princes, and members of the feudal aristocracy were especially charged—or privileged—with specific religious functions.

Yet no priestly class emerged. There were those particularly well versed in ritual whose function it was to assist in its direction. There were professional diviners, experts in the various methods of discovering by lot or oracle the proper course of action. However, no specialized group existed as in ancient Egypt or India which depended for its prestige and power upon a monopoly of the approach to the spirits, gods, and divine forces. Officiation at religious ceremonies formed part of the prerogative of those charged with the civil, military, and social leadership of society.

We have also seen that in the Chou period various schools of thought developed, all of them taking account of religion and some of them with very strong religious elements. There was what Westerners usually call Confucianism, with its three leading exponents and formulators—Confucius, Mencius, and Hsün Tzǔ. There was Taoism, advocating a type of society so simplified that it approached anarchism, and with speculations concerning the nature of things which ever since have fascinated many and were long both an excuse for and an incentive to the search for a means to immortality and for the transmutation of metals. Mo Ti advocated a theory for the organization of society upon the principle of universal love and found justification for it in what he believed to be revealed in nature and in the writings and experience of the ancients—the love of God for men. He was followed by two schools, one of which stressed the religious aspects of his teaching and the other his methods of reasoning. The Legalists wished to govern society by drastic regulations strictly administered. Other schools and independent thinkers of the Chou which have been named earlier do not need even to be mentioned here. The era was one of active and creative thought in which religion could not fail to be involved.

The latter part of the Chou was also a time of political and social turmoil and transition. When the dust had settled what were in many respects a new state and a new society had come into being. Ch'in Shih Huang Ti attempted to reorganize China on the theories which had proved successful in his native state— those of the Legalists. When the brief course of his dynasty had been run, leaving behind it momentous permanent results, the Han followed, won for the Empire a comparative stability, and placed an indelible stamp on the institutions of China. Under the Han Confucianism, greatly modified by the influence of other schools, was eventually established as the philosophy of the state. Taoism, however, continued potent and often numbered among its devotees persons high in court circles. It became something quite different from that disclosed in the great classics it inherited from the Chou. The other schools of the Chou gradually died out, but some of their writings survived and were not without effect, often very lasting and profound, upon the subsequent life and thought of the Empire.

When the Han dynasty went the way of all flesh, approximately four centuries of internal turmoil followed during which a major new religious influence, this time from abroad, made itself felt. Buddhism, it will be recalled, first reached China—at least so far as we are now aware—under the Han. It was, however, in the centuries of the post-Han internal political division of the Empire when there was no single state organized on an intolerant Confucian theory to offer resistance that it achieved its large place in the land.

It was under an Empire revived and unified afresh by the Sui and the T'ang that Buddhism reached its apex. The Chinese made it largely their own and most of the sects through which it has persisted seem to have been of native origin. A wide range of Chinese life has been affected by it. Confucianism, Taoism, folklore, philosophy, popular religious beliefs and practices, and art have never been the same since its years of popularity. It is still a living force. Yet since about the middle of the T'ang Buddhism in China has gradually lost in vitality.

Until very recently Buddhism has been the only foreign religion which has had much effect upon more than a minority of the Chinese. Zoroastrianism, Manichæism, Christianity, Judaism, and Islam have all been present at one time or another, several of them for centuries. Yet the Moslems are the only group which have numbered much more than one per cent. of the population, and even they have been largely apart from the main current of Chinese life and have had but little effect upon it. Of late years, as we have seen, Christianity has had widespread influence and at present is the most vigorous of the religions represented in China.

Beginning with the Han and especially after the Sui and the T'ang, with their revival and strengthening of the civil service examinations based upon the Confucian Classics, Confucianism was, until the twentieth century, usually the philosophy established and supported by the state. It was, therefore, dominant in the life of the nation. Taoism always had its advocates, frequently including those high in official circles, and at times was accorded imperial patronage. Buddhism often enjoyed popularity at court as well as with the masses. Confucianism, however, was the basis on which the Empire was organized.

It is tantalizing to have to pass over the history of the religious life of the Chinese in the fragmentary manner in which it has been touched upon in preceding chapters and in this brief summary. This is all the more so because no satisfactory account is to be found in any language and the subject is one which invites exploration. If and when such a work is written it will treat not only of religious and philosophic thought, but of institutions, ceremonies, the relation of religion to the state and to society in general, and the effect of religion upon art and literature. It will pay attention to religion both as practiced by the ruling and educated classes and by the masses of the people and will record the rise and decline of popular religious cults and the story of the origin and disappearance of the many divinities which for longer or shorter periods have been revered by some or all of the Chinese. Whether such an account can ever be composed is uncertain. Obviously it will have to rest upon many preliminary studies in the vast literary remains of China's past and much, too, must wait upon archæology. Such a history, if it is ever compiled, will be of the greatest interest and value.

GENERAL CHARACTERISTICS OF THE RELIGIOUS LIFE OF THE CHINESE

Unsatisfactory though these brief historical notes are, they may render somewhat more intelligible religion as it was on the eve of the revolution brought by the coming of the Occident and as it exists to-day. They will, moreover, serve to make clear some of the reasons for the religious attitudes of the Chinese.

About these attitudes certain generalizations can be ventured —subject, as generalizations usually are, to exception and qualification. Any picture painted with broad strokes may well fail to portray what religion has meant to any one Chinese. To include this would require a large canvas with detailed portraits of a number of individuals of varying types and would far transcend the proper limits of this chapter. Sweeping outlines may, however, possess a certain rough accuracy.

First of all, then, religiously the Chinese are very eclectic. In proportion to the total population the number of simon pure Buddhists, Confucianists, or Taoists has been and is comparatively small. The average Chinese has long been and still is an animist, a Buddhist, a Confucianist, and a Taoist with no sense of incongruity or inconsistency. For example, in the cult of the dead ceremonies which have come down through the Confucian tradition and others of Buddhist origin have their place, and in domestic rites animism, Confucianism, Buddhism, and Taoism are almost inextricably mixed. Other streams which have not been so potent in China have sometimes mingled their waters in the common current. In this eclecticism the Chinese are by no means always critical. The masses particularly often hold at one and the same time reciprocally contradictory views.

Associated with this eclecticism is a certain tolerance. The statement so commonly made and so widely lauded both in China and the modern West that the Chinese are a religiously tolerant people requires qualification. Again and again there have been persecutions, some initiated and conducted by the state and others popular in their origin. The state, which beginning with the Han and reënforced by the T'ang was until the twentieth century built upon Confucianism, repeatedly sought to stamp out or at least to restrict, other cults. Thus on one memorable occasion in the T'ang the monasteries of several faiths were ordered closed, and in the Sacred Edict which through much of the Ch'ing was officially and widely taught, Buddhism, Taoism, and Christianity were held up to ridicule and the populace exhorted to have nothing to do with any of them. Heterodox faiths and philosophies were condemned, to be sure, not primarily because, from the metaphysical standpoint, they were deemed false, but because they were believed to be injurious to the political and social structure of the Empire, organized as it was on Confucian principles. That, however, has been the argument usually advanced by religious persecutors in other lands. At first sight the course of China's history seems not to have been marred by religious wars as has been much of that of Europe. On the other hand, at least most of the so-called religious wars of Europe have been waged only in part and usually not chiefly from religious motives: the slogans employed have covered personal, dynastic, racial, or national antagonisms and ambitions. In China, too, some of the bloodiest rebellions have appealed to religious sanctions and the frequent sanguinary conflicts between Moslem and non-Moslem portions of the population are notorious.

When these qualifications have been made, however, the fact

remains that in practice there has been much of religious toleration in China. Just why this is so must be in part conjectural. It may have been because the practically minded Chinese have been eager to take advantage of every possible benefit from each of the systems which have come to their attention. It may have been because of a fundamental religious uncertainty—a lurking suspicion that all religions are at least in part false and a lack of confidence in the finality of any one of them—and yet a fear that each may possess elements of truth. It may have been, too, because of the desire to build a mankind-embracing culture, and of the concomitant talent for absorbing other cultures. It seems probable, for example, that many of the divinities which now appear purely indigenous were taken over from other peoples as these were conquered and assimilated.

Still another characteristic of Chinese religious life has been its optimism. There is little of the despair of human existence, of the pessimism about the worth of human life, and of the desire to be rid of personality which one finds in much of Indian thought. This is in spite of the fact that Buddhism, so influential in China, was originally a means of getting rid of desire, and, in the eyes of many interpreters, of the separate entities called persons. It is significant that in Chinese Buddhism nirvana, as a place where desire is at last extinguished, has largely dropped into the background and that heaven and hell, where separate personal existences are pictured as continuing, loom large in popular Buddhist teaching. This optimism, too, is seen in the discussions about the basic quality of human nature which have been prominent in the history of Chinese philosophy. Orthodox Confucianism declares men to be by nature good. Even those who, like Hsün Tzŭ, have denied the truth of this contention have usually regarded human nature as improvable. There is, too, a certain confidence in the moral trustworthiness of the universe. Some have regarded the universe as beyond human understanding and as indifferent to the fate of men, either collectively or as individuals. Others have held that the universe moves according to unvarying law and that nothing like a personal God is at the heart of it. In the main, however, orthodox Confucianism has taught that moral law is part of the essence of things, that when men obey it prosperity ensues and that evil-doing is a cause of calamities. To this confidence in the moral goodness of the forces of the unseen world Buddhism has contributed, for the many buddhas and bodhisattvas to whom it has taught people to look for help are represented as merciful and loving righteousness and as ultimately more powerful than evil.

Closely allied with this optimistic attitude toward the universe is the strong ethical note in much of Chinese religion. Confucianism emphasizes man's duty to man and praises such virtues as sincerity, kindness, loyalty, filial piety, and not doing to another what one does not like to have done to oneself. The Emperor was supposed to rule because of his virtue. National calamities might come as a result of his misdeeds, and in imperial proclamations public confession of lack of righteousness was not unknown. Protestations of the righteousness of the imperial acts and motives were often made. Buddhism has strongly reënforced this ethical note and has taught that suffering is a certain consequence of unrighteousness. Popular Buddhism has vivid representations, both in its literature and in pictures and effigies in some of its shrines, of the tortures which are believed to be meted out in the next life for sin, and speaks also of the joys of its heavens in which the good are rewarded. To be sure, much of popular Buddhism has held that future bliss may be achieved through simple faith or by the correct performance of ritual acts which possess no ethical significance, but the total effect upon the Chinese of its tutelage has probably been to heighten moral sensitivity and strengthen impulses toward good. Taoism has also contributed toward making Chinese religion moral. Some of its treatises, both the abstruse and the popular ones, sound the ethical note.

It must immediately be said that the Chinese, like many other peoples, have had great confidence in ritual and in practice have believed it to be quite as important as an ethically good life. For this the Chou tradition as preserved in the Classics and the state cult has been to no small extent responsible, for, as we have seen, it has set great store by the observance of ceremonies. It must, however, be added that some of the Confucian writings have united ethics and ritual—holding that ceremonies should be performed with a moral purpose and that moral growth is aided by correctly performed ceremonies. Confucius himself, while valuing ritual, placed his major emphasis on ethics. It was, indeed, in this realm that he made his greatest contribution. Buddhism and Taoism, as popularly practiced, have confirmed confidence in ritual. The widespread animism nurtured the conviction that the unseen spiritual beings are to be induced to serve man's will by amoral rites.

Along with this confidence in rites has been what to the modern Westerner seems a kind of slovenliness in the case of temples and in the carrying out of the ceremonies themselves. Numbers of temples and shrines have been well maintained and from time to time some that have become dilapidated have been repaired. Often, too, a shrine is cleaned in preparation for a great ceremony. Even before the anti-religious wave of late years, however, a large proportion of the temples seemed to be in a state of chronic neglect and a visit between important occasions would often find courts weed-grown and the great halls dusty and festooned with cobwebs. While ceremonies have been supposed to conform to prescribed forms, and correct posturing, costuming, and utterance of phrases have been emphasized, yet, as in the case of funerals when beggars are employed to fill out the procession, the wearers of the elaborate clothing may be unwashed and in the less obvious corners of the shrine dust and débris lie undisturbed.

A further characteristic of the religious attitude of the Chinese has been this-worldliness. The earliest religion of the Chinese which we know seems to have had as its primary object the material happiness and prosperity of men here and now. It believed that the dead live on, but its concepts of their state were very vague and its chief concern was the welfare of the living. Several of the schools of thought of the Chou period shared and if anything emphasized this tradition. Their purpose, it will be recalled, was the achievement of an ideal human society. Confucianism possessed this attitude rather strongly and, since it was so long the accepted philosophy of the state, assisted in perpetuating it. Religion, from this standpoint, is a means of keeping the machinery of human society moving smoothly and successfully. In ethical teaching the social duties have been stressed. By its rites religion was believed both to help preserve order in the relations of men to one another and to insure the friendly coöperation with men of the unseen forces, spiritual or otherwise, of the universe. In popular practice this belief has taken rather crass forms. Men have given to the spirits that they may obtain benefits here and now. The boatman may be seen offering incense to ward off danger, and in at least one city the merchant has burned incense and made his *kotow* or bow at the beginning and end of the day to improve his business. If a god has been besought by offerings for a particular favor, such as recovery from illness or success in a business undertaking, and the occasion turns out otherwise than had been hoped, the disappointed worshiper may display an outraged sense of having been defrauded and curse the deity. In time of drought the image of a god may be exposed to the sun to let it feel how hot it is, and may even be fined by the magistrate for allowing the calamity, be condemned, and broken in pieces. It is because of this attitude that some Chinese have accepted Christianity from a belief in its potency to give relief from such present misfortunes as the illness of one's own person or relatives or of one's pigs or oxen.

Utility has by no means been the only motive in Chinese religion. There has been much of a reverence which has had in it no element of self-seeking. Confucius, in extolling awe for Heaven's decrees, touched a responsive chord in the hearts of many of his countrymen. The honors paid to the dead, too, often have had in them self-forgetful respect and affection. Then, too, Chinese religion has displayed much other-worldliness. Taoism early became a channel for the search for immortality and across the centuries one source of its appeal has been the conviction that through it the desired state can be achieved. One of the chief reasons for the strength of Buddhism has been its vivid pictures of the future life and the confidence which it has begotten in many that through its agency the faithful can escape the pains and be assured the blessings of an existence beyond the grave.

Another feature of Chinese religion has been a credulous superstition. In this, of course, the Chinese are by no means unique. Even in this supposed age of enlightenment and in lands where scientific processes have been most fully developed much of unreasoning and unreasonable credulity remains. Witness some of the great office buildings of New York City, equipped with the latest appliances for comfort and efficiency, in which there is a twelfth and a fourteenth but no thirteenth floor. The Chinese, however, have been behind no other people in their anxiety to take advantage of lucky and to avoid unlucky days, hours, and places, in ascribing disease to spirits, and in devices for fending off spirits which are believed to bring misfortune.

Yet, as we have seen more than once in preceding chapters, the Chinese can boast of many robust sceptics. Thinking of them, one modern Chinese has declared—with more enthusiasm than precise accuracy—that the Chinese were the first people to outgrow religion. From at least Yang Chu and Hsün Tzǔ in the Chou there has been a strain of more or less open dissent from currently accepted beliefs. It appears not to have been entirely lacking in Confucius. Certainly some famous passages in the *Lun Yü* have led many of his professed followers to find in him a precedent for their own agnosticism. This scepticism has often contained a good deal of what was at least superficially inconsistent. A Han Yü might denounce most caustically the imperial honors to a miracle-working bone of Buddha and yet write an exhortation to a crocodile to depart from the district in which he had jurisdiction. Again and again officials who have privately expressed disbelief in the existence of spirits, in their public capacity have led in ceremonies which have had as their object the control of these same spirits. In this they were again not without precedent in Confucius, for, even though that revered teacher may have been agnostic concerning at least some of the beliefs of his day, he strongly advocated the meticulous and reverent performance of the traditional rites.

It must also be said, what must have been apparent from much that has been recorded in the historical chapters, that a great deal of profound thought on some of the ultimate philosophic and religious problems is to be found in Chinese literature, and that by no means all of it ends in the denial of the reality of the objects of man's religious faith. Through the centuries many Chinese have been sceptical of much of the popular superstition and yet have been deeply religious and could give a reason for the faith that was in them.

Chinese religion has had both the social and the individual emphasis. According to the Confucian tradition, religion is largely for the salvation of society, for cultivating those relations among men which make for a wholesome social order. Yet Confucianism has had much to say about the cultivation of character, and Buddhism and Taoism have had as at least part of their aim the perfection of the individual.

One last general characteristic of Chinese religion which needs mention is state control. As far back as the Chou and probably earlier, religion was a function of society as expressed in such institutions as the state and the family. When, under the Ch'in, the Empire was organized, the authority of the state in religion was rather rigorously exercised. In theory the state seems to have remained supreme in such matters down through the Ch'ing. The formal declaration of religious liberty under the Republic appears to have been a distinct innovation. The control of the state was not always vigorously asserted. As we have said, a good deal of practical toleration existed. Yet the right was always there and from time to time was emphatically exercised. No great religious organization has ever made an effective bid for superiority over the state in the loyalties of the Chinese. The Buddhist monks, although the richest and most numerous of the religious groups, seem never to have been so closely knit on an Empire-wide scale as the Roman Catholic Church in the West. Nor has the doctrine of the complete separation of church and state much precedent in China. Under the Ch'ing, for example, the state exercised a supervision over the Buddhist monastic communities, appointing officials to control them and designating the monasteries which had the right to admit postulants to the monastic vows. This tradition, it may be remarked, reënforced by contacts with the accentuated powers of the state in the present-day West and by the rise of nationalism, has had to be reckoned with by the groups in China which have sought to build up a Christian society or societies as free as possible from the interference of the state and to exercise functions, such as education, which in China have long been claimed by the government.

THE STATE RELIGION AND CONFUCIANISM

From these general characteristics we must turn to the chief phases of the religious life in China in the nineteenth century on the eve of the changes introduced by the coming of the Occident. In a sense it does violence to the picture to differentiate the several systems. The eclecticism of which we have spoken makes the religious beliefs and practices of most individuals and communities a composite from which only Islam and Christianity have succeeded in standing aloof. However, the separation has a certain validity, for historically, as we have seen, there have been very diverse religions and philosophies which have by no means entirely coalesced.

It would be difficult to defend the logic of any order adopted in presenting the various religions, but the observances fostered by the state and Confucianism as the cult officially sponsored by the government may well be allowed to come first.

Confucianism is largely a Western name, although the Chinese speak of *K'ung Chiao* or the "Confucian Teaching" (or Religion). The designation more commonly employed by the Chinese has been *Ju Chiao*, or the "Teaching of the Learned." *Ju Chia* is also used, but for the Confucian school, or Confucianists. Confucius is revered as the cult's greatest sage, but other teachers and scholars are honored as having shared in its development. To a certain extent, beginning with the Han, Confucianism represented the totality of Chinese philosophic thought outside such special systems as Taoism and Buddhism—and even these strongly influenced it.

The question is sometimes debated of whether Confucianism is a religion. The answer depends in part upon a definition. If one calls religion—as is done by one standard authority—"any system of faith and worship," then Confucianism may be said at least to contain religious elements. As we have repeatedly seen, it has been in large part concerned with the organization of the state and of society and with man's relation to man. However, no thoughtful person can meditate long upon either state or society without encountering problems as to the nature of man and of the universe and the relation of the one to the other. Is man by nature good or bad? What are the criteria by which good and bad are to be distinguished? Is the universe friendly, unfriendly, or indifferent to man? Can man believe in a being or beings who in part or entirely control the course of the universe? If so, can he make such an adjustment to them that he will be reënforced in his efforts to achieve what he believes desirable goals for himself and society? Chinese both in and out of the Confucian school inevitably have raised such questions and in consequence their thinking and acting have shown a religious tinge. Moreover, Confucius, as we have again and again said, set great store by the ceremonial, part of it unmistakably religious, which had come down from the past. The Confucian school, accordingly, has been a bulwark of the religious rites which are supposed to have originated in the Chou dynasty or earlier and of certain others which have developed from or are akin to them. Confucianism, therefore, can certainly be said to contain religious features, even though it includes other elements.

It is the religious rites and beliefs preserved or nourished by Confucianism with which we are here chiefly concerned and not the political and social doctrines—for these have been or will be considered elsewhere. Through the centuries Confucian scholars have differed on the question of the personality of *T'ien* and the existence of spirits, but most of them have agreed that the universe favors righteousness in man and all would maintain religious rites. Even though some, like Hsün Tzŭ, declared that these rites could not alter the course of nature, they contended that they were valuable as a means of educating the people, and so as a form of social control.

It is probable that even without the influence of the Confucian school the state would have supported some kind of religion. Most ancient and many modern governments have done so. Had it not been for Confucianism, however, that religion would probably have been very different from what it was. For instance, it might have been Buddhism or Taoism. It seems to have been due chiefly to Confucianism that the Imperial Government sought to maintain the religious ritual of antiquity which the Sage had endorsed. The government also recognized divinities and permitted or actually supported ceremonies which Confucius had never known but which were believed to be consistent with his teaching.

It must be noted, indeed, that the state cult which is often called Confucianism and in which ceremonies in honor of Confucius and his disciples were accorded an important part, had a long and varied history. Some of this has been hinted at earlier. The resulting product under the later Ch'ing Emperors was a composite of many influences and movements and a large proportion of it would probably have seemed to Confucius and his immediate disciples very strange and quite out of keeping with their teachings.

According to the theory of the Chinese state which was reenforced by Confucianism, the Emperor was the religious as well as the political head of the realm. The Emperor, indeed, was a part of the order of the universe and was commissioned by *T'ien* not only to rule all mankind but to perform certain religious functions. He was a son of *T'ien* and an associate of Heaven and Earth (*T'ien* and *Ti*). A pantheon with ordered ranks was recognized, and to it the Emperor could admit and in it promote and demote divine beings. Repeatedly he conferred titles, usually very resounding ones, on divinities. To the Emperor was reserved the performance of some of the ceremonies conceived of as essential to the smooth coöperation of man and the universe. The chief of these was that at the Altar of Heaven. In connection with it was —and is, for it still stands—a group of imposing buildings of varying dates in a vast enclosure on the southern border of the capital. The altar is a terraced, marble structure, in the open air. It is circular, the traditional form of the symbols of Heaven. Here, on the longest night of the year, the Emperor officiated at a sacrifice to *T'ien*. At the ceremony was a tablet to *Shang Ti*, and tablets to the imperial ancestors, to the sun and moon, the five planets, Ursa Major, the twenty-four constellations, the signs of the zodiac, the God of the Clouds, the God of Rain, the God of Wind, and the God of Thunder. At other times of the year other, less elaborate ceremonies were conducted, in theory by the Emperor. To the north of the capital is an Altar to the Earth where the Emperor, in person or by proxy, sacrificed at the summer solstice. Ceremonies were also conducted there at other times. Here the prevailing form is square, the traditional symbol of Earth. To the east of Peking was an altar to the sun and to the west an altar to the moon—the one round and the other square. The Emperor was also supposed to sacrifice to his ancestors and to the spirits of the ground and of the grain. On occasions of unusual importance, such as the accession of a dynasty or a great crisis in the affairs of state or of the imperial family, the Emperor, by special ceremonies, announced the event to his ancestors and to Heaven and Earth—or perhaps merely to his ancestors. Near the capital were temples to some other spirits of natural objects, where the Emperor officiated at ceremonies either in person or by proxy. At one of them he officially opened the husbandry of the spring by plowing. He was also required to sacrifice to a sacred *yo*, or mountain, when he was near it, or to send a representative to do so. Sacrifices to some other spirits and divinities of lesser rank were performed, not by the Emperor in person but by officials delegated by him.

Many members of the official hierarchy on duty in the provinces were charged with the performance of religious rites. Sacrifices to the spirits of local mountains and streams were expected of them. They also took part in such ceremonies as those in the local temples of Confucius and in the temple of the City God. Officials in the provinces were supposed to offer sacrifices, at the time of the spring planting, to the Gods of the Soil and the Grain. Those of certain grades, including the Viceroy, were required to open the operations of the spring by sacrifices to Shên-nung, the ancient mythical Emperor and patron of husbandry, and by plowing. There were also official ceremonies for neglected ghosts— said to have been ordered by Hung Wu, the founder of the Ming, who, an orphan of destitute parents, is reported not to have known the burial place of his father and mother. Visits of officials, either in person or by proxy, were expected to be paid to other divinities, some of them local and some revered by the various crafts. In other words, within their jurisdiction officials had it as one of their functions to insure by the performance of the proper rites the same smooth coöperation between men and the powerful spirits and forces of the universe which, for the entire realm, the Emperor was expected to maintain.

The pantheon of the spirits and divinities recognized by the state cult was grouped into three grades. In the first were Heaven and Earth, the deceased Emperors, and the Gods of the Ground and the Grain. Near the close of the Ch'ing, Confucius was promoted to this rank. In the second were, among others, the sun and the moon, many famous rulers of antiquity, such as Yao and Shun, the chief disciples of Confucius and the leading exponents of his doctrines, distinguished men and women of virtue and learning, and the Gods of the Sky, of the Clouds, of Rain, Wind, and Thunder. In the third were great physicians of the past, the God of War, the Ruler of the North Star, the God of Fire, the City Gods (Gods of the Walls and Moats), and a number of others.

A few of the divinities honored by the official Confucian cult require special mention. One of these, naturally, was Confucius himself. Every territorial division, such as the *hsien*, the *fu*, and the province, was supposed to have what foreigners call a Confucian temple (usually known to the Chinese as the *K'ung Miao* ("Confucian Temple"), the *Wên Miao* ("Temple of Literature," or perhaps "Temple of Civilization"), or *Hsüeh Kung* ("Temple of Learning"). This meant that in some walled cities such as the capital of a province, which might also be the chief city of a *fu* and contain one or more *hsien*, two or more such temples were found. Especially famous temples were at Ch'ü-fou, the home of the Sage, where a lineal male descendant ennobled in recognition of that fact was (and is) supposed to maintain ceremonies to him and to care for his grave, and at Peking (now Peiping), where was an unusually large structure. The Confucian temple normally consisted of an enclosure containing several courts and buildings. The southern wall was not pierced by a gate until some student of the district had obtained first rank in the examinations for the *chin shih*. The main building had as its chief features (at its northern end, facing south) a tablet to Confucius and, ranged on either hand, on the eastern and western sides, tablets to the chief disciples of Confucius and to men, like Chu Hsi, who through the centuries had added luster to the Confucian virtues or to the Confucian school. Cloisters connected with the main hall contained tablets to others distinguished for adorning the Confucian doctrine. The tablets of the various individuals were placed according to a fixed order, some being in positions of especial honor. New names might be admitted by imperial decree. In a few temples were images of Confucius. In these the Sage was usually represented as swarthy of countenance and garbed in the dress of his period. In a building or a room near the main hall might be tablets to the ancestors of Confucius. On one side of the temple enclosure, too, might be a shrine for tablets to famous scholars and officials who were natives of the locality. The walls of the temple were red, the official color of the Chou, and other features of the equipment and ceremonies associated with the place were supposed to date from that dynasty. Twice a year in each temple formal official ceremonies were held, with an elaborate ritual believed to have come down from antiquity and with offerings of food and the burning of incense. They were usually just before dawn (although they might be held during the day), and with the stately hall, the official costumes of the participants, and the posturing, music, and procedure through which many successive generations had expressed their reverence, could be very impressive. Official visits were supposedly paid to the temples twice each month.

These temples, it may be added, existing as they did throughout the Empire, and maintained officially, were potent in reënforcing and continuing Confucianism. Added to them were halls to Confucius in at least some of the state schools which helped still further to preserve for the Sage and his teachings the loyalty of the powerful official-scholar class.

Another shrine connected with the state cult was the *Ch'êng Huang Miao*, literally the "Temple of the Wall and the Moat," but more freely translated as the Temple of the Tutelar God of the City. Each walled city was supposed to have one. Here was an image of the local *Ch'êng Huang*, or god. He was often represented with two assistants, and sometimes with his wife and concubines and sons, and with other gods. While the image remained constant, the god himself was usually thought of as changed from time to time, much as the local magistrates were transferred. Confirmation of the position was theoretically made by the national head of the Taoist cult, subject to the approval of the Board of Rites. He was often conceived of as a deceased official, and in some cities was a deified local hero and remained constantly at one post. The god and his temple usually played a fairly important part in the life of the city. Magistrates were expected to make them official visits. Semi-monthly ceremonies were held and usually twice a year, in the spring and autumn, the image of the god was carried in procession through the streets. The god and his entourage were often cared for by societies, membership in which might carry with it social prestige. The common people said prayers and made offerings in the temple, and to the god was announced each death in the community. The god was expected to protect the city from harm. He was also believed to watch the deeds of the inhabitants, to report them to Heaven, and to turn over evildoers, on death, to the ruler of purgatory. This latter conception was of Buddhist provenance and an illustration of the fashion in which the faiths of China interpenetrated each other.

The Gods of the Soil and the Grain should also be mentioned. The Gods of the Soil were of very early origin. Theoretically each political unit was under the protection of one of them. In theory the head city of each province, *fu*, and *hsien* had an altar to its local God of the Soil. This was square, the traditional form of objects associated with the cult of the Earth and related deities, and was open to the sky and surrounded by trees. In addition to the large one for the Empire at Peking, the Emperor had an altar of his own in his palace, constructed of earth from various parts of his domains. The God of the Grain was usually closely associated with that of the soil, and throughout the Empire official ceremonies were held and offerings made to the two on the open air altars at stated times each year.

Many villages, too, had each its shrine to the local God of the Soil. The god was supposed to record all village happenings and to report them to Heaven and the ruler of purgatory. Announcements of births and deaths were often made there. The shrine, sometimes very simple, and at others in an elaborate building, was frequently very important in the life of the village. Its upkeep constituted a community interest and in it might be images of other gods.

Another deity prominent in the official cult was the God of Literature, Wên Ti or Wên Ch'ang. His worship had a most interesting development, the full course of which seems not yet to have been accurately traced. He is said actually to have lived, perhaps under the T'ang dynasty, but, if so, that fact appears to have been accidental. Reported incarnations show the influence of Buddhism. He was believed to reside in Ursa Major, a constellation which from very early times had been venerated by the Chinese. He was often represented with several attendants. Whatever the origin and growth of his cult, he had numerous shrines where official ceremonies were conducted in his honor. His temples served as club houses for scholars.

A deity who loomed very prominently in the state cult was Kuan Yü or Kuan Ti, usually, but not with entire accuracy, called the God of War. This latter designation comes from the fact that he was the patron of the military officials, somewhat as Confucius was revered as the Sage of the civil officials. The temple in his honor was called the *Wu Miao,* or "Military Temple" (also the *Wu Shêng Miao*—the "Military Holy Temple"). It will be recalled that Kuan Yü was a commander in the memorable period of the Three Kingdoms, a supporter of Liu Pei, and one of the trio who took the "Peach Garden Oath" so famous in Chinese fiction and drama. His deification and popularity developed slowly and the honors accorded him appear never to have been so great as under the Ch'ing. In the later years of that dynasty, after the T'ai P'ing Rebellion, he was much reverenced. In theory at least, a temple was erected to him in every province, *fu,* and *hsien,* and at periodical intervals official ceremonies with sacrificial offerings were conducted, usually led by the chief military official. Yüan Shih-k'ai particularly honored him and ordered the observance of his cult. In the *Wu Miao* were, at least sometimes, tablets not only to Kuan Yü but to other famous generals, making it a kind of military hall of fame. Especially associated with Kuan Yü has been the name of Yo Fei, a loyal and heroic general of the Sung, who, at least of late years, has often shared the honors with him. Kuan Yü has been popular with more than the soldiers. He has been believed to be skillful in driving out evil spirits and for this reason has been much invoked. He has been regarded as a patron divinity of more than one province, has been looked upon as a god of literature, and has been highly esteemed by merchants.

There were, moreover, temples to the Emperor, *Wan Shou Kung,* where on stated occasions officials were expected to assemble and perform ceremonies. This cult of the monarch, however, was by no means so prominent as in imperial Rome.

Possibly also there should be classified under the state religion deified famous men. Some of these were revered only locally, others more than locally. A popular official, a general, or a martyr to a patriotic cause might have a shrine built to him and there ceremonies be held in his honor and prayers made to him. In its origin, the cult might be unofficial, but if its hero were to attain full status as a recognized god an imperial decree was required ordering his deification and assigning him rank and title.

At least one more type of divinity worshiped under state auspices requires mention—that of the mountains. The spirits of the hills were early revered in China, possibly because, shrouded by clouds and sheltering the sources of springs, eminences were supposed to have some causal connection with the moisture upon which the fruitfulness of the harvest depended. Early, too, five peaks came into especial prominence, each being associated with one of the five directions—east, west, north, south, and the center. Of these the most notable has been for many centuries T'ai Shan—the *Tung Yo,* or Eastern Peak—in Shantung. As the easternmost of the five, it was believed to control the springs of life, to govern man's fate on earth, and to rule the souls of men after death. For a time in its history, T'ai Shan was regarded as an official messenger to *T'ien*—through whom the Emperor offered the special sacrifice *fêng.* Later its functions were modified, yet repeatedly it was sacrificed to by Emperors and given honorary titles. Important events, such as the birth of a son and the choice of an heir to the throne, were officially announced to it. T'ai Shan has been by no means entirely or even chiefly a divinity revered by the state: the spirit or god of T'ai Shan has had wide popularity with the masses. The cult of T'ai Shan is, indeed, another example of the way in which originally separate faiths have mingled. Both Buddhism and Taoism took advantage of and reënforced it. When Buddhism came with its conceptions of the after life, it was not unnatural that T'ai Shan, already regarded as determining the span of men's years and presiding over the spirits of the dead, should be assigned the rulership of one of the Buddhist hells where punishments for certain categories of sins are inflicted. Taoism especially appropriated T'ai Shan and at least some of the many temples to the god scattered over China have belonged more nearly to Taoism than to any other of the major faiths. The mountain has been a favorite objective of pilgrimages. On it are many shrines and through the ages millions have toiled to its summit. As a protection against evil spirits, too, stones professing to be from T'ai Shan have been frequently placed where one street debouches into another to frighten away the demons who seek there a thoroughfare.

To many modern observers the features of the state cult which have to do with sacrifices and religious ritual may well seem uncritically superstitious. Alongside them, however, must be set the ethical emphasis of Confucianism. Officials, from the Emperor down, exhorted those subject to them to observe the moral principles of the sages. Much of this, to be sure, was a platitudinous hypocrisy which deceived no one except the very simple. However, the sincerity which Confucius stressed was by no means entirely lacking. Even though a minority, there were untold numbers, some of them among the educated and powerful and some of them in the humble walks of life, who embodied to a remarkable extent the virtues which the sages had stressed. Throughout the land the Confucian virtues were lauded and set a standard of conduct which exercised a profound influence.

As we have seen, the state had a system of religious and moral education which reached the great bulk of the Chinese. Of this the frequent and regularly performed ceremonies constituted an important part. The preparation for the civil service examinations, based as it was upon the Confucian Classics, directly reached hundreds of thousands in each generation and, by the prestige accorded the holders of literary degrees, invested the Confucian precepts with a halo of sanctity. Official proclamations and, under the later Ch'ing Emperors, the public reading of the Sacred Edict afforded additional channels of familiarizing the populace with orthodox moral standards. Among the duties stressed by the Sacred Edict were care for one's parents, harmony and forbearance in the family and clan, reciprocal helpfulness in the community, the assistance of neighbors in a calamity, courtesy, thrift, foresight, the attempt to reconcile disputants and so to allay litigation, the avoidance of talebearing and of pride, assistance to schools, the eschewal of gambling and thieving, and reverence toward Heaven. The motives appealed to, it may be noted, were largely prudential—the present welfare of oneself and that of society and affection to one's parents. There was no threat of punishment or promise of reward in a future life and no especial appeal to the will of Heaven.

HONORS TO ANCESTORS

It is by no means clear whether what is usually known as the worship of ancestors should be classified under Confucianism. As we have seen, temples to and ceremonies in honor of ancestors long antedated Confucius. Many ideas and practices by no means Confucian in their origin came to be grouped around conceptions of the future life and ritual for the dead. In this development Buddhism and Taoism had a very large share. Popular superstition and animism made extensive contributions. Yet it is probably due more to Confucianism than to any other one factor that the cult of the dead has loomed so large in China. Certainly it is to Confucianism that it has owed a large proportion of its ceremonies and characteristic concepts. Many of the rites for death, mourning, and burial, for instance, have been taken from the ancient writings which Confucianism regards as its Classics and which it had no small share in creating and preserving.

No other phase of Chinese religious life has been more prominent than the ceremonies for the departed. They constitute, indeed, one of the outstanding characteristics of Chinese culture and have been an integral part of that most potent of Chinese social institutions, the family. No attempt to understand the Chinese can be anything but imperfect without at least a brief description of them.

In a country so large as China variations in practices and beliefs associated with the dead are inevitable and even a general description runs the risk of being partially untrue for a particular community or may be such a combination of what has existed in several different localities that it will not give an exact picture of what takes place in any one of them.

In general, the dead have been supposed to be dependent upon the living for their weal or woe. Ceremonies in honor of ancestors, moreover, have had a decided utility in helping to tie together the family and the clan. Their maintenance, therefore, has depended upon a mixture of motives—respect and affection for the departed, fear, the desire for the prosperity of the living, and social usefulness. There have entered, too, the binding influence of custom and the desire so to conduct the ceremonies as to win the good opinion—or perhaps the envy—of one's neighbors. In the hearts of some, respect and affection for the dead have doubtless been the predominant or even the only motive. Possibly a larger number have kept up the ceremonies simply from the desire to conform to the customs of civilized society and have had no confidence that through them good would accrue to the dead or that the dead would be able to bless or injure the living. Probably the majority, however, have been moved by a more or less strong belief that through the prescribed ritual the dead are benefited and are induced to aid the living.

Theories as to the location of the departed have not been uniform, but in general it has been believed that the soul of the deceased is to be found in three places at once, or, perhaps more correctly, that each man has three souls. Each of the dead goes to the future world to be judged and is assigned either to a heaven or to a hell—a conception probably of Buddhist provenance, although likewise to be found in later Taoism. Each also is to be found both in the grave and in the ancestral tablet. The popular idea has it that there are many restless spirits who either because of some ill fortune or crime while still in this life or through neglect of the living wander about doing harm to men. The idea of the transmigration of souls which entered with Buddhism is also to be found, but not so much in the foreground as in India.

The ceremonies for the dead sometimes begin even before life has departed. The dying person may be taken off the bed or *k'ang* on which he is lying, for fear that if this is not done his spirit will later haunt it, and the curtains of the bed may be taken down to prevent his rebirth as a fish. Frequently, too, an attempt has been made to call back, *viva voce,* the soul of the dying. Sometimes a hole has been broken in the roof to facilitate the exit of the soul. Notice of the death is placed on the door, and announcement may formally be sent, possibly by a procession, to the local God of the Soil, and the following day the soul of the dead may be brought back from the shrine.

The coffin has perhaps been prepared months or years in advance (although usually so only in case of the rich). Often, indeed, it has been a mark of affection for one's parents to present them with coffins, and so give them assurance of provision for a worthy burial. The body, properly washed and dressed in mortuary robes, is placed in the coffin with fitting ceremonies and the lid sealed. Near by is set up a temporary tablet.

Buddhist and Taoist priests may be called in and, by chanting from their sacred books, assisted perhaps by a drum or gong or orchestra, help the soul of the deceased through possible sufferings. Visits of condolence are formally paid by friends and ceremoniously received.

The actual burial may be delayed for months or even years, pending the selection of a fortunate site for the grave and the determination of an auspicious day. Upon these is held to depend much of the happiness of the dead, and, in consequence, of the prosperity of the living. The funeral is usually as elaborate as the means and the status of the family allow—or more so. The funeral procession includes the coffin, in some sections a huge image to frighten away evil spirits, Taoist or Buddhist monks, possibly (formerly) the holder of a civil service degree to conduct the ceremonies, musicians, a tablet for the soul, a large picture of the deceased, mourners, and insignia setting forth the honors of the dead. Attendants may include beggars hired for the purpose. In at least some places, indeed, this has been regarded as a prescriptive right of beggars and to disregard it might induce violence. Before the procession starts food and incense may be placed before the coffin and the chief mourners make their ceremonial prostrations to the deceased. Along the route of the cortège paper money may be scattered, presumably to keep evilly disposed spirits from snatching away the soul of the dead. At the grave some of the insignia, a paper house with paper clothes, servants, and other accessories to comfortable living may be burned, the supposition being that these are thus transferred to the spirit world, there to be at the disposal of the deceased. Ceremonies, too, are conducted. A dot is placed on the character 王 on the ancestral tablet, making it 主—preferably (in former days) by some official or holder of a literary degree. The placing of this dot is, presumably, the act which fixes the tablet as a habitation of the soul. These ceremonies, it will be seen, had their origin in various sources. Some of them, however, have been conducted according to the older Confucian works, especially the *I Li* and the *Li Chi*.

Mourning has been governed in part by customs handed down through Confucianism. It has also been partly determined by later traditions and rules. Its duration and intensity have varied with the degree of relationship. For a parent it has theoretically been three years and in current usage a good deal less—running into the third year after death and defined by the *Li Chi* as twenty-five months, but usually in practice about twenty-seven months. For part of this period the hair has been allowed to go uncared for, and marriage, ostensibly forbidden, has taken place only when celebrated with no public festivities. Mourning clothing has been worn. Formerly, as a sign of loyalty and grief the widow might hang or drown herself, and this act, possibly carried out with some ceremony and graced by the presence of a magistrate, might be recognized by the Emperor with an honorary tablet or *p'ai lou* (arch). Some of the Ch'ing rulers attempted to discourage the practice, but they were by no means completely successful.

Prominent in the cult of the dead has been the *shên chu,* called by foreigners the ancestral tablet. In the home of the eldest son and, usually, of the other sons has been customarily a tablet to a deceased father, and on it as well the name of the mother and, perhaps, of the sons. There may also be tablets to other near relatives and to the founder and principal member of the clan. For these there may be a special niche or, if the family can afford it, a room or even a building in the home. Sometimes they are in the main reception room. Before these tablets incense may be burned daily and offerings of food placed on stated occasions. Important family events, such as betrothals, are announced to them, and before them, at a marriage, the wedding couple make their *kotow.* Prayer may be offered them for help in emergencies and lots be cast before them.

Many clans had and have ancestral temples. These, as we have seen, had their prototypes in the religious practices of very early historic times. Many of them are sumptuous. They are managed by the elders or a group elected by the various branches of the clan, and they and the ceremonies in them have usually been maintained by endowments. These endowments may be used not only for the upkeep of the temple but for the support of the aged, the poor, and the widows of the clan and for other family purposes. In the temple may be several halls separated by courts and the whole surrounded by a high wall. In one of the halls are tablets to the deceased male members of the clan. These are arranged on steps, those of the same generation on the same step, the oldest being on the highest with that to the founder of the clan in its center. A poorer member of the clan may be in constant attendance and keep incense continuously burning and light candles before the tablets twice a month. Once a year, at the time of the winter solstice, there is held in the ancestral temple a major ceremony, with a sacrifice. The custom is supposed to go back to pre-Confucian times and its ritual to be of great antiquity. Its perpetuation has formed part of the tradition of the Confucian school. A similar sacrifice may be held on the occasion of a funeral. The clan takes the opportunity of the annual ceremony to meet and transact business. A hall in the temple may be used for a school, and the temple, too, may become a court of justice in which the clan pronounces judgment on one of its members.

Many other practices have been connected with the cult of ancestors. About New Year's time the dead may be welcomed to the homes from the ancestral temples and then, a few days later, be formally sent back to their customary abodes. At Ch'ing Ming, the great spring festival, the graves are cleaned and repaired and offerings made of food and incense. Other occasions, such as the birthday of the deceased, may also be commemorated by a special ceremony and offering.

It can readily be seen that the cult of progenitors has had important social results. It has formed a bulwark of that outstanding social and economic unit, the family, it has made for the conservation of much of the past, it has been a means of moral and social control, and it has acted as a check on individualism. As a factor in molding Chinese life and thought, it can hardly be exaggerated.

BUDDHISM

As we have seen, ever since the T'ang Buddhism in China has been suffering from a slow decline. Up to the very present, however, it has continued to have a prominent place in the life of the country. Its monasteries and shrines are still numbered by the tens of thousands. In Hangchow alone (one of the strongest Buddhist centers, to be sure, and hence not typical) a survey made in 1930–1931 disclosed the existence of nearly a thousand of them. It has been almost inextricably intertwined with folklore and with much of literature and art.

Through the interpenetration of religions by one another and the eclecticism so characteristic of China, the Chinese who can be called exclusively Buddhist have been almost entirely confined to the ranks of the professionals—the monks and the nuns.

The monks, known as *ho shang* or, when a teacher of the Buddhist law, *fa shih*, have been estimated to number between somewhat less than half a million and a million. The total for the nuns is very much less, probably only a few thousand.

The majority of the monks are drawn from the poorer classes, but some come from well-to-do and educated families. Many have been purchased in childhood by the monastery from indigent fathers and mothers who find thus a small fee for themselves and an assured livelihood for the son. Some have entered as the result of a vow made by a parent seeking healing or fearing death. Others enter as adults, drawn by one or more of several motives—the desire for a livelihood or for protection from punishment for crime, the wish in old age to prepare for death, disillusionment and the consequent longing for escape from the world, and the hunger for peace and for light on the mystery of existence.

The novice, on entering the monastery, is given a course of instruction. If a child, he is usually entrusted to the tutelage of one of the monks, is taught to repeat *memoriter* portions of the sacred writings, and learns the services by participating in them. Insistence upon careful instruction varies with the monastery. The majority of monks are content with knowing a greater or smaller portion of the ritual and with being able to repeat some passages from the sacred books. They do not necessarily have much comprehension of the principles of their faith. Many of them, indeed, perhaps the majority, display an abysmal ignorance of them. Some, however, probably a small minority, are very learned, and monks of dignity and beauty of character who have meditated long and earnestly on the problems of life are by no means completely lacking.

Admission to the monastic community, or, as it may be called, ordination, is by three stages. First the candidate is received into what may be termed the novitiate by simple ceremonies in which he takes the ten primary vows—among them the promises not to take life, steal, be unchaste, tell lies, or drink intoxicating liquors. Next he enters, by further vows and ritual, the state of what in Hinayana Buddhism is known as the *arhat* (in Chinese *lohan* or *a-lo-han*), who, it will be recalled, is seeking salvation for himself. Last of all, in accordance with Mahayana conceptions, he assumes the vows of a *bodhisattva* (in Chinese *p'u-t'i-*

sa-t'o or, for short, *p'u-sa*), to seek salvation not only for himself but for others. Part of this last ceremony is a test of the candidate's ability to endure the suffering which he is supposed to have undertaken for others and consists of burning cones of incense in rows on his scalp. The scars of this ordeal, plainly visible on his shaven pate, throughout his life afford tangible evidence of his calling. At least in certain periods of China's history, ordination could be legally administered only by heads of monasteries who had been given imperial permission, and these were comparatively few. The fully qualified monk is given a religious name and a document certifying to his status. The latter assures him a welcome in other Buddhist monasteries. In addition to the ordained monks, the monastic community may include lay brethren who do much of the menial and manual labor.

The monk is supposed to conform to certain standards of conduct. He is to remain unmarried, is to eat no flesh, and, of course, is to observe the vows taken at the various stages of his ordination. His dress is conventional and traditional—grey, orange, or yellowish brown in color, with ornate vestments for some of the services. As a rule, monks have been regarded by the populace with mingled fear and contempt—fear because of their supposed influence over the spirit world and the dead, and contempt in part because they have failed to assume the duties of marrying and rearing children so much honored by Confucianism and so necessary to the maintenance of the family and the ancestral cult. The ignorance and idleness of many of the monks have accentuated the popular disdain—although the occasional scholar or saint commands respect. In moral character some are markedly unworthy, but the average appears not to be much if any below that of the community at large.

A very few monks practice extreme asceticism—perhaps shutting themselves up for years in a small cell with a minimum of food, or inflicting on themselves such a physical mutilation as burning off a finger. The bodies of some of the deceased monks who have practiced asceticism or who have been regarded as especially holy are embalmed, painted, and gilded, and displayed to be reverenced by the faithful. It may be added that usually the corpses of monks are cremated. With interesting conformity to Chinese usage, ancestral tablets may be set up for the dead members of the community and may perhaps be preserved in a special hall.

For support the monks no longer depend upon peripatetic begging with an alms-bowl. Most of them are attached to monasteries, temples, and shrines. Income is derived partly from endowments, partly from offerings, including those of women praying for sons, and partly from fees for the performance of ceremonies, largely for the dead. The endowments are usually in land and some give the impression of being large. Buildings may be erected by gifts from officials and bear the name of the donor prominently inscribed. Collections may be solicited and the name of each giver with the accompanying amount placed on a posted list. The motive appealed to may be merit or fame.

The monasteries may be either in towns and cities or in the country. If in the country, beautiful natural surroundings have usually been chosen for them—perhaps a mountain valley or a hillside—and trees have been encouraged to grow up about them. They vary greatly in size and, naturally, somewhat in interior arrangement. The organization customarily includes a head or *fang chang* who corresponds roughly to the abbot in a Christian monastery, and the division of the monks into two groups, one charged with secular affairs—the reception and care of guests, purchases, and the administration of funds and other property—and the other with the religious duties of the establishment, such as religious instruction, and the ordering of the services and of meditation. The daily services are usually two or three in number—if the latter, one early, one at midday, and one in the evening—and consist of such features as invocations, praises, and the recitation of chapters from the sacred books, as a rule with the assistance of musical instruments, such as bells, drums, cymbals, and especially the "wooden fish" which is a customary part of the equipment of the worship hall. At appropriate times during the service the participants kneel, stand, and march in a processional. Frequently there are sacrificial offerings of rice and tea. Special services are held on stated days, of which there are several each month. Meditation has its part in the life of the monastery, especially since the Ch'an school remains prominent, and often a special hall is devoted to it. However, in spite of the fact that in many instances it is practiced conscientiously, all too often it is formal and perfunctory. The dormitories or other sleeping rooms for the monks are sometimes very comfortable and occasionally, in spite of the rule, the monks have individual possessions.

The number and arrangement of buildings, halls, and images vary from sect to sect and from monastery to monastery. The usual outline of the monastery is a rectangle surrounded by a wall. Along the sides may be cells for the monks, guest-rooms, the dining hall, storerooms, and the like. Crossing the quadrangle transversely and separated by courts may be three halls. In the one nearest the entrance are customarily found four menacing figures, two on each side of the hall, each of a different color, and known collectively as the Four Heavenly Kings (*Ssŭ T'ien Wang*). Each is supposed to govern one of the continents which lie in the direction of the four points of the compass from Mt. Sumeru, the center of the universe. Their fierce demeanor does not inspire fear in the instructed believer, but rather confidence, for they afford protection to and bestow happiness upon the faithful. In the center of this first hall is an image of Maitreya (in Chinese, Mi-lo-fo), fat and laughing, and commonly called by foreigners the Laughing Buddha. This statue, it may be noted, is the conventionalized portrait of a Chinese monk of the tenth century who claimed to be an incarnation of Maitreya. He is the bodhisattva who, after the law has been forgotten and the world become corrupt, is to come and establish on earth the lost truths of Buddhism. Back to back with Mi-lo-fo, usually separated from him by a screen, is Wei-t'o, a bodhisattva, the protector of monasteries, represented as panoplied in full armor and armed with a sword. The worshiper, having passed these encouragements to his faith, now proceeds to the second and main hall, where are represented the leading truths and figures of Buddhism. In the place of honor is generally either one great image, usually that of the historic Gautama Buddha (or, perhaps, Kuan-yin, "The Goddess of Mercy," or O-mi-t'o-fo) or a trinity of images called "The Three Precious Ones" (San Pao) or "The Three Great Venerable Ones." If a trinity, the ideas or persons represented by the images may vary. They may be the historic Buddha flanked by O-mi-t'o-fo (Amitabha, also called A-mi-t'o or A-mi-t'o-fo) and the "Healing Buddha" (Yao-shih-fo) or by two other buddhas or bodhisattvas, or they may be the Buddha, the Law, and the

Community. Gautama Buddha is not always a member of the trinity. Behind the screen which backs these central figures may be an image of Kuan-yin, who is sometimes depicted as rescuing people from peril. Lining the wall of the central hall may be statues of the Eighteen Lohans, or Arhats—listeners to and profiters by the Buddhist doctrine. Or there may be statues representing the thirty-two points of personal beauty attributed to the Buddha, or the Twenty Devas (Gods). The main hall may also contain shrines to other gods, some of them Chinese, or to buddhas or bodhisattvas. Ti Tsang, the so-called Lord of Hell, or Ruler of the Dead, may be one of these. Between the first and second halls may be another one containing a statue of some bodhisattva, such as Kuan-yin or Ti Tsang, or, perhaps, images of the Five Hundred Lohans. As a rule the third hall, in the rear, called the Fa T'ang, or Hall of the Law, has only smaller images and is used by the monks for their regular services or for teaching and preaching to the laity. On the altars in front of the images are likely to be candlesticks, incense-burners, flowers, and dishes for the offerings of food. Some monasteries include a hall for meditation and may have separate buildings for the library and for other purposes. Vivid portrayals of the tortures inflicted in the Buddhist hells may be presented. The heavens with their joys may also be depicted. The Wheel of the Law is often featured. Not infrequently there is a pool stocked with fish, to be fed by the pious as an act of merit and as a symbol of their care for all sentient beings. Such animals as pigs or cows may be kept for the same purpose. The monastery, then, is designed not only for the residence and use of the monks but also to present to them and to the laity the main features of the teaching of Buddhism and thus to be an aid to understanding and practicing its doctrines.

As will have been noticed in the preceding paragraph, the beings revered by the Chinese Buddhists fall into several categories. There are gods, some of them of foreign, usually Indian, origin, and some indigenous. They are not so highly regarded as are many other beings, for they have not attained nirvana and are still subject to metempsychosis. They may even be reborn into a lower state than man. There are the "patriarchs," notable among them Bodhidharma, the reputed founder of the widely prevalent Ch'an school. There are the lohans. The more honored of these number eighteen, earlier sixteen, although the names included in the eighteen vary. As we have seen, however, five hundred of them may be represented in a temple. Those held in greatest reverence and most widely popular are the buddhas and bodhisattvas. It is taught that there have been many buddhas. Naturally the one most generally represented is Gautama or, more frequently in Chinese Shih-chia-fo or Shih Chia-mou-ni (Shakyamuni), the historic founder of the faith. As a rule he is represented as seated on a lotus in the attitude of meditation, sometimes as recumbent (the "Sleeping Buddha") when, at the time of his death, he was entering nirvana, and, less frequently, as an ascetic, emaciated and unkempt. Probably even more popular is the Buddha Amitabha (O-mi-t'o-fo), through faith in whom, according to the widely prevalent teachings of the Pure Land (Ch'ing T'u) sect, entrance is to be had at death into the Pure Land, or Western Heaven. The repeated invocation of his aid is supposed to be efficacious in the achievement of this desired result, so that his name has probably been uttered in China more often than has that of any other honored by Buddhists. P'i-lu-fo (Vairocana), the incarnation of Buddhist doctrine, and early connected with the T'ien T'ai school, is often represented. Yao-shih-fo, revered as the God of Healing, is popular. Kuan-yin, the "Goddess of Mercy," is probably the most widely worshiped of the bodhisattvas. Originally a male figure, an Indian god, Kuan-yin is almost always represented as female, although the male form survives. Mythical stories are told of her life. She is regarded as the embodiment of womanly virtues, of beauty, mercy, and gentleness. Frequently images place a child in her arms. She is especially revered by women, and her statue is often in women's apartments. She is thought, for example, to grant children. Those of any age or of either sex may seek from her deliverance from danger and she is much honored by mariners as their patron. Representations of her often show her rescuing those in peril— from the sea, from wild beasts, or from other distresses. Ti Tsang, rather incorrectly called the God of Hell, is in reality a bodhisattva who has delayed entering nirvana that he may deliver souls from the torments of hell. He is, accordingly, much prayed to. It may be noted in passing that what are called Buddhist hells might better be denominated purgatories, for residence in them is not necessarily permanent, even though prolonged, and souls, having passed through their punishment, may have deliverance from them. The Bodhisattva Wên-shu (Manjusri) is regarded as the embodiment of wisdom. P'u-hsien (Samantabhadra), the "all gracious," usually depicted as riding on an elephant, is a bodhisattva who is highly thought of. The list might be much lengthened.

Both of the two main divisions of Buddhism, Hinayana (Chinese *Hsiao Shêng*) and Mahayana (Chinese *Ta Shêng*), as we have seen, have made their influence felt in China and have more or less coalesced. Mahayana, however, has decidedly predominated. The Chinese enumerate ten schools or sects of Buddhism which either have originated or have gained a following in the country. However, at least four are no longer to be found in China, though their influence is supposed to persist, and no new one has come into existence for centuries. Those that remain have partly interpenetrated one another and have had some of their lines of separation blurred. Professed adherents of more than one school may be found living peaceably together in the same monastery. This failure to produce new divisions and this dimming of distinctions is due chiefly not to carefully reasoned and vigorous tolerance but to haziness in thinking and flabbiness of conviction and is further evidence of the decay of the faith. Accounts of the origin and chief tenets of the more influential of the sects have been given earlier and need no repetition. In monasteries the Ch'an is still the most widespread. A large majority of the monks belong to it. Among the monks T'ien T'ai is probably next in importance. Among the laity the Pure Land school is by far the most popular.

Buddhism in China has a vast literature. Its canon is called in Chinese the *San Tsang* (*Tripitaka*). In the standard collections are both Hinayana and Mahayana works. It is divided into *Ching* (*Sutras*); *Lü* (*Vinaya*), largely on asceticism, ritual, and monastic discipline; *Lun* (*Abhidharma*), largely philosophy; and *Tsa*, miscellaneous works. The *San Tsang* ought probably not to be called a canon in the strict sense of that word, but rather a collection of standard works. Twelve collections have been made by imperial order, the last in the eighteenth century, and each differs somewhat from the others, either through the addition or through the compression or complete deletion of works, or both. The *San Tsang* contains over a thousand works. In addition there is an extensive literature, most of it for popular consumption and much of it ephemeral.

Buddhism has owed part of its appeal to its use of specific mountains as objectives for pilgrimages and as monastic centers. Just how this came about is not quite clear. It may have been due somewhat to Indian tradition, quite possibly it was in part an outgrowth and adaptation of the pre-Buddhist Chinese worship of the spirits of the mountains and the hills, and it is also probably a development from the Buddhist practice of building monasteries on mountain sites where remoteness from other human habitation favors quiet and meditation. Many mountains and hills have been thus utilized by Buddhism, some of them, like T'ai Shan, regarded as peculiarly sacred long before the coming of Buddhism. However, four centers especially have been occupied by Buddhism and are *par excellence* its holy places. These are Wu T'ai Shan, in Shansi, Chiu Hua Shan, south of the Yangtze in Anhui, P'u T'o, an island off the coast of Chêkiang, and Omei Shan, in Szechwan. On Wu T'ai Shan Lamaism is conspicuous, for Mongolia, a stronghold of that cult, is not far away. Wên-shu is the patron bodhisattva. Chiu Hua Shan is sacred to Ti Tsang. On Omei, the highest of the four, P'u-hsien is the most prominent bodhisattva. On one side the summit of Omei breaks off into a precipice thousands of feet deep and from its edge a circular rainbow, the "Glory of Buddha," can sometimes be seen, most impressive to simple pilgrims. P'u T'o is a very attractive mountainous island, held sacred to Kuan-yin.

Buddhism exerts its influence upon the laity in a variety of ways and touches their lives at many points. That it has such a hold is obvious, for the support of the large body of monks and the erection, maintenance, and repair of the shrines depend ultimately upon them. There is a good deal of education of the laity in Buddhist tenets—partly through popular literature, partly through stories which gain currency as folk tales, and partly through pilgrimages and religious ceremonies.

One source of Buddhism's power is the belief that through the friendly offices of Buddhist divinities present evils are to be avoided and desirable goods of this life to be obtained. Thus not many years ago a portion of a monastery was repaired by the funds given by a wealthy man in gratitude for a dream in which Kuan-yin warned him not to take a river steamer on which he was planning to embark and which sank with a heavy loss of life. Such blessings as sons and recovery from illness are prayed for. Another source of its hold is the determining influence which can be exerted through Buddhism upon the soul's lot after death. The reincarnations and, especially, the heavens and hells in which popular Chinese Buddhism believes have been made graphic to the multitude through literature, pictures, sculpture, and ceremonies, and have found their way into folklore.

The incentive to the conduct which Buddhism lauds is largely found in the effects of good and bad deeds upon one's state in a future existence. The acquisition of merit which may later be effective is one of the strong inducements to the founding and maintenance of the many charitable organizations so characteristic of Chinese life—for supporting nurseries, building bridges, repairing roads, giving medicine to or providing coffins for the poor, and the like.

Assurance of a happy state in the life beyond the grave is obtained by repeating prayers and observing vegetarianism. Certificates—passports to heaven—may be purchased from Buddhist clergy by those who have performed these acts of devotion. Souls of the dead may be assisted by the living. Thus services believed to be efficacious in hastening the delivery of the dead from torment are conducted by the monks on payment of a fee. One of the most picturesque of Chinese festivals, that of care for departed spirits, has an especially Buddhist flavor. It may well be of pre-Buddhist origin, and if so is another instance of the manner in which Buddhism has identified itself with native customs. The belief is that once a year, in the summer, on the first day of the seventh month, souls are released from the Buddhist hells or purgatories and come back to earth. In private homes food and paper money are provided and incense and candles burned for them and public ceremonies on their behalf are conducted by the monks. The festival culminates fifteen days after its beginning, when the spirits are supposed to return to whatever abode may now be appropriate for them.

Many homes have a shrine or shrines to Buddhist divinities.

Pilgrimages to Buddhist sacred places are popular, especially to the sacred mountains. Printed directions exist for comportment while engaged in them, a special garb may be worn, incense-burners may be carried, songs may be sung, and, in some instances, the pilgrim may prostrate himself at every step. Societies often exist for the conduct of pilgrimages, aiding and directing the pilgrims and sometimes supported by what in effect is compulsory taxation. By a pilgrimage properly performed special merit is believed to be acquired or a vow fulfilled for the healing of the participant or one of his kin.

Many of the numerous religious associations of lay people to be mentioned later have a partially or even purely Buddhist character. Some are vegetarian, requiring their members to abstain from the taking of life and, as a corollary, from eating meat. Some burn incense. A few enjoin celibacy, and others are for the reading of a particular Buddhist writing or for the repetition of a prayer or prayers or of the name of some divinity.

It is, then, not only among the monks and nuns that Buddhism has an influence, but also upon a large proportion of the masses of the nation. Even those who never support its ceremonies or read its writings are more or less unconsciously influenced by it—possibly in their conceptions of the life after death or in their ethical standards. Even to-day, after all the changes brought to the country by the irruption of the Occident, Buddhism is a force with which to reckon.

TAOISM

In many ways Taoism in the past few generations has been not nearly so vital in China as has Buddhism. Its organization is not so strong, it is much more encumbered by unintelligent superstition, and there has not been so much scholarship in the ranks of its devotees. It has been, too, in many ways a slavish imitation of Buddhism. In its priesthood, its canon, with hundreds of volumes written in the form of Buddhist sutras, and in its acceptance of the idea of transmigration and of karma, Taoism has copied the foreign faith. For all that, however, Taoism has had and still has a profound influence, an influence which its very addiction to popular superstitions has probably strengthened.

As in the case of Buddhism, the only ones who can in the strict sense be termed Taoists are the professionals, or *tao shih*. Some of these are anchorites who through meditation and ascetic practices seek immortality. Others are celibates living in monastic communities. The number of the latter is much smaller than that of the Buddhist monks and nuns. Like Buddhist monks, they may have entered the community either as children through purchase or the donation of parents, or as adults from weariness of the world, or from the hope of escaping the consequences of a crime, or from the desire for an assured livelihood, or from the longing for immortality and a solution to the riddle of existence. Much more numerous than the celibates are those who marry and do not live in communities but in their own homes and who support their families on fees received for saying services for the dead, writing charms, communicating with the dead through automatic writing, or exorcising evil spirits. Entrance to the ranks of the professionals seems usually to be through an apprenticeship to some accredited member.

The *tao shih* have had a sort of national organization. At its head has been one whom foreigners have usually called the "Taoist Pope," but who to the Chinese is known by titles sanctioned by former Emperors, *T'ien Shih* (Heavenly Preceptor), *Chên Chün*, or *Chên Jên*. These *T'ien Shih* claim descent from Chang Taoling, a worthy of the Han dynasty reputed to have been an outstanding expert in Taoism and a master of its alchemy and magic. To the *T'ien Shih* is attributed, among other things, great power over evil spirits, and charms from him are regarded as having extraordinary efficacy in expelling them. The guardian deities of the province and prefecture are supposed to receive their appointment from him. It is said, too, that in each province the *tao shih* have a head man.

Sometimes classified with the Taoists are witches, *wu,* called among other designations *tao nai nai* and *hsien nai nai,* both showing a possible Taoist connection. They are believed to be possessed by familiar spirits, to fall into trances in which they hold communication with spirits, and to be able to cure disease by charms or other devices. It seems probable, however, that they have had an origin quite independent of and earlier than Taoism and that they ought not strictly to be thought of as belonging to it.

One of the characteristics of Taoism is the means which it prescribes for the achievement of immortality. Here Taoism has been much like Buddhism. Primitive Buddhism could hold out hope for salvation only to those who followed the rigorous road of the arhat. Taoism, too, in earlier days offered blissful immortality only to those select few who were willing to pursue the exacting course necessary to its achievement. Even up to our own day there have been those who have sought to follow this way. The regimen has consisted in meditation on Taoist truths, the cultivation of such Taoist attitudes as inaction and placidity, said to be characteristic of the Tao, carefully regulated breathing, diet, discipline, moral living, and partaking of substances supposed to prolong life, such as seeds and resin of evergreens like the pine and fir, products of such other trees and plants as the plum, and certain minerals and jewels—gold, jade, and the pearl. Yet along with the achievement of immortality has gone a belief in hells, derived from Buddhism. The hells, usually closely resembling their Buddhist prototypes, are often vividly depicted in Taoist temples and the ceremonies of the *tao shih* are supposed to be potent in obtaining the release from them of luckless souls.

Taoism, too, has its gods. Many of these it shares with the state cult, partly because some of them have come down from the remote past of China out of which both Taoism and the state religion arose. Its pantheon and iconography have been profoundly influenced by Buddhism. The Taoist gods may be honored in temples, the latter probably originally suggested by Buddhist shrines. The highest god of Taoism is usually said to be Yü Huang ("The Jade Emperor" or, less accurately but more commonly in English, "The Pearly Emperor") or Yü Huang Shang Ti. He has, indeed, been thought of by many of the masses as the supreme god of all the universe. The Taoists also have a trinity, the San Ch'ing ("The Three Pure Ones"), possibly suggested by the Buddhist trinities. The persons in this trinity may vary, as they do in those of Buddhism, being sometimes Lao Tzŭ, Yü Huang, and the ancient mythical ruler P'an Ku, or some other combination. Another Taoist trinity called the San Kuan ("The Three Rulers" or "The Three Officials") is variously said to be composed of Heaven, Earth, and Water, and of the three famous legendary (or perhaps mythical) rulers Yao, Shun, and

Yü. A god sometimes ranked by the Taoists as the Supreme Being is Yüan Shih T'ien Tsun ("The Original Heavenly Revered One"). There is many another god, sometimes a personified idea, such as T'ai I ("The Great Unity") to whom temples are erected, sometimes a purely mythical being, such as the Goddess of the North Star, and sometimes a deified human being. Then, too, the Taoists talk of *Shêng Jên,* or Holy Men, who inhabit the highest heaven, of *Chên Jên,* or Ideal Men, who dwell in the second heaven, and of *Hsien Jên,* or Immortals, whose customary home is the third heaven. The *Hsien Jên* are also said to live in remote corners of the earth, especially on the K'un Lun, in Taoist myth the central mountains of the world. They are represented as having once been real men, and are supposed to appear at unpredictable intervals to perform deeds of mercy, such as the healing of disease. Eight of the Immortals, the *Pa Hsien,* the lists of whose names vary, are held in especial honor and provide favorite subjects for stories and representations in art.

Taoism possesses a voluminous literature from which extensive selections have been published, corresponding roughly to the Buddhist *San Ts'ang.* The *Tao Tê Ching* continues to be a favorite object of study and meditation. Another widely revered work, of which copies have often been gratuitously distributed, is the *Kan Ying P'ien* ("Book of Rewards and Punishments")—although it must be added that many Chinese do not connect this with Taoism. In some of this literature a high standard of morality is taught which reënforces much of that inculcated by Confucianism and Buddhism.

THE RELIGION OF THE MAJORITY

The great majority of the Chinese, as we have repeatedly seen, have not been exclusively Confucian, Buddhist, or Taoist. They have been influenced by all of these systems—in ethical standards, in conceptions of the universe and of divine beings, and in beliefs about the future life. Moreover, there has been much more than Confucianism, Buddhism, and Taoism in the religious ideas and practices which have prevailed among the majority: the religion of the masses has not been just a composite of these three faiths. The additional elements have had in them a great deal of animism. Indeed, more than one foreign observer has declared animism the basic and characteristic religion of the Chinese. They have also contained much of polytheism—a polytheism augmented by the state cult and by Buddhism and Taoism, but which in its list of deities is much larger than the sum of all three of the other pantheons. There has been not a little of divination and of the observance of lucky and unlucky days. It may also be proper to classify with popular religion the pseudo-science, *fêng shui,* although the correctness of this can be challenged.

The belief in and the attempt to propitiate or in other ways to control or ward off spirits is, as we have seen, of great antiquity in China—as in so many other parts of the world. In popular belief *kuei*—evil spirits or demons—are all about us and are of many kinds and shapes. They may have eyes on the tops of their heads. On occasion they may take the forms of animals or even of men and women. A *kuei* may be in a man-eating tiger. Great numbers of stories are told of animals—*kuei*—who can take at will the body of a man or especially of a beautiful woman and in that guise work harm. *Kuei* may be in old trees, or in clothes, in objects of furniture, or in mountains or stones. Leaves driven before the wind may each be a *kuei*. *Kuei* are responsible for all sorts of evils and misfortunes. They lurk in ponds and rivers to draw people in and drown them. Indeed, one theory has it that the *kuei* of a drowned person remains in the place of the tragedy and can obtain release only by luring some hapless wight to a similar fate. The *kuei* of a mother who dies in childbirth wins surcease from anguish by bringing on some other woman the same demise. Insane persons are controlled by *kuei*. An epidemic of *kuei* may visit a city—in the old days cutting queues, and striking people on the streets. By committing suicide a man may, as a *kuei*, haunt the person whom he believes to have hounded him to the act. *Kuei* may be responsible for illnesses of various kinds. They may bring bad crops and famine.

Kuei are associated with the *yin* principle of the universe. It will be remembered that for many centuries—just how long is uncertain—the Chinese have identified with the *yin* and the *yang* the two elements of the dualism which they have regarded as running through all nature. The *yin* and the *yang* have pervaded much not only of popular lore but of the philosophy of the learned. The *yin* stands for Earth, the moon, darkness, evil, and the female sex. On the *yang* side are Heaven, the sun, light, fire, goodness, and the male sex. *Kuei* are, accordingly, supposed to be *yin*. *Kuei* are opposed to *shên*—the latter a name which includes the gods—and *shên* are supposed to be associated with the *yang*. According to a widely prevalent conviction, every man, or practically every man, has in him both a *kuei* and a *shên* corresponding to the *yin* and the *yang* which pervade men as they do the rest of nature. At death, so at least one conception has it, the *shên* goes to the skies while the *kuei* remains earthbound—patently a source of vast numbers of *kuei*.

Since popular belief insists that all about us are these *kuei*, usually invisible, but always a potential cause of all kinds of misfortune and evil, it becomes of the greatest importance to discover and utilize means for warding them off or expelling them. For this there are many devices. Buddhist monks and especially *tao shih* may be called in to exorcise them. For that same purpose the images of gods, particularly of some gods, being *shên* and *yang,* may be carried in procession through the streets or brought to a house. Some of the processions have been community undertakings, the cost being defrayed by popular subscription which custom has made obligatory. Anything associated with *yang* or in which the *yang* element is strong may have potency. Firecrackers and gongs may be employed. The cock, as the morning herald of the sun, is regarded highly and his blood and head are utilized. The peach, as one of the earliest trees to bloom in the spring under the impulse of the returning sun, is also *yang*. Strong and good men are full of *yang* and their pictures or images may put the *kuei* to rout. Officials are supposed to embody the *yang*. Good deeds are a safeguard and passages from the Classics may be recited. Charms may prove effective. Among the latter are papers inscribed—often by a *tao shih*—with magic characters or symbols. They are to be affixed to a door or to some other part of the house, or they may be burned and the ashes mixed in water and drunk. Amulets may be carried, perhaps made of the stone or wood of the peach, and in manufacturing beds peach-wood has often been employed. Mirrors may be worn on the forehead, especially of a child, the theory apparently being that a *kuei*, approaching with evil intent and seeing the reflection of his own ugly face, will be frightened away. Copper cash strung together in the form of a sword may be effective. Certain written characters have been supposed to be particularly efficacious in insuring well-being. Among those frequently employed are *fu*, which may be translated as happiness or good fortune, and *shou* (longevity).

The customs concerned with the *kuei* might be described at great length, for they have entered and, although somewhat weakened in places, still enter extensively into the folklore and life of the masses. For the average man they have probably been fully as important as the more highly rationalized and organized systems of Confucianism, Buddhism, and Taoism.

A belief in certain mythical creatures has had a large place in the popular mind. These do not belong exclusively in the field of religion but at times are objects of reverence and even worship. The *Lung*, or "dragon," is the most familiar. He is regarded as benevolent and is associated with the *yang* and with rain, clouds, and water. As the *Lung Wang*, or "dragon king," the *Lung* has been very widely worshiped and temples have been built to him. There is also the *Fêng-huang* (*Fêng* being the male and *Huang* the female), usually called in English the phoenix, a creature sometimes described as having the head of a hen, the eye of a man, the neck of a serpent, the viscera of a locust, the brow of a swallow, the back of a tortoise, and a tail like that of a fish but with twelve feathers. From time to time in Chinese history it has shown itself, usually as the harbinger of some political event. It is full of *yang*. Then there is the *Ch'i-lin*, *Ch'i* being the male and *Lin* the female. Like the *Fêng-huang*, in appearance it presents a somewhat bizarre composite of several creatures. Because of its single horn it is generally called in English the unicorn. It is gentle by disposition and as a rule is seen only in times of good monarchs. With the *Fêng-huang* it is believed to have a good deal to do with the coming of children and the popular regard for it rests largely upon this phase of its activity. All three—the *Lung*, the *Fêng-huang*, and the *Ch'i-lin*—come down from very early historic and possibly from pre-historic times and so have been long intimately connected with the Chinese mind.

The Chinese have had a great many divinities which do not, strictly speaking, belong to any one of the three major cults, although, with the eclecticism and syncretism so characteristic of China, they may be appropriated by any or all of them. Some are probably of purely native origin, others may be importations, and still others probably were originally local gods in non-Chinese territory but were adopted by the Chinese as the latter extended their domains. Their name is legion, and even to attempt to enumerate them all would not only prolong this chapter unduly but would result in an incomplete list. Many of them have only a local vogue and the representations of and stories about the others vary from place to place. Paper representations of them are popular and have an extensive sale. Among a few that may be mentioned are the Kitchen God (practically universal in the home), the Fire God, the God of Wealth, the God of Medicine, the Goddess of Smallpox, gods adopted as patrons by various crafts and guilds, and a god who is supposed to protect fields against insects and who, accordingly, may be invoked to drive away locusts. Many of these have been represented as historic personages, deified in the course of later generations. In some parts of the country peculiar trees or stones are worshiped.

This account may leave the impression that the religion of the majority has been chaotic, uncritical, and an inconsistent jumble of beliefs and practices of varying origins. This is in part correct. Along with all the diversity, however, has gone a widespread feeling of unity—that the world, both seen and unseen, is, after all, a universe, and that there is one Power or Being who ultimately controls it and to whom appeal may be made. In the will of this One, conceived of as righteous, there has been a good deal of quiet trust. This One has been believed, in the long run, to even up the inequalities of life, in an individual or a group, averaging the bitter with the sweet. For example, the High God of the people, known and revered all over China, is *T'ien Lao Yeh*, or *Lao T'ien Fo Yeh*, or *Lao T'ien Yeh*, personalized Heaven, God, or Providence. This sense of unity may be due to Taoism and Confucianism. Probably, however, it is older than either and owes its perseverence only in part to them. Moreover, there has been a good deal of determinism in the popular mind, a kind of fatalism which bows calmly to the inevitable, conceived of more or less dimly as the will of the inscrutable Power which governs the affairs of men. The determinism seems in part to be a Buddhist contribution—a belief that one's present state is due to the sum of one's deeds in earlier existences. It may also be derived from Confucianism.

FENG SHUI

Whether, as has been said, the set of beliefs and practices called *fêng shui*—literally, wind and water—should be classified under religion may be a matter of debate. Whatever its pigeon-hole in an orderly account, it has played and, to a diminished extent, still plays an important part in Chinese life.

Fêng shui is based upon the belief that in every locality forces exist which act on graves, buildings, cities, and towns, either for the welfare or the ill of the quick and the dead. The object of *fêng shui*, therefore, is to discover the sites where the beneficent influences predominate, or so to alter, by artificial means, the surroundings of existing sites that the same happy results may be achieved. To attain these ends advice is sought from specialists in *fêng shui*.

Among the factors with which *fêng shui* reckons are the *yang* and the *yin;* the *ch'i* (sometimes translated breath) pervading the universe and of which there may be two divisions, the *t'ien ch'i*, or *ch'i* of Heaven, and the *ti ch'i*, or *ch'i* of Earth; the four creatures—the azure dragon, the white tiger, the black tortoise, and the red bird—associated with the four quarters of the heaven; wind (bearing water or drought); and the five traditional elements (metal, earth, fire, water, and wood), especially water. When it comes to the actual choice of a site, experts in *fêng shui* often differ widely as to the worth of a particular locality—a lack of agreement which the sceptical hold up to derision. There appear, however, to be some general principles upon which the decision is supposed to be made. An ideal site is protected on the north (from which the *yin* comes), is open to the south (associated with the *yang*), has water flowing in such a way as partly to encircle it but not so directly away from it as to drain off the good influences, and possesses some natural feature, such as a hill or hummock, in the direction of the dragon (on the east or left) stronger than that of the tiger (on the west or right). Some natural object, such as a hill, or some building, especially a high building, in front of a site—even some distance away—may do serious damage. A straight road, such as a railway, may also work much harm by permitting the good influences to drain away. On the other hand, an otherwise unpropitious site may be improved by such devices as a pool, a hummock of earth, a pagoda, charms, or the picture of a dragon.

Fêng shui has been especially used in determining the locations for interments. Stories abound of families which have been ruined because the grave of an ancestor had an unfavorable *fêng shui* and of others which have prospered because of a fortunate location of ancestral remains. Whole cities, too, are said to have had their fortunes improved by the construction of a pagoda on expert advice, and a neighborhood to have been badly damaged by some high building or flag-pole, such as Westerners have been wont to erect.

DIVINATION AND FORTUNE-TELLING

It is probably also debatable whether such activities as divination, fortune-telling, and the discovery of lucky and unlucky days should be grouped under religion. Here, again, however, whatever their relations, they have long been prominent in Chinese life and, although somewhat shaken by the contacts with the West, remain so.

Each individual is supposed to have his fate in part determined by the year, month, day, and hour, or simply the year, month, and day, on which he was born. Each of these is indicated by a certain combination of one of the ten "heavenly stems" and the twelve "earthly branches." The result is either eight or six characters which must be consulted by the fortune-teller in determining such matters as betrothals. There are lucky and unlucky days for marriages and funerals, for commencing building operations, or for beginning a journey. Among the many factors which may be taken into consideration in determining whether and when to enter upon a particular course of action are the five elements, the animals supposed to be identified with the twelve "earthly branches," and combinations of the two, the calendar with its lucky and unlucky days (formerly published by imperial authority), the *pa kua* (eight trigrams) which form the basis of the *I Ching* and which from prehistoric times have been utilized by diviners, and the *I Ching* itself. There were or are many ways of fortune-telling—among them the inspection of the physiognomy, the choice of a slip of paper by a bird and the interpretation of the picture or characters on the slip by the soothsayer, and the casting of lots by any one of several devices.

RELIGIOUS SOCIETIES

Societies with a religious purpose have been one of the most interesting features of Chinese life. Often they have been secret —partly because proscribed by the state—and many have had a political or social objective in addition to their religious purpose. Some have been very widespread and powerful and have even broken out into violent uprisings. They are often syncretic, combining Buddhist, Taoist, Confucian, and, occasionally of late years, Christian elements. Some of them have insisted upon a high standard of morality for their members and often those in which Buddhism predominates have required vegetarianism and have been the expression of an earnest religious quest. Among the many societies have been the *Pailien Chiao,* or White Lotus (or Lily) Society, which incorporated religious elements but was primarily political and repeatedly gave rise to rebellions; the *Tsai-li Chiao,* which forbade to its members opium, wine, and tobacco, but not meat, and which took over many Buddhist, Taoist, and Confucian features, but was also suspected of being the *Pailien Chiao* under another name; the *Hsien-t'ien Chiao,* or Preceding Heaven Society, which discouraged ancestor worship and idolatry, exacted of its members a pledge to keep the five commandments of Buddhism, including that against the taking of life, and met in small groups for the reading or recitation of Buddhist texts; the *Chin-tan Chiao,* which made much of universal love and the immortality of the soul; and the *Shên Chiao,* also called the *Wu Chiao,* or Sect of the Magicians, which sought to expel *kuei* and to perform acts of magic. Some of them have endured for centuries and others have had a very short existence. The last thirty years have seen a good many founded, flourish for a time, and then wane. Among these have been the *Tao Yüan,* for the cultivation of the inner life, the receiving of messages through the planchette, and philanthropic activities, and the *Tao-tê-hsüeh Shê* which sought to unify all religions, revered the God of All Religions, and met weekly for worship and lectures.

MOHAMMEDANISM

Outside the main stream of Chinese religious life, forming separate religious communities, are the Moslems. In previous chapters we have seen something of the history of Islam in China—

that it first entered in the T'ang but made a very slight impression, and that it became much stronger under the Yüan, thanks largely to foreign soldiers and commanders of that faith who were introduced by the Mongol rulers. During the Yüan it established itself especially in Yünnan, through Moslem commanders. It came in from two directions—brought by way of the sea by merchants to the coast ports, particularly in the South, and overland through the Northwest by Moslems from Central Asia and Sinkiang. Moslems appear to have increased greatly under the Ch'ing—perhaps because of the conquest by that dynasty of so much of the West, where they abounded. Certainly, as we have seen, they rose in several serious rebellions.

Just how many Moslems there are to-day in China is uncertain. Conjectures have ranged all the way from three to eighty millions. What appear to be conservative estimates place the total somewhere between four and ten millions, the true number seeming to be more nearly the latter than the former figure. Moslems are to be found in every province, but are most numerous in Sinkiang and in the North and West of China proper, particularly, as might be expected from their history, in Yünnan, Sinkiang, Hopei (Chihli), and Kansu.

By their fellow Chinese, Moslems are regarded as a distinct and separate group, like the Mongols or the Manchus. They are most frequently called the *Hui-hui,* a name of debatable origin, but possibly derived from Uighur. This classification as a distinct race is not without justification. Some of the Moslems show clearly in their features their non-Chinese ancestry. The majority speak Chinese, but often with some dialectical differences from non-Moslems. Some, too, follow distinctive occupations; in parts of the country, especially the Northwest, the inn-keepers, caravan leaders, those taking charge of horses, and, indeed, any who have to do with transportation, are likely to be Mohammedans. Butchers and leather-workers are often Moslems. However, the cleavage is by no means always distinct. Many converts have come from among the Chinese, partly through the adoption by Moslems of Chinese children, partly through intermarriage, and partly through adult Chinese entering the faith under the influence of Mohammedan officials and of army officers who have had command over them. Nor are occupational and dialectical differences always apparent. The process of assimiliation by which the Chinese have absorbed so many other alien elements is at work.

In religious practices Moslems largely preserve their separation from those of the Chinese about them and maintain those common to their fellow believers in other lands. Usually they do not use pork and tend to abstain from opium and, probably to a less extent, from alcoholic drinks. They repeat the creed, fast during the month of Ramadan, give alms to their own poor, and some few of them make the pilgrimage to Mecca. They refrain from the use of idols and maintain their own worship, in Arabic (although occasionally in Chinese), in mosques. The mosques show the influence of Arab architecture.

Yet even in their religious life the Moslems show marked effects of their Chinese environment. Usually they are not at all fanatical. As a rule only their religious leaders and teachers pray five times a day. Generally, too, it is only these who understand Arabic. In many Moslem families abstention from pork remains the one distinctive practice. A large proportion of the mosques are without minarets and as a rule the public call to prayer is omitted, at times by order of the government. Occasionally Moslems make contributions to pagan observances, such as community processions in which images are carried through the streets. They may use incense in their services. Those who served under the old régime often participated in the religious ceremonies of the state cult which formed part of the duties of their office. Even Mohammed has been represented as a sage of the Confucian type and as conforming to the Confucian virtues.

CHANGES WROUGHT BY THE COMING OF THE OCCIDENT

These, then, are the main outlines of the religious life of the Chinese on the eve of the great changes brought by the impact of the Occident. As has been suggested, much remains but little altered. However, some profound modifications have occurred. Since the chief of these have been mentioned in earlier chapters they need here only be summarized.

Very important has been the growing influence of Christianity. The thousands of Christian foreign missionaries, Roman Catholic and Protestant—with a very few from the Russian Orthodox Church—have been one of the outstanding features of the invasion of the West. In every province missionaries are to be found, and in almost every important city and in many villages churches have been erected, schools organized, and hospitals or dispensaries maintained. Manifold philanthropies have been undertaken and Christian literature has been spread broadcast. The number of professed Christians, while above the three million mark, is less than one per cent. of the total population and is not an adequate measure of the effects of the missionary enterprise. The percentage of Christians, especially of Protestants, prominent in the life of the nation, particularly in politics and education, is far out of proportion to the size of the Chinese church. Through men like Sun Yat-sen, educated at the hands of missionaries and an avowed Christian, Christianity has exercised in the shaping of the new China an influence which it is impossible to measure accurately and yet is certainly very great. The new medical profession owes its foundations chiefly to Protestant missions, and leadership in modern education—especially higher education—was long largely in Christian hands.

Yet upon the religious life, in the strict sense of that term, of the great masses of non-Christians, Christianity seems to have made but slight impress. Here and there a society which seeks to syncretize the various faiths has included Christianity in its purview. In Shansi an organization officially sponsored by the "Model Governor," Yen Hsi-shan, as a substitute for the former state cult as a means of inculcating virtue, strikingly displayed the influence of Christianity. The New Life Movement, sponsored by Chiang Kai-shek, arose in part at Christian suggestion. Some of the methods of the Kuomintang youth corps were taken over from Christians. The impact of Christianity, too, has been in part responsible for the decay of the older forms of polytheism and animism. Yet the non-Christian religious systems display no such extensive adaptation of Christian methods and ideals as do Buddhism in Japan and some forms of Hinduism in India. That may be, of course, because the existing systems in China do not possess as much vitality as do these others and so are not live enough to adjust themselves. Undoubtedly, too, there exist imponderable consequences of Christianity which defy measurement. Whatever the cause, the fact remains that Christianity probably has not had such large results in philosophy and in religion outside the boundaries of its organization as it has upon some other phases of China's life. In these other phases—education, philanthropy, public health, physical education, medicine, and moral and social reform—Christianity is probably the most potent of the religious factors of the China of to-day. In many places in China a marked increase in welfare projects is noted and this, although often not under the Christian name, seems largely due to Christianity.

Another result of the coming of the West, as we have seen, is that the state religion and with it Confucianism have disintegrated. Within the brief compass of less than a decade the abandonment of the civil service examinations followed by the collapse of the monarchy removed two of their strongest supports. Various attempts have been made to bolster up the old system. The new curricula for the schools adopted by the state under the Republic have included attention to the classical books of Confucianism. There have been sporadic revivals of such state sacrifices as have lapsed—and by no means all official sacrifices were immediately discontinued with the coming of the Republic. Yüan Shih-k'ai, for instance, resumed the annual ceremonies on the Altar of Heaven in Peking. For a time, too, much was made of Kuan Yü by the military authorities. Various private associations of scholars long maintained the accustomed ritual in many of the Confucian temples, and vigorous effort was not lacking to win for Confucianism adoption as the official cult of the Republic. An attempt was made by K'ang Yu-wei, followed up especially by Ch'ên Huan-chang, to establish a Confucian church. In Shansi Governor Yen sought new forms of preserving the Confucian ritual and of inculcating the Confucian virtues. None of these efforts, however, has been able more than temporarily and locally to stem the tide. At times even the rites in honor of ancestors have been neglected—the women being much more diligent in maintaining them than are the men. Confucianism as a cult has suffered more than has Buddhism, Taoism, animism, or Islam. Yet as a factor in molding ethical ideals and attitudes toward life it has remained potent and even dominant. Witness many of the public utterances of Chiang Kai-shek.

Buddhism has shown some resilience. Thanks partly to impulses from Japan, where Buddhism is not so nearly moribund as in China, Chinese Buddhism has displayed movements which have sought to purify and revive it. Many monasteries and temples have been renovated, Buddhist societies have been organized, much effort has been expended in circulating literature, the ordination of monks continues, and popular lectures have been delivered. The outstanding leader has been the able and earnest T'ai Hsü.

Since the coming of the Republic, China has experienced a widespread movement away from religion. Some of this is due to a general reaction against old forms and beliefs which is inevitable when a great group of mankind departs from its past. Much of it is to be accounted for by contacts with the religious scepticism and indifference of the modern Occident. Among its leading exponents have been returned students from the West. Many of its leaders have been in France and have been influenced by Positivism. It seeks salvation for this life rather than the life beyond the grave and expects it to be achieved through scientific rather than religious processes. Not a little of it comes from militantly anti-religious Soviet Russia. Some of it is a continuation of the native religious scepticism which has had such a long history. Much of the neglect of religion is due to the disintegration of the social and political institutions and the intellectual patterns with which religion has been associated. Some has been a concomitant of the destruction wrought by civil strife and foreign invasion.

Opposition to religion has come in waves. One of these, at the inception of the Republic, was directed primarily against the native cults. Another, in 1922, was chiefly anti-Christian. Still another came with the rise to power of the Kuomintang, was especially sponsored by the radical elements of that party, and was prominently but by no means entirely anti-Christian. In districts where Communism prevails the lands held as endowments of monasteries and temples have largely been confiscated.

More subtle than open opposition but no less destructive to religion is an indifference which arises from the tacit assumption that the real goods of life are to be won by other than religious means. In this again China is largely conforming to the climate of opinion in much of the modern West.

The movement away from religion has affected all faiths, although in varying degrees. During the fighting of 1926 and 1927 troops occupied many of the buildings belonging to Christian missions. Most of these were later evacuated. The physical equipment of other faiths has not fared so well. Since at least as early as the Revolution of 1911-1912 religious properties of various kinds have been secularized. The diversion of temples to non-religious purposes greatly increased with the political disturbances and anti-religious movement of 1926-1927 and the years immediately thereafter. Some temples simply disappeared. Others were used as schools or barracks. Still others became apartment houses, rice markets, rickshaw stands, or auto terminals. In many the images of the gods were allowed to remain with a few priests to serve them, although most of the building was secularized. In one provincial capital, by 1931 out of one hundred and seventy-five temples examined only three were being used exclusively for worship and only one temple had been erected within three years. In some other sections a revival of religious interest came after 1927 or 1928 and expressed itself in part in the repair or building of temples. The old faiths are hard hit, but none of the major ones is as yet completely dead nor is the early demise of any assured. In many districts most of the customs are observed much as they have been for generations. Especially in rural areas do the traditional religious practices persist. It is in the cities and among the intellectuals that they have been most weakened. It is interesting, too, that partial adaptation to new *mores* is seen in the manufacture and burning of paper automobiles as part of the provision made by relatives for the comfort of the dead.

Fêng shui has also suffered with the influx of Western ideas and practices. Railways and highways have been constructed, streets widened and straightened, graves removed and placed in common cemeteries, and telephone and telegraph poles placed and high buildings erected in utter disregard of its principles. Yet belief in it dies hard, and many instances of its survival can be given.

Nationalism must also be noted among the changes in religion. Much of it has had a religious tinge. The cult of Sun Yat-sen introduced by the Kuomintang but later allowed in large part to fall into abeyance contained religious elements and was the result of the attempt to give unification under the Kuomintang the support of a quasi-religious enthusiasm for a national hero.

The new China lacks such a unifying philosophy as Confucianism once furnished. Nationalism only in part fills the void. The dearth leaves many individuals sadly adrift and unhappy and is imperfectly met by an exaggerated individualism. It may prove a serious handicap to the reintegration of the nation and to the realization of a coherent, creative culture. In the middle of the third decade of the present century, as a phase of the New Tide Movement, or Renaissance, a lively debate over philosophies occurred, although without much that promised the appearance of any new virile school. Even that has largely subsided. Philosophically and religiously young China is wandering and only feebly or uncertainly struggling for a way out, and displays much of shallow, imperfectly thought out materialism and pragmatism. As yet nothing, unless it be Christianity, is emerging from the chaos which holds nearly so much of promise for the future as did the intellectual ferment of the Chou.

BIBLIOGRAPHY

Many of the chief sources in Chinese for the study of the religion of the country have already been mentioned. The main translations of the leading Confucian Classics were given at the end of Chapter II.

Among the translations of Buddhist works are S. Beal, *A Catena of Buddhist Scriptures from the Chinese* (London, 1871), with selections chosen to illustrate various periods in the history of Buddhism; S. Beal, *Texts From the Buddhist Canon Commonly Known as Dhammapada* (London, 1878); T. Suzuki, *A'Svaghosa's Awakening of Faith in the Mahayana Doctrine* (2d edition, Shanghai, 1918); W. E. Soothill, *The Lotus of the Wonderful Law* (Oxford, 1930); and W. Gemmel, *The Diamond Sutra (Chin-kang-chin) or Prajna-Paramita* (London, 1912). Accounts of Chinese Buddhist literature are in Prabodh Chandra Bagchi, *Le Canon Bouddhique en Chine, Vol. I, Les Traducteurs et les Traductions* (Paris, 1926); Bunyiu Nanjio, *A Catalogue of the Chinese Translation of the Buddhist Tripitaka* (Oxford, 1883); E. Chavannes, *Cinq Cent Contes et Apologues. Extraits du Tripitaka Chinois* (3 vols., Paris, 1910, 1911); A. von Staël-Holstein, *Kaçyapaparivarta, A Mahāyānasūtra of the Ratnakūta Class, edited in the Original Sanskrit, in Tibetan and in Chinese* (Shanghai, 1926); R. Gauthiot, P. Pelliot, and E. Benveniste, *Le Sutra des Causes et des Effets du Bien et du Mal, édité et traduit d'après les Textes Sogdien, Chinois, et Tibétain* (2 vols., Paris, 1920, 1926).

Translations of such basic classics of Taoism as the *Tao Tê Ching* and *Chuang Tzŭ* are in James Legge, *The Texts of Taoism* (Oxford,

1891) in *Sacred Books of the East*. There are many translations of the *Tao Tê Ching*. On Chuang Tzŭ see Fung Yu-lan, *Chuang-Tzu* (Shanghai, 1932). H. A. Giles has a rendering of Chuang Tzŭ in *Chuang Tzŭ, Mystic, Moralist and Social Reformer* (2d ed., Shanghai, 1926). L. Wieger, *Taoisme* (2 vols., Hsien hsien, 1911–1913) has translations of the *Tao Tê Ching*, Chuang Tzŭ, and Lieh Tzŭ, and contains a list of the Taoist canon.

Many books in Western languages cover Chinese religion in general. One of the largest is J. J. M. de Groot, *The Religious System of China, Its Ancient Forms, Evolution, History, and Present Aspect* (6 vols., Leyden, 1892–1910), based upon a scholarly study of Chinese texts and upon observations, largely in the vicinity of Amoy. De Groot has two much smaller books, *The Religion of the Chinese* (New York, 1910) and *Religion in China* (New York, 1912). There should also be noted his *Sectarianism and Religious Persecution in China* (2 vols., Amsterdam, 1903, 1904). A brief general survey, largely used, is W. E. Soothill, *The Three Religions of China* (London, 1913). A brief survey, by a Chinese Christian, is in Y. C. Yang, *China's Religious Heritage* (New York, 1943). M. Granet, *La Religion des Chinois* (Paris, 1922) deals chiefly with early Chinese religion. H. A. Giles, *Confucianism and Its Rivals* (New York, 1915) is not always free from bias. Under a somewhat misleading title, J. L. Stewart in *Chinese Culture and Christianity* (New York, 1926) has given a good summary. Henri Doré, *Recherches sur les Superstitions en Chine*, is a sixteen volume work by a Jesuit missionary, largely on current practices and profusely illustrated, and translated in part into English by M. Kennelly as *Researches into Chinese Superstitions* (8 vols., Shanghai, Tusewei Press, 1914–1926). A short popular account of certain phases of popular religion by a distinguished scholar is L. Hodous, *Folkways in China* (London, 1929). A valuable study of some phases of religion in one Chinese city is J. K. Shryock, *The Temples of Anking and Their Cults. A Study of Modern Chinese Religion* (Paris, 1931). E. D. Harvey, *The Mind of China* (New Haven, 1933) deals largely with animism and with popular religious sects and practices. Among other general books deserving mention are J. Legge, *The Religions of China* (London, 1881), C. E. Plopper, *Chinese Religion Seen Through the Proverb* (Shanghai, 1926), W. J. Clennell, *The Historical Development of Religion in China* (London, 1881), E. T. C. Werner, *A Dictionary of Chinese Mythology* (Shanghai, ca. 1932), and E. H. Parker, *Studies in Chinese Religion* (London, 1910). L. Wieger, *Histoire des Croyances Religieuses et des Opinions Philosophiques en Chine* (Hochienfu, 1917), contains a mass of material but is lacking in critical discrimination. An English translation appeared in 1927 at Hochienfu. See articles on China, Confucian Religion, and Taoism in *Encyclopædia of Religion and Ethics* (J. Hastings, editor). E. T. C. Werner, *Myths and Legends of China*, should also be mentioned, as must L. Wieger, *Folk-lore Chinois Moderne* (Hochienfu, 1909). Other interesting studies are Feng Yulan,

A Comparative Study of Life Ideals (Shanghai, 1925); A. Forke, *The World Conception of the Chinese* (London, 1925); and H. G. Creel, *Sinism. A Study of the Evolution of the Chinese World View* (Chicago, 1929). A summary of Chinese philosophic development is in E. V. Zenker, *Geschichte der Chinesischen Philosophie* (2 vols., Reichenberg, 1926). Modern Chinese mythology is treated by Henri Maspero in J. Hackin and others, *Asiatic Mythology,* translated by F. M. Atkinson (New York). A study of popular religion, partly contemporary and from direct observation, is C. B. Day, *Chinese Peasant Cults* (Shanghai, 1940).

On Confucianism and the state religion, in addition to the translation of Confucian texts, mentioned above, and the accounts in the general books already given, see J. K. Shryock, *The Origin and Development of the State Cult of Confucius* (New York, 1932), and T. Watters, *A Guide to the Tablets in a Temple of Confucius* (Shanghai, 1879). On T'ai Shan, see E. Chavannes, *Le T'ai Chan. Essai de Monographie d'un Culte Chinois. Appendice. Le Dieu du Sol dans Chine Antique* (Paris, 1910).

On Buddhism in China there is a large bibliography. Sir Charles Eliot, *Hinduism and Buddhism, An Historical Sketch* (3 vols., London, 1921) contains one of the best historical accounts. K. L. Reichelt, *Truth and Tradition in Chinese Buddhism* (3d edition, Shanghai, 1930) is by a Christian missionary who has made a prolonged and sympathetic study of Buddhism, but in places is uncritical. One of the best brief accounts is L. Hodous, *Buddhism and Buddhists in China* (New York, 1924). Another is in H. Hackmann, *Buddhism as a Religion* (London, 1910). Interestingly written, and by a recognized scholar, is R. F. Johnston, *Buddhist China* (New York, 1913). L. Wieger, *Bouddhisme Chinois* (2 vols., Hochienfu, 1910–1913) contains a great volume of material, some of it very useful, but compiled with little critical acumen. J. B. Pratt, *The Pilgrimage of Buddhism* (New York, 1928) is very readable, devotes a large part of its space to China, is chiefly valuable for current conditions, and, while not by an expert on China, is by an authority on religion. Some of the main members of the Chinese Buddhist pantheon are described in A. Getty, *Gods of Northern Buddhism* (Oxford, 1914). An older, general book by a Christian missionary is J. Edkins, *Chinese Buddhism* (London, 1893). Another is E. J. Eitel, *Handbook of Chinese Buddhism* (Hongkong, 1883). C. H. Hamilton, *Buddhism in India, Ceylon, China and Japan. A Reading Guide* (Chicago, 1931) contains a good outline and a selected bibliography . See also J. Prip-møller, *Chinese Buddhist Monasteries* (London, 1937), by an expert on architecture. For more technical studies there are also E. J. Eitel, *Handbook of Chinese Buddhism. Being a Sanskrit Chinese Dictionary with Vocabularies of Buddhist Terms in Pali, Singhalese, Siamese, Burmese, Tibetan, Mongolian, and Japanese* (2d edition, Hongkong, 1888); O. O. Rosenberg, *Introduction to the Study of Buddhism According to Material Pre-*

served in Japan and China. Part I. Vocabulary: A Survey of Buddhist Terms and Names Arranged According to Radicals with Japanese Readings and Sanskrit Equivalents (Tokyo, 1916); W. E. Soothill and L. Hodous, *A Dictionary of Chinese Buddhist Terms with Sanskrit and English Equivalents and a Sanskrit-Pali Index* (London, 1937); Hôbôgirin, *Dictionnaire Encyclopédique du Bouddhisme d'après les sources Chinoises et Japonaises* (first two fascicles, Tokyo, 1929); J. J. M. de Groot, *Le Code du Mahayana en Chine. Son Influence sur la Vie Monacale et sur le Monde Laique* (Amsterdam, 1893). On the identity of the image of Maitreya with that of a Chinese monk, see Helen B. Chapin, *The Ch'an Master Pu-tai* (*Journal of the American Oriental Society*, March, 1933, Vol. 53, pp. 47–52). A translation of portions of a famous popular Buddhist allegory which was put in the form of a novel is A. Waley, *Monkey. Wu Ch'eng-an* (New York, 1943).

Most of the material on recent Taoism is chiefly either in the general books on religion in China, mentioned above, or in special articles. The same is true of the religion of the masses. On T'ai Shan, see D. C. Baker, *T'ai Shan* (Shanghai, 1925). See, on the Chin Tan Chiao, *The Secret of the Golden Flower* (London), a translation of a German translation (1929) by R. Wilhelm of the *T'ai I Hwa Tsung Chih*.

On Islam in China, in addition to accounts in general books on religion in China, such as E. H. Parker, *China and Religion*, and L. Wieger, *Histoire des Croyances Religieuses et des Opinions Philosophiques en Chine* (of which an English translation has appeared), there are M. Broomhall, *Islam in China* (London, 1910), not especially critical; d'Ollone (and others), *Recherches sur les Musulmans Chinois* (Paris, 1911); I. Mason, *A Chinese Life of Mohammed* (*Journal of the North China Branch of the Royal Asiatic Society*, 1920, pp. 159–180); M. T. Stauffer (editor), *The Christian Occupation of China* (Shanghai, 1922), pp. 353–358; and M. Hartmann, article *China*, in *The Encyclopædia of Islam* (Vol. 1, London and Leyden, 1913, pp. 839–854).

On the Jews in China the best work, containing material from many sources and articles by several authors, is W. C. White, *Chinese Jews* (Toronto, 3 parts, 1942).

On Christianity, K. S. Latourette, *A History of Christian Missions in China* (New York, 1929) contains a comprehensive account and further references may be found in its bibliography and footnotes. Events since the completion of that work may be most conveniently found either in the files of *The Chinese Recorder* (a monthly periodical covering all Protestant missions, published in Shanghai into 1941), the late issues of *The China Christian Year Book* (published annually, with occasional gaps, in Shanghai, through 1939 (and endeavoring to cover all Protestant work), and, for Roman Catholic activities, J. M. Planchet, *Les Missions de Chine et du Japon* (published in Peking about every other year) and *Les Missions de Chine* (Shanghai, 1935–1940).

A satisfactory bibliography of recent religious movements in China outside of Christianity would be long and made up chiefly of articles in periodicals and newspaper despatches. A fairly well-rounded picture can be obtained from articles in *The Christian Occupation of China*, in the files of *The Chinese Recorder*, and in the various issues of *The China Christian Year Book* (before 1926 *The China Mission Year Book*). See also J. C. De Korne, *The Fellowship of Goodness (T'ung Shan She): A Study in Contemporary Chinese Religion* (Grand Rapids, 1941).

CHAPTER XVII

SOCIAL LIFE AND ORGANIZATION

One of the outstanding characteristics of Chinese civilization has been its emphasis upon social relations. Chinese philosophy, as we have seen, has had as a leading objective the achievement and maintenance of an orderly society. Confucianism, so long dominant in the state and in the intellectual and moral life of the Empire, has laid great stress upon right relations among human beings. In the course of the centuries the Chinese have developed many institutions and customs to conserve and perpetuate society, to give joint protection to individuals, and to facilitate the intercourse of the many millions who have formed the population of the Empire. The most extensive of these organizations, the Government, has been described in a previous chapter. Some others, especially the guilds, have also been portrayed. It remains to give an account of the more important institutions which thus far have been only mentioned. It would also seem to be in place to associate with these some of the customs and principles of social intercourse and some of the features of collective life, such as recreation and holidays, which are not readily grouped elsewhere.

It must be said at the outset that it is difficult and in many instances quite impossible to formulate generalizations which will prove applicable to all China. In spite of the tendency to uniformity throughout the country, amazing for so huge a mass of mankind, almost any statement may prove to be untrue for a particular locality. This is especially the case today, for one must reckon not only with the variations which formerly existed but with the changes induced by the coming of the Occident and which have by no means uniformly affected different districts and classes. What, therefore, may be a correct description of one community may not fit elsewhere and what may be an accurate picture of one class or individual may be quite inappropriate for another, even in the same city or *hsien*.

THE FAMILY

The basic and most characteristic Chinese institution has been and is the family. The family, of course, constitutes an outstanding feature of the life of every nation. Among the Chinese, however, it has been emphasized more than among most peoples. It has had a leading part in economic life, in social control, in moral education, and in government. The members of a family have been supposed to stand by one another in trial and distress. The indigent and the aged have been expected to be cared for by their more prosperous and younger relatives. To a greater or less extent the family has performed the functions which in the modern Occident are associated with sickness and unemployment insurance, old age pensions, and life insurance. Magistrates have held the entire family responsible for the conduct of its members. The family has been looked upon as a model for the government, and the state has been thought of as a large family. Moral education has been given largely through the family and the leading although not the only motives appealed to have been family affection, loyalty, and pride. Through the rites in honor of ancestors the family has been an important religious unit.

As we have seen, this emphasis upon the family goes back to remote ages. In historic times much of it has been due to Confucianism, for this school has made much of the institution and of the duties of relatives to one another. The organization of the family, however, has not remained constant through the centuries, but has undergone important modifications, apparently especially in pre-Han times before Confucianism became dominant. Its history would prove interesting, but too little of it is known, or at least has been put into easily accessible form, to warrant venturing into even a brief summary. However, the main outlines of the family system can be pictured as they were on the eve of the great changes brought about by the Occident and as they remain in many places to-day.

Under the term family may be included various types of organizations. There is what may be called the small family, made up of husband, wife, and children. At present this is not much if any larger than the corresponding unit in the Occident. In one market town in North China studied not many years ago it averaged a fraction under five members. Also as in the West it has not been uncommon for such a group to live by itself as a distinct household although perhaps with one or more servants and relatives as additional members. Much more generally than in the Occident, however, what may be called a family has been much larger. It has not been uncommon for several of the smaller families to dwell together under one roof or in one enclosure and have a common life. Here four generations may sometimes be found—great-grand-parents with their sons, daughters-in-law, grandsons, grand-daughters-in-law, and great-grandchildren. In this case each of the smaller units may preserve a certain amount of individual identity, with its own bedrooms and kitchen, but inevitably there has been a degree of community life, with a head of the whole, possibly a common ancestral hall, and—although this is not uniform—a common purse. The head of such a family may have autocratic power. The leadership normally passes to the eldest son, but by common consent it may be entrusted to the son adjudged most worthy. Elders, including a widowed mother or grandmother, may exert marked influence. Such large family groups have been found especially in rural areas but have by no means been unknown in towns and cities. Frequently, moreover, whole villages are made up of those claiming descent from one male ancestor and its members bear the same surname.

In a community composed of blood relations the village government may be purely a family matter, the family elder being the chairman of the village assembly, and other offices going to various branches of the family in turn. In these circumstances the public endowments used for such objects as the maintenance of roads and schools are to all intents and purposes family possessions.

Moreover, still larger groups exist, made up of those tracing their descent from one progenitor, having a common patronymic, perhaps united through an ancestral temple, but not necessarily living in one community or even in the same province.

The two latter types, and especially the last, are sometimes denominated clans, but from the standpoint of scientific exactitude the definitions of this term differ so greatly that the word must be used with caution. Each "clan" is, in turn, made up of smaller family groups.

The cohesion of the groups usually varies inversely with the size, but even in the largest there is often a strength of coöperation, social control, and community feeling unknown in the corresponding units of the modern West. For Occidental parallels one must go back to much earlier days and to such regions as the highlands of Scotland.

Of the three characters which usually make up a Chinese name, the one designating the family is written first, the second is frequently identical for all cousins of the same generation, and the third is peculiar to the individual. Sometimes the third character rather than the second is common to the same generation. Not infrequently the individual has only a second character in addition to his patronymic. Whatever the names, they are listed in the family records. It may be added that the Chinese generally bears a cognomen given him in infancy and a number of other designations, bestowed on him or assumed by him from time to time—in a manner often most confusing to the foreigner. Placing the family name first, rather than the "given name" as in the West, may indicate the manner in which in the old China the family was exalted—in contrast with the individualism of the Occident.

It must also be noted that a large number of terms have come into use corresponding to uncle, aunt, cousin, and the like, for the many degrees of relationship. These likewise are often most mystifying to the Westerner. For instance, different ones exist for relatives on the husband's and on the wife's side of the house —as, for a father's older brother, a father's younger brother, a mother's older brother, and a mother's younger brother.

The family has not been, nor is it now, of uniform strength throughout China. Nor are the forms and the customs associated with it everywhere the same. In the North, for example, the "clan" is not, on the whole, so powerful as in the South. Then, too, even before contact with the Occident brought the startling changes of the past few years with their many variations from older *mores*, some other differences existed. However, while uniformity was not complete, customs and ideals tended to be the same the country over. The almost universal acceptance of Confucianism operated powerfully in this direction, for Confucian standards of family ethics and relationships were regarded as authoritative and customs contained in the classical books which Confucianism so highly esteems were thought of as normal.

The ties binding the family together have been many. So numerous and so strong are they that it is not strange that the family has been prominent and enduring. First of all, the family has exercised certain important functions. Through it have been perpetuated the honors to ancestors stressed by Confucianism and ancient custom. Upon the maintenance of these ceremonies, as we have seen, has been believed to depend the welfare of the dead and the living. The family, too, has constituted a kind of mutual protective association. China has been a nation in which the individual has found it difficult to stand alone. In a keenly competitive society organized by groups the man who attempts to make his way unassisted is more likely than not to be crushed. The family has been and is the most widely spread of these groups. It is especially adapted to rural areas and to the villages and small towns whose affiliations with the soil are very close. Since China was and is predominantly agricultural by occupation, it is not surprising that the family has been prominent. In the larger cities it has not usually been so outstanding, and other forms of association, such as the guild, have tended to take over some of its functions. When, as has often been the case, a family has risen to importance in an urban center, not infrequently it has continued rooted in the soil through membership in a "clan" whose seat is in the country, or through possession of the favorite form of investment, farming lands. In the North, where the larger family, or "clan," generally has not been so prominent as in the South, secret societies—another form of mutual protection—have flourished. The family also, as we have seen, has often exercised some of the functions which in the modern Occident are performed by the government—such as the settlement of disputes among its members, poor relief, and the maintenance of schools. In many instances, it will be recalled, the village government itself has been a family affair.

Ethical concepts have contributed to the strength of the family. Of the five relations emphasized by traditional moral standards and reënforced by Confucianism—those between prince and minister, father and son, older brother and younger brother, husband and wife, and friend and friend—three are in the family.

Hsiao, usually translated as "filial piety," is exalted by Confucianism as one of the cardinal virtues. While it includes much more than the family, loyalty to one's parents is part of its essence. Older brothers have obligations to younger brothers, and younger brothers owe deference to older brothers. That official Confucian tract of the Ch'ing dynasty, the so-called *Sacred Edict*, was true to tradition when it made family duties primary and urged as a motive toward self-control and a righteous life not allegiance to God but to one's parents.

In such a society, the institution of marriage has been of surpassing importance. Sons are so indispensable in carrying on the family line and in maintaining the honors to ancestors that failure to have them has been regarded as a major offence against filial piety. Without sons the rites to parents cannot be continued and not only will the living be disgraced, but the spirits of the dead, deprived of such service, will be in misery. Marriage has, accordingly, been practically universal except for a few of the very poor and such special groups as Buddhist monks and nuns and Taoist ascetics. Even some of these have been married before entering the religious life. Judged by modern Western standards, moreover, marriage has taken place early. In one village in South China where customs have probably not changed greatly, a few years ago the average age for boys at marriage was seventeen and a half years and for girls about eighteen years. In a town in the North at about the same time the average age was twenty, and was less for girls than for boys. Here again the social pressure for male progeny has made itself felt, for as soon as possible sons must beget sons if family honor is to be maintained and parents be assured of a continuation of the line and of proper honor to themselves after death.

Since marriage has been so largely for the purpose of perpetuating the family and the ancestral rites, the mating of couples has been regarded as a concern of the elders and of the family even more than of the two most immediately involved. Betrothals have been arranged by the head or other members of the family, perhaps the eldest brother, and not infrequently as a result of consultation among the more influential relatives. Generally the prospective bride and groom have had no voice whatever in the arrangement and have not even seen each other until the wedding day. Betrothals have often been made when the children are very small and cannot easily be broken. They have, indeed, been almost as binding as marriage. In probably the majority of instances they have been negotiated through go-betweens. As a rule they have been contracts with provisions about property— such as the gifts which are to pass between the two n‘ ie   and the amount of furniture and clothing which the br⋯ with her. Usually, too, the gifts from the groom'⋯ e been supposed to pay for the bride's equipment. No⋯ re- quently they have been of the nature of a bride price. A wealthy father may refuse gifts from the groom's family and send his daughter to marriage with property which her husband is to manage but which is to be used toward the support of her children and the unconsumed balance of which is to go to them after her death. In the case of the poor the betrothed girl may go to her future husband's home as a servant, her parents being thus relieved of her support. A marriage cannot be contracted between persons of the same surname, even though no blood relationship exists. Provided patronymics are different, a marriage can be entered into between near relatives, as, for example, between a girl and the son of her father's sister. Some types of consanguineous marriages, however, are forbidden. For instance, even distant relatives cannot marry if they belong to different generations. Often two influential families have been allied to each other by marriage generation after generation. Usually parents have attempted to obtain for a son a wife from a family of equal or superior social standing and wealth.

Through marriage the bride becomes a member of her husband's family. She is taken to her husband's home for the wedding ceremony and part of the rite consists in an obeisance by the two before the groom's ancestral tablets. To be sure, the two make a return visit to her home where they do reverence to the tablets of her family's ancestors and soon after the wedding she makes a ceremonial visit to her old home. Her relatives, too, may bring pressure to bear upon her husband's kinfolk if she is treated with especial injustice. For better or for worse, however, a wife is linked with her husband's family. She is especially subject to her husband's mother. While that rule may prove salutary, particularly in view of the immaturity of the bride, her need of guidance and control, and the necessity of having a recognized arbiter in households which may include the wives and children of several sons, mothers-in-law can be tyrannical and make bitter the lot of their daughters-in-law.

According to the age-old standards, a husband may divorce his wife for certain specific causes—failure to bear him a male heir, neglect of his parents, a shrewish tongue, theft, jealousy, an incurable disease, and adultery. But restrictions placed by law made divorce, in practice, very rare. A wife could not divorce her husband, and divorce by her husband has been regarded as a deep disgrace. In case she has living blood relatives with considerable influence they may prevent a divorce—perhaps often more from the fear of loss of "face" or of having to support her than from affection. The divorced husband may remarry, but the divorced wife seldom if ever can do so. Both widows and widowers may remarry, but it has been considered a virtue for a widow not to do so. Then, too, a widow with sons occupies in the household a position of especial importance and usually is not tempted to sacrifice it, except because of poverty, by venturing again upon matrimony.

A man can have only one legal wife. Until recently, however, he might take as many concubines as he wished and could afford. While the new codes forbid concubinage without the wife's consent, they are not yet universally enforced. Concubinage has been and is, therefore, frequent among the well-to-do. It seems to have been most common in the families of merchants—at least in some localities. On occasion officials have been dismissed for concubinage. One of two motives has usually been responsible for the acquisition of a concubine: a man may take one in case his wife has failed to bear him a son or in case his wife's sons have died, or, his marriage having been a matter of family convenience and having failed to result in binding love, he may acquire concubines because of their personal attractiveness. Sometimes a husband has taken one or more of his wife's sisters as concubine. As a rule, however, concubines have been from families socially and economically inferior to that of the wife. Many have been prostitutes and in that capacity have first attracted the attention of their future spouse. Sometimes a concubine may be held largely as a servant. To prevent the coming of a rival a wife without male children may bring about the adoption of a son. However, concubinage, while by no means uncommon, has been practiced only in a small minority of families. The approximately equal number of men and women in the population and the poverty of the vast majority would have militated against it even had public opinion been altogether favorable. Promiscuity has been and is far more common among all classes—among the humbler with women of neighbors' families, among the prosperous with paid prostitutes.

The dissensions and jealousies which frequently accompany concubinage have been familiar features of Chinese households, even though the first and legal wife is recognized as mistress. However, a man may maintain entirely separate establishments in different places for his wife and each concubine, and if all are housed within one enclosure each woman usually has her distinct apartment and, perhaps, a somewhat separate menage. An able concubine may exert a good deal of influence, especially if she bears a son and if she has her own establishment in which she can be undisputed mistress. Usually, however, she has been regarded by the community with a certain amount of contempt and often there has been a feeling that apology must be made for her. Concubinage, while formerly legal, was often regarded as the result of moral weakness on the part of the husband or as a misfortune, even before the strong convictions which many of the younger Chinese of modern ideas have developed against it.

As has been suggested, adoption has been frequently practiced as a means of continuing the family line and perpetuating the honors to ancestors. A device by no means unknown has been to take a male child into the family after the death of an unmarried son, to go through the form of marrying the deceased son to a living bride, or, perhaps, to a dead bride, and then to regard the adopted child as the son of the departed. In this manner the family line can be maintained unbroken and the deceased be provided with an heir to carry on the rites in his honor.

As in all other nations, family life in practice has had both its lights and its shadows. In many homes the pressure of convention and the fear of public opinion have kept an outward semblance of unity, but no love has existed between husband and wife, the husband has been tyrannical and the wife a dispirited patient drudge, or the wife has been a termagant and luckless daughters-in-law have been led a life little better than slavery. There have been homes into which the husband has brought concubine after concubine, adding a fresh one as his passion has cooled toward the last, where children have grown up undisciplined and high ideals have been ignored. The arranging of marriages by the elders without consultation with the couple immediately concerned has led to unhappy situations in which the husband and wife have at best never more than tolerated each other and at the worst have lived continuously at swords' points. The practical universality of marriage has forced some, as an alternative to an unhappy and socially maladjusted celibacy, into an unfortunate union, perhaps with a physically or mentally defective mate. The communal holding of property by large families has often led to continuous friction, and the division of the property, when finally effected, has frequently left an aftermath of bitterness. When families made up of several smaller ones live together in one homestead, friction between brothers, between sisters-in-law, and between children is almost inevitable and at times becomes both chronic and acute. Moreover, not infrequently filial piety has scarcely been rendered even lip service and parents have been neglected. Then, too, the family is by no means always stable. In the case of the very poor a famine or some other economic calamity may scatter its members. Civil or foreign war may lay waste whole provinces and annihilate or break up homes. The death of a parent, especially of the father, may have something of the same effect. In the case of poorer families, daughters may be sold into what is little better than slavery, or even into prostitution.

On the other hand, there have been and are many homes in which husband and wife hold each other in profound respect and deep affection. Nor has this been so uncommon as might be expected by the Westerner who regards marriage as a relationship entered into freely by the bride and groom. In a society in which boys and girls have been prepared by their rearing to expect their elders to arrange for their mating, and in which education—especially of the girl—has fitted each to fulfill his or her part in wedded life, the existence of happy homes is not surprising. Moreover, parents with the affection for their children which has existed in China, as elsewhere, have, probably more frequently than when change has meant improvement. Along with the political organization of the Empire and its maintenance of Confucian orthodoxy, the family has been a chief factor making for a relatively static civilization. We need not here enter upon a discussion of the relative merits of such a society and of a rapidly changing one, like the modern Occident, or debate whether that movement which the West calls "progress" is really such. The difference between the two civilizations which has repeatedly been apparent in the preceding chapters is due in no small degree to the strength and nature of the Chinese family. The family, moreover, has discouraged individualism. Chinese life, as we have seen, has been in groups of many kinds, each of which has exercised a restraining influence upon its members. Of these none has been quite so strong the country over as the family. The contrast between the individualism of the modern Occident and the lack of it in the old China is striking. In China the individual did not make his own decisions. Social determinism prevented any marked development of private conscience or of moral will. With so much of life confined to and controlled by the family, adjustment to the established group and to its opinion was the supreme requirement. It was not abstract right, of which the individual must be the judge and for which he must ultimately be responsible, but expediency which governed action. The family has been a major obstacle in adopting and making effective in China some of the institutions of the modern Occident. For example, as we have seen, loyalty to the family has stood and often still stands in the way of operating efficiently such typical Western devices as the stock company and a strong government. The traditional ethics which stress devotion to one's family have often made it seem natural and moral for an official in a business concern to bring into lucrative positions as many of his relatives as possible, regardless of whether they are fitted for them. It has also made it seem right to use public office to restore the family fortunes and appoint relatives to public posts, even when to do so has jeopardized the well-being of the state. In the fierce international competition of the modern world the state tends to insist more and more upon primary allegiance to itself. Anything short of this, it believes, imperils its existence. In China the relation of prince to minister has been only one of five and not necessarily the chief. That supremacy of loyalty to the state as personified in the Emperor which has been one of the strongest elements making for the stability of the modern Japan has been conspicuously lacking. The weakening of the family which has set in here and there in modern China has not yet proceeded far enough to alter in any very large proportion of the population the impress which the institution has made.

THE POSITION OF WOMEN AND RELATIONS BETWEEN MEN AND WOMEN

Closely associated with the family system, and possibly as one of its corollaries, have been the relations between men and women and the position of women. The ceremonies in honor of ancestors have constituted a cornerstone of the Chinese family. Male progeny has been necessary if these were to be continued. For this reason boys have been regarded as more valuable than girls. To the high esteem for men other factors have contributed. From the economic standpoint boys have been preferable. Remaining in the family as they do, they are producers who throughout their working lives aid its prosperity. On the other hand, after marriage a girl is lost to the family which has been to the expense of rearing her. The centuries-old doctrine of the *yin* and *yang* has made for the higher status of men, because the *yang*, associated with good fortune and all that is desirable, has been identified with the male, and the *yin*, the element of darkness and evil, is female. Confucianism has tended in the same direction, for in addition to its emphasis upon the rites to ancestors its world has been one which men control. To be sure, Confucius paid great honor to the memory of his mother—a precedent which has helped to accord to motherhood and especially to those bearing male children a dignified and honored status. However, his example made for a separate social life for men and women and for confining to men public offices and the type of education which he gave to his disciples. It was not that he felt women to be necessarily inferior to men, but that, conforming to the existing practices of his times, he thought of the sexes as moving in quite different realms.

Social life knew no free mingling of the sexes on the basis of equality and respectability. After early childhood, boys and girls did not play together or have an opportunity to meet in any recognized and proper way. As a result prostitutes were the only women with whom men could have free and easy social intercourse. At least of late years and in one large city, this fact has tended to drive into that life some girls of ability and education who, restive under the old taboos, have sought escape from them.

Girls have been generally regarded as much less valuable than boys and sayings in common circulation appraise sons as infinitely preferable to daughters. One such proverb states in effect that the most beautiful and gifted girl is not so desirable as a deformed boy. Boys, as children, have sometimes been given girls' names to protect them from evil spirits, who, thereby supposedly deceived into believing that the child is actually a girl, and less valuable, will pass him by. Among the very poor, the killing of female infants has been by no means unknown. While statistics are lacking, it seems, indeed, to have been very common. Girls were formerly given a type of education very different from that for boys. Only relatively infrequently were they taught to read. In some families with scholarly traditions and social and official standing a tutor might be employed for the girls and a father might take pride in the literary attainments of a daughter. Schools, however, were for boys. This was only natural, for they had as their primary objective preparation for the civil service examinations—to which girls were ineligible. The education of the daughter was given in the home, usually, if there were time, by the mother, and consisted of such matters as the management of a household and the duties owed to a husband, a mother-in-law, and others of the husband's relations. Often a girl was permitted to grow up with but very little care, and such training as she had, even in her essential domestic duties, was acquired casually and incidentally, through hard experience, or under the tutelage, often harsh, of a mother-in-law. In theory the husband has been the head of his wife and the master of the home. The wife has had no property of her own, except, perhaps, some which has been assigned to her by her family at her wedding, and even that has been for the support of her offspring, has been managed by her husband, and on her death has gone to her children. In practice a wife of vigorous character has often been dominant. By bearing a son a woman acquires greater importance and as, in the normal course of events, she becomes a mother-in-law and a grandmother, she is regarded as being of more and more consequence and is treated with increasing respect. After death she shares with her husband the honors paid by her sons. A woman without a son, however, is a reproach among her neighbors and to her husband, and often without honor or provision for support in her old age. In ordinary homes, especially of most of the farmers and of the poor, girls and women have led a life of hard labor. In such households—the vast majority in China—from their earliest possible years children, both boys and girls, have been trained to work, at such tasks as watching the cattle and gathering fuel. To her duties of bearing and rearing children and caring for the home the wife has often added those of helping in the heavy labor in the fields. The wives of the well-to-do have led a somewhat easier and even luxurious existence—but have not therefore necessarily been happier. Their seclusion and idleness have encouraged them to seek solace in gambling, opium smoking, and other vices.

A custom of the old China, now fortunately passing, was binding the feet of women. The practice was almost universal—although the Hakkas, the Manchus, non-Chinese tribes, the boat population in the South, and some of the very poor did not conform with it. Its origin seems very uncertain, but it is at least several centuries old. The requirement was in no sense religious but purely a matter of social convention. A woman without small feet was regarded as disgraced and it was impossible to get a desirable husband for her. The process of binding the feet was very painful, involving as it did the compression of those members by tight bandages into as small a compass as possible. Infection and gangrene might set in and the girl might even lose her life. When the binding had once been completed the pain largely ceased, but walking was difficult, especially for those with very small feet, and the general effect upon the health deleterious. At least one of the Ch'ing Emperors tried to stop the practice, but without avail. It was not until the disintegration of old customs wrought by the coming of the West that the practice began to fall into abeyance.

SECRET SOCIETIES

The family has been the strongest universal social unit in China. However, as we have seen, it has been and is but one of several types of units. Another has been the secret societies. These have played and continue to play a very important part in the life of China, probably much more so than do the numerous fraternal organizations in the United States. Often they have had an active and influential part in politics. It is estimated that to-day about half the adult males who can lay claim to any influence are members. Almost everywhere they must be reckoned with by those who would understand the life of a community. Just how ancient are those now in existence is a matter of doubt, although some of them claim to have begun hundreds of years ago. Certainly organizations of this general type have long had a share in Chinese life. The Red Eyebrows and Yellow Turbans, prominent in civil wars in Han times, appear to have been fraternal bodies. Repeatedly in seasons of disorder others have come to the fore. Since the societies are secret, it is impossible to give a full and satisfactory account of them. Sometimes, as we have seen, they have religious features. Often they have solemn and binding vows of brotherhood, and they may have secret codes. Frequently, too, their discipline is very severe, exacting of members strict obedience to the commands of their officers. Some are to be found among the Chinese abroad and fill a prominent rôle in the lives of the emigrants. Such, for example are the *tongs* among the Chinese in the United States. These *tongs,* it may be added, seem to be peculiar to Chinese colonies in America and were, perhaps, originally organizations for legal and benevolent services to their members.

One of the most famous and powerful of the secret societies has been the *Ko Lao Hui,* or Association of Elder Brothers. It is said to have an elaborate ritual and its members are reported to take an oath of brotherhood. It is believed to have been responsible for numerous outbreaks and riots from time to time and of late years sometimes to have taken to banditry. It has been much feared and revenge visited for any violence to its members has added to the dread felt for it. Chapters of another, the Red Spears, were often started as a farmer's protective society. Then ruffians frequently obtained the weapons and the power, compelled all residents to join and pay fees or submit to their demands, struggles ensued with adjacent groups or with the authorities, and disorder was accentuated. Still another has been the Triad Society (*San Ho Hui*), also known as the *Hung* Society and the Society of Heaven and Earth. Just how far back it goes is uncertain, but it has been implicated in more than one rebellion and has probably appeared under various guises and aliases. It is organized by individual chapters as well as by a general brotherhood. Opposed to the Manchus, it was associated with the beginnings of the T'ai P'ing Rebellion. The White Lily and the White Cloud Societies are also famous. Both probably originated near the beginning of the twelfth century. Both appear to have been founded by Buddhist monks and were originally religious and Buddhist in character. Both repeatedly fell afoul of the state and were responsible for outbreaks, some of them of serious dimensions.

Secret societies have played an important part in recent politics. A large proportion of the leaders of the country belong to them. Indeed, it is said to be impossible for an aspirant for power in the state long to be successful without membership in one of them. As a rule a man joins only one and not many—contrary to the practice in the United States. A connection with more than one is said to work disadvantageously for him.

Numbers of the societies at the outset possessed no political purpose. They were religious associations, or business or benevolent organizations, for the benefit and reciprocal protection of their members. Inevitably, however, many were sooner or later drawn into politics—perhaps captured by some ambitious leader who wished to use them for his ends or regarded with suspicion by the state and proscribed and so forced into revolt, or, wishing to protect a member or members, compelled by force of circumstances to exert political pressure.

OTHER FORMS OF ASSOCIATION

There were and are associations which have remained largely or entirely non-political in character. Such have been the many societies where the religious purpose has continued dominant, the guilds, the groups for the coöperative saving and lending of money (in which every member puts in a sum—perhaps in monthly installments—and the total principal is loaned to each in turn, the order being often determined by lot), the clubs whose purpose it is to make pilgrimages to sacred mountains and to accumulate funds to make these pilgrimages possible for their members, the very widespread organizations of farmers for the protection of growing crops, the associations by which farmers aid each other in the irrigation of their fields, the coöperatives formed to assist their members in financing and performing the rites connected with death and burial, and the benevolent societies of many kinds—for maintaining soup kitchens and lodging houses for the needy, for providing coffins and burial for the very poor, for resuscitating drowning people, and for the relief of indigent widows. The benevolent societies have been largely, although by no means entirely, of Buddhist origin. For instance, the Shanghai General Benevolent Society, run by Buddhists, had an annual budget of about 500,000 *yüan* each year, buried about 30,000 bodies found in the streets and the river, and maintained "homes," hospitals, and schools.

The Chinese have, indeed, a traditional capacity for organization and mass action. Dissension there may be and often is in their many associations, but coöperation has long been the rule and they have come to act almost instinctively in that manner. Even the thieves and the beggars possess their groupings. Officials, through their underlings, have kept in touch with the thieves' "guild" in each community and have been able, on occasion, to exert sufficient pressure on it to bring about the restoration of stolen property. Experience with the boycott long antedates the nation-wide extension of the practice which of late years has been so effective against foreigners. Sometimes beggars have picketed and so prevented customers from entering a shop which has refused to contribute the customary fee to their guild. On at least two occasions the fishermen of Ningpo have been able, by blockading the river and cutting off all entrance and egress by water, to compel the officials to withdraw a tax to which they have objected. Several times a guild has used a strike or a riot to force the public authorities to rescind a regulation or an assessment which it has believed to be unjust. Group opinion, often general enough to deserve the title of public opinion, repeatedly has brought irresistible pressure upon the individual or the government. At times even the throne has had to bow to it.

Clearly, therefore, the individual who attempts to stand alone finds his path thorny. Chinese society has been and is an interplay of groups, some of them united by blood, some by economic ties, and some by political, professional, or religious interests. By the custom of "sworn brotherhood" men not otherwise bound to each other pledge reciprocal fidelity, perhaps professing to hark back for a precedent to the famous "Peach Garden Oath" taken during the Three Kingdoms by Lui Pei, Chang Fei, and Kuan Yü. It is believed that it was such a relationship which in 1898 led Yüan Shih-k'ai to reveal to Jung Lu Kuang Hsü's plan of action and so precipitated the fateful *coup d'état* of September of that year.

All these many kinds of associations make Chinese society extraordinarily complex. They are one reason why the uninitiated foreigner finds particular problems and situations in politics and business so difficult to understand. Even an intelligent Chinese frequently fails to know all the elements involved.

It is also apparent that such a society develops marked skill in effecting compromises and adjustments among its many groups and that secret parleys and intrigues flourish. Not only must the individual, if he is to succeed and often if he is even to survive, associate himself with as strong a group or groups as possible, but he must frequently be an adept at playing off one against another and at diplomacy, perhaps underhanded and tortuous. This may help to account for that foreign policy for which the Chinese Government has been noted in the nineteenth and twentieth centuries—of seeking to save itself by pitting powers against each other and entering into secret treaties. It is part of the struggle for survival in which the Chinese have been drilled from infancy. In such a society, moreover, the forthright person has often been at a disadvantage and he who would stand against convention and the group may be given short shrift.

Still another side of the picture must not be forgotten. Many, both foreigners and Chinese, regard the Chinese as rather unsuccessful at coöperation. They point out that much of existing concerted action is under the pressure of strong necessity, that in such matters as schools, bridges, and roads coöperation is either weak or entirely lacking, that many associations are inaugurated only to disintegrate almost before they have begun, that reciprocal distrust exists, that most Chinese find it impossible to believe that the organizer is acting from sincere public spirit, that joint action is fully as often for destruction or self-protection as for public welfare, and that stable working-together for purposes of public value is discouragingly rare. All this is undoubtedly true and must be remembered in an appraisal of present day China. However, the successes in coöperation are also facts. The Chinese, like other peoples, often display contradictory traits.

THE STRATIFICATIONS OF SOCIETY

In spite of the strength of the family tie and of all these many organizations, Chinese society has been characterized by a remarkable minimum of hard and fast class divisions. The sharp distinction between the aristocrat and the commoner which seems to have existed at the dawn of China's history largely disappeared long ago, probably shattered in the prolonged disorders which brought the Chou dynasty to an end and further erased by the autocrats who built the Ch'in and the Han. An hereditary aristocracy was manifestly an obstacle to the absolutism which these latter sought to establish. The bureaucracy of the Ch'in displaced the old hereditary feudalism. Feudal states tended to appear once more during the initial years of the Han, but the creation by the monarchs of that dynasty, especially by Wu Ti, of a ruling bureaucracy appointment to which was on the basis of worth rather than birth checked the movement. The continued development under later dynasties of a system of choosing officials from those who had proven their worth in the free competition of the public examinations militated against the formation of an hereditary ruling caste. At least under the Ch'ing these tests were open to the majority regardless of birth. Only members of a few occupations, such as actors, were excluded. Admission to the aristocracy of intellect which so dominated the life of the nation could be had by rich and poor alike. Incidentally, the entire family and even the city of a successful scholar shared in his fame. Under a system by which—in theory—wealth, social position, and power went to the ablest, a certain amount of fluidity existed and a general and continuous leveling process which discouraged class lines. Even when, as was usually the case, the relatives of the Emperor formed a privileged group, the whirligig of fate displaced them with another governing line. The rebellions and civil strife so characteristic of Chinese history provided an additional avenue by which men of force could come to the front, regardless of birth and even of education.

The system did not entirely eliminate the divisions wrought by heredity. Many families possessed traditions of education, good breeding, inherited wealth, and devotion to public service from which their scions derived a decided advantage in the competition in the examination stalls and in obtaining office. Members of these houses naturally were inclined to intermarry. Under the Later Han, it will be recalled, certain powerful families rooted in the Confucian tradition and interlocked by marriage for a time formed a kind of ruling class. A somewhat similar aristocracy arose in the period of division between the Han and the T'ang. Apparently through the centuries almost every community has had its "first families" who have been looked up to and accorded leadership in local affairs. This has fluctuated, as in all countries, and it is an exceptional district or town which has not known instances of the rise and fall of a great house. Indeed, it has been so usual as to become proverbial. On the other hand, a few paternal lines have been accorded recognition over the course of the centuries. Such has been that of Confucius. Moreover, the Han and succeeding dynasties by no means entirely abolished all hereditary rank. For example, the Ch'ing, although it made a fairly clean sweep of claims to titles existing at its accession, had its own nobles. A large proportion of these were Manchus, but some were Chinese. However, apparently as a safeguard against sedition through an hereditary caste, only some of the titles were granted in perpetuity, and most of these were held by Manchus. While as a rule high offices in the Empire carried with them a title or titles, and in some instances the recipient's forefathers were made to share in the award by the posthumous grant of rank for several generations back, the honors usually did not descend to the sons. The heirs either were commoners or were given titles of progressively lower degree for each succeeding generation until the family found itself once more among the undistinguished.

Major occupational groups were accorded a certain traditional gradation. Scholars came first, as might be expected in an order whose theory it was that society should be controlled by those educated in the lore and the virtues of civilized humanity. Teachers were regarded as one of the five objects of worship—the others being Heaven, Earth, the Emperor, and parents. In ancient times the soldier and the scholar were ranked together under the same term. Next came the farmers, for they produced the food upon which mankind depended for sustenance. Third were the artisans, for they also were producers. Merchants were classified as fourth, for they made their profits by exchanging the fruits of other men's toil. Officials belonged to the scholar class and often felt it beneath them to intermarry with families engaged in trade.

The population which lived in boats on the south coast, actors, prostitutes, eunuchs, the underlings or "runners" in official yamens, and slaves were held to be markedly inferior socially.

Slavery seems never to have been so extensive or prominent as in the Roman Empire. At least on the eve of the changes brought by the Occident it was almost entirely domestic. Few if any great estates were cultivated by non-free labor. Slaves were used, if at all, chiefly in household service. Moreover, slavery was not associated with a racial distinction, as in the case of the American Negro. Most of the slaves seem to have been individuals of Chinese stock who through some misfortune, usually economic, had fallen to that status. The poor, for example, might sell their daughters, especially in time of famine. Household slaves were predominantly women and girls. It was because girls were regarded less highly than boys that they were the members the family sold first. They led a hard life, but public opinion generally acted as a restraint on excessive cruelty. Slave girls might be taken as concubines, or, more frequently, be married off to poorer men of the neighborhood.

Beggars have been a fairly numerous and well recognized portion of the community. As a rule their plight has been miserable. People have been driven into mendicancy by a variety of causes. In the case of many, illness or an accident has incapacitated the sufferers for ordinary employment and in default of friends or family who could give financial support the beggar's life has offered the only escape from starvation. The blind have been peculiarly unfortunate. They have been very numerous and no public institutions cared for them and no schools existed where they could be taught to read. Indeed, it was not until Christian missionaries devised a system for them that they could read at all. At best they could only eke out a precarious existence as public entertainers, story tellers, or musicians. Many beggars have become such because of the famines so prevalent in China. Sometimes mendicancy has been only temporary. In other instances it has become permanent and professional.

Some other divisions there were. We have seen the distinctions between the Hakkas and their neighbors, between Moslems and non-Moslems, and between the Chinese and the aboriginal tribes. Moreover, a great deal of local feeling has existed. Natives of one province living in another have often been regarded almost as foreigners. Provincial consciousness is stronger in some quarters—in Hupeh and Kwangtung, for instance—than in others.

In spite of all these divisions, the Chinese, as we have said more than once, have never developed such hard and fast caste lines as exist in India. Intermarriages have occurred between many of the groups. Even from the most despised classes escape was possible.

Some public and private attention was given to the unfortunate members of society, but philanthropy did not construct such large institutions as it has in the modern West or even as in the Europe of the Middle Ages. In a good many cities there have been hospitals for foundlings, some of them supported both by private subscriptions and by state funds. Soup kitchens have frequently been maintained for the destitute. Famine relief has been carried on both by private agencies and by the government. The state granaries especially were long a means of relieving acute distress. Some refuges have been maintained where lepers could be segregated and given care. Beggars have been recognized as possessing a claim on the community and custom has accorded their organizations a right to regular contributions from such property-holders as shopkeepers.

On the other hand, a great deal of callousness to human suffering and much cruelty have existed—reminiscent of the West before the humanitarian movement of the eighteenth and nineteenth centuries.

The motives impelling to assist relief activities have been mixed—in part the native milk of human kindness, in part the hope of accumulating merit in a future life (a Buddhist importation), in part the standards inculcated by Confucianism, and in part (as in the case of payments to the beggars' guilds) the desire to be relieved of further requests from the unfortunates.

RULES AND PRINCIPLES OF SOCIAL INTERCOURSE

The Chinese, like every other civilized people, have developed conventions for social intercourse, for easing the jars which are inevitable where human beings have to live with one another, and for promoting those amenities which are among the marks of culture.

Underneath the many conventions have been certain principles. One of these is an emphasis upon correct form. We have seen that from very early times the Chinese have stressed ceremonies. Confucianism especially made for the perpetuation and strengthening of this tradition. The *Li Chi,* or Book of Rites, was one of the five *Ching,* or Classics, most honored by the Confucian school, and other ancient collections on ritual, the *I Li* and the *Chou Li,* were highly esteemed. *Li,* which included not only religious ceremonies but many social conventions, was regarded as one of the distinguishing characteristics of civilization. Right motives in carrying out the *li* were looked upon as important, but careful observance of form was valued fully as highly. The correct performance of the *li* was believed to have important moral values and to be an indispensable feature of education and social control. The disregard of Westerners for Chinese *li* and the differences between the conventions of the Occident and China were long among the major factors making for irritation in official and unofficial intercourse between Westerners and Chinese. Even to-day, when the precise forms of the older *li* are passing into desuetude, the abruptness of Westerners and their seeming—and often actual—disregard for some of the general attitudes of mind engendered by the *li* are not infrequently sources of more or less serious friction.

Another important principle is "face." "Face" in the Chinese sense is not always easy of definition. It can be best described through specific illustrations. A servant in a foreign household is told that the sugar under his charge is disappearing rather more rapidly than it ought. He sees that he is being accused—very indirectly—of appropriating it. He suggests a device for safeguarding it against possible intruders from the street—although he knows that his master is aware that no such pilfering by strangers is possible. Both he and his master, however, act as though the suggestion were made in good faith, and the desired results are accomplished. The sugar no longer disappears and the servant's face is saved. In one of the kaleidoscopic political changes of the past three decades the personnel of a committee in charge of a public fund becomes objectionable to a new government. To save the face of its members, the committee is induced to meet and to offer its resignation. Then, in open session, the official most responsible for the resignation presides and urges the members to reconsider and retain their posts. They insist on adhering to their original decision, and, with outward reluctance, their resignations are accepted. Every one recognizes that the procedure has been staged to save the face of those dismissed, but the amenities have been observed. A distinguished Chinese who speaks no English is unavoidably placed at dinner next to a foreign host who knows very little Chinese. The host does his best to maintain a conversation. The Chinese, without giving the least appearance of amusement, annoyance, or condescension, quickly adjusts himself to his host's limited vocabulary and speaks slowly. An intermittent if somewhat restricted conversation is carried on, an embarrassing situation is eased, and the host's face is saved. None of this is so very different from what is repeatedly done in other lands. It arises in part from a respect for personality and from the principle that an essential of good manners is sparing one's neighbor from injured feelings and public humiliation. In China, however, it has been carried to a greater extreme than in some other countries. Certainly it has had to be reckoned with as a prime factor in the intercourse between China and the powers. In the long controversy in the last century over the reception of foreign envoys at court the Chinese were chiefly concerned that the appearance should be preserved of the traditional superiority of the Emperor over all other monarchs—although all informed officials knew it to be a fiction. In the more recent conflicts over the "unequal" clauses in the treaties, especially extraterritoriality, it is the loss of face involved which has been most galling to the Chinese. If only face can be preserved, all sorts of adjustments and compromises can be privately and unobtrusively agreed upon. So, too, in the insistence of Chinese spokesmen that the Nanking Government represented the entire country and was able to guarantee protection to aliens, even when much of the interior was known to be in chaos and the central authorities all but impotent, it was face which had to be observed.

This emphasis on the face of the nation is accentuated by the intense pride of the Chinese. They long regarded themselves as the dispensers of civilization and most of the rest of mankind as barbarians. It has involved much humiliation to confess, even tacitly, that the old culture must be modified or abandoned. Even among Western-trained men there still remains some contempt for the Westerner and a feeling that the latter can never fully understand or rightly interpret the Chinese civilization which is passing.

The emphasis on face may be due to the fact that the Chinese, even more than some other peoples, seem to have the attitude of actors. The theatre has long been one of their favorite recreations, and even the humblest laborer is skilled in assuming a rôle. Two coolies may have an altercation, storming at each other and seemingly intent on flying at each other's throats, and yet allow the bystanders to hold them back and eventually to make peace between them.

Another possible reason for face is the fact that in a crowded, relatively immobile society such as was the old China, a man's future depends on preserving a satisfactory station. It was not easy for him to go elsewhere—as he might in a fluid frontier society—and make a new start. Moreover, his family shared in any disgrace which might come to him.

The importance given to face may, too, be the result of the sensitivity of the Chinese. Some observers have declared that Chinese men seem to have many of the temperamental qualities which in the Occident are deemed feminine. However, this distinction may not be so great as appears at first sight. After all, Westerners attach an immense amount of importance to what they call "honor."

In such a society the place of the middleman has been important. A neighbor or a group of neighbors may tender their good offices in adjusting a quarrel in which each antagonist would be sacrificing his face by taking the first step in approaching the other. The wise intermediary can effect the reconciliation while preserving the dignity of both.

It is obvious, too, that compromise must be a major feature of the social relations of such a people. In any dispute the reputations of both parties must, if possible, be preserved. Public opinion would regard unkindly a contestant who caused an adversary too great loss of face. To bring a difference into court would prove expensive and might be ruinous to both litigants. If possible, then, a settlement must be reached by private, extra-legal means. Several peacemakers may offer their services and the final adjustment will probably be a modification of the original demands, with some reward, possibly in the form of a feast, for the middleman at the expense of one of the parties.

The regard for face may be responsible for the dislike of the Chinese for the use of physical violence. Such violence is by no means unknown (for instance, hospitals continually get cases of knife-wounds inflicted in personal encounters), but it has not been held in the honor that it has in some countries of the Occident. Dueling has not been a polite art. Boxing and fencing exist, but rather as forms of physical exercise for one person and as gymnastic exhibitions than real fighting. A man gives great offence by laying hold on another with the object of exerting force. Two members of the lower classes may revile each other, publicly, for half an hour or more, and even spit on each other, and yet without coming to blows.

While the Chinese regard the use of physical violence in a quarrel as a breach of good breeding, they think of suicide as an honorable means of protest. By committing suicide an aggrieved party can bring opprobrium upon his enemy and cause the latter costly embarrassment with officials and neighbors.

Dignity has been regarded as one of the marks of a gentleman. Rapid walking, loud talking, and violently abusive language have been thought of as derogatory to it. A Chinese may be bland and affable even to a person whom he heartily dislikes, and it is often difficult to know from his calm or even genial exterior what are his real thoughts. However, in this, it may be noted again, he is no different from cultivated members of other civilized communities.

The Chinese are, as has been suggested, extremely sensitive. There are, to be sure, phlegmatic souls. Physicians in China testify to the relative insensitivity and physiological-neurological stolidity of the great majority of their patients. Much cheerfulness exists, even among the very poor, and an immense amount of patient persistence in the face of hardship and discouragement. Without these qualities the present disintegration of life in China would be very much greater. A vivid illustration of this is repeatedly seen in the return of farmers to fields which have been wasted by flood, drought, civil strife, or foreign invasion, and the resolute resumption of the normal processes of cultivation. Particularly in the South, however, and among the educated, there is much quickness of response to an emotional stimulus. A keen sense of humor gives a hearty reaction to the funny or the ridiculous. There is, also, an equally strong dislike of a loss of face through seeming to be ridiculous. Many Chinese are, moreover, subject to spasms of anger. The educated may keep these under control, but those without the restraints of convention and training not infrequently give way to them. Such a seizure usually vents itself in violently pouring forth voluble and explicit denunciations and characterizations of the morals and qualities of the offending party and of his or her ancestors, and in calling down on the head of the offender the unhappiest and most lurid fate which the imagination of the injured can invent. Two women or two men may thus berate each other until each is exhausted.

Chinese are extremely subject to mob psychology. Mass feeling develops very quickly—fear, hostility, or mere excitement. Individuals often find it difficult to stand out against the crowd. Chinese, indeed, are sometimes accused of cowardice. However, many exceptions to the rule could be instanced by any experienced observer. So far as failure boldly to dissent from the group exists—and it is very common—it may in part arise from a lack of individual self-reliance, from habituated fear of collective social pressure, and from the absence of strong motives apart from conventional ones.

It may be due to this regard for face and this sensitiveness that another characteristic of Chinese intercourse has developed, a dislike for bluntness and abruptness and the consequent indirect approach to a subject. A caller coming with a request to prefer or an awkward subject to broach may talk at length about entirely irrelevant matters before stating the main object of his visit and then perhaps leave it to be inferred by more or less delicate hints. Or an educated man, feeling it to be beneath his dignity to show anger at an offence, may express his displeasure or return an insult through an obscure literary allusion. All this may prove costly in time, but that is regarded as of small consequence. The foreigners' directness of speech and anxious economy of hours and minutes seem to a Chinese crude and curious Westernisms—unless he himself, as is the case with many young Chinese, has become so Occidentalized as to have acquired them.

The etiquette which the Chinese developed for social intercourse was, as it existed before the changes by contact with the West, elaborate and intricate. To the uninstructed foreigner it was often bewildering. It is needless to try to describe it in any detail, partly because much of it is disappearing. In the chief cities and for many of the younger generation a large proportion of the old customs have largely passed. However, they have by no means entirely disappeared, and some remain unimpaired and in universal use. There has been the custom of speaking deprecatingly of anything connected with oneself and in praise of everything belonging to the person with whom one is talking. Thus in meeting a stranger it is still proper to ask his "honorable name," and in response to a similar inquiry to apprize him of one's "unworthy name." In addressing a superior or one older than oneself, it has been good form to remove one's glasses. One did not shake hands with those whom he met, but clasped his own hands, possibly shaking them and making a bow—more or less profound as the occasion demanded. The Chinese bow, especially of the more profound kind, required practice and was a work of art. In offering or receiving objects it has been proper to do so only with both hands. The seat of honor is on the left of the host, but he who is asked to take it, especially if others are present, must do so, if at all, only after protesting his unworthiness and after one or more refusals. So with going through doors: it has been proper to urge the other to proceed first. Affability and genial good temper have been expected in social intercourse and any departure from them considered boorish. Self-control has been highly esteemed, even though temperamentally so many of the Chinese are excitable. The serving of tea is part of the ritual of every call, whether for business or pleasure. Usually a request from one's host to drink one's tea has been a sign that the interview is at an end. Certain inquiries have been considered proper which in the Occident are usually thought of as impertinent, such as one's age and income. In meeting a friend or acquaintance in the street, if he is mounted or in a sedan chair courtesy has required that recognition be avoided. Otherwise good form would necessitate his stopping, dismounting, and going through the greetings which convention prescribes. The giving and receiving of presents have been regulated by conventions which indicate when a gift should be offered or accepted and, if accepted, how much of it should be sent back and what should be given in return. In eating, spoons and what the foreigner calls chopsticks are used and the food brought on in such a state that it can be easily handled by these implements. To the Chinese of the old school the Western custom of bringing meat to the table in great lumps and then dismembering it with knife and fork must have appeared quite barbarous. Calling cards were formerly much larger than those now in use in the West. The possession of one by a person other than the owner has been supposed to be evidence of authorization to act as a messenger or agent. Dress has been carefully regulated, various forms of garb being prescribed for different occasions. Some of the customs are confusing to the foreigner and even amusing, but they have been means, as are polite conventions in all lands, of keeping society moving pleasantly and with the minimum of friction.

Perhaps here should also be mentioned the custom of gratuities to servants and to those in other positions who have been of use to one. Such gifts have been and are expected. It was and is customary for servants and others to take a proportion of what passes through their hands—"squeeze," as the foreigner has denominated it. The proportion is not always standardized, and the practice easily admits of abuses. Squeeze, however, has been regarded as a legitimate perquisite of position, from that of a servant to that of an official high in the public service, and unless excessive has not been regarded as in any way dishonest.

RECREATION AND AMUSEMENTS

Closely associated with social intercourse and, indeed, often as phases of it, have been recreations and amusements. They have, moreover, profoundly affected the characteristics of the nation—or, perhaps, they have been expressions of these characteristics or have been both cause and effect.

One of the features of the life of the China of the nineteenth century which impressed the Westerner was the slight emphasis upon athletics. Archery held a recognized place, especially in the preparation and drill of the soldier, hunting had its devotees, there were professional acrobats, and shadow boxing was much enjoyed. Many boys displayed skill in keeping a shuttlecock in the air with their feet, and engaged in swimming, wrestling, boxing, flying kites, and fishing. However, archery was regarded as primarily an occupation of the warrior. Hunting as a vigorous sport was largely confined to the Manchus—a heritage from energetic days before their conquest of China—and died out among them as the influence of sedentary life and of Chinese environment progressively became more potent. For the great majority of the Chinese physical exertion was associated with labor and escape from it deemed desirable. Games involving vigorous physical effort were not widely approved. Sports which in the Occident have been thought of as befitting the aristocracy—such as hunting, football, cricket, and tennis—would have been frowned upon in China in recent centuries. This was not always true. In more than one dynasty hunting constituted a favorite diversion of the court and aristocracy. Polo, of foreign origin, in T'ang times was followed ardently in imperial circles by both men and women. However, by the latter part of the nineteenth century interest in such strenuous diversion had largely died out even among the once hardy Manchus. For the decay of such exercises the Manchu rulers seem, at least in part, responsible. They discouraged Chinese from pursuing manly sports for fear that thus preparation might be made for throwing off the Ch'ing yoke. While, in spite of supposed taboos on such activities, some survived, they did not enjoy the prominence in China that they have in Anglo-Saxon lands.

The rapid growth in popularity of athletics in the past two or three decades is one phase of the influence of the Occident. The passion for such spectacles as the Olympic games of Greece, the gladiatorial contests of ancient Rome, the tourneys of the European Middle Ages, and the bull fights and the football and baseball matches of modern Europe and America have been quite alien to Chinese custom.

This contrast between China and the West may be due in part to a difference in the ideals of the dominant classes. In the West the aristocracy has traditionally been the military. Preparation for fighting and the bodily skill and fitness derived from appropriate sports have been accepted as an essential part of the training and life of the gentleman. The lower classes have naturally taken their cue from the aristocracy and the tradition has passed over to the influential middle classes and democracies of recent years. In China, on the other hand, it was the Confucian scholar who set the standard and the fighting man and his works were at best regarded as necessary evils. By tradition the Confucian scholar did not take kindly to vigorous physical exertion—even though Confucius himself practiced archery and is said to have hunted. The scholar usually confined his exercise to a slow, dignified walk, or he might engage in such an unenergetic diversion as taking a pet bird out for an airing, possibly throwing seeds for it to catch.

With this kind of example set from above, the amusements of the populace tended to be of the same sort. Flying kites was popular, at least in certain places and seasons. Crickets were induced to fight one another.

Gambling provided one of the most prevalent forms of diversion and for it many devices existed. The contests between the gladiatorial crickets usually have had wagers placed on the outcome. There have been many games of chance. Counters or cards roughly resembling dominoes in size have been used for several of them. In the Occident not many years ago one, *mah jong*, enjoyed a sudden popularity and suffered almost as sudden a demise. Sets of cards have been employed for centuries and have been of several varieties. *Fantan* is played with coins. A pile of them is covered with a bowl and the participants register wagers on the remainder—three, two, one, nothing—which will be left after the whole has been divided by four. From time to time the government has attempted to stamp out gambling, but its efforts have been in vain. All classes, from the highest official circles to the poorest laborers, have indulged in it. Travellers in the interior will not soon forget how the coolies who have carried their burdens by day have spent the night in gambling, often in the next room separated only by a thin partition—to the great annoyance of their employer. Some other games have not been so frequently associated with gambling. One of these is much like Western chess and very possibly has a common origin. As is well known, chess has been found in many different countries and ages and may go back to an Indian prototype.

A center of gossip and a place for spending the idle and lighter hours has been the tea shop. Here, over a cup of that innocuous beverage, neighbors or casual acquaintances exchange news. Here, too, comes the professional story-teller with his entertaining narratives.

It may be noted that the Chinese have not been so violently addicted to the excessive consumption of alcoholic drinks as have been some of the Northern European peoples. Fermented liquors have been used widely and for centuries. That most generally seen is derived from rice and is distilled—once, and for stronger brands twice and even three times. Drunkenness has been by no means unknown. There even seem to have been periods, as under the T'ang, when it has been fairly prevalent. In the nineteenth century, however, it was not nearly so common as in the England or the United States of that time. In the nineteenth and twentieth centuries opium has played a part in China somewhat like that which liquor has had in Anglo-Saxon lands. Its moderate use has been very widespread and excessive indulgence in it all too common—to the moral, physical, and financial undoing of its victims and the sorrow and suffering of their relatives and dependents. As has been noted in earlier chapters, the rapid rise in the consumption of opium was due in large part to trade with Westerners and was associated with the commercial invasion of the Occident. Opium has been produced extensively in China, however, and of late years the growth of the opium poppy has become once more a major problem. Some estimates indicate that the total production may be ten times that of the rest of the world. The reason for this popularity of opium in China—greater than in any other large nation—is not entirely clear. Obviously it is at least partly because it provides a temporary escape from unpleasant realities and a surcease from care, much as alcoholic beverages do for many other folk.

Tobacco has been and is extensively smoked—although formerly the total quantity was much less than to-day. The familiar Chinese pipe has a very small bowl, holding only enough of the weed for a whiff or two. Men and women, especially elderly people, formerly sat by the hour alternately filling their pipes (or having it done for them by servants), lighting them, smoking, and then knocking out the ashes.

Still other types of recreation have been feasting (an accompaniment of many social events, such as weddings, and of many business transactions), watching processions, reading novels and stories, singing with or without the accompaniment of musical instruments, retailing and exchanging gossip, resorting to clairvoyants, watching marionettes and jugglers, attending village fairs (at which plays are often shown), visiting temples, automatic writing through what corresponds to the planchette, and simply frequenting crowded places.

Before the days when Western customs made their influence felt, and when social intercourse between men and respectable women was still impossible, many men found diversion with girls, usually of easy morals, who were professional entertainers. The changing customs by which, in the cities, men and women of the same rank now often associate freely seem not to have reduced prostitution. Dance halls of a new type in the ports have added to the problem and many hotels have been frankly in the business.

THE THEATRE

The drama has had a great fascination for the Chinese and has been and is a familiar feature of their life. We have already seen something of its history. Pantomimes with music were already in existence in early historic times as a means of commemorating the deeds and the memory of ancestors. There were plays in the Han, probably of a simple type, and a further development occurred in the T'ang and the Sung. A noteworthy and rather sudden flowering of dramatic genius came under the Mongols. Both under the Ming and the Ch'ing new styles of plays and of the accompanying music appeared. A very large number of plays were written in the nineteenth century.

The theatre has been one of the most potent agencies for popular education. To the masses, almost or entirely illiterate as the large majority of them have been, the written character cannot provide a direct medium of instruction. Every one, however, could and can see a play. In the cities and large towns buildings have been constructed specifically for the drama. These, however, have not been so numerous as might be supposed. In Nanking, for example, before the days of the cinema, only two theatres existed and these were not regularly open. Temples have often been used for dramatic performances, even when the plays have contained little or nothing immediately connected with religion. Frequently a raised platform over a street or in a field has served for a stage. At the periodical fairs in market towns and on other special occasions a performance or series of performances by a dramatic troupe has been a usual part of the program. Since many of the plays have historical themes and the great virtues, such as filial piety, are often extolled and vividly illustrated, and vice has been represented as punished, the populace has obtained some idea, even though in distorted and more than semi-fictional form, of their country's past, and has seen orthodox morals held up for praise.

The main features of the theatre can be fairly quickly described. The buildings designed especially for the theatre have been Elizabethan in their simplicity, except when, as in some instances in recent years, they have been affected by the modern West. At one end of the building is a raised platform for the stage. In front of this is the main floor; with benches, or with backless chairs clustered around little tables, and on three sides a gallery, also with seats. Formerly men and women were usually—although not always—in different parts of the house. Now in the cities this separation has largely ceased. During the progress of the play attendants move about the audience with tea and food or with the familiar towels wrung out of hot water, with which hands and face are wiped. Individuals enter and leave at will and carry on conversations during the performance.

Very little scenery is employed—perhaps a table and a few chairs and at times a rude painting of a city wall and gate. Much is left to the imagination of the audience assisted by conventional and therefore well understood motions of the actors. As the actor stoops the audience perceives that he is entering a door, even though no building is apparent. Certain gestures indicate that he is mounting his steed, although no horse is there. In contrast with the scenery, the costumes are often rich and elaborate, and masks are much in evidence. Here again convention has been followed. A character carrying a wand tipped with white horse-tail hair is known to represent a supernatural being. A red mask proclaims the wearer to be of an upright character and a black one is worn by those of cruel and severe dispositions. The painting of faces is closely governed by custom and the audience resents any departure from what is expected in the make-up of a particular character. During the course of the play attendants move about the stage rearranging the chairs and tables and perhaps serving the actors with tea. Much of the acting consists of postures and gestures which again are governed by convention. To perform them correctly and gracefully in a manner acceptable to a critical audience requires both ability and practice.

The themes of the plays vary greatly. They include comedy and tragedy, avowed fiction and historical episodes. A favorite period from which to draw stories is the Three Kingdoms, perhaps in part because of the popularity of the famous novel with that title. Some of the plays are long but others are very short. Performances may be given afternoon and evening and may last for six or seven hours. In both, however, it is usual to present several plays, or, perhaps, famous scenes from some of the longer ones. In a play singing, spoken dialogue, and dancing (or posturing) may all be found. There is, too, a type of acrobatic posturing representing fighting. It seems probable that the types of programs now seen on the stage spring from a variety of origins—that the military plays symbolizing fighting (for instance) have come from one set of early ceremonials and that the others have grown up quite distinct from them. To-day both may be seen on the same stage.

Some of the theatrical troupes are large, with fifty or a hundred members. Others, usually itinerant, are small, sometimes with only two members. Although actors are regarded as socially inferior and are usually recruited from the lower classes, some achieve great popularity. The training is prolonged and exacting. Usually it is begun in early youth, and those who take it serve a kind of apprenticeship. At least during the nineteenth century women did not customarily appear on the stage—a ruling which is said to date from the time of Ch'ien Lung—and men took women's parts. Some men became extraordinarily skillful in female rôles. Fairly recently there have been companies made up entirely of women in which the members have displayed marked talent in portraying men.

There has also been a kind of little theatre in the form of puppet shows, in which marionettes are moved about by the operator and the various parts are spoken by the same expert individual. Some marionettes are controlled by strings, some are costumed dolls, and others are translucent and painted, a kind of "shadow doll."

The theatre has been immensely popular, and while in other days an occasional magistrate attempted to prohibit performances, presumably because he believed the money spent on them might more profitably have been invested elsewhere, such efforts have seldom if ever received the support of the public. Perhaps as a result Chinese seem to take almost instinctively to acting a part in social intercourse, and have a penchant for dramatizing themselves and incidents in which they are vitally concerned.

With all this emphasis on the theatre, however, it must be noted that drama in China appears never to have risen to the heights in the portrayal of character and in dealing with some of the persistent problems of human life and destiny that it did in ancient Greece and that it has in some countries of the modern West. The Chinese have not been blind to these questions, as we have repeatedly seen, and have thought on them profoundly and with acumen. For an expression of their meditations and conclusions on these issues, however, they have chosen other vehicles, notably philosophy. Drama, therefore, has not occupied the prominent place in serious Chinese literature that it has held in some lands of the Occident. In China the theatre has remained more exclusively a diversion.

Closely akin to the theatre has been the professional storyteller. For many centuries his seems to have been an accepted occupation. He finds his audiences at tea shops, where the proprietors pay him for his services as a means of drawing patrons, and in other places where people congregate—in streets, on market days, and in opium dens. His themes are often taken from the famous historical romances, such as *The Three Kingdoms*. Indeed, some of the greatest novels appear to have grown out of these narratives as they were told for generations by these experts in popular entertainment. The story-teller may accompany his recital with a musical instrument. Along with the theatre, he has been a potent if unintentional agent of popular education in the history—highly colored and in semi-fictional form—and in the folklore of the nation.

Somewhat akin also to the theatre have been jugglers and acrobats. The Chinese have rejoiced in them and have produced unusually skillful ones. Then, too, the processions which are so important in funerals, weddings, and religious festivals both give expression and provide incentive to the passion for the dramatic.

It would not be correct to classify music under the diversions of the Chinese, for although in some of its aspects it has undoubtedly been such, it has played a much larger rôle than providing recreation. Yet music has had and still has a prominent place in the theatre and this phase of it should probably be mentioned here rather than among the arts.

A regular part of the equipment of the theatre is the orchestra. There are a number of instruments, among them flutes, balloon guitars, drums, gongs, cymbals, pieces of hollow wood beaten with sticks, some of them resembling violins with two strings, another a clarinet, and still another a castanet. Usually an orchestra is made up of eight or ten instruments. Moreover, singing has had a large place on the stage, for a great many of the parts are sung rather than spoken. The songs heard in the theatre have often caught the popular fancy and can be heard on the streets for days after. The singing is in a high or falsetto voice and to Western ears is either excruciating or amusing. Here, however, as in so many other conventions, Occidental standards are not necessarily either universal or final.

FESTIVALS AND SPECIAL DAYS

Before the impact of the Occident Chinese life was entirely lacking in the week with its recurring day of rest. It was not, however, without an alternation between days of recreation and rest and days of work. This was largely because of the standard festivals of the Chinese year, which, in spite of some modifications and additions made in the past few years by the coming of the West, still persist.

The most important has been and in the vast majority of localities still is the New Year. This event does not fall regularly on the same days of the Gregorian calendar, for the older Chinese measurement of time has been both by the lunar month and the solar year, and to make the two somewhat nearly coincide—since the lunar year of twelve months is only 354 days—some years are regarded as made up of twelve months and to others an additional or intercalary month is added. The date does not fall earlier than January 21st or later than February 19th. A few days before the New Year the Kitchen God is supposed to return to heaven to report the conduct of the members of the family since the last anniversary. This is signaled by burning the image of the god, perhaps after smearing his lips with molasses—to insure that the deity carries with him a final good impression of the household. On the last day of the old year he is welcomed back and a fresh picture of him is pasted above the kitchen stove. The New Year has been the time for the settlement of debts, and it has been considered bad form to enter it without having paid them. The day itself and the several following ones are devoted to feasting and visiting, and all but the most necessary labor ceases. Honors are paid to ancestors and there are family reunions. When old customs are followed, children make their obeisances to their parents, pupils pay their respects to their teachers, and friends call on one another and exchange good wishes. With the anniversary, another year is added to the reckoning of the ages of all members of the family. While birthdays are observed, according to Chinese reckoning a child is one year old at its birth and two years of age after it passes into its first New Year. Thus an infant born in the last month of the year is in the succeeding month said to be two years old.

For the very poor and, perhaps, the majority of the population the New Year's celebration lasts but three or four days. Theoretically, however, and practically for many the period is regarded as ending on the fifteenth day of the first month with the Feast of

Lanterns. In some parts of the country this is a very gay occasion. Huge paper dragons are carried about the streets, each draped over several men. In the evening lanterns of many shapes and kinds are displayed by the populace. There is also the inevitable firecracker—so widely employed on occasions of jollification and worship.

Ch'ing Ming has been the chief spring festival. It has especially been a time for commemorating the dead—a sort of "Memorial Day"—by repairing and cleaning graves and placing offerings before the ancestral tablets and on the tombs. It is also incidentally for picnicking and feasting. Recent changes have altered it but little, if at all—although the modern schools have in places attempted to graft on it an Arbor Day.

What has been regarded as the opening of summer has been popularly observed, although not so prominently as some of the other great days of the year.

The Dragon Boat festival, on the fifth day of the fifth moon, may originally have been associated with the summer solstice and have been for the purpose of obtaining rain. It certainly had for one of its objectives assistance in harmonizing the *yin* and the *yang*. The *yang* increases between the winter and the summer solstice. With the advent of the latter, the *yin* begins to grow in power. Precautions are therefore taken against evil spirits, particularly those which cause disease, by cleansing the home, especially by hanging up herbs and by drinking a specially prepared wine and sprinkling the house with it. In many parts of the country a favorite public event of the day has been races between "dragon-boats." The craft are long and narrow and at the bow each has a dragon's head. In theory the contests are commemorative of the search for the dead body of Ch'u Yüan, a statesman, it will be recalled, who is reputed to have committed suicide by drowning in the third century before Christ, but it seems highly probable that the custom had its origin quite independently of that event.

On the seventh day of the seventh month is the festival of the weaver maid and the herdsman. The story told in connection with it is that the weaver maid (who is identified with Vega and two other stars) and the herdsman (identified with three stars in Aquila) so neglected their respective duties after their marriage that they were separated by divine decree, but that once a year, on this night, if it does not rain, magpies build with their wings a bridge across the Milky Way and over it the weaver passes to her spouse and spends a day with him. It is peculiarly a woman's festival.

Also in the seventh month is the festival for the departed spirits, mentioned in the preceding chapter.

The harvest festival is celebrated in the eighth month and culminates on the fifteenth day of that month, at the full moon. It is a time when debts are supposed to be paid, although this is not so necessary as at the beginning of the New Year. It is sometimes called the moon's birthday and at least in some parts of the country moon cakes are made, with a crescent on them and perhaps the image of a pagoda or an effigy of the rabbit which to Chinese imagination is supposed to be seen on the face of the full orb. It is a time of rejoicing and feasting for all ages and is very much a children's festival. Many quaint and pretty customs have been connected with it.

Confucius's birthday has been observed, especially by the schools, on the twenty-seventh day of the eighth month, but since 1931 according to the solar calendar. Of late the commemoration has been perfunctory and little popular interest attaches to it.

A festival on the ninth day of the ninth month may represent the coming of the first frosts in the North where the custom seems to have originated. As a precaution against calamity (so at least some have believed) people betake themselves to a high place—the top of a hill or the city wall. It is a time of happy excursions and picnics.

The last great festival of the year is that of the winter solstice. It is devoted especially to family gatherings and honors to ancestors. Formerly it was also the occasion for the major one of the annual sacrifices at which the Emperor officiated, that on the Altar of Heaven.

In addition to the holidays in which the majority of the population have participated, other events have brought diversion into the routine of life—birthdays, religious pilgrimages, market days in towns where these are customary, and festivals peculiar to a particular religion, especially those of Buddhism. Life has by no means gone on without variation.

In spite of all the many forms of diversion, however, for a large proportion of the masses life has been fairly circumscribed and monotonous. Particularly has this been true of the women and girls, to whom many of the amusements open to men are not available. For the farmers an interval occurs between the harvest and the spring planting—a hiatus which is longest in the North—when there is a good deal of enforced idleness. The monotony is augmented for the artisan, merchant, common laborer, and many others by the steadiness of toil. Some know of no release from work, not even (as in the case of food shops) on New Year's Day. Many have off only four or five days a year. The hours of labor are usually long, and while the pace is slow, little leisure exists for genuine rest or recreation. For instance, hand looms can often be heard going at almost any hour of the day or night.

To the Westerner of the modern rushing age much of the life of the farm and village and even of the towns seems peculiarly drab and lacking in variety. It must be remembered, however, that such an observer would probably have made the same comment on rural life in Europe in the eighteenth and even in much of the nineteenth century. Moreover, foreigner after foreigner has commented on the cheerfulness of the Chinese masses, and on their ability to find joy in little things, to laugh in the face of hardship, and to be patient under crushing natural disasters.

CHANGES WROUGHT BY THE COMING OF THE WEST

The West with which China has come into collision in the nineteenth and twentieth centuries differs radically in social organization, ideals, and customs from the Middle Kingdom. Since the Occident has been the aggressor, it is China which has been most affected. The West, as we have suggested, has not been appreciably modified—not even so much as by the contacts of the eighteenth century. The change in China has been all the more violent because the West with which the Orient has collided in the past two generations is itself in rapid transition, with institutions and customs in which every decade sees striking and bewildering alterations.

The contrasts between the two cultures in the phases of life dealt with in this chapter have been especially great and the results of the collision correspondingly disruptive. The Chinese large family, with its early marriages arranged by the elders, has been brought into touch with a family which is small and in which the young people choose their own mates. Moreover, the family of the Occident is itself being dealt staggering blows, particularly by the mechanization and urbanization of modern life. Divorce has rapidly increased, the average number of children has declined, and contraceptive practices and devices are widely, even if surreptitiously, employed. The restraint exercised on children by elders has sharply decreased, and the family as a social and economic unit is threatened. It is a family life with such characteristics which has impinged upon China.

The West which China has known is one in which the relations between the sexes are not only strikingly different from those insisted upon by Chinese custom, but have also been rapidly changing. Men and women have traditionally mingled freely. There has been added in the course of the past hundred years or so the feminist movement with much greater liberty for women. This has been in startling contrast with the separation of the social life of the sexes in China and with the subordination of women to men and the sharp occupational divergences between them.

The sacrifice of the individual to the group in the older China has been quite the opposite of the individualism of the Occident of the nineteenth and the early part of the twentieth century. That individualism is now threatened by such systems as fascism, communism, and socialism, but it still characterizes much of the West.

Moreover, the differences between the relative social status of classes in China and the Occident are very great. In the West, as has been remarked, by tradition the soldier is the ruler and the aristocracy is militaristic in its traditions and moral ideals. At times that supremacy has been challenged and modified by the Church and of late years by democratically elected civil authorities and by merchant and industrial magnates, especially in such newer countries as the United States, Canada, and Australia. It still remains, however, even though shaken. In China in theory the scholar has been the most highly esteemed and the soldier has been tolerated only as a necessary evil. It must be added, however, that practically all Chinese dynasties have been founded by successful warriors, and that repeatedly the military have been supreme—including the more than two decades since the downfall of the Ch'ing.

In recreation the Occident—especially the Anglo-Saxon portion of it—has stressed athletics and China has not. Western forms of amusement in which both sexes participate, especially dancing, are quite alien to the Chinese tradition and to old-fashioned Chinese even seem immoral. Such recent Occidental inventions as the "movie" and the "talkie" are also a marked innovation.

This Western social life, so different from that of the Middle Kingdom of the nineteenth century, has been pouring into China through many channels. For more than a century, as we have seen, foreign merchants, consuls, diplomats, and members of the customs service have been living in the great ports and in some of the smaller ones and have been travelling through the interior. Christian missionaries have been widely scattered, not only in the cities but in the towns, and in the interior as well as on the coast and the main rivers. Chinese students have been going abroad by the thousands and a large proportion of them have seen Occidental life, not in smaller university centers, where the changes affecting the West are not so obvious, but in such cities as New York, Paris, Berlin, and London, where all the new forces affecting the Occident are the most powerful. It is this ultra-modern Western life which they tend to reproduce when once more in China. Chinese emigrants to America and to the lands to the south of China have been returning with new ideas. Their influence is felt most markedly on the south coast. The "movies" and especially those of American origin, with their bizarre exaggeration of certain phases of Western life—usually the less desirable—have been immensely popular and have been an agency for the spread of Western ideals and institutions in badly distorted forms. Translations of foreign literature of many types have been issued in quantities. Some of the large cities are centers from which the new forces stream out into the surrounding country. This is particularly true of the commercial and financial metropolis, Shanghai—that hybrid of the West and China, with the Occidental elements obvious and dominant. The result of these varied influences from the West is that China has been brought in touch with many different types of Occidental life, including, and often especially, those in which the recent changes are most apparent.

The revolution in Chinese social life has been hastened by the introduction of many of the mechanical devices which have had so large a share in altering the West. As we have seen, the factory has made its appearance, particularly in the region of Shanghai, and industrialism has begun to have its effect. In the North iron stoves are often taking the place of the *k'ang*. The candle or crude oil lamp has been widely displaced by the kerosene lamp. The automobile, by drawing towns and villages nearer together, has begun to work some of the alterations which rapid transportation has wrought in the West, including the breaking down of the relative isolation and economic and social self-sufficiency of the village and small town and the spread of customs and ideas from the urban centers. In some places the extensive use of the bicycle has brought changes, although not so marked as those which follow in the wake of the automobile.

In view of all these factors it is not surprising that Chinese social life and institutions have been partly overturned. Some of the innovations have been mentioned. For the sake of a complete picture, however, the entire range must here be summarized.

Marked changes are in progress in the family. In some districts the large families, in which three generations or even four live together in one compound, are diminishing in number, and the small families, made up of a husband and wife and their children, are increasing. The religious functions of the family are in places disappearing—the old forms connected with it falling here and there into desuetude. In the cities the economic ties which once held the family together are often being dissolved. The authority which the family has over its members is also weakening.

Even more radical are the innovations in the institution of marriage. Many young people are insisting upon arranging their own engagements—although probably in the large majority of instances these are still negotiated by parents. The object of modern youth in marriage, moreover, is less and less the continuation of the family line and the succession of male heirs to perpetuate the traditional honors to ancestors and is more and more their own happiness. There has entered as a controlling factor for many the romanticism so prevalent in the modern Occident, with its idea that marriage should be based upon reciprocal attraction and the ability of two souls to supplement each other, that its primary object is to satisfy the desires, both physical and spiritual, of a man and a woman, and that children and the family line are quite secondary and perhaps even an unwelcome interference. Marriage ceremonies have also often been altered by "modern" young people. It must be noted, however, that with all his talk of romantic love, a modern Chinese young man, when he comes actually to the choice of a wife, bases his selection upon much the same grounds as his parents would have done—such as education, earning capacity, and the ability to run a house.

The relations between men and women are being modified. The sexes enjoy much freer social intercourse. The Western dance has even come into some advanced groups—usually centering in "returned students." Among students particularly a great amount of interest in sex is displayed, with much discussion and no little experimentation. The assertive individualism which is one of the outstanding concomitants of the disintegration of the old order insists upon the right of each, whether man or woman, to consult first his or her personal interests.

Especially are women declaring that they have a right to their own careers and to a share in occupations and diversions formerly monopolized by men. Coëducation is becoming the rule in higher education. The feminism of the Occident is making itself felt. In no other country in Asia, unless it may be Turkey and Russia, is the status of women changing so rapidly and are women making greater strides toward equality with men.

The extent of these innovations in the family, in the relations of the sexes, and in the position of women must not be exaggerated. Students are usually the ones most deeply involved and they form only a minority even of the sections of the population within their own age groups. Factory workers are affected, but the industrial revolution so far has touched only a small proportion of the Chinese. For the masses, particularly in the country, the old family and the old customs and ideals are fairly generally maintained. China is still predominantly rural and not only are agricultural districts notoriously conservative the world over, but in Chinese farming communities most of the economic, social, and religious factors remain which have given strength to the traditional family. In many cities the innovations, while coming in rapidly, have not yet prevailed. Even in the cities on the coast and on the main rivers and railroads, where the changes are most marked, and among those with a modern education there are conservatives who cling to the old ways.

It is inevitable that the introduction of the new *mores* should be accompanied by much maladjustment and unhappiness. In breaking with the old some men and women come to moral and physical shipwreck. Many marriages are made unhappy. In numerous instances a boy who has received a modern training is betrothed or married to a girl who has been reared in the old manner and the two not only have little in common but fail to understand and help each other. Some such couples succeed in making a satisfactory adjustment and achieve a happy family life. Others simply endure each other. In instances, probably very much in the minority, a divorce is effected—but except in a few limited circles most influenced by the West that is still regarded with high disfavor and the divorced wife is thought of as irreparably disgraced. Divorce usually is much more of a hardship on the woman than on the man, for her old style training has not fitted her for economic or social independence, remarriage is generally out of the question, and if her own family has a place for her, which is not always, it is likely to be one of sufferance. Some women with a modern training fail to find a man whom they are content to marry and live a celibate existence—although that is still very much more rare, even among the most Westernized, than in the Occident. Occasionally extra-marital relations are entered upon. Concubinage, which for men of the old school offered a partial way out of an unsatisfactory marriage, is now not only illegal without the wife's consent but is regarded with disfavor by those of a Western training and so is not available as a solution. Yet it would not be true to the facts to fail to recognize the existence of many happy homes formed and lived under the new conditions and according to the new ideals.

The individualism of the nineteenth century Occident has entered China. It has been accentuated by the weakening of many of the old forms of social control and of traditional moral standards, and by the political and economic distress which have set so many adrift from their former moorings. The sudden release from these restraints and the collapse for many of the former methods of obtaining a livelihood have led to much exaggerated and unregulated individualism. Often, however, there has been a great dearth of initiative and of capacity for leadership. Chinese, accustomed to act under old forms, have not yet learned how to lead and coöperate under the new. They are often willing to follow, sheeplike, any resolute man who seems to know his own mind. At the same time and in contradiction to this individualism new forms of mass action have emerged. Anti-foreign boycotts have repeatedly been nation-wide and very effective. Labor unions and the strike have appeared. The Kuomintang with its many local and provincial units and its national organization modeled to a great extent on the Communist Party of Russia has been coërcive. The new China, therefore, presents a strange mixture of assertive individualism and of group action which is most tyrannical.

A modification has come in the traditional relative social standing of the various occupations and in the ideals of some of them. Under the Republic the military authorities have usually been dominant. While the rank and file of the soldiers are about as much despised and feared as ever, many of their officers have acquired prestige and some have been men of education. Moreover, some students have been entering the army. Many of them enlisted in the Kuomintang forces in 1926 and 1927, believing that thus they could best serve their country. Military drill is finding a place on the school curriculum and in some instances is demanded by the students. It is even given in some girls' schools, although nurses' training is more common. Many students and educational authorities, seeing their country prostrate before a militarized Occident and Japan and being intensely nationalistic, are convinced that salvation can come only as China adopts the methods of the Occident and Japan and defeats her oppressors with their own weapons. A proportion of the male youth pass through the training given by the Boy Scouts. Indeed, the government has attempted to make it compulsory for junior middle schools boys. It differs from the movement in Anglo-Saxon lands in being pretty thoroughly militarized. It places added emphasis on political service and on assisting the police. However, the degree of the militarization of education can easily be exaggerated. Usually in the schools only two or three hours a week have been assigned to drill and these often are loosely managed or covered by lectures. Only in regions or periods of excitement—such as in the recent Sino-Japanese crises—has it received much serious attention.

The characteristics, then, of the intelligentsia are changing. Scholars trained by the old methods are passing off the scene and are being replaced by those educated in the Occident or Japan, or in China by Western or semi-Western methods. To be sure, the educated class of the new régime retains some of the characteristics of the old. The civil officials are still largely recruited from its ranks, and a large proportion of the students look forward to taking service under the state. Students, too, are actively interested in politics, both national and international. Repeatedly they have joined in boycotts directed against an obnoxious nation, especially Japan. In 1926 and 1927, when it was seeking to unify the country, the Kuomintang found among them some of its most enthusiastic supporters. In the autumn of 1931 they thronged into Nanking by the thousands demanding war against the Japanese. Some of them attacked and did physical violence to C. T. Wang, then Minister of Foreign Affairs, and precipitated his retirement. They also had a share in forcing the resignation of Chiang Kai-shek in December of that year, and later in bringing him back to power. In most of this political activity, it must be noted, students have been swayed and manipulated by skillful agitators of more mature years. For example, in 1931 they were largely the tools of political agitators in Shanghai. However, the student class of the present day shows marked differences from that of the nineteenth century. The education of the schools no longer has as its sole objective preparation for civil service examinations and employment under the state. A large proportion of the students are consciously looking forward to other occupations. With the decay of Confucianism and the smaller part occupied by the older literature in the curriculum, the moral standards of present-day students tend to vary from those of other years. The customs and ethics of the nation have been so largely shaped by Confucianism that the influence of that school is still potent, but it is diminishing. As a result, many students are morally adrift with no dominant philosophy except nationalism. Since the majority of those vocal in politics are in secondary schools, they are usually immature, subject to waves of emotion, and can often be manipulated by astute elders. Some of the ablest have been attracted by Communism, believing that in the midst of desperately confusing and discouraging circumstances it offers an apparently decisive program and an early way out of the nation's difficulties.

It must also be noted that the weakening of some of the old groups has tended to dislocate the traditional order of society. The abolition of the civil service examinations has led to the progressive disappearance of that official-scholar class which for many centuries set the standard in customs and morals. The banditry, the civil wars, the foreign invasion, and the Communism of the past few years, combined with flood and drought, have impoverished many prominent families and have wiped some of them out. In many communities, therefore, the elements which formerly made for social as well as economic and political stability have been obliterated or greatly weakened. In this respect China has suffered much more than did Japan in its days of transition. In the latter country a large proportion of the "new men" who have controlled the nation in the past fifty or sixty years have sprung from the *samurai* and even from the ancient court nobility. This may help to account for the much greater comparative order and lack of civil war with which Japan accomplished her Westernization and for the disorder which in China has accompanied the same process.

The old forms of etiquette are passing. Those who adhere to them are at the best thought of as gentlemen of the old school and at the worst as hopelessly out of date. Less respect is shown for age and for teachers. Hand-shaking after the Western fashion has become good form, and the old profound bow has usually been replaced by a more moderate one. The elaborate polite terminology has been abbreviated. Not unnaturally, in the transition some individuals display an absence of any kind of good manners and a good deal of rudeness.

There has been widespread adoption of Western dress among the upper economic and social groups, especially for school uniforms and by the military—although, with waves of nationalism, occasional reactions toward Chinese costumes have been seen. Recently the agitation has been not so much against foreign styles as against foreign materials. The queue began passing before 1911 and after the revolution of that year rapidly disappeared in much of the land—although even now it persists in many places. Of late women and especially school girls have taken to bobbing their hair. The custom of binding the feet of girls has by no means ceased, especially in the interior, but for many it is lapsing.

Marked innovations have come in recreation. Athletics are now good form, particularly in the schools. They are still far from being so popular and so universal as in modern Japan or in Anglo-Saxon lands. There is not the same absorption in them as in Great Britain, Australia, or the United States. Nor is there yet so high an average of skill or of adherence to what in the West is called good sportsmanship. The old *mores* of face and the Western *mores* of accepting defeat smilingly and without complaint are in conflict. It has not been easy to subordinate individual pride to the good of the team. However, physical sports attract much more attention from the educated than they did thirty years ago and men can be found who not only have participated in them in student days but have carried over an enthusiasm for them into mature life. Such games as tennis, requiring quickness and accuracy, are popular. Soccer football and basketball are played by even a larger number. Active sports have been taken up in the schools for girls and the contrast is almost bewildering between many of the young women who are the products of modern education, with their skill in tennis and swimming, and their mothers and grandmothers, swaying painfully along on their bound feet. In Nanking before 1937 a National Stadium was constructed, seating twenty-five thousand. The trend toward athletics has been somewhat reënforced by the introduction of military training in the schools and the desire for physical fitness in the army, but it long preceded them.

Moving pictures have achieved popularity. With their passion for the theatre, the Chinese have taken quickly to the cinema. The Western style of theatrical performance and stage setting has been introduced, although to a limited extent and without supplanting the old. Western music has come in somewhat through the churches but chiefly through "brass bands" which often form a prominent feature of processions and of the entourage of a high official. The phonograph has also been widely introduced. The

Chinese themselves have been producing extensively for the cinema and the phonograph, and the radio is widely spread.

The old style tobacco pipe is being supplanted by the cigarette and the consumption of tobacco in this new form has enormously increased. This has been partly due to the nationwide propaganda of advertising and selling conducted for the past three decades or so by the British-American Tobacco Company, but other houses, both foreign and Chinese, have shared in the promotion and the manufacture.

A good deal of change has come in the rhythm of vacation and work. The Western Sunday is now usually observed as a day of rest by government offices, by some government institutions such as post offices and state banks, by schools, and by a few private business houses. This is not, of course, because of the religious significance of the day, but must be ascribed to Western secular practice. The government, too, has adopted the Western solar calendar and has endeavored to discourage and even to forbid the observance of the old New Year. The attempt has by no means met with universal success, but in some localities it has had some effect. Moreover, new holidays have been brought into the calendar, such as the observance of the "Double Tenth," the anniversary of the first Revolution (October 10th, 1911), and of Sun Yat-sen's death (March 12th). Certain "Humiliation Days" have been observed, chiefly by students, notably those in May commemorating the forcing on China of the Sino-Japanese treaties and notes of 1915 and the shooting of students in Shanghai on May 30th, 1925. Some of the old festival customs are falling into abeyance, as, for example, the dragon-boat races on the fifth day of the fifth moon.

A good deal of dislocation has been brought into the routine of Chinese life by Western mechanical inventions, such as the electric light, the automobile, the kerosene lamp, and even modern water systems with their conveyance of a larger supply of that commodity than formerly and by pipes and faucets rather than by the water-carrier and his pails. The wider and straighter streets driven through many of the cities in imitation of the Occident and the removal of some of the city walls tend to produce changes in urban customs. Here again, however, the extent of the innovations can easily be exaggerated, especially by those familiar with only the chief coast ports. Very few cities have had any kind of public water supply—not even the capital, Nanking, with its population of more than half a million. Comparatively few walls have been destroyed, although many have been pierced for the convenience of traffic.

SUMMARY

In conclusion it must be repeated that in spite of great changes in the social institutions and customs of China, in most communities those features which survive from the old quite outnumber the new. So huge a body of mankind with so matured a life is not easily or quickly dislocated. It will be recalled that the revolution in culture did not really begin until after 1895 and did not get fully under way until after 1900—much later than in India and Japan. Even though the revolution has been accompanied by a great deal of chaos, not a little of the old China abides. This is especially true outside those cities which are on the main arteries of communication with the West. China's population is predominately rural and while alterations have come in agricultural communities and in some places sweepingly and violently, much of the ancient life, ideals, and customs persist. For the masses the transition is still in its early stages. The traveller who has seen only such centers as Shanghai, Nanking, and Tientsin or who has met chiefly English-speaking students, many of whom have studied abroad, may easily believe that the disintegration of the old has proceeded much further than it really has. In the offices of at least some high officials, with their Occidental furniture and procedure and their staffs in Western garb, one might believe oneself to be in Washington or New York. However, Shanghai, Tientsin, and Nanking are not typical of all China, and even in these cities no small amount of the old survives and the new is either localized or superficial.

Yet it would also be a mistake to suppose that outside of these and a few other centers the old China remains as it was under the Ch'ing. Through semi-Occidentalized cities and through many another channel the culture of the West is pouring in and it is a very rare community indeed which does not give some evidence of transformation. Prophecy is notoriously fallible, but it seems probable that before many decades life even in the districts most remote from the coast will be fairly thoroughly altered.

BIBLIOGRAPHY

A good many books contain descriptions of Chinese social institutions and customs as they were in the latter half of the nineteenth century and the first decade of the twentieth, before the changes produced by the West became very apparent. Two giving an unduly pessimistic and sombre picture, but very readable and by one who had opportunity for ample and intimate knowledge, are Arthur H. Smith, *Chinese Characteristics* (New York, 1894), and Arthur H. Smith, *Village Life in China* (New York, 1899). At almost the other extreme, idealizing its subject, is Y. K. Leong and L. K. Tao, *Village and Town Life in China* (London, 1915). See, too, Fei Hsiao-tung, *Peasant Life in China. A Field Study of Country Life in the Yangtze Valley* (London, 1939), excellent. A description of life as it was about the middle of the last century in and near Foochow is J. Doolittle, *Social Life of the Chinese* (2 vols., New York, 1867). There is a great deal of material culled from various books in Chinese and European languages in *Descriptive Sociology, or Groups of Sociological Facts, Classified and Arranged by Herbert Spencer, Chinese,* by E. T. C. Werner, edited by H. R. Tedder (London, 1910). A shorter work by E. T. C. Werner is *China of the Chinese* (London and New York, 1919). J. H. Gray, *China, A History of the Laws, Manners, and Customs of the People* (2 vols., London, 1878) contains a great deal of information on the China of the mid-nineteenth century. See also S. D. Gamble, *Hsin Chuang. A Study of Chinese Village Finance* (*Harvard Journal of Asiatic Studies,* Vol. 8, pp. 1–33).

An excellent book on Chinese women, old and new, is F. Ayscough, *Chinese Women Yesterday and Today* (Boston, 1937).

Books portraying family life and customs of the old style but as they have been altered to a certain extent by contact with the West are D. H. Kulp, *Country Life in South China. The Sociology of Familism* (New York, 1925), a description, by trained observers, one of them Chinese, of a village not very far from Swatow; Lady Hosie, *Two Gentlemen of China* (London, 1924), an account, by a sympathetic Englishwoman, of two families, both wealthy and of high official rank, with which she had been intimate; The Princess Der Ling, *Kowtow* (New York, 1929), an autobiography of a Manchu lady of high rank, especially of her childhood and youth, with charming accounts of her home; Pierre Hoang, *Le Mariage Chinois au Point de Vue Legal* (2d ed., Shanghai, 1916); E. T. Williams, *China, Yesterday and Today* (New York, 3d ed., 1927), by one who knew China and the Chinese well for many years and writes of them with sympathy; Pearl S. Buck, *The Good Earth* (New York, 1931), although fiction, a remarkably vivid and accurate description of life on a farm and in an old-fashioned city; *Ching Ho, The Report of a Preliminary Survey of the Town of Ching Ho, Hopei, North China* (Peiping, 1931), done by members of the department of Sociology of Yenching University; Sheng-cheng,

A Son of China (translated from the French by M. M. E. Lowes, New York, 1930); H. D. Lamson, *Social Pathology in China* (Shanghai, 1935); and Lin Yueh-hwa, *The Golden Wing, a Family Chronicle* (New York, 1944).

A voluminous account of one of the greatest of the secret societies, the Triads, largely as it was not long ago among the Chinese community at Singapore, is in J. S. M. Ward and W. G. Sterling, *The Hung Society, or The Society of Heaven and Earth* (2 vols., London, 1925).

On etiquette of the old days a brief treatise is W. G. Walshe, *"Ways that are Dark," Some Chapters on Chinese Etiquette and Social Procedure* (Shanghai, 1906). Another on the same subject is Simon Kiong, *Quelques Mots sur la Politesse Chinoise* (*Variétés Sinologiques*, No. 25, Shanghai, 1906).

There are several books on the theatre in China. Three of the best are L. C. Arlington, *The Chinese Drama from the Earliest Times until Today* (Shanghai, 1930), George Soulié de Morant, *Théâtre et Musique Moderne en Chine* (Paris, 1926), and R. F. Johnston, *The Chinese Theatre* (1921). Others, less adequate, are Chu Chia-chien, *The Chinese Theatre*, translated from the French by James A. Graham, with illustrations . . . by A. Jacovleff (London, 1922), A. E. Zucker, *The Chinese Theatre* (London, 1925), and B. S. Allen, *Chinese Theatres Handbook* (Tientsin, no date). There is also an interesting monograph on one phase of dramatic art, W. Grube, translator, *Chinesische Schattenspiele. Auf Grund des Nachlasses durchgesehen und abgeschlossen von Emil Krebs. Herausgegeben und eingeleitet von Berthold Laufer* (2 vols., Munich, 1915).

On music, see bibliography at close of Chapter XVIII.

A good deal of material on Chinese festivals is in L. Hodous, *Folkways in China* (London, 1929). Other books on the festivals are Juliet Bredon and I. Mitrophanow, *The Moon Year, a Record of Chinese Customs and Festivals* (Shanghai, 1927) and J. J. M. de Groot, *Les fêtes annuellement célébrées a Emoui* (*Amoy*) (2 vols., Paris, 1886).

On fighting crickets, there is a brief popular account by Henry Peterson, *Gladiators an Inch Long*, in *Asia*, Oct., 1930 (Vol. 30, pp. 720, 721).

Accounts of the changes during the last few years are to be found in many books and articles. Some of the innovations in family life and relations between the sexes and the problems attendant on them are described in Lady Hosie, *Portrait of a Chinese Lady and Certain of Her Contemporaries* (New York, 1930), in an excellent piece of fiction by Pearl S. Buck, *East Wind, West Wind* (New York, 1930), in Pearl S. Buck, *China, the Eternal* (*International Review of Missions*, 1924, Vol. 13, pp. 573–584), in Pearl S. Buck, *Chinese Women* (*Pacific Affairs*, Oct., 1931, pp. 905–909), in Pearl S. Buck, *Sons* (New York, 1932), and in a short story by Pearl S. Buck, *The First*

Wife (*Asia*, Dec., 1931, Jan., 1932). E. A. Ross, *The Changing Chinese, The Conflict of Oriental and Western Cultures in China* (New York, 1911), is a readable and discerning description by a well known sociologist who was in China on the eve of the Revolution of 1911. An interesting autobiography of a Young Chinese woman affected by the new ways is Helena Kuo, *I've Come a Long Way* (New York, 1942). Glimpses of Chinese Life in the disturbances of the 1930's are in W. Galbraith, *In China Now* (New York, 1941).

CHAPTER XVIII

ART

CONTRARY to an impression widespread in the West, China is a land of beauty. Hills and mountains, valleys and gorges, some of them of surpassing grandeur, characterize much of her landscape. For those who have ever felt her charm, China holds an inescapable fascination. In spite of the grey, dusty plains of her North, the dirt of many of her streets, the poverty of her masses, and the disrepair into which the relics of her past have often been allowed to drift, she casts her spell over those who are long within her borders and are at all sensitive to beauty. No one who has travelled much in China can easily escape the haunting memories of sights and sounds which have stirred him to the depths—the glow of the sunset on distant bare peaks, thundercaps over mountains and fertile plains, evening twilight on a pagoda-crowned hill above the quiet reaches of a river, the solid lines of an ancient city wall, the boom of a distant temple bell coming through the stillness of the night, the antiphonal, wordless chanting of laboring coolies in the drowsy heat of a summer afternoon, the sweep of the Yangtze, the glimpse of a monastery half-hidden in a wooded glen, the charm of an old painting which a succession of faithful hands now long since gone have handed down through many generations, the well-proportioned contours of a garden, or the impressively silent courts and magnificent, time-mellowed colors of the palaces of Peiping.

HISTORICAL SUMMARY

In earlier chapters we have recorded something of the history of Chinese art and have noted how varied and rich has been that phase of the culture of the Empire. We have seen, too, that art has been by no means uniform either in quality or in characteristics, but that it has had distinct periods. Here, as in so many other respects, over the course of the centuries the civilization of China has exhibited anything but a uniform or monotonous aspect.

There is the pottery of prehistoric times with its markings and colored surfaces, some of it reminiscent of early ceramics to the west of China. Between it and the surviving examples of the artistic genius of the Shang dynasty a gap may have intervened—although the two may have overlapped. From the Shang are still extant "oracle bones," the writing on which shows skill and taste, and some jade. There are also bronzes—weapons and vessels of various kinds—although some experts are reluctant confidently to assign to the Shang many of the objects usually attributed to it. While obviously archaic, they possess vigor as well as grace of outline, with geometrical designs and more or less conventionalized animal forms, and bear witness to a civilization which was no longer primitive.

From the Chou, with its long duration and lasting into the third century B.C., a large number of objects remain, many of them disclosed by accidental exhumation. Systematic archeological excavations on a large scale would certainly bring to light quantities of additional examples. Bronze weapons, vessels of many shapes, and bells are fairly numerous. On some is seen the favorite design of an ogre, or glutton, the *t'ao t'ieh*. There are pieces of jade, many of them symbols of Heaven and Earth. For centuries the Confucian Temple in the capital has housed the famous ten stone drums, boulders roughly hewn and bearing inscriptions in archaic characters. Much of the art of the Chou was apparently a continuation of that of the Shang, but with modifications. Especially toward the latter part of the dynasty new influences entered, possibly Scythian, from that great region in Central Europe-Asia with which the Chinese have through the centuries been closely in touch and from which have repeatedly come contributions to Chinese culture.

Artistically the Ch'in was in large part an extension of the latter part of the Chou, but with increasing liveliness of style and a certain exuberance and flamboyance which may have been due in part to the general temper of the times and in part to contacts with the outside world. Influences may have entered through the conquest of Ch'u, whose culture in some respects differed from that of the North.

With the Han great changes occurred. Unlike the Ch'in, a simplicity and severity of decoration and of outline were often seen. A tendency was displayed to return to the styles of the Chou—as was to be expected from the revival and study of ancient literature. At the same time much more of movement entered and of the attempt to portray life and the forms of animals and men as they really are. Surviving stone sculptures depict battles and scenes at court, hunting, processions, and animals, men, and gods in groups or singly, with a naturalness and a freedom of action which are in striking contrast with the work of artists of preceding centuries and which still help to make vivid the life and the mythology of the age. A similar naturalness and delight in action are seen in the figures on bronzes and jades and in terra cotta funerary figurines. Marked development was registered in ceramics, both plain and glazed. A few examples of the lacquer ware of the dynasty survive. Painting and its closely allied art, calligraphy, were represented. We begin to get some clear ideas of architecture, partly from contemporary terra cotta models, partly from sculptures on the walls of tombs, and partly from a few extant examples, such as walls and forts on the Western frontiers.

Some of the artistic developments and innovations of the Han can be proved to have been due to stimulus from the outside. Certain Han *motifs*, for example, are similar to those in the Central and Western Asia and in the Europe of the time. What are known as Scytho-Sarmatian influences were present. Part of the Han artistic novelty, however, was probably due to that new burst of life and that prosperity which characterized so much of the China under the Han.

In the period of disunion and civil strife which intervened between the Han and the Sui art by no means disappeared. No sudden break occurred and it is often difficult to know whether to assign surviving objects to the Han or to the immediately post-Han centuries. However, modifications and innovations were made. In the states ruled by the barbarians from the North and West it was to be expected that new influences would be at work. Buddhism especially brought with it much that was revolutionary. With Buddhism came many buddhas and bodhisattvas and new gods. With it, too, entered vivid ideas of the future life, of heavens and hells, and many stories of the worthies of the faith which inspired images, carvings, and paintings. Moreover, with the foreign religion came exotic artistic traditions and techniques. We have seen that much of the early Buddhist iconography—the Gandhara School—evolved under the influence of Greek art was transmitted to China. Other, more distinctly Indian influences also entered—notably that of the Gupta era (fourth and fifth centuries). Statues and frescoes, some of gigantic proportions on cliffs and in grottoes, and others smaller and even in miniature were produced. Especially notable are the sculptures of the Northern Wei dynasty, that state founded by the T'u Pa (or Toba) conquerors. One of the greatest of Chinese painters, Ku K'ai-chih, belongs to the period and the canons of Chinese pictorial art as then defined have remained standard. Lay as well as religious subjects were portrayed. New forms of architecture appeared in monasteries and pagodas.

Buddhism was by no means the only foreign influence which entered during the centuries of division. In that Central Asia with which China was in touch were other currents. For example, Persia, through the powerful Sassanid rule, was making itself felt. While these varied strands are seen most distinctly in remains disclosed in recent decades in the ruins on Western frontiers of the then China, in what is now Sinkiang, at least some are distinguishable in China proper.

With the unification of China under the Sui and the T'ang the Empire entered upon a new period of artistic development. Again no sharp break severed the old from the new. The T'ang saw Chinese Buddhism reach its apex and begin its decline. The Chinese soul, stirred profoundly by the Indian faith, expressed itself æsthetically to no small degree in Buddhist forms, although the older Chinese tradition, represented by a vigorous Taoism and a revived Confucianism, remained strong. Much of the impulse seen in the Northern Wei carried over into the Sui. Chinese pilgrims, returning from their pious journeys, helped to keep their native land in touch with the religious art of India. The wealth and power of China under the T'ang naturally favored extensive artistic production. T'ang conquests in Central Asia strengthened contacts with the diverse artistic traditions and movements of that region. There was much Buddhist sculpture. The realistic reproduction of movement and of the human form contribute to the distinctiveness of the work of the era. The depiction of actual life is very marked in such kinds of objects as were becoming emancipated from religious influences, notably funerary earthenware figures. From them, so full of expression and of pulsing action, it is possible to reproduce much of the customs and the dress of the period. Bronzes continued to be produced, among them, as under the Han, decorated mirrors. The traditional popularity of jade persisted, and many were the forms in which this semi-precious stone was painstakingly carved. Painting flourished, with religious (chiefly Buddhist and Taoist) and secular subjects. He who is sometimes regarded as the greatest Chinese painter of all time, Wu Tao Tzŭ, belongs, it will be remembered, to the T'ang. Calligraphy probably reached its height. Marked development was made in pottery: glazes were more skillfully used than heretofore, there was an improvement in the forms of vases, and true porcelain first appeared.

Under the Sung sculpture declined, but painting, and especially landscapes, attained new heights. In an earlier chapter we have seen some of the reasons for the emphasis upon this type of painting and have noticed that the landscapes of subsequent periods have never surpassed and have seldom if ever equalled those of the Sung masters. We have also seen that porcelains of fine quality, predominantly with monochrome glazes, were produced in great quantities.

The Yüan dynasty, being that of Mongol conquerors who furthered contacts with aliens, brought a fresh influx of foreign impulses. These are especially seen in a reaction from landscapes and in a vivid portrayal of action, notably in the horses which the Mongol riders of the steppes and deserts so much admired. Persian influences were also present. As was to be expected, however, older forms and schools persisted, for the rule of the Mongols over all China spanned scarcely two generations.

Under the Ming it was secular art in which the greatest achievements were registered. Religious art continued, but the fervor and vigor of both Buddhism and Taoism were declining and inspiration and creative genius were disappearing from the portrayal of religious subjects. Painting remained popular, with landscapes, flowers, birds, animals, and scenes from everyday life among its leading subjects, but while it was often elaborate and painstaking, with a highly developed technique, it did not equal the best of the Sung. Porcelain was made in large quantities, polychrome decoration, often rich and varied, predominating. Articles of luxury—rugs, embroideries, bronzes, jades, lacquers, ivory, and the like—were produced, often with cunning and a lavish expenditure of time and labor, for the wealthy and powerful, for under the Ming and the Ch'ing, except for the disorders of the seventeenth century and the latter half of the nineteenth, China was as prosperous as it had ever been. The Ming, too, was an age of building, when many of the walls, bridges, and palaces were constructed which constituted the chief architectural features of the China of the nineteenth and twentieth centuries. The Ch'ing made no marked departure from the Ming.

This brief sketch, inadequate though it is, will at least show that the course of Chinese art has been marked by great periods, each with its distinct characteristics.

Yet through all the centuries has run a continuity. With their admiration for the past, the Chinese have loved and tended to reproduce the forms of the earliest ages. In the bronzes of the Ch'ing are objects which obviously take their inspiration from those of the Chou and the Shang and the porcelain and pewter of the Ming and the Ch'ing often show respect for antiquity. The architecture of the Han, as we see it depicted in grave sculptures and pottery, is obviously in the ancestral line of the palaces, walls, and temples of the nineteenth and twentieth centuries. When, as often, the Chinese accepted foreign contributions, they were seldom slavish imitators but placed their own stamp upon them. The Chinese artistic genius has distinct features and characteristics.

If, as some maintain, art is the expression of a people's soul, and if a civilization can be epitomized in its æsthetic forms, then Chinese culture is most varied. The magnificence of its imperial ideal, a single state governing all mankind, is set forth in the imposing walls and impressive palaces of its capital. The long struggle to defend the prosperous plains from the barbarian is pictured by the Great Wall. The sense of moderation, so prized in its Confucian philosophy, is made vivid by the repose of well proportioned courts and buildings. The desire to be at one with the soul back of the visible universe is seen in the landscapes of Sung masters, and the vision of a life beyond the grave is given by

Buddhism in many paintings and sculptures. The delicate, almost feminine sensitiveness of the race may be divined in many a picture of flowers and animals and in intricate carving. In some of the temple representations of hell is the coarse vigor of Chinese popular life.

To do as we have in several of the immediately preceding chapters, and describe this phase of Chinese life as it was in the nineteenth century on the eve of the great change brought by the impact of the Occident, would scarcely be adequate. The decadence of the Ch'ing which helped cast a blight over much of Chinese genius was reflected as clearly in art as in any phase of culture. We must, rather, attempt to show the main characteristics and the total achievement of the Chinese in the chief divisions of art and then indicate something of the effect of the West upon them.

ARCHITECTURE

Although for more than two thousand years the Chinese have been erecting buildings and walls, some of them of gigantic proportions, a surprisingly small proportion of the structures are very old. In their present form comparatively few go back as far as the T'ang and the Sung or even to the Yüan. Most of those which can boast of more than a century of age were put up, at least substantially as they are now, only in the Ming or in the prosperous first century and a half of the Ch'ing. To be sure, some walls of the Han are extant—largely because they have been preserved in the desert air of the Western frontiers. There are many tombs from the Han and even earlier. A few rockhewn temples have come down from T'ang and even pre-T'ang times, and a number of pagodas built under the Sung and T'ang can still be seen. Here and there are a very few temples which were probably erected before the T'ang. So, too, there are ancient stone bridges. Compared with the extent and richness of Chinese culture, however, the archeologist interested in architecture has available much less surviving material than in such sites of old civilizations as Mesopotamia, the Nile Valley, and the shores of the Mediterranean.

This dearth of structures of pre-Ming times is not due to the absence of building in these centuries. From books and paintings we know that then as now the land had palaces and temples, some of them as huge as could be found in the world of their time. The great wall built on the northern marches of Ch'in Shih Huang Ti must have dwarfed the seven wonders of the Mediterranean world, and the imperial residence which he erected at his capital was enormous. So, too, the palaces of Han and the T'ang must have been very extensive. At the height of these dynasties Ch'angan could probably have stood comparison with the other metropolises of those eras in the number of its dwellings and in the spaciousness and dignity of its walls and palaces. Marco Polo, who had been in many of the great cities of his day, saw Hangchow only a few years after it had ceased to be the capital of the Sung and described it as preëminent "to all others in the world, in point of grandeur and beauty." From the extent of its walls, which can even now be traced, from the accounts of contemporary travellers, and from such a surviving monument as the Drum Tower, we can form some conception of the extent and architectural magnificence of Cambaluc under the Mongols.

The lack of buildings and walls from ancient times is due largely to the perishable nature of the materials. Wood has been extensively employed. As a rule, indeed, it has been the chief reliance for the framework not only of private houses but of palaces and temples. Brick has been utilized to fill in walls or for supporting platforms, and not to hold up roofs. Stone appears chiefly in ornamental trimmings. Since, moreover, the great frontier ramparts and the walls of cities have usually been of rubble lined with brick, and sometimes even of tamped unbaked earth, they have not stood up as well as though they had been of stone.

In spite of the paucity of ancient monuments, it is possible to learn a good deal of the architecture of pre-Ming centuries and to know something of the main stages of its development. Japan possesses very old wooden buildings which have escaped the ravages of fire and war and since some of these caught their inspiration from Chinese models we can form an idea of what the latter were like. Wall sculptures from the Han and later dynasties not infrequently portray buildings, and paintings of the T'ang and Sung of which we have either the originals or copies often include pictures of buildings, from simple huts to palaces and temples. The great wealth of Chinese literature which has come down to us from previous centuries contains useful information. There is at least one detailed treatise on architecture from as early as the Sung.

We cannot here go into this history. It must be noted, however, that non-Chinese influences entered, with marked results. Buddhism particularly brought new forms, some of them Indian and others Tibetan or of other provenance. Yet, although factors from abroad were often potent, architecture remained distinctively Chinese. In time even alien patterns were altered to fit the national tradition.

Without attempting to arrange them in any logical order, the main characteristics which run through most of Chinese architecture may be enumerated about as follows. First of all may be mentioned the desire to make the works of man accord with the universe. From early times it has been felt that if man is to prosper he must not antagonize or even strive to master the world about him but must seek to put himself in harmony with it. This conviction has expressed itself in part in *fêng shui*. As we have seen, the latter often determines the location of houses and especially of tombs and the arrangement of the units of these structures.

Walls are prominent. Every city has had one, and many survive. Although the passion to conform to Western example has torn down a few of them, others have recently been repaired. Their primary purpose has been defence, and this they have fulfilled most usefully. Even villages may be surrounded by mud ramparts as a protection against robbers. The city walls are often imposing. They are usually, as has just been said, of clay or earth faced with brick and in some instances are trimmed with stone. Many average twenty-five or thirty feet in height and at the top are twenty feet or more in breadth. A circumference of five or six miles is not unusual. In some of the chief cities, such as Peiping, the walls are higher and enclose a larger area. City walls are pierced by gates which usually are closed at nightfall and opened at dawn. Over the gates rise towers, many of them several stories in height, and in front are sometimes secondary, curtaining walls, with a gate or gates entering obliquely. The wall is often surrounded by a moat, and its top is crenelated.

As we have seen, the Great Wall, called by the Chinese the *Wan-li-ch'ang-ch'êng*, "the Ten Thousand Li Long Wall," along the northern frontier of China proper, has a long history. Sections of it were in existence before Ch'in Shih Huang Ti, and that great monarch completed the barrier. It was repaired and rebuilt again and again, sometimes not on the original course of the old. As it exists now it dates from several periods and is of more than one type of construction. The latest thorough-going repairs seem to have been given it under the Ming, and two hundred miles or more were added under that dynasty. The Ch'ing being masters of Manchuria and Mongolia, against inroads from which it was a protection, presumably did not have as much need for it as did the Ming. The Wall stretches from Shanhaikuan into Kansu, a distance of about twelve hundred and fifty miles in a straight line, and with all its windings probably over fifteen hundred miles. In several places it is double and even triple, thus affording more than one line of defence. Sometimes the successive barriers are many miles apart. Built with an eye for strategic positions, the Great Wall follows mountain crests and takes advantage of narrow gorges. In height it ranges from fifteen to fifty feet, with towers rising at intervals above it. At its base its width is from fifteen to thirty feet and at its top twelve feet or more. On its outer side, for much of the distance, is a moat. The material varies. On the eastern reaches, where it is in the best repair, the Wall usually has an earth or rubble core faced with either brick or stone, bound together by an excellent mortar. Many of the stones are huge hewn granite blocks, some of them fourteen feet long and three or four feet thick. In the western sections the Wall is often carved out of the loess and faced with stone, or made of loess watered and tamped into wooden forms. In much of Kansu it is simply an earthern bank. Behind it at intervals were permanent camps for the garrisons.

Walls have been used not only for cities and for imperial defence, but to enclose temples, palaces, and private homes. From the outside, nearly every such Chinese structure presents the aspect of a blank screen, at proper places pierced by gates which in turn are often shielded by curtaining walls. The wall may show a little variation and some of the interior buildings may rise above the parapet, but the exterior frequently gives little clue to the quiet courts and gardens within.

Another feature of Chinese architecture is the enclosed court.

In temples, palaces, and dwellings of any size the individual units are as a rule grouped about quadrangles, sometimes square and sometimes elongated. Most buildings are one or two stories in height, and more space is usually obtained, not by adding stories, as is so often done in the Occident, but courts. The best of Chinese buildings preserve a proportion between the width of courts and the heights and forms of buildings which is both impressive and restful.

A characteristic already hinted at is the extensive use of wood. A few buildings have stone pillars, but in the vast majority the framework is timber. Wooden pillars are used to support the roof and the entire structure is tied together by beams of the same material. The walls—of brick or wood or sometimes of plastered wattled or tamped earth—are simply for purposes of enclosure. In this respect the Chinese house is not unlike the steel construction of a modern Occidental office-building.

Many of the beams are left exposed. The walls may be built around the inner row of pillars and the outer row be left unenclosed. The supporting pillars may be painted or coated with lacquer and the beams carved or painted in conventional designs of various colors. In this manner the exposed wooden framework becomes an ornamental feature and the view upward, toward the beams and rafters which support the roof, can be made very attractive.

Chinese pillars are without capitals in the Western sense of that word. Often wooden brackets at the top give the appearance of helping to support the beam above and so prevent the transition from seeming abrupt. Usually, too, there are pedestals, some of them small, but many of them large and highly ornamented.

As a rule important buildings are placed on platforms faced with brick or stone. Some of the platforms are low, requiring only one or two steps to mount them. Many, however, are quite high, necessitating a dozen or more steps. The platforms and the stairways are often set off by balustrades of stone, brick, or wood, in numerous instances elaborately carved. The stairways themselves may be broad, and frequently two rows of steps are separated by an inclined face displaying an elaborately carved dragon. There may be three sets of steps mounting the platform, especially if, as is so often the case, the surmounting building has three doorways.

One of the most prominent features of a Chinese building is the roof. It is possible that the platform is designed to preserve a balance and to keep the roof from seeming out of proportion. Sometimes roofs are double or even triple, the eaves of the second and the third being set back from the one below, and each upper one being raised above the one underneath by a wall or a kind of clerestory with supporting pillars. They are usually tiled, although thatch may be employed in poorer houses. In many instances, especially in such structures as temples and palaces, the tiles are covered with a colored glaze. No one who has seen them can forget the yellow roofs of the imperial palaces of Peiping or the blue of the Temple of Heaven. Often the main lines of the roofs are emphasized by tiles curiously shaped in conventional geometric patterns or in the form of dragons or of other animals mythical or real. Sometimes the decorations are in bronze or iron. Often the crown of the roofs is mounted by especially elaborate decorations of designs of varying history and origin. The eaves are usually prominent and terminated by ornate tiles. The curved eaves are familiar to all who know anything at all about Chinese buildings. The origin of the curve is uncertain. The surviving representations of Han buildings do not have it, and it seems not to have entered until the first millennium of our era. It may have been adopted to afford relief from the severely straight lines which the heavy projecting roof would otherwise present, or it may have been devised to let in more light.

Not much is made of the gable ends, although these are often decorated. Most Chinese buildings are elongated rectangles and are intended to be viewed from the side rather than the end. It is the broad façade in which the door or doors are placed and from which the sweep of the roof can be seen to best advantage.

Much color is employed, and generally, even to the uninitiated Westerner, with pleasing effect. When it is said baldly that the roofs of some buildings are yellow and their walls red, and that the timbers are ornamented with elaborate designs in bright and variegated colors, to one who has never seen them the results might be thought rather bizarre. When actually viewed, however, they usually seem eminently fitting and in excellent taste.

Many buildings have a great deal of lattice-work, some of it elaborately carved. To this Chinese construction lends itself, for since the weight of the roof is carried by pillars the walls need not be substantial but can be perforated as much as the architect desires.

Chinese buildings display more variety than the preceding account with its impressions of rectilinear courts and flanking structures might indicate. The Chinese have often employed the octagonal pavilion, generally for decorative purposes. Even walls of cities and rectangular courts and buildings lend themselves to many combinations.

The architecture of much of the Yangtze Valley and the South differs in part from that of the North. The former shows a greater tendency to flamboyance, and to exaggerated curves in the roof.

The pagoda has been prominent. As we now see it, it is a Chinese development. It came, however, from Buddhism. It appears to have taken its inspiration, at least in part, from the stupa, a structure which seems originally to have been for the housing of relics of Buddhist saints, and is of Indian provenance. Pagodas began to be built in China not long after the introduction of Buddhism. At least one is extant which dates from early in the sixth century and several can be seen which were built during the T'ang and the Sung. Pagodas seldom have more than fifteen stories. The total is always uneven, for popular Buddhism sets more value by odd than by even numbers. Pagodas may be very high. One is known which towers to three hundred and sixty feet. The material varies. In some instances it has been wood, but, naturally, the structures which survive are mostly of brick or stone. Often they are octagonal and frequently they are square, but the shape and size vary greatly. The pagoda has largely lost its close connection with Buddhism and has come to be associated with *fêng shui*. It was generally under the guidance of this pseudo-science and to insure good fortune to a city or a site that the pagodas—at least the later ones—were erected. While very few, if any, have been built in recent decades, hundreds of those constructed by earlier generations are still to be seen, picturesque features of many a landscape.

Bridges are another characteristic work of the Chinese builder. A large proportion are of stone. Many have a single arch, some of them, perhaps for the purpose of allowing boats to pass, made high and ascended by steps. Others have several arches. Many are constructed of huge stones laid longitudinally and supported by piers. There are some suspension bridges, but these are usually over the mountain torrents in the West.

A familiar feature of Chinese cities is the *p'ai lou* or *p'ai fang*, the memorial arch. At least under the Ch'ing, these could be erected only by imperial permission. They are in honor of distinguished officials, of local worthies noted for their virtue or learning, for centenarians, for families who have lived together for several generations, for women who won celebrity by a life of virtuous widowhood from youth to old age, or for those memorable for other meritorious action. Sometimes they are not commemorative, but simply decorative. As a rule they consist of four pillars supporting transverse stones and presenting three passages, the central one wider than the others. Often, however, they have only one passage, and a good many have five.

Graves are inevitable concomitants of a Chinese landscape. Some are quite elaborate. Imperial tombs generally cover a fairly large area, and with their great courts, their avenues, their numerous buildings, and their sense of dignified repose, are very impressive, even in decay.

Many travellers declare Peiping to be architecturally the most majestic city they have ever seen. That is not solely or perhaps entirely because to the Westerner it appears exotic. It is rather because it is so fittingly constructed for the capital of an Empire which professed to rule all of civilized humanity. Its high walls with the higher towers above the gates seem in themselves symbols of dignity and power. Its distances and its broad main streets, some of them straight, so in contrast to many of the other old cities of the world, give a sense of spaciousness which dust, dirt, and squalor cannot obscure. Its temples, especially that constructed for the worship of Heaven, bespeak an order which sought to harmonize the forces of all nature for the welfare of all mankind. But especially do the imperial palaces, even in their present emptiness and air of departed glory, create the impression of empire. Placed in the center of a city which in itself is imposing, they symbolize a power to which all the rest is but ancillary. To the envoy bringing the homage of a tributary state the entire setting must have inspired awe—the entrance through the towering city wall, the broad avenue leading to the Imperial City, progress through an imposing gateway which formed the main entrance to the imperial precincts, then a succession of great courts flanked by well-proportioned buildings, resplendent in their yellow-tiled roofs and highly colored walls, and at last, after passage across a huge court, the imperial throne-room and the imperial presence. It must all have been most telling, especially when, as on important occasions, the courts were the scene of stately ceremonial and were flanked by the many dignitaries in their gorgeous official robes and by uniformed servants and soldiers. Through centuries of experience the Chinese learned to construct a capital to conform to their vision of a world-embracing rule and civilization.

GARDENS

With the Chinese, the art of garden-planting has been closely related to architecture. Not only are buildings often designed to fit into rather than to dominate nature, but through gardens that adjustment is furthered. Buddhist and Taoist monasteries and temples are often placed in mountain valleys. Trees and shrubs are encouraged to grow about them so that the buildings are half hidden and harmonize with their natural surroundings. Paths make accessible the chief beauty spots of the grounds. The Summer Palace outside Peiping, although built in the years of the decay of the Ch'ing, displays remarkable success in the arrangement of buildings to fit in with the landscape and in the alteration of the landscape by roads, bridges, trees, and bodies of water in such a fashion that, without seeming to do violence to it, it is made to contribute to the buildings and to the pleasure of the Court. So, too, the imperial palaces and their grounds in Peiping, with their pools and artificial hills and their planting of shrubs, are examples of harmonious planning. The way in which the builder has utilized the West Lake at Hangchow with its guardian hills is still another instance of Chinese skill in taking advantage of attractive scenery and enhancing its beauty and accessibility.

Many a private home has its gardens. These are usually formal and numbers of them have artificial rockeries which to the uninitiated Westerner seem somewhat bizarre and grotesque. The garden is often a miniature landscape, with hills, grottoes, crags, streams, trees, and lakes. Frequently doorways, some of them circular, afford vistas of other sections of the garden. Walls with or without lattice work are added to the picture. Water is essential and is directed into pools, often lotus-covered, or into running streams. The Chinese gardener is a master of the art of dwarfing trees and of training them into shapes to suit his purposes. He rejoices, too, in little hills crowned with small pavilions. Summer-houses, rustic bridges, and walks laid out in zigzag or winding designs are customary.

The range of flowers and decorative shrubs and trees utilized by the Chinese is not so wide as the rich flora of the country would give reason to expect. The Chinese, however, cultivate a fairly large variety. Even in the poorest homes a flowering plant or two will often be seen, and the courtyards of inns and shops frequently have one or more of them. Avenues of trees are often planted as an approach to a tomb or a temple, many a tree is protected from the woodsman's ax by a wayside shrine, and, as we have seen, Buddhist and Taoist monasteries are usually embowered in groves. The Chinese have floral calendars and watch eagerly for the appearance of the first blossoms on certain trees and shrubs and may go in parties into the country to see them. Flowers have been favorite subjects for poems and paintings.

SCULPTURE

In China sculpture has not usually been regarded so highly as have been some other branches of art—as, for example, painting. Few names of sculptors have, accordingly, come down to us, unless they are famous for other reasons. Yet much of Chinese sculpture, even though the work of unknown artisans, has been noteworthy, and the total quantity is enormous.

Chinese sculpture, as we have seen, reached its apex in the T'ang, under the inspiration of Buddhism. However, it has not been confined to Buddhist subjects nor is it entirely a Buddhist creation. It was found at least as early as the Shang and a good many examples have survived from the Han, before Chinese art had been much affected by the foreign faith.

In themes Chinese sculptors have shown a great variety. They have not been much interested in the human form as such. Of course they have depicted it extensively, and there have been many portrait statues. However, they have taken no such joy in it as did the artists of the ancient Graeco-Roman world and of the European Renaissance. As a rule the human body has been for them simply a means of expressing action or an idea or has been an object on which to drape clothing. Many Chinese sculptors, however, have rejoiced in depicting animals. They have shown them in motion and at rest and have delighted in their play of muscles.

Some surviving examples of ancient sculpture are connected with graves. From the Han we have pillars which once formed a kind of entrance to the tomb enclosure. We have huge stone animals which were associated with tombs, vivid carvings on the walls of the tombs themselves of scenes from real life or from mythology, and earthen figures, some of them shaped in molds and others fashioned directly by the hands of the craftsmen. These general types were not confined to the Han, but persisted through several dynasties. Such were the terra cotta figurines, of which we have particularly beautiful examples from the T'ang. Such, too, were the monolithic figures, of animals and men, arranged in pairs on either side of a "spirit way" leading southward from the tomb. Apparently they were for the purpose of protecting it from evil influences, including malevolent spirits.

Some of the *motifs* of early tomb-statues are clearly foreign importations. Prominent among them is the lion, a beast which seems not to have existed in China, at least in large numbers, for some were sent as tribute, obviously as rarities. The idea of depicting the lion in stone appears to have been of non-Chinese origin. There are even some winged beasts, reminiscent of the great figures in the Tigris-Euphrates Valley, and very possibly historically connected with them. Central Asiatic influences, perhaps Iranian and Sarmatian, also entered. We hear of huge bronze statues under the Ch'in and the Han, but all of these seem to have disappeared.

Most of the greatest Chinese sculpture has been produced under the inspiration of Buddhism. That faith, as we have repeatedly seen, first made itself powerfully felt in the period of disunion between the Han and the Sui. With it came a rich iconography—of buddhas, bodhisattvas, gods, the lotus, and many another symbolic design. The impulses under which this Buddhist art had taken form were, as we have seen, varied. Some, notably those adopted on the northwestern borders of India, were Greek. Others were more fully Indian. Persian art, through the Sassanian Empire, made its influence felt, especially on minor decorations. Buddhist iconography had conventions—among them draperies and symbolic gestures and postures—which were rather inflexible and allowed the craftsman less freedom for the expression of individual genius than have some other artistic traditions. Yet the Chinese sculptor took over these alien forms and at his best greatly improved them. Often he seems to have been a lay artisan who worked from a description rather than a model. Certainly he sometimes took liberties with tradition. He more nearly humanized the revered figures and gave them greater variety. In time, too, he made the mantle folds on the images more flowing and graceful. At its highest, Chinese Buddhist sculpture is of a better quality as an expression of artistic genius and even of religious feeling and conviction than are its Indian prototypes. The characteristic Buddhist statue shows repose, relaxation, meditation, and unperturbed calm. Into it can go much of the idealism and aspiration which Buddhism fosters.

Chinese Buddhist sculptors ventured on innovations. The *stelae*, for example, which they executed either were Chinese in origin or had been sinicized in form and design. Memorial *stelae* seem first to have appeared in Han times and were elaborated in subsequent centuries. They bore inscriptions and sometimes figures, and often were mounted on tortoises and crowned with entwined dragons.

Since the greatest of Chinese Buddhist sculpture was executed in the first century of the T'ang and in pre-T'ang times, most of it has probably perished. There remain, however, numerous examples, notably on cliffs and in grottoes. Prominent among these are the ones at Ta-t'ung, in Shansi, once a capital of the Northern Wei, at Tun-huang, in Kansu, and at Lung Mên, in Honan. Through extant specimens experts trace various periods. In the sculptures of the Northern Wei the Hellenistic influences which found such marked expression at Gandhara are strong, into a transitional period shortly before the Sui and under the Sui a new wave from India entered, and the early years of the T'ang are characterized by a strength and a richness and exuberance of decoration in keeping with the vigorous years of that dynasty.

By the close of the seventh century Chinese Buddhist sculpture was declining both in quantity and quality. This is probably attributable in part to the fact that Chinese Buddhism was itself passing its zenith. Secular influences began to make themselves felt. More portrait statues appeared among them of monks and some of them obviously excellent likenesses. Even bodhisattvas were more humanized.

Under the Five Dynasties and the Sung, painting reached its greatest heights and absorbed much of the artistic genius of the Empire. Sculpture responded to the change and showed the effects of the popularity of the rival art. The sculptor worked less exclusively in stone and bronze, used more wood, clay, iron, and lacquer, and tended to treat his images with color. Kuan-yin, originally male, became female in form and acquired her now characteristic expression of womanly mercy and compassion.

Under the dynasties which conquered the North during the latter centuries of the Sung a revival of Buddhist sculpture occurred—from what cause is uncertain. The Yüan brought modifications but no marked development or improvement.

Under the Ming quantities of religious figures were produced, for Buddhism was still popular. Probably because the faith was largely dependent on the momentum acquired in earlier, more pious generations and no longer attracted genius and quickened the imagination as it had in its years of greatest prosperity, most of the Buddhist images were now the uninspired reproduction of stereotyped forms. Ming sculptors seem to have become enthusiastic only when they dealt with real life—as they did at times in a rather incidental fashion. They devoted much energy to the carving of columns and of architectural details, and usually were here at their best. Ch'ing Buddhist sculpture was chiefly a continuation of that of the Ming.

It must again be noted that, great as was its debt to Buddhism and the foreign influences of which Buddhism was the vehicle, Chinese sculpture, even in the most flourishing days of that faith, was by no means exclusively Buddhist. Secular monolithic figures were still carved to adorn tombs. Memorial *stelae* were erected for non-Buddhist as well as Buddhist purposes. Taoism, heavily indebted to and often slavishly imitative of Buddhism, evolved its own more or less stereotyped iconography. Statues of Confucius were produced. Purely secular sculpture increased with the waning of Buddhist vitality. Naturally it never attained to the spiritual qualities of the best of the Buddhist statues, nor did it loom so large in creative art.

Buddhist and Taoist images, at least in later centuries, were usually in much more perishable material than stone or bronze. Chiefly of clay, they were molded and then painted or gilded. Moreover, as was to be expected, even at the period of richest genius many examples of crude and uninspired craftmanship were perpetrated. Certainly this was true in the centuries of decadence. For instance, the Buddhist and Taoist "hells" whose tortures have been presented in such stark realism in some modern temples seldom display much true artistic feeling. Yet in our own time Buddhist shrines are to be found whose images show religious conviction and give even to the non-Buddhist visitor something of an inkling of the calmness, the repose, and the serenity which are part of the Buddhist ideal.

Closely related to the work of the sculptor was that of the craftsmen who carved wood or ivory. Since the supporting timbers of a Chinese building are so largely utilized for decorative purposes and are often incised as well as painted or lacquered, the Chinese wood carver has found much occupation and has developed not a little skill. He has had many designs—from the flora and fauna of China, and from mythology and religious symbolism. Wood has been carved, too, for furniture and for ornamental objects. China itself produces several kinds of timber which have been used for this purpose and others have been imported. From early times ivory has been prized as a material in which the skilled craftsman could work. Of late years Canton has been a noted center for it. Rhinoceros horns have been favorite objects for the tools of the carver.

PAINTING

If sculpture has not been ranked high by the Chinese as an art, that is not true of painting. They judge painting to have been among their greatest forms of artistic expression. In this appraisal Western connoisseurs are more and more concurring. In the last few decades especially the Occident has been discovering Chinese pictures and notable collections have been gathered in both Europe and America. Many experts freely assert that at its best Chinese painting is one of the outstanding expressions of man's ability to create beauty.

Yet most of the best paintings have long since been lost. This is partly because the most famous artists lived centuries ago—under the Sung, the T'ang, and even earlier. It is partly, too, because the materials employed are extremely perishable. Silk has been the favorite, although paper has also been used, and frescoes have not been uncommon. It is also partly due to the many wars which have swept China. Frail pictures, usually housed in the almost equally inflammable palaces, temples, and private homes, have been calamitously subject not only to the ordinary vicissitudes of fire but to the destruction wrought by civil strife, rebellion, and foreign invasion.

Yet in spite of the perishability of Chinese paintings and the many dangers to which they have been exposed, numerous examples are extant of Sung, T'ang, and even of pre-T'ang masters. A very few are original productions of these periods. Their preservation is due to the high esteem in which they have been held and the care bestowed upon them. More are copies, or copies of copies, for the works of the leading painters have been reproduced again and again. The copy seldom quite equals the original and in quality is often far below it, but at least it transmits something of the conception of the creator. Then, too, since the Japanese have been warm admirers of Chinese art, many examples have been preserved for us in the Island Empire, some of them originals, but more of them copies, or themes treated in the spirit of the great Chinese artists.

This is not the place to attempt a history of Chinese painting. Some of its epochs have been noted in the narrative chapters. It is possible, however, to give some of the outstanding characteristics of the art, together with the names of a few of the greatest of the masters.

Chinese painting is with a brush and by ink and watercolors and by the Chinese is regarded as closely akin to calligraphy. Painting and calligraphy have moved hand in hand since the invention of the brush pen in the Ch'in or the Han. The brush strokes are thought of as providing the framework of the picture and are regarded as of fundamental importance. Perfect control of the brush combined with lofty and discerning thought are held to insure a good picture. Skill in wielding the brush is generally acquired only through prolonged practice. The correct use of the wrist is essential. This is usually a free movement, a support being employed only for the finer strokes.

Before the T'ang, painting was largely by artisans rather than by artists and its strokes lacked variety. However, some great painters emerged and it was in the sixth century that Hsieh Ho laid down the famous canons which are supposed to govern the art. Under the T'ang both calligraphy and painting developed markedly. All the principles of calligraphy were applied to painting and many types of strokes were evolved. It was, however, after the T'ang that the widest variety of strokes appeared. Especially were the artists of the Ming and the Ch'ing masters of technique. They lavished time and energy on it, and developed many schools of employing the brush. The Ming and the Ch'ing painters are, it must be confessed, usually regarded as having been more expert as technicians than great as artists, for in the latter capacity they are commonly judged to have been outranked by their predecessors of the Sung and the T'ang. They were numerous, however, and many of them unquestionably deserve to be remembered.

There have been many mural pictures, but as a rule the work of the Chinese painter is not intended to be displayed continuously in the home or in a public place. It is often in the form of a scroll which is meant to be progressively unrolled and rolled bit by bit, and so not to be viewed in its entirety at once. Even though many paintings are designed to be seen as a whole, they are usually mounted—on heavy paper—in such a way that they can be rolled up and brought out for display only on occasion. Often the scroll bears the seals of the various owners and perhaps a poetic comment on the picture or a note attesting its authenticity. In the case of some older works of art the seals and the comments occupy more space than the picture itself. These seals, it may be added, are obviously one way of tracing the history of a painting—although they are not always genuine and may deceive even the experts.

The subjects of Chinese paintings are many. As we have seen in earlier chapters, the Chinese were the first to paint landscapes extensively. Religious themes have been favorites, especially in the heyday of Buddhism, and both Buddhist and Taoist figures and mythological and historical incidents have been frequent objects of representation. Flowers and trees have been used again and again. Especially has the bamboo been regarded as the test of an artist's ability. The bamboo is at once so employable by man in a wide variety of ways, such a common feature of the Chinese landscape, and so graceful, that it has made a marked appeal to the painter. Depicting the bamboo calls for the utmost skill in the application of the brush strokes which are the basis of Chinese pictorial technique. Only the master can do it well, and, naturally, many have made it a starting point of their endeavors. Birds, insects, fish, and animals have often served as models. Many, too, have rejoiced in portraying scenes from court life, famous historical incidents, and views of the life of humbler folk. There is a marked recurrence of themes: artists have often tested themselves by treating famous subjects and scenes.

The purpose of the Chinese artist has not been to give a photographic reproduction of a landscape or an object. In China poetry and painting have been closely associated. A painter often wrote poetry, and a distinguished poet was also often a painter. Buddhism and Taoism, both of them so largely subjective in their effects, have profoundly influenced painting. Perhaps it is for these reasons that the Chinese artist has attempted to give his own interpretation of what he has seen—to catch the spirit of his subject and to reproduce it, or to seek to put down the impression which has been made on his own soul. In this, to be sure, he has not been unlike many Western artists.

Perhaps because of the Chinese philosophic attitude, man has been subordinated to nature, or, rather, he has been conceived of as part and parcel of the universe—not as dominating it but ideally as harmonizing with it. Many portraits have been made, and human figures have often been introduced into landscapes. Religious pictures, too, have included man. However, the attitude toward man has been quite different from that of the art of the ancient Graeco-Roman world and of European humanism of the Renaissance and modern times.

To some Westerners Chinese paintings at first sight seem lacking in perspective. Judged by Occidental standards this impression is largely justified. Any attempt to represent three dimensions on a two-dimensional surface must have recourse to conventions. The Westerner has accomplished this in part by reproducing lights and shadows and in part by the use of lines. A landscape or object is represented as viewed by an observer from a particular point. By lines and the use of shading and colors the attempt is made to reproduce what the eye has seen from that point. The Chinese, however, have not been unaware of the problem. One of the famous six canons of Hsieh Ho of the sixth century was that proportion (or what may perhaps be translated "perspective") should be correctly conceived or observed. The Chinese painter has employed several devices to convey perspective. Apparently he has often wished the observer to look at his landscape from several angles. In many instances, too, he has thought of the observer as viewing a landscape from a height. At his best the Chinese painter has succeeded in avoiding flatness and in conveying a sense of distance. This he has achieved partly by his use of colors. Often, too, he has done it by reproducing the mists which in the Yangtze Valley and the South are so frequently seen.

Color has played a large part in Chinese paintings. To be sure, there has been much use of monochrome, but in many paintings two or more colors have been employed, often with delicacy and feeling. Again one of the famous six canons of Hsieh Ho was that the tints should be suitable.

Chinese paintings, like those of any other people, must be seen to be appreciated. Even the best of printed reproductions cannot do them full justice. Fortunately many examples are now in the galleries and museums of Europe and North America. Even the amateur cannot fail to be moved by the best of them and finds himself returning to them again and again. Though Buddhism and Taoism are alien to his own spiritual experience, he is impressed by the buddhas, bodhisattvas, and immortals, or perhaps especially by the pictures of a hermit in meditation in a mountain fastness. The landscapes move him. The flowers, the trees, the horses, the birds, and the other living creatures in which the Chinese artists rejoice speak a universal language. So, too, the scenes from the life of court and of commoners are often so full of action and so obviously have caught the spirit of the original that the Westerner to whom the civilization depicted is exotic finds in them the appeal which, when it is well portrayed, human character in its varying moods always makes.

CALLIGRAPHY

As we have seen, the Chinese have thought of calligraphy and painting as closely allied. The two have been regarded as branches of the same art. Expertness in the use of the brush pen is basic to both. It has been maintained, indeed, that it can be better seen in calligraphy than in painting, for in the former it is not modified or obscured by the necessity of portraying objects. Calligraphy has been highly honored, perhaps as much as or more so than any other branch of art.

Examples of calligraphy are more widespread than paintings. In the old system of education specimens of the work of noted calligraphers were reproduced in the form of copy books. Inscriptions were and are to be found almost everywhere—in tablets over city gates, in temples, in government offices and palaces, as shop signs, on the honorary arches or *p'ai lou,* on votive or memorial tablets, on the supporting pillars of a building, and in homes. Scrolls—to be hung in pairs and bearing inscriptions which match each other—are almost universal. They are customary forms of gifts and may be purchased, or, if he is a skilled calligrapher, written by the donor himself. The famous or the powerful may honor their friends by presenting them with scrolls or tablets written by their own hand.

There have been many noted calligraphers. Probably as distinguished as any was Wang Hsi-chih (A.D. 321–379). Much attention was paid by T'ang scholars and artists to calligraphy, but the dynasty did not produce as many outstanding masters of the art as did some others, notably the Sung. Probably the ranking Sung experts were Su Shih (1036–1101) and the eccentric painter Mi Fei (1051–1107). To mention even the most noted of the various dynasties, however, would prove tedious.

The best examples of the calligrapher's work have been treasured as carefully as have been great paintings. Like paintings, too, they have been copied again and again. Moreover, they have been mechanically reproduced. The Chinese form of block printing has allowed them to be multiplied. Some of the most famous have been transferred to stone, and can thence be almost endlessly copied by rubbings—a practice much employed by the Chinese.

Also as in the case of paintings, certain themes have been treated many times. One of the most popular has been the Thousand Character Classic (*Ch'ien Tzŭ Wên*). It is attributed to a scholar of the sixth century A.D. and contains a thousand different characters, no one of which is repeated, arranged four in a line in complete sentences. It was, it may be noted, long used as an elementary text in the schools. Still another has been a famous example of Wang Hsi-chih's penmanship, the Orchard Pavilion of Ting Wu (*Ting Wu Lan T'ing*).

Again as in the case of painting, canons have been laid down for calligraphy. Probably sometime in the Sui or T'ang—although they were attributed to a famous calligrapher of the Han—eight rules were set forth, illustrated in writing the character *yung*. Under later dynasties these were multiplied and elaborated.

Many styles of writing have been developed. At least ten are recognized, and in recent times at least six have been in use—some of them for special purposes only. The four most frequently seen are that which is usually adopted for books, with each stroke clearly written, the "pattern style" for formal and official documents, a running hand, and the *ts'ao* or "grass" hand which is even more abbreviated than the latter.

With their emphasis upon calligraphy, the Chinese have naturally given a great deal of attention to writing materials—paper, pen, ink, and ink-stone. Paper is of several grades and is made of a number of materials. Rice straw, rags, bamboo, what is sometimes known as "paper mulberry," and at least two other plants are employed. In each case, of course, a different kind of paper is produced. Some grades are entirely of plant fibre. Others are treated with sizing—perhaps impregnated with starch. Some, in spite of their apparent fragility, have been very enduring. Not only have specimens of Han times been preserved in the dry desert air of the Western frontier, but entire printed books have come down from the Sung, and there are examples from earlier dynasties. The ink is made from soot resulting from the burning of pine, fir, or oil, mixed with one form or another of glutinous substance, beaten fine and then put into molds. The better kinds may be scented and have gold leaf mixed in them. Ink is put on the market in cakes or cylinders and is inscribed with characters, usually in gold. To prepare it for use by the writer it is rubbed with water on a stone. Some of these stones are regarded as very valuable. Pens are made from the hair of various animals and in such form that when moistened they can be easily pointed.

JADE

What is collectively called jade by Westerners and *yü* by the Chinese comprises more than one kind of rock. It includes nephrite and jadeite, the former a silicate of calcium and magnesium and the latter a silicate of aluminum and sodium. Many peoples have regarded jade as valuable, but it has been especially prized by the Chinese. Under the Chou and part of the Han it was quarried in what is now Shensi and perhaps was found in other parts of the older China. As the domestic sources became exhausted, however, it was imported from Turkestan and later from Yünnan and Burma.

Jade has served many purposes. Jade implements, apparently for secular occupations, have come down from the Chou and perhaps from earlier times. Out of it ceremonial utensils have been made. Under the Chou special kinds of insignia of power were carved from it. In ancient times, too, it was frequently employed in the worship of Heaven, Earth, and other divinities. For instance, a circular jade disc pierced by a round hole was a symbol of Heaven. Tablets of jade have been utilized for writing—but apparently only for imperial purposes. They were used in the ceremonies of *fêng* and *shan*, and even in the Ch'ing dynasty some important documents were incised on them. Jade has been employed for amulets, and jade objects have been buried with the dead, partly because they have been supposed to protect the body from decay and partly because they have been believed to promote immortality. Jade, it has been held by Taoists, is the food of spirits, and at one time it was believed that one's chances of immortality could be improved by eating from jade bowls. Jade has been and is extensively employed in the manufacture of ornaments of many kinds—earrings, hairpins, pendants, clasps, buckles, and the like. From it have been carved vases, bells, resonant stones, ornamental screens, and artificial flowers. Some of its former functions have dropped into abeyance, but it is still greatly valued.

Chinese lapidaries have shown marked skill in working in jade. They have also applied their art to agates, rock crystals, and other stones.

CERAMICS

Another characteristic feature of Chinese æsthetic life has been ceramics. In one phase, porcelain, China long led the rest of the world and in common parlance China and porcelain ware have been almost synonymous. Yet, compared with the Occident, the Chinese potters did not become masters of their craft until comparatively late. Not until the T'ang and Sung did they deserve high rank as artists. In this phase the ancient Mediterranean civilizations were far ahead of the contemporary China of the Chou and the Han.

Something of the history of the potter's art in China has been narrated in earlier chapters. Since, however, it there appeared in piecemeal fashion, a brief recapitulation may help to show the main features of the development and the outstanding characteristics of Chinese ceramics.

What is probably the earliest extant pottery known in China belongs to the Yang Shao and related cultures—that neolithic civilization which was on the edge of the bronze age. What may be the oldest of this earthenware is well shaped, thoroughly baked, painted in various designs and colors, and seems to be akin to forms widely scattered through neolithic Asia. It is quite impossible yet to determine exact dates, but one estimate declares that it cannot be later than 3000 B.C. Along with this painted pottery are remnants of a grey ware of coarser texture and less skilled workmanship and of a type which persisted into the Han. There is also a hard, black pottery. Fragments of a white, hard, carved pottery have been discovered which probably belong to the Shang. The surviving pottery of Chou times is not of particularly high quality.

With the Han, glazed ware began to appear, the art of manufacturing it possibly having been transmitted from the Western world. Moreover, a good deal of attention was paid to ornamentation of other kinds, and there are vessels whose forms show no inconsiderable taste. Most of the examples of Han pottery which we know have been obtained from graves. As we have seen, some of this funerary ware pictures in most interesting and informing fashion the architecture, costumes, and customs of the time. Men, animals, houses, implements, and even fortresses are reproduced in miniature.

In the interval between the Han and the T'ang pottery of Han types persisted, much of it for funerary purposes. New designs entered, some of them possibly of Hellenistic provenance. There appeared, too, a hard ware which is a kind of proto-porcelain. It is within the realm of possibility that true porcelain was developed some time between the Han and the T'ang.

It is certain that under the T'ang porcelain was being manufactured, and from fragments discovered in Western Asia we may assume that it was being exported. Moreover, in the T'ang not only were lead glazes in vogue, but marked development was registered in the harder, feldspathic glazes whose firing requires higher temperatures and which had begun to appear in pre-T'ang times. Glazes of more than one color were sometimes applied to an object and paint might be used. Under the T'ang, indeed, much more color was employed in pottery. Improvement was made in the artistic forms of the earthenware. Numerous figures of burned clay, akin to those of preceding centuries, have been recovered from T'ang tombs. Some of them are glazed and many show marked artistic feeling and skill. The grace and lively vigor of statuettes of dancing girls and horses are unforgettable.

The political turmoil of the five decades which immediately followed the downfall of the T'ang did not prevent improvements in pottery. Chinese literature tells of a remarkably fine ware manufactured for a few years in the present Honan and of a "secret color" made in the present Chêkiang.

The Sung period, so noted for its achievements in painting and in other refined forms of culture, is also distinguished for its ceramics. This was, not unnaturally, of varying quality. Some was heavy stoneware, some semi-porcelainlike, and some the most delicate and beautiful porcelain. A number of different types were produced. Several are peculiar to the Sung and some were made as well under other dynasties—earlier or later, or both—so that even experts are often at a loss to know whether a particular specimen is of Sung or of earlier or of subsequent origin. Both state-directed and private potteries existed. Each important center of manufacture produced a distinct type—although not all the differences are discernible to the layman. Among the most noted of the Sung types is a pure white, somewhat translucent porcelain, often with carved or incised designs, and with a cream or ivory tinted glaze. Frequently the rim of the mouth is not covered by glaze but by a band of copper or silver. Another class with many subdivisions is celadon. Celadon is porcelain or porcelaneous ware, usually with a grey or greyish white body, covered heavily with a translucent glaze of varying shades of green—bluish, greyish, and even grass-green. Sometimes the celadon ware has carved or incised designs, sometimes designs in relief, and sometimes figures which were purposely left uncovered by the glaze and so in baking turned red or reddish brown. These celadons, as we have seen, were widely scattered by commerce and either in Sung or in later times made their way to Mesopotamia, the Near East, and even to Western Europe and as far south as Zanzibar. There was also crackle ware—although this was by no means confined to the Sung. By it is meant objects whose glazes are a network of cracks, sometimes accentuated by coloring. While the cracks were probably at first accidental, Chinese potters eventually learned how to produce and control them, chiefly by modifying the components of the glaze and by methods of applying it. Still another type of ware was characterized by rich and varied colors which were due to the changes wrought by the fire of the kilns in the copper oxide and in the trace of iron which entered into the composition. These by no means exhaust the kinds of pottery and porcelain of the Sung, but they are outstanding.

In general, and somewhat regardless of the particular centers in which they worked, the Sung potters tended to simplicity and yet elegance of form and decoration. Occasionally they departed from these standards, especially when copying old bronzes, but in the main they held to them. The shapes of the vessels were graceful or at times sturdy without being elaborate. Often only one color of glaze was used. Such figures as were painted, incised, or embossed on the surfaces were also usually far from being complex or multi-colored. In this the Sung potters formed a striking contrast to many of their successors of the Ming and the Ch'ing.

The Yüan dynasty made no noteworthy contribution to ceramics. The Sung models and techniques were continued, but with diminished vigor and skill. The Ming, however, witnessed distinct innovations and ushered in a new period. The industry tended to center at the vast imperial works at Ching-tê Chên, in Kiangsi, not far from the P'o-yang Lake. Here was an extensive supply of the materials most needed for the manufacture of porcelain—*kaolin* and *petuntse*—and a cobalt-bearing manganese ore which provided the blues in which the Ming potters delighted. Moreover, Ching-tê Chên was conveniently located for the transportation and distribution of its wares. It was on a stream which communicated with the P'o-yang Lake and thus had easy access to the Yangtze and the vast network of China's waterways. The porcelain characteristic of Ching-tê Chên possessed a white body and since the output was enormous and was at the maximum in the years when the Occident was making its first extensive contacts with China, it was this which was most widely distributed and which in the West was thought of as china or chinaware. It formed, moreover, an important item in the trade of China with its Asiatic neighbors.

In their designs the Ming craftsmen tended to depart from the restrained yet elegant simplicity of their Sung predecessors. Monochrome wares were still produced—pure white, blues, celadon green, and red being among them, and it is not always easy to tell whether a particular specimen is of Sung or of Ming origin. However, the potters of the Ming delighted in cobalt blue, a color which would withstand the high temperatures needed to melt the porcelain glaze. They also paid much attention to elaborate scenes and designs in more than one color. Some of their colors were applied as a kind of enamel to the surface of the glaze and were fixed by refiring at a low temperature. In this richness of painstaking and elaborate decoration Ming potters were but giving expression to the artistic spirit of an age which revelled in details and technique in painting and in ornate sculpture of the pillars, beams, and balustrades of buildings.

The great Emperors of the Ch'ing continued their patronage of Ching-tê Chên. Never have Chinese potters had better command of their materials than in the latter part of the seventeenth and the early part of the eighteenth century. Originality may have been sacrificed to mass production. Certainly no revolutionary departure was made from the Ming traditions and there was some continuation of Sung forms. However, toward the latter part of the eighteenth century new colors were introduced and with them came new types of decoration. Many pieces and sets, moreover, were produced for the Occidental trade and often had Western designs. With the decay of the dynasty in the nineteenth century the artistic quality of the porcelain ware declined—as did so much else of China's culture. The rebellions of the middle of the century dealt ceramics a blow from which they have never recovered. Ching-tê Chên especially was ravaged by the T'ai P'ings and its famous works have never been fully restored. By no means all the porcelain of the Ch'ing period was produced by Ching-tê Chên. There were potteries in a number of other places, and in some of them work of excellent quality was done. However, Ching-tê Chên was the main center and with its decay ceramics fell to a low level.

This sketch of the history of the work of the Chinese potter has incidentally included several of the main characteristics of the more artistically meritorious portions of Chinese ceramics. It must be added that pottery and porcelain have been employed in enormous quantities and for a great variety of purposes. Utensils in daily use for common purposes have, as in many another land, been of earthenware, and their production has consumed much of the energy of the potter. The prominence of the tiled roof in Chinese architecture has given work to many thousands of craftsmen. Most of the tiles have been of undecorated baked clay, but those for the more pretentious structures have usually been glazed—at least in recent years—and the highly ornamental ones, some of them with grotesque figures, used to accentuate the more prominent features of the roof, have given opportunity for the craftsman to express himself with originality. The funerary earthenware figures of earlier centuries and especially the porcelains have afforded scope for artistic expression which has often been of a very high order.

The work of the potter, like that of other artists and craftsmen, has its conventions. Folklore, mythology, and religion have had marked effect. Designs, indeed, are often highly symbolic and frequently give opportunity for that delicate expression by a donor of wishes for good fortune in which the Chinese have been and are adepts. Pottery and porcelain, therefore, have combined utility with an opportunity for æsthetic and even religious feeling and have occupied a large part in the life of the Chinese.

BRONZE

Rather more than with some peoples, bronze has had among the Chinese an important rôle as a means of artistic expression. In this there may be additional evidence of Chinese conservatism. Under the Shang and the Chou, when bronze was the metal most commonly in use, it naturally loomed large as an art material. Inevitably, moreover, a larger number of objects of bronze survived than of those made of more perishable substances. The Chinese, therefore, with their admiration for antiquity, have highly prized the bronzes of their early centuries, have devoted much study to them, and have continued to employ the metal for many of their art objects. In numbers of these they have copied ancient designs, either with a good deal of fidelity or with more or less freedom in detail, and in others they have branched out into new forms. Artistically China has continued in no small degree to live in the bronze age.

Even in the Han the chance exhumation of an antique bronze vessel was considered a notable event. Many books on ancient bronzes have been written and valued collections of the original objects have been made. The Sung is the first dynasty in which these treatises seem to have been composed in fairly large numbers, but we know that one was written as far back as the sixth century of our era and in still earlier works on ritual the names and dimensions of many bronze vessels are carefully noted. Chinese have prized their older bronzes not only for their age and their beauty but because many contain inscriptions. The reverence for the written character and the zeal for discovering its earliest forms have enhanced the value placed upon inscribed vessels.

Recent archeology has disclosed bronzes which are indubitably from the Shang, but many specimens attributed to that dynasty do not certainly go back that far. Undoubtedly, however, many of the objects now in Chinese and Occidental collections are of at least as early origin as the Chou. These include weapons, the trimmings of chariots, and ceremonial utensils. The vigorous, massive, dignified, and often graceful and well-proportioned lines of many of the vessels are indicative of skill and taste of no mean order. Shang bronzes especially give evidence of superb workmanship. Under the Han new designs entered, both in form and decoration, and again many of the surviving examples display artistic merit of a high level. In bronzes, as in so many other phases of Chinese art, Buddhism was the vehicle for new *motifs* which were of foreign origin or showed alien influence. Buddhist images, large and small, were cast in bronze, and the metal was used in numerous objects connected with Buddhist worship. Bells were cast, not only after the advent of Buddhism and for Buddhist uses, but centuries earlier. The Sung workers in bronze rejoiced in copying archaic designs, but also created forms of their own. Under the Ming and the Ch'ing, as in so many other phases of art, the bronzes were often characterized by elaborate decoration. Æsthetically some of them, even though huge, are vastly inferior to the best products of earlier dynasties. There was, too, much imitation of antique forms. The bronzes which were being made when contacts with the West first became important were, then, usually much below the level of those of many of the preceding centuries.

Bronze is not the only metal in which Chinese artistic feeling has expressed itself. Silver has been widely used, not only for jewelery but for other objects. Gold has been employed—although not so lavishly as in some other lands—perhaps because it has been relatively scarce. Pewter has been much utilized, and even iron objects have sometimes shown æsthetic taste.

LACQUER

Lacquer was early seen in China. Lacquered objects made in the present Szechwan during the Han have been found in Korea. Because of its perishability, lacquer has not stood the ravages of time as well as has bronze or jade, but specimens probably of T'ang origin are preserved in Japan and we have descriptions of it as it was handled under the Sung and know that by then much care and artistic skill were being devoted to it. We know, too, that it was extensively produced under the Ming and the Ch'ing.

The lacquer of China is prepared from the sap of a particular kind of native tree. The sap is collected from incisions, darkens with exposure to the air, is strained, and then is ground to improve its grain and to give it uniform consistency. It is colored by mixing it with various substances. For instance, a red frequently seen is obtained through cinnabar.

Lacquer is applied with spatula and brush to the article to be decorated. Several and sometimes many layers are spread, each being allowed to dry before the next is put on. The base to be covered may be wood, metal, porcelain, or even cloth. The objects generally need special preparation for the lacquer, and the entire process, if well carried out, requires great skill. Succeeding layers may be of varying composition, consistency, and color, and the drying and polishing demand experience and care. The surface may be decorated in a number of ways, and the designs may be very elaborate—landscapes, groups of figures, mythological and religious incidents or symbols, or flowers and trees. The surface may be painted, often with gold or silver gilt; it may have the pattern placed on it in relief; it may be inlaid with mother of pearl or semi-precious stones; or it may be carved, sometimes very deeply. For carved objects layers of different colors may be applied, and the carving done in such a manner as to bring out the colors. Or the lacquer may be mixed with fine particles of gold and the polished surface left with no other ornamentation. Many different objects have been lacquered—boxes, screens, fans, trays, ewers, vases, chairs and thrones, and even the pillars of buildings, large as well as small.

There have, too, been many different centers of manufacture. Often each has been noted for a particular kind of workmanship and type of decoration. In recent years Canton, Foochow, and Peiping have been prominent.

ENAMELS

The art of applying enamels appears to have been of non-Chinese origin. It may have come in both by the sea and by the overland routes. Certainly we do not hear of it much if at all before the Yüan. Beautiful enameled ware was produced under the Ming and the great Ch'ing Emperors of the seventeenth and eighteenth centuries, some of it in imperial workshops at Peking (Peiping).

Chinese have utilized enamel in three processes—cloisonné, champlevé, and painting. In cloisonné, it will be recalled, the pattern is outlined by thin metal strips which are soldered upon the surface to be decorated. In the cells thus formed the powdered enamel is placed and then the entire object is fired. After firing, the surface is smoothed and polished. In champlevé the pattern is incised, the resulting depressions are filled with the enamel, and the whole is fired and later smoothed and polished as in the case of cloisonné. In both cloisonné and champlevé unskillful or careless technique leaves pitted surfaces and small spaces imperfectly filled. In both, too, gilding is often applied to the exposed metal. Probably the most nearly perfect technique was attained under Ch'ien Lung, but somewhat at the cost of vividness in coloring and vigor of design. Enamel may be spread, like paint, either on metal or on porcelain and the whole be then heated. The Chinese have used porcelain more than metal for this purpose. Canton seems to have been the chief center for the manufacture of painted enamel objects.

GLASS

Glass is not certainly a native invention. It was imported as early as the Han—from Ta Ch'in, as the Chinese then denominated what we now with equal inexactness call the Near East. It was manufactured in China as early as the fifth century and a good many artistic objects have been made from it. The Chinese have not esteemed it so highly as porcelain and so have not devoted the same amount of skill to its production. They have, however, long known and practised the chief processes by which it is manipulated in the Occident, among them blowing, casting, and molding. It has usually been for smaller objects that the Chinese have employed glass. Often they have used it to imitate jade. They have known and utilized a good many colors. It is in carving glass that the Chinese are at their best, for to this they bring the technique acquired in the cutting of the much harder stones and gems with which they have long worked. Here they have shown craftsmanship equal to the best of its kind in any other part of the world.

JEWELRY

Like most other civilized peoples, the Chinese have developed jewelry. Jewelry has been, naturally, chiefly for purposes of ornamentation, but, although by no means to the same extent as in India, it has also been a means of saving capital against the proverbial rainy day. In its manufacture, Chinese craftsmen have developed no little taste. Neither by foreigners nor by the Chinese, however, has it been ranked as a major class of the fine arts. It is interesting that some of the stones regarded as most precious in other parts of the world, among them the diamond, have not been esteemed so very highly.

TEXTILES

It is not surprising that a people who have used silk for so long have developed marked skill in the manufacture of textiles. Certainly for many centuries the Chinese have been producing silk cloths of many different kinds. They have made brocades, they have interwoven silk with gold threads, and they have manufactured velvets and satins. They have incorporated many designs into their cloth—flowers, birds, elaborate geometrical patterns, and even landscapes and scenes from life or from mythology and religion. Embroideries, large and small, have been produced, some of them for clothes and some for screens and hangings. Portraits and congratulatory inscriptions may be embroidered. Many beautiful garments have been made, for, if they can afford it, both men and women wear silk, often of varied colors and of exquisite design. Official robes for state occasions were especially ornate, and a formal court gathering was gorgeous in its dress. Tapestries have been produced, although the art of weaving them seems to have come in from abroad. In the case of at least some kinds of carpets and rugs the methods and models appear to have been of foreign origin.

Silk was by no means the only material utilized for textiles. The fibers of several kinds of plants were employed. It will be recalled that the nankeens much prized by our great-grand-parents were cotton fabrics imported from China. Wool, too, has been woven, much of it going into rugs, and camel's hair has been used for the same purpose. The "Peking rugs" so popular among West-

MUSIC

The Chinese, like other peoples, have found in music an expression of their æsthetic sense. Music in China has had a long history and into it many influences have entered. We hear a good deal of the music of the Chou. At least some of it was used to accompany worship, and the instruments employed in certain religious ceremonies of later times, notably in Confucian temples, have been supposedly modeled on those of that period. Confucius himself is said to have been particularly interested in music. Buddhism has its special compositions. There are folk songs. Traveling minstrels sing their rhymes to the accompaniment of an instrument. As we have seen, singing and an orchestra accompany the universally popular theatre. There are, then, several kinds of music, and some of them are either of foreign provenance or show foreign influence. Many different types of instruments are or have been in use—among them drums, flutes, reeds, a variety of string instruments, metal bells, and resonant stones. So, too, a number of different scales have been known. The pentatonic which is so much heard in Chinese folk music is only one of several.

CHANGES WROUGHT BY THE COMING OF THE OCCIDENT

As in so many other phases of Chinese culture, artistically contact with the Occident has been disintegrating and disruptive. Also as in them, the disorder has been accentuated by the fact that the Westerner came in force at a time when, because of the decaying vigor of the ruling house, the processes of creative civilization were in decline.

The Occident has proved disturbing in many ways and for a number of reasons. Several Western products have displaced those of domestic manufacture in part or entirely. Thus cotton goods from Lancashire, Japan, and the new factories of Shanghai have tended to drive out some of the native cloths, and cups from Japan and teapots from Birmingham have partially superseded the corresponding indigenous earthenware. Then, too, the political chaos resulting from the impact of the West and the collapse of the Ch'ing has weakened or eliminated several of the centers of the production of artistic objects. Added to this has been the demand in the West for certain types of Chinese products. To meet it the handicraftsman has often yielded to the temptation to hurried and therefore careless work or to use cheap materials. Probably even more devastating has been the undiscriminating popularity in China of things Western. Thus the Chinese, and especially the educated Chinese, often abandons his old costume for Occidental garb, studies Western music, attempts to paint in European fashion, and discards his older forms of architecture for those of the West or attempts to combine the two in strange hybrids which violate the canons of both.

Reconstruction has only barely begun, but here and there are encouraging movements. Among the educated nationalistic spirit has brought sporadic waves of return to native garb. It has also stimulated attention to the remains of the older culture. It has accentuated an interest in archeology and has led to the collection of some of the folk songs. In architecture there are successful examples of an effort to adapt native forms to modern uses. Among these are the mausoleum of Sun Yat-sen at Nanking and buildings in some of the colleges and universities, notably several of those maintained by the Christian forces. It is interesting that much of the most satisfactory utilization of Chinese models has been by Western architects and by Chinese whom they have trained.

In no other realm of contemporary Chinese culture is it more difficult to forecast the future. The old traditions are being so weakened and such scanty beginnings are being made toward something new that the friends of China can only be patient and hope. Whether the Chinese æsthetic sense will in time be stimulated to fresh creative expression of a high order no one knows. Still less ought one to essay the rôle of a prophet in predicting the forms which, if it appears, the renaissance will take. One can only express the wish that the heritage of the past will not be completely abandoned, and that it will form the basis and provide much of the inspiration for whatever is to come.

BIBLIOGRAPHY

This is not the place to list even the more important works which the Chinese themselves have written on art. Space must be taken, however, to say that there is a voluminous literature. Some of the titles may be found in A. Wylie, *Notes on Chinese Literature* (new edition, Shanghai, 1902), pp. 135-142, in George Soulié de Morant, *Histoire de l'Art Chinois* (Paris, 1928), pp. 283-290, in S. W. Bushell, *Chinese Art* (second edition, 2 vols., London, 1910), and in B. Laufer, *Jade* (Chicago, 1912).

There is a large and rapidly increasing literature in European languages, some of it in the form of sumptuous volumes, for Chinese art has recently been arousing much enthusiasm among Western collectors. Among the books covering all or a large portion of the field are the two small volumes by Bushell mentioned above which, though now in some sections in part superseded by later works, are still useful, especially because they cover so wide a scope. D. Carter, *China Magnificent* (New York, 1936) is an excellent popular survey. There are O. Sirén, *A History of Early Chinese Art* (4 vols., London, 1929-1930 and also in French) which deals with the prehistoric and pre-Han period, the Han period, sculpture, and architecture; M. I. Rostovtzeff, *The Animal Style in South Russia and China* (Princeton, 1929), which deals with relationships of art *motifs* in those regions; H. d'Ardenne de Tizac, *L'Art Chinois Classique* (Paris, 1926), which brings the story down through the Han; René Grousset, *Les Civilisations de l'Orient, Tome III, La Chine* (Paris, 1930), which is an historical sketch of Chinese art, principally of painting, sculpture, ceramics, and bronzes; O. Münsterberg, *Chinesische Kunstgeschichte* (2 vols., Esslingen, 1910), quite detailed and well illustrated; George Soulié de Morant, *Histoire de l'Art Chinois* (Paris, 1928), well illustrated, short, and popular, and of which there is an English translation; an even shorter popular sketch, with a large number of illustrations—William Cohn, *Chinese Art* (London, 1930); and E. F. Fenollosa, *Epochs of Chinese and Japanese Art* (2 vols., London, 1912), much fuller for Japan than for China. There is also a series of introductory sketches by several authors and with beautiful illustrations in *Chinese Art, An Introductory Review of Painting, Ceramics, Textiles, Bronzes, Sculpture, Jade, etc.* (*Burlington Magazine Monographs*, London, 1925). On symbolism, see C. A. S. Williams, *Outlines of Chinese Symbolism* (Peiping, ca. 1931).

On architecture there is an excellent sketch by Oswald Sirén, *Chinese Architecture*, in the *Encyclopædia Britannica*, 14th edition, vol. 5, pp. 556-565. There are also several substantial volumes, including Ernst Boerschmann, *Chinesische Architektur* (2 vols., Berlin, 1925), most of which is illustrations; volume four, *Architecture*, of O. Sirén, *A History of Early Chinese Art* (London, 1930, also in French, Paris,

1929–1930), profusely illustrated; A. Hubrecht, *Grandeur et Suprématie de Péking* (Peking, 1928), profusely illustrated; O. Sirén, *The Walls and Gates of Peking* (London, 1924); a long, detailed review by M. P. Demieville of a reissue of the 1925 edition of *Ying-tsao-fa-shih* ("Methods of Architecture") by Li Ming-chung, based on Sung wood block editions, in *Bulletin de l'École Française d'Extrême-Orient* (1925, Vol. 25, pp. 213–264); and O. Sirén, *The Imperial Palaces of Peking* (3 vols., Paris, 1926). A sketch of the literature, Chinese and Western, on Chinese architecture, compiled by W. P. Yetts is in the *Burlington Magazine*, Vol. 50 (1927), pp. 116–131.

On the Great Wall there is an excellent travel article by F. G. Clapp, *Along and Across the Great Wall of China* (*Geographic Review*, 1920, Vol. 9, pp. 221–249). The book by W. E. Geil, *The Great Wall of China* (London, 1909), has excellent illustrations and fairly good travel notes, but from the standpoint of history and archeology is unreliable.

On gardens there is a short popular article, Matilda C. Thurston, *Beauty in Chinese Garden Courts* (*Asia*, Aug., 1931, Vol. 31, pp. 514 et seq.). E. H. Wilson, *China, Mother of Gardens* (Boston, 1929), while dealing chiefly with the author's travels in China in search of plants, has important information on the flora of China and a few notes on Chinese gardens.

On Chinese sculpture, there is again an excellent summary, well illustrated, by Oswald Sirén, *Chinese Sculpture,* in the *Encyclopædia Britannica,* 14th edition, Vol. 5, pp. 579–588. O. Sirén has a massive work on the subject, *Chinese Sculpture from the Fifth to the Fourteenth Century* (4 vols., of which one is text, London, 1925). E. Chavannes, whose name guarantees work of a high scholarly order, has *Six Monuments de la Sculpture Chinoise* (Brussels and Paris, 1914) and *Mission Archéologique dans la Chine Septentrionale* (Paris, 1909–1915), with two albums of plates and one volume of text in two parts, *La Sculpture à l'Époque des Han* and *La Sculpture Bouddhique.* There is V. Segalen, G. de Voisins, and J. Lartique, *Mission Archéologique en Chine* (*1914 et 1917*) (Paris, 1923–1924), with an atlas and two portfolios on *La Sculpture et les Monuments Funéraires* (*Provinces du Chan-si et du Sseu-tch'ouen*), *Monuments Funéraires* (*Region de Nankin*), and *Monuments Bouddhiques* (*Province du Sseu-tch'ouen*). There is also L. Ashton, *Introduction to the Study of Chinese Sculpture* (London, 1924). O. Sirén has *Studien zur Chinesischen Plastik der Post-T'ang Zeit* (1927), and a volume on sculpture in his *A History of Early Chinese Art* (London, 1930. Also in French). On ancient sculpture on the Western borders of China there are P. Pelliot, *Les Grottes de Touen-Houang. Peintures et Sculptures Bouddhiques des Époques des Wei, des T'ang et des Song* (six portfolios, Paris, 1920–1924) and von Le Coq, *Die Buddhistische Spätantike in Mittel-Asien,* Vol. 1, *Die Plastik* (Berlin, 1922).

On figures buried in tombs, in addition to material contained in works which do not specialize on them, there are B. Laufer, *Chinese Clay Figures. Part I, Prologomena on the History of Defensive Armor* (Chicago, 1914) and C. Hentze, *Chinese Tomb Figures. A Study in the Beliefs and Folklore of Ancient China* (London, 1928)—profusely illustrated.

Painting has called out a good many special works in addition to the accounts given in general treatises of Chinese art. L. Binyon has an excellent though brief summary in the 14th edition of the *Encyclopædia Britannica*, Vol. 5, pp. 575–579. H. A. Giles has a small volume on *An Introduction to the History of Chinese Pictorial Art* (London, 1918). There are also J. C. Ferguson, *Chinese Painting* (Chicago, 1927), largely a description of individual painters and their works arranged by dynasties; F. Hirth, *Scraps from a Collector's Notebook: Some Chinese Painters of the Present Dynasty* (Leiden, 1905); Arthur Waley, *An Introduction to the Study of Chinese Painting* (London, 1923),—an historical account with excellent illustrations, some of which are in color; R. Petrucci, translator, *Kiai-Tseu-Yuan Houa Tchouan. Les Enseignements de la Peinture du Jardin Grand comme un Grain de Moutarde. Encyclopedie de la Peinture Chinoise* (Paris, 1918); R. Petrucci, *Les Peintres Chinois* (Paris, 1912), of which there is an English translation; O. Fischer, *Chinesische Landschaftsmalerei* (Munich, 1921)—an historical and descriptive account with a good many illustrations in monochrome; O. Fischer, *Die Chinesische Malerei der Han-Dynastie* (Berlin, 1931); E. Chavannes and R. Petrucci, *La Peinture Chinoise au Musée Cernuschi* (Paris, 1914); A. Waley, *An Index of Chinese Artists Represented in the Sub-Department of Oriental Prints and Drawings in the British Museum* (London, 1922); L. Binyon, *Painting in the Far East. An Introduction to the History of Pictorial Art in Asia, Especially China and Japan* (London, 1908); B. March, *Some Technical Terms of Chinese Painting* (Baltimore, 1935); O. Sirén, *A History of Early Chinese Painting* (London, 2 vols., 1933); and L. Binyon, *Chinese Paintings in English Collections* (Paris, 1927).

On calligraphy there are brief notes in J. C. Ferguson, *Outlines of Chinese Art* (Chicago, 1919) and in S. W. Williams, *The Middle Kingdom* (New York, 1882), Vol. I, pp. 592–600.

On jade there are B. Laufer, *Jade, A Study in Chinese Archaeology and Religion* (Chicago, 1912); U. B. Pope-Hennessy, *Early Chinese Jades* (London, 1923); and P. Pelliot, *Jades Archaiques de Chine Appertenant à C. T. Loo* (Paris, 1925).

Westerners have also given much attention to Chinese ceramics. Volume 9 of F. Brinkley, *China: Its History, Arts, and Literature* (Boston and Tokyo, 1902) is devoted to the subject. There are also R. L. Hobson, *Chinese Pottery and Porcelain* (2 vols., New York and London, 1915); A. D. Brankston, *Early Ming Wares of Ching-te Chên* (Shanghai, 1938?); R. L. Hobson, *The Wares of the Ming Dynasty* (London, 1923); R. L. Hobson, *The Later Ceramic Wares of China*

(London, 1925); R. L. Hobson, *George Eumorfopoulos Collection: Guide of the Chinese, Corean and Persian Pottery and Porcelain* (6 vols., London, 1927–1928), most of which is on China; A. L. Hetherington, *The Early Ceramic Wares of China* (London, 1922); R. L. Hobson and A. L. Hetherington, *The Art of the Chinese Potter from the Han Dynasty to the End of the Ming* (London, 1923)—made up mostly of illustrations; B. Laufer, *Chinese Pottery of the Han Dynasty* (Leiden, 1909); B. Laufer, *The Beginnings of Porcelain in China* (Chicago, 1917); S. W. Bushell, translator, *Description of Chinese Pottery and Porcelain, Being a Translation of T'ao Shuo* (Oxford, 1910); S. W. Bushell, *Oriental Ceramic Art, Illustrated by Examples from the Collection of W. T. Walters* (10 vols., New York, 1897); and an excellent article in *Encyclopædia Britannica*, 14th edition, Vol. 18, pp. 360–369.

On bronzes there are C. K. Kelley in *Encyclopædia Britannica*, 14th edition, vol. 4, pp. 245–249; E. A. Voretzsch, *Altchinesische Bronzen* (Berlin, 1924); M. I. Rostovtzeff, *Inlaid Bronzes of the Han Dynasty in the Collection of C. T. Loo* (Paris, 1927); A. J. Koop, *Early Chinese Bronzes* (London, 1924); and W. P. Yetts, *The George Eumorfopoulos Collection: Catalogue of the Chinese and Corean Bronzes, Sculpture, Jades, Jewellery and Miscellaneous Objects* (2 vols., London, 1929, 1930); B. Laufer, *Archaic Chinese Bronzes of the Shang, Chou and Han Periods in the Collection of Mr. Parish-Watson* (New York, 1922).

On lacquer there are E. F. Strange, *Catalogue of Chinese Lacquer* (London, 1925); E. F. Strange, *Chinese Lacquer* (London, 1926); and A. A. Breuer, *Chinese Inlaid Lacquer* and *Chinese Incised Lacquer* in *Burlington Magazine*, 1914, vol. 25, pp. 176–182, 280–285.

On enamels, jewelry, and textiles, see Bushell, *Chinese Art*, where there are short sketches of each.

On music there are J. A. Van Aalst, *Chinese Music* (Shanghai. 1884); L. Laloy, *La Musique Chinoise* (Paris, 1910); M. Courant, *Essai Historique sur la Musique Classique des Chinoise avec un Appendice Relatif à la Musique Coréenne* (Paris, 1912); G. Soulié de Morant, *Théâtre et Musique Modernes en Chine avec un Étude Technique de la Musique Chinoise et Transcriptions pour Piano* by André Gailhard (Paris, 1926); R. Wilhelm, *Chinesische Musik* (Frankfurt am Main, 1927); E. Chavannes, *Les Mémoires Historiques de Se-ma Ts'ien*, Vol. 3 (Paris, 1898), pp. 230–319, 630–645; A. C. Moule, *A List of the Musical and Other Sound-Producing Instruments of the Chinese* (*Journal of the North China Branch of the Royal Asiatic Society*, 1908, pp. 1–160); and T. W. Kingsmill, *The Music of China* (*ibid.*, 1910, pp. 25–56).

CHAPTER XIX

LANGUAGE, LITERATURE, AND EDUCATION

One range of topics remains to be treated in our survey of Chinese history and culture—namely, language, literature, and education. Part of the proper contents of this chapter has been included earlier, under other subjects. More than one phase of literature has already been discussed and education has been touched upon both in the chapter on government, where the civil service examinations, the goal of so much of the educational system, were described, and in that on religion, where the preparation given Buddhist monks was briefly summarized. The present chapter, therefore, will describe only those features of the subjects which head it as have not been covered elsewhere.

THE SPOKEN LANGUAGE

The Chinese language is the mother tongue of more people than is any other on the face of the earth, and, indeed, of more than have spoken any other language at any one time in the history of the race. Even its most prevalent form, *mandarin*, probably surpasses all other tongues in the number of those who employ it in the daily affairs of life. English, French, and possibly Russian have a wider geographic spread, but none is the primary language of so large a proportion of the world's population.

To the Westerner the Chinese language is at the outset most disconcerting, for it does not fit into many of the patterns to which he is accustomed. One of the most striking of the dissimilarities is that which exists between the spoken and much of the written language. The vernacular may be and more than once has been reduced to writing. An interesting and influential movement of the present day, as we have seen, is toward the production of a much larger proportion of the literature in a standardized form of the most widely spoken of the colloquials. On the other hand, since some time before the Christian era and possibly from the remote period when literature first began to be written, most of that which has been regarded as of high quality has differed markedly in style from ordinary conversation.

The original relationships of the Chinese spoken language are still somewhat doubtful. Chinese is often regarded as one of a group of which Siamese, Tibetan, and Burmese are other important representatives. For example, Siamese belongs to the Tai languages and at least one distinguished authority has declared proto-Tai to be the most archaic known form of Chinese. However, to-day Chinese differs so much from these other tongues that if it was ever identical or nearly identical with them the separation must have occurred very long ago.

The history of the Chinese spoken language cannot be clearly traced, partly because of the fact that during much of its course, due to differences between the usual written and spoken forms, it was not reduced to writing. However, it is possible to amass a good deal of evidence giving either clues or exact information about it in various stages of its existence. Thus, some of the dialects now spoken in the South are usually regarded as being more archaic than those in the North. The Japanese, too, have taken over many words from the Chinese. There were periods when this borrowing was on a much larger scale than at others. Chinese entered by various routes, so that the two major forms in which its pronunciation survives represent chronological and regional variations. Japanese is fundamentally different from Chinese, and Chinese words were modified when spoken with the inevitable Japanese accent. However, the alterations are often detectable. Korean and Annamese, too, borrowed wholesale from Chinese and are of help to the philologist who wishes to reconstruct earlier stages of the colloquial. Moreover, the Chinese sometimes wrote in the vernacular. Pre-Sung examples of the colloquial are rare, but we have a few from the T'ang. The rhyming dictionaries, as they are called, give important information. A famous one of these, surviving only in fragments, was composed in the sixth century of our era, and another in the eleventh century. Characters were grouped according to the sounds with which their pronunciations began and ended. By comparison with modern pronunciations of the same characters it is possible in many instances to know what values were given them at the time the dictionaries were compiled. The transliteration of Indian Buddhist terms and names, much of which took place in T'ang times on a large and accurate scale (and previously somewhat casually), also affords useful evidence.

It is clear that extensive changes have taken place in the colloquial. In many instances final consonants have been elided and initial consonants altered. It is possible, too, that at one time the Chinese language possessed some inflections, at least with differences in case. One theory has it that spoken Chinese gives evidence of being an old language. It declares that while English has gone part way toward ridding itself of inflections, Chinese by completely eliminating all conjugations and declensions has departed even further from its youth.

The causes for the changes are at least four. Chinese has not been recorded by a type of writing fitted to preserve existing sounds. The invasions which periodically overwhelmed the North and left more or less permanent deposits of immigration led to the kind of alterations which occur when foreigners acquire a new tongue. The migrations of the Chinese themselves, principally southward, in some instances have made for variation. For instance, the Hakkas, settlers in the South from the North, have kept themselves distinct in dialect from those around them. Then there are the modifications which the years seem always to bring in a living language, just from the fact that it is being spoken.

It is to be expected that a language used by so many people over so wide an area and over so many centuries will develop dialects. Chinese has a great many of them, of which numbers are mutually unintelligible. They are especially prevalent in the coast provinces from Shanghai south. A man from Canton, for instance, who knows only his own dialect, cannot understand a man from Peiping or Nanking. The dominant form is that called *mandarin* by foreigners and known in Chinese as *kuan hua*, literally "the official speech." Technically *kuan hua* is the language of the court and its capital—Pekingese under most of the Ming and all of the Ch'ing. However, while the Peking dialect was long standard, variations of the *mandarin* are spoken over the major portion of China proper and Manchuria and by a large majority of the Chinese. While some of the patois, especially in rural districts, may be almost or entirely incomprehensible to one who knows only the standard Pekingese, most of its forms are mutually intelligible—at least with a little practice. For example, a foreigner who has learned spoken Chinese toward the extreme southern limits of the *mandarin* area, say in Changsha in Hunan, can understand and make himself understood as far east as Nanking and even in Hangchow (but not in the rural districts around Hangchow), as far west as the western borders of Szechwan or Kansu, and as far north as Heilungchiang. It is a form of *mandarin*, the *kuo yü,* or "national speech," it will be recalled, which the Chinese are now trying to make standard and to spread throughout the country, especially in non-*mandarin* speaking areas.

We have said that the Chinese spoken language differs in several ways from the tongues of the Occident. We have already noted the sharp distinction between it and what until recently was the most esteemed and generally used form of the written language. We have seen that it is without inflections of case or tense. It is also without words formed by derivative affixes, such as *teach-er, coward-ice,* and *strict-ness*. In a sense it is monosyllabic. The number of vocables, moreover, is greatly limited. There are no consonant groups, such as *scr* in *screech,* but only single consonants. It has been suggested, partly on the basis of the occurrence of consonant groups in modern Siamese and Tibetan, which are usually regarded as related to Chinese, that Chinese once had them. If it did, it has lost them and thereby has reduced the opportunity for multiplying the number of its vocables. Moreover, in *mandarin* words can be ended only with vowels and a limited number of the consonants—roughly, *n*, *ng*, and *r*. This means that the number of vocables is very small—in Peking *mandarin* only about four hundred and thirty and in other forms, such as the dialects of Canton and Amoy, where a wider range of final consonants permits a greater variety, less than a thousand.

With this exclusive use of uninflected monosyllables and this paucity of available vocables, it is obvious that much confusion might arise, for many quite diverse objects and ideas must be represented by the same vocable. Precision is sought by several interesting devices. Auxiliary words, both in the written and in the spoken language, when added to other words, make clear the case or the sense and so give the effect of inflection. Sentences have a fixed word order—such as subject, verb, and object. Then there is the use of tones. Peking *mandarin* has four, some other types of *mandarin* five, and other dialects still more—Cantonese nine. A given syllable may be pronounced in any one of the tones permitted by the particular dialect of the region. This, therefore, at once multiplies by four or more the number of vocables. Moreover, any given meaning has only one appropriate tone (although in speaking the sound may, in actual practice, be varied) and the tone is an integral part of the word. Here, however, room exists for confusion between dialects: although the Chinese have names for each of the tones and a given word is pronounced with what the Chinese call the same tone, even in different varieties of *mandarin* the musical representations (so far as that is possible) of the four or five tones differ. Thus what is called the "rising" tone as spoken in Changsha sounds quite different from that of Hankow.

Another effective device for avoiding confusion—as in many other languages—is the context. Still another is the use of what are sometimes known as classifiers. Thus in *mandarin* one never speaks of "a man" as *i jên*, but as *i ko jên*, *i* being "one," *ko* the classifier, and *jên* "man." There are a number of classifiers, often a special one being inseparable from a certain type of objects, somewhat as we say "a strip of paper" or "a chunk of wood." The classifier frequently gives a clue to the nature of the noun which follows. Thus *k'ou*, or "mouth," is used before words meaning "well" and "pot" and some other objects having a round opening.

Then the Chinese often use together two words of approximately or exactly the same meaning. Thus *k'an*, meaning "see," and *chien*, also meaning "see," are combined into *k'an chien*. While *k'an* and *chien* each has several meanings, there is little likelihood of ambiguity when the two are joined. Little misunderstanding arises if the phœnix is called *fêng huang*, *fêng* being the male and *huang* the female, for while *fêng* and *huang* separately have several meanings, the combination is not likely to be mistaken for something else.

A descriptive word may be prefixed. Thus a tiger is not called simply *hu,* for many meanings attach to that vocable, but *lao hu,* an "old tiger." Or a descriptive word may be added. Thus *shih,* meaning "stone," could be very readily confused with several other widely different meanings for the same vocable and tone. To it, however, is added *t'ou,* meaning "head," and one has *shih t'ou,* which is less easily mistaken. "A stone" in translation becomes *i k'uai shih t'ou, i* being "one" or "a" and *k'uai* the classifier.

The Chinese employ what in effect are compound words. For example, this is seen when, as in late years, they have been under the necessity of finding terms for new ideas and objects. Thus electricity is *tien ch'i,* the "breath of lightning," an electric car *tien ch'ê,* "lightning carriage," an automobile *ch'i ch'ê,* "breath carriage," and a steamboat *huo lun ch'üan,* "fire wheel boat" or "fire turn boat."

THE WRITTEN CHARACTER

If the spoken language of China is, as we have said, the native tongue of more people than any other used by mankind, the written language is the acceptable literary medium of an even larger proportion of the world's population. It is employed not only by the Chinese but by the Japanese and Koreans. The Japanese have, to be sure, usually put into it only their more erudite productions, but even in such ephemeral publications as newspapers they resort to Chinese characters to express part of their ideas. The Koreans, too, although they have their own phonetic form of writing, until the close of the nineteenth century thought of the Chinese character as the only dignified literary medium. Geographically some other written languages have been more widely spread, notably Latin and English, and the forms of the alphabet used most generally in the modern Occident are probably understood by more millions of people—although this may be debatable. However, measured by the population for whom it is the sole literary vehicle the Chinese written language outranks all others.

Moreover, as we shall shortly see, both in quantity and in quality the literature produced in the Chinese written character stands well when compared with that in other languages. In sheer bulk it is possible that in 1700 and even in 1800 more pages, written and printed, existed in Chinese than in all other languages put together. For grace and skill in literary expression the choicest of Chinese poetry and prose can be placed, unashamed, beside the rest of the world's best.

The Chinese characters seem to be an indigenous invention. Certainly, in spite of theories to the contrary, no conclusive proof has yet been given of a foreign origin. We have seen that primitive types were in use as far back as the Shang. Even then they were often so complex and so skillfully inscribed that they may have had back of them a long history. It is usually impossible to ascertain the most archaic form of a given character, for in the early days of the script a character was often written in a variety of ways and it is not feasible to determine the original with certainty. However, at least some of the methods in which characters were created seem clear.

A number of characters are conventionalized pictures of objects. It is not difficult to see in the present 日 and an older predecessor ⊙, a portrayal of the sun, and in 月, in an older form ☾, the moon for which it stands. So, too, 魚 is not unlike a fish, 馬 formerly 馬, suggests a horse, and in 羊, earlier 羊 and 羊, meaning "sheep," the horns and legs of a ram are clearly seen. 田 is a little less obviously a field, and even the present character for door or gate 門 shows the two leaves and posts of that useful object. Some hundreds of characters could and did come into existence in this way.

Some are attempts to put ideas into picture form. Thus 中 is a convenient representation of "middle" or "center," and 三 is obviously the numeral "three." Often abstract ideas were presented to the eye by combining characters which originally were pictures of objects. Thus the verb "to sit" is written 坐, which is probably two men 人 on the ground 土, although in some early forms this is not indisputable. 明 "bright" or "brilliant" is a combination of characters for the sun and moon. Sometimes the scribes employed the picture for an object with which the abstract idea was associated. Thus "high" is 高, apparently in an early form meant to portray a tower. It seems probable, too, that in some instances the spoken word for an abstract idea which had the same sound as a word for a concrete object might be written with the character which had been devised for the latter. Thus one authority accounts for *wan* 萬, meaning "ten thousand," on the theory that the character was originally the picture of a scorpion (one older form being 𧋸, a picture of that troublesome insect) and that the word for scorpion once had the same pronunciation as the present *wan*.

While by these methods a large number of characters could and did come into existence, the majority were brought into being through a form of phonetic writing. This at once took advantage of the fact that Chinese possesses many words having the same sound but different connotations and framed a device for preventing confusion between the written representations of these words. Thus in the early days there were a number of words with quite diverse meanings which have come down to us under the common pronunciation of *fang*. There is an ancient symbol 方, apparently once a picture, meaning "square" and now pronounced *fang*. When one wished to write the word *fang* meaning "to ask" it seemed simple and logical to preface 方 by a character for "words," 言, and so to obtain 訪. When it was wished to write the name of a particular kind of wood pronounced *fang* it was not unnatural to prefix 方 with the character for tree 木, which in an early form was 朮 (the picture of a plant with its roots and branches) and so to obtain 枋. *Fang*, meaning "kettle" was written 鈁, which is 方 prefaced by 金, an ancient symbol for "metal." Similarly "spin" was written 紡, a combination of 方 and 糸, meaning "silk." It is clear that in this fashion one part of the character gives a clue to the pronunciation and another to the meaning. One modern Occidental terminology calls the former the "phonetic" and the latter the "radical."

It is on this principle of the composition of characters by phonetics and radicals that some Chinese and many Western dictionaries of Chinese have been compiled. The Chinese have enumerated and placed in a fixed order, in accordance with the number of strokes of the pen which it takes to write them, two hundred and fourteen radicals. Theoretically each character in the language either is a radical or contains a radical. Each character, therefore, is listed under its appropriate radical in the order of the number of strokes of the brush pen required to write it. It must be noted that the number of radicals has not always been the same. The earliest etymological dictionary, the *Shuo Wên*, of the Han, had five hundred and forty. In the sixth century there were over five hundred, and later three hundred and sixty. It was not until the latter part of the Ming that the most frequently used present list of two hundred and fourteen was established.

It is not always that the phonetic gives so exact a clue to the modern pronunciation as in the case of the various characters for *fang*. This may in part be due to failures to abide by the principle when the characters were first formed and so at times to use a phonetic to write sounds which were similar but not identical. It is certainly largely attributable to the fact that in the course of the centuries words once identical in pronunciation have come to differ—in some instances only slightly but in others almost past recognition.

The changes in pronunciation result to no small extent from an outstanding feature of the written character—its appeal to the eye rather than to the ear. While a phonetic quality entered into the origin of most characters, it is not inseparable from the character. A given character may be pronounced in any one of many quite different ways and its meaning be unaffected. It can thus be used to write dialects and even widely different languages. For example, the character 山, in any early form ⛰ (apparently the picture of three peaks) may be called *shan,* as in modern *mandarin,* or *sang* as in Foochow, or *sa* as in Wenchow, or *san* and *yama* as in Japanese, without altering the meaning which it conveys to the eye. Similarly the 方 mentioned a few lines above has the same connotation to the eye whether it be called *fang* as in *mandarin, hwong* as in Foochow, *foa* as in Wenchow, or *ho* as in Japanese.

Given the various ways in which characters can be created, it is not strange that the number has been greatly multiplied. The *Shuo Wên* contains slightly over ten thousand, and the *K'ang Hsi Tzŭ Tien,* the dictionary compiled by order of the Emperor K'ang Hsi, and long standard, has about forty-nine thousand. A large proportion of these, however, are mere variants of other characters, for it must be noted that many can be written in more than one way.

Reverence for the classical literature and for the characters in which it was written discouraged for many centuries the creation of fresh characters. New ideas and objects are customarily represented by what are in effect compound words.

The burden imposed on students by having to learn the characters may seem unnecessarily onerous. However, the task is by no means so formidable as at first appears. Only slightly more than four thousand characters are in common use, few scholars are said to cumber their memories with more than six thousand, radicals and phonetics afford mnemonic assistance, and even the uninitiated foreigner can, with diligence, commit two or three thousand to memory in the course of a year's time.

Several forms of simpler phonetic writing have been devised, some of them involving the use of Roman letters. None, however, has gained wide currency. There seems to be no immediate prospect of relegating the traditional script to the discard. Perhaps it is just as well that the Chinese are clinging to it. To abandon it would close the enormous and worthy literature of China's past to the average literate person and so to all but a relatively few scholars.

THE WRITTEN LANGUAGE

The characters can be used to write any of the dialects of the vernacular—although in some of the latter are words for which no special written equivalents exist. However, the larger proportion of Chinese literature has been composed in what may be called the classical style—that which foreigners, with scant Chinese precedent, denominate *wên li*. It is not certain that this ever exactly reproduced any form of the spoken language. Some maintain that, for the sake of economy in the labor of writing, especially before the days of the invention of paper and the brush pen, it was always more condensed than the vernacular. However, there seems to have been a time in the days of the Chou when it at least approximated to the colloquial. Even to-day it is obviously related to the vernacular in structure and form. It has greatly influenced the latter, especially by contributing to it quotations, words, and phrases. It has, however, marked contrasts with the speech of every day. Several of its auxiliary words differ from those of *mandarin*, some of its characters, among them the pronouns, are not the same as those commonly used to write the vernacular, and the two are often at variance in the rules of composition. The most striking dissimilarity, however, is in the fact that the literary language employs fewer words to express the same thought. It can do this because it is meant for the eye and not for the ear. While it may be and is read aloud, even a scholar usually cannot understand an unfamiliar passage when it comes only through the ear.

It may seem that so artificial a language is an unmitigated handicap and that the Chinese would do well to abandon it for one more nearly in accord with the colloquial. However, much can be said for it. Being independent of any one form of the vernacular it has been understood by scholars all over the Empire and so has helped to give unity to the Chinese. Then, too, although the classical style should not be written in the singular, but in the plural, for there have been various forms of it, a scholar who has mastered it has opened to him all the literature of past generations. It has not changed so rapidly as have the vernaculars.

Still, the Chinese classical language presents difficulties. It is highly artificial. It is often replete with allusions and quotations and to appreciate and even to understand much of it the reader has to bring to it a vast store of knowledge of existing literature. Many individual characters have several widely different meanings and frequently in a particular passage only the context determines which one is intended. Although there are initial, terminal, and transitional words and phrases, the paucity of other punctuation in most of the texts is often confusing. Then, too, the presence of proper names with nothing to distinguish them as such except the context and the knowledge of the reader not infrequently leads to ambiguity. The confusion is heightened by the fact that a Chinese often has a number of given names or designations. It is only by going through a prodigious amount of literature and especially by memorizing quantities of it that the scholar obtains a kind of sixth sense which enables him to divine which of several readings is correct. Even the perusal of the classical language, therefore, requires long preparation.

Composition is still more of a task. Few Occidentals have achieved an acceptable style and many a modern Chinese who is the finished product of the present-day curriculum is far from adept. Composition in the literary language is so difficult partly because of the skill required in the use of the various auxiliary particles, partly on account of the fine distinctions which must be made in the choice of words and phrases, partly because of the wealth of quotation and allusion which it is necessary to have at one's command, and partly by reason of the requirement that the accepted order of words be followed intelligently and with taste. To achieve a worthy style it is necessary not only to possess a certain amount of native ability but to have mastered the needed technique. This latter can be acquired only through long and concentrated practice and discipline. It seems improbable that in the new age, when the Chinese student must familiarize himself with so many different fields of knowledge, any large number will find the time to become really proficient in the older methods of writing. The literary language, except in vastly simplified forms, must inevitably pass out of general use even by scholars. The modern emphasis on literature in the vernacular is the logical and unavoidable concomitant of the influx of Western branches of learning.

It may be added that the different styles in which the literary language has been written number about thirty. One group is denominated the *ku wên,* or "ancient literature." In general it has sought to follow the terse, antithetical models found in the Chou Classics. Han Yü of the T'ang was a master of it and it was used extensively by the great authors of the Sung—although possibly with less originality than under the T'ang. It was also employed in other dynasties, including, of course, the Han. As it came from the pens of its most distinguished exponents it had vivacity, brevity, energy, and grace. Another group of literary forms includes what may be called rhythmic prose—from the Western standpoint about half-way between poetry and prose.

LITERATURE

The greater part of the voluminous literature in Chinese has been written in the classical style. Literature in the vernacular has not been lacking. Not only has a good deal of it appeared in print, but there has been much of what may be called unwritten literature, in the form of folklore and multitudinous proverbs. Until very recently, however, composition in the speech of every day was considered beneath the dignity of scholars. When men of scholarly training wrote in the colloquial they often did so anonymously lest their standing in the world of letters be impaired. Until after 1911 any work which would lay claim to serious consideration as a piece of literature and worthy of any other purpose than of whiling away a leisure hour or of educating the masses had to be in *wên li*.

This literature has dealt with many kinds of subjects and can be placed under several headings. First in order of esteem by the Chinese have been the classical books. They are popularly supposed to come down from Chou and pre-Han times, although, as we have seen, large portions of them originated in the Han. The list of those regarded by Confucianism as of highest worth—to which the term "canonical" may be applied—varied at different times. Beginning with the great neo-Confucian scholars of the Sung the Classics *par excellence* have been nine in number and in two groups. The *Wu Ching* or Five Classics are the *I Ching*, or Classic of Changes, the *Shu Ching*, or Classic of History, the *Shih Ching*, or Classic of Poetry, the *Li Chi*, or Record of Rites, and the *Ch'un Ch'iu*, or Spring and Autumn (Annals). All of these, it will be recalled, were described in the second chapter. The *Ssŭ Shu*, or Four Books, the second group, are the *Lun Yü*, or Analects, containing many of the sayings attributed to Confucius and his immediate disciples, the *Ta Hsüeh*, or Great Learning, ascribed to a disciple of Confucius, the *Chung Yung*, or Doctrine of the Mean, supposedly by a grandson of Confucius, and *Mêng Tzŭ*, or the discourses of Mencius. Both the *Ta Hsüeh* and the *Chung Yung* are sections of the *Li Chi*, but were singled out from it by the Sung scholars of the dominant school as of especial importance.

In addition to these, other early works have been highly regarded, some of them having been included in the canonical lists of pre-Sung dynasties. The most important are the *Chou Li*, or Rites of Chou, the *I Li*, another collection of rites, the *Êrh Ya*, an early dictionary, and the *Hsiao Ching*, or Classic of Filial Piety, held to be the record of a conversation between Confucius and one of his disciples.

We need not enter into the moot question of the authenticity, dates, and authorship of these various works. Something of that has been touched upon earlier. Here it need only be said that none of the Classics has escaped searching critical tests and that the traditional ascriptions of authorship and accounts of composition or compilation have all been challenged, some of them successfully.

As we have noted, numerous dictionaries have been compiled and under various dynasties. In some of these the characters are classified according to their initial and final sounds, in others according to radicals, and in still others by subjects. The Chinese have devoted much attention to philology, including the study of ancient pronunciations and forms of characters.

In marked contrast with the peoples of India the Chinese have been historically minded. Indeed, no other people in the history of the human race has over so long a period displayed so much zeal for recording in detail the events which it has deemed important. As a result no other nation possesses such voluminous records of so long a past. We have seen something of the dynastic histories, which, beginning with the *Shih Chi* of Ssŭ-ma Ch'ien, have continued the chronicles of the Empire through the Ch'ing. In a certain sense, each is a continuation and is built on the general plan of Ssŭ-ma Ch'ien's *magnum opus*.

The *Ch'un Ch'iu*, including the work traditionally associated with it, the *Tso Chuan*, provided the model for another type of history, largely in the form of a chronicle by years. This was in large part due to the prestige which its reputed Confucian authorship gave it. Perhaps the most famous of the group is the *Tzŭ Chih T'ung Chien*, by Ssŭ-ma Kuang, of the Sung, with supplementary compilations by the same author. It covered the course of China's development from late in the Chou to the beginning of the Sung, and, condensed by Chu Hsi and his disciples as the *T'ung Chien Kang Mu* and continued by later pens, became the best known and most highly esteemed single history of the Empire. The *T'ung Chien Kang Mu* has itself been the subject or the incentive of a number of studies, some of them supplementary and some critical. There have been many scores of other historical studies, a number of them extensive and displaying a high order of ability and originality of plan and conception. Some cover long periods and others only a comparatively brief time. Many specialize on particular phases of history. Collections have been made of state papers, among them compilations of memorials to the throne. There are hundreds of biographical works, some of them of single individuals, others bringing together the lives of several scholars and statesmen, and still others travel diaries and journals of thrilling events. Accounts have been written of particular sections of China, especially of the states which have been more or less independent of the dynasties considered legitimate. Of these states there have been a large number, some, as we have seen, having been very important.

China possesses an extraordinarily voluminous group of what may be called local histories or gazeteers. A few of them cover the entire Empire and are in the nature of descriptive and statistical geographies. More treat of special sections of the Empire. Each of the major subdivisions of the country—the provinces, the *fu,* the *hsien,* and the main cities—is normally provided with a work which is both a local history and a description, often very minute, of the region as it was at a particular time. Many of the chief hills, mountains, and monasteries of the country have been made the subject of similar works. There are accounts, too, of some of the chief rivers and of the engineering measures which have been taken to control their waters. Treatises exist on the outlying dependencies of the Empire, on several of the non-Chinese peoples within the Empire, and on what the Chinese of a particular time knew of one or more of the foreign countries. Of the gazeteers about five thousand are still in existence. Many of them are very detailed and extend to large dimensions.

China also has numerous descriptions of her governmental machinery. Some portray the entire imperial structure by which the country was ruled and others only certain phases or functions of the state. Some are historical and others chiefly or entirely devoted to what was contemporary with the author.

The Chinese have long been attracted by certain phases of archeology. Inscriptions have absorbed much attention and numerous collections of transcriptions or exact reproductions of them—by rubbings—have been compiled and treatises written on them.

There have, too, been essays and more extensive treatises of what may be called historical criticism, a large proportion of them dealing with individual works or series of histories. The Chinese have also written a good many books in which prodigies and the marvelous have held the chief place and which to the modern historian are of interest mainly because of the light which they shed upon the beliefs of the writers and their contemporaries. Many catalogues of existing works have been produced, usually in the form of lists of private or imperial collections, which possess great value for the historian.

Much of the historical writing of the past was of excellent quality, even when judged by the exacting standards of modern scholarship. On the other hand, a large proportion of it was of lesser worth. The student of China's history, therefore, is confronted by an embarrassment of riches. His plight is made worse by the absence of adequate guides through the huge maze. Indices and other implements indispensable to him who would find all the material pertinent to a given subject are largely lacking. Since each generation tends to write history from its own standpoint, to a historiographer of our times much of the information contained even in the standard works seems trivial and uninteresting and the number of volumes which must be gone through to glean what is germane to one's special interest is often discouraging. To huge masses, too, must be applied the tests for accuracy and dependability without which no writing can be done that will satisfy the historical conscience. All this prodigious body of records, then, is at once the despair and the joy of the scholar.

The Chinese have what they call *lei shu*, often rather loosely translated as "encyclopædias." Some cover only a limited range of subjects, such as the origin and history of family names, and others embrace the entire scope of Chinese knowledge. Usually instead of being, like Western encyclopædias, made up of articles written especially for them, the *lei shu* are composed of longer or shorter excerpts from existing works. Some *lei shu* have attained huge proportions. The largest was the *Yung Lo Ta Tien*—although it is said not to fall under the *lei shu* in the strictest sense of that term. It was compiled by order of the third Emperor of the Ming, ran to nearly twelve thousand volumes (each, moreover, in two separate fascicles) and, since the expense of printing was discouraging even to the exchequer of one of the most powerful and energetic rulers of China's history, it existed only in three manuscript copies, now represented by a few widely scattered folios. Others of the *lei shu* were printed, and some of these were very voluminous. Often they have preserved more or less extensive fragments of works which except for them have entirely disappeared. The *Ssŭ K'u Ch'üan Shu,* compiled under Ch'ien Lung, existed in seven manuscript copies. It was utilized in the compilation of the *Ssŭ K'u Ch'üan Shu Tsung Mu, Ch'in Ting,* an important annotated bibliography. The latter also included thousands of titles not represented in the former.

The *ts'ung shu* must also be mentioned. The term does not exactly fit into any Western category but it may be translated as collectanea. *Ts'ung shu* are made up of works, usually on several subjects and by several authors, some of which may have appeared elsewhere and others of which are here printed for the first time. The entire range of knowledge is covered by them—geography, philosophy, agriculture, medicine, history, etc. They are still produced in large numbers.

So much has been said in earlier chapters of the development of philosophic and religious thought that not much space need be given to it here. Each of the great schools has produced a literature. Confucianism, Buddhism, and Taoism have been responsible for adding thousands of volumes to the libraries of the land. All three have treated of morals, and Confucianism naturally also spread into the field of political science. Buddhism developed its own logic and technical terms. Its literature, therefore, is one through which only the expert can hope to thread his way with any assurance of understanding. This is particularly so since there are many Buddhist schools, some of which have delved with profundity and acumen into the issues that perennially perplex the thoughtful mind, and since a knowledge of much of Indian thought and some of the Indian languages is prerequisite to a full comprehension of them. Much of Taoist literature, too, cannot be understood without a knowledge of Buddhism, so that any extended research in it is not for the amateur. In spite of much which is shallow and trivial, in these three great philosophies the Chinese at their best have displayed a variety and a quality of thought and insight which can be compared without apology with the intellectual product of any other people.

We have also spoken so frequently of poetry and have given the names of so many of the chief poets that this important branch of literature need here be but little more than mentioned. It must be noted, however, that from the earliest times the Chinese have been greatly interested in verse. Some of the resulting collections are those of a particular author. Others are anthologies in the poems of many writers. The Chinese have developed no lyric or epic poetry.

What we in English would classify under poetry occurs in Chinese under many forms. Ballads have been multitudinous. Much of the text of plays for the theatres is in what we would call verse. Many historical romances, some of which run to great length, are in rhythmic style. Mosaics of characters have been put together in such a fashion that when read in different directions they form poems. The characters contained in the Thousand Character Classic have been arranged into verse by several different authors. There is rhythmic prose which from the Western standpoint is really poetry, and a whole division of literature is made up of poems of irregular lines and of many patterns.

What the Chinese themselves include under *shih*—usually translated as "poetry"—is much more limited. It embraces, however, a number of forms. Some of these, in the so-called "ancient" style, allow a good deal of latitude. Others, in what is denominated the "modern" style—really many centuries old—are more fixed. In poems of the "modern" style the length of line, the arrangement of characters by tones and rhymes, and the parallelism of characters follow strict conventions—although even here many patterns have been used. The "modern" style, for instance, permits verses of four lines of five characters each, of four lines of seven characters each, of eight lines of five characters each, and of eight lines of seven characters each. In this style characters must be made to fit particular tone patterns—that is to say, only characters of a given tone can be put in a particular place in a line and must be matched by the tones of the characters in the succeeding line. For this purpose the five tones of *mandarin* are divided into two groups, the first two being called "even" and the other three "uneven." An "even tone" in one line must be countered by an "uneven tone" in the corresponding character in the line with which it is paired. Rhymes must also be observed, a frequent rule being that the final characters of every other line must match. They are regulated by a standard rhyming dictionary, compiled more than a millennium ago, so that, due to changes in pronunciation wrought by the centuries, according to the present pronunciation rhyme may often seem absent. Then, too, another form of parallelism must be observed, by which parts of speech—adjectives, verbs, and nouns—must be matched by the same parts of speech in the next line. Moreover, a given character must not be used twice in the same poem. Obviously such forms are much less elastic than those of most other peoples. A genius is able to express himself through them with beauty, but for the majority who have conformed to them—as have a large proportion of Chinese scholars—they are apt to lead to somewhat mechanical results.

Fiction has been mentioned more than once in preceding chapters and, accordingly, requires here no elaborate statement. Since stories were usually written in the vernacular, the Chinese scholar, with his exclusive esteem for the classical style, formerly did not regard them worthy of admission to the ranks of literature. Of late years, however, with the use of the vernacular for all literary purposes, an increasing interest has developed in fiction and its history, especially since in some of it are to be found examples, rare elsewhere, of the colloquial of past centuries. At least as early as the Sung stories were being composed in the language of every day. Under the Mongols what are usually called novels were written in large quantities, and the output continued under the Ming and the Ch'ing. Some fiction is made up of short stories. Much of it, however, is in long narratives. Part of it is in the form of historical romances, of which the *San Kuo Chih,* or the "History of the Three Kingdoms" is probably the most famous. The *San Kuo Chih* arose out of tales which must have been related for centuries, somewhat like the Arthurian legends, before they were put in their present standard literary dress. Historical romances have been made the basis of many plays and from them has been drawn much of the repertoire of the strolling storytellers. Several of the novels, among them the *Hung Lou Mêng,* are of high literary quality, with excellent delineation of character and with intimate and informing pictures of Chinese life and customs. Fiction has sometimes been made the vehicle for portraying utopias and advocating reform. It also contains much of the supernatural, with a good deal about the actions of spirits. The love which is exalted is usually extramarital and sex is often badly dealt with. Some stories belong as much to pornography as to fiction, but that criticism cannot be leveled against most of the best of the novels. To the Westerner one of the great values of Chinese fiction is the insight which much of it gives into the folklore and *mores* of the days of its composition.

SCIENTIFIC LITERATURE

One of the interesting characteristics of the older Chinese culture is the rudimentary nature of most of the knowledge which was accumulated in the field of mathematics and the natural sciences. The hypothetical visitor from Mars might well have expected the Industrial Revolution and the modern scientific approach to have made their first appearance in China rather than the Occident. The Chinese have directed so much of their energy toward attaining this-worldly ends, are so industrious, and have shown such ingenuity in invention and by empirical processes have forestalled the West in arriving at so much useful agricultural and medical lore that they, rather than the nations of the West, might have been looked to as the forerunners and leaders in what is termed the scientific approach toward the understanding and mastery of man's natural environment. It is little short of amazing that a people who pioneered in the invention of paper, printing, gunpowder, and the compass—to speak only of some of their best known innovations—did not also take precedence in devising the power loom, the steam engine, and the other revolutionary machines of the eighteenth and nineteenth centuries.

The reason for the failure to achieve this priority must be in large measure a matter of conjecture. It may have been because under the Confucian state with its system of education and its civil service examinations the best of the trained minds were absorbed in government, ethics, history, and *belles-lettres*. It may have been that China failed to develop a system of logic the equal of that which Western Europe owes to the Greek mind. The cause may need to be sought in obscure and debatable climatic factors or in biological and racial inheritance. It is conceivable that it can be discovered in differences of religious background. One suggestion has it that the Chinese are practical and that science is first of all theoretical—as in Copernicus and Newton. One thoughtful modern Chinese attributes it to the fact that, under the influence of Taoism, Buddhism, and Confucianism, especially as seen in the Sung philosophers, Chinese thinkers devoted their attention to developing techniques for knowing and controlling the mind—in contrast with the West which has sought techniques for knowing and controlling matter. To this generalization exception can easily be taken, but it may well be that in the subjectivity of so much of Chinese philosophy, particularly after the advent of Buddhism, is to be found the secret of the arrested development in the mastery of nature.

Whatever the cause, the backwardness of the Chinese in the mathematical and the natural sciences and in mechanical devices when compared with the Western Europeans and Americans of the past century and a half is indisputable. In mathematics, astronomy, and in some mechanical appliances, indeed, China was notably behind the Europe of even the sixteenth and seventeenth centuries. Quite a literature was produced on mathematics and astronomy, but much of the knowledge which lies back of it originated in the West. This was true even before the great enrichment which came through the Jesuits in the late Ming and the early Ch'ing. Moslems were responsible for some of it and there may have been importations as early as the Chou.

However, in some phases of what may be called scientific literature there was a large output—apparently chiefly and perhaps almost entirely independent of stimulus from abroad. This was particularly marked in agriculture and medicine. Agriculture has a very extensive literature, some of it dating back as far as the T'ang. Many phases of the subject are dealt with—such as the implements utilized, fruits, vegetables, bamboo, ploughing, sowing, hydraulics, the planting of mulberry trees, the rearing of silkworms, and the breeding of cattle. The Chinese had here acquired a vast amount of information and had developed many ingenious devices.

We know that medical literature existed as early as the Han, and it is probable that some was written even before that time. The *Nei Ching*, said to be the oldest Chinese medical classic, is ascribed to the end of the Chou or the beginning of the Ch'in, and some other works are said to be fully as ancient. A number of extant treatises were composed by Sung physicians, a voluminous literature, including a famous materia medica, dates from the Ming, and Ch'ing physicians were prolific authors.

The traditional Chinese medical lore compares favorably with that of the pre-nineteenth century West. In it has been much of superstition, but that was also the case in the Occident. Charms have been extensively employed and gods have been asked to indicate which of several medicines shall be taken. Dissection was not practised, at least of late centuries, and the knowledge of anatomy was correspondingly imperfect. Anæsthetics are said to have been used in surgery as early as the Han. For many centuries what is known as acupuncture has been extensively followed—a procedure by which the flesh is pierced with needles for many different illnesses. Another favorite therapeutic measure, very ancient, has been burning on the body cones of *artemesia moxa* or common mugwort and thus raising blisters with the effect of counter-irritation or cauterization. Massage has long been employed. Inoculation against smallpox (not vaccination) is said to have been known as early as the Sung. The *yin* and the *yang* permeated both theory and practice. So also did the theory of the five elements. Much, too, was made of the pulse in obtaining a diagnosis, the belief being that by taking it in different ways the state of the principal internal organs of the body could be determined. Certain readings could be made from the pulse in the left wrist and others from that in the right wrist. At least in the Sung and the Yüan imperial medical colleges were conducted. As a rule, however, medical education was by apprenticeship and no state or privately administered examinations existed to standardize the profession. Practitioners, accordingly, varied widely in preparation, traveling quacks abounded, and the patient often suffered more from the treatment than from the disease. The pharmacopoeia included many remedies which depended for their supposed efficacy upon thoroughly fanciful theories. It is highly doubtful, for example, whether the much esteemed ginseng has any value beyond that of mental suggestion. But for the fact that the Chinese, by long contact with many virulent diseases, had developed a partial immunity to some of them, the death rate would have been much higher than it was. Yet when all is said which can be brought as an indictment against the traditional medical literature and practice, and it is much, the fact remains that the Chinese acquired and transmitted a great deal of valuable lore. Their pharmacopoeia contained many useful drugs and their methods of treatment not infrequently produced excellent results. It has not been uncommon after the introduction of modern Western medicine for the Chinese to acknowledge the superiority of Occidental surgery but for internal remedies to prefer practitioners trained in the native fashion. Western physicians have reported rather remarkable cures wrought by old-style Chinese physicians.

It is impossible to say, however, whether much of permanent value will be found in the vast store of older Chinese medical literature and whether any of it will be retained by the newer medical profession which is arising under Western tutelage.

PRINTING

For centuries the normal process by which literature has been reproduced in the Middle Kingdom has been printing. We have already seen that this epoch-making invention was developed in China hundreds of years before it was known in Europe, and, indeed—although as yet this is unproved—may have been transmitted from China to the West. Printing from movable type was known, but the preferred method and the one most extensively employed has been by incised wooden blocks. These blocks or plates are usually the size of two pages. The surface is prepared by smoothing it and then spreading over it a paste. While this surface is still moist there is placed on it, face down, a sheet of thin paper on which has been previously written the passage to be reproduced. The paper is rubbed off, leaving, in reverse form, the ink of the text. An artisan with a sharp tool cuts away all the surface but that marked by the characters and the result is a woodcut of the double page. Ink is then applied with a brush, a piece of paper is placed on the block, is made to lie smoothly and take the impression by applying a dry brush to its back, is removed, the block is reinked, and the operation is repeated. The paper is usually thin and is printed only on one side. In binding, the leaves are folded and stitched together. The process can be very rapidly carried out, and the most skillful products are beautiful examples of the printer's art. A cheaper form of block printing was the use of clay or wax blocks, on which the text was incised. The clay or wax could be remolded and used again and again. The resulting product was artistically less desirable than that of the wooden blocks and so was used chiefly for inexpensive editions of the Peking Gazette and the corresponding provincial sheets, and for placards.

LIBRARIES

Chinese have valued books very highly and libraries, some of them of vast extent, have been assembled. The largest have been collected under imperial auspices. We have repeatedly seen how the destruction of successive imperial libraries in the vicissitudes of civil war and foreign invasion has been one of the major sources of loss to scholarship. Buddhist monasteries often have considerable libraries, but these specialize in the literature of that faith. Many private collections have also been assembled and some of them handed down for generations. Again the hazards of war and of changing family fortunes have sooner or later led to their destruction or dispersion. But for the art of printing which made possible the production of many copies of a single edition, most of the ancient books would long since have disappeared. Even as it is, a large proportion of the literary treasures of the past have vanished in whole or in part, leaving at most no traces but a title and perhaps a few quotations. However, fragile though Chinese paper may appear to be, Sung editions are by no means unknown, and many examples have come down to us of the work of Yüan and Ming printers.

EDUCATION

Formal education in China before the close of the nineteenth century was dominated by the preparation for the two chief learned professions—the service of the state and the Buddhist priesthood. The training for the latter was conducted only in monasteries and for the novitiate which led to membership in a monastic community. Except indirectly, through the instruction which the monks gave the laity and through Buddhist services and literature, it exerted no influence upon the life of the Empire as a whole. On the other hand, the type of education which in theory led to the civil service examinations and which was controlled by the requirements for these ordeals was entered upon by many who either did not aspire to compete or who were never successful. The large majority of those who received some training in the elementary schools remained outside the charmed circle of the holders of degrees.

It would, however, give an incomplete picture of the older educational system of China to focus attention exclusively on the instruction imparted in monasteries and schools. Much was acquired in other ways. Members of the guilds, through their apprenticeships, conducted a good deal of what would now be called vocational education. It was largely thus that skill in handicrafts and in commercial methods was transmitted. Apprentices, too, in the course of their training often picked up a knowledge of some of the written characters most necessary to their occupations. Farmers passed on to their sons such lore as they had acquired in agriculture. Women, moreover, although not eligible for public office and hence not admitted either to the civil service examinations or to the schools which prepared for them, were by no means always uneducated. Illiterate most of them were, but in better families a very considerable number were initiated by private tutors into the mysteries of the printed page. China, indeed, has not been without women who have been noted for their literary attainment. In well regulated homes, moreover, the daughters were given a careful education by their mothers in the management of a household, in courtesy and the ceremonial and proprieties which helped to make Chinese society run smoothly (if and when it did), and in their duties toward their future husbands and parents-in-law. Woman's sphere was believed to be the home, and the training deemed proper for that sphere was often very conscientiously conducted.

The schools which led up to the civil service examinations had a long history and may go back to Chou dynasty prototypes. It is clear that schools existed in Chou times. Certainly, too, in the Han there were schools, both government and private. Institutions, indeed, for the study of the recognized classics were an essential corollary of the Confucianism then being adopted by the state, for if, as it demanded, the Empire was to be governed through educated men, centers must be maintained where this training could be given. Han Wu Ti did much to inaugurate an imperial system of education, and government schools were multiplied under the Later Han—perhaps in part because of an impetus given by that energetic, utopian innovator, Wang Mang. In the years of disunion between the Han and the Sui mention is made, at intervals, of government schools in some of the states which flourished in that kaleidoscopic era. Under the Sui the system was renewed and under the T'ang it was reorganized and greatly extended. It is not surprising that during the Sung, with its Confucian revival, a structure existed which constituted—at least on paper—a kind of pyramid beginning with a school in each administrative subdivision and culminating in institutions in the capital. Even under the Mongols there were government schools. The Ming, with its emphasis upon Confucianism and its thoroughgoing strengthening of the civil service examinations, not unnaturally still further elaborated the educational program. In theory its system contemplated a school in each village, *hsien, chou,* and *fu,* and a national institution in the capital. Some of the students were to be subsidized from the public revenues. The Ch'ing followed the Ming, with modifications, and had a paper plan which called for schools of several kinds in the capital, including some for the Manchu nobles and Bannermen and what might loosely be termed a national university, a college in each of the provinces, and a school in every *fu, chou, hsien,* and village.

In practice the system outlined by the Ch'ing was only imperfectly put into operation. To be sure, several schools existed in the capital. There were, too, provincial and some prefectural colleges. The majority of the students in these institutions were supported at public expense, the income to maintain them coming from endowments or from official subsidies. Village schools were largely left to local initiative. The Imperial Government for the most part contented itself with conducting the civil service examinations and with maintaining a few schools in Peking and the provinces (often halfheartedly), and left the student, with such aid as the local authorities or the village or family might give him, to obtain his preparation where and as he could. The high esteem in which degrees were held prevented any dearth of candidates for the examinations. The Central and Provincial Governments could be sure that an ample number of aspirants would appear, well equipped in the type of education demanded by the tests, without much, if any, financial aid from imperial officialdom. At least under the Ch'ing, then, and possibly through most of China's history, primary education was left to local and private initiative.

When they could afford it, families seem usually to have employed private tutors for their children. Often, too, a scholar father or grandfather himself undertook the task of guiding the studies of the youths of the household. Almost if not quite invariably, however, this was only after the primary stages had been passed, for classical precedent frowned upon a father teaching his own son. Often a large family or clan maintained a school for its boys, housing it in the ancestral temple. Frequently several families in a village joined in hiring a teacher, or a benevolent person or persons of means financed a free school. Almost never was a building erected for the purpose, but a temple or the room of a house was borrowed or rented.

The teacher had no special training in pedagogy. Books existed which held up standards for the conduct of the pupil but the instructor received no formal preparation in his art. He tended to follow rather slavishly the methods by which he himself had been taught. In theory teachers were highly respected, but in practice the majority suffered from poor pay and precarious tenure. Often they were recruited from among the unsuccessful aspirants for the civil service examinations and the training of many had not proceeded far enough to warrant even the attempt to compete in them. Here and there, however, men in the profession could show respectable scholarly attainments or displayed skill in the art of instruction.

The method of the primary school consisted largely in committing to memory texts which were beyond the comprehension of the child and which were not explained to him until after the process of memorization had stored his mind with quite an array of literature. Even then the interpretation vouchsafed was either in the form of traditional commentaries, perhaps of Chu Hsi, or in a style more calculated to display the teacher's erudition than to enlighten the student. The pupil repeated aloud after the instructor the text to be learned. Then, at the top of his voice, he went over the passage again and again until he had fixed it in mind. He was tested by being required to recite the lesson with his back to the teacher and without looking at his book. Thirty or forty boys thus engaged sounded like bedlam. The student was also taught to write characters. The hours were long, from early morning until late in the afternoon, and the intermissions were not for recreation of even unorganized forms. Discipline was supposed to be strict and the teacher was generous in his use of the ferule.

The texts memorized were designed to fit the pupil for the state examinations. For the beginner they included first the *San Tzŭ Ching,* or "Three Character Classic," a short compendium in rhymed lines of three characters each of standard Confucian philosophy and ethics and of Chinese history, concluding with incentives to study in the form of noteworthy examples of past ages. Then followed the *Pai Chia Hsing,* or "Hundred Family Names" (in reality more than four hundred surnames), the famous *Ch'ien Tzŭ Wên,* or "Thousand Character Essay," in which none of the thousand characters occurred twice, a series of "Odes for Children," and the *Hsiao Ching,* or "Classic of Filial Piety." These were succeeded by the famous Four Books and Five Classics of the Confucian Canon. Poetry might also be studied, perhaps as copy for learning to write the characters.

By no means all who entered the elementary schools remained long enough to complete the curriculum. The majority usually dropped out after a year or two. They had acquired the ability to read and to write a number of characters and returned to the fields or went into a store or a handicraft. It was only the rare boy who possessed the ability or whose family could provide the means to pursue the course long enough to be prepared to compete in the state examinations.

The secondary schools gave their students additional training in composition and literature and in the study of essays selected from those which had won recognition in the civil service examinations.

The faults of the system are obvious. A curriculum designed to prepare applicants for the government examinations was pursued by all, even though only a minority of those who began it had any serious thought of qualifying for these tests. It was confined to limited phases of human knowledge. The lack of physical education and of training in hygiene took a heavy toll in life and health. The method of instruction emphasized memory and discouraged independent thought. Even the finished products were very limited in their range of information and were inclined to be blind to the existence of other realms of knowledge and to have a bigoted pride in their own attainments and in the finality and sufficiency of the literary culture of their class. Little or no preparation was given for meeting the problems with which most of the pupils would later be confronted. Many were actually unfitted for life and eked out an uncertain living, too proud to demean themselves by manual labor and unadapted to most remunerative occupations. The program had glaring deficiencies even as a training for the task of the government administrator—the profession to which it was supposed to lead. Much of the political weakness of China in the nineteenth and twentieth centuries can be traced to it.

Yet the system also had its virtues. Although the majority of those who entered upon it never reached the examination stalls, a fairly large proportion of the male population acquired through it some knowledge of the written character. No statistics for literacy are available for the Empire, and the proportion varied between town and country and from district to district. In some cities, however, nearly if not fully half of the adult men could read some characters. Although in other places, particularly in rural sections, the proportion was very much smaller, it was a rare community which did not contain some one who could read and write. The emphasis upon memory had its faults, but it at least supplied those who had gone far in the course with the command of the text of a large body of literature, much of it of very high quality, and so helped to maintain standards of taste. Even though the system did not give direct training in the technique of government, it grounded future officials in the principles which Confucianism held to underlie ordered society and trusted the individual, with the assistance of laws and precedents, to apply them. Its purpose was the growth of men and not the impartation of information. Its aim was cultural, not utilitarian, the self-development of the individual who was supposed to set an example. So, in theory at least, it made government almost unnecessary. Then, too, education of the traditional type proved of immeasurable assistance in perpetuating Chinese culture and in promoting the unity of the Empire. We have repeatedly seen that the remarkable coherence of China and the ability of the country to come together after periods of civil strife and division were due not primarily to force, although that nearly always was an important factor, but to a uniformity of social institutions and the general acceptance of basic ethical, political, and social ideals. This universality of cultural forms and principles must be ascribed largely to an education which inculcated a common body of literature and a particular philosophy of life. The establishment and maintenance of the system, chiefly through the device of the civil service examinations, constituted one of the most noteworthy achievements of the Chinese.

CHANGES WROUGHT BY THE COMING OF THE WEST

In no other phase of Chinese life has the revolution wrought by the impact of the Occident been more thorough-going than in what may be called the realm of the intellect—language, literature, and education. The old depended for its continuance upon a type of political organization which could not survive in the modern world. When the Confucian imperial state system collapsed, as it did early in the present century, its associated institutions and ideals were dealt a staggering blow. Moreover, under the new circumstances the specialization and rigidity which were part of the strength of the accepted forms of literature and thought proved a weakness. The Chinese have had to take account of and to acquire a competency in great fields of learning in which the Occident has led and through which it has overwhelmed them. To do so they have had to give over concentrating on their older literature and entirely to reorganize their education. Many of the resulting changes have been recounted earlier (in Chapter IX). They must, however, be summarized here—in a somewhat different form but with a certain amount of repetition.

The language has undergone great modifications. The many new ideas and objects which have been introduced in the past generation have had to be named. Usually this has been done by coining compound words out of existing vocables and characters—a process to which Chinese readily lends itself. Thus a telegram is *tien pao*—"a lightning report." In this the Japanese have led the way. Many of the new terms, indeed, were made in the Island Empire, where Chinese characters have been used for centuries and where the wholesale adoption of Western culture preceded the corresponding movement in China by a generation. Some terms have been taken over almost bodily from foreign tongues by transliteration. English has been the chief source of such loan words, for it is the Western language most widely studied. So many educated Chinese use it readily and so much of the teaching in higher schools has English as a medium and employs English texts that it is not surprising to find English words in Chinese speech. Such terms as "democracy" and "dictator" are among them. As in modern Japanese, quite a list might be compiled of foreign words which, modified by a more or less marked accent, are in current use. Such a device, however, is probably only temporary, for all such words will presumably be supplanted later by indigenous terms, compounds of existing Chinese vocables, suited to the genius of the language.

That strange hybrid, "Pidgin English," which arose as a *linqua franca* for foreign commerce, persists, but in limited circles and in declining use. It is made up largely of English words arranged in the order of Chinese idiom. It is not the English which the educated use, nor is it taught in the schools.

Although the taboo has been removed from the invention of characters, not a great many new ones have appeared. It is simpler and less confusing to make compound words or to transliterate foreign terms than to devise characters. However, a few have been coined. For instance, the pronoun of the third person was formerly written by a character which did not have any variation for gender. Now new ones have been framed to make possible a differentiation between "he," "she," and "it." So, too, punctuation is more freely used than formerly, several marks of Western origin having been adopted.

Attempts have not been lacking to do away entirely with the old written characters and to substitute for them a small number of phonetic signs. Some of these experiments have been by Protestant missionaries in their zeal to teach Christians to read—a desire actuated by the purpose of making the Bible an open book to every church member. Missionaries have often employed the Roman letters and in a few instances have invented new scripts. These alphabets are chiefly represented by the Bible in whole or in part and by a few books and pamphlets, mostly of a religious character, but their use has not extended appreciably outside the Christian communities or beyond those who otherwise would be illiterate. So limited a range of literature has been produced in them that none of them appears to give promise of early widespread adoption. A few phonetic systems have been devised by Chinese, but these have met the fate of those originated by foreigners. At least one has been utilized fairly widely by Protestant missionaries in making accessible the Bible and a rather restricted literature to those, particularly women, previously unable to read. None, however, seems to be making any great headway. The famous Mass Education Movement, the most widespread of the private purely Chinese enterprises for the removal of illiteracy, employs the historic characters. Indeed, any attempt to substitute a phonetic script for the time-honored forms must face the fact that the larger part of the existing literature would be unintelligible if transcribed in an alphabet or syllabary. If one were ever adopted by the entire nation, most of the literary treasures of the past would be closed to all except a few specialists. The chief reason for the failure of phonetic scripts to achieve widespread adoption has been that they have offered a kind of education which the literate do not need and which, consequently, the illiterate have not wanted. Effort is better expended in learning a limited number of the characters which the scholars themselves use.

Although efforts to introduce a simpler form of written character thus far have affected only a minority and give little promise of permanent success, extensive modifications have been made in the written language. We have previously noted that about 1917 a dignified form of the *mandarin*, as the *pai hua*, began to be prominent. It is written with the old characters, but it much more closely approximates the speech of every day than does the classical style. Such a change was obviously necessary. Imported Western democratic ideals demanded that the masses be educated, and this would be all but impossible if all scholarly writing were to continue in *wên li*. Moreover, with the many new subjects with which youth must now perforce become acquainted, for most students time does not permit the attainment of facility in the classical forms of composition. It is a choice between a debased or greatly simplified *wên li* and a worthy vernacular. The latter alternative has been decided upon.

If, however, this *pai hua* is to be easily intelligible throughout the nation it is obvious that there must be a general understanding of the vernacular upon which it is based. It is clear, too, that this type of linguistic unity must be achieved if that reënforcement to cultural and national unity heretofore given by the Empire-wide use of the classical language is not to be lost. Accordingly a vigorous effort has been made to have a form of *mandarin* adopted as the *kuo yü,* or "national speech." It is taught in the schools and has made headway among the educated in at least some of the non-*mandarin* speaking areas on the south coast. Although as late as thirty years ago a public address in *mandarin* would not have been understood by an educated audience in Canton or Foochow, of recent years a lecturer using it can expect an intelligent hearing in almost any school assembly. The local dialects persist, but the standard national vernacular is spreading.

In literature the changes wrought by the coming of the West are especially marked. Not only has it become good form to write in the *pai hua,* but the scope of literature is being modified and widened. In scholarly circles historical criticism is popular. The Han School of the seventeenth and eighteenth centuries with its courageous and original investigation of the authenticity of the accepted texts of the ancient Classics has once more come into vogue and has been reënforced and enriched by contact with the historical methodology of the modern West. Aided by the tools thus made available, stimulated by the efforts of Western sinologists, and freed from the shackles of the older state-supported orthodoxy, Chinese scholars are eagerly investigating afresh the records of antiquity. For example, Hu Shih has been writing the history of Chinese philosophy and in this and in other realms has been challenging the accuracy of traditional views. Much attention is being devoted to the Chou and pre-Chou period and the books ascribed to those centuries are being subjected to critical scrutiny with conclusions which are often very sceptical. A good deal of study is being directed toward the archeology of Sinkiang and of China's West. A record of the Ch'ing has been compiled on the general pattern of the other dynastic histories in the hope that it will be admitted to that notable series. As is natural in a time of energetic agitation to rid China of the "unequal treaties" much attention has been given to the history of the nation's diplomatic relations with the Occident.

The range of Chinese literary forms has been extended by contact with the West. Poetry, drama, and fiction often show the effects of Occidental influence. Newspapers and magazines are being issued in great quantities. Most of the newspapers are bitterly partisan and propagandist, but some of the magazines are of better quality. Perhaps in part as a development from the placards which for years have been employed to arouse public opinion, propagandists have made extensive use of cartoons and printed slogans which, often in glaring colors, have been affixed to walls in public places. Under Russian tutelage this type of agitation was given an especial impetus in the northward march of the Kuomintang armies in 1926–1927. It has been effective in anti-foreign boycotts and provides a favorite medium for a type of popular education.

The scope of Chinese thought has also been broadened. Western books covering a wide range of subjects have been translated in large numbers. Natural science especially has become popular. At first sight it seems strange that the Chinese, who for a highly civilized people have long been so backward in mathematics and the natural sciences, should suddenly adopt with enthusiasm scientific processes and results. Indeed, not a few of the younger men have shown marked skill in scientific research. However, the this-worldly attitude encouraged by Confucianism, the practical outlook of much of Chinese philosophy, and the ingenuity long displayed in the invention of mechanical appliances have probably been a preparation for the scientific approach.

Printing is now more and more by movable type, although the older methods are still employed. Great publishing houses have arisen, the most notable being the Commercial Press. It was given a severe blow by the destruction of its central plant in Shanghai in 1932 by the Japanese and by the enhanced Japanese invasion which began in 1937, but it has branches in all the more important Chinese cities.

With their love of books the Chinese have paid a good deal of attention to libraries. In spite of civil wars, a number have been assembled, some of them public. For example, the various collections in the old imperial palaces in the capital have been brought together, and a new National Library building has been erected in Peking, embodying much of the equipment and the methods of modern Western libraries.

In an earlier chapter something has been said about the history and recent status of the education of the new type. It will be recalled that Protestant missionaries were its leading pioneers. Before the China-Japanese War of 1894–1895 their schools enjoyed no wide patronage, for they were not of the kind to which boys would go for preparation for the civil service examinations. Their students were recruited largely from church members or from those too poverty-stricken to afford an education elsewhere. Their graduates usually found employment either in the service of a Christian mission or in business houses engaged in foreign trade. With the "reform movement" which began about 1895, mission schools, as the best places in China in which the now highly desired Western education could be acquired, rose quickly to popularity. In the twenty-five years after the defeat of China by the powers in 1900 they had a very rapid growth, for in mental and moral discipline and as a place in which to acquire Western learning the best of them, especially the secondary and higher institutions, were equal and usually superior to the best non-Christian ones in their communities. In the meantime private and government schools of the new type have increased even more rapidly. Their growth has been retarded by the civil strife and foreign invasions of the past fifteen or twenty years, but in places continues. Indeed, it has had a phenomenal expansion in "free" China. For a time the rising tide of nationalism regarded the mission schools as part of a foreign, "imperialistic" invasion, agitated for the "recovery of educational rights," and between 1926 and 1932 compelled most of them to register with the Government —the terms being state supervision, the placing of all religious teaching on a voluntary and extra-curricular basis, and the direction of each by a Chinese principal and by a board a majority of whose members are Chinese. As government and private schools have multiplied in numbers and improved in efficiency, mission schools have declined in relative importance.

It will also be recalled that thousands of Chinese youth have studied or are studying abroad—in Japan, Europe, and America—as large a student migration from any one country as the world has ever seen.

It will be remembered, too, that students have taken an active part in politics, sometimes as the tools of older manipulators, but more than once prominently and decisively—notably in the pressure which brought about the resignation of Chiang Kai-shek and C. T. Wang in the latter part of 1931.

In a number of ways the new schools have made radical innovations. The most sweeping is in the purpose of education. No longer are schools dominated by the idea of preparing candidates for the civil service examinations. That is partly because the latter have passed into oblivion. It is also because the objectives of education have broadened. They are still conceived of as being in part preparation for the service of the state. Education is regarded as a function of government and is dominated by nationalistic purposes. The duty of a patriot, however, is thought of as discharged not only in holding office but also in tne capacity of private citizenship. The ideal has been adopted of universal primary education. To be sure, this has been only partially attained. The country is too poor and too racked by civil division, foreign war, and banditry to permit it to be reached at present. Like the other novelties in modern Chinese education, it is an importation from the West. Yet it must sometime be approximated if the nation is to achieve a stable government of a Western type and is to compete successfully with the Occident and Japan in commerce, industry, and agriculture.

Associated with the extension of formal education to groups for which hitherto it has not been designed is the inclusion of girls in the schools. The beginnings must be ascribed to the Protestant missionary—as must so many other features of education and social reform. In higher education for women Protestant Christian institutions still predominate. More and more, however, government and non-Christian private schools are being opened to girls or organized especially for them. Coëducation of the sexes is increasingly common.

Adult education likewise is being conducted. In its inception the Mass Education Movement was primarily for those of mature years and its program still includes them. Protestant missions have been doing much to teach illiterate adults, particularly women, to read.

The curriculum has been broadened. Not only does that of ordinary primary and secondary schools now include many subjects undreamed of two generations ago, but technical schools have been founded to give the training which, if available at all, was formerly to be had only through the apprentice system or in the home. All this, it will be observed, is of Occidental provenance. So, too, is the idea of a university. Numbers of institutions have been founded which seek, some of them with increasing success, to be true universities in the Western sense of that term. Often the equipment for the modern school is pitifully behind that of its Western contemporaries and frequently apparatus, when acquired, is unintelligently used. This is not surprising, because formerly all except the higher schools needed merely a bare room with a few desks and even the higher schools required only a library. Such Western devices as laboratories and playing fields are more and more being installed and, in spite of the destruction brought by war, are being increasingly utilized.

The new system of schools is still decidedly in process of formation. It displays several different types of educational theory and is not fully integrated into a national organization. Nor is it yet thoroughly adapted to Chinese needs. Much in it is an incompletely digested importation from foreign lands, especially from the United States. It is accused of being top-heavy and of training its graduates to live too remote from the actualities of Chinese life. Too scanty funds are expended on it and the distribution of its advantages by provinces is decidedly uneven. Yet, considering the problems which China has had to face, marked progress has been made. For instance, the number of pupils in primary schools more than doubled between 1916 and 1930, in spite of civil strife, and in 1930 totaled nearly nine millions—although this was still only about one-fifth of the children of primary school age. Real progress has been made in secondary and higher education.

The intellectual atmosphere of China is, then, being profoundly altered. The scholar of the old school, thoroughly drilled in the Classics but knowing little else, is passing. The product of the new education usually knows much less of the ancient literature than did his predecessor. At his worst he is shallowly trained in Western subjects as well. At his best he has at least some familiarity with the older literature of his country, uses easily one or more foreign languages, is acquainted with the broad range of ancient and modern Western knowledge, and is a specialist in some one segment of it. The typical product of the new age is sceptical of the traditionally accepted beliefs and customs both of his own and of other lands, but is inclined to dogmatism, is intensely nationalistic, and has an almost naïve confidence in the findings of modern science and in the scientific method. The New Tide, or Renaissance Movement, of which much was said about two decades ago, is now less prominent, but the attitude of mind of which it was an expression persists and, if anything, is growing. More than in any other time in recorded history, the Chinese educated classes have moved out of one age into another. It is a mental world which is largely adrift. The West, by which it is molded, is itself in process of rapid change and is abandoning old standards in search of new. The situation is one with great possibilities both for good and for evil.

BIBLIOGRAPHY

Good introductory handbooks to the nature and history of the Chinese language, written and spoken, are B. Karlgren, *Sound and Symbol in Chinese* (London, 1923) and B. Karlgren, *Philology and Ancient China* (Oslo, 1926). A longer work by the same author is *Études sur la Phonologie Chinoise* (Leiden and Upsala, 1915–1926). On the ancient forms of the written character there is a monograph, now largely obsolete, by Frank H. Chalfant, *Early Chinese Writing* (*Memoirs of the Carnegie Museum*, Vol. 4, No. 1, Sept. 1906). On the same subject, see also L. Wieger, *Chinese Characters* (2 vols., 2d edition, translated from the 4th French edition, Hsien-hsien, 1927) and G. D. Wilder and J. H. Ingram, *Analysis of Chinese Characters* (North China Language School, Peiping). See also Chiu Bien-ming, *The Phonetic Structure and Tone Behavior in Hagu* (*Commonly Known as the Amoy Dialect*) *and Their Relation to Certain Questions in Chinese Linguistics* (*T'oung Pao*, 1931, Vol. 28, pp. 245–343).

Standard Chinese-English dictionaries are H. A. Giles, *A Chinese-English Dictionary* (2d edition, revised and enlarged, Shanghai and London, 1912) and S. W. Williams, *A Syllabic Dictionary of the Chinese Language* (Shanghai, 1874), the former being usually considered the better. Smaller, but useful, especially to the specialist, is B. Karlgren, *Analytic Dictionary of Chinese and Sino-Chinese* (Paris, 1923).

Many handbooks have been prepared for the purpose of introducing the foreigner to Chinese. Among those for an English-speaking constituency there are, for *mandarin,* Sir Walter Hillier, *The Chinese Language and How to Learn It* (2 vols., London, 1907), fairly simple; C. W. Mateer, *A Course of Mandarin Lessons, Based on Idiom* (revised edition, Shanghai, 1900), long standard but embracing the colloquial as it was before the recent changes; and J. P. Ratay, *Current Chinese* (2 vols., one the Chinese text and the other an English translation with a glossary of terms and phrases, Shanghai, 1927). For the literary language there are J. Brandt, *Introduction to Literary Chinese* (Peking, North China Union Language School, 1927); F. W. Baller, *Lessons in Elementary Wen-li* (Shanghai, 1912); T. L. Bullock, *Progressive Exercises in the Chinese Written Language* (Shanghai, 1902), and H. G. Creel, T. C. Chang, and R. C. Rudolph, *Literary Chinese by the Inductive Method* (Chicago, 2 vols., 1938, 1939). Selections from various types of Chinese prose in the literary language, together with translations and notes, are in Evan Morgan, *A Guide to Wenli Styles and Chinese Ideals* (London, 1912). The entrance of the United States into the Far Eastern war in 1941 made necessary the introduction of hundreds to Chinese. For this many new methods and text-books were devised. These have been so numerous that no attempt has here been made to list and evaluate them.

On one of the most widely used forms of the literary prose style see G. Margouliès, *Le Kou-Wen Chinois. Recueil de Textes avec Introduction et Notes* (Paris, 1926), and G. Margouliès, *Évolution de la Prose Artistique Chinoise* (Munich, 1929). On poetic forms see G. Margouliès, *Le "Fou" dans le Wen-Siuan, Étude et Textes* (Paris, 1926), and the introduction in Witter Bynner and Kiang Kang-hu, *The Jade Mountain. A Chinese Anthology, Being Three Hundred Poems of the T'ang Dynasty, 618–906* (New York, 1929).

The standard book on printing in China is T. F. Carter, *The Invention of Printing in China and Its Spread Westward* (revised edition, New York, 1931). See also B. Laufer, *Paper and Printing in Ancient China* (Chicago, 1931).

Of general works on Chinese literature probably the most useful is A. Wylie, *Notes on Chinese Literature* (new edition, Shanghai, 1902). An excellent introduction is Ssŭ-yü Têng and K. Biggerstaff, *An Annotated Bibliography of Selected Chinese Reference Works* (Peiping, 1936). Disappointing and unsatisfactory is H. A. Giles, *A History of Chinese Literature* (New York, 1901). R. Wilhelm, *Die Chinesische Literatur* (Wildpark-Potsdam, 1930) is semi-popular and with translations of many selections. There is also W. Grube, *Geschichte der Chinesischen Literatur* (Leipzig, 1902). On the *ts'ung shu* A. W. Hummel has a short but important article—*Ts'ung Shu* (*Journal of the American Oriental Society*, Vol. 51, March, 1931, pp. 40–47).

Translations have been made of a number of Chinese works, in whole or in part—although, of course, by far the greater proportion of Chinese literature has not been put into any European language. The most notable translations of the classical works of the Chou period have been given in the bibliography at the end of chapter two, and of the Han works at the end of chapter three. Several others have been mentioned at the end of chapters five to nine inclusive. Among those covering more than one period are H. A. Giles, trans., *Gems from Chinese Literature* (second edition, two vols., Shanghai, 1923); A. Waley, trans., *A Hundred and Seventy Chinese Poems* (second edition, London, 1923); A. Waley, *More Translations from the Chinese* (New York, 1919); A. Waley, *The Temple and Other Poems* (London, 1923); H. H. Hart, *The Hundred Names. A Short Introduction to the Study of Chinese Poetry with Illustrative Translations* (Berkeley, 1933); Florence Ayscough and Amy Lowell, trans., *Fir-Flower Tablets, Poems* (Boston, 1921); G. C. Stent, *Entombed Alive and Other Songs, Ballads, &c. (From the Chinese)* (London, 1878); H. A. Giles, *Chinese Poetry in English Verse* (London, 1898); R. K. Douglas, *Chinese Stories* (Edinburgh and London, 1893); C. C. Wang, translator, *Contemporary Chinese Stories* (New York, 1944); C. C. Wang, translator, *Traditional Chinese Tales* (New York, 1944); Ts'ai T'ing-kan, *Chinese Poems in English Rhyme* (Chicago, 1932); *Selections from the Work of Su Tung P'o*, by C. D. Le Gros Clark (London, 1932). See also P. S. Buck, *All Men Are Brothers [Shui Hu Chuan]* (New York, 2 vols., 1933), a translation of a famous novel of the Ming dynasty, and E. Clement, *The Golden Lotus, A Translation from the Chinese Original of the Novel Chi'n P'ing Mei* (London, 4 vols., 1939).

Some Chinese proverbs are in H. H. Hart, translator, *Seven Hundred Chinese Proverbs* (Stanford, 1937), W. Scarborough, *A Collection of Chinese Proverbs* (Shanghai, 1875), and A. H. Smith, *Proverbs and Common Sayings from the Chinese* (new edition, Shanghai, 1914).

Some of the material in Western languages on Chinese medicine is in Fr. Hübotter, *Die Chinesische Medizin zu Beginn des XX. Jahrhunderts und ihr historischer Entwicklungsgang* (Leipzig, 1929); Fr. Hübotter, *A Guide through the Labyrinth of Chinese Medical Writers and Medical Writings and Bibliographical Sketch* (Kumamoto, Japan, 1924); H. A. Giles, *The Hsi Yüan Lu, or Instructions to Coroners* (*Proceedings of the Royal Society of Medicine*, Vol. 17, pp. 59–107); A. G. Vorderman, *The Chinese Treatment of Diphtheritis* (*T'oung Pao*, 1890, pp. 173 ff., 349 ff.); F. P. Smith, *Contributions towards the Materia Medica & Natural History of China* (Shanghai, 1871); Bernard E. Read, *Chinese Materia Medica;* K. C. Wong and Wu Lien-teh, *History of Chinese Medicine* (Tientsin, 1932); E. H. Hume, *The Chinese Way in Medicine* (Baltimore, 1940); and I. Snapper, *Chinese Lessons to Western Medicine* (New York, 1941).

On the backwardness of natural science in China, see Fung Yu-lan, *Why China Has No Science* (*International Journal of Ethics*, Apr. 1922, Vol. 32, pp. 237–263).

On the older education in China, the standard history in a Western language is E. Biot, *Essai sur l'Histoire de l'Instruction Publique en Chine et de la Corporation des Lettres depuis les Anciens Temps jusqu'à Nos Jours* (Paris, 1847). The old style village school is graphically and somewhat pessimistically described in A. H. Smith, *Village Life in China* (New York, 1899), pp. 70–110. Much information concerning education in the T'ang is contained in Robert des Rotours, *Le Traité des Examens Traduit de la Nouvelle Histoire des T'ang* (Paris, 1932).

On the Chinese writing of history see an excellent study, C. S.

Gardner, *Chinese Traditional Historiography* (Harvard University Press, 1938).

Some of the new terms in the Chinese language are in Evan Morgan, *Chinese New Terms* (Shanghai, 1926). A brief account of the movement to write in the *pai hua* by the one who is credited with having more influence in initiating it than any other is Hu Shih, *The Literary Renaissance* (in Sophia H. Chen Zen, editor, *Symposium on Chinese Culture*, Shanghai, 1931). There is an account of changes in the theatre in George Kin Leung, *Hsin Ch'ao (The New Tide). New Trends in the Traditional Chinese Drama (Pacific Affairs*, 1929, pp. 175–183). A popular description of some of the attempts to find a simpler way of writing Chinese than the traditional characters is C. C. Wang, *A Roman Alphabet for Modern China (Asia*, June, 1930, pp. 437–439, 459–464).

A good deal has been written on modern education in China. P. W. Kuo, *The Chinese System of Public Education* (New York, 1915) tells of the earlier years of the changes. So, too, for education for girls, does Ida Belle Lewis, *The Education of Girls in China* (New York, 1919). A somewhat later account of women's education is Lin Paotchin, *L'Instruction Féminine en Chine (Après la Revolution de 1911)* (Paris, 1926). D. H. Kulp, *Country Life in South China* (New York, 1925) has a chapter on education valuable for its description of a particular community. Paul Monroe, the distinguished American educator who has been an adviser of the Chinese authorities, has a chapter on modern education and the student movement in his *China, A Nation in Evolution* (New York, 1928). There is also a summary in one chapter of H. A. Van Dorn, *Twenty Years of the Chinese Republic* (New York, 1932). King Chu has a chapter on education in Zen, *Symposium on Chinese Culture* (Shanghai, 1931). The various issues of *The China Mission Year Book* (beginning with 1926 *The China Christian Year Book*) and *The China Year Book* usually contain summaries of education and often statements about the New Tide Movement. *Bulletins on Chinese Education, 1923* (Shanghai, 1923) contains a number of informing papers. *Educational Review*, a quarterly published in Shanghai by the China Christian Educational Association, contains information on secular as well as Christian education. *Christian Education in China* (Shanghai, 1922) is the report of an important educational commission and is very comprehensive. C. H. Peake, *Nationalism and Education in Modern China* (New York, 1932) is partly a brief historical account of educational changes since 1860 and partly a summary of the nationalistic program of that education. See also *The Reorganization of Education in China*, by the League of Nations Mission of Educational Experts (Paris, 1932), a volume which has been commented on unfavorably by several reviewers.

On the press see Lin Yutang, *A History of the Press and Public Opinion in China* (Chicago, 1936).

CHAPTER XX

BY WAY OF SUMMARY

The outstanding characteristic of the China of to-day is, as we have seen, the clash of two cultures, with the partial and progressive disintegration of the one which we think of as traditionally Chinese.

The civilization which at present seems in process of disappearing was the product of a long evolution. Its development was marked by great stages, each with its distinct characteristics. In spite of the fact that certain features occur again and again through much of its course, Chinese history is by no means, as some would have us think, a repetition of movements identical except for the names of the actors.

As is the case with most cultures of ancient origin, the beginnings of that of the Chinese are veiled in obscurity. We first catch glimpses of its outlines sometime in the second millennium before Christ in what is known as the Shang dynasty. There was then living on the fertile plains of North China, on the lower course of the Yellow River, a race whose blood appears to be the dominant strain in the population which still inhabits that region. It had written characters (an archaic form of the present script), depended upon agriculture for subsistence, used bronze for some of its weapons, implements, and utensils, had a vigorous and by no means crude art, and already possessed a political organization of some complexity. How much of the culture was autochthonous and how much an importation from the West or South is still a matter of conjecture and debate. We know that many centuries and perhaps millenniums before the Shang, primitive man inhabited what is now North China and that at a time not very remote from and perhaps contemporary with the Shang men on the edge of the bronze age and using polished stone implements and a painted pottery lived in the valley of the Yellow

River and in Manchuria. There was also a black pottery culture. The precise connections between the continuous development of which the Shang constitutes the earliest known phase and these primitive cultures have still to be determined.

The Shang was replaced by the Chou. The latter triumphed in a trial of arms, the traditional date being toward the close of the second millennium before the Christian era. The Chou was possibly a new invader from the West seeking control of the fertile North China plain and differing somewhat in culture from the Shang. Apparently the advent of the Chou was accompanied by no marked revolution in culture. However, in the course of the centuries in which the Chou supplied the titular rulers, striking developments occurred. The area within the purview of the Chinese political organization expanded, reaching south into the valley of the Yangtze and north into the highlands of Shansi. The authority of the Chou monarchs diminished almost to the vanishing point, although long after they ceased to have an effective military control those who inherited the Chou title of *wang* continued to hold a religious preëminence and by a convenient fiction were still the fountain of titles and of legitimacy. The actual power passed more and more into the hands of a varying number of territorial magnates and the political structure resembled that of European feudalism. Much of the time the feudal states waged war on one another and on the neighboring non-Chinese peoples. There were cities, commerce, money, art, and a certain degree of luxury for the ruling classes. A sharp distinction existed between the aristocracy and the proletariat. Original thinking emerged, some of it profound, and the third quarter of the first millennium before Christ spanned one of the most creative periods in the intellectual history of China. The philosophers chiefly, but by no means exclusively, centered their attention upon the achievement of an ideal human society. Political and economic theories were, accordingly, warmly debated. The chief schools were four in number. The Confucianists insisted upon the maintenance of the traditional religious and political ceremonies and organization, but purified and kept just through the example of educated and righteous rulers and officials who had the welfare of the populace at heart. The Taoists believed in having mankind conform to what was denominated the Tao. The Tao, as they conceived it, may be defined as the way of the Universe. This they thought to be simplicity itself. Accordingly they wished to reduce government and economic organization to the minimum. To them the elaborate ceremonies and meticulous ethics of the Confucianists were anathema. Then there were the Mohists. Mo Ti, their founder, was intensely religious. He believed that T'ien or Shang Ti, the traditional Supreme God of his day, loved all men. All men, therefore, so he held, should love one another and should seek one another's welfare. He condemned aggressive war as contrary to love and held that costly funerals were wasteful of materials needed for the living and should be discouraged. His followers divided into two groups, one emphasizing his religious views and the other stressing his dialectic. A fourth main school, the Legalists, sought to create economically self-sufficient states under autocratic monarchs—each a centralized fighting machine in command of a ruler who strictly controlled his subjects under impartially administered law. In and out of these four schools a good deal of religious and metaphysical speculation went on, some of it marked by daring and acute scepticism and some of it by reasoned faith.

In the fifth century before the Christian era the wars between the states which made up the then China increased in intensity. Eventually, out of the sorrows of these years, in the middle of the third century B.C. a decisive transition occurred. The old order passed away and a new China emerged, more widely extended, but with a culture largely based on that of the past. Ch'in, with its seat in the valley of the Wei in the Northwest, conquered its rivals and founded the Chinese Empire. Its great leader and autocrat, Shih Huang Ti, extended his rule over the major portion of what is now China proper, sought to stamp out the remnants of the Chou feudalism, and administered his realm through a centralized bureaucracy, which, under rulers and ministers who had adopted the Legalist theory, had been developed in his native state of Ch'in. To make his power secure, Shih Huang Ti endeavored to curb the non-Legalist philosophic schools which criticized the political theory and the attendant organization on which he depended.

The structure which Ch'in Shih Huang Ti had so triumphantly erected was disrupted shortly after his death. A successful warrior, however, soon succeeded in founding a new dynasty, the Han, under which, with one interruption about the time of Christ, the Empire was ruled from the close of the third century B.C. to the beginning of the third century A.D. While for a time the Han reverted in part to the feudal forms of the Chou, it increasingly governed through a bureaucracy some of whose main principles it derived from the Ch'in. However, instead of Legalism the Han eventually adopted Confucianism as the theory on which to build the state. The Confucianism which prevailed was a syncretism in which the Confucianism of the Chou was the dominant element, but to which Mohism, Taoism, and the Legalists contributed. It was on the basis of the Confucian principle that the realm should be governed by the ablest and the best, regardless of birth, that, after the first few reigns, the Han rulers more and more recruited the members of the bureaucracy. To this end they established schools in which Confucianism was dominant and instituted the beginnings of a system of civil service examinations through which some members of the bureaucracy were chosen. The structure so erected provided machinery by which autocratic Emperors could govern their vast domains without recourse to an hereditary nobility and the consequent threat of decentralizing feudalism. This Confucian state system, greatly elaborated by later dynasties, persisted until in the twentieth century it collapsed under pressure from the Occident.

The other main philosophic schools of the Chou not only left their impress on the dominant school but did not immediately die out as separate entities. Taoism, greatly changed, continued popular, even and perhaps particularly in court circles. Some Legalist measures of state control of phases of economic life were warmly debated and adopted, and the Mohists did not at once disappear. Yet philosophic speculation became less original and the debates over it less marked. The intellectual ferment of the Chou was passing.

Territorially the Han was characterized by expansion. The Han arms were carried southward into the present Annam, northward into the present Korea, and westward into Central Asia as far as what is now Russian territory. Contacts with foreign peoples multiplied and more or less indirect intercourse was had even with the Roman Empire. Art was profoundly altered, in part because of influences from abroad. Its figures became more lifelike and showed more vigorous action. There arrived, too, the first waves of Buddhism—that faith which was to be the vehicle for more profound foreign influences on the Chinese than came from any other single source in historic times until almost our own day.

With the end of the Han, in the third century A.D., a period of political disunion began which lasted for not far from four centuries. During much of this time non-Chinese peoples from the North and West ruled great sections of the North. Numbers of families claimed imperial power, but no one of them was able to command the allegiance of so much of the country as had acknowledged the Han—although in the third century one nearly succeeded in doing so. Most of them ruled over what were only fragments of the former Han domains. Thanks in part to the weakening of the administrative system inherited from the Han and the consequent feebleness of its accompanying Confucianism, Buddhism made great headway and established itself as a major religion of the land. With it came new and varied art forms, some of them of Greek origin, and it inspired marked artistic and literary activity. By the end of the period the Chinese had begun to make Buddhism their own and to think it through in terms of their experience. The result was Buddhist sects which, while often claiming Indian nativity, usually displayed marks of their Chinese environment. Yet the older religious systems—Confucianism and Taoism—did not disappear, even though both, especially Taoism, were profoundly modified by competition with their rival.

In spite of the nearly four centuries of division, the dream of political unity for all the inheritors of Chinese culture did not die. At the close of the sixth century it was once more realized by the Sui dynasty. The Sui was quickly followed by the T'ang. During the T'ang, which led China from early in the seventh to early in the tenth century A.D., the Empire reached a new level of power and prosperity, but with a culture which in some respects differed decidedly from that of its greatest predecessor, the Han. Like the Han it extended the geographical boundaries of the Empire toward the south and north, and especially toward the west. The outer limits of the two were not far from the same. Like the

Han it built its political structure on the Confucian theory. Indeed, it carried still further the system which the Han had originated of recruiting the staff of its bureaucracy through civil service examinations based largely although not entirely upon Confucian literature. To prepare for these examinations it expanded the state system of schools. Under the T'ang Confucianism revived and once more became powerful. Taoism, modified by Buddhism, was popular. Yet the T'ang showed marked contrasts with the Han, and under it fresh advances were made. Chinese Buddhism attained the height of its vigor and entered upon a slow decline. Sculpture reached its apex and there were noted painters. Many of the art *motifs* were very different from those of the Han. Later generations have regarded the poetry and the calligraphy of the T'ang as the finest that the Chinese have produced. Printing and porcelain appeared, probably for the first time. Other foreign faiths—Christianity, Zoroastrianism, Manichæism, and Islam—entered, and one of them, Islam, persisted to our own day. More than at any time previously, too, Japan was brought within the circle of Chinese cultural influence.

Following the T'ang, after a half-century or so of disorder, came the Sung. During much of its course the North was ruled by aliens, but the native culture of the period was rich and had its distinct developments. For many years debate over a political experiment somewhat akin to the modern state socialism of the Occident disturbed the realm. Buddhism, while still strong, gave additional evidences of decay. Confucianism, although more than ever the accepted philosophy of the educated and ruling classes and enforced through a further development of government schools and civil service examinations, was extensively modified. It was thought through afresh and restated, and much of Taoism and Buddhism were more or less unconsciously incorporated in it. The form then given it remained orthodox until the twentieth century. Landscape painting was the crowning achievement of the art of the Sung and the best of it has never been equaled in China before or since. Printing and porcelain were improved. Sung editions are valued for their beauty as well as their antiquity and Sung porcelains, largely monochrome and simple of design, are highly esteemed.

In the fourth quarter of the thirteenth century the last of the

Sung rulers succumbed to the rising tide of foreign conquest and for nearly a century all China submitted to the Mongols. However, the latter did not seek to displace Chinese culture and ruled largely under the accustomed machinery and in the guise of Chinese Emperors, with the dynastic name of Yüan. Many foreigners entered China as merchants, soldiers, and officials. Western Europeans reached the Empire for the first time, most of them as merchants and missionaries, and carried back glowing reports of the wealth and culture of Cathay. Novels and the theatre became prominent.

In the second half of the fourteenth century Chinese armies drove out the Mongols and one of their generals placed his family on the throne as a dynasty, the Ming, which ruled the Empire until the middle of the seventeenth century. The Neo-Confucianism of the Sung remained the official philosophy in which the educated were drilled and on which the state continued to be based. The administrative machinery and the civil service examinations which had come down from the Han were further elaborated and strengthened. Yet even the Ming, which sought so earnestly to restore the traditional culture, saw distinctive developments. Buddhism became more somnolent than ever, and art, deprived in part of its inspiration, grew more and more secular. Landscape painting declined in quality, but the technique of painting was elaborated. Porcelains were enriched by the use of more colors and polychrome designs. There was even a revolt (although affecting only a few) against the dominant Neo-Confucianism of the Sung, partly in the school of Wang Yang-ming and partly in the beginnings of the attempt to get back of the interpretations of the Sung philosophers to the primitive documents of the accepted Classics as they had come from the hands of the Han editors.

In the seventeenth century the native Emperors gave way before another group of foreign conquerors. These, the Manchus, established the Ch'ing dynasty and held the throne until 1912. Under the rule of the greatest of the Ch'ing, in the seventeenth and eighteenth centuries, the territory controlled reached the widest extent in the history of the Empire. Population attained new high levels and the Chinese race spread over a larger area than ever before. In culture, however, the Ch'ing era was almost entirely a continuation of the Ming. Important innovations from within in art, literature, religion, philosophy, and political organization were almost entirely lacking. To be sure, the Han school of literary and historical criticism came to fruition, but it had begun in the Ming. Until the Ch'ing the course of Chinese cultural development, while marked by certain fairly constant factors and characteristics, had shown progressive change. One dynasty was by no means a complete repetition of its predecessor. Ever since the Yüan, however, creativity and originality had been slowing down and the Chinese were more and more content to repeat old customs and forms. For this the enforced conformity to Sung Neo-Confucianism and the lack of stirring contacts with other cultures seem to have been at least in part responsible.

However, under the Ming and the Ch'ing those intimate contacts with an expanding Occident began which in the nineteenth and twentieth centuries were to have revolutionary results. The comparatively brief touch of a few Europeans with China under the Yüan had its main permanent results in kindling in the hearts of adventurous Westerners the desire to reach the rich and populous Cathay of which Marco Polo wrote. Not until the sixteenth century were those relations established which have continued and grown. Moreover, not until nearly the middle of the nineteenth century was China seriously affected by them. The collapse of the structure of Chinese life before the invasion of the West was probably more overwhelming than it otherwise would have been and the resulting chaos more marked because the increasing pressure of that invasion synchronized with the decline in vigor of the Ch'ing rulers. It was a China with incompetent and decadent leadership at the top which had to face the most serious combination of crises in its history.

The contrasts between the Chinese culture whose disruption the present generation has witnessed and the civilization of the West which brought about the revolution are numerous and striking. Both are notable achievements of the human genius and it would be difficult to decide which is the more admirable. However, since it is the West which has conquered, Chinese rather than Occidental civilization has suffered and the disintegration in the former is greater than would have been the case had the background of the two been more nearly similar. On the one hand was a culture where changes, once frequent, were occurring more and more slowly. On the other was a civilization in which a machine age and applied science were working alterations with constantly accelerated speed. The Chinese idea of the state was that of an empire embracing all civilized mankind, owing allegiance to one sovereign Son of Heaven and governed through scholars trained in the Confucian theories of life. Unity was as much cultural as political and wide variations from Confucianism were decried. The Western conception is a commonwealth of nations, each theoretically sovereign in its own territory and guided in its relations to others by an international law. This difference has been the cause of frequent misunderstandings and friction. For instance, the signature of a treaty has not had the same connotation to Chinese as to Occidentals. Moreover, while the Occident possesses a certain unity of cultural background, wide national variations from it have occurred and have been accepted and even praised. In Western nations until recently the warrior was dominant and set the standards of political life. Such political theories as democracy and latterly socialism and communism are transforming political institutions. In China the scholar administered the government and crowned the social ladder. In China a people that has been culturally but not nationally self-conscious has collided with a West in which the tides of nationalism are running strong. China's trade and industry have been organized by guilds. Those of the West are by stock companies which tend ever to coalesce into larger and larger units. Chinese currency has not been uniform throughout the country and has been based on copper and silver. Western currencies usually employ the gold standard and the central government establishes uniform measures of fineness and weight. Chinese industry has been in the handicraft stage. By the time it began seriously to affect China that of the Occident had been made over by the Industrial Revolution and had entered the factory era. The transportation of China has been by the sailing craft, the wheelbarrow, the cart, and on the backs of men and beasts of burden. That of the West is by the steamship, the railway, and the automobile. The Occident which has forced itself on China is in possession of the ocean cable and the telegraph and of nationally and internationally organized postal systems and has added the radio and the cinema.

A China primarily agricultural and rural has been forced into a world which is increasingly industrial and urban. Religiously China has been Confucian, Taoist, and Buddhist, with a strong admixture of animism and with occasional scepticism. It has had to face an Occident which in philosophy and religion is the heir of Greek, Hebrew, and Christian traditions and which at present displays a strong tendency to discredit and discard all religion. A people organized in part on the patriarchal basis and in which the individual and even the state have been subordinated to the family has been invaded by *mores* from a huge section of the world where the individual has been exalted, where the family is disintegrating, and where subordination of the individual, when it occurs, as it does increasingly, is to the state. An intellectual culture of a very high order but in which literary form, ethical and social content, and a subjective philosophy—which looks within to the human spirit—have been the chief preoccupations has had to face a world which has created the scientific method, is in possession of an amazing and rapidly growing knowledge and control of its physical environment and in which the premium is upon discoveries in the natural sciences. A people among whom the education of the schools was the privilege of the few and was primarily for the purpose of training state officials has been thrown into competition with a world in which the ideal is an elementary school education for all. Artistic traditions hallowed by centuries of development and of high achievement have been rudely challenged by the products of quite different historical processes. A people whose socially dominant classes have been uninterested in the development of the body and in athletic sports has been forced into an age whose standards are set by those who rejoice in a sound body and in games involving physical competition. The contrasts between the two civilizations could be multiplied. One world of traditions and customs has been rudely entered and mastered by another with quite a different background.

Some similarities, to be sure, exist between the old China and the modern West. The Chinese have been this-worldly and interested in constructing a civilization which will bring physical comfort to all its members. So increasingly is the Occident. By tradition the Chinese are disposed to take kindly to the scientific processes and the mechanical devices of the West and to enter into successful competition in its commercial life. It seems fairly clear that the Chinese have more in common with the modern West than they have with India.

When the similarities between China and the Occident have been pointed out, however, the fact remains that in many basic characteristics the two civilizations are antipathetic. As a consequence Chinese culture has been disrupted and thrown into chaos, with great suffering to millions of Chinese and with danger to the rest of the world. It is a spectacle the like of which in sheer magnitude human beings have never before seen. The largest fairly homogeneous group of mankind is experiencing the most thorough-going and destructive revolution in its history. The outcome remains uncertain. The Chinese may be stimulated to fresh originality and build a civilization which will integrate in partially or entirely new forms some of the old with many of the features of the Occident. On the other hand they may sink more or less permanently into chaos, become more than ever politically and economically subject to foreign peoples, and retain only enfeebled remnants of their older culture unsuccessfully combined with unintelligently adopted institutions and ideas from the Occident. At the best there is every indication that the full outcome will not be clearly seen for at least a generation and probably very much longer. So shattering an experience to so large a body of mankind cannot be passed through quickly.

The world should not lose faith in China if the process requires centuries. Many of us who have known and loved the Chinese have a hopeful confidence in the ultimate result and base it upon what we know of Chinese history and of individual Chinese of to-day. We see no clear signs of degeneration in the native capacity of the race. Remembering as we do the ability which the Chinese have shown in the past to construct a civilization we believe that they will ultimately recover from the stunning blows dealt them and will once more create a worthy culture. It is improbable, however, that we or our children's children will live to see our faith fully justified. The next century or more probably has in store as intense sufferings as the Chinese have ever known. Some of us, however, are not without faith that these will prove the birth pangs of a new and greater China—even though we cannot now clearly discern its features.

PROPER NAMES AND CHINESE WORDS USED IN THE TEXT AND THEIR CORRESPONDING CHINESE CHARACTERS

Achmach (in Chinese A-ho-ma 阿合馬)
Ahmad (in Chinese A-ho-ma 阿合馬)
A-lo-han 阿羅漢
A-lo-pên 阿羅本
Amban (Chinese An-pan 諳版) (Manchu word meaning Ta Ch'ên 大臣)
A-mi-t'o (same as O-mi-t'o)
A-mi-t'o-fo (same as O-mi-t'o-fo)
Amoy (Hsia mên) 厦門
Amur (Heilungchiang 黑龍江)
Amursana (Chinese A-mu-êhr-sa-na 阿睦爾撒納)
Anfu (Club) 安福
Anhsi 安西
Anhui 安徽
An Lu-shan 安祿山
Annam 安南
An-shih-kao 安世高
Burma (Chinese Mien 緬 or Mien-tien 緬甸)
Canton (Kwangchow) 廣州
Ch'ahar 察哈爾
Champa (in Chinese formerly Lin-i 林邑 and later Chan-ch'êng 占城)

Ch'an (sect of Buddhism) 禪
Ch'ang-an 長安
Chang Ch'ien 張騫
Ch'ang Chien 常建
Chang Chih-tung 張之洞
Ch'angchow 常州
Chang Fei 張飛
Chang Hsüeh-liang 張學良
Chang Hsün 張勳
Chang I 張儀
Chang Pang-ch'ang 張邦昌
Chang Tao-ling 張道陵
Chang Tsai 張載
Chang Tso-lin 張作霖
Chan Kuo ("Contending States") 戰國
Chan Kuo Tsê 戰國策
Chao (dynasty) 趙
Chao (state in Chou dynasty, formerly part of Chin 晉) 趙
Ch'aochow 潮州
Ch'aohsien 朝鮮
Chao-hui 兆惠
Chao Kao 趙高
Chao K'uang-yin 趙匡胤
Chao mêng-fu 趙孟頫
Chefoo 芝罘
Chêkiang 浙江

Ch'ên (dynasty) 陳
Chên Chün 眞君
Chêng (Shih Huang Ti) 政
Chêng Ch'êng-kung 鄭成功
Chêng Ch'iao 鄭樵
Ch'êng Hao 程顥
Chêng Ho 鄭和
Ch'êng Huang Miao 城隍廟
Ch'êng I 程頤
Ch'êng I-ch'uan 程伊川
Ch'êng Ming-tao 程明道
Ch'êng Tsu 成祖
Chengtu 成都
Ch'êng Wang 成王
Ch'ên Huan-chang 陳煥章
Chên Jên 眞人
Ch'ên Pa-hsien 陳霸先
Ch'ên Shou 陳壽
Ch'ên Shu 陳書
Ch'ên Tu-hsiu 陳獨秀
Ch'ên Tzŭ-ang 陳子昂
Chên-yen (Buddhist sect) 眞言
ch'i (in Sung philosophy and in fêng-shui) 氣
Ch'i (state in Chou dynasty) 齊
Ch'i (dynasty) 齊
Chia Ch'ing 嘉慶
Chiang Kai-shek (Chiang Chieh-shih) 蔣介石
Chia Ssŭ-tao 賈似道
Chieh 桀
Ch'ien Chao (dynasty) 前趙
Ch'ien Ch'in (dynasty) 前秦
Ch'ien Han Shu 前漢書
Chien-k'ang (later Nanking) 建康
Ch'ien Liang (dynasty) 前涼
Ch'ien Lung 乾隆
Ch'ien-t'ang 錢塘
Ch'ien Tzŭ Wên 千字文
Chien-yeh 建業
chih chou 知州
chih chün 制軍
chih fu 知府
chih hsien 知縣
Chih I 智顗
Chihli 直隸
Ch'i Hsiung ("seven martial" [states] of Chou dynasty) 七雄
chih t'ai 制台
Ch'i-lin 麒麟
chin (catty) 斤
Ch'in (dynasty, 3d century B.C.) 秦
Chin (dynasty, 3d and 4th centuries A.D.) 晉
Chin (state of—in Chou dynasty) 晉
Chin (dynasty, 12th and 13th centuries A.D.) 金
Ching (Classic or Sutra) 經
Ch'ing (Manchu dynasty) 清
Ch'ing Hai (Kokonor) 青海
Ch'ing ming (festival) 清明
Ching Pao 京報
Ch'ing Shih Kao 清史稿
Ching Tê 景德
Ching-tê Chên 景德鎮
Ching Ti 景帝
ching t'ien ("well field" system) 井田

Ch'ing T'u (sect of Buddhism) 淨土
Chinkiang 鎮江
Ch'in Kuei 秦檜
chin shih (literary degree) 進士
Chin Shih (History of the Chin dynasty 12th and 13th centuries A.D.) 金史
Chin Shu (History of the Chin dynasty, 3d and 4th centuries A.D.) 晉書
Chin-tan Chiao 金丹教
Chin Wu Ti 晉武帝
Ch'i-tan (Khitan) 契丹
Chiu Hua Shan 九華山
Chiu T'ang Shu 舊唐書
Chiu Wu Tai Shih 舊五代史
Chou (dynasty) 周
chou (prefectures under T'ang T'ai Tsung) 州
chou (administrative division) 州
Chou Hsin 紂辛
Chou Kuan 周官
Chou Kung 周公
Chou Li 周禮
Chou Shu 周書
Chou Tun-i 周敦頤
Ch'u (state of—in Chou dynasty) 楚
Ch'u (state at beginning of Sung) 楚
Ch'üanchow 泉州
Chuang Tzǔ 莊子
Chu Chiu-t'ao 朱九濤
Ch'ü fou 曲阜
Chu Hsi 朱熹

chü jên 舉人
Chu-ko Liang 諸葛亮
chün (provinces in Ch'in dynasty) 郡
Chün Chi Ch'u 軍機處
Ch'un Ch'iu 春秋
Chung Chia 独家
Ch'ung Êrh 重耳
Chung Hua Min Kuo 中華民國
Chung Kuo 中國
Chung-kuo Li-shih Yen-chiu Fa 中國歷史研究法
Chung Yung 中庸
chün tzǔ 君子
Chusan (archipelago) 舟山
Chu Shu Chi Nien 竹書紀年
Chu Ti 朱棣
Chu Wên 朱溫
Ch'ü Yüan 屈原
Chu Yüan-chang 朱元章
Chu Yün-wên 朱允炆
Co-hong 公行
Confucius (K'ung Fu Tzǔ) 孔夫子
Dairen, see Talienwan 大連灣
Dalai Lama (Chinese ta-lai-la-ma 達賴喇嘛 also Chin-kang Ta-shih 金岡大師)
Dalny, see Talienwan
Eleuths (Chinese O-lu-t'ê 厄魯特)
Êrh Shih Huang Ti 二世皇帝
Êrh Ya 爾雅
Fa Chia 法家
Fa-hsiang (Buddhist sect) 法相

Fa Hsien 法顯
Fanch'êng 樊城
fang chang 方丈
fan t'ai 藩台
fantan 番攤
Fan Yeh 范曄
fa-shih 法師
Fa T'ang 法堂
Fên (River) 汾
fêng (a sacrifice) 封
Fêng-huang 鳳凰
Fêng Kuo-chang 馮國璋
Fêng Tao 馮道
Fêngtien 奉天
Fêng Yü-hsiang 馮玉祥
Fêng Yün-shan 馮雲山
Foochow 福州
Formosa (T'aiwan 臺灣)
fu (administrative division) 府
fu (good fortune or happiness) 福
Fu Chien 苻堅
Fu Hsi 伏羲
Fukien 福建
Fulin 拂菻 or 拂懍
Fushun 撫順
fu t'ai 撫台
fu yüan 撫院
Galdan (Chinese Ka-êhr-tan 噶爾丹)
Gobi 戈壁 (also called Sha Mo 沙漠)
Golden Sand, River of the (upper reaches of the Yangtze) Chin-sha Chiang 金沙江

Gurkhas (Chinese K'uo-êhr-k'o 廓爾喀)
Hainan 海南
Hakka 客家
Hami 哈密
Han (dynasty) 漢
Han (state in Chou dynasty, formerly part of Ch'in 晉)漢
Han (state) 韓
Han (River in Kwangtung) 韓
Han (River in Hupeh) 漢
Han Chi 漢紀
Han Fei Tzŭ 韓非子
Hangchow 杭州
Han Hsüeh 漢學
Han Jên 漢人
Han Kan 韓幹
Hankow 漢口
Han Learning (School) (Han Hsüeh P'ai) 漢學派
Hanlin 翰林
Hanlin Yüan 翰林院
Han Wên-kung 韓文公
Hanyang 漢陽
Hanyehp'ing 漢冶萍
Han Yü 韓愈
Heilungkiang 黑龍江
Hei Miao 黑苗
Hochienfu 河間府
ho lun ch'üan 火輪船
Honan 河南
Honanfu 河南府
Hongkong 香港
Hopei 河北
ho shang 和尚
Ho Shên 和珅

Hou Chao (dynasty) 後趙
Hou Ch'in (dynasty) 後秦
Hou Chin (dynasty) 後晉
Hou Chou (dynasty) 後周
Hou Han (dynasty) 後漢
Hou Han Shu 後漢書
Hou Liang (dynasty, 4th century, founded by Lü Kuang) 後涼
Hou Liang (dynasty, 10th century) 後梁
Hou Shu (dynasty) 後蜀
Hou T'ang (dynasty) 後唐
Hou T'u 后土
Hsia (dynasty) 夏
Hsia (state) 夏
Hsianfu 西安府
Hsiang (River) 湘
Hsiang Chi 項籍
Hsiang Liang 項梁
Hsiangyang 襄陽
Hsiang Yü 項羽
Hsiao (duke or prince of Ch'in) 孝
hsiao (filial piety) 孝
Hsiao Shêng (Hinayana) 小乘
Hsiao Ching 孝經
Hsiao Tao-ch'êng 蕭道成
Hsiao Tzǔ-hsien 蕭子顯
Hsiao Yen 蕭衍
Hsieh Ho 謝赫
hsien (administrative division) 縣
Hsien Fêng 咸豐
Hsien Nai Nai 仙奶奶
Hsien Pei 鮮卑

Hsien-t'ien Chiao 先天敎
Hsien Yang 咸陽
Hsi Hsia 西夏
Hsi K'ang 西康
Hsi Kiang (West River) 西江
Hsin (name of Wang Mang's dynasty) 新
Hsin Chiang, same as Sinkiang 新疆
Hsin Ch'ing Nien Tsa Chih 新青年雜誌
Hsinganling (Khingan) 興安嶺
Hsing Pu 刑部
Hsin Huang Ti 新皇帝
Hsin T'ang Shu 新唐書
Hsin Wu Tai Shih 新五代史
Hsin Yüan Shih 新元史
hsi ssǔ 細絲
Hsi Ti 西帝
Hsiung Nu 匈奴
hsiu ts'ai 秀才
Hsi Wang Mu 西王母
Hsi Wei (dynasty) 西魏
Hsüan Tê 宣德
Hsüan Tsang 玄奘
Hsüan Tsung 玄宗
Hsüan T'ung 宣統
Hsüan Wang 宣王
Hsüeh Kung 學宮
Hsüeh Shu Chiang Yen Chi 學術講演集
Hsü Hsia-k'o 徐霞客
hsün fu 巡撫
Hsün K'uang 荀況
Hsün Tzǔ 荀子
Hsün Yüeh 荀悅

Hsü Shih-ch'ang 徐世昌
Hsü Ta 徐達
Huai Ho 淮河
Huai-nan Tzǔ 淮南子
Hua Miao 花苗
Huan (Huan [Kung 公] of Ch'i) 桓
Huang Ch'ao 黃巢
Huang Ho 黃河
Huang-p'u 黃浦
Huang Shang 皇上
Huang Ti (legendary Yellow Emperor) 黃帝
Huang Ti (imperial title) 皇帝
Huan Wên 桓溫
Hua-yen 華嚴
Hu Hai 胡亥
Hui-hui 回回
Hui-nêng 慧能
Hui Ssǔ 慧思
Hui Ti 惠帝
Hui Tsung 徽宗
Hui Tzǔ 惠子
Hui Yüan 慧遠
Hulutao 葫蘆島
Hunan 湖南
Hung 洪
Hung Hsiu-ch'üan 洪秀全
Hung Jên 洪仁
Hung Lou Mêng 紅樓夢
Hung Wu 洪武
Hupeh 湖北
Hu Pu 戶部
Hu Shih 胡適
Hu Wei 胡渭
I Ching (Classic) 易經

I Ching (Buddhist pilgrim) 義淨
I Ho Ch'üan 義和拳
I Ho T'uan 義和團
i jen 一人
i ko jên 一個人
i ko shih t'ou 一個石頭
Ili (territory) 伊犁
I Li (book) 儀禮
I Ti 義帝
Japan (in Chinese Jih-pên) 日本
Jehol 熱河 or Jê-ho-êrh 熱河兒
Jenghiz Khan (in Chinese Ch'êng-chi-ssǔ 成吉思). Also known by his dynastic title, T'ai Tsu 太祖
Jên Huang 人皇
Juan Juan 蠕蠕
Ju Chia 儒家
Ju Chiao 儒教
Jung Lu 榮祿
Kachin (Chinese Yeh-jên 野人 or Shan t'ou 山頭)
K'aifêng 開封
K'ailan 開灤
Kan (River) 贛
k'an chien 看見
k'ang 炕
K'ang Hsi 康熙
K'ang Hsi Tzǔ Tien 康熙字典
K'ang Yu-wei 康有爲
Kansu 甘肅
Kan Ying P'ien 感應篇
Kao Hsien-chih 高仙芝
kaoliang 高粱
kaolin 高嶺
Kao P'ien 高駢
Kao Ti 高帝

Kao Tsu 高祖
Kao Tsung 高宗
Karakorum (in Chinese K'o-la-k'u-lun 喀拉庫倫
　also K'o-la-ho-lin 喀喇和林)
Kashgar (in Chinese K'o-shih-ka-êhr 喀什噶爾
　Also Shu-fu-hsien 疏附縣)
Keh-Lao (Ch'i-lao 犵狫)
Kêng Ching-chung 耿精忠
Khalkhas (Chinese K'o-êhr-k'o 喀爾喀)
Khoten (in Chinese Yü-t'ien 于闐)
Khubilai (in Chinese Hu-pi-lieh 忽必烈 or Hsieh-ch'an 薛禪)
　Also known by his dynastic title Shih Tsu 世祖)
Kiangsi 江西
Kiangsu 江蘇
Kiaochow 膠州
Kirin 吉林
Kiukiang 九江
Kokonor (Ch'ing Hai 青海)
Ko Lao Hui 哥老會
Korea (Chaohsien 朝鮮)
kotow (k'o-t'ou) 磕頭
k'ou 口
K'ou Ch'ien-chih 寇謙之
Kuan Chung 管仲
Kuang Hsü 光緒
Kuang Wu Ti 光武帝
kuan hua 官話
Kuan Ti 關帝
Kuan-yin 觀音
Kuan Yü 關羽

Ku Chieh-kang 顧頡剛
kuei 鬼
Kuei-ku Tzǔ 鬼谷子
Kuei Wang 桂王
Ku K'ai-chih 顧愷之
Kuldja (Ilifu 伊犁府)
Kung (Prince) 恭
K'ung Chiao 孔教
K'ung, H. H. (K'ung Hsiang-hsi) 孔祥熙
K'ung Miao 孔廟
Kung Pu 工部
Kung-sun Hung 公孫弘
Kung-sun Lung 公孫龍
Kung-sun Yang 公孫鞅
K'un Lun (Mountains) 崑崙
Kuo Chung-shu 郭忠恕
Kuo Hsi 郭熙
Kuominchun 國民軍
Kuomintang 國民黨
Kuo Tzǔ-i 郭子儀
kuo-yü 國語
Ku Shih Pien 古史辨
Ku T'ing-lin 顧亭林
ku wên 古文
Ku Yen-wu 顧炎武
Kwangchow (bay) 廣州
Kwangsi 廣西
Kwangtung 廣東
Kweichow 貴州
Kyushu (Chinese Chiu-chou 九州)
Lanchow 蘭州
lao hu 老虎
Lao T'ien Fo Yeh 老天佛爺
Lao T'ien Yeh 老天爺

Lao Tzǔ 老子
lei shu 類書
li (law) 例
li (abstract right, the eternal fitness of things) 理
Liang (dynasty) 梁
liang (tael) 兩
Liang Ch'i-ch'ao 梁啟超
Liang Shu 梁書
Liang Wu Ti 梁武帝
Liao (dynasty) 遼
Liao (River) 遼
Liao Chai Chih I 聊齋誌異
Liaoning 遼寧
Liao Shih 遼史
Liaotung (Peninsula) 遼東
Li Chao-tao 李昭道
li chee 荔枝
Li Chi 禮記
Li Fan Yüan 理藩院
Li Hung-chang 李鴻章
Likin 釐金
Li K'o 李克
Li K'o-yung 李克用
Li Kuang-li 李廣利
Li Kuang-pi 李光弼
Li K'uei 李悝
Li Lin-fu 李林甫
Li Lung-chi 李隆基
Li Lung-mien 李龍眠
Lin-an 臨安
Ling-hu Tê-fên 令狐德棻
Lin Tzê-hsü 林則徐
Li Ping 李冰
Li Po 李白
Li Po-yao 李百藥

Li Pu (Board of Civil Office) 吏部
Li Pu (Board of Rites) 禮部
Li Sao 離騷
Li Shih-chên 李時珍
Li Shih-min 李世民
Li Ssǔ 李斯
Li Ssǔ-hsün 李思訓
Li T'ai-po 李太白
Li Tê-lin 李德林
Li Ts'un-hsü 李存勗
Li Tung-yang 李東陽
Li Tzǔ-ch'êng 李自成
Liu (ruling family of Han dynasty) 劉
Liu An 劉安
Liu Chih-chi 劉知幾
Liu Chih-yüan 劉知遠
Liu Ch'iu (Islands) 琉球
Liu Hsiang 劉向
Liu Hsin 劉歆
Liu Pang 劉邦
Liu Pei 劉備
Liu Sung (dynasty) 劉宋
Liu Ts'ung 劉聰
Liu Tsung-yüan 柳宗元
Liu Yü (founder of Liu Sung dynasty) 劉裕
Liu Yü (12th century) 劉豫
Liu Yüan 劉淵
Li Yen-shou 李延壽
Li Yüan 李淵
Li Yüan-hung 黎元洪
Lohan (arhat) 羅漢
Loi (li 黎

THEIR HISTORY AND CULTURE 825

Lo-lo 玀玀 Also written Lao-lao 狫狫 and Liao-liao 獠獠
Loyang 洛陽
lü 律
Lü (Empress of Ch'ien Han dynasty) 呂
Lu (state in Chou dynasty) 魯
Lu Chia 陸賈
Lu Chiu-yüan 陸九淵
Lü Hou 呂后
Lü Kuang 呂光
Lun 論
lung 龍
Lung Mên 龍門
Lung Wang 龍王
Lun Yü 論語
Lü Pu-wei 呂不韋
Lü Shih 呂氏
Lü-tsung 律宗
Lü Yen 呂嵒
Man Chia 蠻家
Manchuria (Tung san shêng 東三省 Three Eastern Provinces, or simply Tung shêng 東省 The Eastern Provinces)
Mangu (in Chinese Mêng-ko 蒙哥)
Man Tzŭ 蠻子
Ma Tuan-lin 馬端臨
Ma Yüan (1st century B.C.—1st century A.D.) 馬援
Ma Yüan (Sung dynasty artist) 馬遠
Mei Tsŭ 梅鷟
Mencius 孟子

Mêng T'ien 蒙恬
Mêng Tzŭ 孟子
Mêng Tzŭ Shu 孟子書
Miao (aboriginal people) 苗
miao (temple) 廟
Miao Chia 苗家
Miaotzŭ 苗子
Mi-Chiao 密教
Mi Fei 米芾
Mi-lo-fo 彌勒佛
Min (River, in Fukien) 閩
Min (River, in Szechwan) 岷
Min (state at beginning of Sung) 閩
Ming (dynasty) 明
Ming Chia 名家
Ming Huang Ti 明皇帝
Ming Shih 明史
Ming Ti 明帝
Mongol (Mêng ku) 蒙古
Mongolia (Mêng ku) 蒙古
Mo-so 摩些
Mo Ti 墨翟
Mo Tzŭ 墨子
mou (measure of land) 畝
Mu (prince of Ch'in) 穆
Mu Ch'i 牧溪
Mu-jung 慕容
Mu Wang 穆王
Nan Chao 南詔
Nan Ch'i Shu 南齊書
Nan Han 南漢
Nanking 南京
Nan Pei Ch'ao 南北朝
Nan P'ing 南平
Nan Shan 南山

Nan Shih 南史
Nan T'ang 南唐
Nan Wang 赧王
Nan Yüeh 南越
Nayan (in Chinese Nai-yen 乃顏)
Nei Ching 內經
Nei Ko 內閣
Newchwang 牛莊
nieh t'ai 臬台
Nienfei 撚匪
nien hao 年號
Ninghsia 寧夏
Ningpo 寧波
Nonni (nên-kiang 嫩江)
Nüchên 女眞 (better Jûchen)
Nü Kua 女媧
Nurhachu (in Chinese Nu-êhr-ha-ch'ih 努爾哈赤
  His dynastic title was T'ai Tsu Kao 太祖高 and his reign title T'ien Ming 天命)
Ogotai (in Chinese Wo-k'uo-t'ai 窩闊台) His dynastic title was T'ai Tsung 太京)
O Mei Shan 峨嵋山
O-mi-t'o 阿彌陀
O-mi-t'o-fo 阿彌陀佛
Ordos (Ho t'ao) 河套
Ou-yang Hsiu 歐陽修
Pa Hsien 八仙
Pai Chia Hsing 百家姓
p'ai fang 牌坊
Pai Ho 白河
pai hua 白話
Pai-lien Chiao 白蓮敎
Pai-lien Hui 白蓮會

p'ai lou 牌樓
pa kua 八卦
Panch'an Lama 班禪喇嘛
Pan Chao 班昭
Pan Ch'ao 班超
Pan Ku 班固
P'an Ku 盤古
Pan Piao 班彪
Pan Yung 班勇
Pei Ch'i (dynasty, 6th century A.D.) 北齊
Pei Ch'i Shu 北齊書
Pei Chou (dynasty, 6th century A.D. 北周)
Pei Han (dynasty) 北漢
Peiping 北平
Pei Shih 北史
Peit'ing 北庭
Peking 北京
Pên-t'sao-kang-mu 本草綱目
Petuntse 白墪子
Pien Liang 汴梁
P'ien t'i (a style of writing) 駢體
P'i-lu-fo 毗盧佛
P'ing Ch'êng 平城
Ping Pu 兵部
P'ingyang 平壤
Po Chü-i 白居易
P'o-yang (Lake) 鄱陽
P'u-hsien 普賢
p'u-sa 菩薩
P'u Sung-ling 蒲松齡
p'u-t'i-sa-to 菩提薩埵
P'u-t'o 普陀
P'u-t'o Shan 普陀山

P'u-yi (P'u-i), Henry 溥儀
(the last Manchu Emperor)
San Ch'ing 三清
San Fan (rebellion) 三藩
San Ho Hui 三合會
San Kuan 三官
San Kuo Chih 三國志
San Kuo Chih Yen I 三國志演義
San Min Chu I 三民主義
San Pao 三寶
San Tsang 三藏
San Tzŭ Ching 三字經
Shameen 沙面
Shan (a sacrifice) 禪
Shang (dynasty) 商
Shang Chih-hsin 尙之信
Shang-ch'uan (island) 上川
Shanghai 上海
Shang K'o-hsi 尙可喜
Shang Shu Ku Wên Shu Chêng
　　尙書古文疏證
Shang Ti 上帝
Shang Yang (also called Wei Yang) 商鞅
Shanhaikuan 山海關
Shansi 山西
Shantung 山東
Shao Yung 邵雍
Shê 社
Shên 神
Shên Chiao 神敎
shên chu 神主
shêng 省
Shêng Jên 聖人
Shêngking 盛京
Shêng Tsŭ Jên 聖祖仁

Shêng Yü 聖諭
Shên Nung 神農
Shensi 陝西
Shên Yo 沈約
shih (poetry) 詩
shih (stone) 石
Shih Chi 史記
Shih-chia-fo 釋迦佛
Shih-chia-mou-ni 釋迦牟尼
Shih Ching 詩經
Shih Ching-t'ang 石敬塘
Shih Huang Ti (of Ch'in dynasty) 始皇帝
Shih Ssŭ-ming 史思明
shih t'ou 石頭
Shih T'ung 史通
shou 壽
Shu (state in present Szechwan) 蜀
Shu Ching 書經
Shu Han 蜀漢
Shun 舜
Shun Chih 順治
Shuo Wên 說文
shu yüan 書院
Sinkiang 新疆
Soochow 蘇州
Soong, T.V. (Sung Tzŭ-wên)
　　宋子文
Ssŭ-ma Ch'ien 司馬遷
Ssŭ-ma Kuang 司馬光
Ssŭ-ma T'an 司馬談
Ssŭ-ma Yen 司馬炎
Ssŭ Shu 四書
Ssŭ T'ien Wang 四天王
suan p'an (abacus) 算盤

Su Ch'in 蘇秦
Sui (dynasty) 隋
Sui Jên 燧人
Sui Shu 隋書
Suiyüan 綏遠
Sun Ch'üan 孫權
Sun Ch'üan-fang 孫傳芳
Sung (state of—in Chou dynasty) 宋
Sung (dynasty) 宋
Sungari (Sunghua-kiang 松花江)
Sung Chih-wên 宋之問
Sung Shih 宋史
Sung Shu 宋書
Sung Yün 宋雲
Sun Wên 孫文
Sun Yat-sen 孫逸仙
Su Shih 蘇軾
Su Tung-p'o 蘇東坡
Swatow 汕頭
Szechwan 四川
Ta Shêng (Mahayana) 大乘
Ta Ch'i 大齊
Ta Ch'in 大秦
Ta Ch'ing (dynasty) 大清
Ta Ch'ing Hui Tien 大清會典
Ta Ch'ing Lü Li 大清律例
Ta Hsüeh 大學
t'ai chi 太極
T'ai Hsü 太虛
T'ai Hu 太湖
T'ai I 太一
T'ai P'ing 太平
T'ai P'ing Yü Lan 太平御覽
T'ai Shan 泰山
T'ai Tsu 太祖

T'ai Tsung 太宗
T'ai Wan (see Formosa) 臺灣
T'aiyüan 太原
Talai Lama 達賴喇嘛
Talienwan (Dalny, or Dairen) 大連灣
Talifu 大理府
Ta Li Ssŭ 大理寺
tan (picul) 擔
T'ang (dynasty) 唐
T'ang Jên 唐人
Tangpu 黨部
T'ang T'ai Tsung 唐太宗
Tao (of Taoism) 道
tao (provinces under T'ang T'ai Tsung) 道
T'ao Ch'ien 陶潛
T'ao Han 陶翰
Tao Hsüan 道宣
Tao Kuang 道光
Tao Nai Nai 道奶奶
Tao Shêng 道生
tao shih 道士
T'ao Shuo 陶說
tao t'ai 道台
Tao Tê Ching 道德經
Tao-tê-hsüeh-shê 道德學社
t'ao t'ieh 饕餮
Tao Yüan 道院
T'ao Yüan-ming 陶淵明
Tarim River (T'a-li-mu-ho 塔里木河)
Tat'ung 大同
Ta Yü 大禹
Tê (virtue) 德
Têngchow (Shantung) 登州

Ti (an imperial title) 帝
Ti (Earth) 地
tiao 吊
'Tibet (Tsang 藏 or Hsi Tsang 西藏)
ti ch'i 地氣
tien (lightning) 電
tien (hall) 殿
T'ien (Heaven) 天
tien ch'ê 電車
tien ch'i 電氣
t'ien ch'i 天氣
T'ien Hsia 天下
T'ien Huang 天皇
T'ien Lao Yeh 天老爺
T'ien Li 天理
T'ien Ming (Heaven's decree) 天命
tien pao 電報
T'ien Shan 天山
T'ien Shih 天師
T'ien T'ai (sect of Buddhism) 天台
Tientsin 天津
T'ien Tzǔ 天子
Ti Huang 地皇
t'ing 廳
Ting Wu Lan T'ing 定武蘭亭
ti-pao 地保
Ti-tsang 地藏
Tongking 東京
T'o Pa (Toba) 拓跋
T'o-t'o 脫脫
T'oung Pao 通報
Tsa 雜
Ts'ai Ching 蔡京

Tsai Li Chiao 在理教
Ts'ai T'ing-kan 蔡廷幹
Ts'ai Yüan-p'ei 蔡元培
ts'ao (grass) 草
Ts'ao Hsüeh-ch'in 曹雪芹
Ts'ao Kun 曹錕
Ts'ao P'ei 曹丕
Ts'ao Ts'ao 曹操
Tsêng Kuo-fan 曾國藩
Tsin (dynasty) 晉
Tsinanfu 濟南府
Tso Chuan 左傳
Tso Tsung-t'ang 左宗棠
Ts'ui Shu 崔述
Tsung K'apa 宗喀巴
Tsungli Yamen 總理衙門
ts'ung shu 叢書
tsung tu 總督
Tuan Ch'i-jui 段祺瑞
Tu Ch'a Yüan 都察院
T'u Chüeh 突厥
tuchün 督軍
Tu Fu 杜甫
T'ung Ch'êng 桐城
T'ung Chêng Ssŭ 通政司
T'ung Chien Chi Shih Pên Mo 通鑑紀史本末
T'ung Chien Kang Mu 通鑑綱目
T'ung Chih (a history) 通志
T'ung Chih (Ch'ing Emperor) 同治
t'ung chih (sub-prefect) 同知
Tung Cho 董卓
Tung Chou Chün 東周君
Tung Chung-shu 董仲舒
Tung Han (dynasty) 東漢

Tung Ti 東帝
T'ung Tien 通典
T'ung-t'ing (Lake) 洞庭
Tung Wei (dynasty) 東魏
Tung Yo 東嶽
Tun-huang 敦煌
Turfan (T'u-lu-fan t'ing) 吐魯番廳
Turgut (Chinese T'u-êhr-hu-t'ê 土爾扈特)
Tu Wên-hsiu 杜文秀
Tu Yu 杜佑
Tzŭ Chih T'ung Chien 資治通鑒
Tz'ŭ-ên-tsung 慈恩宗
Tz'ŭ Hsi 慈禧
Tzŭ Ying 子嬰
Uighurs (Chinese Hui-ho 廻紇 or 回紇 Also 袁紇, 烏紇, 韋紇, 紇國)
Urga (Chinese K'u-lun 庫倫)
Ussuri (Wu-su-li 烏蘇利)
Wai Wu Pu 外務部
Wang 王
Wang An-shih 王安石
Wang Ch'ung 王充
Wang Hsi-chih 王羲之
Wang Mang 王莽
Wang Pi 王弼
Wang Wei 王維
Wang Yang-ming 王陽明
Wanhsien 萬縣
Wan Li 萬歷
Wan-li-ch'ang-ch'êng 萬里長城
Wan Shou Kung 萬壽宮
Wan Sui Yeh 萬歲爺
Wei (dynasty) 魏
Wei (state in Chou dynasty formerly part of Chin 晉) 魏
Wei (River) 渭
Wei-shih-hsiang-chiao 唯識相教
Wei Shou 魏收
Wei Shu 魏書
Wei-t'o 韋陀
Wei Yang (also called Shang Yang) 衛鞅
Wên (personal name Ch'ung Êhr 重耳) 文
Wên Ch'ang 文昌
Wên Hsien T'ung K'ao 文獻通考
wên li 文理
Wên Miao 文廟
Wên-shu 文殊
Wên Ti 文帝
Wên Wang 文王
wu (witch) 巫
Wu (dynasty in Yangtze Valley) 吳
Wu (state in Chou dynasty) 吳
Wuchang 武昌
Wu Chiao 巫教
Wu Ching 五經
Wuhan 武漢
Wu Hou 武后
Wuhu 蕪湖
Wu Miao 武廟
Wu P'ei-fu 吳佩孚
Wu San-kuei 吳三桂
Wu Shêng Miao 武聖廟
Wusih 無錫
Wu T'ai Shan 五臺山
Wu Tao-hsüan 吳道玄
Wu Tao-tzŭ 吳道子

Wu Tao-yüan 吳道元
Wu Ti (title of several emperors) 武帝
Wu Ti (The Five Sovereigns) 五帝
Wu Tsê T'ien 武則天
Wu Wang 武王
Wu Wei 無為
Wu Yüeh 吳越
Yakub Beg (Chinese Ya-ku-po-k'o 牙固伯克)
Yalu 鴨綠
Yang (of Yin Yang) 陽
Yang Chien 楊堅
Yangchow 揚州
Yang Chu 楊朱
Yang Hsiung 楊雄
Yang Kuang 楊廣
Yang Kuei-fei 楊貴妃
Yang Shao (culture) 仰韶
Yang Ti 煬帝
Yangtze Kiang 揚子江
Yang Yen 楊炎
Yao (a non-Chinese people in the South) 猺
Yao (ruler, before the Hsia dynasty) 堯
Yao Ch'a 姚察
Yao Chien 姚簡
Yao Chi-hêng 姚際恆
Yao-shih-fo 藥師佛
Yarkand (in Chinse Yeh-êhr-ch'iang 葉爾羌 or So-ch'ê-fu 莎車府)
Yeh-lü Ch'u-ts'ai 耶律楚才
Yeh Ming-shên 葉名琛

Yehonala 葉赫耶拉
Yen (state in the North in 4th and 5th centuries A.D.) 燕
Yenching 燕京
Yen Hsi-chai 顏習齋
Yen Hsi-shan 閻錫山
Yen Hui 顏回
Yen, James Y.C. (Yen Yang-ch'u) 晏陽初
Yen Jo-chü 閻若璩
Yen Li-pên 閻立本
Yen Li-tê 閻立德
Yen Yüan 顏元
Yin (of Yin Yang) 陰
Yin (dynasty) 殷
Yo 嶽
Yo Fei 岳飛
yü (jade) 玉
Yü 禹 (or Ta Yü 大禹) (founder of the Hsia dynasty)
Yüan 院
Yüan (dollar) 元
Yüan (dynasty) 元
Yüan Chao Pi Shih 元朝祕史
Yüan Ch'u 袁樞
Yüan Shih 元史
Yüan Shih-k'ai 袁世凱
Yüan Shih T'ien Tsun 元始天尊
Yüan Wei (dynasty in 4th to 6th centuries A.D.) 元魏
Yüan Yu 元祐
Yüan Yüan 阮元
Yu Ch'ao 有巢
Yüeh (state in Chou dynasty) 越
Yüeh (peoples on the south coast in Ch'in and Han times and earlier) 越

Yüeh Chih 月氏
Yü Hsien 毓賢
Yü Huang 玉皇
Yü Huang Shang Ti 玉皇上帝
Yü Mên 玉門
yung 永

Yung Chêng 雍正
Yung Lo 永樂
Yung Lo Ta Tien 永樂大典
Yung Wing 容閎
Yünnan 雲南
Yu Wang 幽王

INDEX

Abhidharma, 640
Acrobats, 703
Acupuncture, 786
Adoption, 673
Agriculture, under the Chou, 56, 57; general description, 558–575, 602, 603
Aigun, treaty of, 353
Air transport, 450, 451, 462
Alans, 276
Albazin, 317
Alexander the Great, 105, 123, 128
Alfalfa, 106
A-lo-pên, 198
Altar, 56
Amban, 323
Amitabha, 637, 639
Amoy, 11
Amur River, 19, 353
Amursana, 322
Ancestors, honors to, 628–633
Anfu Club, 405
Anglo-Japanese Alliance, 394, 396
Anhui, 5, 10
An Lu-shan, 189, 208
Annam, 94, 191; invaded by Mongols, 265, 266; and Ch'ien Lung, 324; 368
Anshan, 439
An-shih-kao, 129
Anti-comintern pact, 438
Antimony, 15
Anti-religious movement, 466, 467, 471, 658, 659
Apricot, 125
Arabs, 184, 187, 199
Archery, 696
Architecture, 15, 728–736, 761
Arhat, 129, 634
Aristocracy, 56, 58
Armenians, 276
Army, 540, 541, 546
Arrow, 349
Art, under the Chou, 62; under the T'ang, 210–212, 220; in general, 722–764
Artemesia moxa, 786
Asiatic Petroleum Company, 457
Athletics, 696, 697, 716
Australia, 507
Automobiles, 441, 461, 573

Bactria, 105
Bamboo, as subject for painters, 744
Bamboo slips, 40
Banca Italiana per la Cina, 426
Bandits, 412
Bangkok, 506
Bank of China, 598, 600
Bank of Communications, 598, 600
Banks, 591–593, 598, 605
Banners, 540, 543
Banque Industrielle de Chine, 425
Barley, 55
Beans and bean cake, 457
Beggars, 687, 688
Benevolent societies, 683
Berthemy convention, 352
Betrothals, 671
Biot, 33
Bishops, Chinese, 472, 473
Bodhidharma, 166, 170
Bodhisattva, 128, 634
Bones, Oracle, 34, 40
Books, burning of the, 91, 92
Borodin, Michael, 407
Boxer Protocol, 392, 393
Boxer Rebellion, 389–394, 486
Boycott, 420, 421, 426, 458
Boy Scouts, 713
Bridges, 734, 735
Bronzes, 41, 62, 126, 754, 755, 764
Buddhism, its origin and introduction to China, 126–130, 141; growth between the Han and the Sui, 161–172, 175, 176; under the T'ang, 195, 196;

INDEX

200–203, 219; general description, 633–643, 660, 662
Burial, 631
Burlingame, Anson, 366, 367
Burma, 20; invaded by Mongols, 266; 323, 324, 368, 506
Burma Road, 446, 449

Cairo conference, 452
Calendar, 41
Calligraphy, 212, 746–748, 763
Cambaluc, 234, 269, 271, 275, 276
Canada, 508
Canals, 111, 594
Candareen, 591
Canton, 194, 333, 344–348
Capital investments of foreigners, 459
Cartoons, 798
Carts, 594
Cash, 590, 599
Cash shops, 592
Cattle, 40
Catty, 588
Celadon, 751
Censorate, 523, 524
Central Bank, 598
Ceramics, 749–754, 763
Ceremonies, 608, 614
Chahar, 18, 440
Chalcolithic culture, 34
Chamber of commerce, 597
Champa, invaded by Mongols, 265
Champlevé, 757
Chan Kuo, 50–54
Chan Kuo Ts'ê, 65
Ch'an Buddhism, 170, 202, 246, 247
Chang Ch'ien, 105, 106
Chang Chih-tung, 386
Changchun, 435
Chang Fei, 145
Chang Hêng, 136
Chang Hsüeh-liang, 410, 411, 434, 442
Chang Hsün, 404
Chang I, 52, 75
Chang Pang-ch'ang, 228
Chang Tsai, 245
Chang Tso-lin, 405, 407, 410, 424
Ch'angan, 43, 90, 102, 119, 120, 190, 192, 197, 214
Ch'ang Chien, 209
Chao Kao, 96–98
Chao K'uang-yin, 225, 226

Chao Mêng-fu, 278
Chao Wang, 44
Ch'aohsien, 106
Chapdelaine, 350
Characters, 771–774; general description, 633–643, 660, 662
Chariot, 41, 61, 108
Chefoo Convention, 367
Chêkiang, 11
Chên Chün, 644
Chên Jên, 644, 646
Chên-yen, 202
Ch'ên dynasty, 154
Ch'ên Huan-chang, 657
Ch'ên Shu, 173
Ch'ên Tu-hsiu, 478, 480
Ch'ên Tzŭ-ang, 209
Chêng. *See* Shih Huang Ti
Chêng Ch'êng-kung, 293
Chêng Ch'iao, 251
Chêng-ho, 288
Ch'êng Hao, 245
Ch'êng Huang Miao, 624
Ch'êng I-ch'uan, 245
Ch'êng Ming-tao, 245
Ch'êng Tsu, 287
Ch'êng Wang, 43
Ch'i, 47, 48, 51–54
Ch'i, 248
Ch'i Hsiung, 51
Ch'i-lin, 649
Ch'i-tan, 223
Chia Ch'ing, 326, 327
Chiang Chieh-shih. *See* Chiang Kai-shek
Chiang Kai-shek, 408–413, 441, 442, 450, 452, 470, 489, 656, 657
Chicken, 55
Chien-k'ang, 147
Chien-yeh, 147
Ch'ien Chao, 151
Ch'ien Ch'in, 151
Ch'ien Han. *See* Former Han
Ch'ien Han Shu, 136, 138
Ch'ien Lung, 321–326
Ch'ien-t'ang, 11
Ch'ien Tzŭ Wên, 747, 792
Chih Chou, 526
Chih Chün, 526
Chih Fu, 526
Chih Hsien, 526
Chih I, 171

INDEX

Chih K'ai, 171
Chihli, 5
Chih T'ai, 526
Chin, 588
Chin (Juchên), 228–232
Chin dynasty, 146, 147
Chin, state of, 48–50
Chin shih, 179, 205, 258, 531
Chin shu, 173
Chin-tan Chiao, 653
Ch'in, state of, 47–54, 78–80
Ch'in dynasty, 88–98
Ch'in Kuei, 229
China proper, described, 3–16
China Inland Mission, 369
Chinese Eastern Railway, 382, 423–425
Ching Pao, 525
Ching-tê-chên, 255, 306, 328, 752, 753
Ching Ti, 103
Ching t'ien, 38, 56, 57, 78
Ch'ing dynasty, 309–401
Ch'ing Ming, 705
Ch'ing Shih Kao, 336
Ch'ing T'u, 171
Chinkiang, 10
Chiu Hua Shan, 641
Chiu T'ang Shu, 216
Chiu Wu Tai Shih, 258
Chou, 181, 526
Chou dynasty, 42–81
Chou Hsin, 42
Chou Kuan, 65
Chou Kung, 43, 44, 64
Chou Li, 43, 65, 82, 117, 135, 242, 331
Chou Shu, 173
Chou Tun-i, 245
Christianity, under the T'ang, 197, 198; under the Mongols, 275, 276, 281; under the Ming, 298, 299; under K'ang Hsi and Ch'ien Lung, 317–319, 325; in the nineteenth century, 347, 369–371; after 1894, 467–473; in general, 655–658, 663
Chu Chiu-t'ao, 355
Chu Hsi, 245–250, 300, 301, 330
Chu-ko Liang, 145, 146
Chu Shu Chi Nien, 81
Chu Ti, 287–289
Chu Wên, 192, 224
Chu Yüan-chang, 271, 283–286
Chu Yün-wên, 286, 287
Ch'u, 47–49, 51–54, 87, 99

Ch'u Yüan, 705
Chü jên, 530, 531
Ch'ü-fou, 623
Ch'ü Yüan, 52, 66
Chuang Tzŭ, 73, 83
Ch'üanchow, 11, 194, 237, 272
Ch'un Ch'iu, 63, 135
Chün, 89
Chün Chi Ch'u, 320, 522
Chün tzŭ, 71
Chung Chia, 498
Chung Hua Min Kuo, 3
Chungking, 444, 450
Chung Kuo, 3
Chung Yung, 249
Ch'ung Erh, 48
Chusan archipelago, 11
Civil service examinations, begun, 109; under the T'ang, 182, 205; in the Ch'ing period, 529–533, 552
Clan, 667–669
Classic of Change. See *I Ching*
Classic of History. See *Shu Ching*
Classic of Poetry. See *Shih Ching*
Classifier, 769
Climate, 12–15, 25
Cloisonné, 757
Coal, 15, 584, 585
Coffin, 630
Co-hong, 333, 346
Commerce, under the Han, 111, 123–125; between the Han and Sui, 159, 160; under the T'ang, 193, 194; under the Sung, 237–239, 260; under the Mongols, 272–274; under the Ming, 205–299; after 1894, 454–460, 586–589
Commercial Press, 470
Communists, 407–412, 441, 442, 450
Compradore, 458, 597
Concessions, in open ports, 372, 384, 427, 436, 453
Concubinage, 672, 673, 712
Confucianism, under the Chou, 70–72; under the Han, 101–136, 141; between the Han and Sui, 157; under the T'ang, 182, 204–206; under the Sung, 243–250, 260; under the Ming, 286, 300; after 1894, 466, 515, 516; in general, 618–628, 662
Confucius, 70, 71
Contending States, 50–54

Co-prosperity Sphere, 443
Cormorants, 570
Cotton goods, 457, 458, 462
Cotton mills, 580, 581
Cowry, 40
Crickets, fighting, 720
Currency, 117, 464
Cushing, Caleb, 346
Customs service, 365, 366, 384, 428

Dalai Lama, 315, 316, 323
Dead, honors to, 628–633
Deutsche-Asiatische Bank, 381
Dharmaraksha, 165
Diet, 566, 567
Divination, 41, 64, 69, 652
Divorce, 672, 712
Dog, 55
Dollars, 599
Double Tenth, 717
Dragon, 649
Dragon Boat Festival, 52, 66, 705
Dream of the Red Chamber, 329
Dress, 715
Drums, stone, 723
Drunkenness, 698
Dzassak, 543

Earlier Han dynasty, 99–115
Earth, Altar of, 621
Eastern Chin, 147, 148
Eclecticism, 611
Economic history, 491
Economic life and organization, 555–606
Education, 473–480, 788–793, 799, 800, 804, 805
Eight Immortals of the Wine Cup, 208
Eighth Route Army, 443
Elder Brothers, Association of, 681
Eleuths, 314, 320–322
Emperor, 519–522, 621
Empress Dowager. *See* Tz'ŭ Hsi
Enamels, 756, 757
Encyclopædias, 780
England. *See* Great Britain
Êrh Shih Huang Ti, 97, 98
Êrh Ya, 135, 777
Etiquette, 694, 695, 715, 720
Eunuchs, 120
Europe, effect of China on, in eighteenth century, 334, 335, 339

Ever Victorious Army, 362
Examinations. *See* Civil Service Examinations
Extraterritoriality, 346, 423, 428–430

Face, 689–693
Fa Chia. See Legalists
Factories, grow, 462, 463
Factory legislation, 582
Fa-hsiang, 202
Fa-hsien, 166
Family, 665–678
Famines, 464
Fanch'êng, 234
Fang chang, 636
Fantan, 697
Fan Yeh, 138
Farms, size of, 559, 560
Fa Shih, 634
Fêng, 113, 114, 140, 185
Fêng-huang, 649
Fêng Kuo-chang, 404
Fêng shui, 585, 651, 652, 659
Fêng Tao, 225
Fengtien, 19
Fêng Yü-hsiang, 405, 407, 410, 411, 470
Fêng Yün-shan, 355
Ferghana, 106, 190
Fertilizers, 567, 568
Festivals, 703–707, 717, 720
Feudalism, under the Chou, 59–61
Fiction, 209, 210, 279, 783
Filatures, 462
Filial piety, 670, 674, 675
Five Classics, 777
Five Dynasties, 222–225
Foochow, 11
Football, 716
Foot-binding, 680
Forestry, 570
Former Han dynasty, 99–115
Formosa, 21, 293, 314, 377, 379, 505
Four Heavenly Kings, 637
Four Power Treaty, 421
France, 346, 350, 354, 368, 381, 382
Franciscans, 275
Fu, 526
Fu Chien, 151
Fu Hsi, 37
Fukien, 11
Fulin, 183
Funeral, 631

Fu T'ai, 526
Fu Yüan, 526

Galdan, 315
Gambling, 697
Gandhara, 168, 210
Gardens, 736, 737, 762
Gautama, 130
Gazeteers, 779
Germany, in Shantung, 381
Glass, 124–126, 757
Glaze, 749
Gobi, 18
Goddess of Mercy. *See* Kuan Yin
Gods, 621, 622
Gold, 15
Gordon, Charles George, 362
Government, 513–554
Governor, 526
Græco-Buddhist art, 168, 169, 210
Grand Canal, 10, 179, 269, 289
Grape, 106
Grass hand, 747
Great Britain, first war with, 344–347; second war with, 350–352; sphere of influence in the Yangtze Valley, 381, 382, in Weihaiwei, 382; in China's trade, 459, 460; in Tibet, 413, 414
Greater East Asia, 443
Great Wall, first built, 95; under the Ming, 305, 730, 762
Green Standard, 541
Guilds, 463, 577–581, 586, 587, 604
Gurkhas, 323

Hainan, 11, 382
Hakkàs, 237, 497
Han Chi, 138
Han dynasty, 99–137
Han Fei Tzŭ, 78, 88, 92
Hangchow, 11, 229
Han Hsüeh, 331, 332, 339
Han Kan, 212
Hankow, 10, 384
Han Learning, 331, 332, 339
Hanlin Yüan, 187, 286, 524, 531
Han River, 9
Han Wên Kung, 206
Hanyehp'ing Company, 416, 585
Han Yü. 206, 776
Hart, Robert, 365
Harvest festival, 706

Hawaii, 508
Hay, John, 385
Heaven, Altar of, 621, 657
Heilungchiang, 19
Hei Miao, 498
Hexagrams, 64
Hideyoshi, 290
Hinayana, 128, 167, 640
Histories, 778
Honan, 5
Honesty, 589
Hongkong, ceded to Great Britain, 346; captured by Japanese, 449
Hongkong and Shanghai Banking Corporation, 381, 459, 598
Hopei, 5
Horse, 40
Ho Shang, 634
Ho Shên, 326, 327
Hou Chao, 151
Hou Chin, 224
Hou Ch'in, 151
Hou Chou, 225
Hou Han, 119–122, 224
Hou Han Shu, 138
Hou Liang, 151
Hou Shu, 226
Hou T'ang, 224
Hou T'u, 68
Hsi Hsia, 227, 230
Hsi Kiang, 4, 11
Hsi Ti, 52
Hsi Wang Mu, 44
Hsia dynasty, 38, 39, 86
Hsia, fifth century dynasty, 152
Hsia Kuei, 257
Hsianfu, 43, 392
Hsiang Chi, 99, 100
Hsiang Liang, 99
Hsiang River, 9
Hsiangyang, 149, 234
Hsiang Yü, 99, 100
Hsiao, 670
Hsiao Ching, 135, 792
Hsiao Shêng, 640
Hsiao Tao-ch'êng, 148
Hsiao Yen, 149
Hsieh Ho, 745
Hsien, 89, 181, 435, 526
Hsien Fêng, 358
Hsien Jên, 646
Hsien nãi nai, 644

Hsien Pei, 152
Hsien-t'ien Chiao, 653
Hsien Yang, 90
Hsin dynasty, 116
Hsin Ch'ing Nien Tsa Chih, 478
Hsin Huang Ti, 116
Hsin T'ang Shu, 216
Hsin Wu Tai Shih, 258
Hsin Yüan Shih, 280
Hsinganling, 19
Hsing Pu, 522
Hsiu ts'ai, 529, 530
Hsiung Nu, 94, 95, 104–106, 115, 118, 121, 125, 150, 151
Hsü Hsia-k'o, 303
Hsü Kuang-ch'i, 304
Hsü Shih-ch'ang, 405
Hsü Ta, 271, 284
Hsüan-tsang, 195, 202
Hsüan Tsung, 186–189
Hsüan T'ung, 400, 401, 435
Hsüan Wang, 45
Hsüeh Kung, 623
Hsün Fu, 526
Hsün K'uang, 72, 73
Hsün Tzŭ, 72, 73, 78, 83, 88
Hsün Yüeh, 138
Hu Hai, 97
Hu Pu, 522
Hu Shih, 478, 480, 797
Hu Wei, 331
Hua-yen, 202
Huai River, 5, 8
Huai style, 62
Huai-nan Tzŭ, 130, 142
Huan, 47, 48
Huan Wên, 147
Huang Ch'ao, 192
Huang Ho. See Yellow River
Huang Shang, 520
Huang Ti, 37, 39
Huang Tsung-hsi, 330
Hui hui, 654
Hui-nêng, 202
Hui Ssŭ, 171
Hui Ti, 103, 134
Hui Tsung, 228, 254
Hui Tzŭ, 76
Hui Yüan, 170, 171
Hulagu, 233
Humiliation Days, 717
Hunan, 9

Hundred Family Names, 792
Hung Hsiu-ch'uan, 354–356, 361
Hung Lou Mêng, 329, 783
Hung Society, 682
Hung Wu, 283–286
Hutukhtu, 414

Ibn Batuta, 272
I-ching, 196
I Ching, 64, 77, 81, 135, 157, 245, 248, 252
I Ho T'üan, 390
Ili, 18, 368
I Li, 65, 82, 135, 140
Immortals, 646
Imperial Maritime Customs, 365, 366, 384
Indemnity, Boxer, 393, 423, 425, 475
Individualism, 712, 713
Indo-China, 20, 354
Industrial coöperatives, 444
Industrialization, 462, 463
Industry, 575–584, 605
Inflation, 449, 450, 476
Ink, 747, 748
Inner Mongolia, 440
Inns, 595
International Settlement in Shanghai, 348, 426, 427, 453
Iron, 15, 56, 111
Irrigation, 56, 57, 111
Islam, 194, 199, 219, 277, 654, 655, 663
Italy, 384
I Ti, 99

Jade, 748, 763
Jade Gate, 104
Japan, influenced by China, 160, 161; influenced by the T'ang, 214, 215, 221; by the Sung, 238; invaded by Mongols, 264, 265; and the Ming, 285, 287, 290; clash with, before 1894, 377, 378; war with (1894–1895), 379, 380; war with Russia, 394–396; in World War I, 415–419; and the Kuomintang, 431, 432; attacks China in 1931, 433–439; further invasion of China after July, 1937, 442–453
Java, 238; invaded by Mongols, 266
Jehol, 18, 19

INDEX

Jên Huang, 37
Jenghiz Khan, 231, 232, 235
Jesuits, 298, 299, 317–319, 325, 347
Jewelry, 758
Jews, 238
Juan Juan, 153
Juchên, 228–232
Ju Chia, 619
Ju Chiao, 619
Jugglers, 703
Jung-lu, 360, 389
Justinian, 159

Kachins, 498
Kaidu, 264
K'aifêng, 228
Kailan Mining Administration, 585
Kalmuks, 314, 315
Kan River, 9
Kan Ying P'ien, 646
Kang Tê, 439
K'ang, 569, 710
K'ang Hsi, 311–320
K'ang Yu-Wei, 387–389, 478, 657
Kanishka, 128
Kansu, 5
Kao Hsien-chih, 187, 188
Kaoliang, 564
Kao P'ien, 191
Kao Ti, 101, 102
Kao Tsu, Han, 101, 102
Kao Tsu, T'ang, 180
Kao Tsung, T'ang, 184, 185
Kao Tsung, Sung, 228, 229
Karakorum, 233, 264
Karma, 128, 163
Kashgar, 183
Kashmir, 187
Keh-lao, 498
Kêng Ching-chung, 313
Keraits, 276
Kerosene, 456
Kerosene lamp, 710
Khalkhas, 314, 315, 322
Khanfu, 237
Khingan, 19
Khitan, 188, 223, 224, 226, 227
Khubilai, 233, 234, 264–269
Kiakhta, treaty of, 321
Kiangsi, 9
Kiangsu, 5, 10

Kiaochow Bay, 381, 415, 416, 419, 422
Kirghiz, 192
Kirin, 19
Kitchen God, 650, 704
Kite flying, 697
Ko Lao Hui, 681
Korea, 95, 106, 125, 180, 184, 185; under the Ming, 284; Japan and China clash over, 378, 379; Russia withdraws from, 395
Koreans, in Manchuria, 432, 434
Kotow, 327
K'ou Ch'ien-chih, 168
Koxinga, 293, 314
Ku Chieh-kang, 82
Ku K'ai-chih, 169
Ku T'ing-lin, 330
Ku wên, 776
Ku Yen-wu, 330, 331
Kuan Chung, 47, 48
Kuan hua, 767
Kuan Hsü, 361, 366, 388, 389, 399, 400
Kuan Ti, 625
Kuan-yin, 637, 638, 641, 642
Kuan Yü, 145, 625, 626, 657
Kuang Wu Ti, 119
Kucha, 160
Kuei, 647, 648
Kuci-ku Tzŭ, 75
Kuei Wang, 293, 299, 312
Kuldja, 18
Kumarajiva, 165, 170
Kung, Prince, 360
Kung Pu, 522
K'ung Chiao, 619
K'ung, H. H., 410
Kung-sun Hung, 110
Kung-sun Lung, 76
Kung-sun Yang, 51, 78
Kuo Chung-shu, 256
Kuo Hsi, 256
Kuominchun, 410
Kuomintang, 403, 407–412, 445, 452, 548, 549, 582, 714
Kuomintang Youth Corps, 477, 656
Kuo Yü, 65
Kuo yü, 479, 768, 797
Kushan dynasty, 105, 123, 128
Kwangchow, leased to France, 382
Kwangsi, 11
Kwangtung, 11
Kweichow, 9

Labor unions, 463, 581, 582
Lacquer, 126, 755, 756, 764
Language, spoken, 766–770; written, 770–776
Lansing-Ishii Agreement, 418
Lao T'ien Fo Yeh, 650
Lao T'ien Yeh, 650
Lao Tzŭ, 73
Later Chin, 224
Later Chou, 225
Later Han dynasty, 119–122, 224
Later Liang, 192, 224
Later T'ang, 224
Laws, 61, 535–538, 552
League of Nations, 431, 436–438, 441
League of states, in the Chou dynasty, 48, 51
Legalists, 77–80, 83, 84, 88–98, 109, 110, 130
Legation quarter, 391, 393
Lei shu, 252, 780
Lenses, 197
Lesser Seal, 93
Lhasa, 316, 322
Li, 248, 523, 535, 689
Li Chao-tao, 212
Li Chi, 65, 81, 135, 247
Li Fan Yüan, 524, 543
Li Hung-chang, 362, 363, 378
Li K'o, 78
Li K'o-yung, 224
Li Kuang-li, 106
Li Kuang-pi, 190
Li K'uei, 78
Li Lin-fu, 188
Li Lung-chi, 186–189
Li Lung-mien, 257
Li Ping, 91
Li Po, 207, 208
Li Po-yao, 173
Li Pu, 522, 523
Li Sao, 66, 82
Li Shih-chên, 304
Li Shih-min, 180–184
Li Ssŭ, 88–98, 135, 139
Li Ssŭ-hsün, 212
Li Tê-lin, 173
Li Tsun-hsü, 224
Li Tung-yang, 304
Li Tzŭ-ch'êng, 292
Li Yen-shou, 173, 216
Li Yüan, 180
Li Yüan-hung, 400, 401, 403–406
Liang Ch'i-ch'ao, 478
Liang Shu, 173
Liang Wu Ti, 149, 167
Liaoning, 19
Liao River, 19
Liao Shih, 258
Liaotung Peninsula, 19, 379, 380, 395
Libraries, 787, 798
Likin, 547
Lin-an, 229
Literature, under the Chou, 62–66; under the Ming, 302–304
Liu An, 130
Liu Chih-chi, 206
Liu Chih-yüan, 224
Liu Ch'iu, 284, 377
Liu Hsiang, 134
Liu Hsiang-shan, 250
Liu Hsin, 117, 134
Liu Pang, 100–102
Liu Pei, 145
Liu Sung, 148
Liu Ts'ung, 151
Liu Tsung-yüan, 209
Liu Yü, 147, 229
Liu Yüan, 151
Lob Nor, 18
Local government, 533–535
Loess, 6, 7
Lohan, 634
Loi, 498
Lo-lo, 498
Loyang, 45, 120, 124, 129
Lu Chia, 101
Lu Chiu-yüan, 250
Lü, 536
Lü Hou, 102, 103
Lü Kuang, 151
Lü Pu-wei, 53, 54, 57, 85, 87
Lü-tsung, 202
Lun Yü, 71, 83, 135, 249, 331
Lung, 649
Lung Mên, 739
Lung Wang, 649
Lytton, Earl of, 437

Ma Tuan-lin, 252, 501
Ma Yüan, 119, 257
Macao, 296–298, 316, 368, 449, 591
Macartney Embassy, 324
Magellan, 297

INDEX 841

Mahayana, 128, 164, 167, 640
Mah jong, 697
Maitreya, 637
Man Chia, 498
Manchoukuo, 19, 435, 439
Manchuria, 19, 20; Russia in, 382, 394, 395; Japan in, 395, 396; ruled by Chang Tso-lin, 411; and the Twenty-one Demands, 416; controlled by Japan, 431, 432, 433-439, 490, 491; migration to, 504, 505; 542
Manchus, conquer China, 291-294; rule China, 309-401
Mandarin, 479, 767-769
Mangu, 233
Manichæism, 198, 199
Manjusri, 640
Marcus Aurelius Antoninus, 124
Margery, 367
Marriage, 670-673, 710-712
Mass Education Movement, 476, 796, 800
Mazdaism, 199, 200
Medicine, 785-787, 804
Meditation, 636
Mei Tzŭ, 304
Mencius, 71, 72
Mêng T'ien, 93, 95
Mêng Tzŭ Shu, 73, 135
Merchants, 57
Mercy, Goddess of. *See* Kuan-yin
Mezzabarba, Jean Ambrose Charles, 318
Miao, 498
Miaotsŭ, 326
Mi-chiao, 202
Middleman, 692
Mi Fei, 257, 746
Migration, of the Chinese, 503-510
Military Governor, 549
Millet, 35, 41, 55, 564
Mi-lo-fu, 637
Min River, 91
Minerals, 15
Ming dynasty, 283, 308
Ming Huang, 186-189, 208
Ming Shih, 307
Ming Ti, 120, 129
Mining, 584
Missionaries, Christian. *See* Christianity
Mo Ti, 75, 76, 83, 111, 130
Mo Tzŭ. *See* Mo Ti

Mohammedanism. *See* Islam
Monasteries, Buddhist, 633-639
Money, 40, 589-591, 599, 605
Mongolia, 18, 26, 543
Mongolia, Inner, 440
Mongolia, Outer, 414, 423
Mongols, 152; conquer China, 230-234; rule China, 262-280; and the Ming, 289
Monks, Buddhist, 633-636
Montecorvino, John of, 275
Morrison, Robert, 333
Moslems. *See* Islam
Mo-so, 498
Mou, 588
Mountains, sacred, 626, 627
Mourning, 631
Moving pictures, 478, 709, 716
Mu, 49
Mu Ch'i, 257
Mu-jung, 152
Mu Wang, 44
Mukden incident, 1931, 434
Music, 160, 703, 759, 764

Nan Chao, 188, 191, 226, 227, 233
Nan Ch'i Shu, 173
Nan Han, 226
Nanking, 147, 148, 285; treaty of (1842), 346; capital of the Republic, 401, 410, 411; incident, March, 1927, 430; taken by Japanese, 1937, 444
Nan P'ing, 226
Nan Shih, 173
Nan Wang, 53
Nan Yüeh, 107
Narcotics, 446
Nationalist Party. *See* Kuomintang
Nayan, 264
Nei Ching, 785
Nei Ko, 285, 320, 522
Neo-Confucianism of the Sung, 243-250, 260
Nepal, 323
Nerchinsk, treaty of, 317
Nestorians, 197, 198, 276
New Dominion. *See* Sinkiang
New Life Movement, 656
Newspapers, 798
New Tide, 479, 480
New Year, 704
New Zealand, 507

Nieh T'ai, 526
Nienfei, 357, 363
Nien hao, 520
Nine Power Treaty, 421
Ninghsia, 5, 18
Nirvana, 127, 163
Nonni, 19
North China Plain, 5, 6, 34
Northern Han, 226, 227
Novel, under the Mongols, 279
Nüchên, 228
Nü Kua, 37
Nurhachu, 291

Ocean, its effects, 28, 29
Ogodai, 232, 233
Old Buddha, 360, 361
Omei, 641
O-mi-t'o-fo, 637–639
Open Door policy, 384, 385
Opium, 345, 348, 456
Optimism, 613
Oracle bones, 34, 40, 86
Orchard Pavilion of Ting Wu, 747
Ordos, 7
Outer Mongolia, 414, 423
Ou-yang Hsiu, 242, 258

Pa Hsien, 646
Pa kua, 37, 324
Pagoda, 734
Pai Chia Hsing, 792
Pai Ho, 5
Pai hua, 478, 796, 797
Pai-lien Chiao, 324, 653
Pai Lien Hui, 270
P'ai fang, 735
P'ai lou, 632, 735
Painting, under the T'ang, 211, 212; under the Sung, 256, 257; under the Mongols, 278; in general, 741–746, 763
Paleolithic man, 35
Panch'an Lama, 315
Pan Chao, 136
Pan Ch'ao, 121, 122
Pan Ku, 136
Pan Piao, 136
Pan Yung, 122
P'an Ku, 37, 39
Panay incident, 448

Panthay Rebellion, 363
Paper, 135, 214, 747
Parkes, Harry, 349
Parthians, 123, 129
Pattern style, 747
Peach, 125
Peach Garden Oath, 145, 684
Pearly Emperor, 645
Pei Ch'i, 154
Pei Ch'i Shu, 173
Pei Chou, 154
Pei Han, 151
Peiping, 411, 735, 736
Pei Shih, 173, 216
Peking. *See also* Peiping
Peking, 13, 288; and the Boxers, 390–393; architecture, 735, 736
Peking Gazette, 525
Peking man, 35, 36
Pen, 93
Pên ts'ao kang mu, 304
People's Political Council, 452
Persians, 194
Perspective, 745
Pescadores Islands, 379
Petroleum, 15
Philippines, 297, 506
Philosophy, under the Chou, 67–80
Phoenix, 649
Phonetic, 772
P'i-lu-fo, 639
Picul, 588
Pidgin English, 795
Pien Liang, 228
P'ien t'i, 158, 332
Pig, 40, 56
Pillars, 732
Pingch'êng, 153
Ping Pu, 522
P'ingyang, 106
Pirès, 296
Plano Carpini, John of, 275
Platforms, 732
Plow, 55
Po Chü-i, 209
Poetry, under the Han, 136; under the T'ang, 206–209; in general, 782, 783
Polo, 696
Polo, Marco, Nicolo, and Maffeo, 274
Pomegranate, 160
Pope, Taoist, 644
Population, figures, 500–502

INDEX 843

Porcelain, under the Sung, 254–256; under the Ming, 305, 306; under Ch'ien Lung, 328; in general, 750–754
Port Arthur, 379, 382
Portsmouth, Treaty of, 395
Portuguese, 296
Postal service, 595
Pottery, early, 35; in general, 749–754
P'o-yang Lake, 9
Prices, 464
Printing, begun, 212, 213; under the Sung, 253, 254; in general, 787, 798, 803
Protestants, after 1894, 467–472
Proverbs, 804
Provinces, 526–529
Provincial Judge, 526
Punitive Expedition, 403
Pure Land Buddhism, 171
P'u-hsien, 640, 641
P'u-i, 435, 439
P'u-sa, 635
P'u-t'o, 11, 641

Queue, 481, 716

Rabban Cauma, 273
Radical, 772
Race, 495, 496
Railroads, begun, 373; concessions for, 383, 384; more building, 441, 460
Rainfall, 12–14
Ramie, 566
Recreation, 696, 697, 716
Red Basin, 8, 9
Red Eyebrows, 118, 681
Red Sect, 315, 316
Red Spears, 681
Reform movement, of 1898, 386–389
Religion, under the Shang, 41; under the Chou, 67–69; under the Ch'in, 95, 96; under the Han, 110, 111, 113, 114; under the Mongols, 267, 268, 275–277, 281; after 1894, 465–473; in general, 607–664
Renaissance, 479, 480
Republic, 400–483
Ricci, Matthew, 298, 299
Rice, 55, 564
Richard, Timothy, 386
Rites Controversy, 318
Roads, 23, 24

Roman Catholics, after 1894, 468–473. *See also* Christianity
Roman Empire, 124
Romanization, 795
Roof, 733
Rubruck, William of, 275
Russia, ceded land north of the Amur, 353; and Ili, 368; in Manchuria, 382; war with Japan, 394–396; in Outer Mongolia, 414; relations with, 1917–1930, 422–425; and Japan, after 1931, 438, 439; after 1941, 446, 447
Russians, 297, 317, 321, 327
Russo-Japanese War, 394–396, 486

Sacred Edict, 319, 612, 670
Salt, 111
Salt tax, 538
Samantabhadra, 640
San Ch'ing, 645
San Fan, 313
San Ho Hui, 682
San Kuan, 645
San Kuo Chih, 173, 783
San Kuo Chih Yen I, 145
San Min Chu I, 408
San Tsang, 640
San Tzŭ Ching, 792
Sarmatians, 126
Schall, 299, 317
Science, backwardness in, 784, 785, 804
Sculpture, 737–741, 762, 763
Scythian influence, 55
Secret societies, 550, 587, 681, 682, 720
Seven Sages of the Bamboo Grove, 157
Shakyamuni, 639
Shan, 113, 114, 140, 185
Shang dynasty, 35, 38–42, 86
Shang Chih-hsin, 313
Shanghai, 348
Shanghai General Benevolent Society, 683
Shang K'o-hsi, 312
Shang Shu Ku Wên Shu Chêng, 331
Shang Ti, 41, 68, 75, 607, 608, 621
Shang Yang, 51, 78
Shansi, 5, 7
Shansi bankers, 592
Shantung, 5–7, 419
Shao Yung, 245
Shên, 648
Shên Chiao, 653

Shên Nung, 37
Shên Yo, 173
Shêng, 526
Shêng Jên, 646
Shengking, 19
Shêng Yü, 319
Shensi, 5
Shih Chi, 84, 112, 113, 138, 303
Shih-chia-fo, 639
Shih Ching, 32, 39, 44, 62, 81, 92, 117, 135, 252
Shih Ching-t'ang, 224
Shih Huang Ti, 53, 54, 88–98
Shih Ssŭ-ming, 189
Shih T'ung, 206
Shimonoseki, treaty of, 379
Shu, 51
Shu Ching, 32, 63, 81, 82, 92, 117, 135, 252, 304, 331
Shu Han, 145, 146
Shu school, 250
Shun, 38
Shun Chih, 311
Shuo Wên, 136, 772
Siam, 506
Silk, 55, 124, 125, 456, 565
Silla, 185
Singapore, 449, 507
Sinkiang, 17, 26, 27, 322, 425, 543
Six Boards, 522
Six Kingdoms, 52
Slavery, 142, 195, 687
Soil, God of the, 625
Soong, T. V., 410
Sorghum, 278
Southern Ch'i, 149
Soy bean, 564
Spain, 354
Spaniards, 297
Spring and Autumn Annals. See *Ch'un Ch'iu*
Squeeze, 589, 695
Ssŭ K'u Ch'üan Shu, 781
Ssŭ K'u Ch'üan Shu Tsung Mu, Ch'in Ting, 781
Ssŭ-ma Ch'ien, 84, 97, 112, 113, 138, 303
Ssŭ-ma Kuang, 251
Ssŭ-ma Yen, 146
Ssŭ T'ien Wang, 637
Standard Oil Company, 457
State cult, 618–628
Steam navigation, 461

Stelae, 739
Stimson Doctrine, 436, 437, 448
Story-teller, 702, 703
Student movements, 476, 477, 713, 714
Su Ch'in, 52, 75
Su Shih, 250, 253, 746
Su Tung-p'o, 253
Sugar, 197
Sui dynasty, 177–180
Sui Jên, 37
Sui Shu, 216
Suiyüan, 5, 18
Sumatra, 238
Summer Palace, 736
Sun Ch'üan, 145
Sun Ch'üan-fang, 408
Sun Fo, 489
Sun Yat-sen, 362, 386 387, 401, 403, 405, 407, 408, 470
Sung, 48
Sung Chih-wên, 209
Sung dynasty, 225–258
Sung, pottery, 750, 751
Sung Shih, 258
Sung Shu, 173
Sung-yün, 166
Sungari River, 19
Sutras, 640
Swatow, 11
Sycee, 591
Szechwan, 9

Ta Ch'i, 192
Ta Ch'in, 124, 146, 159
Ta Ch'ing Lü Li, 536
Ta Hsüeh, 247
Ta Li Ssŭ, 524
Ta Shêng, 640
Tablet, ancestral, 631, 632
Tael, 591
Tai Chên, 331
T'ai chi, 248
T'ai Hu, 10
T'ai I, 114, 646
T'ai P'ing Rebellion, 354–356, 359, 361 363
T'ai P'ing Yü Lan, 252
T'ai Shan, 627
T'ai Tsu, 225, 226
T'ai Tsung, Sung, 227
T'ai Tsung, T'ang, 180–184
Taku forts, 350, 390, 393

INDEX

Talienwan, 382
Tamerlane, 284, 285
Tan, 588
T'ang, 38
T'ang dynasty, 180–216
Tangku truce, 440
Tangut, 227
Tangpu, 411, 548
Tao, 73, 74, 77
Tao-hsüan, 202
Taoism, 73, 74, 120; under the Han, 130, 131; between the Han and the Sui, 168, 169, 171; under the Tang, 204; in general, 643–646, 660, 661, 663
Tao Kuang, 357
Tao nai nai, 644
Tao Shêng, 170
Tao shih, 644, 645
Tao T'ai, 526
Tao Tê Ching, 73, 83, 157, 646
Tao Yüan, 467, 653
T'ao Ch'ien, 157
T'ao Han, 209
T'ao t'ieh, 723
Tariff autonomy regained, 428
Tarim River, 18, 27
Tat'ung, 153, 739
Taylor, J. Hudson, 369
Taxes, 111, 112, 140, 538, 547
Tea, 456, 457, 565
Tea shop, 698, 702
Temple, Confucian, 623; ancestral, 632
Temuchin, 231
Tenantry, 561
Tennis, 716
Terrien de Lacouperie, 33
Textiles, 758
Theatre, under the Mongols, 278; in general, 699–702, 720
Thousand Character Classic, 747, 792
Three Character Classic, 792
Three Dynasties, 43
Three Feudatories, 313
Three Kingdoms, 145, 146
Ti, 52
Ti Huang, 37
Ti pao, 534
Ti Tsang, 638, 639, 641
Tiao, 590
Tibet, 17, 315, 316, 322, 323, 413, 414
Tibetans, 122, 188, 190
Tientsin, treaties of (1858), 351, 352

Tientsin massacre, 371
T'ien, 68, 75, 249, 607, 608, 621
T'ien Hsia, 3
T'ien Huang, 37
T'ien Lao Yeh, 650
T'ien Li, 327
T'ien Shan, 18
T'ien Shih, 644
T'ien T'ai, 170, 171
T'ien Tzŭ, 520
Tiles, 753
Tin, 15
Ting Wu Lan T'ing, 747
T'ing, 526
Toba, 152–154
Tobacco, 699
Tochari, 104
Tolerance, 612
Tones, 769
Tongs, 681
Tortoise shells, 40
T'o-t'o, 258
Tournon, Charles Maillard de, 318
Towns, growth of, 57
Transportation, 594, 595, 600
Triad Society, 682
Tripitaka, 640
True Word, 202
Tsai-li Chiao, 653
Ts'ai Ching, 243
Ts'ai Yüan-p'ei, 480
Ts'ao Chan, 329
Ts'ao hand, 747
Ts'ao Hsüeh-ch'in, 329
Ts'ao Kun, 405, 406
Ts'ao P'ei, 120, 145
Ts'ao Ts'ao, 120, 145
Tsêng Kuo-fan, 361–363, 365
Tsin dynasty, 146, 147
Tsinan incident, 1928, 431
Tsing Hua, 475
Tsingtao, 416; restored to China, 422
Tso Chuan, 65, 82, 117, 140
Tso Tsung-t'ang, 363, 365, 368
Ts'ui Shu, 331
Tsung K'apa, 315
Tsung Tu, 526
Tsungli Yamen, 366, 393
Ts'ung shu, 781
Tu Ch'a Yüan, 523
Tu Fu, 208, 209
Tu Yu, 205, 252

INDEX

T'u Chüeh, 153, 178
T'u Pa, 152–154
Tuan Ch'i-jui, 404–406
Tuchüns' Parliament, 405
Tung Cho, 120
Tung Chou Chun, 53
Tung Chung-shu, 110, 133
Tung Han, 119–122
Tung Ti, 52
Tung Ti, 188
Tung Yo, 627
T'ung Chien Chi Shih Pên Mo, 251
T'ung Chien Kang Mu, 84, 251, 778
T'ung Chih, 251, 361, 366, 526
T'ung Tien, 206, 252
T'ung-t'ing Lake, 9
Tungsten, 15
Tunhuang, 212
Turfan, 17
Turguts, 322
Turks, 153, 178, 183, 187, 188
Twenty-one Demands, 416
Tzŭ Chih T'ung Chien, 216, 251, 778
Tzŭ Ying, 98
Tz'ŭ-ên-tsung, 202
Tz'u Hsi, 360, 361, 389–391, 394, 399, 400

Uighurs, 184, 187, 190, 192
Ungern, Baron, 423
Unicorn, 649
United States, and the Open Door, 384, 385; and World War I, 417–419; and Manchoukuo, 436, 437; enters war against Japan, 447–452; immigration of Chinese, 508
Ussuri River, 19

Vairocana, 639
Vegetables, 565
Vegetarians, 643
Verbiest, 317
Versailles, Treaty of, 419
Viceroy, 526–528
Village, 534, 604
Vinaya, 640

Wai Wu Pu, 393
Walls, 730
Walnut, 159
Wan Li, 290, 291
Wan-li-ch'ang-ch'êng, 730, 731

Wan Shou Kung, 626
Wan Sui Yeh, 520
Wang, 40, 59, 60, 69, 90, 103, 108, 285
Wang An-shih, 239–243, 260
Wang Ch'ing-wei, 445
Wang, C. T., 714, 800
Wang Ch'ung, 133, 137, 142
Wang Fu-chih, 330
Wang Hsi-chih, 157, 746, 747
Wang Mang, 115–119, 139
Wang Pi, 157
Wang Wei, 209, 211
Wang Yang-ming, 301, 302, 308
War, God of, 625
Ward, Frederick T., 362
Washington Conference, 421, 422
Water mill, 158
Weaver maid and herdsman, 705
Wei dynasty, 121, 145, 152–154
Weihaiwei, 379, 382, 422
Wei River, 6, 42, 90, 102, 111
Wei Shou, 173
Wei Shu, 173
Wei-t'o, 637
Wei Yang, 51, 78, 79, 83, 89–92
Weights and measures, 588
Well-field system, 56, 57
Wên, 48, 49
Wên Ch'ang, 625
Wên Hsien T'ung K'ao, 252
Wên li, 774, 796
Wên Miao, 623
Wên-shu, 640
Wên Ti, 103, 148, 625
Wên Wang, 42–44, 64
West Lake, 11, 736
West River. *See* Hsi Kiang
Western Chin, 150, 151
Wheat, 41, 55, 564
Wheelbarrow, 158, 594, 595
White Cloud Society, 682
White Lotus Society, 270, 324, 326, 633
Wine, 197
Winter solstice, 706
Women, 678–680, 711, 719
World War I, 415–419
Writing, 40, 62, 93, 135
Wu, 49, 50
Wu dynasty, 145, 146
Wuchang, 400
Wu Chiao, 653
Wu Ching, 777

INDEX

Wuhan, 10
Wu Hou, 185, 186
Wu Miao, 626
Wu P'ei-fu, 405, 406, 408
Wu San-kuei, 292, 312, 313, 337
Wu Shêng Miao, 626
Wu T'ai Shan, 7, 641
Wu Tao-hsüan, 211
Wu Tao Tzǔ, 211
Wu Tao-yüan, 211
Wu Ti, Chin, 146
Wu Ti, Han, 103–114
Wu Tsê T'ien, 185, 186
Wu Wang, 42–44
Wu Yüeh, 226, 227

Xavier, Francis, 298

Yakub Beg, 363
Yalu River, 19
Yang, 64, 77, 647, 648, 651, 678
Yang Chien, 150, 154, 178
Yangchow, 292
Yang Chu, 76, 77, 84
Yang Hsiung, 133
Yang Kuang, 179, 180
Yang Kuei-fei, 189, 208
Yang Shao culture, 35
Yang Ti, 179, 180
Yangtze River, 4, 8–10
Yao, 38, 498
Yao Ch'a, 173
Yao Chi-hêng, 331
Yao Chien, 173
Yarkand, 183
Yeh-lü Ch'u-ts'ai, 236
Yeh Ming-shên, 349, 350
Yellow Emperor, 37
Yellow River, 4–7, 34
Yellow Sect, 315, 316
Yellow Turbans, 120, 681
Yen, 51, 152
Yen, James Y. C., 476

Yenan, 442, 450
Yenching, 232
Yen Hsi-shan, 410, 411, 656
Yen Hui, 270
Yen Jo-chü, 331
Yen Li-pên, 212
Yen Li-tê, 212
Yen Yüan, 330
Yin, 64, 77, 647, 651, 678
Yin dynasty, 38–42
Yo Fei, 229, 626
Yoshimitsu, 287
Young Men's Christian Association, 470
Yu Ch'ao, 37
Yu Wang, 45
Yü, 38, 39
Yü Hsien, 390, 391
Yü Huang, 645
Yü Huang Shang Ti, 645
Yü Mên, 104
Yüan (branch of government), 549, 550
Yüan (money), 599
Yüan Ch'u, 251
Yüan dynasty, 262–280
Yüan Shih, 280
Yüan Shih-k'ai, 378, 379, 389, 390, 400–403, 656
Yüan Shih T'ien Tsun, 646
Yüan Yu Party, 242
Yüan Yüan, 332
Yüan Wei, 152
Yüeh, 49–51, 94
Yüeh Chih, 104, 105, 123, 128
Yung Chêng, 320, 321
Yung Lo, 287–289
Yung Lo Ta Tien, 289, 780
Yung Wing, 373, 375
Yünnan, 8

Zaitun, 272, **275**
Zen, 170
Zungaria, 18